PROTECTION OF CIVILIANS

OXFORD
UNIVERSITY PRESS

Great Clarendon Street, Oxford, OX2 6DP,
United Kingdom

Oxford University Press is a department of the University of Oxford.
It furthers the University's objective of excellence in research, scholarship,
and education by publishing worldwide. Oxford is a registered trade mark of
Oxford University Press in the UK and in certain other countries

First Edition published in 2016
Impression: 1

Published in the United States of America by Oxford University Press
198 Madison Avenue, New York, NY 10016, United States of America

British Library Cataloguing in Publication Data
Data available

Library of Congress Control Number: 2015959953

ISBN 978–0–19–872926–6

Printed and bound by
CPI Group (UK) Ltd, Croydon, CR0 4YY

Erratum

Protection of Civilians
Edited by Haidi Willmot, Ralph Mamiya, Scott Sheeran, and Marc Weller
9780198729266

The title of chapter 8 was incorrectly printed as "Displacement and the Protection of Civilians under International Refugee Law."

The correct title of chapter 8 is "Displacement and the Protection of Civilians under International Law."

Oxford University Press apologizes for this error.

This book is dedicated to the civilians whose lives are threatened by war—victims and survivors. And to those who fight to protect them—on the ground and in the halls of power.

Foreword

Protecting civilians is at the heart of the work of the United Nations. Our founders had lived through a war in which millions upon millions of civilians perished. Even though they could not have anticipated the ways in which the United Nations or indeed warfare would evolve in the subsequent seventy years, they knew in their hearts what one of our guiding purposes would be and would remain: protecting people caught up in war. It is thus a pleasure to introduce this remarkable collection of essays, which tells the story of the ways in which we have sought to live up to this most fundamental of goals.

The world has put in place an extensive normative framework to protect civilians from war, starting with the three great pillars of the post-war world—the Charter of the United Nations, the Geneva Conventions of 1949 and their Additional Protocols, and the Universal Declaration of Human Rights.

There is also a strong practical framework. Through preventive diplomacy, the deployment of peacekeepers, human rights investigations, and other forms of advocacy and accountability, many of our most important international institutions have protection at their core.

In the past twenty years, there has been a marked growth in the doctrine and practice of putting people at the centre of what we do. In 1991, the Security Council first recognized a humanitarian crisis as a threat to international peace and security. In 1999, a peacekeeping operation was given a mandate to protect civilians for the first time. More recently, the Secretary-General has launched his Human Rights Up Front initiative to bring about a culture change throughout the United Nations so that we are guided in everything we do by the call to protect the most vulnerable.

These developments suggest that politicians, humanitarian actors, human rights activists, and peacekeepers are learning from the past and pushing the boundaries of a people-centred approach.

Yet despite this progress, we continue to witness massive civilian suffering. We have recently marked the twentieth anniversaries of the genocides in Rwanda and Srebrenica. But we have hardly put such situations behind us. At the time of writing, the war in Syria is well into its fifth year, the Central African Republic and South Sudan are marked by sectarian violence, and more than 60 million people have been forcibly displaced from their homes by armed conflict, persecution, and instability. Despite all we have witnessed and learned, protection needs remain appallingly high.

When we talk about protection, it is often through the silos and prisms of international bureaucracy. Humanitarians tend to focus on 'protection'; human rights advocates promote 'rights'. Moreover, the protection of civilians is frequently associated with the intervention of international forces, creating a paternalistic picture that bears little resemblance to reality. Similarly, too often we view protection as something in which the civilians themselves are passive participants, yet those who work in protection know that this is never the case. It is time to put people at the centre of our actions and our words.

This volume marks an important step on an important subject. I appeal to the reader, the student, the interested practitioner, to treat this as more than a discussion of law, concept, or policy. We are running out of words of regret and statements of good intentions. Now is the time for action. My hope is that this volume can help make us more clear-eyed and ready to act when people turn to the United Nations for help and hope in their time of need.

Jan Eliasson
Deputy Secretary-General of the United Nations

Acknowledgements

The editors would like to thank each of the contributors for the analysis, insight, and passion captured in the chapters of this book. They would also like to thank Jikita de Schot, José Luengo-Cabrera, Ryan D'Souza, and Alexander Simon-Fox for their invaluable editorial assistance. Above all, they would like to thank Eric and Suzie Willmot, Alexandra Sicotte-Levesque, Lawrence and May Mamiya, Mae Lawson, and Loretta Sheeran for their intellectual partnership and their unwavering love and support throughout the production of this volume, as always.

Table of Contents

Table of Cases xiii
Table of Legislation xv
List of Abbreviations xxiii
List of Contributors xxvii

Introduction 1
Haidi Willmot, Ralph Mamiya, Scott Sheeran, and Marc Weller

PART I
CONCEPTUAL AND HISTORICAL FOUNDATIONS

1. Civilians, Distinction, and the Compassionate View of War 11
   Hugo Slim
2. Protection of Civilians, Responsibility to Protect, and Humanitarian Intervention: Conceptual and Normative Interactions 29
   Scott Sheeran and Catherine Kent
3. A History and Conceptual Development of the Protection of Civilians 63
   Ralph Mamiya
4. Protecting Civilians: Comparing Organizational Approaches 88
   Stian Kjeksrud, Jacob Aasland Ravndal, Andreas Øien Stensland, Cedric de Coning, and Walter Lotze
5. The Evolution of the UN Collective Security System 109
   Haidi Willmot

PART II
LEGAL FRAMEWORK

6. Protection of Civilians under International Human Rights Law 141
   Andrew Clapham
7. Protection of Civilians under International Humanitarian Law 160
   Jamie A Williamson
8. Displacement and the Protection of Civilians under International Refugee Law 177
   Erin Mooney

9. Legal Aspects of the Use of Force by United Nations Peacekeepers for the Protection of Civilians 205
Mona Ali Khalil

10. International Responsibility for Ensuring the Protection of Civilians 224
Siobhán Wills

PART III
POLITICS AND PRACTICE

11. The United Nations and the Protection of Civilians 257
Jean-Marie Guéhenno

12. The African Union and the Protection of Civilians 275
Ben Kioko and Lydia Wambugu

13. Security Council Diplomacy on the Protection of Civilians: A Convoluted History 292
Bruno Stagno Ugarte

14. Using Force to Protect Civilians in United Nations Peacekeeping Operations 309
Fiona Blyth and Patrick Cammaert

15. The Utility of Force for Protecting Civilians 329
Stian Kjeksrud

16. The Contribution of Human Rights to Protecting People in Conflict 350
Michael Keating and Richard Bennett

17. Humanitarian Protection—Moving beyond the Tried and Tested 372
Sara Pantuliano and Eva Svoboda

18. The Problems and Dilemmas of Helping to Build Protection Capacities 391
Lise Grande

19. Community Self-protection 409
Aditi Gorur and Nils Carstensen

Conclusion 428
Haidi Willmot, Ralph Mamiya, Scott Sheeran, and Marc Weller

Index 439

Table of Cases

ICJ

Applicability of Article VI, Section 22, of the Convention on the Privileges and Immunities of the United Nations (Advisory Opinion) [1989] ICJ Rep 177 249

Application of the Convention on the Prevention and Punishment of the Crime of Genocide (Bosnia and Herzegovina v Serbia and Montenegro) (Judgment) [2007] ICJ Rep 43 247

Case Concerning the Application of the Convention on the Prevention and Punishment of the Crime of Genocide (Bosnia and Herzegovina v Serbia and Montenegro) (Judgment) [2007] ICJ Rep 43 56–7

Case Concerning Armed Activities on the Territory of the Congo (DRC v Uganda) (Judgment) [2005] ICJ Rep 168 . . . . 238, 241

Case Concerning Military Activities and Paramilitary Activities In and Against Nicaragua (Nicaragua v United States of America) (Judgment) [1986] ICJ Rep 14 . . . . 35, 168

Difference Relating to Immunity from Legal Process of a Special Rapporteur of the Commission on Human Rights (Advisory Opinion) [1999] ICJ Rep 62 249

Legal Consequences of the Construction of a Wall in Occupied Palestinian Territory (Advisory Opinion) [2004] ICJ Rep 136 . . . . 239, 241, 245–6

Military and Paramilitary Activities in and against Nicaragua (Nicaragua v United States of America) (Judgment) [1986] ICJ Rep 14 244

Nuclear Tests Case (Australia and New Zealand v France) [1974] ICJ Rep 253 228

Prosecutor v Tadić, Judgment (Decision on the Defence Motion for Interlocutory Appeal on Jurisdiction) (2 October 1995) IT–94–1–AR72 33

IAC

Velásquez Rodriquez v Honduras, Judgment (Merits) (29 July 1988) IntAmCtHR (Series C) No 4 56

IACHR

Neira Alegría et al. v Peru, IAHCR Series C No. 20 (1995) 3 237

Velasquez–Rodriguez v Honduras, Inter-American CtHum Rts (IACHR) Series C, Case 4 (1988) 237

ECHR

Al–Jedda v The United Kingdom Application 27021/08 (ECtHR, 2011) 229, 239

Al–Skeini and Others v The United Kingdom Application 55721/07 (ECtHR, 7 July 2011). 239

Behrami and Behrami v France and Saramati v France, Germany and Norway Application nos. 71412/01 and 78166/01 (ECtHR, 2 May 2007) 239

Jordan v The United Kingdom Application 24746/94 (2001) ECtHR 237

McCann et al. v The United Kingdom Application 1998/91 (1995) ECtHR................ 237
Mahmout Kaya v Turkey, 22535/93 [2000] ECHR 129 (28 March 2000).................. 253
Osman v The United Kingdom 23452/94 [1998] ECHR 101 (28 October 1998) 56, 253
PF and EF v United Kingdom (Application no. 28326/09) [2010] ECHR 2015............. 253

USA

D Georges v United Nations et al., US (2013) 250
Jean-Robert et al. v United Nations, US (2014) 250
LaVenture et al. v United Nations, US (2014)... 250
Delma Georges, et al. v United Nations (Brief) No 1:13-cv-07146 (JPO) 250

ACTHPR

African Commission on Human and Peoples' Rights v The Great Socialist Libyan Arab Jamahiriya [2011] AHRLR 175 (AfCtHPR, 2011)........................ 284, 287
African Commission on Human and Peoples' Rights v The Republic of Kenya, App No 006/2012 (ACtHPR, 2012).. 284

THE NETHERLANDS

Mothers of Srebrenica v. The Netherlands and the United Nations, Case No C/09/295247/ HA ZA 07–2973 (District Court of the Hague, the Netherlands, Judgment of 16 July 2014).................................. 153, 215, 229, 240, 251
The State of the Netherlands v Mustafic 12/03329 (Supreme Court of the Netherlands, 2013).. 239–40
The State of the Netherlands v Nuhanovic 12/03324 (Supreme Court of the Netherlands, 2013).. 239

Table of Legislation

STATUTES

USA

Lieber Code of 1863 . . . . 15, 186
Art 15 15
Art 16 15
Art 23 186

INTERNATIONAL TREATIES AND CONVENTIONS

Additional Protocols to the Geneva Conventions 1977 . . . . 55, 65
African (Banjul) Charter on Human and Peoples' Rights (adopted 27 June 1981, entered into force 21 October 1986) 21 ILM 58 282
Art 61 284
African Charter on the Rights and Welfare of the Child (adopted 11 July 1990, entered into force 29 November 1999) OAU Doc CAB/ LEG/24.9/49 . . . . 143, 237, 277, 285
Art 32 285
African Union Convention for the Protection and Assistance of Internally Displaced Persons in Africa (adopted 22 October 2009, entered into force 6 December 2012) 52 ILM 397 . . . . 143, 200, 277, 283, 285, 373
Arts 2–4 283
Art 6 283
Art 7 283
Art 9 283
Arts 11–3 283
African Union Protocol to the African Charter on Human and People's Rights on the Rights of Women in Africa (signed 11 July 2003, entered into force 5 November 2005) 143, 277
Agreement for the establishment of an International Military Tribunal for the prosecution and punishment of the major war criminals of the European Axis (8 August 1945) 82 UNTS 279
Art 6(b) 187
Art 6(c) 187
American Convention on Human Rights 1969 56
Art 1(1) 56
American Convention on Human Rights (adopted 22 January 1969, entered into force 18 July 1978) 1144 UNTS 123 237
Art 27(2) 237
Cartagena Declaration on Refugees (published 22 November 1984) OAS Doc OEA/ Ser.L/V/II.66/doc.10 193
Charter of the Organization of African Unity (OAU) of 1963 276
Charter of the United Nations (UN Charter) (adopted 26 June 1945, entered into force 24 October 1945) 1 UNTS XVI 2, 30, 32, 34, 36–7, 46, 49, 54, 61–2, 68, 70, 79, 90, 110, 117–19, 142, 209, 222, 234, 236, 245, 248, 251, 257–8, 291, 351, 438
Ch VIII 32–3, 51, 53, 57, 60, 70, 85, 126, 128, 142, 208, 210, 219, 222, 233–4, 252, 262, 317, 325–6
Art 1 117
Art 1(1) 49
Art 1(3) 33, 49, 351
Art 2(1) 49
Art 2(3) 233
Art 2(4) 32, 35, 49, 117, 122–3
Art 2(5) 117
Art 2(7) 33, 38, 49, 53, 122–3
Art 10 121
Art 11 306

Art 12 . . . 121
Art 24(1) . . . 32, 121
Art 25 . . . 59, 219, 232
Art 27(3) . . . 120
Art 29 . . . 302
Art 30 . . . 302
Art 39 . . . 32, 35, 117, 122, 125
Art 41 . . . 125
Art 42 . . . 32, 35, 117, 309
Arts 43–7 . . . 33, 58
Art 43 . . . 33, 117
Art 45 . . . 117
Art 51 . . . 32, 35, 51, 117–18
Art 54 . . . 247
Art 55(c) . . . 32
Art 99 . . . 304, 358
Art 109 . . . 119

Constitutive Act of the African Union (adopted 1 July 2000, entered into force on 26 May 2001) OAU Doc CAB/LEG/23.15 . . . 94–5, 276–7
Art 4(h) . . . 276–8, 282, 291
Art 4(j) . . . 278, 282
Art 4(m) . . . 276
Art 4(o) . . . 276
Art 5(2) . . . 285
Art 9(g) . . . 282
Art 10 . . . 283
Art 17 . . . 282
Art 22 . . . 286

Convention for the Amelioration of the Condition of the Wounded in Armies in the Field (adopted 22 August 1864, in force from 22 June 1865 to 16 August 1966) 11 LNTS 440 . . . 160–1, 173
Art 5 . . . 161
Art 8 . . . 161

Convention on the Elimination of All Forms of Discrimination against Women (adopted 18 December 1979, entered into force 3 September 1981) 1249 UNTS 13 . . . 143

Convention on the Prevention and Punishment of the Crime of Genocide (adopted 9 December 1948, entered into force 12 January 1951) 78 UNTS 277 . . . 56, 69
Art 1 . . . 247

Convention on the Privileges and Immunities of the United Nations (adopted 13 February 1946, entry into force 17 September 1946) 1 UNTS 15 . . . 249

Convention on the Rights of Persons with Disabilities (adopted 13 December 2006, entered into force 30 March 2007) . . . 143

Convention on the Safety and Security of United Nations and Associated Personnel (adopted 9 December 1994, entered into force 15 January 1999) . . . 80, 216

Convention Governing the Specific Aspects of Refugee Problems in Africa (adopted 10 September 1969, entered into force 20 June 1974) 1001 UNTS 45 . . . 193

Convention relating to the Status of Refugees (adopted 28 July 1951, entered into force 22 April 1954) 189 UNTS 137 (1951 Refugee Convention) . . . 55, 195
Art 1 . . . 193
Art 1A . . . 192
Art 1F . . . 193
Art 9 . . . 195
Art 33 . . . 194–5

Council of Europe Convention on Preventing and Combating Violence against Women and Domestic Violence (adopted 11May 2011, entered into force 1 August 2014) CETS No 210 . . . 143

Covenant of the League of Nations (adopted 28 April 1919, entered into force 10 January 1920) UKTS 4 . . . 32
Art 4 . . . 32
Art 8 . . . 32
Arts 10–12 . . . 32
Arts 15–16 . . . 32

Convention for the Amelioration of the Condition of the Wounded in Armies in the Field (adopted 22 August 1864, replaced by the Geneva Conventions of 1906, 1929 and 1949) . . . 14–5

Convention for the Protection of Human Rights and Fundamental Freedoms (adopted 4 November 1950, entry into force 3 September 1953) 213 UNTS 222 . . . 236
Art 2 . . . 239
Art 3 . . . 239
Art 15 . . . 237

Convention relative to the Treatment of Prisoners of War (adopted 27 July 1929, replaced by the third Geneva Convention of 12 August 1949) . . . 18

Geneva Conventions (I-IV) adopted 1949 . . . 165, 171, 244, 247, 306

Geneva Convention for the Amelioration of the Condition of the Wounded and Sick in Armed Forces in the Field (adopted 12 August 1949, entered into force 21 October 1950) 75 UNTS 31 (First Geneva Convention) 55, 65–6, 166–7, 171
Art 1 . . . . 56, 243–7
Art 3 . . . . 166–8, 172, 241, 252
Art 8 171
Art 47 167
Art 52 171
Geneva Convention for the Amelioration of the Condition of Wounded, Sick and Shipwrecked Members of Armed Forces at Sea (adopted 12 August 1949, entered into force 21 October 1950) 75 UNTS 85 (Second Geneva Convention) 171
Art 1 243–7
Art 3 . . . . 167–8, 172, 241, 252
Art 8 171
Art 48 167
Art 53 171
Geneva Convention relative to the Treatment of Prisoners of War (adopted 12 August 1949, entered into force 21 October 1950) 75 UNTS 135, Article 124 (Third Geneva Convention) 171
Art 1 243–7
Art 3 . . . . 167–8, 172, 241, 252
Art 8 171
Art 132 171
Geneva Convention relative to the Protection of Civilian Persons in Time of War (adopted 12 August 1949, entered into force 21 October 1950) 75 UNTS 287 (Fourth Geneva Convention) 65, 73, 162–3, 171, 246
Art 1 243–7
Art 3 . . . . 167–8, 172, 241, 252
Art 4 194
Arts 9–12 67
Art 9 171
Art 11 67
Art 23 414
Art 23(c) 413
Art 24 67
Art 26 194
Art 27 67
Art 28 67
Art 31 67
Art 33 67
Arts 35–46 194
Art 38 67
Art 44 193
Art 45 194
Art 46 67
Art 49 187–8
Art 49(1) 189
Art 49(2) 201
Art 54 67
Art 67 67
Art 70 194
Art 75 67
Art 144 167
Art 147 . . . . 67, 187
Art 149 171
Hague Convention 1899 186
Hague Convention 1907 . . . . 15, 66, 186
Inter-American Convention on the Forced Disappearance of Persons (adopted 9 June 1994, entered into force 28 March 1996)
Art IV 144
Inter-American Convention on the Prevention, Punishment and Eradication of Violence against Women (adopted 9 June 1994, entered into force 5 March 1995) 33 ILM 1534 143
Inter-American Convention to Prevent and Punish Torture (adopted 9 December 1985, entered into force 28 February 1987) OAS Treaty Series No 67
Art 3 144
International Convention for the Protection of All Persons from Enforced Disappearance (adopted 20 December 2006, entered into force 23 December 2010)
Art 11 144
International Convention on Civil and Political Rights 1966 . . . . 55–6, 144, 147, 236, 238–40
Art 2(1) 56, 148
Art 4 . . . . 143, 237
Art 6 . . . . 157, 239, 352
Art 7 . . . . 157, 239, 352
Art 9 352
International Convention on Economic, Social and Cultural Rights 1966 . . . . 55, 144
International Convention on the Protection of the Rights of All Migrant Workers and Members of Their Families (adopted 18 December 1990, entered into force 1 July 2003) 2220 UNTS 3 143

Kigali Principles on the Protection of Civilians, as issued from the International Conference on the Protection of Civilians held in Rwanda (1 June 2015) 135
OAU/AU Convention Governing the Specific Aspects of Refugee Problems in Africa of 1969 (adopted 10 September 1969, entered into force 20 June 1974) 1001 UNTS 45 277
Optional protocol to the Convention on the Rights of the Child on the involvement of children in armed conflict (adopted 20 May 2000, entered into force 12 February 2002) 2173 UNTS 222 . . . . . 143, 171
Art 8 171
Protocol Additional to the Geneva Conventions of 12 August 1949, and relating to the Adoption of an Additional Distinctive Emblem (Protocol III) (adopted 8 December 2005, entered into force 14 January 2007) 45 ILM 558 160
Protocol Additional to the Geneva Conventions of 12 August 1949, and relating the Protection of Victims of International Armed Conflicts (adopted 8 June 1977, entered into force 7 December 1978) 1125 UNTS 3 (Additional Protocol I) 164, 166, 171–2, 187, 201, 243
Art 1 243
Art 50 24
Art 52 164
Art 57 164
Art 70 164
Art 73 193–4
Art 74 194
Art 85(4)(b) 201
Art 90 171
Protocol Additional to the Geneva Conventions of 12 August 1949, and relating the Protection of Victims of Non-International Armed Conflicts (adopted 8 June 1977, entered into force 7 December 1978) 1125 UNTS 609 (Additional Protocol II) 164, 166–7
Art 4(3)(b) 188
Art 18 164
Art 17 188
Art 17(1) 188
Art 17(2) 189
Protocol to the African Charter of Human and Peoples' Rights on the Establishment of the African Court on Human and Peoples' Rights (adopted 10 June 1998, entered into force 24 January 2004) OAU Doc OAU/LEG/EXP/AFCHPR/PROT 283
Art 5 286
Art 30 283
Protocol to the Treaty Establishing the African Economic Community Relating to the Pan-African Parliament (adopted 2 March 2001, adopted 14 December 2003) AU Doc CM/2198
Art 2(3) 282
Protocol Relating to the Establishment of the Peace and Security Council of the African Union (signed 9 July 2002, entered into force 26 December 2003) 277, 280
Art 2 280
Art 6(a) 282
Art 6(d) 282
Art 7 280
Art 7(1)(e) 277
Art 7(1)(f) 277
Art 13(3)(f) 279
Protocol relating to the Status of Refugees (adopted 31 January 1967, entered into force 4 October 1967) 606 UNTS 267 193
Art 1(2) 193
Regulations respecting the Laws and Customs of War on Land, annexed to the Hague Convention (II) with Respect to the Laws and Customs of War on Land (adopted 29 July 1899, entered into force 4 September 1900) 161
Art 25 161
Art 27 161
Regulations respecting the Laws and Customs of War on Land, annexed to Convention (IV) respecting the Laws and Customs of War on Land (adopted 18 October 1907, entered into force 26 January 1910) 161
Rome Statute of the International Criminal Court (adopted, entered into force 1 July 2002) 2187 UNTS 90 . . . . . 55, 69, 154
Art 5 69
Art 7(1)(d) 190
Art 8 216
Art 8(2)(b)(viii) 187
Art 8(2)(c)(viii) 189

Statute of the International Court of Justice
Art 38 41
Statute of the International Tribunal for the Prosecution of Persons Responsible for Serious Violations of International Humanitarian Law in the Territory of the Former Yugoslavia since 1991
Art 5(d). 190
Statute of the International Tribunal for Rwanda
Art 3(d). 190
Treaties of Westphalia 1648. 31
Treaty Establishing the African Economic Community (adopted 3 June 1991, entered into force 12 May 1994)
30 ILM 1241 282
Art 7(1)(c) 282
UN Convention against Torture and Other Cruel, Inhuman or Degrading Treatment or Punishment (adopted 10 December 1984, entered into force 26 June 1987)
1465 UNTS 85. . . . . 55–6, 171
Art 1 157
Art 2(1). 56
Art 13 144
UN Convention on the Rights of the Child (adopted 20 November 1989, entered into force 2 September 1990)
1577 UNTS 3 . . . . 55, 143
Arts 43–5 171
Universal Declaration on Human Rights 1948 . . . . 55, 144, 158, 234, 306, 351
Art 12 200
Art 14 192

UNITED NATIONS RESOLUTIONS

UN SECURITY COUNCIL

UNSC Res 54 (1948)
UN Doc S/RES/54 123
UNSC Res 82 (1950)
UN Doc S/RES/82 120
UNSC Res 83 (1950)
UN Doc S/RES/83 120
UNSC Res 84 (1950)
UN Doc S/RES/84 120
UNSC Res 85 (1950)
UN Doc S/RES/85 120
UNSC Res 93 (1951)
UN Doc S/RES/93 293
UNSC Res 161 (1960)
UN Doc S/4741 . . . . 71, 207
UNSC Res 169 (1960)
UN Doc S/5002 . . . . 71, 207
UNSC Res 217 (1965)
UN Doc S/RES/217 124
UNSC Res 678 (1990)
UN Doc S/RES/678 33
UNSC Res 688 (1991)
UN Doc S/RES/0688 . . . . 33, 72, 124, 181–2
UNSC Res 731 (1992)
UN Doc S/RES/731 124
UNSC Res 743 (1992)
UN Doc S/RES/743. . . . . 44, 128
UNSC Res 758 (1992)
UN Doc S/RES/758 44
UNSC Res 775 (1992)
UN Doc S/RES/775 129
UNSC Res 776 (1992)
UN Doc S/RES/776 44
UNSC Res 794 (1992)
UN Doc S/RES/794. . . . . 33, 124–5
UNSC Res 814 (1993)
UN Doc S/RES/814 129
UNSC Res 827 (1993)
UN Doc S/RES/827. . . . . . 125, 190, 297
UNSC Res 836 (1993)
UN Doc S/RES/836 44
UNSC Res 841 (1993)
UN Doc S/RES/841 124
UNSC Res 872 (1993)
UN Doc S/RES/872 44
UNSC Res 912 (1994)
UN Doc S/RES/912. . . . . 44, 295
UNSC Res 918 (1994)
UN Doc S/RES/918. . . . . 44, 123
UNSC Res 929 (1994)
UN Doc S/RES/929 . . . . 33, 124–5, 295
UNSC Res 940 (1994)
UN Doc S/RES/940. . . . . . . 33, 125, 313
UNSC Res 955 (1994)
UN Doc S/RES/955. . . . . . 125, 190, 297
UNSC Res 1054 (1996)
UN Doc S/RES/1054 124
UNSC Res 1101 (1997)
UN Doc S/RES/1101. . . . . 123, 125
UNSC Res 1132 (1997)
UN Doc S/RES/1132 124
UNSC Res 1208 (1998)
UN Doc S/RES/1208 182
UNSC Res 1261 (1999)
UN Doc S/RES/1261 298

UNSC Res 1265 (1999)
UN Doc S/RES/1265 . . . 12, 44, 84, 141, 259, 292, 298
UNSC Res 1267 (1999)
UN Doc S/RES/1267 125
UNSC Res 1270 (1999)
UN Doc S/RES/1270 . . . . . 44, 77–8, 90, 124, 129, 208, 262, 298
UNSC Res 1272 (1999)
UN Doc S/RES/1272 78
UNSC Res 1291 (2000)
UN Doc S/RES/1291. . . . 90, 123–4, 129
UNSC Res 1296 (2000)
UN Doc S/RES/1296 . . . . . 12, 33, 44–5, 131, 141, 183, 208, 259, 292
UNSC Res 1325 (2000)
UN Doc S/RES/1325 130
UNSC Res 1373 (2001)
UN Doc S/RES/1373 383
UNSC Res 1386 (2001)
UN Doc S/RES/1386. . . . . 125, 358
UNSC Res 1401 (2002)
UN Doc S/RES/1401 359
UNSC Res 1464 (2003)
UN Doc S/RES/1464. . . . . . 125, 129–30
UNSC Res 1483 (2003)
UN Doc S/RES/1483 125
UNSC Res 1484 (2003)
UN Doc S/RES/1484 129
UNSC Res 1502 (2003)
UN Doc S/RES/1502. . . . . 12, 216
UNSC Res 1509 (2003)
UN Doc S/RES/1509 . . . . . . 44, 78, 124, 202, 208, 299, 310
UNSC Res 1528 (2004)
UN Doc S/RES/1528 . . . . 44, 78, 90, 123–5, 129–30, 208, 267, 310, 313
UNSC Res 1542 (2004)
UN Doc S/RES/1542 . . . . 44, 66, 78, 90, 124, 208, 299
UNSC Res 1545 (2004)
UN Doc S/RES/1545 . . . . 44, 90, 124, 129
UNSC Res 1574 (2004)
UN Doc S/RES/1574 130
UNSC Res 1590 (2005)
UN Doc S/RES/1590 . . 44, 90, 123, 393
UNSC Res 1612 (2005)
UN Doc S/RES/1612. . . . . 130, 152, 298
UNSC Res 1671 (2006)
UN Doc S/RES/1671 130
UNSC Res 1674 (2006)
UN Doc S/RES/1674 . . . . 44, 49–50, 60, 131, 141, 259, 292
UNSC Res 1690 (2006)
UN Doc S/RES/1690 125
UNSC Res 1701 (2006)
UN Doc S/RES/1701 . . . . 44, 78, 90, 124, 208, 299, 310
UNSC Res 1706 (2006)
UN Doc S/RES/1706. . . . . . . 46, 50, 124
UNSC Res 1738 (2006)
UN Doc S/RES/1738 . . . . 44, 131, 141, 292
UNSC Res 1746 (2007)
UN Doc S/RES/1746 359
UNSC Res 1769 (2007)
UN Doc S/RES/1769 . . . . 44, 46, 78, 90, 129, 131, 184, 202, 208, 219, 262, 299–300, 310
UNSC Res 1778 (2007)
UN Doc S/RES/1778. . . . 90, 130–1, 299
UNSC Res 1794 (2007)
UN Doc S/RES/1794 315
UNSC Res 1820 (2008)
UN Doc S/RES/1820 315
UNSC Res 1856 (2008)
UN Doc S/RES/1856 129
UNSC Res 1861 (2009)
UN Doc S/RES/1861 . . . . 44, 124, 129, 184
UNSC Res 1882 (2009)
UN Doc S/RES/1882 151
UNSC Res 1888 (2009)
UN Doc S/RES/1888 351
UNSC Res 1894 (2009)
UN Doc S/RES/1894 . . . . . 12, 44–5, 49, 131, 185, 211, 231, 234, 237, 253, 259, 292, 315, 320, 322
UNSC Res 1906 (2009)
UN Doc S/RES/1906 45
UNSC Res 1925 (2010)
UN Doc S/RES/1925 . . . . 44, 78, 90, 129, 202, 208, 310, 373
UNSC Res 1970 (2011). 287–9, 291, 299
UNSC Res 1973 (2011)
UN Doc S/RES/1973 . . . . 41, 59, 93, 123, 128, 229, 231, 270, 287–9, 291, 306
UNSC Res 1975 (2011)
UN Doc S/RES/1975. . . . . 81, 230
UNSC Res 1990 (2011)
UN Doc S/RES/1990 . . . . 44, 78, 90, 124, 129, 184, 208

UNSC Res 1996 (2011)
UN Doc S/RES/1996 . . . . . . 44, 90, 123, 129, 202, 232, 299, 324, 362–3, 369, 373, 394
UNSC Res 1997 (2011)
UN Doc S/RES/1997 362
UNSC Res 2003 (2011)
UN Doc S/RES/2003. . . . . 131, 134, 314
UNSC Res 2016 (2011)
UN Doc S/RES/2016 59
UNSC Res 2048 (2012)
UN Doc S/RES/2048 270
UNSC Res 2053 (2012)
UN Doc S/RES/2053 184
UNSC Res 2066 (2012)
UN Doc S/RES/2066 131
UNSC Res 2068 (2012)
UN Doc S/RES/2068 292
UNSC Res 2085 (2012)
UN Doc S/RES/2085. . . . . 125, 130, 300
UNSC Res 2086 (2013)
UN Doc S/RES/2086 44
UNSC Res 2089 (2013)
UN Doc S/RES/2089 316
UNSC Res 2096 (2013)
UN Doc S/RES/2096 202
UNSC Res 2098 (2013)
UN Doc S/RES/2098 . . . . . 46, 80–2, 92, 103, 133–4, 184, 202, 217, 299, 324, 331
UNSC Res 2100 (2013)
UN Doc S/RES/2100 . . . . 78, 80, 82, 90, 202, 208, 299–300, 317, 397
UNSC Res 2106 (2013)
UN Doc S/RES/2106 292
UNSC Res 2113 (2013)
UN Doc S/RES/2113 184
UNSC Res 2116 (2013)
UN Doc S/RES/2116 184
UNSC Res 2117 (2013)
UN Doc S/RES/2117 305
UNSC Res 2118 (2013)
S/RES/2118 301
UNSC Res 2122 (2013)
UN Doc S/RES/2122 292
UNSC Res 2127 (2013)
UN Doc S/RES/2127 . . . . 125, 130, 267, 299–300
UNSC Res 2132 (2013)
UN Res S/RES/2132. 394
UNSC Res 2134 (2014)
UN Doc S/RES/2134 270
UNSC Res 2139 (2014)
UN Doc S/RES/2139. . . . . 292, 302
UNSC Res 2145 (2014)
UN Doc S/RES/2145. . . . . 299, 359
UNSC Res 2147 (2014)
UN Doc S/RES/2147. . . . . . 46, 210, 259
UNSC Res 2149 (2014)
UN Doc S/RES/2149 . . . . . 45–6, 72, 78, 90, 124, 129, 131, 134, 144, 153, 184, 208, 210, 219, 300, 310, 327
UNSC Res 2151 (2004)
UN Doc S/RES/2151 403
UNSC Res 2155 (2014)
UN Doc S/RES/2155 . . . . . 78, 124, 134, 185, 208, 210, 212, 221, 232, 259, 293, 363, 368, 396
UNSC Res 2161 (2014)
UN Doc S/RES/2161 270
UNSC Res 2162 (2014)
UN Doc S/RES/2162 46
UNSC Res 2164 (2014)
UN Doc S/RES/2164 . . . . 44–5, 131, 134, 210, 232
UNSC Res 2165 (2014)
UN Doc S/RES/2165 . . . . 84–5, 185, 202, 292, 302, 382
UNSC Res 2170 (2014) 191–2
UNSC Res 2175 (2014)
UN Doc S/RES/2175. . . . . 131, 185
UNSC Res 2185 (2014)
UN Doc S/RES/2185 . . . . 80, 82

UN GENERAL ASSEMBLY

UNGA Res 377 A(V) (1950)
UN Doc A/RES/377 A(V) 121
UNGA Res 998 (ES–I) (1956)
UN Doc A/RES/998(ES–I) 121
UNGA Res 1474 (ES–IV) (1960)
UN Doc A/RES/1474(ES–IV) 121
UNGA Res 34/179 (1979) UN Doc A/RES/34/179. 154–5
Art 5 154
UNGA Res 39/46 (1984)
UN Doc A/RES/39/46 195
UNGA Res 43/173 (1988) UN Doc A/43/173 154
UNGA Res 45/594 (1990) UN Doc A/45/594 . . . . 215, 220
UNGA Res 46/182 (1991)
UN Doc A/RES/46/182 411
UNGA Res 48/57 (1993)
UN Doc A/RES/48/57 411
UNGA Res 49/59 (1994)
UN Doc A/RES/49/59 80

UNGA Res 51/77 (1997) UN Doc A/RES/51/77 351
UNGA Res 52/130 (1998) UN Doc A/RES/52/130 197
UNGA Res 52/247 (1998) UN Doc A/RES/52/247 249
UNGA Res 53/35 (1998) UN Doc A/RES/53/35 . . . . 76, 206
UNGA Res 60/1 (2005) UN Doc A/RES/60/1 . . . . 210, 391, 420
UNGA Res 61/106 (2007) UN Doc A/61/106 143
UNGA Res 63/280 (2009) UN Doc A/RES/63/280 45
UNGA Res 64/266 (2010) UN Doc A/RES/64/266 45
UNGA Res 65/310 (2011) UN Doc A/RES/65/310 45
UNGA Res 66/253 (2012) UN Doc A/RES/66/253 122
UNGA Res 66/297 (2012) UN Doc A/RES/66/297 45
UNGA Res 68/277 (2014) UN Doc A/RES/68/277 . . . . 80, 82

UN COMMISSION ON HUMAN RIGHTS (CHR)

CHR Res 1991/25 (1991) UN Doc E/CN.4/RES/1991/25. 181
CHR Res 1992/73 (1992) UN Doc E/CN.4/RES/1992/73 181–2
CHR Res 1997/39 (1997) UN Doc E/CN.4/RES/1997/39. 197
CHR Res 2000/61 (2000) UN Doc E/CN.4/RES/2000/61. 351

UN HUMAN RIGHTS COMMITTEE/ UN HUMAN RIGHTS COUNCIL (HRC)

Camargo (on behalf of Suarez de Guerrero) v Colombia, Human Rights Committee, Communication No. 45/197 (1982) UN Doc Supp No 40 (A/37/40) 137 237
HRC Res 14/6 (2010) UN Doc A/HRC/14/6 183
HRC Res 25/L.1/Rev.1 (2014) UN Doc A/HRC/25/L.1/Rev.1 355

MISCELLANEOUS UN INSTRUMENTS

Basic Principles on the Use of Force and Firearms by Law Enforcement Officials (adopted by the Eighth United Nations Congress on the Prevention of Crime and the Treatment of Offenders, Havana, Cuba) . . . . 27 August to 7 September 1990) 154–5
Principle 4. 155
Principle 8. 154
Principle 9. 155

List of Abbreviations

ADF-NALU	Allied Democratic Forces–National Army for the Liberation of Uganda
AFISMA	African-led International Support Mission to Mali
ALNAP	Active Learning Network for Accountability and Performance in Humanitarian Action
AU	African Union
AUCISS	Report of the Commission of Inquiry on South Sudan
CAN	Community Alert Networks
CAR	Central African Republic
CONOPS	Concept of Operations
CPA	Comprehensive Peace Agreement
CSDP	European Common Security and Defence Policy
CWGs	UNMISS Community Watch Groups
DARSIWA	2001 Draft Articles on the Responsibility of States for Internationally Wrongful Acts
DFS	United Nations Department of Field Support
DPKO	United Nations Department of Peacekeeping Operations
DRAIO	2011 Draft Articles on the Responsibilities of International Organisations
DRC	Democratic Republic of the Congo
ERDC	Enhanced Rapidly Deployable Capacity
EU	European Union
FARDC	Forces Armées de la République Démocratique du Congo—Armed Forces of the Democratic Republic of the Congo
FDLR	Democratic Forces for the Liberation of Rwanda
FIB	MONUSCO Force Intervention Brigade
HPG	Humanitarian Policy Group
HRW	Human Rights Watch
ICCPR	1966 International Covenant on Civil and Political Rights
ICESCR	1966 International Covenant on Economic Social and Cultural Rights
ICISS	International Commission on Intervention and State Sovereignty
ICJ	International Court of Justice
ICRC	International Committee of the Red Cross
ICTR	International Criminal Tribunal on Rwanda
ICTY	International Criminal Tribunal for the former Yugoslavia
IDP	Internally displaced person
IEDs	Improvised explosive devices
IHL	International humanitarian law
IHRL	International human rights law
ILC	International Law Commission
INCAF	International Network on Conflict and Stability
IRL	International refugee law
ISAF	International Security Assistance Force in Afghanistan
ISIL	Islamic State in Syria and the Levant

ISIS	Islamic State of Iraq and al-Sham
JMAC	United Nations Joint Mission Analysis Centre
L2GP	Local to Global Protection Initiative
LTTE	Liberation Tigers of Tamil Eelam
MINURCAT	United Nations Mission in the Central African Republic and Chad
MINURSO	United Nations Mission for the Referendum in Western Sahara
MINUSCA	United Nations Multidimensional Integrated Stabilization Mission in the Central African Republic
MINUSMA	United Nations Multidimensional Integrated Stabilization Mission in Mali
MINUSTAH	United Nations Stabilization Mission in Haiti
MISCA	African-led Support Mission to the Central African Republic
MONUC	United Nations Organization Mission in the Democratic Republic of the Congo
MONUSCO	United Nations Organization Stabilization Mission in the Democratic Republic of the Congo
NATO	North Atlantic Treaty Organization
NGO	Non-governmental organizations
OAU	Organization of African Unity
OCHA	United Nations Office for the Coordination of Humanitarian Affairs
OHCHR	United Nations Office of the High Commissioner for Human Rights
OIOS	United Nations Office of Internal Oversight Services
OSCE	Organization for Security and Cooperation in Europe
PoC	Protection of Civilians
PSC	African Union Peace and Security Council
ROE	Rules of engagement
RtoP	Responsibility to Protect
RwP	Responsibility while Protecting
SACEUR	North Atlantic Treaty Organization Supreme Allied Commander Europe
SADC	South African Development Community
SHIRBRIG	United Nations Standing High Readiness Brigade
SOFA	Status of Force Agreement
SPLA	Sudan People's Liberation Army
SRSG	Special Representative of the United Nations Secretary-General
SSPS	South Sudan Police Service
TCCs	Troop contributing countries
UDHR	1948 Universal Declaration of Human Rights
UN	United Nations
UNAMA	United Nations Mission in Afghanistan
UNAMID	African Union–United Nations Hybrid Operation in Darfur
UNAMIR	United Nations Assistance Mission in Rwanda
UNAMSIL	United Nations Mission in Sierra Leone
UNDOF	United Nations Disengagement Observer Force
UNFICYP	United Nations Peacekeeping Force in Cyprus
UNGA	United Nations General Assembly
UNHCR	United Nations High Commissioner for Refugees
UNIFIL	United Nations Interim Force in Lebanon

UNISFA	United Nations Interim Security Force for Abyei
UNMIK	United Nations Mission in Kosovo
UNMIL	United Nations Mission in Liberia
UNMIS	United Nations Mission in the Sudan
UNMISS	United Nations Mission in South Sudan
UNMOGIP	United Nations Military Observer Group in India and Pakistan.
UNOCI	United Nations Operation in Côte d'Ivoire
UNPROFOR	United Nations Protection Force for the Former Yugoslavia
UNRWA	United Nations Relief and Works Agency
UNSC	United Nations Security Council
UNTAET	United Nations Transitional Administration in East Timor
UNTSO	United Nations Truce Supervision Organization
UPR	Universal Periodic Review
WFP	World Food Programme

List of Contributors

Richard Bennett Richard Bennett served with the United Nations in senior human rights posts from 2000 to 2013. He headed human rights components of peacekeeping operations in Sierra Leone, Timor-Leste, Afghanistan, and South Sudan. From 2007 to 2010 Mr Bennett was the Representative of the United Nations High Commissioner for Human Rights in Nepal and head of the United Nations Office of the High Commissioner for Refugees office. He has also been Chief of Staff for the Secretary-General's Panel of Experts on Sri Lanka and Special Adviser to the Assistant Secretary-General for Human Rights in New York. Currently he is Amnesty International's Representative in New York. A national of New Zealand and the United Kingdom, Mr Bennett graduated from the University of Auckland with an MA (hons.1) in Social Anthropology.

Fiona Blyth Fiona Blyth has been a Policy Advisor on the United Kingdom's Security Council team at the United Kingdom Mission to the United Nations since 2013. She leads on Mali and the Central African Republic dossiers, with a particular focus on the UN peacekeeping missions in both countries. Fiona holds a Masters degree in Modern History from the University of St Andrews in Scotland and a Master of Letters in Terrorism Studies from the Centre for the Study of Terrorism and Political Violence, also at the University of St Andrews. Ms Blyth commissioned into the Intelligence Corps of the British Army from the Royal Military Academy Sandhurst. Since leaving the military, she has provided security consultancy and worked at the United Kingdom's Foreign and Commonwealth Office in London and New York. Fiona has also conducted research on African peace and security issues and the deployment of the United Nations' Force Intervention Brigade in the Democratic Republic of Congo for the International Peace Institute.

Patrick Cammaert Major-General (rtd) Patrick Cammaert joined the Royal Netherlands Marine Corps in 1968. He has served in many United Nations peacekeeping operations, including the United Nations Transitional Authority in Cambodia (UNTAC) and the United Nations Protection Force (UNPROFOR) in Bosnia. Major-General Cammaert was Force Commander of the UN Mission in Ethiopia and Eritrea (UNMEE) from October 2000 until November 2002, after which he was appointed by the United Nations Secretary-General as the Military Adviser in the Department of Peacekeeping Operations. On 1 February 2005 he was appointed as Division Commander of the United Nations Forces in the eastern part of the Democratic Republic of Congo (MONUC). Major-General Cammaert retired from active duty in 2007. Since that time he has consulted governments and multinational organizations extensively on UN peacekeeping, and in particular on the protection of civilians. He recently published an International Peace Institute issue brief, *The UN Intervention Brigade in the Democratic Republic of the Congo.*

Nils Carstensen Nils Carstensen is a writer, documentarist, and senior humanitarian adviser. He has worked with humanitarian crisis response in Sudan, South Sudan, Palestine, Syria, Myanmar, Haiti, the Balkans, Somalia, Ethiopia, Eritrea, North Korea, and other major humanitarian crises since the late 1980s. Mr Carstensen is a co-founder and manager of the Local to Global Protection (L2GP) initiative and a senior humanitarian advisor to DanChurchAid (DCA)—a member of the ACT Alliance. L2GP focuses on documenting and promoting local communities' perceptions of protection and survival as well as analysing the dynamics between affected individuals and communities, and the perceptions and actions of external actors such as aid agencies, authorities, and armed groups.

Andrew Clapham Andrew Clapham is Professor of International Law at the Graduate Institute of International and Development Studies, and served as the first Director of the Geneva Academy of International Humanitarian Law and Human Rights from 2006 to 2014. He is also a Commissioner of the International Commission of Jurists. Professor Clapham worked as the academic advisor on international humanitarian law to the Special Representative of the United Nations Secretary-General in Iraq in 2003, and as a special advisor on business and human rights to United Nations High Commissioner for Human Rights Mary Robinson. His publications include *Brierly's Law of Nations: An Introduction to the Role of International Law in International Relations* (7th edn) (2012), *Human Rights Obligations of Non-State Actors* (2006), *The Oxford Handbook on International Law in Armed Conflict*, co-edited with Paola Gaeta, and most recently, co-edited with Paola Gaeta and Marco Sassòli, *Commentary to the 1949 Geneva Conventions* (2015).

Cedric de Coning Cedric de Coning is a Senior Researcher with the Peace Operations and Peacebuilding Research Group at the Norwegian Institute of International Affairs (NUPI) and a Senior Advisor on Peacekeeping and Peacebuilding for ACCORD. He serves on the editorial boards of the journals *Global Governance* and *Peacebuilding*. Dr de Coning has a PhD from the Department of Philosophy at the University of Stellenbosch in South Africa. His research focus is on peace operations and peacebuilding policies and practices. Recent publications include *The BRICS and Coexistence* (Routledge, 2014), *Rising Powers and the Future of Peacekeeping and Peacebuilding* (NOREF, 2013), 'Understanding Peacebuilding as Essentially Local' (*Stability Journal*, 2013), 'Coherence & Coordination: The Limits of the Comprehensive Approach' (*Journal of International Peacekeeping*, 2011), and *The Unintended Consequences of Peacekeeping* (UN University Press, 2007).

Aditi Gorur Aditi Gorur is a research analyst and acting Deputy Director of the Future of Peace Operations programme at the Stimson Center, an independent research institute based in Washington, DC. Her primary research focus is on preventing and responding to violence against civilians, particularly in the context of peace operations. Before joining Stimson, Ms Gorur worked with the Indian Institute for Human Settlements in India, the Asia Foundation and the Center for Liberty in the Middle East in Washington, DC, and the Melbourne University Law School in Australia. She holds a Bachelor of Arts in international development and a Bachelor of Laws with honours from the University of Melbourne. She is completing a Master of Arts in international security at Georgetown University.

Lise Grande Lise Grande has worked for the United Nations for twenty years, serving in India, South Sudan, Democratic Republic of Congo, Armenia, Angola, East Timor, Tajikistan, Sudan, Occupied Palestine, and Haiti. Ms Grande's experience spans development, humanitarian action, and peacekeeping. She is currently serving as the Deputy Special Representative of the Secretary-General to the United Nations Assistance Mission for Iraq (UNAMI).

Jean-Marie Guéhenno Jean-Marie Guéhenno is President of the International Crisis Group. Until taking up that post he was the Arnold Saltzman Professor of Professional Practice at Columbia University and the director of its centre for international conflict resolution (School of International and Public Affairs). He is also a non-resident Senior Fellow at the Brookings Institution. In 2012, Mr Guéhenno was appointed deputy joint special envoy of the United Nations and the Arab League for Syria. He left that position to chair the commission appointed by President François Hollande to review the French defence and national security posture. Between 2000 and 2008, he served as the United Nations' Under-Secretary-General for Peacekeeping Operations. A former French diplomat, he held the position of Chairman of the Institut des Hautes Études de Défense Nationale between 1998 and 2000, and served as director of the French policy planning staff and as ambassador to the Western European Union.

Michael Keating Michael Keating is the United Nations Secretary-General's Special Representative for Somalia and Head of the United Nations Assistance Mission in Somalia (UNSOM). At the time of writing his chapter for this book he was Associate Director, Research Partnerships at Chatham House. Mr Keating served as the head of the team that drafted the 'Human Rights Up Front' plan of action that was issued by the United Nations Secretary-General in 2013. Prior to that, he served in senior United Nations posts in Afghanistan, Jerusalem, Gaza, and New York. Mr Keating was Executive Director of the Africa Progress Panel, has worked as an adviser on conflict resolution issues, and served on a number of boards and non-profit organizations addressing humanitarian, environmental, and energy issues.

Catherine Kent Catherine Kent earned her LLM degree in International Human Rights and Humanitarian Law from the University of Essex, where she was also a Research Associate for the Human Rights in Iran Unit, providing support to the United Nations Special Rapporteur for Iran. Prior to that, she served as a legal intern in the Appeals Chamber of the International Criminal Tribunals for the former Yugoslavia and Rwanda. Ms Kent has recently returned from the Occupied Palestinian Territories, where she was facilitating advocacy and capacity-building for projects focusing on food security and women's rights.

Mona Ali Khalil Mona Ali Khalil is currently on special leave from her position as a Senior Legal Officer in the United Nations Office of the Legal Counsel and is working as a Legal Advisor with Independent Diplomat, the international diplomatic advisory group. She holds a BA in International Relations and a Masters in

Middle East Studies from Harvard University. She also holds a Masters in Foreign Service and a Juris Doctorate from Georgetown University. She has served in the United Nations Office of the Legal Counsel since 1993, most recently as the head of the peacekeeping team and the sanctions team. Ms Khalil also served as the legal adviser to the United Nations Mission to Investigate Allegations of the Use of Chemical Weapons in the Syrian Arab Republic and the Joint OPCW–UN Mission for the Elimination of the Syrian chemical weapons programme. From 2005 to 2009 she was seconded to the International Atomic Energy Agency, where she provided advice on a broad range of public international law issues arising out of the international nuclear security and counter-terrorism regime as well as on non-proliferation sanctions. Her article 'Afghanistan, Iraq and the War on Terrorism: Winning the Battles and Losing the War' was published in the *Georgia Journal of International and Comparative Law* in 2004.

Ben Kioko Ben Kioko was elected by the Executive Council of the African Union and appointed by the Assembly of Heads of State & Government as a judge of the African Court on Human and Peoples' Rights in July 2012, for a six-year term. Previously, he served in various capacities in the legal service of the Organization of African Unity and subsequently the African Union Commission, rising to become the Chief Legal Counsel and Director of the Legal Department. Justice Kioko was actively involved in all aspects of conceptualization, drafting and steering the process of negotiations of at least twenty-five treaties adopted under the aegis of the Organization of African Unity/African Union. He is a member of several professional bodies and serves in various international advisory boards for academic, legal, and research institutions. He has published on various subjects, including international human rights, humanitarian law, peace and security, governance, rule of law, and regional integration. Justice Kioko is a recipient of two high-level state awards in Kenya for his dedicated service and contribution to the development of the rule of law.

Stian Kjeksrud Stian Kjeksrud is a Senior Researcher at the Norwegian Defence Research Establishment (FFI) and a PhD candidate at the University of Oslo. He holds a Master of International Affairs from Columbia University. His research focus is contemporary United Nations peacekeeping operations in Africa, and the role and utility of military force to protect civilians. Among his articles and book chapters on these topics, the most recent are *Protecting Governments from Insurgencies: The Democratic Republic of the Congo and Mali* with Lotte Vermeij in *UN Peacekeeping Doctrine in the Post-Brahimi Era* (forthcoming), *The Future of UN Peacekeeping Operations* in *International Military Operations in the 21st Century* (2015), and, *Emerging Lessons from MONUC* with Jacob Ravndal in *The Protection of Civilians in UN Peacekeeping* (2013). He is a former police officer, soldier, and military officer with experience in operations in Afghanistan, Kosovo, Macedonia, and Lebanon.

Walter Lotze Walter Lotze is a Senior Researcher at the Centre for International Peace Operations (ZIF). Prior to joining ZIF he was a Special Advisor to the Head of Mission for the African Union Mission in Somalia (AMISOM), before which he worked in the Peace Support Operations Division of the African Union. Prior to joining the African Union he was a Visiting Fellow with the Norwegian Institute of International Relations (NUPI), and prior to that he headed the Peacebuilding Unit of the African Centre for the Constructive Resolution of Disputes (ACCORD). He holds a PhD in International Relations from the University of St Andrews, and an MA in International Relations from the University of Stellenbosch.

Ralph Mamiya Ralph Mamiya leads the Protection of Civilians Team in the United Nations Department Peacekeeping Operations/Department of Field Support. He has spent more than seven years working on peacekeeping and protection issues, including tours with United Nations missions in Sudan and South Sudan. He has published articles on international law and international relations in journals and in edited volumes, including the *Oxford Handbook on the Use of Force in International Law* (2015). Mr Mamiya holds a Juris Doctor from Cornell Law School.

Erin Mooney Erin Mooney is a researcher, policy adviser, and field practitioner on forced migration, human rights, and humanitarian issues, specializing since 1992 in the protection of internally displaced persons (IDPs) and other civilians at risk in their own countries. She has worked extensively throughout Africa as well as in the Americas, Asia, the Balkans, and the Caucasus. Ms Mooney has worked with the United Nations High Commissioner for Refugees, the Representative of the United Nations Secretary-General on IDPs, the United Nations High Commissioner for Human Rights, the United Nations Secretary-General's Special Representative on Children and Armed Conflict, the United Nations Departments of Political Affairs and Peacekeeping Operations, the International Organization for Migration, U.S. Agency for International Development, the Canadian Armed Forces, and international NGOs. She also served as the first Deputy Director of the Brookings Institution Project on Internal Displacement. In addition to publishing widely in scholarly publications, Ms Mooney has authored numerous international, regional, and national policy and strategy documents, as well as operational guidance for field staff and tools for legislators and policy-makers on a wide range of IDP issues. She has been a member of the Editorial Advisory Board of *Forced Migration Review* since 1999.

Sara Pantuliano Sara Pantuliano is the Director of the Humanitarian Policy Group at the Overseas Development Institute (ODI) in London. She is a political scientist with extensive experience in conflict and post-conflict contexts. Prior to ODI, Sara led the United Nations Development Programme (UNDP) Sudan Peace Building Unit, managed a high-profile post-conflict response in the Nuba Mountains, and was an observer at the Intergovernmental Authority on Development (IGAD) Sudan peace process and a lecturer at the University of Dar es Salaam. She holds a PhD in Politics and has written widely on Sudan, South Sudan, the Middle East, and humanitarian affairs, and is a recognized public speaker on these issues. Ms Pantuliano is Managing Editor of the *Disasters* journal and a member of the World Economic Forum's Global Agenda Council on Risk and Resilience. She is the Chair of the Board of Integrated Regional Information Networks (IRIN) news, a Trustee of SOS Sahel, and serves on the advisory boards of the Refugees Studies Centre and the United Nations Association of the United Kingdom, amongst others.

Jacob Aasland Ravndal Jacob Aasland Ravndal is a Research Fellow at the Norwegian Defence Research Establishment (FFI). He currently studies right-wing terrorism and militancy in post-Second World War western Europe. Previously he has conducted research on strategic cybersecurity, the protection of civilians in United Nations peacekeeping, and intelligence analysis in international peace operations. Mr Ravndal has also carried out field work to study the United Nations Joint Mission Analysis Centers (JMACs) in Haiti, the Democratic Republic of the Congo, and Liberia. He holds an MPhil in Peace and Conflict Studies from the University of Oslo.

Scott Sheeran Scott Sheeran is Senior Legal Counsel and Leader of the Peace Operations and Sanctions Teams for the New Zealand Permanent Mission to the United Nations, in its delegation on the Security Council. He is also a Senior Lecturer (on leave) at the School of Law and Human Rights Centre at the University of Essex. He is a graduate of Cambridge University and was a United Nations Institute for Training and Research (UNITAR) Fellow at Columbia Law School. Mr Sheeran has previously worked as a diplomat, legal adviser, and United Nations and human rights adviser, including in New York and Geneva, and has served on the advisory council of human rights NGOs including Universal Rights Group. While posted in New York, he was Vice Chair of the United Nations Legal (Sixth) Committee. Mr Sheeran has published widely on the law of the United Nations, peacekeeping, international human rights law, and public international law.

Hugo Slim Hugo Slim is Head of Policy at the International Committee of the Red Cross (ICRC). At the time of writing his chapter for this book he was Senior Research Fellow at the University of Oxford's Institute for Ethics, Law, and Armed Conflict. Dr Slim is an Associate Lecturer at the Graduate Institute in Geneva and has been a Visiting Professor at the University of Oregon. Through Oxford University Press, he has published *Humanitarian Ethics: A Guide to the Morality of Aid in War and Disaster* and *Killing Civilians: Method, Madness and Morality in War*. From 1983 to 1994 Dr Slim served as a humanitarian worker in Sudan, Morocco, Ethiopia, Bangladesh, and the Palestinian Territories. From 2003 to 2007 he was Chief Scholar at the Centre for Humanitarian Dialogue in Geneva, leading policy work on civilian protection and political mediation.

Andreas Øien Stensland Andreas Øien Stensland currently works at the Norwegian Refugee Council on the deployment of expert personnel to United Nations and national agencies. He was formerly a research assistant at the Norwegian Institute of International Affairs (NUPI), Department of Security and Conflict Management. His academic interests include the protection of civilians in peace operations, human rights, and security policy in the African Union and the Southern African Development Community (SADC), and norms and practices in international organizations. Mr Stensland has undertaken field work in South Sudan and Ethiopia. He received his master's degree in Peace and Conflict Studies from the University of Oslo.

Eva Svoboda Eva Svoboda has been working as a Research Fellow with the Humanitarian Policy Group of the Overseas Development Institute (ODI), London, since June 2012. She holds a Masters in Middle Eastern Studies and Philology, and a Masters in Public International Law. Following her studies she worked for various NGOs in the Occupied Palestinian Territories, held a position as liaison officer in a peacekeeping mission, and provided consultancy work for the Swiss Development Agency in Jerusalem, before joining the International Committee of the Red Cross (ICRC) in 1999. Ms Svoboda's assignments with the ICRC were predominantly field-based, in countries including Iraq, the Democratic Republic of the Congo, Myanmar, East Timor, Algeria, and Sudan. They included positions as head of delegation, head of office, and protection co-ordinator. Ms Svoboda's areas of research include the protection of civilians, civil–military interaction, the engagement of regional organizations in humanitarian response, and issues related to access by humanitarian agencies to populations in need.

Bruno Stagno Ugarte Bruno Stagno Ugarte has been Deputy Executive Director at Human Rights Watch since September 2014. Previously, he served as the Executive Director of Security Council Report (2011–14), Foreign Minister of Costa Rica (2006–10), Ambassador-Permanent Representative of Costa Rica to the United Nations in New York (2002–6), and Chief of Staff of the Costa Rican Foreign Ministry (1998–2000), among other foreign service postings. Mr Stagno has also served as the President of the Assembly of States Parties of the International Criminal Court (2005–8) and Co-President of the Comprehensive Test Ban Treaty Article 14 Conferences (2007–9). He was a founding member of several multilateral groupings including the Small Five (S5), the Coalition of Rainforest Nations, and the Forest-11 (F11). He is a graduate of Georgetown University, the Sorbonne, and Princeton University and author or editor of several books, chapters and articles, including most recently *The UN Security Council in the Age of Human Rights* (Cambridge University Press, 2014) and *The UN Security Council in the 21st Century* (Lynne Rienner Publishers, 2015). As of 2015, he is also a Visiting Professor at SciencesPo-PSIA. In 2011 he was made an Officier de la Légion d'Honneur.

Lydia Wambugu Lydia Wambugu is a pan-African researcher with extensive experience and expertise in peace and security, governance, gender, and development in Africa. She has served with various research and academic institutions, United Nations agencies (including UNDP, UNECA, UNFPA, UNHCR, and UNICEF), inter-governmental organizations (including the African Union and the Inter-governmental Authority on Development), and government institutions and civil society bodies. Dr Wambugu has conducted research projects and assessments in post-conflict settings within the Great Lakes Region and the Horn of Africa, including the Democratic Republic of the Congo, Darfur, northern Uganda, and South Sudan. She also has experience dealing with displaced populations residing in Ethiopia, Kenya, South Africa, and western Tanzania. Much of Dr Wambugu's research work has adopted a policy-oriented approach and was undertaken in order to provide policy recommendations to governments and inter-governmental organizations, among others. She holds a PhD from the faculty of Commerce, Law, and Management, University of the Witwatersrand, Johannesburg, South Africa and has published on peace and security, governance, gender, and development.

Marc Weller Marc Weller is Professor of International Law and International Constitutional Studies in the University of Cambridge and the Director of the Lauterpacht Centre for International Law. He became a member of the Faculty of Law of the University of Cambridge in 1990. From 1997 to 2000 he was Deputy Director of the Centre of International Studies. During 2011/12 he served in the Department of Political Affairs of the United Nations Secretariat in New York, in the role of Senior Mediation Expert. He advised on the transitions in Cote d'Ivoire and Egypt, and supported mediation efforts during the armed conflict in Libya and the transition in Yemen. He also contributed to the mediation efforts of the Joint Special Envoy for Syria, Kofi Annan. Professor Weller served as an adviser in the Doha negotiations on a peaceful settlement of the Darfur crisis, and advised on constitutional reform in Bosnia and Herzegovina. He is the author, editor, or co-editor of some twenty-five books and a large number of academic journal articles and book chapters. Professor Weller holds Masters degrees from the Fletcher School of Law and Diplomacy and the University of Cambridge, and Doctorates in Law, in Economic and Social Sciences, and in International Law from the Universities of Frankfurt, Hamburg, and Cambridge respectively.

Jamie A Williamson Jamie A Williamson works with the International Committee of the Red Cross (ICRC) as its Head of Unit for relations with militaries, security forces, and armed groups. He has previously served in Geneva as ICRC Legal Advisor on International Humanitarian Law for Common Law countries and as Legal Advisor at the ICRC Washington D.C. Regional Delegation, where he was responsible for ICRC legal activities in the United States and Canada, with particular focus on Guantanamo and military operations in Afghanistan and Iraq. He has also served as the ICRC regional legal adviser in Pretoria, South Africa. Before joining the ICRC, Mr Williamson worked for nearly ten years with the United Nations ad hoc international criminal tribunals in Tanzania and the Netherlands, and the Special Court for Sierra Leone. Mr Williamson is on the faculty of the Academy on Human Rights and Humanitarian Law at the American University Washington College of Law and has been a visiting professor at the New England School of Law. He has published numerous papers on repression of war crimes, international justice, the laws of war, and challenges to international humanitarian law in contemporary armed conflicts.

Haidi Willmot Haidi Willmot has held a number of positions in the United Nations Secretariat, including in the United Nations Operations and Crisis Centre and the Department of Peacekeeping Operations Office of the Chief of Staff and

Office of Military Affairs. Prior to joining the Secretariat, Ms Willmot was the Peacekeeping Policy Officer at the Australian Mission to the United Nations, and worked as an analyst with the New Zealand government. She previously worked in Vanuatu with the Australian Agency for International Development (AusAid) and in legal practice in Australia and throughout the island nations of the South Pacific. Ms Willmot holds an BA/LLB (hons) from the Australian National University and a MPhil in International Relations from the University of Cambridge. She has published academic work in peer-reviewed journals, in edited volumes and with the International Peace Institute.

Siobhán Wills Siobhán Wills is Professor of Law at the Transitional Justice Institute/Law School, University of Ulster. She is currently the recipient of a British Academy Mid-Career Fellowship, awarded in 2015 to enable her to work on a project on the use of lethal force by peacekeepers. In 2013 she held the Ariel Sallows Chair of Human Rights at the University of Saskatchewan and prior to that she was co-Director of the Centre for Criminal Justice and Human Rights at University College Cork. Her primary research area is public international law, particularly the law of armed conflict, human rights law, and the law relevant to peacekeeping operations. Professor Wills spent time as a Fulbright Fellow at Harvard Law School on the Human Rights Program, and at New York University Law School on the Hauser Global Fellowship Program. In addition to her book *Protecting Civilians: The Obligations of Peacekeepers* published by Oxford University Press in 2009, Professor Wills has published numerous journal articles and contributed to the *British Yearbook of International Law 2006*. She obtained her LLB from National University of Ireland, Galway, her LLM from Yale, and her doctorate from the University of Oxford.

Introduction

Haidi Willmot, Ralph Mamiya,
Scott Sheeran, and Marc Weller

The protection of civilians is a highly topical issue, which has been of increasing importance in international relations discourse for some time. It is at the heart of United Nations (UN) peacekeeping deployments, including to Darfur, South Sudan, the Democratic Republic of the Congo, the Central African Republic, and Mali; it was central to the North Atlantic Treaty Organization (NATO) intervention in Libya; and it is a part of the debates on the failures of the international community in Sri Lanka and Syria. Variously described as a moral responsibility, a legal obligation, a mandated peacekeeping task, and the culmination of humanitarian and development activity, it has become a high-profile concern of international organizations, governments, and civil society. Yet, the concept remains unclear and confusion persists regarding the legal framework, both of which undermine the effective protection of civilians in practice.

This volume was conceived in an effort to develop a holistic and coherent understanding of the protection of civilians. That intent is reflected in its structure and the spectrum of contributors. The first section probes deeply into the academic roots of the issue, examining it from ethical, theoretical, conceptual, and historical perspectives. The following section attempts to draw together a cohesive international legal framework, exploring the treatment of civilian protection within the bodies of international law governing the use of force (*jus ad bellum*), the conduct of hostilities (*jus in bello*), human rights, and refugees. The final section examines civilian protection practice across a number of fields including diplomacy, military, human rights, humanitarian, development, and community self-protection. Providing this multidisciplinary analysis are experts drawn from academia and practice, including ethicists, international lawyers, diplomats, UN officials, and military, humanitarian, human rights, and development professionals.

Hugo Slim, who was at the time of writing Senior Research Fellow at the University of Oxford's Institute for Ethics, Law and Armed Conflict, opens the volume with a consideration of the ethical basis for the protection of civilians. He examines the ethical background of the compassionate view of war as it is epitomized in the 'doctrine of civilians' that has emerged in modern times, and the distinction between those who fight and those who do not. He explores the two traditions of ruthless and limited war and the strong rhetorical and operational emergence of compassion and restraint in international society in modern history.

He also considers the victimhood and agency that characterizes the civilian experience of war to see how this can cause ethical and legal ambiguity that queries a simplistic notion of distinction. Dr Slim then examines why most war ideologues still opt for a more ruthless form of violence than the espoused norm, and how that poses ethical and legal problems for the wider project of restraint. Finally, he argues for continued normative and legal consolidation around the ethics of compassionate war, supporting a generous definition of 'civilian'.

Scott Sheeran, Senior Legal Adviser at the New Zealand Permanent Mission to the UN, and Catherine Kent, a human rights specialist, consider the related concepts of protection of civilians, responsibility to protect, humanitarian intervention, and responsibility while protecting, analysing their development and interactions on legal, political, and operational levels. The authors find that humanitarian intervention is now a largely abandoned idea, but one still necessary to retain in the absence of Security Council reform. They argue that the responsibility to protect has failed to lead to real change, the selectivity of its application has fuelled mistrust, and it is not capable of crystallizing into an effective obligation in light of the veto embedded in the UN Charter. Protection of civilians has, however, had some successes where the responsibility to protect has been less able. Due to the acceptance among the UN membership of the protection of civilians peacekeeping mandate, it has become the foundation stone for the use of force under the Charter, and has made the UN's intervention in conflicts more palatable. The authors argue that it represents a fundamental trend in global governance and use of force for humanitarian and human rights purposes by the UN, and a recalibration of the Security Council's powers under the Charter.

Ralph Mamiya, the head of the protection of civilians team in the UN Department of Peacekeeping Operations, outlines the historical evolution of civilian protection concepts. He considers key developmental drivers and explores the various modern conceptions of civilian protection, comparing and contrasting how it is understood and applied in humanitarian, human rights, and military contexts. Mr Mamiya contrasts the conception and practice of the protection of civilians during the inter-war period, which focused heavily on neutral and impartial action, with the concept and practice latterly developed by the Security Council, incorporating greater focus on international human rights law and the use of force. He concludes by examining the responsibility to protect and the use of protection of civilians language in the Security Council resolution authorizing the 2011 intervention in Libya.

Under the auspices of the Norwegian Defence Research Establishment (Forsvarets forskningsinstitutt (FFI)), Stian Kjeksrud, Jacob Aasland Ravndal, Andreas Øien Stensland, Cedric de Coning, and Walter Lotze compare organizational approaches to the protection of civilians. Focusing on military activities to protect civilians, the authors analyse the approaches taken by the UN, the European Union (EU), NATO, and the African Union (AU). They address the inter-related aspects of protection discourses, concepts, and operational practices. The authors find that despite the unprecedented concern with improving the physical security of civilians under threat, none of the four organizations does so effectively. The UN knows what it takes to protect, but seldom displays the will to apply military force for this purpose. NATO is willing to use force to protect, but is less aware of how it should be done when civilians are directly targeted. The AU has the knowledge, experience, and willingness to apply force to protect, but remains highly dependent on external resources to do so consistently. And the EU has both concepts and relevant capabilities, but struggles to generate troops in time, when needed. The authors posit that understanding the limitations and comparative advantages of each organization is an important step towards more effective protection in the future.

Haidi Willmot, a UN Secretariat official, explores the impact of the protection of civilians on the evolution of the UN collective security system, framing this analysis within international relations theory. She examines changes in three key aspects of the collective security system: (a) the *mechanism* for determining aggression and deciding response measures; (b) the *determination* of threats to the peace; and (c) the *measures* used to address such threats. Ms Willmot finds that the system recognizes the legitimacy of civilians as a group to be protected irrespective of their polity, but at the same time remains committed to States as the primary security actors, and therefore seeks to execute protection within that paradigm. In doing so, the system creates two distinct but closely linked communities—a society of individuals and a society of States—both of which civilians are simultaneously members of, and that, it is argued, represents a trajectory toward a cosmopolitan idea of the ordering of global society.

Opening the section on the international legal framework, Andrew Clapham, Professor of Public International Law at the Graduate Institute of International and Development Studies, Geneva, considers the protection of civilians under international human rights law. He notes that the role of international human rights in protecting civilians is complex. Unlike international humanitarian law, international human rights law does not distinguish between civilians and others. Professor Clapham elucidates the debates regarding whether certain human rights obligations apply to a State and their troops when operating outside of their own territory. He examines whether armed non-State actors owe human rights obligations to those who find themselves under their control. He also considers the related problem of the international legal responsibility and accountability of the UN itself for human rights violations. In the wake of the UN's failure to avert the genocide and atrocities in Rwanda and Srebrenica, or address the human rights violations in Sri Lanka, Professor Clapham notes a realization that human rights warnings should not be ignored, and yet there remains apprehension about what the duties are of those who become aware of human rights atrocities. He finds that UN peacekeeping missions are obliged to observe human rights standards and to halt human rights violations whether or not the operation has a protection of civilians mandate.

Jamie Williamson, the head of the International Committee of the Red Cross (ICRC) unit for relations with militaries, security forces, and armed groups, considers the protection of civilians under international humanitarian law. Mr Williamson notes that sixty-five years after the adoption of the Fourth Geneva

Convention, the number of civilian casualties remains alarmingly high in many armed conflicts. He concludes that too often belligerents seem to act with utter disregard for the protection of civilians, with many of the most egregious attacks against civilians committed by non-State actors. His chapter considers whether that state of affairs can be apportioned to the conceptual limitations of international humanitarian law, or whether it is simply a result of the challenges posed by the complex dynamics of many contemporary armed conflicts. He argues that improving the protection of civilians through compliance with international humanitarian law requires more integrated efforts by the international community, not only in preventing harm from occurring, but also to address the root causes of today's humanitarian challenges.

Erin Mooney, an academic at York University, considers the state of the protection of civilians under international refugee law. She situates the protection of displaced persons in the broader challenge of protection of civilians, considering the place that displacement occupies in the protection agenda of the Security Council. Ms Mooney examines the protection that international law affords civilians who are at risk of, or experiencing, displacement in situations of armed conflict. In her analysis, she focuses on three elements: (a) protection against the act of forced displacement; (b) protection when displaced, both cross-border and internally; and (c) safe and sustainable solutions to displacement. Ms Mooney illustrates her legal analysis by reference to actual situations of displacement in contemporary conflicts.

Mona Khalil, a Senior Legal Officer with the Office of the Legal Counsel, provides a cross-cutting analysis of the legal aspects of the protection of civilians in UN peacekeeping operations. She examines the evolution and *raison d'être* of the protection of civilians mandate and elaborates the legal framework governing the use of force by UN peacekeepers to protect civilians from the imminent threat of physical violence. Ms Khalil finds that the legal framework for the protection of civilians mandate and the authority to use all necessary means, up to and including deadly force, is both broad and deeply founded. However, she concludes that a number of factors may have an inhibiting effect on the use of force by UN peacekeepers beyond self-defence and for the protection of civilians. These factors include: confusion regarding the meaning and scope of the legal terminology; concerns regarding the host State's consent; lack of clarity around the mission leadership's roles and responsibilities; the potential for criminal accountability and/or becoming a party to the conflict; the duality of contingent and mission command structures; and the 'basic principles' of peacekeeping. She concludes that the use of force for the protection of civilians is a right afforded to, and a duty expected from, UN peacekeepers.

Concluding the legal section, Siobhàn Wills, Professor of Law at the University of Ulster, explores a specific aspect of the international legal framework, namely international responsibility and accountability for failure to protect civilians. She focuses specifically on protection obligations of UN Security Council-mandated missions. Professor Wills notes that civilian protection norms have developed in an ad hoc manner through a combination of legal and political enterprises. Consequently, although peacekeeping mandates authorize protection activities there is little established guidance as to what a force is *expected* to do, and even less as to what it is *obliged* to do, to carry out its mandate. She argues that there are legal obligations to protect that are derived largely from international human rights law, international humanitarian law, and the International Law Commission's Draft Articles on the Responsibilities of International Organizations. These obligations are comparatively weak because they depend on a narrow intersection of developing (or debatable) law, practice, and circumstance, but nevertheless, they have important operational implications for UN missions.

Opening the discussion on politics and practice, Jean-Marie Guéhenno, President of the International Crisis Group and former Under-Secretary-General of the UN Department of Peacekeeping Operations, analyses the UN's practice on the protection of civilians, primarily in the UN peacekeeping context. He questions whether the UN has effectively used the range of tools at its disposal to protect civilians in conflict and considers the role that the UN, the international community, individual States, and civilian populations can and should play to protect civilians. Mr Guéhenno finds that both the UN's efforts to provide physical protection and to build State capacity have revealed the Organization's limitations. Noting the shallow political consensus for dealing with protection issues, he suggests that protection of civilians peacekeeping mandates may simply reflect Security Council recourse to a concept adopted from international humanitarian law, used to mask continuing political divisions. For the protection of civilians to truly serve people on the ground, and be more than a temporary response to an emergency, he argues that UN efforts need to go beyond the superficial and address the creation of a lasting protective environment, which ultimately empowers communities.

Ben Kioko, Justice of the African Court on Human and Peoples' Rights and former AU Legal Counsel, and Lydia Wambugu, an independent researcher, together consider the protection of civilians within the framework of the AU. Conflicts in Africa, and the international community's response to those conflicts, have played a large role in shaping the legal and operational framework for civilian protection activity. The AU recognizes and supports a right to intervention to stop mass violations of international humanitarian and human rights law. The authors provide an overview of the AU framework for the protection of civilians, based on an examination of relevant AU organs and actual regional responses. They also address the NATO intervention in Libya in 2011, finding that international or regional intervention for the protection of civilians would be more likely to be embraced by African States if the duties and responsibilities of intervening States were more clearly articulated. The authors conclude that the most effective measure for ensuring civilian protection on the continent would be for the AU to operationalize its unique normative framework for intervention, so that it becomes a living instrument for protecting civilians and arresting violations of international humanitarian, human rights, and refugee law.

Bruno Stagno Ugarte, Deputy Assistant Director of Human Rights Watch, former Executive Director of Security Council Report, former Foreign Minister of Costa Rica, and former Ambassador on the UN Security Council, examines Security Council diplomacy on protection. He tracks the practice of the Security

Council in addressing the protection of civilians, presenting an 'inside story' of protection of civilians diplomacy within the Council. Mr Stagno also considers Council interaction with other stakeholders, including host States and troop contributing countries, the UN Secretariat, and regional and sub-regional organizations. He draws conclusions about the benefits and limitations of Security Council engagement on protection issues given its composition and function as prescribed by the UN Charter as well as its working methods, highlighting the fundamental importance of political will and the role of non-permanent Security Council members.

Fiona Blyth, a member of the Permanent Mission of the United Kingdom to the UN, and Patrick Cammaert, a former UN Military Adviser and Force Commander, together consider the use of force to protect civilians in UN peacekeeping operations. The authors examine the framework under which force is authorized to protect civilians, the role that force can play in the protection of civilian populations, and the challenges facing the UN when deploying forces with protection mandates. Using examples drawn from the authors' respective operational experiences, they argue that for force to be effectively employed, troops must be well trained and equipped, supported by adequate assets, and led by visionary and proactive commanders at all levels. To allow adequate resources to be mobilized, there must be political cohesion at the strategic level among UN Member States and within the Secretariat with a focus on effects-based force generation. The authors also consider a number of political challenges, including differing interpretations by troop contributors of protection of civilians mandates, a lack of political will to implement such mandates to their fullest extent, and the need to hold troop contributors accountable for mandate implementation. Above all, they assert that that there must be a political peace process in place, without which the impact of any military operations will be transitory.

Stian Kjeksrud, a researcher at the Norwegian Defence Research Establishment (FFI) and at the time of writing resident at the University of Cape Town, uses empirical analysis to consider the utility of military force to protect civilians. He seeks to develop conclusions about the utility of the use of force, drawing on an assessment of 188 military protection operations across ten UN peacekeeping missions in Africa during the period 1999–2014. Based on analysis of data, he tests a theory regarding the effective use of force for the protection of civilians. Mr Kjeksrud concludes that the ways in which UN peacekeepers apply force to protect civilians can be improved. Not only do UN forces seldom respond to 'force with force', but when they do, in most cases they seem unable to effectively protect civilians. Presenting typologies of force used by protectors and perpetrators, he argues that there is substantive support for claiming that if the types of force employed by UN peacekeepers were better suited to address the types of violence exerted by the perpetrators, more civilians would be protected in the majority of cases.

Michael Keating, at the time of writing Associate Director, Research Partnerships at Chatham House, and Richard Bennett, Amnesty International's Representative in New York, examine the contribution of human rights to protecting people in conflict. The authors consider the link between human rights and the protection of civilians and describe human rights protection practice, using examples from

Sri Lanka, Afghanistan, and South Sudan. Drawing on the three case studies, the authors conclude that UN human rights protection practice can significantly contribute to overarching civilian protection objectives before, during, and after conflicts. However, they find that despite a strong normative basis and renewed determination by the UN, serious challenges persist with regard to operationalizing human rights standards and ensuring that human rights work plays a full part in protection strategies on the ground.

Sara Pantuliano and Eva Svoboda, both from the Humanitarian Policy Group at the Overseas Development Institute (ODI), discuss the humanitarian elements of protection. The authors describe the humanitarian protection policy framework and humanitarian protection practice, noting a significant gap between the two. They argue that the lack of definitional clarity of the concept of humanitarian protection, a proliferation of protection actors, and differing mandates and objectives have all contributed to disjointed humanitarian protection activity, even as mechanisms such as the Inter-Agency Standing Committee (IASC) aim to counter this effect. Humanitarian actors recognize that an improved collective analysis of protection threats and needs is critical for protection work to influence the behaviour of armed actors and thus better protect affected communities. The authors assert that too often local actors are insufficiently incorporated into the humanitarian response, and improved collective analysis needs to reflect the role of local actors who have knowledge of and networks among communities. They conclude that, regardless of protection actors' involvement, the local population ultimately constitutes the first line of defence when people are threatened. Civilians' own activities are frequently the most important element of their survival based on an often sophisticated and intricate understanding of the threats they face.

Lise Grande, who currently serves as the Deputy Special Representative of the Secretary-General for the UN Assistance Mission in Iraq and has been a UN Development Programme (UNDP) Resident Coordinator in India and South Sudan, considers the problems and dilemmas of building national capacity to protect civilians. Although most international effort to protect civilians focuses on military intervention, humanitarian relief, or promotion of human rights, State responsibility for the security and safety of the people who live within their borders is the end-goal of the 'protection chain'. Ms Grande examines the strategies that international actors use to help build the capacity of States to protect their own people, questioning whether the approaches being used are effective and, if not, what the preferred alternatives are. She describes capacity-building practice and notes that there are two primary competing approaches: rapidly and rigorously pursuing the security and safety of civilians, or working to establish institutions of governance and justice as State-building priorities. While recognizing the risks, the author assesses that a 'security-first' approach, giving priority to building the capacity of a State to ensure the safety of its population is the most pragmatic means of achieving the end-goal of the protection chain.

Concluding the politics and practice section, Aditi Gorur, a research analyst at the Stimson Center, and Nils Carstensen, of the Local to Global Protection Initiative, consider community self-protection. Discussions on the protection of civilians frequently focus on what the international community, governments, or armed groups do or fail to do to protect civilians. Yet often it is civilians themselves who do the most to guarantee their own safety, and the safety of their families and communities. The authors explore the importance of understanding local perspectives on protection and review current efforts to support individual self-protection and community-based protection strategies. Based on research in several major crises, they seek to demonstrate how understanding and supporting community-based protection strategies in a flexible and sensitive manner can significantly improve the impact of protection interventions by both affected communities themselves and external humanitarian, human rights, or peacekeeping protection actors.

Informed by the rich analysis provided by our contributors, we conclude this volume with a humble attempt to offer a holistic vision of the protection of civilians, in particular, to reconcile definitions, identify a cohesive legal framework, and find complementarities in protection activities. The issue is as complicated and diverse as the conflicts in which it arises. But it is imperative to clear the extraneous political machinations and institutional skirmishes, to focus cleanly and clearly on saving civilian lives. It is as difficult and as simple as that.

PART I

CONCEPTUAL AND HISTORICAL FOUNDATIONS

1

Civilians, Distinction, and the Compassionate View of War

Hugo Slim[1]

I. Introduction

The idea of the civilian in war arises from an enduring human conviction that there should be some compassion and restraint in armed conflict. This view of war reaches far back in time and seems to hold a permanent, if fragile, place within the human conscience. It can be found in most ancient religious texts and many epic stories, which tell tales of mercy bestowed by warriors and kings on individuals and groups. It is widely held that there is virtue in restraint. War is not always required to be extremely brutal. War's violence need not be heaped upon everyone but can be properly confined to a warrior class and to what we today might call 'green on green', in which men (and increasingly women) in combat battle-dress fight other men and women also in khaki.

Although persistent, this restrained and compassionate view of war struggles to prevail against a more violent view. Compassion has very seldom dominated the actual practice of war around the globe. It may do so occasionally in wars of choice or in counter-insurgencies that are more concerned with maintaining global influence than ensuring national survival. Such campaigns prioritize winning the support of strategic civilian populations and so tend to be kinder to them. However, in existential wars when our very homes, families, and nations are at stake and we have no tactical reason to court an enemy population, our standards tend to drop and the infliction of widespread suffering becomes strategic or cathartic. In this, democracies showed themselves no different to anybody else during the Second World War and the Vietnam War. It is as if we humans have two ways of doing war: nicely or nastily, compassionately or ruthlessly. Yet, the past sixty years have seen a dramatic surge in international norms and laws that prioritize compassion and seem to place the individual as the main object of concern in war, over and above

[1] *The research leading to this chapter has received funding from the European Research Council under the European Union's Seventh Framework Agreement (FP/2007-2013)/ERC Grant Agreement n. [340956].*

the strategic purpose of the State.[2] Resolutions of the United Nations (UN) Security Council since the first Iraq War in 1991 have become preoccupied with the treatment of civilians in conflicts within and between its Member States.[3]

In this chapter, I examine the ethical background to this compassionate view of war as it is epitomized in the strong doctrine of civilians that has emerged in modern times, and the distinction between those who fight and those who don't. I explore the two traditions of ruthless and limited war and the strong rhetorical and operational emergence of compassion and restraint in international society in modern history. I also explore the victimhood and agency that characterizes civilian experience to see how this can cause ethical and legal ambiguity that rightly queries a simplistic notion of distinction. I then examine why most war ideologues still opt for a more ruthless form of violence than the espoused norm and how this poses several ethical and legal problems for the wider project of restraint. Finally, I argue for continued normative and legal consolidation around the ethics of compassionate war, even if sometimes fighting a losing battle with actual practice. In doing so, I support a generous and forgiving definition of the civilian that goes beyond the norm of giving ambiguous civilians the benefit of the doubt to actually recognizing the certainty of their role as enemies sometimes. Accepting civilian identity means knowing that civilians are involved against us. It is not a moral label we grant them only when we feel they are neutral or are not sure if they are acting against us. 'Civilian' is an identity primarily based on our enemy's humanity as well as on the extent of their involvement in violence against us.

II. Two Traditions

In human history there has always been a range of views about the limits that should be placed on human violence. More often than not, organized human violence—as war, rebellion, or raid—has been content to set no moral limits. The majority of military, political, religious, and moral cultures across the world have often found it right and reasonable to kill and hurt extensively. Ancient and modern tribal raids alike have made common practice of killing unarmed men, women, and children, burning their houses, destroying their crops, and stealing their livestock and possessions. In urban wars, conquered cities have been customarily ransacked, with men murdered, women and children enslaved, and a policy of pillage that traditionally served as military reward. Rape, torture, ransom, and imprisonment have almost always been routine wherever war has been pursued. Violence against

[2] Gabriella Blum, 'The Individualization of War: From War to Policing in the Regulation of Armed Conflicts', in Austin Sarat, Lawrence Douglas, and Martha Merrill Umphreys (eds), *War and Law* (Stanford, USA: Stanford University Press, 2013) 48–83; Hugo Slim, 'Protecting Civilians: Putting the Individual at the Centre', in *The Humanitarian Decade: Challenges for Humanitarian Assistance in the Last Decade and into the Future* (New York: United Nations, 2004) 154–70.

[3] For example, see United Nations Security Council Resolution (UNSC Res) 1265 (1999) UN Doc S/RES/1265; UNSC Res 1296 (2000) UN Doc S/RES/1296; UNSC Res 1502 (2003) UN Doc S/RES/1502; UNSC Res 1894 (2009) UN Doc S/RES/1894.

non-combatants has been largely unlimited and usually encouraged in the history of war.[4]

Cross-cultural continuity in this tradition of limitless violence in war is striking. Very few cultures, old and new, can boast a military tradition that is a consistent exception to this norm of extreme and limitless violence.[5] Mostly male political leaders and their military subordinates have either embraced such violence as essential to an ethic of war, or found strong reasons to argue for its application as exceptional necessity.[6] Yet, alongside the blood and horror of this predominant ideology and practice of war, there has always co-existed a weaker but resilient ethic of restraint, which argues for clear boundaries to killing, hurting, stealing, and destroying. This different moral view of organized human violence insists that we should kill and hurt each other as little as possible in war as well as peace. A spirit of compassion rather than domination drives this view of the ethics of war. It is a moral tradition that takes ethical account of human suffering. The compassionate ideologues of war see suffering as a profound problem in war, and not simply an objective or inevitable consequence of war.

In human history this compassionate view has been cherished in religious and secular ethics. However, all the big global religions have an intellectual and moral history of ambivalence around restraint in war. They routinely espouse compassionate war but can also abandon it in favour of religiously justified brutality. Nevertheless, religious ideals insist on political and personal restraint in war. Politically, they argue that war should only ever be a last resort. This principle was a keystone of rather minimal medieval Christian ideas of a 'just war' that also insisted on just cause, just means, legitimate authority, and a reasonable prospect of success.[7] The rights and wrongs of going to war became termed *ad bellum* ethics. *Ad bellum* decisions turned on whether or not the use of force could be morally and legally justified. If force was deployed, religious recommendations on personal good conduct to the warrior emphasized mercy alongside courage and self-sacrifice. These restraints were commonly developed into codes of honour that idealized a certain kind of virtuous warrior in all global faiths. These codes concerned *in bello* ethics, the right things to do once engaged in war. In the European Christian tradition, it took shape in codes of chivalry for Christian knights, which framed their fighting role as pious and protective of the weak.[8] These early *in bello* ethics have developed into modern *in bello* legal concerns regarding the 'conduct of hostilities'.

As early modern Europe began its imperial expansions, the encounter with what later post-modernists would grimly call the global 'other' raised new questions about restraint in war. These turned on whether people wickedly termed 'savages' by Europeans should be considered as humans in war. European Christianity was

[4] Hugo Slim, *Killing Civilians: Method, Madness and Morality in War* (London: Hurst, 2007) 37–120.

[5] Ibid.

[6] Ibid., 121–80; see also, Alexander Downes, *Targeting Civilians in War* (Ithaca, USA: Cornell University Press, 2008).

[7] Alex Bellamy, *Just Wars from Cicero to Iraq* (Cambridge: Polity, 2006) 117–34; Nigel Biggar, *In Defence of War* (Oxford: Oxford University Press, 2014) 3.

[8] Maurice Keen, *Chivalry* (New Haven, USA: Yale University Press, 2005) 162–78.

torn on this point. Gradually, determined Catholic priests such as Francisco de Vitoria and Francisco Suarez argued for the same rights of all people to be treated as human. This universalist thinking was then taken up in the rise of secularism. New thinkers of the Enlightenment (such as Vattel, Grotius, Voltaire, and Rousseau) won the day to extend compassion to all in an updated doctrine of Just War and the beginnings of the international regulation of war.

Legally, this more compassionate ideology of war now emerged forcefully in Enlightenment Europe to dictate the rhetoric of modern international laws of war as they were developed in political conferences in St Petersburg, The Hague, Geneva, and New York, from the late nineteenth century to the early twenty-first century.[9] This shift in emphasis in the espoused ethics of war in international relations is signified in our own times by recent changes in the nomenclature of this particular body of ethics and its laws. More traditionally described as 'the laws of war', with the emphasis on the violence of the field, these various conventions are now more commonly called 'international humanitarian law', a term which puts the emphasis on compassion in war. Bizarrely, this new title gives no hint of violence and no clue as to the law's specific field of concern. The shift in international terminology from 'war' to 'armed conflict' is similarly revealing. Armed conflict emphasizes the idea of a dispute with weapons, but still a dispute that is subject to the logic and restraint of human reason. This is very different to war, which resonates in our consciousness as a terrible force of nature—primordial, epic, and beyond human control once it is unleashed. Despite the hope placed in the restraining influence of a new more reasonable name, politically organized human violence remains awful for most civilians. Like Shakespeare's rose, a name change does not bring about a category change. A war by any other name is still as bad.

III. Wounded and Combatants First

A major element in this formal compassionate turn in the ethics of war has been a move in international morality and law away from an original emphasis on the individual combatant to a gradual concern for the individual non-combatant or, as he and she would come to be called, the 'civilian'. Contrary to popular adage, the development of the laws of war did not start with women and children first, but with a primary concern for wounded combatants. In the modern legal development of the laws of war, there was for some time a curious blind spot over the suffering and involvement of non-combatants. The First Geneva Convention of 1864 expressed a compassionate concern for the individual wounded soldier. Subsequent Hague conventions were primarily concerned with the excessive effects of particular armaments on the individual combatant. This was an ethics and a set of laws about protecting individual soldiers in armies at war, and not about protecting

[9] See generally, Geoffrey Best, *Humanity in Warfare* (London: Weidenfeld and Nicholson, 1980); Geoffrey Best, *War and Law Since 1945* (Oxford, UK: Oxford University Press, 1945).

ordinary people in the much larger population that were negatively affected by these armies in a wide variety of ways.

This early, singular focus on military suffering did not develop because there was very little non-combatant suffering. There surely was extensive civilian suffering in many nineteenth-century European wars, and certainly had been in previous centuries. In the century before the Hague conferences, the Napoleonic Wars often took a heavy toll on non-combatant populations as food and housing were requisitioned, soldiers were billeted with local families, and insurgency and counter-insurgency in the Peninsular Wars saw scorched-earth policies and atrocities against the wider population by French and British forces. Pillage was customary, and so too were rape and punitive measures to coerce popular support for invading or occupying armies.[10]

Despite all this non-combatant suffering, concerns about the individual non-combatant never achieved significant traction in the modern ethics of war and its nascent international laws in the nineteenth century. The various Hague Conventions of the late nineteenth century remained mesmerized by combatants, with only very few articles about the rights of non-combatants under occupation or bombardment, and the consistent outlawing of pillage.

Much more explicit about non-combatants, however, was the American Lieber Code of 1863, albeit drafted by a former Prussian officer.[11] It was produced for Unionist forces in the bitter struggle of the American Civil War, which saw considerable civilian suffering.[12] This national military code was no simple civilians' charter. While Lieber recognized the place of morality and crimes in war and the need to avoid wanton violence, rape, and pillage of the non-combatant population, he also inserted the stern principle of military necessity. The demands of victory could rightly require policies of starvation or forced movement, and the lives and property of non-combatants could not be taken for granted if their destruction became essential to winning.[13]

In the Lieber Code, rather than the early Hague and Geneva conventions, the modern laws of war finally began to recover much earlier and more nuanced principles that valued limit and restraint, but also arguments of necessity that justified a moral breach of such restraint. Medieval principles of protection for the weak and non-combatant population in war had been developed to protect the peasant population of Europe from a marauding and perpetually belligerent nobility, especially in France, where non-combatant protection became central to

[10] Gregory Fremont-Barnes, *The Napoleonic Wars: The Peninsular War 1807–1814* (Oxford, UK: Osprey Publishing, 2002) 8, 36–8, 53–74, 85; see generally, Alan I Forrest, Karen Hagemann, and Jane Rendall (eds), *Soldiers, Citizens and Civilians: Experiences and Perceptions of the Revolutionary and Napoleonic Wars, 1790–1820* (New York: Palgrave Macmillan, 2009).

[11] United States, 'General Orders No. 100, Adjutant General's Office, 1863' (Washington: US Government Printing Office, 1898) <www.icrc.org/ihl/INTRO/110> (the Lieber Code).

[12] See generally, Mark Grimsley, *The Hard Hand of War: Union Military Policy toward Southern Civilians, 1861–1865* (Cambridge, UK: Cambridge University Press, 1997); and Joan E Cashin (ed.), *The War Was You and Me: Civilians in the American Civil War* (Princeton, USA: Princeton University Press, 2002).

[13] Lieber Code (1863), see n 11, Articles 15 and 16.

the Peace of God negotiated between the Church and nobility.[14] The Latin word 'innocens', meaning not harming, was chosen to describe this wider group who deserved immunity from conflicts in which they played no active part.[15] This principle of separation and protection on the basis of harmlessness continued to be fostered by significant parts of the Church in European conflicts, if not in its own crusading wars against the 'infidel' in the Near East or Spanish wars of conquest against 'savages' in the Americas, where standards were evidently lower.[16] Lieber grappled with the moral tensions within the compassionate tradition in a way that his contemporary European tradition did not.

IV. The First World War and the Advent of the Civilian

Although there were always some provisions favouring non-combatants in nineteenth and very early twentieth-century laws of war, the big international step change towards a significant focus on non-combatant populations in the modern world emerged in the First World War. This global war simultaneously threw new light on two hard truths in the ethics of non-combatant experience in war, one simple and one rather more complex. The simple truth was that the non-combatant population of Europe, Central Asia, Africa, and the Middle East suffered extremely as a result of war. In her impressive analysis of civilian experience in the First World War, Tammy Proctor shows how individual atrocity, massacre, bombardment, displacement, starvation, forced labour, hostage taking, detention, and rape were marked features of the war.[17] Some ten million people were displaced between 1914 and 1918. Hundreds of thousands of displaced people and deprived populations from the Central Powers died from war-related disease and starvation. Civilians were massacred in numerous different places and Armenians in Anatolia were targeted *en masse* in what would later be recognized as genocide. There were sharp rises in organized prostitution, which sent the rates of venereal disease soaring across Europe and the Middle East. Many thousands of 'enemy aliens' were detained in prison camps by both sides for the duration of the war. People's houses, horses, and food were requisitioned on a grand scale. Many thousands of rural East African men were coerced into war-related wage labour, leaving a dangerous lack of agricultural labour. This combined with crop requisitioning to create a devastating famine in what is contemporary Tanzania.

In response to this widespread suffering, international practice in support of non-combatants during the war steamed ahead of existing international norms and legal rules. Proctor's work also reveals how the First World War saw the coming of age of international humanitarian relief to non-combatant victims of war, and the

[14] Robert Schütte, *Civilian Protection in Armed Conflicts: Evolution, Challenges and Implementation* (Berlin: Springer, VS, 2015) 51–3.

[15] Slim, see n 4, 13.

[16] See generally Ross Hassig, *Mexico and the Spanish Conquest* (Norman, USA: University of Oklahoma Press, 2006).

[17] See generally Tammy Proctor, *Civilians in a World at War 1914–1918* (New York: New York University Press, 2010).

extension of the principle of humanitarian neutrality to relief work with non-combatants as well as combatants. State and private relief societies boomed and the non-combatant became a central ethical focus in the war. The American government led unprecedented food relief operations while it was still neutral before entering the war in 1917. The International Committee of the Red Cross (ICRC) came of age and was transformed from a staff of 10 to 1,500. Red Cross and Red Crescent societies reached out beyond their core mission to wounded combatants and prisoners of war, to help sick, hungry, and detained non-combatants. The Quakers and the Young Men's Christian Association (YMCA) expanded dramatically, and Save the Children was born in 1919 as a post-war response to continuing starvation in Austria and Germany.

The simple truth about non-combatants made plain by the First World War was that, in modern war as well, the non-combatant population fell victim to the effects of armies and armed conflict to an extreme and easily observable degree. Therefore, their suffering and their relief must also be of concern to the ethics of war, and to any new laws of war. Civilians rightly became central moral subjects in the ethics and practice of war.

The more complex truth about non-combatants to emerge from the First World War was that they did not simply suffer in war and inhabit some politically neutral space. Many also took sides in the war, played supporting roles, and were often anything but neutral.[18] This truth was not a new one but it was now a very obvious one in the first 'total war' in which strong central governments could mobilize and orchestrate their whole nation for war. War work became the norm for most people on what was described explicitly as 'the home front'. Some women worked in bomb factories or as farmers to increase food production for the war. Other women and children prepared millions of 'comfort packages' for soldiers on the front line. Many men, women, and children campaigned vocally for victory. Others campaigned for peace, and might be arrested for doing so. Many male non-combatants were formed into volunteer defence forces, carrying weapons but not wearing uniforms. As airpower and marine artillery enabled both sides to reach behind enemy lines, these non-combatants actively supporting military activity increasingly appeared as ever more legitimate targets in war.

Here was complexity indeed for an ethical and legal understanding of non-combatants, which would require significant attention in the developing ethics and laws of war. This hard truth raised important questions about the ambiguity of non-combatant identity and the uncomfortable fact that participation in war can take several different forms. This truth, combined with Lieber's consequentialist recognition that it might sometimes be necessary to breach non-combatant ethics in order to meet the greater moral goal of victory, meant that the law and ethics of non-combatant protection would never be as simple as it seemed.

The term 'civilian' was not used in any medieval or renaissance discussions of the ethics of war, or in any nineteenth and early twentieth-century conventions on the

[18] Ibid., chapter 3; and Peter Cooksley, *Home Front: Civilian Life in World War One* (Stroud, UK: The History Press, 2006).

ethics and laws of war. Instead, the wider population in a war was described as unarmed inhabitants, peasantry, non-combatants, the enemy population, or the occupied population. It is important to realize, therefore, that when we use the term 'civilian' referring to people before the First World War, we use it anachronistically. It was only in the 1920s that the ICRC began to take a systematic interest in a possible law relating to 'civilians'. In 1929, States party to the Geneva Conventions asked the ICRC to set up a commission on civilians.[19] This produced the first draft convention on civilians, which was dismissed by the major powers at the Red Cross conference in Tokyo in 1934.[20]

So, the world went into the Second World War with no major international convention protecting 'civilians'. This was a war that saw civilians deliberately targeted in massive industrial-scale attacks that included the Nazi genocide against Europe's Jewish communities and extensive aerial bombardment, blockade, and siege by all sides. Japanese atrocities against civilians in Asia were extensive, as were the Japanese army's industrial-scale policies of women's sexual enslavement. Millions of people were displaced, destitute, hungry, and dramatically impoverished. Millions of families were broken up, many forever. At the end of the war, there were an estimated thirteen million unaccompanied children roaming around Europe.[21]

V. Civilian Experience in War

In its extraordinary global scale, the Second World War epitomized the variety of ways in which civilians experience war and always have done. They experience it as both victims and agents. As victims, they suffer its effects directly and indirectly in a number of ways. As agents of their own survival, they are extremely busy doing a variety of things to ensure that they and their families cope with what are often extreme changes imposed upon them.

A. Civilian victims

Civilian suffering can be conveniently—if a little simplistically—summarized into seven spheres.[22] The first sphere is suffering inflicted directly upon the body as death or injury from physical attack of some kind. This might be from bombardment, gunfire, a machete, or torture. The second form of suffering is the experience of rape and sexual violence. This is another direct assault upon a person's body. Such personalized violence also qualifies as torture and is often deliberately administered as such. It also often involves enslavement of some kind. It is now more openly

[19] Slim, see n 4, 19.

[20] Phillipe Abplanalp, 'The International Conferences of the Red Cross as a Factor for the Development of International Humanitarian Law and the Cohesion of the International Red Cross and Red Crescent Movement' (1995) 35 IRRC 520.

[21] Nicholas Stargardt, *Witnesses of War: Children's Lives Under the Nazis* (London: Jonathan Cape, 2005) 357.

[22] Slim, see n 4, 37–120.

acknowledged that rape and sexual violence in war are inflicted upon women and men, girls and boys, very young and very old.[23]

These bodily attacks on civilians are a terrible feature of most wars. However, with some exceptions, these direct physical assaults do not usually account for the most common forms of civilian suffering or the highest civilian mortality rates in most wars. In genocides or wars in middle-income countries like Syria or Bosnia which have more robust economies, these direct forms of suffering do tend to account for the highest number of deaths. In much poorer societies where people routinely live much closer to subsistence, people tend to suffer and die more often from a damaging spiral of movement and impoverishment than they do from shrapnel, bullet, or blade.

The third form of civilian suffering sets this spiral in train and is best described as spatial suffering. The first casualty of war is not usually truth, as the proverb would have it, but space. In some form or other, war is typically a struggle for territory. A key military and political goal in war is to dominate space by force or fear. Attacks, threats, checkpoints, mines, improvised explosive devices (IEDs), terror tactics, infrastructure destruction, or deliberate policies of forceful population clearance create sudden and sustained changes in civilian space. The habitual social, economic, and cultural space of civilian populations is typically transformed by war. Schools, markets, and workplaces no longer exist or are simply too dangerous to visit. Travel of any kind can become life-threatening. Flight can become the wisest option, so that people's space is suddenly extended by hundreds of miles. They arrive in a strange place where they are usually confined in a humanitarian camp of some kind or held within the generosity of a host family. Both spaces may be life-saving but they are also life-changing.

These spatial changes usually bring with them impoverishment and often destitution of some kind, which is the fourth sphere of civilian suffering. With no job or no livelihood, people sell precious assets and gradually become much poorer so that impoverishment becomes the fourth sphere of suffering. Sometimes this impoverishment can be corrected or relieved by strong humanitarian programmes or access to new work. In many poor societies at war, however, impoverishment often leads fast to destitution. Humanitarian programmes can be under-funded, logistically difficult, late, or politically blocked—as they have been recently in Syria, in Somalia in 2011, in South Sudan in 2014, and, most famously perhaps, in Ethiopia in 1985.[24] In such cases, poor people's destitution can soon become catastrophic. Hunger follows fast. Hard on its heels comes disease, which always accompanies hunger, frequently to deal its deathblow. These two debilitating conditions make up the fifth sphere of civilian suffering. In most rural wars in poor countries, it is deaths from starvation and disease that lead the mortality rates in

[23] See Sandesh Sivakumaran, 'Sexual Violence Against Men in Armed Conflict' (2007) 8 EJIL 253.

[24] Hugo Slim and Lorenzo Trombetta, 'Syria Common Context Analysis, Report for the Inter-Agency Standing Committee' (New York: United Nations, 2014) <docs. unocha. org/sites/dms/Documents/Syria%20Crisis%20Common%20Context%20Analysis_June%202014. pdf>; Hugo Slim, 'Inter-Agency Standing Committee Synthesis Report of the Real-Time Evaluation of the Humanitarian Response to the Horn of Africa Crisis' (New York: United Nations, 2012) <ochanet. unocha. org/p/Documents/RTE_HoA_SynthesisReport_FINAL. Pdf>.

civilian suffering. In poor wars, the great majority of people are not killed by violent hands but die from war's socio-economic effects. Such deaths are the terrible structural violence of war and are frequently designed as strategy by warring parties eager to ethnically cleanse, punish, or break an enemy population.

The sixth sphere of civilian suffering is emotional distress and long-term loss. It hurts to lose family, friends, home, job, professional identity, and an anticipated future. Grief is deep and the change in personal horizon is permanent. No more are the people you loved, and who loved you. No more is the future that you had in mind. Now there is only starting again. Queuing at a water pump in an internally displaced persons (IDPs) camp in the only clothes you have when you used to be a primary school teacher, farmer, shopkeeper, or civil servant can be bewildering. War also reduces the future post-conflict life chances of civilians. This future damage is the seventh form of civilian suffering. Years of schooling can be lost forever for a generation of children whose schools were destroyed or for whom it was too dangerous to go to school. People may never be as well or live as long as they might have done because they have been badly wounded, starved, or are simply much poorer than they were before the war.

These patterns of suffering encompass the essential concept of civilians being victims of war. As a result, the modern definition of war crimes focuses on the deliberate infliction of such suffering. The fundamental objective of preventing such suffering forms the basis of the 'protection of civilians' concept and the 'responsibility to protect' doctrine. Preventing, mitigating, or remedying these main forms of suffering have come to be key areas of focus in the provision of international humanitarian assistance, human rights advocacy, military activity, and international litigation. The many recent manuals and guides on protecting civilians through humanitarian assistance concern themselves with these dynamics of civilian victimhood.[25]

B. Civilian agency

But civilians are not only victims of war. They are also agents of survival, resistance, and peace. The significance of civilian agency has been rightly highlighted by important fieldwork in recent African wars by Erin Baines and Emily Paddon.[26] An understanding of this aspect of the civilian experience is equally important to any meaningful development of the ethics and laws of war. Civilian agency seems to come in six main forms: personal survival, business activity, humanitarian and

[25] For further discussion, see Hugo Slim and Andrew Bonwick, *Protection: A Guide for Humanitarian Agencies* (London: Overseas Development Institute, 2005); Hugh Breakey et al., 'Enhancing Protection Capacity: Policy Guide to the Responsibility to Protect and the Protection of Civilians in Armed Conflicts' (Brisbane: Griffith University, 2012) <isp.unu. edu/publications/files/R2P_POC_Policy_Guide.pdf>; and Global Center for the Responsibility to Protect, 'The Relationship Between the Responsibility to Protect and the Protection of Civilians in Armed Conflict' (New York: Global Center for the Responsibility to Protect, 2009) <www.globalr2p.org/media/files/the-relationship-between-r2p-and-poc-in-armed-conflict-brief-21-june-2012.pdf>.

[26] Erin Baines and Emily Paddon, '"This is how we survived": Civilian Agency and Humanitarian Protection' (2012) 43 Security Dialogue 231.

human rights activism, civil resistance and support, peace activism, and coerced involvement in military activity.

Personal and family survival is the primary motivation of most civilians. Rightly, they feel it an ethical imperative to do the best for their family and community, and to ensure the maximum protection of human life and personal dignity. As a result, the search for safety, food, health, and income become matters of great urgency and activism. In contrast to what most aid agencies show us in the photographic constructs of their fundraising advertisements, civilians in war are typically extremely busy, innovative, and active—the prime movers and makers of their own survival.[27] We tend to see people in front of a camera but getting to that camera may well have involved hard decisions about when and how to flee, followed by a two-week walk, the judicious sale of assets, careful avoidance or accommodation of armed forces, and significant stamina and courage. Humanitarians rightly distinguish between positive and negative coping strategies in their understanding of civilian self-protection. Positive strategies involve flight, collaborative resource sharing, the division of risk across family units, innovative trading relations, sustained livelihoods, and dignified engagement with humanitarian aid. Negative coping strategies include last-resort measures like survival sex, criminality, violence, and unfair exploitation of humanitarian services.

Many civilian businesses manage to survive in war, and some adapt and thrive as key suppliers to the military or humanitarian agencies.[28] In this way, civilian businesses provide supplies that are critical to the war economy, the humanitarian economy, or both. Hoteliers, landlords, banks, moneychangers, food and pharmaceutical suppliers, fuel companies, trucking businesses, and security companies all support the big end of the humanitarian sector. Petty traders, moneylenders, and mobile phone companies all become central to the survival of individuals within the civilian population. Many of these businesses are run by civilians, employ civilians, and enable the survivalist agency of the general civilian population[29]—although, of course, ownership of strategic businesses in any war economy is often captured by big military or political players who function more as military profiteers than as legitimate civilian business people.

Many civilians also adopt formal or informal humanitarian or human rights roles in war. They form vital community initiatives that may offer shelter, food, and water to neighbours, or take part in various early warning activities to alert people to violent raids and threats of various kinds. Local humanitarian and human rights activism has been a hallmark of the Syrian civil war, especially in hard-to-reach areas where international agencies have been denied access.[30] Many thousands of civilians also join the staff of formal humanitarian agencies to work to protect and relieve their fellow citizens or refugees from neighbouring countries. These roles

[27] Ibid., 231.

[28] Hugo Slim, 'Business Actors in Armed Conflict: Understanding Roles and Responsibilities' (2012) 94 IRRC 903.

[29] Gilles Carbonnier, *Humanitarian Economics: War, Disaster and the Global Aid Market* (Hurst/Oxford University Press, 2015), chapter 3.

[30] Slim and Trombetta, see n 24, 43, 57–8.

provide humanitarian assistance to others, an important salary, and an element of international protection for their own families.

Many civilians often go one step further than survival, business, and humanitarian activism to engage in civil resistance or support of some kind. Resistance may include explicit protests against the political logic and practice of war or occupation. This kind of confrontational civil resistance has been most obvious in conflicts against dictatorships like Argentina's.[31] It is also common in continuing Palestinian and Israeli protests in their conflict over State formation and occupation. Israelis and Palestinian civilians alike protest frequently and publicly within this conflict as an instrument of resistance against occupation. In its *intifada* culture, Palestinian protest typically moves from non-violent to violent activity using small rocks and petrol bombs that change the military and legal dynamic of the confrontation. When overt protest and resistance becomes too dangerous (as it usually does), civil resistance is often more subtle and covert, its aim being to subvert rather than confront. In most wars which involve forces moving through or occupying enemy territory, civilians will co-operate frostily in a way that signals their resistance without endangering their lives. They will stall and delay their response to enemy requests, cook bad food for occupying troops, use silence to render enemies uncomfortable, write resistant graffiti, or make small gestures and tell jokes that safely ridicule the enemy.

In wars that have a high level of popular support, civilian communities often engage in active war work or solidarity movements of some kind to support their community's war effort. The Syrian civil war has seen a wide variety of opposition efforts by the civilian community to support the military uprising with cash, food, and international campaigning through social media. In Britain, the wars in Iraq and Afghanistan have generated a range of support movements akin to those that developed in the First World War. New fundraising efforts like 'Help for Heroes' have mobilized popular support for wounded soldiers.[32] Journalists and commentators have written in support of the war (and against it) and radio programmes have played requests for fighting men and women. The national flag and bumper stickers have been paraded in support of 'our boys'. In some conflicts, it is clear that large numbers of civilians have taken sides so that there is majority or near-unanimous support for war. But many wars are also deeply disputed across a civilian population, as the Afghan and Iraq wars have been in the UK. Scholars have rightly noted that it is a humanitarian conceit to pretend that civilians are somehow only political objects and not political subjects in war.[33] They are usually very much the latter. In some elite-led wars, such as African civil wars, the majority of civilians take no sides and wish a plague on both houses of governments and armed groups. But in most wars, civilians have a view and are part of the socio-political movement that constructs and resources one or other side of the conflict.

[31] Robert Adams and Timothy Garton Ash, *Civil Resistance and Power Politics: The Experience of Non-Violent Action from Gandhi to the Present Day* (Oxford, UK: Oxford University Press, 2011) 14.

[32] See 'Help for Heroes' (Help for Heroes, undated) <www. helpforheroes.org.uk>.

[33] Helen Kinsella, *The Image before the Weapon: A Critical History of the Distinction Between Combatant and Civilian* (Ithaca, USA: Cornell University Press, 2011) 5.

Peace activism is another way in which civilians take up specific agency in an effort to transform a war's politics and practice. A recent example of such a movement is the mobilization and success of the Liberian women's peace movement and the role it played in forcing and sustaining a UN peace process.[34] In many other conflicts, civilians join in peace efforts as non-governmental organizations (NGOs) and are increasingly funded to do so by international aid from western governments.

Finally, civilian agency is frequently coerced. It is hard to say 'no' if an armed group is taking cover in your village, an occupying force is controlling your city, or units of your national army are positioned in your offices or billeted in your house. Civilians are often forced into some form of involvement in war: giving information, making food, offering shelter, and having sex. All these are not easily or wisely refused. There is also the force of love. Wondrously and dangerously enemies can fall in love in war, a phenomenon that is often hushed up but has been beautifully evoked by Jean Renoir and Irene Nemirovsky, among others.[35] Perhaps falling in love across the lines of conflict is also coerced in some way and beyond our control, imposed on us by Cupid's power if not by a conventional force. But romance is certainly another way in which we cannot help blurring lines in war.

Many of these forms of civilian agency are part of our more primary survival strategy. We seek safety, do business, help others, resist, support, work for peace, co-operate with the enemy, and make love because we think it gives us and those we love our best chance to survive, and later to thrive. Yet, some of these things can look like an unreasonable involvement in war, one that verges on participation. This ambiguity threatens one of the ancient pillars of the compassionate view of war—the principle of distinction.

VI. Challenging Distinction

The core principle of distinction in the compassionate view of war rests upon the simple moral premise that one should never harm someone who has no means of harming you. To do so would be a disproportionate and unjust use of violence. This principle turns on the medieval notion of innocence as 'not harming'. It sits at the heart of the modern ethics of war and is entrenched within the prohibitions and injunctions of international humanitarian law. But in her critical history of distinction, Helen Kinsella reminds us that we have created the categories of combatant and civilian, and that we tend to recreate them anew in each conflict as we determine who is innocent and how. As she points out, 'the persistence of this question [of the indeterminacy of distinction] and the historical attempts to resolve it are remarkable in their consistency, arising not only during attempts to codify war but also during the practice of war'.[36] Determining who is innocent and so what makes

[34] *Pray the Devil Back to Hell* (Fork Films, 2008) <praythedevilbacktohell.com/impact.php>.

[35] *La Grande Illusion* (Réalisations d'Art Cinématographique, 1937); *Suite Francaise* (Chatto and Windus, 2004).

[36] Kinsella, see n 33, 68.

for a proper distinction continues to be problematic: 'innocence is, paradoxically perhaps, premised on passivity, an apolitical and dependent status that may be both impossible and dangerous to maintain in times of war.'[37] As we have seen, civilians engage in a range of different kinds of agency in war. They are not simple two-dimensional caricatures that simply suffer violence and receive aid. Most civilians are not passive but are involved in many aspects of a war. In every war, this means that the discussion of what constitutes distinction is a highly contextual determination usually made first by those inside the war. In practice, distinction is not best understood as a fixed and given principle. Instead, it is a 'productive' principle that raises a range of questions that must be answered fairly in every context, and requires a certain 'performance' by civilians themselves if they want to be counted as such.[38]

The insights of critical Foucauldian theorists like Kinsella are important upstream prompts to practical decision-making about civilian identity and the conduct of hostilities. She reminds us that in matters of civilian determination, 'doubt becomes an integral attribute of the category itself as well as the basis for an injunction to extend the category'.[39] Here she is referring to the famous clause in Article 50 of Additional Protocol I of the Geneva Conventions, which states that ' . . . in case of doubt whether a person is a civilian, that person shall be considered a civilian'. This clause reveals the chronic scepticism that exists around the determination of civilian status in every war. This scepticism is deadly to many people who should be rightly counted as civilians because most ideologues of war do not err on the side of caution and compassion, but of ruthlessness.

The limitless ideologies of war are all too content to challenge distinction as a false and sentimental conceit. This explains the wide range of anti-civilian ideologies in the ruthless tradition of war that find good reason for rejecting the category outright.[40] These ideologies include: genocidal and dualist thinking; power dominance and subjugation; visceral policies of revenge; collective punishment and forced compliance; consequentialist arguments of necessity; and deep ideas of human sacrifice.[41] In his impressive quantitative study of civilian killing in inter-State wars, Alexander Downes contributes a statistical analysis to improve our understanding of why and under what circumstances the norms protecting civilians break down. His findings identify the desperation to win and the appetite for territorial conquest as the key variables in civilian victimization.[42] A 'desperation logic' drives leaders to punish an enemy population and deny the enemy's military machine the wider civil capacity needed to win. While this is typically a strategy of last resort, civilian victimization is usually a first resort in territorial conquests when invading or annexing powers attempt to destroy resistance and fifth columns, or pursue a policy of ethnic cleansing that leaves no rationale for the enemy to retake the area.

[37] Ibid., 193, 196. [38] Ibid., 195–8. [39] Ibid., 5. [40] Slim, see n 4, 121–80.

[41] Alex Bellamy, *Massacres and Morality: Mass Atrocities in an Age of Civilian Immunity* (Oxford: Oxford University Press, 2012) 17–41; see also Jacques Sémelin, *Purify and Destroy: The Political Uses of Massacre and Genocide* (London: Hurst, 2007).

[42] See Downes, n 6.

If these various logics explain why people reject the principle of distinction and pursue limitless civilian killing, it is also necessary to explain how leaders persuade others to follow them in such policies: in other words, how it is possible to make others actually do the killing.[43] In his recent work on the 'justificatory mechanisms' of mass atrocity, Jonathan Leader Maynard combines a range of recent scholarship to systematize the many different ideological traits that leaders deploy to reject the distinction between civilians and combatants, and mobilize their population to support a policy of killing without limit.[44] His boiled-down list comes to six main ideological features. 'Dehumanization' is by now well understood as a way in which certain ideologies can deliberately erode the humanity of a particular group of enemy people, so that killing them seems to count for little. 'Guilt attribution' is the way in which ideology and false narrative load collective guilt upon a whole group, so framing victims as legitimate targets. In 'threat construction', ideology exaggerates the physical threat posed by the whole of this group that therefore demands their destruction. 'Deagentification' of the killers comes up with natural, necessary, or inevitable forces that account for civilian destruction: forces of history beyond the control of the killers which means that 'no other option but violence exists'. 'Virtue talk' then encourages killers of civilians to see a stern ethic in their actions, which leaves no room for sentiment or squeamishness and must put party or country first. A 'future bias' exists in all anti-civilian ideologies, which tend to make an extreme consequentialist and often utopian case for doing terrible things now in order to usher in a glorious future.

Violent ideologues are not the only ones challenging the idea of legitimate distinction. Revisionist just war theorists such as Jeff McMahan are also dissolving the easy case for distinction. McMahan has developed a new ethics of war that is based on personal liability and human rights responsibility.[45] To his mind, if there are just wars and unjust wars, then there are just combatants and unjust combatants. There are even just civilians and unjust civilians. McMahan argues that the distinction between just cause and just means becomes morally meaningful above all others in the ethics of war, and he introduces the principle of personal liability into just war theory. In doing so, McMahan significantly widens the net for combatant identity in war: 'all those who pose a threat in war are—by definition, it seems—combatants in the moral sense: that is in the sense of being morally legitimate targets of attack.'[46] More than this, he finds many cases supporting the idea of civilian liability.[47] Thus, many people not in uniform and not carrying arms pose a threat as bomb designers, planners, orchestrators, supporters, and so forth. And, paradoxically in current just war theory, some people in uniform do not pose a threat, such as the military legal advisors who constantly work to restrain their country's military attacks and so protect more than they harm.[48]

McMahan's theory is unnerving to people from the humanitarian tradition in which distinction and civilian protection are fixed and last-ditch points of

[43] Slim, see n 4, 213–50.

[44] Jonathan Leader Maynard, 'Rethinking the Role of Ideologies in Mass Atrocities' (2014) 26 Terrorism and Political Violence 821.

[45] Jeff McMahan, *Killing in War* (Oxford: Oxford University Press, 2008).

[46] Ibid., 12. [47] Ibid., 203–35. [48] Ibid., 12–13.

principle. His theory is especially disquieting where he cites George Orwell supporting a principle of wider targeting in war and dispelling what he considers the myth of distinction. Writing in 1944, Orwell argued that 'it does not seem a bad thing that others should be killed besides young men'.[49] In the middle of a terrible war for civilians, Orwell found wider notions of civilian liability and targeting more egalitarian, more fairly retributive, and more gender-neutral. He also thought that the more civilians suffer, the less they are likely to support and enable war in future.

Today's just war revisionists seem to be heading in the same direction as Orwell, even if, like McMahan, they still hold the line that the principle of civilian immunity remains 'a legal necessity' despite being 'false as a moral doctrine'.[50] Janina Dill and other critics of this ethical revisionism and its emphasis on individual liability are rightly concerned about the feasibility of this morality. They point out that it is highly impractical to attempt to regulate war on the same lines as peacetime justice, as during the latter evidence and due process allow us to make sound judgements on individual liability. It is simply not feasible to impose an individualist paradigm of human rights law and liability in war around the development of targeting and strategy. Such a scheme is operationally impossible most of the time, especially in large-scale attacks and in the face of threats that force an immediate response that has no certainty of outcome. Dill notes that military actions in war are often made within the moral context of an 'epistemically cloaked forced-choice' in which we have to act without clear knowledge of the outcome of our actions.[51] In such a situation, it must make sense to be guided by a broad moral distinction of civilian immunity when precise verdicts of individual liability are not possible. In other words, it makes sense to give a civilian population the benefit of the doubt in any plan of attack and protect them as a whole as much as you can.

The moral reframing of war by just war revisionists encourages a paradigm error in the ethics of war before we have evolved the necessary paradigm shift in our understanding and practice of war that is required by their theory. At this point in human affairs, it is too risky to pretend that war is similar to peace and allows sufficient time, space, and knowledge to separate the liable from the innocent before each and every attack. Playing God in this way is extremely difficult, as God himself discovered in his discussions with Abraham over the destruction of Sodom.[52] As Abraham negotiated with God, he pleaded: 'Surely you are not going to destroy the innocent along with the impious, so that the innocent will be just like the impious?' In response, God initially promised not to destroy Sodom even if there were only ten innocent people left within it. But in the end God does destroy the whole city and Abraham looks on. The compassionate view of war and its strong doctrine of the civilian rightly demands that we aim to show more restraint than God. If he can't separate the pious from the impious before a major attack, then we certainly cannot.

49 Ibid., 210. 50 Ibid., 235.

51 Janina Dill, 'Should International Law Ensure the Moral Acceptability of War?' (2013) 26 Leiden J Intl L 253.

52 *Bible* (New International Version) Genesis 18:17–33.

VII. Arguing for Civilian Protection

The various anti-civilian ideologies in the ruthless tradition of war and the new revisionism in just war theory all make the case that distinction and civilian immunity is a conceptual error, a doctrine that is more a myth rather than a right. This sceptical view of civilian identity and protection can be a persuasive one, but is misguided in my view. It is especially persuasive if you are a soldier walking through crowded streets of hostile civilians, many of whom insult you and some of whom you worry may have their finger on the button of an IED and be on the point of relinquishing their civilian status by trying to kill you. It is also a persuasive argument if you are a member of a civilian population threatened or entrapped by an enemy force and can hear the opposing civilian population baying for your blood. How can these people be innocent and uninvolved in war, and entitled to protection when they are so desirous of other people's deaths?

This ambiguity in claims to civilian identity is the challenge that the ethical and legal doctrine of the distinction of civilians from military forces has to meet. Like most important political challenges, the matter will not be settled once and for all in law or ethics but must be struggled for anew in every war. The struggle for compassionate war has to be made on the ground in practical strategies of legal enforcement by responsible governments, in compliant practice by military forces and armed groups, in effective humanitarian action, and in responsible civilian behaviour that does not set out deliberately to breach the principles of civilian immunity. On this last point, international humanitarian law and ICRC commentary as it stands must surely be right to determine that civilian status remains intact until such time as a person takes a direct part in hostilities by picking up a weapon of some kind and trying to kill or harm another person.[53]

Underwriting all this protective law and action, there is also the need for some headline ethics that can justify the international society's increasing move to the protective and compassionate practice of war, and which can cast doubt on the doubters of civilian protection. Here there is need for something simple that chimes with people's moral intuition. It is this. We all need the moral and legal principle of civilian protection because we know we should kill and hurt each other as little as possible. We also know that each of us is vulnerable to the violence of war and to its tendency to make us hate and kill people who, like us, are prone as we are to bellicose influence, group loyalty, and people of power. The doctrine of civilian protection does not emerge from doubt as a precautionary measure. Rather, it emerges from the certainty that non-combatant people in war are bound to be involved in war in various ways. But, unless they actually take up arms and try to hurt us directly, we can tolerate the political and military ambiguity in an enemy population because otherwise we would have to kill them all, which would be wrong.

The doctrine of the civilian needs to be as generous and forgiving as possible, for three main reasons. Practically, because we cannot be sure that we have the precise

[53] Nils Melzer, *Direct Participation in Hostilities Under International Humanitarian Law* (Geneva: International Committee of the Red Cross, 2009).

means to separate the innocent from the guilty as we attack people and places. Ethically, because many of the brutal things done to civilians (like rape, torture, murder, pillage, and starvation) are done without good reason and are terribly wrong. Personally, because we need the civilian label for ourselves and for our children when we too become involved in wars that may be just or unjust and are usually beyond our control.

2

Protection of Civilians, Responsibility to Protect, and Humanitarian Intervention

Conceptual and Normative Interactions

Scott Sheeran and Catherine Kent

I. Introduction

The concepts of humanitarian intervention, responsibility to protect (RtoP), and protection of civilians (PoC) are related but distinct. Each one is nourished by a range of disciplines, including international relations, philosophy, ethics, and international law. The three concepts monopolize the international legal and political lexicon for intervention and the use of force in the name of addressing human suffering. They concern not just an *authority* to act, but the *expectation*, and some might suggest *obligation*, to do so.

Each concept has a unique genesis, rationale, history, development, and acceptability, as well as discrete 'interpretive communities'.[1] PoC is best understood by peacekeeping and humanitarian communities, in contrast to humanitarian intervention and RtoP, which are better known in the political field and civil society.[2] In practical terms, PoC is the most widespread and influential of the ideas. At the time of writing, there were over 125,000 United Nations (UN) peacekeepers acting under a PoC mandate in ten countries, and humanitarian actors undertaking protection activity in many more conflicts.[3] PoC is embraced by the wider UN membership, including the Global South, as is not the case with the rejection of humanitarian intervention, or the caution associated with RtoP. Yet academic literature, policy discussions, and non-governmental organization activism have favoured a stronger focus on RtoP and, at times, even humanitarian intervention.

[1] See Stanley Fish, *Is There a Text in This Class? The Authority of Interpretive Communities* (Cambridge, USA: Harvard University Press, 1982) 167–73.

[2] See, for example, Alexander Bellamy, 'Responsibility to Protect or Trojan Horse? The Crisis in Darfur and Humanitarian Intervention after Iraq (2005) 19 Ethics and Intl Affairs 31–54; Gareth Evans, 'The Responsibility to Protect: Rethinking Humanitarian Intervention' (2004) 98 ASIL Proceedings 78–89; 'About Us' (*Global Centre for the Responsibility to Protect*, undated) <www.globalr2p.org/about_us>.

[3] United Nations Peacekeeping, *Peacekeeping Fact Sheet* (31 March 2015) <www.un.org/en/peacekeeping/resources/statistics/factsheet.shtml>.

The concepts clearly overlap, and consequently are sometimes used interchangeably, as well as differently, by various communities. All three concepts are intertwined with the law of the UN Charter, as the quasi-constitutional system governing the international use of force.[4] RtoP and PoC are particularly central in the work of the Security Council. The comparison and contrast of these concepts, and the search for their distinct meanings, reveals at a deeper level the fissures and weaknesses of the current international system. Despite being extremely powerful ideas, each concept faces significant challenges in light of the existing international framework of politics and law.

Even in light of the challenges, humanitarian intervention, RtoP, and PoC are concepts that have and will continue to play an important role in the arc of history. This is particularly so in providing normative content to international discourse, and the role of humanism in international law and politics concerning the *jus ad bellum*. They are part of the long journey since 1945. When the Charter was adopted with its original *raison d'être* of the maintenance of international peace and security, the Organization was not yet imbued with the power or authority to protect individuals.

To understand PoC at a deeper level, including its limitations and trajectory, it is necessary to analyse and consider it together with its conceptual brethren of humanitarian intervention and RtoP. The relationships and interactions, which are both broad and complex, need to be analysed at legal, political, and operational levels. In this regard, this chapter considers the history and development of all three concepts, as well as the 'responsibility while protecting' (RwP), before turning to consider the three concepts' common foundations and different foci, and their varied constraints and shared pathologies.

II. History and Development

The history and development of the three concepts—humanitarian intervention, RtoP, and PoC—is intertwined and inherently multidisciplinary since it engages international relations, political and legal dimensions. Given the close relationship to the use of force, it also includes conceptual antecedents such as historical just war theories, as well as contemporary constructs such as the collective security system. This history and development reveals the strong interrelationships between the three concepts, which have developed in reaction to international issues and events and, to a certain extent, in response to each other.

[4] Pierre-Marie Dupuy, 'The Constitutional Dimension of the Charter of the United Nations Revisited', in Armin von Bogdandy and Rüdiger Wolfrum (eds), *Max Planck Yearbook of United Nations Law: Volume 1* (Leiden, the Netherlands: Martinus Nijhoff, 1997) 1–33; Bardo Fassbender, *The United Nations Charter as the Constitution of the International Community* (Leiden, Netherlands: Brill, 2009); Nicholas Tsagourias and Nigel D White, *Collective Security: Theory, Law and Practice* (Cambridge: Cambridge University Press, 2013) 32–8.

A. Historical use of force: Just war theory

Historically, the normative rationale for use of force was found in the just war theories of the Middle Ages.[5] This justification derived from both religion and natural law. A *religious* basis for just war theory was first reflected in the work of Saint Augustine of Hippo.[6] This was later built upon and systematized by Saint Thomas Aquinas, who argued that just war could be waged in self-defence and to restore peace and promote Christianity.[7] Aquinas proposed three core conditions for a just war: right authority, just cause, and right intention.[8]

A *natural law* basis for just war theory was subsequently proposed by Hugo Grotius, a leading figure in the development of modern international law in the seventeenth century. This was based on war on behalf of the oppressed, and war as punishment.[9] In relation to war on behalf of the oppressed, Grotius argued that natural law granted the power to assert the rights of others.[10] For war as punishment, sovereign States were deemed to have a right to demand punishment for injuries that 'excessively violate the law of nature or of nations in regard to any person whatsoever'.[11] The importance of this natural law doctrine lay in its secular basis[12] in contrast to the prevailing context at that time, which focused on divisive 'just' religious wars against the 'wicked'.[13] Such secularism was also reflected in the 1648 *Treaties of Westphalia*, which transformed medieval Europe into a horizontally organized system of sovereign States independent of the Holy Roman Empire, with the freedom for each to choose their own religion.

While the just war theories included aspects of civilian protection, it would be an overstatement to suggest that safeguarding the population's welfare was central to the thinking of most philosophers, jurists, and ecclesiastics at the time. However, just war theory, regardless of a religious or natural law foundation, fell victim in the twentieth century to the growth of positivism in international legal theory. Positivists rejected the just war concept due to fears of doctrinal abuse, given the inherent subjectivity of its core underpinnings (e.g.

[5] Simon Chesterman, *Just War or Just Peace? Humanitarian Intervention and International Law* (Oxford: Oxford University Press, 2001) 9.

[6] St Augustine, *The City of God [De Civitate Dei]* [413–426 AD] (Marcus Dods, trans.) (Peabody, USA: Hendrickson Publishers, 2008) Part II, Book XIX; Mary Ellen O'Connell, 'Peace and War', in Bardo Fassbender and Anne Peters (eds), *The Oxford Handbook of the History of International Law* (Oxford: Oxford University Press, 2012) 274–5; John Mark Mattox, *St. Augustine and the Theory of Just War* (London: A&C Black, 2009) 44–91.

[7] Thomas Aquinas, *The Summa Theologica of St Thomas Acquinas* [1265–1274] (Fathers of the English Dominican Province, trans.) (New York: Christian Classics, 1981) Part II, Section II, Question 40: 'Of War'; Thomas Aquinas, *St Thomas Aquinas on Politics and Ethics* (Paul E Sigmund, ed., trans.) (New York: Norton Critical Editions, 1987); Mary Ellen O'Connell, see n 6, 274–5.

[8] O'Connell, see n 6, 275.

[9] H Grotius, *De Jure Belli Ac Pacis Libri Tres* [1646] (Francis W Kelsey, trans.); Clarendon Press 1925) II, xx: 'On Punishment'; xxv: 'On Undertaking War on Behalf of Others'.

[10] Ibid., II, xxv: 'On Undertaking War on Behalf of Others', para. 1(1).

[11] Ibid., II, xx: 'On Punishment', para. 40(1). Grotius went on to argue: 'wars are justly waged against those who act with impiety towards their parents, [and] . . . against those who feed on human flesh', para. 40(3).

[12] Ibid., II, xx: 'On Punishment', para. 48, 50.

[13] Chesterman, see n 5, 10.

'justness').[14] As Simon Chesterman notes, the development of positivism, alongside the dominance of the 'balance of power' concept in European international relations, led to State sovereignty emerging as the constituent and inviolable element of international law.[15] A leader of that discourse, Emmerich de Vattel, consequently argued in his influential work *The Law of Nations* (1758) that just war theory must be relegated to an ethical rather than legal domain.[16]

B. The modern paradigm for use of force: Collective security

The modern paradigm on the use of force under international law is based on the collective security agreement.[17] This is manifest in the Covenant of the League of Nations (1919) and the UN Charter (1945). Both treaties codified the conditions for the use of force in the name of international peace and security, and placed the maintenance of that peace and security in the hands of a select council of States.[18] Under both of these collective security agreements, recourse to war and the use of force was prohibited.[19]

The UN Charter provided two main exceptions to the prohibition on the use of force: self-defence and collective enforcement action authorized by the Security Council under Chapter VII ('collective action') to maintain or restore international peace and security.[20] Beyond the need for self-defence, which is interpreted by the State concerned, the collective framework placed the authorization for the use of force in the hands of the Security Council as a multilateral and legitimate organ. In theory, this significantly limited the space for national interest and *realpolitik*, which lent themselves to subjective notions as reflected in just war theories.

Collective action under the UN Charter is predicated on a threat to international peace and security, as reflected in Article 39 of Chapter VII.[21] Traditionally, the Security Council took a State-centric approach to this determination, which focussed on inter-State conflict. This was in furtherance of the principle of the UN's

[14] Ibid., 13.

[15] Ibid., 17. See Christian Wolff, *Jus Gentium Methodo Scientifica Pertractatum* [1764] (Joseph H Drake, trans.) (Oxford: Clarendon Press, 1934) xxxviii; Emer de Vattel, *The Law of Nations: Principles of the Law of Nature, Applied to the Conduct and Affairs of Nations and Sovereign* [1758] (Edward Ingram, ed.) (Joseph Chitty, trans.) (Philadelphia, USA: Johnson & Co, 1883); Immanuel Kant, 'Toward Perpetual Peace', in Immanuel Kant, *Practical Philosophy* [1795] (Mary J Gregor, trans.) (Cambridge: Cambridge University Press, 1996) 8:346 [trans 319–20]; Nicholas Tsagourias, 'Self-Defence, Protection of Humanitarian Values and the Doctrine of Impartiality and Neutrality in Enforcement Mandates' in M Weller (ed.), *The Oxford Handbook of the Use of Force in International Law* (Oxford University Press 2015) 400–1.

[16] E de Vattel, see n 15, para. 190.

[17] Tsagourias and White, see n 4.

[18] Charter of the United Nations (UN Charter) (adopted 26 June 1945, entered into force 24 October 1945) 1 UNTS XVI, Articles 2(4) and 24(1); Covenant of the League of Nations (adopted 28 April 1919, entered into force 10 January 1920) UKTS 4 (Cmd 153), Articles 4, 8 10–12 and 15–16.

[19] For more on collective security, see Haidi Willmot, Chapter 5 in this volume.

[20] UN Charter, see n 18, Articles 39, 42, 51.

[21] Article 39 reads: 'The Security Council shall determine the existence of any threat to the peace, breach of the peace, or act of aggression and shall make recommendations, or decide what measures shall be taken in accordance with Articles 41 and 42, to maintain or restore international peace and security.'

non-intervention in domestic affairs, referred to in Article 2(7) of the Charter, and also as a natural corollary of State sovereignty. By contrast, a narrow interpretation was given, at least initially, to the UN Charter's provisions that promoted human rights.[22]

However, the interpretation of a threat to international peace and security was expanded over time, especially following the conclusion of the Cold War. In practice, the Security Council's agenda began to reflect atrocity situations and those characterized by serious internal humanitarian and human rights abuses and violations.[23] This change was justified by the transboundary effects of ever-increasing civil wars, alongside the express or implied consent of the affected States.[24] As Nigel Rodley suggests, it was 'artificial, if not unconscionable, for the happenstance of geography to determine the international reaction to the fate of a particular population'.[25] In the 1990s the Security Council authorized military action under Chapter VII in conflict situations such as Northern Iraq, Somalia, Haiti, and Rwanda.[26] This was clearly more about addressing intra-State conflict and suffering than due to transboundary effects, State consent, or requests for assistance.[27]

Despite the expanding interpretation of a 'threat to international peace and security', the collective security system faced numerous hurdles to authorizing intervention. There were no standing UN forces, as envisaged and required under Articles 43–47 of the Charter.[28] In the absence of this, UN peacekeeping crystallized as a distinct form of intervention during the Cold War period, with forces contributed voluntarily, and acting as a substitute for Chapter VII action.[29] However, over time it proved difficult to convince States to offer their military forces to UN peacekeeping operations deployed in hostile situations.[30] Furthermore, the use or threat of the veto hampered action by the Security Council in places such as Rwanda and the

22 UN Charter, see n 18, Articles 1(3) and 55(c). See Nigel Rodley, 'Collective Intervention to Protect Human Rights and Civilians Populations: The Legal Framework' in Nigel Rodley (ed.), *To Loose the Bands of Wickedness: International Intervention in Defence of Human Rights* (London: Brassey's (UK), 1992) 18. For human rights promotion clauses see UN Charter, n 18, 1(2), 1(3), 55–6.

23 See, for example, *Prosecutor v Tadić*, Judgment (Decision on the Defence Motion for Interlocutory Appeal on Jurisdiction) (2 October 1995) IT-94-1-AR72, para. 30; United Nations Security Council (UNSC) Resolution (Res) 688 (1991) UN Doc S/RES/0688; UNSC Res 1296 (2000) UN Doc S/RES/1296 (2000), para. 5.

24 S Chesterman, see n 5, 139.

25 Nigel Rodley, 'Collective Intervention to Protect Human Rights and Civilians Populations: The Legal Framework', in Rodley, see n 22, 35.

26 Northern Iraq: UNSC Res 678 (1990) UN Doc S/RES/678, para. 2; Somalia: UNSC Res 794 (1992) UN Doc S/RES/794, para. 10; Haiti: UNSC Res 940 (1994) UN Doc S/RES/940, para. 4; Rwanda: UNSC Res 929 (1994) UN Doc S/RES/929, para. 3.

27 Jennifer Welsh, 'The Security Council and Humanitarian Intervention' in Vaughan Lowe, Adam Roberts, Jennifer Welsh, and Dominik Zaum, *The United Nations Security Council and War: The Evolution of Thought and Practice since 1945* (Oxford: Oxford University Press, 2008) 538–46.

28 Pursuant to Article 43 of the UN Charter, see n 18, UN Member States undertake to 'make available to the [UNSC] . . . armed forces, assistance, and facilities . . . necessary for the purpose of maintaining international peace and security'.

29 Mats Berdal, 'The Council and Peacekeeping' in Lowe, Roberts, Welsh, and Zaum, see n 27, 177; Chesterman, see n 5, 172.

30 See Jean-Marie Guehenno, Chapter 11, and Fiona Blyth and Patrick Cammaert, Chapter 14, in this volume.

Balkans, as today in Syria, the Ukraine, and Palestine.[31] Martti Koskenniemi, a former Finnish legal adviser in the Security Council, notes that the 'politically possible' determined the outcome of Council issues on intervention.[32]

C. Humanitarian intervention

Despite examples from the nineteenth century,[33] the concept of 'humanitarian intervention' has been mainly invoked in response to the limits of the UN collective security agreement. Humanitarian intervention has been most often raised in the context of proposed military intervention in another sovereign State for humanitarian purposes, without Security Council authorization (i.e. 'unilateral action')—often necessary due to the casting or threat of the veto. As recently as 2013, the United Kingdom cited humanitarian intervention as a legal basis for potential military intervention in Syria, in light of Russia and China's vetoes, both actual and threatened, of Security Council action.[34]

The precise legal basis for humanitarian intervention is unclear; as Ian Brownlie noted, the doctrine is 'inherently vague'.[35] General concepts of humanity and dictates of human conscience may provide a potential foundation, but this does not reflect a positivist legal basis. Commentators such as Rodley suggest that the concept arose more from 'a humanitarian impulse to alleviate a human disaster than an attempt to uphold individual *rights* as against the oppressive state authorities'.[36] Others, such as Chesterman, suggest that humanitarian intervention is a modern equivalent of Grotius' right to wage war on behalf of the oppressed,[37] providing a linkage back to just war theory.

A justification for humanitarian intervention under the UN Charter and international law is difficult to establish. The Charter prohibits the use or threat of

[31] Rwanda: Céline Nahory, 'The Hidden Veto' (*Global Policy Forum*, 2004) <www.globalpolicy.org/security-council/42656-the-hidden-veto.html>; the Balkans: UNSC, *Draft Resolution 1358 (1994)* (2 December 1994) UN Doc S/1994/1358 (regarding unimpeded access to humanitarian assistance); Syria: UNSC, Draft Resolution 348 (2014) (22 May 2014) UN Doc S/2014/348 (regarding the referral of the situation in the Syrian Arab Republic to the Prosecutor of the International Criminal Court); Ukraine: UNSC, Draft Resolution 189 (2014) (15 March 2014) UN Doc S/2014/189 (regarding the proposed referendum on the status of Crimea); Palestine: UNSC, Draft Resolution 24 (2011) (18 February 2011) UN Doc S/2011/24 (regarding the illegality of Israeli settlements in the Occupied Palestinian Territories).

[32] Martti Koskenniemi, 'The Police in the Temple: Order, Justice and the UN: A Dialectical View' (1995) 6 EJIL 325, 327. He also noted that, where the will exists, the textual constraint of the UN Charter is 'practically non-existent'.

[33] S Chesterman, see n 5, 66. See also Anne Orford, *International Authority and the Responsibility to Protect* (Cambridge: Cambridge University Press, 2011) 32–4.

[34] Marko Milanović, 'Breaking: UK Government Discloses Legal Rationale for Syria Intervention' (*EJIL: Talk!* 29 August 2013) <www.ejiltalk.org/breaking-uk-government-discloses-legal-rationale-for-syria-intervention/>. See also Caroline Kennedy-Pipe and Rhiannon Vickers, '"Blowback" for Britain?: Blair, Bush and the War in Iraq' (2007) 33 Rev of Intl Studies 205, 211; Foreign and Commonwealth Office, *Saddam Hussein: Crimes and Human Rights Abuses: A Report on the Human Cost of Saddam's Policies by the Foreign and Commonwealth Office* (November 2002) <image.guardian.co.uk/sys-files/Guardian/documents/2002/12/02/hrdossierenglish.pdf>.

[35] Ian Brownlie, *International Law and the Use of Force by States* (Oxford: Clarendon Press, 1963) 338. See also Rodley, n 22, 20.

[36] Rodley, see n 22, 20.

[37] Chesterman, see n 5, 37.

force in Article 2(4) except in cases of self-defence under Article 51 or Security Council enforcement action authorized under Chapter VII to maintain or restore international peace and security.[38] Therefore, a *right* of humanitarian intervention prima facie challenges the collective security system of the UN Charter. To uphold such a right, it is necessary to establish either that it can be read into the UN Charter without violating Article 2(4), or that it exists separately as a parallel rule of customary international law.[39] Whichever avenue is taken, to accept the concept of humanitarian intervention, essentially a unilateral right, as a legal basis for intervention requires a strained or extra-textual interpretation of the UN Charter,[40] and therefore undermines the sanctity of the collective security agreement.

In relation to the customary international law argument, some instances of humanitarian interventions have been tolerated by the international community 'apparently out of recognition of the relatively benign motives and positive consequences of those interventions'.[41] However, many of the States involved in such interventions (e.g. India in respect of Bangladesh in 1971, Vietnam in Kampuchea 1978–9, Tanzania in Uganda 1978–9) were hesitant to invoke it as a legal justification for their actions.[42] Furthermore, the International Court of Justice (ICJ) in the *Military Activities in Nicaragua* case asserted that human rights violations could not be invoked to justify military interventions,[43] which confirmed some scholars' view that unilateral armed humanitarian intervention cannot be legally justified.[44]

With the greater consensus in the Security Council after the Cold War, international intervention by the UN increased and the Council often framed its justifications as humanitarian.[45] The peak of the debate on humanitarian intervention was NATO's intervention in Kosovo in 1999, which sidestepped institutional Security Council authorization in the face of Russian intransigence and threatened use of the veto.[46] As Koskenniemi notes, many Western lawyers took the inventive or ambivalent position that the intervention was 'both formally illegal and morally

[38] UN Charter, see n 18, Articles 39, 42, and 51.

[39] Chesterman, see n 5, 48–62. [40] Ibid., 47–53. [41] Ibid., 47.

[42] Nigel Rodley, 'Human Rights and Humanitarian Intervention: The Case Law of the World Court' (1989) 38 Intl and Comparative L Q 326, 332; Chesterman, see n 5, 71–5, 77–81, 84; Nicholas J Wheeler, *Saving Strangers: Humanitarian Intervention and International Society* (Oxford: Oxford University Press, 2000) Chapters 2 and 3.

[43] *Case Concerning Military Activities and Paramilitary Activities In and Against Nicaragua (Nicaragua v United States of America)* (Judgment) [1986] ICJ Rep 14, para. 268.

[44] Rodley, see n 42, 330. See and compare: even upon a restrictive interpretation of the *ratio decidendi* whereby the judgment is limited to its statements on the *disproportionate* use of force, the judgment is only at best 'not incompatible with a narrow right of humanitarian intervention': Chesterman, see n 5, 62. See Sean D Murphy, *Humanitarian Intervention: The United Nations in an Evolving World Order* (Philadelphia, USA: University of Pennsylvania Press, 1996) 129–30; Fernando Tesón, *Humanitarian Intervention: An Inquiry into Law and Morality* (3rd ed.) (Dobbs Ferry, NY: Transnational Publishers, 2005) 366–72.

[45] For example, see Adam Roberts, 'Humanitarian Issues and Agencies as Triggers for International Military Action', in Simon Chesterman, *Civilians in War* (Boulder, USA: Lynne Rienner Publishers, 2001) 177, 180–6.

[46] Chesterman, see n 5, 211; Martti Koskenniemi, '"The Lady Doth Protest Too Much": Kosovo, and the Turn to Ethics in International Law' (2002) 65 Modern L Rev 159, 170. Note: China, Belarus, and India also opposed NATO action as a violation of the UN Charter.

necessary'.[47] Only the United Kingdom and Netherlands claimed that the action was a *legal* response to the humanitarian disaster.[48] Other NATO States asserted a mix of legal and humanitarian justifications for their actions.[49] The 'exceptional' nature of NATO's action was highlighted by many political leaders. Chesterman notes that this raised questions as to whether it was 'an admission that it violated international law and a plea for mitigation, or merely a reference to the frequency with which such actions might take place in the future'.[50]

The juxtaposition of *unlawful* yet *legitimate* in relation to the Kosovo intervention raises numerous problems. In effect it reduces Security Council authorization to the formalistic or procedural, rather than legally determinative for the use of force.[51] This in turn negatively impacts the credibility of the UN Charter and the collective security system, especially in the eyes of moderate States and Non-Aligned Movement (NAM) members.[52] Furthermore, the taxonomical distinction (legality vs. legitimacy) offers little guidance to political decision-makers about what action to take in cases involving such difficult circumstances.[53]

Today, humanitarian intervention continues to be controversial due to an association with an imperialistic or Western agenda. This is because of the perception, or reality, that powerful States only intervene due to tangible national interests and *realpolitik*, including sometimes as part of a post-colonial agenda.[54] International society theory, for example, objects to humanitarian intervention on the grounds that absent international consensus on the governing rules, States will act according to their own moral principles and thereby undermine the international order based on the principles of State sovereignty and non-use of force.[55] Realists, as well as neo-Marxists such as Noam Chomsky, also raise objections, notably, that States do not intervene primarily for humanitarian reasons and are instead motivated by considerations of national self-interest, cloaked in the rhetoric of humanitarian intervention.[56]

Despite the possibility of safeguards, humanitarian intervention occupies a narrow space in contemporary discourse on the use of force and international law, and its support by States and scholars is exceptional.[57] The fundamental problem is that

47 Koskenniemi, see n 46, 162. See also Chesterman, n 5, 231–2.
48 Chesterman, see n 5, 212. 49 Ibid., 207.
50 Ibid., 217. See also M Koskenniemi, n 46. 51 Chesterman, see n 5, 5, 218.
52 Evans, see n 2, 88. 53 Ibid., 79.
54 International Commission on Intervention and State Sovereignty, *The Responsibility to Protect: Report of the International Commission on Intervention and State Sovereignty* (ICISS Report) (Ottawa: International Development Research Centre, 2001) <responsibilitytoprotect.org/ICISS%20Report.pdf>, para. 6.9. For example, the 1960 Belgian intervention in the Congo was cited as an example of humanitarian intervention. However, the main justifications were the protection of *Belgian* nationals and concerns over access to copper mines, rather than genuine 'humanitarian' concerns. See Chesterman, n 5, 66. See also Orford, n 33, 29–30.
55 Wheeler, see n 42, 28.
56 Noam Chomsky, *The New Military Humanism: Lessons from Kosovo* (London: Pluto Press, 1999) 10–11; Wheeler, see n 42, 29–30; Thomas Franck and Nigel Rodley, 'After Bangladesh: The Law of Humanitarian Intervention by Military Force' (1973) 67 AJIL 275, 290.
57 Nigel Rodley and Başak Çali, 'Kosovo Revisited: Humanitarian Intervention on the Fault Lines of International Law' (2007) 7 Human Rights L Rev 275, 276 n 1, n 2; Tesón, see n 44, 187 n 49, 189 n 51; Security Council Report, *Cross-Cutting Report: Protection of Civilians in Armed Conflict* (New

the concept conflicts with the UN Charter, which embodies both international law and the collective security agreement. As Chesterman notes, unilateral enforcement action 'is not a substitute for, but the opposite of, collective action: as unilateral assertions of humanitarianism come to displace multilateral institutional legality, so the normative restraints on the recourse to force weaken'.[58] By shifting the determination of the legality of an intervention from the Security Council (i.e. as an authoritative, legitimate, and multilateral process) to individual States and/or groups of States, the constraints on the use of force become more subjective and shaped by national interest. To permit a right of humanitarian intervention will likely lead to abuse by the powerful and its selective application.[59]

D. Responsibility to protect

The responsibility to protect is contextualized as a reaction to the atrocities of the 1990s in Somalia, Rwanda, Srebrenica, and Kosovo, as well as to the political and normative failure of humanitarian intervention.[60] This sentiment was well captured in a 1999 report of the UN Secretary-General, Kofi Annan, in which he called for the 'use of coercive action ... as a mechanism of last resort to protect the civilian population from immediate threats to their lives'.[61] In 2001 the International Commission on Intervention and State Sovereignty (ICISS) published the seminal report on RtoP in direct response to NATO's unauthorized intervention in Kosovo and calls by the UN Secretary-General.[62]

Yet, as Carsten Stahn noted, RtoP 'is not a completely novel idea'; it built on, inter alia, historical notions of just war theory and the maxim that sovereignty exists for the protection of people.[63] This latter idea, in the form that sovereign power was held on trust for the people and could be removed, was present in Jean Bodin's original theory of absolute, perpetual, and undivided sovereignty.[64] Vattel's application

York: Security Council Report, 2010) <www.securitycouncilreport.org/atf/cf/{65BFCF9B-6D27-4E9C-8CD3-CF6E4FF96FF9}/XCutting%20POC%202010.pdf> 4.

58 Chesterman, see n 5, 236.

59 Wheeler, see n 42, 29–30; Franck and Rodley, see n 56, 288, 290; Rodley, see n 22, 20.

60 Anne Peters, 'Humanity as the A and Ω of Sovereignty' (2009) 20 EJIL 513, 522; UN General Assembly (UNGA), 'Supplement to an Agenda for Peace: Position Paper of the Secretary-General on the Occasion of the Fiftieth Anniversary of the United Nations' (1995) UN Doc A/50/60-S/1995/1.

61 UNSC, 'Report of the Secretary-General on the Protection of Civilians in Armed Conflict' (1999) UN Doc S/1999/957, para. 67. The report states: 'In situations where the parties to the conflict commit *systematic and widespread breaches* of international humanitarian and human rights law, causing threats of *genocide, crimes against humanity* and *war crimes*, the Security Council should be prepared to intervene under Chapter VII of the Charter. The use of coercive action should be seen as a mechanism of *last resort* to protect the civilian population from immediate threats to their lives and to ensure the safe passage of humanitarian convoys.' See also ICISS Report, n 54, xii–xiii.

62 Ibid.

63 See Carsten Stahn, 'Responsibility to Protect: Political Rhetoric or Emerging Legal Norm?' (2007) 101 AJIL 99, 111–14.

64 Stéphane Beaulac and Phillip Allott, *Power of Language in the Making of International Law: The Word 'Sovereignty' in Bodin and Vattel and the Myth of Westphalia* (Leiden, the Netherlands: Brill Academic, 2004) 106–12. See Jean Bodin, *On Sovereignty: For Chapters from the Six Books of the Commonwealth* [1576] (Julian H Franklin, trans.) (Cambridge: Cambridge University Press, 1992) Book I, Chapter 8: On Sovereignty, 1–45.

of sovereignty to public international law was the externalization or transposition of the concept, and broke down the symmetry of power over, and responsibility to, the people. As Stephane Beaulac and Philip Allot suggest, this resulted in a 'power which is *incorporated* and *independent*, as opposed to a power which is *personal* and *interconnected*'.[65] As such, the 'sovereign state and not the individual man are henceforth the criterion by which all relations in the international sphere are judged'.[66]

The central idea for RtoP was established in a study co-authored by Francis Deng on conflict management in Africa, which was subsequently built upon by the ICISS Report.[67] The key innovation was the reconceptualization of State sovereignty from the Westphalian notion of 'sovereignty as *control*' to 'sovereignty as *responsibility*'.[68] Gareth Evans, a leading figure among the ICISS Report's authors, noted that this was justified 'by the ever-increasing impact of international human rights norms and the increasing impact in international discourse of the concept of human security'.[69] Where a State is unwilling or unable to uphold such responsibility, external military intervention is justified, as a last resort, by the international community. This reassessment of sovereignty is more conceptually defendable, and represents an innovative response to the limitations of humanitarian intervention.

The ICISS Report focused on intervention as 'action taken against a state or its leaders, without its or their consent, for purposes which are claimed to be humanitarian or protective'.[70] The ICISS articulation of RtoP, conceptually broader and more ambitious than humanitarian intervention, is composed of three interrelated sets of responsibilities: responsibility to prevent, responsibility to react, and responsibility to rebuild.[71] The concept of 'sovereignty' implies both an external responsibility to 'respect the sovereignty of other states', as enshrined in Article 2(7) of the Charter,[72] and an internal responsibility 'to respect the dignity and basic rights of all the people within the state'.[73]

This dual understanding transcends sovereignty as reflected in Vattel's transposition to the international plane (including the principle of non-interference in domestic affairs) and Bodin's original conception, which included aspects of a responsibility to the population.[74] As Anne Peters notes, RtoP 'infuses external sovereignty with elements of internal sovereignty, because it conditions non-intervention (a consequence or corollary of external sovereignty) on the capability properly to discharge the internal functions of a sovereign'.[75]

[65] Beaulac and Allott, see n 64, 137.

[66] Peter Pavel Remec, *The Position of the Individual in International Law According to Grotius and Vattel* (Leiden, the Netherlands: Martinus Nijhoff, 1960) 180.

[67] Francis Deng, Sadikiel Kimaro, Terrence Lyons, Donald Rothchild, and I William Zartman, *Sovereignty as Responsibility: Conflict Management in Africa* (Washington, DC: Brookings Institution Press, 1996). For commentary on the Deng Study, see Orford, n 33, 13–15.

[68] ICISS Report, see n 54, para. 2.14.

[69] Evans, see n 2, 82. Note that the concept of 'human security' here differs to that articulated in the 1994 United Nations Development Programme's Human Development Report, which 'provides a philosophical base for identifying problems from the perspective of individuals *holistically* and includes hunger, disease, inequality, violence, disasters and poverty': Security Council Report, see n 57, 4.

[70] ICISS Report, see n 54, para. 1.38. [71] Ibid., paras 3.1–5.31. [72] Ibid., para. 2.8.

[73] Ibid., para. 1.35. [74] See Beaulac and Allott, n 54, 150–6.

[75] Peters, see n 60, 517.

The ICISS Report states that the international community has a residual responsibility to protect when a State 'is clearly either unwilling or unable to fulfil its responsibility to protect or is itself the actual perpetrator of crimes or atrocities'.[76] The responsibility includes, as a last resort, military intervention, but this is subject to numerous precautionary principles, including just cause, right intention, and proportionality of means.[77] The 'just cause' threshold was elaborated in the ICISS Report as:

> [L]arge scale loss of life, actual or apprehended, with genocidal intent or not, which is the product either of deliberate state action, or state neglect or inability to act, or a failed state situation; or large scale 'ethnic cleansing,' actual or apprehended, whether carried out by killing, forced expulsion, acts of terror or rape.[78]

This more sophisticated substantive test still shared some commonality with the underlying drivers of humanitarian intervention and its own 'just cause' rationale. However, the ICISS Report situated RtoP in multilateral institutions and processes, namely the Security Council, in order to provide legitimacy and greater impartiality.[79] Notably, it omitted to take a stance on the legality of an intervention not authorized by the Council.[80]

The period between the ICISS Report (2001) and the World Summit (2005) saw a flurry of discussions and reports regarding RtoP, the use of force, and the veto. The two intermediate seminal texts were the UN High Level Panel on Threats, Challenges and Change report *A More Secure World: Our Shared Responsibility* (2004),[81] and the UN Secretary-General's report *In Larger Freedom* (2005).[82] The latter report declared that RtoP 'was no longer exclusively viewed as a surrogate for humanitarian intervention but as a strategy to promote the commitment of all nations to the rule of law and human security'.[83]

The final text of the UN World Summit Outcome Document ('World Summit Outcome') in 2005 represented a political compromise that broadly endorsed RtoP but whittled it down to its minimalist core.[84] First, regarding the just cause threshold, the World Summit Outcome defined RtoP as engaged in respect of genocide, war crimes, ethnic cleansing, and crimes against humanity, but at the same time moved away from language that provided for a threshold (e.g. from 'large scale loss of life' to simply protecting populations from war crimes, crimes against humanity,

[76] ICISS Report, see n 54, para. 2.31.

[77] Ibid., para. 2.25, 4.1; Hugh Breakey, Angus Francis, Vesselin Popovski, Charles Sampford, Michael G Smith, and Ramesh Thakur, *Enhancing Protection Capacity: Policy Guide to the Responsibility to Protect and the Protection of Civilians in Armed Conflict* (Griffith University: Institute for Ethics, Governance and Law, undated) 10 <www.griffith.edu.au/__data/assets/pdf_file/0016/471301/R2P-POC-Policy-Guide.pdf>.

ICISS Report, see n 54, para. 4.19.

[78] Ibid., para. 4.19. [79] Ibid., paras 6.9, 6.14, 6.15. [80] Ibid., para. 6.36–6.40.

[81] UNGA, 'A More Secure World: Our Shared Responsibility' (2004) UN Doc A/59/565. See Stahn, n 63, 105–6.

[82] UNGA, 'In Larger Freedom: Towards Development, Security and Human Rights for All' (2005) UN Doc A/59/2005. See Stahn, n 63, 107–8.

[83] Stahn, see n 63, 107; UNGA (2005) UN Doc A/59/2005, paras 133–5.

[84] Ibid., 108.

etc).[85] Second, the residual responsibility of the international community was framed in narrower terms.[86] The Security Council was deemed the '*exclusive* authority for mandating any RtoP coercive use of force'.[87] Third, whereas under the ICISS Report's notion of RtoP the international community's responsibility was triggered when a State is 'unable or unwilling to act', under the World Summit Outcome the State must be 'manifestly failing to prevent', introducing a higher threshold.[88] And finally, it failed to address the use, or threat of, the veto.

The period after 2005 saw numerous invocations of RtoP, especially by Western countries. For example, France took a broad approach towards RtoP concerning Myanmar after Cyclone Nargis in May 2008, based on the government's refusal to accept international assistance.[89] A few months later, Russia claimed that its invasion of Georgia was justified by RtoP in order to prevent genocide in South Ossetia.[90] Such claims quickly raised the spectre of interventionism, and were resisted or viewed cynically by many. Perhaps receptive to such a risk, the advocacy of RtoP since the World Summit Outcome has reflected a progression in presentation from coercive to less coercive measures.[91] The Secretary-General's *Report on the Implementation of the Responsibility to Protect* (2009), for example, sought to find common political ground by introducing three pillars for RtoP:

1. Preventative—The primary responsibility of the *State to protect its population* from genocide, war crimes, ethnic cleansing and crimes against humanity and from their incitement;
2. Assistance—The *international community's responsibility to assist* and encourage States to fulfil their responsibility to protect;
3. Response—The *international community's responsibility* to take a *timely and decisive response*.[92]

The implementation of RtoP still failed, however, to gain the unequivocal support of the majority of UN Member States, reflecting the increasing cracks in the edifice of the World Summit Outcome and its agreement by all UN Member States.[93] In 2011 the Security Council's authorization by vote (ten in favour, five abstentions)

[85] UNGA Res 60/1, '2005 World Summit Outcome' (2005) UN Doc A/RES/60/1, para. 138 (World Summit Outcome).

[86] Stahn, see n 63, 108; World Summit Outcome, see n 85, para. 139; Welsh, see n 27, 558.

[87] Breakey, Francis, Popovski, Sampford, Smith, and Thakur, see n 77, 7. Note the contrary arguments of: Stahn, see n 63, 109; World Summit Outcome, see n 85, para. 139; Welsh, see n 27, 558.

[88] World Summit Outcome, see n 85, para. 139; Welsh, see n 27, 558.

[89] Asia-Pacific Centre for the Responsibility to Protect, *Cyclone Nargis and the Responsibility to Protect: Myanmar/Burma Briefing No. 2* (16 May 2008) <www.r2pasiapacific.org/docs/R2P%20Reports/Cyclone%20Nargis%20and%20R2P%20Myanmar_Burma_Brief2%202008.pdf>.

[90] Alex J Bellamy, 'The Responsibility to Protect: Towards a "Living Reality"' (United Nations Association-UK, April 2013) 18 <www.r2pasiapacific.org/docs/In%20the%20Media/UNA-UK%20Alex%20J%20Bellamy%20R2P%20Briefing%20Report%20no.%201.pdf>.

[91] N Tsagourias, see n 15, 408.

[92] UNGA, 'Implementing the Responsibility to Protect: Report of the Secretary-General' (2009) UN Doc A/63/677. Emphasis added.

[93] Bellamy, see n 90, 25–6.

to intervene in Libya appeared to be the application of RtoP, namely, the use of force to protect civilians without the consent of the State concerned.[94] The Council's resolution 1973 (2011) did not expressly mention RtoP, and this intervention has since become a controversial example, with allegations that the mandate became a vehicle for regime change.[95]

While RtoP has not reached the status of customary international law, the ICISS Report argued that growing State and regional organization practice and Security Council precedent suggested that RtoP was an 'emerging guiding principle'.[96] Yet, as Stahn notes, even subsequent to the four seminal RtoP-related documents—the ICISS Report, High Level Panel Report, Secretary-General's Report, and World Summit Outcome—a positivist perspective does not support RtoP as an emergent *legal* norm.[97] The World Summit Outcome is arguably the most legally authoritative, as a declaration of all UN Member States. However, there remains doubt as to 'whether and to what extent States intended to create a legal norm', especially one that was intended to override the UN Charter and veto (e.g. an *obligation* rather than *authority* to intervene).[98] It is very difficult within the bounds of the current paradigm, practice, and structure of the Charter to convincingly argue that RtoP is part of international *law*.

In scholarship, the concept of RtoP has been extended by implication through the reconceptualization of sovereignty as the protection and promotion of human rights. Evan Criddle and Evan Fox-Decent argue that sovereignty is conditional upon respecting and ensuring human rights, since a State's assumption of sovereign power places it in a fiduciary relationship with its subjects.[99] Building on this point, Criddle and Fox-Decent further propose that *jus cogens* norms express constitutive elements of the normative dimension of sovereignty, and that the fiduciary model explains their peremptory status.[100] In a similar vein, Peters argues that State sovereignty is no longer the first principle of international law. She suggests that, as evidenced by the international endorsement of RtoP, a State's entitlement to such power must be justified. The normative value of sovereignty is derived from, and conditioned on, the principle that human rights must be respected, protected, and fulfilled.[101] Applying this logic to a situation in which a State fails to discharge its

[94] See discussion in Justin Morris, 'Libya and Syria: R2P and the Spectre of the Swinging Pendulum' (2013) 89 Intl Affairs 1265, at 1272–3.

[95] For example, see Alex J Bellamy and Paul D Williams, 'The New Politics of Protection? Côte d'Ivoire, Libya and the Responsibility to Protect' (2011) 87 Intl Affairs 825.

[96] ICISS Report, see n 54, para. 2.24. See also Evans, n 2, 83.

[97] This is insofar as none of these documents constitute binding sources of international law as per Article 38, Statute of the International Court of Justice. See Stahn, n 63, 101.

[98] See Stahn, n 63, 101. It is more emphatic of 'a growing tendency to recognise that the principle of state sovereignty finds its limits in the protection of "human security"'.

[99] Evan J Criddle and Evan Fox-Decent, 'The Fiduciary Constitution of Human Rights' (2009) 15(4) Legal Theory 301–36.

[100] Ibid., 331–87. In this article, Criddle and Fox-Decent propound that 'the fiduciary structure of international order might supply a basis for [collective] humanitarian intervention in extreme cases where states systematically violate peremptory norms', at page 383.

[101] Therefore, sovereignty exists only in function of humanity, resulting in the humanization of sovereignty, and any conflict between the two should be resolved in favour of the latter. See Peters, n 60, 513–44.

human rights responsibilities, its external sovereignty is then suspended, thereby permitting intervention.[102]

While such arguments add to the theoretical rationale for limiting State sovereignty, they fail to address the practical challenges in law and politics that RtoP continues to face. The concept has not brought the degree of change envisaged, especially in respect of Security Council action in dire situations for civilians.[103] Indeed, it has failed to be respected in various international crises, notably the conflict in Syria, which was estimated to have killed at least 210,000 people by early 2015.[104] Once RtoP is overlaid with international legal rules and procedure, the veto becomes central to the reticence about the concept. Many countries in the Global South, especially in the NAM, are cautious about RtoP.[105] This is because RtoP can justify action by great powers, but not realistically compel that action. For this reason, attempts to date to secure a General Assembly resolution on implementation of RtoP have been unsuccessful. Furthermore, there is a lack of compulsion among UN Member States to assume the burden and costs of collective action. RtoP has regrettably struggled to overcome the status quo, and has not significantly addressed the problems that informed its development.

E. Protection of civilians

As mentioned above, UN peacekeeping arose out of the failure of the collective security system during the Cold War.[106] A critical development in UN peacekeeping since the late 1990s has been the inclusion of the use of force to protect civilians as a mission task within Security Council-mandated operations. This represented a practical manifestation of the reconceptualization of threats to international peace and security grounded in human rights and humanitarian principles.[107] Despite PoC gaining traction within UN peacekeeping, there is no universally accepted

[102] Ibid., 513–44. However, the humanization of sovereignty does not 'imply unfettered interventionism'. Ibid., 543.

[103] Alex J Bellamy, *Global Politics and the Responsibility to Protect: From Words to Deeds* (London: Routledge, 2011) 51–70. RtoP is conceptually defensible, yet, while it has been invoked in at least eight humanitarian crises to date, it has not been used in several significant cases, notably Somalia (2006–ongoing) and Sudan (2008–9).

[104] Suleiman Al-Khalidi, 'Syria Death Toll Now Exceeds 210,000: Rights Group' *Reuters* (London, 7 February 2015) <www.reuters.com/article/2015/02/07/us-mideast-crisis-toll-idUSKBN0LB0DY20150207>. See also Megan Price, Anita Gohdes, and Patrick Ball, 'Updated Statistical Analysis of Documentation of Killings in the Syrian Arab Republic' (Human Rights Data Analysis Group, August 2014) <www.ohchr.org/Documents/Countries/SY/HRDAGUpdatedReportAug2014.pdf>.

[105] Orford, see n 33, 20, 180; Bellamy, see n 103, 26–7, 28–31. The ICISS Report recognized the 'capricious use of the veto, or threat of its use, as ... the principal obstacle to effective international action', stating that 'it is unconscionable that one veto can override the rest of humanity on matters of grave humanitarian concern'. See ICISS Report, n 54, para. 6.20.

[106] Bellamy, see n 103; Scott Sheeran, 'The Use of Force in United Nations Peacekeeping Operations', in Weller, see n 15, 350.

[107] Haidi Willmot and Scott Sheeran, 'The Protection of Civilians Mandate in UN Peacekeeping Operations: Reconciling Protection Concepts and Practices' (2013) 95 IRRC 517, 529; Katherine E Cox, 'Beyond Self-Defense: United Nations Peacekeeping Operations and the Use of Force' (1999) 27 Denver J of Intl L and Policy 239, 258.

definition and insufficient guidance on implementation.[108] In this environment, conflicting conceptions of 'protection' have developed among the human rights, humanitarian, and peacekeeping communities.[109] While some argue that PoC entails protection from physical harm as the concept's core,[110] others employ a rights-based approach, and expand the concept to incorporate the protection and promotion of human rights, humanitarian relief, and development activity.[111]

The development and growth of PoC has occurred with relatively modest fanfare. Despite its comparative dominance and engagement at the level of policy-makers, practitioners, and think tanks,[112] the concept's prevalence is not as well addressed in academic literature as RtoP and humanitarian intervention. The genesis of PoC lies in the well-documented failures of UN peacekeeping in the 1990s and, most notably, concerning the atrocities within so-called 'safe havens' in the former Yugoslavia and the genocide in Rwanda.[113] It may be seen as a reaction to the deficiencies of the principles of UN peacekeeping, namely, consent of the parties, impartiality, and non-use of force except in self-defence (and now in defence of the mandate).[114] The principles were developed *ex post facto* in 1958, after deployment of the UN Emergency Force (UNEF I) in the Suez Canal, the first armed UN peacekeeping operation.[115] This 'traditional' peacekeeping, characterized by ceasefire monitoring and passive observance, differed greatly from the complex, robust, multidimensional missions of the twenty-first century, leading to strain upon the peacekeeping model, and subsequent failure in cases such as Srebrenica and Rwanda.[116] As the seminal *Brahimi Report* on UN peacekeeping noted in 2000, there are situations where 'local parties consist not of moral equals but of obvious aggressors and victims' and, therefore, 'continued equal treatment of all

[108] William Durch and Alison Giffen, *Challenges of Strengthening the Protection Of Civilians in Multidimensional Peace Operations* (October 2010) 4 <www.stimson.org/images/uploads/research-pdfs/Challenges_of_Strengthening_POC_in_Peace_OperationsDurchGiffenFINALOct2010.pdf>; Victoria Holt and Glyn Taylor with Max Kelly, *Protecting Civilians in the Context of UN Peacekeeping Operations: Successes, Setbacks and Remaining Challenges* (New York: United Nations, 2009) 57; Department of Peacekeeping Operations (DPKO) and Department of Field Support (DFS), Draft Operational Concept on the Protection of Civilians in UN Peacekeeping Operations (Draft Operational Concept on PoC) (January 2010) <www.peacekeeping.org.uk/wp-content/uploads/2013/02/100129-DPKO-DFS-POC-Operational-Concept.pdf> 4.

[109] See Willmot and Sheeran, n 107, 531–5.

[110] Draft Operational Concept on PoC, see n 108, para. 10; Willmot and Sheeran, see n 107, 534.

[111] See Michael Keating and Richard Bennett, Chapter 16 in this volume; Sara Pantuliano and Eva Svoboda, Chapter 17 in this volume; and Lise Grande, Chapter 18 in this volume. See also the Draft Operational Concept on PoC, see n 108, para. 10. See also Inter-Agency Standing Committee, 'Protection of Internally Displaced Persons' (New York: Inter-Agency Standing Committee, 2000) 4.

[112] See Holt and Taylor with Kelly, n 108.

[113] UNGA, 'Report of the Secretary-General Pursuant to General Assembly Resolution 53/35' (1999) UN Doc A/54/549, para. 502; UNSC, 'Letter Dated 15 December 1999 from the Secretary-General Addressed to the President of the Security Council' (1999) UN Doc S/1999/1257, 50.

[114] DPKO and DFS, *United Nations Peacekeeping Operations: Principles and Guidelines* (New York: United Nations, 2008) (Capstone Doctrine) <pbpu.unlb.org/pbps/Library/Capstone_Doctrine_ENG.pdf> 31.

[115] UNGA, 'Summary Study of the Experience Derived from the Establishment and Operation of the Force: Report of the Secretary-General' (1958) UN Doc A/3943, para. 154-193.

[116] Scott Sheeran, 'A Constitutional Moment?: United Nations Peacekeeping in the Democratic Republic of Congo' (2011) 8 Intl Organizations L Rev 55, 130.

parties by the United Nations can in the best case result in ineffectiveness and in the worst may amount to complicity with evil'.[117]

The UN Secretary-General, Kofi Annan, first referred to PoC in his *Report on Causes of Conflict and the Promotion of Durable Peace in Africa* (1998).[118] Prior to the ICISS Report on RtoP (2001), the Security Council took up PoC both thematically and through country-specific peacekeeping mandates, the latter combining PoC with authorization for the use of force.[119] In the early 1990s, the UN's use of force was not focused on 'protection of civilians', despite this being manifest in peacekeepers' authority relating to humanitarian assistance and safe havens.[120] The UN Mission in Sierra Leone (UNAMSIL) was the first peacekeeping operation to be provided a PoC mandate, which authorized it to 'take the necessary action ... to afford protection to civilians under imminent threat of physical violence'.[121] This was recognized by the Security Council's members as the commencement of a new dimension of UN peacekeeping operations.[122] At the time of writing, fourteen UN peacekeeping operations have been provided a PoC mandate,[123] demonstrating the essential nature of PoC within such operations.

[117] UNGA and UNSC, 'Report of the Panel on United Nations Peace Operations' (2000) UN Doc A/55/305-S/2000/809, ix (Brahimi Report). In an attempt to amend this, the principles were modified in subsequent doctrine to account for contemporary peacekeeping contexts. See Brahimi Report, ibid., para. 48, 50; Capstone Doctrine, see n 114, 31–5.

[118] UNGA and UNSC, 'The Causes of Conflict and the Promotion of Durable Peace and Sustainable Development in Africa: Report of the Secretary-General' (1998) UN Doc A/52/871–S/1998/318, paras 49–52.

[119] See UNSC, Res 1265 (1999) UN Doc S/RES/1265; UNSC Res 1296 (2000) UN Doc S/RES/1296; UNSC Res 1674 (2006) UN Doc S/RES/1674; UNSC Res 1738 (2006) UN Doc S/RES/1738; UNSC Res 1894 (2009) UN Doc S/RES/1894; UNSC Res 2086 (2013) UN Doc S/RES/2086 (2013); Haidi Willmot and R Mamiya, 'Mandated to Protect: Security Council Practice on the Protection of Civilians' in Weller, see n 15, 388.

[120] In relation to the former Yugoslavia, see, for example, UNSC Res 743 (1992) UN Doc S/RES/743; UNSC Res 758 (1992) UN Doc S/RES/758; UNSC Res 776 (1992) UN Doc S/RES/776; UNSC Res 836 (1993) UN Doc S/RES/836. In relation to Rwanda, see, for example, UNSC Res 872 (1993) UN Doc S/RES/872; UNSC Res 912 (1994) UN Doc S/RES/912; UNSC Res 918 (1994) UN Doc S/RES/918.

[121] UNSC Res 1270 (1999) UN Doc S/RES/1270, para. 14.

[122] Willmot and Sheeran, see n 107, 521.

[123] The United Nations Observer Mission in the Democratic Republic of the Congo (MONUC), see UNSC Res 1291 (2000) UN Doc S/RES/1291, para. 8; the United Nations Mission in Liberia (UNMIL), see UNSC Res 1509 (2003) UN Doc S/RES/1509, para. 3(j); the United Nations Operation in Côte d'Ivoire (UNOCI), see UNSC Res 1528 (2004) UN Doc S/RES/1528, para. 6(i); the United Nations Stabilization Mission in Haiti (MINUSTAH), see UNSC Res 1542 (2004) UN Doc S/RES/1542, para. 7(I)(f); the United Nations Operation in Burundi (ONUB), see UNSC Res 1545 (2004) UN Doc S/RES/1545, para. 5; the United Nations Mission in Sudan (UNMIS), see UNSC Res 1590 (2005) UN Doc S/RES/1590, para. 16(i); the United Nations Interim Force in Lebanon (UNIFIL), see UNSC Res 1701 (2006) UN Doc S/RES/1701, para. 12; the African Union/United Nations Hybrid Operation in Darfur (UNAMID), see UNSC Res 1769 (2007) UN Doc S/RES/1769, para. 15(a)(ii); the United Nations Mission in the Central African Republic and Chad (MINURCAT), see UNSC Res 1861 (2009) UN Doc S/RES/1861, para. 7(a)(i); the United Nations Stabilization Mission in the Democratic Republic of the Congo (MONUSCO), see UNSC Res 1925 (2010) UN Doc S/RES/1925, para. 11, 12(a); the United Nations Interim Security Force for Abyei (UNISFA), see UNSC Res 1990 (2011) UN Doc S/RES/1990, para. 3(d); the United Nations Mission in South Sudan (UNMISS), see UNSC Res 1996 (2011) UN Doc S/RES/1996, para. 3(b); the United Nations Multidimensional Integrated Stabilisation Mission in Mali (MINUSMA), see UNSC Res 2164 (2014)

From the inception of the concept, the Security Council has made PoC a priority of its work. In 2000, the Council affirmed 'its intention to ensure, where appropriate and feasible, that peacekeeping missions are given suitable mandates and adequate resources to protect civilians under imminent threat of physical danger'.[124] Despite a hiatus in the advancement of PoC between 2002 and 2006 due to, inter alia, a shift in thematic focus to specific groups at risk,[125] protection was again prioritized from 2007 onwards.[126] In 2009, the Council determined that 'mandated protection activities must be given priority in decisions about the use of available capacity and resources'.[127] For example, Security Council resolution 1906 (2009) on the UN mission in the Democratic Republic of the Congo (MONUC) explicitly prioritized PoC over all other mandate tasks and unequivocally stated that it 'must be given priority in decisions about the use of available capacity and resources, over any of the other tasks described'.[128]

Further support for PoC was developed through the UN General Assembly's Special Committee on Peacekeeping Operations (C-34), which has included PoC language in its regular session reports since 2009.[129] The C-34's reports are adopted by the General Assembly, reflecting a level of support for PoC in the wider UN membership.[130] Since 2011, the Security Council has appeared to be exploring the boundaries of PoC mandates in the context of the missions in Libya, Mali, and the Democratic Republic of the Congo.[131] The fact that PoC's mainstream acceptance was not tarnished by controversy over the coalition operation's liberal use of the PoC mandate in Libya, discussed in more detail later in the chapter, is evidence of the concept's resilience and its deep political support.

While PoC is strongly supported, it faces several problems. A significant one is that the UN Secretariat and troop contributing countries (TCCs) do not appear to have the same understanding and expectations of PoC including its relation to, and the constraints imposed upon it by, the principles of UN peacekeeping. TCCs are often unwilling or unable to use force in a way that mirrors the mandate and needs and expectations on the ground.[132] This is reflected in a highly critical 2014 UN Office of Internal Oversight Services (OIOS) report on PoC in UN

UN Doc S/RES/2164, para. 13(a)(ii); the United Nations Multidimensional Integrated Stabilization Mission in the Central African Republic (MINUSCA), see UNSC Res 2149 (2014) UN Doc S/RES/2149, para. 30(a).

124 UNSC Res 1296 (2000) UN Doc S/RES/2000, para. 13.

125 Willmot and Mamiya, see n 119, 389–90.

126 Ibid., 390–1.

127 UNSC Res 1894 (2009) UN Doc S/RES/1894, para. 19.

128 UNSC Res 1906 (2009) UN Doc S/RES/1906, para. 5(a), 7.

129 UNGA, 'Report of the Special Committee on Peacekeeping Operations and its Working Group' (2009) UN Doc A/63/19; UNGA, 'Report of the Special Committee on Peacekeeping Operations' UN Doc A/64/19; UNGA, 'Report of the Special Committee on Peacekeeping Operations' (2011) UN Doc A/65/19; UNGA, 'Report of the Special Committee on Peacekeeping Operations' (2012) UN Doc A/66/19.

130 See UNGA, 'Resolution adopted by the General Assembly on 8 May 2009' (2009) UN Doc A/RES/63/280; UNGA, 'Resolution adopted by the General Assembly on 21 May 2010' (2010) UN Doc A/RES/64/266; UNGA, 'Resolution adopted by the General Assembly on 19 July 2011' (2011) UN Doc A/RES/65/310; UNGA, 'Resolution adopted by the General Assembly on 17 September 2012' (2012) UN Doc A/RES/66/297.

131 Willmot and Mamiya, see n 119, 391–5.

132 Mona Ali Khalil, Chapter 9 in this volume.

peacekeeping.[133] The OIOS report concludes that PoC mandates are often not properly implemented, constituting a 'continuing and systematic failure'.[134] In practice, force is almost never used to protect civilians under attack.[135] UN peacekeepers tend to focus on prevention and mitigation activities, rather than physical protection.[136] This is, inter alia, a matter of the political will of TCCs and a problem of the gap between UN peacekeeping mandates and the resources deployed into often difficult and volatile environments.[137] The Security Council's reaction to implementation problems has been narrow and not holistic, as reflected in responses such as the removal of the qualifying term 'imminent' in the mandates of UN missions in Sudan (UNMIS), Darfur (UNAMID), Central African Republic (MINUSCA), Côte d'Ivoire (UNOCI), and the Democratic Republic of the Congo (MONUSCO),[138] and the addition of a Force Intervention Brigade with a more robust mandate to MONUSCO.[139]

It is important to recognize the challenge in conceiving PoC as an *obligation* rather than a legal *authority* to use force.[140] Legal arguments have been made to support this view,[141] but State and UN practice clearly does not treat PoC as a legal obligation. PoC manifests itself more as a mission task, activity, and authority, thereby creating a methodology for the use of force. It is thus rendered less *normative* in nature than humanitarian intervention and RtoP. Usually, it is only seen as engaged for UN peacekeeping missions in which the Council has expressly prescribed it in the mandate.

A related question is whether UN peacekeepers have an *inherent* authority to use force to protect civilians, which is *independent* of the express grant of authority by the UNSC.[142] The Brahimi report suggests that, at least at a moral level, UN peacekeepers should act under a presumption of authorization, when faced with such a situation 'in support of basic United Nations principles and ... consistent with

133 UNGA, 'Evaluation of the Implementation and Results of Protection of Civilians Mandates in United Nations Peacekeeping Operations: Report of the Office of Internal Oversight Services' (2014) UN Doc A/68/787 (OIOS Report).

134 Ibid., para. 80. 135 Ibid., paras 17, 20, 22, 79. 136 Ibid., para. 79.

137 Ibid., paras 30–2. For additional reasons why peacekeeping missions fail to understand and/or exercise the authority to use force to protect civilians, see Khalil, Chapter 9 in this volume.

138 See UNSC Res 1706 (2006) UN Doc S/RES/1706, para. 12(a); UNSC Res 1769 (2007) UN Doc S/RES/1769, para. 15(a)(ii); UNSC Res 2149 (2149) UN Doc S/RES/2149, para. 30(a)(i); UNSC Res 2162 (2014) UN Doc S/RES/2162, para. 19(a)(i); UNSC Res 2147 (2014) UN Doc S/RES/2147, para. 4(a)(i).

139 UNSC Res 2098 (2013) UN Doc S/RES/2098, paras 9–10, 12. See Scott Sheeran and Stephanie Case, 'The Intervention Brigade: Legal Issues for the UN in the Democratic Republic of the Congo' (New York: International Peace Institute, 2014) <www.ipinst.org/wp-content/uploads/publications/ipi_e_pub_legal_issues_the_brigade.pdf>.

140 Willmot and Sheeran, see n 107, 531; Sheeran, see n 106, 369–70.

141 See Section IV(B) of this chapter.

142 Such authorization comes from implied powers within the UN Charter for the defence of its purposes and principles. Thus, by protecting civilians in this context, the UN does not resemble an intervening State, but rather upholds the Charter's norms and values. This is, broadly speaking, consistent with the underlying rationale for action by the international community within the prism of RtoP. See *Guidelines for Rules of Engagement: UN Master List of Numbered Rules of Engagement* (2000) <www.peacekeepingbestpractices.unlb.org/pbps/Library/GLINES_DEVELOPING_ROE_2000.pdf>; Sheeran, see n 106, 362; Willmot and Sheeran, see n 107, 530–1.

"the perception and the expectation of protection created by [an operation's] very presence"'.[143]

F. Responsibility while protecting

Responsibility while protecting (RwP) is a relatively new concept, but worth mentioning in light of linkages between the three other concepts and international practice. It was developed by Brazil, an elected Security Council member at the time, in response to the emerging view that coalition forces in Libya had abused the scope of their PoC mandate provided by the Council, and potentially as a means to appeal to the global South. The concept was introduced during the 2011 Security Council open debate on PoC, and was later reiterated by Brazil in the 2011 general debate of the General Assembly.[144]

RwP is designed essentially as an attempt to constrain the powers of the Security Council and those acting under its authority.[145] The underlying premise is that in exercising RtoP, the international community must exercise its responsibility to intervene within constraints.[146] Furthermore, both 'concepts should evolve together, based on an agreed set of fundamental principles, parameters and procedures'.[147] RwP focuses on developing consensus on the use of force under RtoP through a set of principles to protect civilians. These principles include, inter alia, prevention as the preferable policy, limitations on the use of force to protect civilians, and accountability of those who are authorized to use force.[148] The Secretary-General, in his 2012 report on RtoP implementation, stated that RwP in essence is 'doing the right thing, in the right place, at the right time and for the right reasons'.[149]

Despite the RwP principle being welcomed in overly broad terms by the Secretary-General,[150] it has not gained much traction among the wider UN membership.[151] Its introduction has garnered little political support and had minimal impact, partly because of its misconception of the key problem. The issue

[143] Brahimi Report, see n 117, para. 62, quoting UNSC, 'Report of the Independent Inquiry into the Actions of the UN during the 1994 Genocide in Rwanda' (1999) UN Doc S/1999/1257, 51. See also *Guidelines for Rules of Engagement: UN Master List of Numbered Rules of Engagement* (2000), n 142; Sheeran, see n 106, 367–8.

[144] UNSC (2011) UN Doc S/PV.6650; UNGA and UNSC, 'Letter Dated 9 November 2011 from the Permanent Representative of Brazil to the United Nations Addressed to the Secretary-General' (Brazilian RwP Letter) (2011) UN Doc A/66/551-S/2011/701; Statement by Dilma Rousseff, President of the Federative Republic of Brazil at the Opening of the General Debate of the 66th Session of the United Nations General Assembly (New York, 21 September 2011) <gadebate.un.org/sites/default/files/gastatements/66/BR_en_0.pdf>.

[145] Thorsten Benner, 'Brazil as a Norm Entrepreneur: the "Responsibility While Protecting" Initiative' (Berlin: Global Public Policy Institute, 2013) 3–4 <www.gppi.net/fileadmin/media/pub/2013/Benner_2013_Working-Paper_Brazil-RWP.pdf>.

[146] Brazilian RwP Letter, see n 145, para. 11.

[147] Ibid.

[148] Ibid., para. 11(a)–(b), (c)–(f), (i); Security Council Report, *Cross-Cutting Report: Protection of Civilians in Armed Conflict* (New York: Security Council Report, 2012) 5 <www.securitycouncilreport.org/atf/cf/{65BFCF9B-6D27-4E9C-8CD3-CF6E4FF96FF9}/XCutting%20POC%202012.pdf>.

[149] UNGA and UNSC, 'Responsibility to Protect: Timely and Decisive Response: Report of the Secretary-General' (2012) UN Doc A/66/874—S/2012/578, para. 53.

[150] Ibid., paras 49–53.

[151] Benner, see n 146, 4–9.

is not the overuse, but the underuse, of RtoP for a justified intervention. While RtoP intervention requires Security Council approval, the main challenge in practice is not an overly zealous Council, but rather one that exercises its power selectively and is hampered by the threat or use of the veto. In other words, the Libya coalition intervention was the exception and not the norm for PoC, and there are contrasting problems concerning UN peacekeeping and RtoP situations in which the veto is threatened or used, such as Syria. In UN peacekeeping operations the troops tend to be overly cautious or lack resources to implement PoC especially with robust use of force.[152] The RwP concept fails to tackle that very real problem.

III. A Common Foundation: A Different Focus

A. Commonalities of RtoP and PoC

As demonstrated above, humanitarian intervention, RtoP, and PoC share a common normative and ethical *raison d'être*, namely, the protection of human beings.[153] However, despite the conceptual commonalities, there are also disparities, as each concept has its own distinct focus. The discrepancies are most obvious between humanitarian intervention on the one hand, and RtoP and PoC on the other. Unlike humanitarian intervention, PoC and RtoP as articulated in the World Summit Outcome are responsive to the concerns of national interest and imperialism. The UN's collective security agreement is central for both RtoP and PoC, by virtue of their invocation essentially requiring the authorization or endorsement by the Security Council.[154] The centrality of the UN and multilateral decision-making within both concepts reinforces the legitimacy of global governance and collective security, and acts as a bulwark against *realpolitik*.[155]

Furthermore, while humanitarian intervention focuses on a *right* of intervention by those who carry out such action, RtoP and PoC focus on the *responsibilities* of the State concerned and international community to address the needs of the vulnerable.[156] Building on this dichotomy, RtoP and PoC, unlike humanitarian intervention, are not necessarily synonymous with military intervention and both concepts can be constituted by a wide variety of multifaceted protection activities.[157] RtoP has been conceived to include human rights (preventive) and

152 OIOS Report, see n 134, para. 79.

153 Security Council Report, see n 57, 4.

154 ICISS Report, see n 54, para. 6.14–6.15; UNGA, see n 81, para. 203; UNGA, see n 82, paras 122–6

155 ICISS Report, see n 54, para. 6.9. Collective intervention helps to ensure that the RtoP criterion of 'Right Intention', namely halting or averting human suffering, is satisfied. See Evans, n 2, 85.

156 Breakey, Francis, Popovski, Sampford, Smith, and Thakur, see n 77, 10; Stahn, see n 63, 103; Evans, see n 2, 83.

157 The Global Centre for the Responsibility to Protect, 'The Relationship between the Responsibility to Protect and the Protection of Civilians in Armed Conflict' (New York: City University of New York, 2012) 2<www.globalr2p.org/media/files/the_relationship_between_r2p_and_poc_in_armed_conflict_brief_21_june_2012.pdf>; Breakey, Francis, Popovski, Sampford, Smith, and Thakur, see n 77, 9.

development (assistance) pillars, in addition to the military (response) pillars.[158] As explored in detail elsewhere in this volume, PoC has also been conceived to include the protection and promotion of human rights,[159] humanitarian relief efforts,[160] and development activity,[161] in addition to the use of force by peacekeepers.[162] Humanitarian intervention lacks such a holistic approach, and despite purportedly being for humanitarian purposes, it also lacks a victim-centric approach, focussing strongly on the rights of the intervener.

Both RtoP and PoC represent a promotion of the UN Charter, and the Organization's Purposes set out in Article 1, particularly those associated with 'respect for human rights'. Both concepts also pose a challenge to the Principles in Article 2 associated with State sovereignty and non-intervention, and to the traditional, Westphalian international legal order.[163] The development of RtoP and PoC has marked a departure from a textualist or originalist approach to the UN Charter, especially Chapter VII, under which the use of force was focused on inter-State wars only. RtoP and PoC accordingly represent a change in the international community's understanding of international peace and security, and are twin pillars of a conceptual and normative shift in global governance and use of force for humanitarian purposes. However, central to the acceptance and effectiveness of both concepts is the legitimacy of Security Council decisions on use of force, and the impartiality and effectiveness of UN peacekeeping operations under the ultimate command and control of the Secretary-General.

B. UN attempts to define the relationship: Political vs legal?

RtoP and PoC are interrelated subsets of the same objectives, for example protection of human rights, and are complimentary and mutually reinforcing. Yet, their relationship to each other has not been extensively considered at the conceptual or doctrinal level in the literature, and consequently, there has been discernible confusion regarding their precise correlation. The interrelationship has been recognized in Security Council thematic and country-specific resolutions and in the Secretary-General's reports. For example, the World Summit Outcome's articulation of RtoP has been incorporated in the PoC context in thematic Security Council resolutions 1674 (2006) and 1894 (2009).[164] Regarding country-specific

158 See generally UNGA, 'Implementing the Responsibility to Protect: Report of the Secretary-General' (2009) UN Doc A/63/677.

159 For example, see Michael Keating and Richard Bennett, Chapter 16 in this volume.

160 For example, see Sara Pantuliano and Eva Svoboda, Chapter 17 in this volume.

161 For example, see Lise Grande, Chapter 18 in this volume.

162 For example, see also Fiona Blyth and Patrick Cammaert, Chapter 14, and Stian Kjeksrud, Chapter 15, in this volume.

163 UN Charter, see n 18, Articles 1(1) and (3), and see and compare Articles 2(1), (4), (7); Tsagourias, see n 15, 409.

164 UNSC Res 1674 (2006) UN Doc S/RES/1674, para. 4: 'Reaffirms the provisions of paragraphs 138 and 139 of the 2005 World Summit Outcome Document regarding the responsibility to protect populations from genocide, war crimes, ethnic cleansing and crimes against humanity.' UNSC RES 1894 (2009) UN Doc S/RES/1894, preambular para. 7: 'Reaffirming the relevant provisions of the 2005 World Summit Outcome Document regarding the protection of civilians in armed conflict,

resolutions, resolution 1706 (2006) on Darfur reaffirms RtoP and the thematic resolution 1674 on PoC in armed conflict, and then goes on to authorize the use of force to protect civilians under threat of violence.[165] In his 2007 *Report on the Protection of Civilians in Armed Conflict*, the UN Secretary-General suggested that RtoP, as manifest in the World Summit Outcome, has advanced the normative framework of PoC.[166] The Secretary-General also recognized an explicit connection between the two concepts in his 2009 report on implementing RtoP, and called for the mainstreaming of RtoP through UN peacekeeping operations.

However, confusion over the relationship between RtoP and PoC became apparent in the Secretary-General's report on PoC in 2012, which asserted that PoC was a *legal* concept and RtoP a *political* concept.[167] The Secretary-General's report on RtoP in 2012, published only two months later, backtracked and reinstated RtoP to its traditional grounding in international law.[168] However, political nuances remain within this 2012 RtoP report. While RtoP is referred to as 'a concept based on fundamental principles of international law as set out, in particular, in international humanitarian, refugee and human rights law',[169] it is also described as providing 'a political framework based on [such] principles ... for preventing and responding to genocide, war crimes, ethnic cleansing and crimes against humanity'.[170] In fact, RtoP and PoC both in the wider sense contain normative aspects and policy, as well as operational and institutional elements.[171]

As Nicholas Tsagourias notes, because peacekeeping is a central tool used by the UN to realize its objectives, the connections between RtoP and PoC are 'not only normative, but also institutional and operational'.[172] Within both RtoP and PoC, the primary or initial responsibility rests with the State concerned.[173] In this sense, PoC is a mechanism that enables peacekeeping operations to assist States in fulfilling their primary responsibility.[174] Insofar as a UN mission is established with host State consent, PoC could fall within the second pillar of RtoP, namely, supporting host States in fulfilling their protection responsibilities.[175] Indeed, both RtoP and PoC embody implementation measures with overlapping preventative and capacity-building aspects.[176] This preventative and capacity-building connection is considered in the Secretary-General's 2012 report on RtoP:

including paragraphs 138 and 139 thereof regarding the responsibility to protect populations from genocide, war crimes, ethnic cleansing and crimes against humanity.'

[165] UNSC Res 1706 (2006) UN Doc S/RES/1706, preambular para. 2, para. 12(a).

[166] UNSC, 'Report of the Secretary-General on the Protection of Civilians in Armed Conflict' (2007) UN Doc S/2007/643, para. 11.

[167] UNSC, 'Report of the Secretary-General on the Protection of Civilians in Armed Conflict' (2012) UN Doc S/2012/376, para. 21.

[168] UNGA and UNSC, see n 150, paras 9, 59. [169] Ibid., para. 9.

[170] Ibid., para. 59.

[171] Breakey, Francis, Popovski, Sampford, Smith, and Thakur, see n 77, 44.

[172] Tsagourias, see n 15, 409–10.

[173] ICISS Report, see n 54, para. 2.29; UNSC Res 1674 (2006) UN Doc S/RES/1674, preambular para. 9; UNSC Res 1590 (2005) UN Doc S/RES/1590, para. 16.

[174] Khalil, Chapter 9 in this volume.

[175] Willmot and Mamiya, see n 119, 382. For the normative content of the second pillar, see UNGA, see n 159, paras 28–48; Bellamy, see n 103, 37.

[176] Tsagourias, see n 15, 409.

United Nations peacekeeping missions are based on the principle of consent and generally deploy in support of and with the overall consent of the host State. As such, they fall under pillar two [assistance] and are to be distinguished from pillar three tools [response/intervention].[177]

However, as Alex Bellamy notes, the UN's engagement 'has not perceptibly changed as a result' of PoC being seen through an RtoP prism, for example, in Darfur and eastern DRC.[178] Furthermore, the Secretary-General qualified the connection, stating that: 'While the work of peacekeepers may contribute to the achievement of [RtoP] goals, the two concepts . . . have separate and distinct prerequisites and objectives.'[179] No further reasoning is provided to supplement this point, perhaps reflecting a lack of impetus or clarity within the Secretariat on the relationship between RtoP and PoC, or a desire to keep PoC distinct from its more controversial cousin.

C. A vertical rather than horizontal relationship constituted by the use of force

Hugh Breakey articulates the distinction that humanitarian intervention and RtoP endeavour to protect *populations* facing the four main atrocity crimes, whereas PoC endeavours to protect *individuals* facing physical violence.[180] This usefully suggests a more *vertical* relationship than the *horizontal* relationship often implied by others, such as the Secretary-General with his political and legal dichotomy. However, the distinction that Breakey posits is blurred, as the four atrocity crimes are constituted in theory and practice by violence against the individual, making the distinction more one of scale and aggregation.

The nature of the three concepts can be better understood through the prism of different types of use of force—strategic, operational, and tactical. In a basic sense, strategic use of force refers to the macro level of intervention in a State, for example, the mandating of a peace enforcement mission under Chapter VII or an act of self-defence under Article 51.[181] Operational use of force pertains to the planning level, such as development of a UN peacekeeping mission's military concept of operations. Tactical use of force refers to the micro level, such as use of force by individual soldiers or army units based on a particular factual circumstance such as a patrol.

RtoP and humanitarian intervention relate significantly to the strategic use of force and, indeed, directly confront the issue of military intervention.[182] PoC is

[177] UNGA and UNSC, (2012) UN Doc A/66/874—S/2012/578, para. 16.

[178] Alex J Bellamy, *Global Politics and the Responsibility to Protect: From Words to Deeds* (Routledge 2011) 89.

[179] UNGA and UNSC (2012) UN Doc A/66/874—S/2012/578, para. 16.

[180] Breakey, Francis, Popovski, Sampford, Smith, and Thakur, see n 77, 10, 16; Jon Harald Sande Lie, *Protection of Civilians, the Responsibility to Protect and Peace Operations* (Oslo: Norwegian Institute of International Affairs, 2008) 5 <english.nupi.no/content/download/8505/85101/version/2/file/R2P-4-Sande+Lie.pdf>.

[181] Capstone Doctrine, see n 114, 34–5.

[182] Willmot and Mamiya, see n 119, 381–2.

more concerned with the operational and tactical use of force through the mission's tasking usually in the context of host State consent, genuine or coerced, to the mission's deployment.[183] Indeed, within the PoC rubric the use of force is arguably not a primary aim, but rather a result of the mandate.[184] This distinction is recognized in the ICISS Report as 'the responsibility to protect means that human protection operations will be different from both the traditional operational concepts for waging war and for UN peacekeeping operations'.[185] This distinction—humanitarian intervention and RtoP as strategic and PoC as operational and tactical—illustrates the differing foci of the concepts.

A similar yet nuanced dichotomy is recognized in the 2008 *UN Peacekeeping Operations: Principles and Guidelines* (also known as the Capstone Doctrine), which argues that the strategic use of force defines peace enforcement operations, and the tactical use of force defines peacekeeping operations.[186] While this distinction receives scant attention within the Capstone Doctrine, the use of force at the tactical level would certainly cover physical protection of individuals under a PoC mandate. However, the distinction between peacekeeping and peace enforcement has gradually blurred as peacekeeping mandates have become more 'muscular'.[187] Victoria Holt and Tobias Berkman argue that coercive PoC missions, whereby protection is the major objective of the operation, come close to crossing the line into RtoP's intervention approach and that 'modifying traditional peacekeeping operations is an inadequate answer for upholding protection mandates in extreme circumstances such as large-scale violence or genocide'.[188] The central challenge in protecting civilians is operating in the grey area between traditional peacekeeping and RtoP's intervention force.[189] However, the Department of Peacekeeping Operations has historically tried to avoid placing itself in a position where its missions are expected to respond to mass atrocity crimes. This is due to expectation management and limited resources and capacity to respond to RtoP situations.[190]

While PoC doctrine does not explicitly confront military intervention, it is difficult to assert that it avoids the issue in practice.[191] Whereas RtoP faces political and operational criticisms and challenges, PoC is generally accepted throughout the UN.[192] PoC is innovative in that it represents the most legitimate use of force at the operational level,[193] and therefore makes more legitimate the use of force at the

183 Willmot and Sheeran, see n 107, 523; Willmot and Mamiya, see n 119, 381–2.

184 Tsagourias, see n 15, 404, 410–11.

185 ICISS Report, see n 54, para. 7.50.

186 Capstone Doctrine, see n 114, 19, 34–5.

187 Chesterman, see n 5, 173.

188 Victoria Holt and Tobias Berkman, *The Impossible Mandate? Military Preparedness, the Responsibility to Protect and Modern Peace Operations* (Washington, DC: The Stimson Center, 2006) 50–1 <www.stimson.org/images/uploads/research-pdfs/Complete_Document-TheImpossible_Mandate-Holt_Berkman.pdf>. See also Breakey, Francis, Popovski, Sampford, Smith, and Thakur, n 77, 87.

189 Holt and Berkman, see n 189, 178.

190 Breakey, Francis, Popovski, Sampford, Smith, and Thakur, see n 77, 87.

191 Ibid., 11.

192 Lie, see n 180, 17; Breakey, Francis, Popovski, Sampford, Smith, and Thakur, see n 77, 16.

193 Sheeran, 'The Use of Force in United Nations Peacekeeping Operations', see n 106, 368; Daphna Shraga and Ralph Zacklin, 'The Applicability of International Humanitarian Law to United Nations Peace-Keeping Operations: Conceptual, Legal and Practical Issues' in Umesh Palwankar (ed.),

strategic level. Consequently, the Security Council uses PoC to frame the way in which force may be used, regarding the mission's task (operational use of force) but also the legal authority (strategic use of force). The acceptability of the strategic intervention, that is, the UN peacekeeping mission and host State consent thereto, is closely linked to the nature of the use of force it is authorized to use. Consequently, PoC mandates represent a 'new legal and moral dimension' to the use of force.[194]

D. A challenge to state sovereignty and UN membership support

Humanitarian intervention, RtoP, and PoC, both separately and collectively, are a challenge to the Westphalian notion of State sovereignty and the principle of non-intervention articulated in Article 2(7) of the UN Charter. Furthermore, both RtoP and PoC move away from the idea of 'sovereignty as *control*' whereby the State has 'capacity to make authoritative/decisions about the people and resources within [its] territory'.[195] The three concepts did not initiate the trend to degrade sovereignty, but rather crystallized currents of discourse that already existed. For example, a foundation current has been the Security Council's reconceptualization of Article 39 of the Charter, to include internal violations of human rights and humanitarian law as the basis for Chapter VII action.

As Breakey notes, at a general level, 'PoC is more neutral and respectful of sovereignty than RtoP'.[196] PoC functions on the basis of the concerned State's consent and also complementarity, as action is only authorized where the host State is unwilling or unable to protect civilians. Consequently, PoC is accepted by the wider UN membership as is evident in C-34 resolutions, not having been cast in the North–South divide to the extent that RtoP and humanitarian intervention have.[197] However, there are concerns that PoC is becoming more politicized through the introduction of RtoP into Security Council resolutions on PoC.[198]

In addition, Mona Khalil suggests that the Security Council has created a 'misleading impression' that a PoC mandate is an enforcement action through explicit Chapter VII references in the chapeau of establishing resolutions, thereby obscuring the fact that peacekeeping missions are established with host State consent and show respect for State sovereignty.[199] The reality may be different, however, as while host State consent is politically emphasized it is often coerced, and is also rendered technically irrelevant *ex post facto* by virtue of a Chapter VII authorization, at least until the mandate's renewal. There are numerous examples, in the context of

International Committee of the Red Cross Symposium on Humanitarian Action and Peacekeeping Operations (Geneva: International Committee of the Red Cross, 1994) 39, 43; Cox, see n 107, 258; Willmot and Mamiya, see n 119, 396–7.

[194] Christine Gray, *International Law and the Use of Force* (3rd edition) (Oxford: Oxford University Press, 2008) 313; Willmot and Mamiya, see n 119, 376.

[195] Evans, see n 2, 81–2.

[196] Breakey, Francis, Popovski, Sampford, Smith, and Thakur, see n 77, 24.

[197] Willmot and Mamiya, see n 119, 381.

[198] The Global Centre for the Responsibility to Protect, see n 158, 1.

[199] Khalil, see Chapter 9 in this volume.

'consent-based' UN peacekeeping operations, of host State government behaviour that suggests an absence of real consent and consistent and determined undermining of the UN mandate and effective protection of civilians.

IV. Constraints and Shared Pathologies

When put to the test in the international legal and political environment, humanitarian intervention, RtoP, and PoC have had varied levels of success, and faced many constraints and hurdles. Humanitarian intervention is a concept that has not been accepted by the international community as a legal exception to the UN Charter's prohibition on the use of force. Instead, it is regarded as the preserve of the powerful. While conceptually cogent, rational, and defendable, RtoP in practice is more politicized and controversial than PoC among the wider UN membership and particularly the NAM countries. This is evidenced by difficulties the Secretary-General has faced in obtaining a General Assembly resolution to support his implementation of RtoP. Despite challenges to PoC posed by the Security Council's authorization of coalition forces in Libya, this concept has flourished in UN peacekeeping operations as the most prevalent international tool for the contemporary use of force.

A. Definitional ambiguity

Humanitarian intervention is criticized for its lack of substantive and procedural clarity—a critical view being it is simply 'just war' in the eyes of the (powerful) beholder. Both RtoP and PoC though also suffer from definitional ambiguity. The four seminal documents on RtoP all embody slightly differing versions of the concept.[200] For example, all four documents take different approaches to the use of force when it is not authorized by the international community through the Security Council, despite their common denominator that the collective security system should be the primary forum to support military intervention.[201] While this divergence promoted the popularity of RtoP by enabling 'different bodies to promote different goals',[202] it contributed to normative uncertainty and the rendering of the concept as more 'a political catchword rather than a legal norm'.[203]

A similar fate has befallen PoC, whereby there is 'a disconnect between mandates, intentions, expectations, interpretations and real implementation capacity'.[204] Such mandates remain 'largely undefined as both a military task and as a mission-wide task', meaning '[e]ach mission interprets its protection mandate as best it can in its specific context'.[205] Furthermore, the use of protection lexicon varies further across the interpretive communities of humanitarian assistance, human rights, and peacekeeping, resulting in fragmented and conflicting conceptions of and a lack of a

[200] Stahn, see n 63, 118. [201] Ibid., 119–20. [202] Ibid., 118. [203] Ibid., 120.
[204] UNSC, 'Report of the Secretary-General on the Protection of Civilians in Armed Conflict' (2009) UN Doc S/2009/277, para. 51.
[205] Ibid., para. 52. [206] Willmot and Sheeran, see n 107, 518, 531–5.

coherent strategy towards civilian 'protection'.[206] Some commentators distinguish between narrow PoC, with its origins in international humanitarian law,[207] and broad PoC, which takes a human rights-based approach to protecting individuals.[208] This has occurred to the detriment of the practical implementation of PoC mandates in peacekeeping operations: for example, where peacekeeping missions use force against government forces, it can result in retaliatory restrictions for humanitarian access.[209] Consequently, the concept of PoC is diluted and the 'focus and effectiveness of the use of force to protect civilians' is undermined.[210]

The focus on physical protection and human needs in the UN Secretariat's conceptualization of PoC has at times misconstrued these aspects as being distinct from human rights.[211] This is reflected in the UN Secretariat's major initiative, the Human Rights Up Front Plan of Action. The Plan of Action represents an attempt to better orientate the Secretariat's work towards human rights and operationalize human rights across the Organization. The Plan delineates PoC to a narrower context than human rights by stating in the Preamble that '[w]here conflict occurs nevertheless, the imperative for the UN System is the protection of civilians'.[212] This is the sole reference to PoC in the Plan of Action, reinforcing the Secretariat's distinction between PoC and human rights.

Nonetheless, the Human Rights Up Front Plan of Action may be seen as an attempt to assist in the implementation of RtoP and PoC. It sets out an 'action' for the UN to provide 'Member States with candid information with respect to peoples at risk of, or subject to, serious violations of human rights or humanitarian law'.[213] This action provides greater transparency to civilian protection needs but runs against State sovereignty and the risk that, within a peacekeeping context, the host State's consent will be withdrawn if government actors are identified as committing human rights violations.[214] It is unclear how this action can be achieved within the context of the Security Council, given the unlikelihood of all members agreeing to mandate changes or other actions to seriously promote this objective. Yet, all this said, international debate and action without the RtoP and PoC concepts is difficult to imagine in today's context, despite the lack of clarity, or even confusion, over their definition and relationships.

B. An expectation without a corresponding positive obligation to act

A common problem facing humanitarian intervention, RtoP, and PoC is that conceptually they suggest the need for action, but normatively they do not create a

207 Security Council Report, see n 57, 5.

208 This approach draws from the 1949 Geneva Conventions and their 1977 Additional Protocols, the 1948 Universal Declaration on Human Rights, the 1966 International Convention on Civil and Political Rights, the 1966 International Convention on Economic, Social and Cultural Rights, the 1951 Convention relating to the Status of Refugees, the 1984 Convention against Torture, the 1989 Convention on the Rights of the Child, and the 1998 Statute of the International Criminal Court.

209 Willmot and Sheeran, see n 107, 518, 535–7.

210 Ibid., 518.

211 See Siobhán Wills, Chapter 10 in this volume.

212 'Rights Up Front' (May 2014) United Nations Secretary-General www.un.org/sg/rightsupfront/doc/RuFAP-summary-General-Assembly.htm.

213 Ibid.

214 Willmot and Sheeran, see n 107, 536.

firm obligation to act. There is limited authority for the imposition of positive obligations under international law. Under international human rights law, the State has a positive obligation to respect and promote the human rights of its people.[215] This is a substantive and procedural obligation of due diligence.[216] With regard to international humanitarian law, it is argued that common Article 1 of the Geneva Conventions (1949) provides a prima facie positive obligation to 'ensure respect' for international humanitarian law, whether by one's own forces or other actors in the armed conflict.[217] However, others grant this rule a narrower interpretation and cite consistent State practice to the contrary.[218] There is also the positive obligation to prevent genocide. This is enshrined in Article 1 of the Genocide Convention (1948) and is to some extent recognized in the International Law Commission's (ILC) Draft Articles on State Responsibility and International Organizations.[219]

In relation to PoC, while mandates provide a right to use force, whether they imply an *obligation* as such is unclear.[220] Some scholars argue that PoC creates an affirmative obligation to act.[221] Khalil argues that this duty entails prevention, preemption, deterrence, and response, once there is a 'reasonable belief that a potential aggressor has the intent and capacity to inflict physical violence'.[222] Some support for this is found in the Department of Peacekeeping Operations and Department of Field Support's *Concept of Protection of Civilians Operations*, which envisages a holistic, proactive approach to PoC.[223] Khalil argues that a 'failure to use authorised force may … amount to a failure to fulfil the PoC mandate',[224] an argument framed in policy terms but with legal undertones. Similarly, Siobhán Wills suggests that, under international human rights and humanitarian law, peacekeeping forces are *obliged* to protect people in 'their immediate care, insofar as they are capable of doing so; and to take reasonable precautions, where feasible, to prevent attacks

215 International Covenant on Civil and Political Rights (adopted 16 December 1966, entered into force 23 March 1976) 999 UNTS 171, Article 2(1); American Convention on Human Rights (adopted 22 January 1969, entered into force 18 July 1978) 1144 UNTS 123, Article 1(1); UN Convention against Torture and Other Cruel, Inhuman or Degrading Treatment or Punishment (adopted 10 December 1984, entered into force 26 June 1987) 1465 UNTS 85, Article 2(1).

216 See, for example, *Velásquez Rodriquez v Honduras*, Judgment (Merits) (29 July 1988) IntAmCtHR (Series C) No 4, paras 172–5; *Osman v The United Kingdom* 23452/94 [1998] ECHR 101 (28 October 1998), paras 115–16.

217 Siobhán Wills, *Protecting Civilians: The Obligations of Peacekeepers* (Oxford: Oxford University Press, 2009) 100–10. See, for example, Louise Arbour, 'The Responsibility to Protect as a Duty of Care in International Law and Practice' (2008) 34 Rev of Intl Studies 445, 445, 453.

218 Laurence Boisson de Chazournes and Luigi Condorelli, 'Common Article 1 of the Geneva Conventions Revisited: Protecting Collective Interests' (2000) 82 IRRC 67; Carlo Focarelli, 'Common Article 1 of the 1949 Geneva Conventions: A Soap Bubble?' (2010) 21 EJIL 125.

219 International Law Commission, Draft Articles on the Responsibility of States for Internationally Wrongful Acts (DARSIWA), in UNGA, 'Report of the International Law Commission' (2001) UN Doc A/56/10, Article 41, paras 2–3; Draft articles on the responsibility of international organizations, in UNGA, 'Report of the International Law Commission' (2011) UN Doc A/66/10, Article 42; see and compare *Case Concerning the Application of the Convention on the Prevention and Punishment of the Crime of Genocide (Bosnia and Herzegovina v Serbia and Montenegro)* (Judgment) [2007] ICJ Rep 43, para. 429.

220 Willmot and Mamiya, see n 119, 377–8.

221 Khalil, Chapter 9 in this volume.

222 Ibid.

223 *Draft Operational Concept on PoC*, see n 108.

224 Khalil, Chapter 9 in this volume.

where these are clearly foreseeable'.[225] However, such an *obligation*, and by definition potential legal responsibility for failure to use force that is authorized, is not generally articulated or accepted by Member States or the Organization. In relation to RtoP, the ICISS Report's language of a *responsibility* to act, which is 'more than an *option* to protect', is diluted by qualifiers that 'support action, but do not suggest it is a requirement'.[226] Furthermore, the ICISS Report refers simply to the 'residual responsibility' of the international community, a term that lacks legal specificity.[227] The World Summit Outcome subjects the responsibility for collective action, via the Security Council under Chapter VII, to a double qualifier reflecting a more reserved approach.[228] First, Member States simply reaffirm the international community's *preparedness* to take collective action,[229] suggesting a voluntary rather than mandatory intervention.[230] Second, action is to be taken on a 'case-by-case basis',[231] undermining the assumption of a systematic duty.[232] Furthermore, the uncertainty regarding the implications of inaction by States creates doubt as to whether RtoP was sufficiently crafted to be an emerging hard principle of international law, rather than merely soft law or a political or policy goal.[233]

In the ICJ's judgment on the *Application of the Convention on the Prevention and Punishment of the Crime of Genocide (Bosnia and Herzegovina v Serbia and Montenegro)* (2007) the Court clarified that the obligation to prevent genocide is one of conduct, not of result, the standard of which is *due diligence*, and in practice not particularly forward-leaning.[234] Despite a clear factual picture of Serbian support to Bosnian Serb forces operating in Bosnia and at Srebrenica, the Court held that Serbia was not responsible itself for the genocide, only that it had violated the general obligation to prevent the genocide.[235] Even though the Court specifically limited its judgment to the narrow scope of the Genocide Convention,[236] it is debated whether the rationale will ultimately be applicable to RtoP crimes more generally, thereby providing legal substance to central aspects of RtoP.[237]

Stahn argues that the World Summit Outcome understanding of RtoP is partially a progressive development of the law. This is to the extent that collective responsibility is understood in the sense of a positive obligation under Article 41(1) of the ILC's Draft Articles on State Responsibility.[238] Article 41(1) entails a positive duty of co-operation in order to lawfully bring to an end any *serious* breach of a *peremptory* norm of general international law, which is applicable to States regardless of whether or not they are affected.[239] The ILC's commentary indicates 'a joint and coordinated effort by all States to counteract the effects of these

[225] Wills, *Protecting Civilians: The Obligations of Peacekeepers*, see n 218, 266–7.
[226] Holt and Berkman, see n 189, 32. [227] Stahn, see n 63, 120. [228] Ibid., 109.
[229] World Summit Outcome, see n 85, para. 139. [230] Stahn, see n 63, 109.
[231] World Summit Outcome, see n 85, para. 139. [232] Stahn, see n 63, 109.
[233] Ibid., 118.
[234] *Bosnia and Herzegovina v Serbia and Montenegro*, see n 219, para. 430.
[235] Ibid., para. 433–8. [236] Ibid., para. 429.
[237] Breakey, Francis, Popovski, Sampford, Smith, and Thakur, see n 77, 85.
[238] Stahn, see n 63, 115–16. [239] DARSIWA, Article 41, paras 2–3.

breaches'.[240] The commentaries also recognize that such co-operation could be organized within a UN framework.[241]

However, it is debatable whether current general international law fully embraces a positive duty of co-operation and, therefore, Article 41(1) may reflect a progressive development of the law.[242] This issue will be fleshed out should the draft Articles proceed to a diplomatic conference for negotiation and adoption as a treaty. The World Summit Outcome understanding of RtoP stretches the notion of responsibility even further by modifying the ILC draft Articles threshold. In the Outcome, all forms of genocide, war crimes, ethnic cleansing, and crimes against humanity, which are without a threshold of scale, replace the double qualifier of *serious* breaches of *peremptory* norms.[243] Furthermore, the obligation on the international community is broadened from co-operating to end the breach to a general obligation to 'use diplomatic, humanitarian or other peaceful means' or coercive action to 'protect populations from atrocities'.[244]

C. Political selectivity and inability to overcome state sovereignty

As indicated earlier, RtoP and PoC both seek to provide, at different levels, a degree of impartiality and automaticity to use force for humanitarian purposes. The concepts have also progressively shaped the international community's understanding of State sovereignty and international peace and security as reflected in the Charter.[245] However, despite normative and political support, they have not been able to overcome the problems of selectivity and State sovereignty that they set out to counteract.

RtoP and PoC create an expectation to act, which may be met with a corresponding action and justification if the political landscape is favourable. The veto is the nucleus of decision-making in the Security Council, and its use, or threat of use, based on political self-interest has hobbled the response to many international conflicts and atrocities, notably the Rwandan genocide and Syrian conflict. The Security Council, including the major contributors to the UN budget such as the US, has demonstrated that it will not be compelled to mandate a mission and provide the necessary forces.

The system of standing UN forces and the Military Staff Committee under Articles 43–47 of the Charter never materialized. As such, Member States cannot be required or coerced to provide troops for peacekeeping operations, which in turn impacts on incentives for those on the ground—providing forces for UN peacekeeping is a 'seller's market'. This introduces elements of selectivity and inconsistency that undermine RtoP and PoC in the UN context. This is apparent in the international community's ongoing response, or lack thereof, to the civil war in Syria. Although pursuing the purposes of the Charter, RtoP and PoC have been unable to pierce the shield provided by another Charter construct, the veto of Permanent Members.

240 Ibid., Article 41, para. 3.
241 Ibid., Article 41, para. 2.
242 Ibid., Article 41, para. 3.
243 Stahn, see n 63, 116.
244 Ibid., 116.
245 See Haidi Willmot, Chapter 5 in this volume.

In criticizing the veto, Permanent Members, and a lack of intervention in the face of atrocities, care should be taken to avoid being didactic or simplistic. As the 2015 UN High Level Panel on Peace Operations concludes, a political strategy is necessary for any operation and therefore the use of force.[246] RtoP and PoC are primarily attuned to avoiding human suffering rather than resolving a current political and armed conflict that causes that suffering, at least in the narrow sense. Those Member States in favour of intervention sometimes do not support the kind of political compromise necessary for consensus in the Security Council to resolve or manage a conflict.

In addition, RtoP and PoC have not significantly altered the international willingness to undertake interventions, nor the objectivity of the justifications. Pursuant to Article 25 of the Charter, the government of the host State is presumptively required to accept and respect Security Council decisions and UN peacekeepers' mandates once their express or implied consent is established.[247] However, despite this, the strategic consent of the host State is difficult to sustain when peacekeeping operations consider acting against elements of the government's armed forces, or government-backed elements, that pose a threat to civilians.[248] The need to retain host State consent, in order to enable the practical implementation of the mandate more broadly, imposes political and military constraints on peacekeeping operations. Consequently, UN missions have consistently failed to act in the face of human rights and humanitarian law violations by host States, including in Darfur, South Sudan, and eastern DRC.[249] This leads to practical and legal implications for a mission's real or perceived impartiality and constitutes a failure to act in accordance with the mandate.[250]

A converse problem is evident in the less frequent situations in which there is a surplus of political will and interest. This was evident in the battle for Security Council support for the strategic use of force in Libya, which was the sole occasion on which the Council entrusted PoC to a coalition force rather than a UN peacekeeping mission, and authorized it in the absence of host State consent. The controversial resolution 1973 (2011), which authorized Member States 'to take all necessary measures ... to protect civilians and civilian populated areas under threat of attack',[251] was passed with only ten votes in favour.[252] The result was that PoC language was used as a tool to authorize what was essentially an RtoP intervention[253] despite no explicit invocation.[254] This resulted in

[246] High-Level Independent Panel on United Nations Peace Operations, *Uniting Our Strengths for Peace: Politics, Partnerships and People* (16 June 2015) paras 39(i), 100, 177(1) <www.un.org/sg/pdf/HIPPO_Report_1_June_2015.pdf>.

[247] Khalil, Chapter 9 in this volume.

[248] Ibid. See also Willmot and Mamiya, n 119, 381.

[249] OIOS Report, see n 134, paras 45, 70.

[250] Khalil, see Chapter 9 in this volume.

[251] UNSC Res 1973 (2011) UN Doc S/RES/1973, para. 4. This authorization was terminated on 27 October 2011 when the UNSC adopted Resolution 2016 (2011) (UN Doc S/RES/2016).

[252] Security Council Report, *Cross-Cutting Report: Protection of Civilians in Armed Conflict* (New York: Security Council Report, 2011) 18.

[253] Willmot and Sheeran, see n 107, 523; Tsagourias, see n 15, 411; Breakey, Francis, Popovski, Sampford, Smith, and Thakur, see n 77, 11; Statement by the Secretary-General on Libya (17 March 2011) <www.un.org/sg/statements/?nid=5145>; Willmot and Mamiya, see n 119, 392.

[254] The resolution merely reiterates the Libyan authorities' RtoP in its Preamble (see preambular para. 4), omitting reference to the international community's role therein and to the UNSC's

'RtoP in substance and [PoC] in name'[255] and led to conceptual and political problems.

Criticism has arisen where PoC was politically overextended through the alleged use of force for the purpose of regime change. It is arguable that the UNOCI mission's PoC mandate in Cote d'Ivoire was exceeded when UN peacekeepers used force, underpinned by a separate French military deployment, to dislodge the former President from power in a political stalemate.[256] The risk of such action occurring is higher in UN-authorized enforcement actions compared to UN peacekeeping operations, due to the greater injection of national interest and partial leadership.

This was the case in Libya, with controversy surrounding the mandate on whether its interpretation permitted strikes against those ordering attacks on rebel-held towns, rendering Qaddafi a military target.[257] Concerns were raised both within and outside the Council that the NATO operation exceeded the Council mandate and became aimed at regime change rather than PoC.[258] As a result, it is possible that future action may face long-term implications, such as increased reluctance on the part of those States placing their sovereignty at the apex of the international legal system to authorize PoC mandates for non UN-led operations under Chapter VII, other than in the most exceptional cases.[259]

RtoP and PoC draw meaning and strength from their implied and inherent place in the Charter. The problem is that they cannot overcome the fundamental deficiencies in the structure of the UN collective security system, as evident in the veto, non-compulsion to provide military forces, and limited incentives for those who constitute the forces on the ground. Regardless of the Security Council's 'uneven performance, its unrepresentative membership, and its inherent institutional double standards with the Permanent Five veto power', absent a fundamental change in the international system, the Council remains the most appropriate body and *locus* for an international response.[260] There is some truth in Orford's claim that RtoP and PoC are tools of 'international executive rule', with all that is positive and negative about that, and mark the gradual reorganization of international power.[261]

V. Conclusion

The history, relationship, and interaction of humanitarian intervention, RtoP, and PoC reveal much about their meaning and limitations. The first concept developed

affirmation of RtoP in Resolution 1674, which reflects the UNSC's continuing anxiety about the principle and potential precedent-setting. See Breakey, Francis, Popovski, Sampford, Smith, and Thakur, n 77, 83.

255 Breakey, Francis, Popovski, Sampford, Smith, and Thakur, see n 77, 11.

256 Tsagourias, see n 15, 413.

257 Security Council Report, see n 253, 18.

258 Ibid., 20; Security Council Report, see n 8; Alex Bellamy, *The Responsibility to Protect and the Problem of Regime Change* (e-International Relations, 27 September 2011) <www.e-ir.info/2011/09/27/the-responsibility-to-protect-and-the-problem-of-regime-change/>; Bellamy and Williams, see n 95; N Blokker, 'Outsourcing the Use of Force: Towards More Security Council Control of Authorised Operations?' in Weller, see n 15, 214–15.

259 Security Council Report, see n 253, 20, 25.

260 Evans, see n 2, 87.

261 Orford, see n 33, 90–108.

among the three, namely humanitarian intervention, is now a largely abandoned idea but one still necessary to retain in the absence of Security Council reform, including of the veto. The original components that constituted a 'just war', such as just cause and right authority, continue to have relevance today. These components help feed the juxtaposition of *illegality* with *legitimacy* found in humanitarian intervention, as in NATO's actions in Kosovo, a flawed cure for the concept's conflict with the UN Charter and *jus ad bellum*.

RtoP was designed and carefully crafted to respond to failures of international law and politics, as evident in Rwanda and Srebrenica. It is also a direct response to the shortcomings of humanitarian intervention, with its inherent subjectivity and focus on the intervener. RtoP reconceived sovereignty as responsibility, thereby making the shield conditional, and empowering the Security Council with greater legitimacy to act. However, once grafted onto the international system and discourse, it too has failed to lead to real change. The Security Council veto and UN membership's reticence to shoulder the military and financial burdens of acting have stymied its operation. The consequent selectivity has fuelled mistrust, particularly in the Global South. RtoP is regrettably not capable of crystallizing into an effective *obligation* in light of the veto embedded in the UN Charter, which has a lapidary or quasi-constitutional status in the international legal system.

PoC by contrast has been a relatively modest and low-profile concept, developed in response to the crises of UN peacekeeping experience. In this sense, PoC's current extensive impact, measured by predominance in UN peace operation mandates, has been organic and driven from a 'bottom-up' rather than 'top down' model, a contrast to RtoP. PoC's ostensible containment or isolation from divisive debates on intervention and the strategic use of force, and its place within UN missions that have strategic consent, has fed a more healthy acceptance and reception. It is justified to note that PoC has had some successes where RtoP has been less able. Due to PoC's acceptance among the wider UN membership, including across the North–South divide, it has developed into the modern foundation stone for use of force under the Charter. This is manifest in its practical uptake and consistent inclusion in Chapter VII mandates provided by the Security Council.

PoC has also subtly influenced the strategic level use of force and intervention. In theory, a basic principle of peacekeeping is consent, for both mission and mandate, but this is a fiction, as many host States have such operations imposed upon them, with 'consent' politically or even financially coerced. PoC has made the UN's intervention in the form of peacekeeping more compelling for States in which there is mass human suffering in armed conflict. It also represents a fundamental trend in global governance and use of force for humanitarian and human rights purposes by the UN, and a recalibration of the Security Council's powers under the Charter.

There are, however, downsides in the narrative. In the hands of coalitions of States authorized by the Security Council, as in Libya, the PoC mandate has been tarnished. It has succumbed to abuse by powerful States, the key criticism and warning that can be drawn from the experience of humanitarian intervention. In addition, in UN peacekeeping operations the mandate is consistently and tragically under-implemented, including against host State forces that threaten and actually harm civilians. This is due to the sovereignty of both host States and TCCs, and the inability to create real incentives for enforcement of the collective security agreement in the absence of the Charter's original machinery of a standing UN force.

The Security Council's role in engaging RtoP and PoC provides procedural and substantive legitimacy, in theory by acting as a bulwark against unilateral subjectivity and national interest. However, action by the Council faces many significant hurdles, such as the use or threat of use of the veto, the lack of compulsion among UN Member States to assume the burden of military action, and the fact that mandates only amount to an authority to act, rather than an obligation. Despite all that RtoP and PoC have achieved and represent, they have no answer to the absolute block against action that the Permanent Members' veto can provide. This supports a realist perspective that humanitarian intervention, RtoP, and even PoC are able to provide a cloak for self-interest or indifference of the Security Council Permanent Members, their allies, and other powerful States. The active prevention and curtailment of atrocities against civilians should be paramount, and also transcend national sovereignty and interests. However, until the structures of the UN Charter system, especially the Security Council and Permanent Members' veto, are addressed, it will be very difficult to change this reality and further advance the protection of civilians.

3

A History and Conceptual Development of the Protection of Civilians

Ralph Mamiya[1]

I. Introduction

'The protection of civilians' is a phrase regularly invoked by humanitarians and diplomats, political activists and military commanders. Now the centrepiece of major debates within the Security Council, protection language has become key—and controversial—in resolutions on conflicts in Libya and Syria, and in almost every United Nations (UN) peacekeeping mandate since 1999. The international community has united behind the language of civilian protection in an unprecedented manner, despite regular laments that civilians continue to suffer. It is often claimed that the 'normative' content of protection is clear but that there is a 'protection gap' with regard to implementation.[2] This chapter argues, through drawing on the history and development of the protection of civilians as concept and practice, that the implementation gap is traceable, in substantial part, to a normative gap. The principles of promoting and enforcing protection standards remain contested. First, there is an approach rooted in the pre-1945 State-centric system, in which international humanitarian law (IHL) formatively developed—a system in which neutrality and impartiality were constitutive aspects of the international system and of protection. Second, there is the approach of the post-war world of the UN, in which the Security Council may authorize enforcement actions in the name of nearly two hundred States, but where neutrality and impartiality are increasingly considered anachronistic.

[1] The author is the Team Leader for the Protection of Civilians Team in the UN Department of Peacekeeping Operations (DPKO). He writes here in his own capacity and his views do not necessarily represent those of the UN or DPKO. He is deeply indebted to Jonathan Horowitz, Keith Stanski, and Jehanne Henry for their comments on many drafts of this piece, and is grateful to Alexandra Sicotte-Levesque, Ernesto Mauricio Granillo, Damian Lilly, and Conor Foley for their comments and support.

[2] See, for example, Security Council Report, 'Protection of Civilians in Armed Conflict' (New York: Security Council Report, 2013) 3; Ashley Jackson, 'Protecting Civilians: The Gap between Norms and Practice' (London: Overseas Development Institute, 2014) <www.humanitarianresponse.info/system/files/documents/files/HPG_Protecing_Civilians_Gap_2014.pdf>.

The following pages chart a history of the protection of civilians as concept and practice. This task is complicated by the nature of the term 'protection of civilians', which simultaneously encompasses an enormous array of activities and yet appears elusive at times, consistently confounding attempts at concrete definition. Two important studies of the concept find no less than six separate meanings of the term.[3] Approached broadly, a history of the protection of civilians could very easily become a complete history of the human rights, humanitarian, peacekeeping, and international governance movements. Approached narrowly, it becomes a disjointed, technical history, framed by disagreements in terminology, policy, and doctrine within fields of practice. Rather than attempting to resolve such competing positions, which often owe as much to bureaucratic as to conceptual differences, this chapter traces uses of the term 'protection' and the 'protection of civilians', examining each usage within its own field of practice and in its own context while also seeking a narrative of influence between independent developments; for instance, humanitarian protection, the protection of civilians in peacekeeping, and the responsibility to protect (RtoP) are all addressed in what follows.

The narrative traces the evolution of both the standards of protection and the practices used to enforce and promote those standards. While the history of ideas of protection can be traced far back in European history and that of other cultures, the protection of civilians as it is understood today begins with the codification of IHL in the late nineteenth and early twentieth centuries. These standards were later complemented by international human rights law (IHRL) and international refugee law (IRL). The practices of enforcement of the pre-war origins of these legal regimes, seen most strongly in IHL, were based upon a system in which international armed conflict was an accepted way of resolving disputes.[4] In this system, neutrality was not only a disposition, as commonly professed by numerous humanitarian non-governmental organizations (NGOs) today, but also a legal status with obligations. The end of the Second World War and the establishment of the UN fundamentally altered this system, building a new legal regime to regulate when war was acceptable (*jus ad bellum*), further to the manner in which it should be waged (*jus in bello*). The UN, particularly the Security Council, would play an important role in promoting the protection of civilians and utilizing its authority to deploy peacekeepers, sanctions, and other interventions to that end.

As Council action to protect civilians has developed, however, it has also moved farther from the principles of neutrality and impartiality upon which humanitarians and early peacekeepers founded their work; this evolution includes the authorization of intervention in Libya, ostensibly on the grounds of civilian protection.

[3] See Victoria K Holt and Tobias C Berkman, *The Impossible Mandate? Military Preparedness, the Responsibility to Protect and Modern Peace Operations* (Washington, DC: The Stimson Center, 2006) 35–42; Hugh Breakey, 'The Protection of Civilians in Armed Conflict: Four Concepts', in Angus Francis, Vesselin Popovski, and Charles Sampford (eds), *Norms of Protection: Responsibility to Protect, Protection of Civilians and their Interaction* (New York: United Nations University Press, 2012) 40–59.

[4] The League of Nations introduced the prohibition of a resort to force but was short-lived in the face of a lack of support from great powers at the time. See Robert Kolb and Richard Hyde, *An Introduction to the International Law of Armed Conflicts* (Portland, USA: Hart Publishing, 2008) 10, 23.

The tensions between these approaches are real and have influenced Council inaction over Syria. At the same time, this chapter argues that the history of the protection of civilians shows that there is nothing inherently incompatible between Council action on protection and the work of more traditional protection actors, such as the International Committee of the Red Cross (ICRC). Yet effective and sustainable action on protection may require greater attention by the Council to the idea of principled action.

II. The Rise of Legal Protections for Civilians in Conflict

Any history of the protection of civilians is tied fundamentally to the history of IHL. This international legal regime established the language of protection, as well as important standards for protection—standards that were later built upon by human rights and refugee law. Today, there is consensus on these standards as norms by which civilians should be treated during armed conflict. But IHL spoke far less to the ways in which those standards would be enforced. The structures described in the Geneva Conventions to ensure the protection of civilians are grounded in concepts of neutrality and impartiality remain highly influential in notions of protection today. The influence of IHL is also evident, both in the elaboration of protection standards by the international community and in multilateral efforts to enforce such standards.

A. Foundations in international humanitarian law and international refugee law

The modern concept of civilian protection can be traced to IHL[5] during and after the First World War.[6] After unsuccessful attempts to conclude a convention on the protection of civilians in the 1930s,[7] the Fourth Geneva Convention of 1949, titled the 'Geneva Convention relative to the Protection of Civilian Persons in Time of

[5] For ease of reference, this chapter will use the term 'international humanitarian law' (IHL) to describe the laws of war, including 'Hague Law' and 'Geneva Law', while recognizing that the term IHL was rare before the 1949 Geneva Conventions.

[6] Note also that the phrase 'protection of civilians' or 'protection des civils' is found at least as early as 1923, with peaks in usage that roughly correspond to the 1949 Geneva Conventions, the 1977 Additional Protocols, and the 1999 Security Council discussion; since 1999, usage has continued to rise each year. See F Ferière, 'Projet d'une Convention internationale réglant la situation des civils tombés à la guerre au pouvoir de l'ennemi' (1923) 5 Intl Rev of the Red Cross 560, 566–7; see also Google Books Ngram Viewer, available at: books.google.com/ngrams. Analysis through this tool is not a rigorous scientific measure, but the tool provides an informative analysis of the phrases over time. It is also worth noting that concepts of chivalry and the welfare of individuals (rather than states) are evident in the military practices of many cultures and writings at least as early as Grotius. See Heinz Duchhart, 'From the Peace of Westphalia to the Congress of Vienna', in Bardo Fassbender and Ann Peters (eds), *The Oxford Handbook of the History of International Law* (Oxford: Oxford University Press, 2012) 639; and Robert Kolb, 'The Protection of the Individual in Times of War and Peace', in Fassbender and Peters, see n 6, 318. See also in this volume Hugo Slim, Chapter 1, and Jamie Williamson, Chapter 7.

[7] See Draft Convention on the Condition and Protection of Civilians of enemy nationality who are on territory belonging to or occupied by a belligerent (adopted by the XVth International Conference

War', provided an important set of rules for the status and treatment of civilians in wartime.[8]

International humanitarian law first gave legal meaning to terms such as 'civilian',[9] but it would be a significant oversimplification to view the concept of the protection of civilians under IHL as straightforward. The 1949 Geneva Conventions refer to 'protection' several times without defining the term. 'Protection' also became a prominent term for the work of refugee advocates during the inter-war period. As noted with regard to protection under IRL, which arose during the same period and has numerous similarities with protection under IHL,[10] '[t]he word "protection" has become something of a term of art, obscuring something that ought to be fundamentally clear'.[11]

The language of protection in these documents is likely, and in the case of refugee law almost certainly,[12] drawn from 'diplomatic protection' in international law.[13] Diplomatic protection was one of the only areas of international law during the nineteenth century that dealt with wrongs done to an individual in a foreign

of the Red Cross, 29 October 1934, never entered into force) <hwww.icrc.org/applic/ihl/ihl.nsf/Treaty.xsp?action=openDocument&documentId=85EE9A58C871B072C12563CD002D6A15>.

[8] Geneva Convention relative to the Protection of Civilian Persons in Time of War (adopted 12 August 1949, entered into force 21 October 1950) 75 UNTS 287 (Fourth Geneva Convention). Earlier humanitarian law instruments, such as the Lieber Code, the second Hague Convention of 1899, and the fourth Hague Convention of 1907 are important predecessors of civilian protection in humanitarian law. For an overview of these sources, see Waldemar A Solf, 'Protection of Civilians from the Effects of Hostilities under Customary International Law and Protocol I' (1986) 1 American U J of Intl L & Policy 117.

[9] As many scholars and practitioners have noted, despite an abundance of law, separating 'civilians' from 'combatants' in many armed conflicts is both a legal and practical challenge. See, for example, Hans-Peter Gasser, 'Protection of the Civilian Population', in Dieter Fleck (ed.), *The Handbook of International Humanitarian Law* (second edition, Kindle edition) (Oxford: Oxford University Press, 2008) 6123–64; and see generally Helen M Kinsella, *The Image Before the Weapon: A Critical History of the Distinction Between Combatant and Civilian* (Ithaca, USA: Cornell University Press, 2011). Also of note, Hugo Slim has argued that over-legalizing the concept of 'civilian' in discussions of protection is not necessarily helpful from an ethical perspective. See Hugo Slim, *Killing Civilians: Method, Madness and Morality in War* (New York: Columbia University Press, 2010), 259. It is, perhaps, for this latter reason that contemporary usage of 'protection of civilians' by the Security Council is not strictly limited to IHL's boundaries of armed conflict, such as the protection mandate provided to peacekeepers in Haiti. See UN Security Council (UNSC) Resolution (Res) 1542 (2004) UN Doc S/RES/1542, para. 7(I)(f).

[10] Guy S Goodwin-Gill, 'The Language of Protection' (1989) 1 Intl J of Refugee L 6, 7, 10–11. Goodwin-Gill compares the very similar roles of UNHCR and ICRC under the refugee and IHL regimes, respectively—in particular their dual functions as officially recognized, impartial facilitators of protection provisions under the relevant conventions, as well as humanitarian advocates with a 'right of initiative'. In the context of this chapter, it may also be added that the situation of refugees and civilians in conflict (not exclusive categories, of course) is similar in that both face a loss of traditional protections under domestic law: the former because he or she may be a non citizen in a foreign country, the latter because traditional rule of law precepts beak down in situations of conflict.

[11] Ibid., 6.

[12] See Antonio Fortin, 'The Meaning of "Protection" in the Refugee Definition' (2000) 12 Intl J of Refugee L 548.

[13] The link between the language of protection in diplomatic protection and IHL cannot be drawn as clearly as in refugee law, but the complementarity of the systems, particularly with regard to protecting powers, makes a compelling case. See Michael Bothe, Karl Josef Partsch, and Waldemar A Solf, with the collaboration of Martin Eaton, *New Rules for Victims of Armed Conflicts: Commentary on the Two 1977 Protocols Additional to the Geneva Conventions of 1949* (Second edition) (Leiden: Nijhoff, 2013),

country, establishing a role for an expatriate's home State to intercede on his or her behalf.[14] Yet diplomatic protection in the nineteenth and early twentieth centuries was, despite its name, ultimately dependent upon the complainant State. It was frequently a belligerent endeavour, serving as the pretext for the invasion of weaker countries by stronger ones.[15] Diplomatic protection was thus a very State-centric concept, lacking a focus on or respect for the individual, but it likely propagated the language of 'protection' that we continue to use.

IHL established protective standards for civilians composed of negative obligations, such as rules regarding the conduct of hostilities that limit harm to civilians, and positive obligations, particularly where detainees and civilians in occupied territory are concerned.[16] In both of these cases, impartial enforcement, whether through military superiors or domestic courts, was a primary method to ensure compliance. The Geneva Conventions also included the possibility of ensuring compliance through neutral or impartial third parties, including protecting powers—third states designated to safeguard the interests of a conflict party's civilians and prisoners of war[17]—and the ICRC. The Geneva Conventions arose from a legal landscape of: the law of peace, in which traditional international law regulated relations between States, and national governments provided protection to their people; the law of war, when relations between States broke down, internal governance was often chaotic, and IHL provided minimal standards for civilian protection; and the law of neutrality, whereby neutral States and their people remained governed by the law of peace so long as the government respected the rights and duties of neutrality.[18]

The emphasis on neutrality and impartiality for third parties engaged in protection was not an accident but rather fundamental to the system on which the early international legal protection regimes were based. The custodians of IHL and IRL, the ICRC and the High Commissioner for Refugees (first under the League of Nations, later under the UN as UNHCR), respectively, could not, of course, rely on martial strength. The practice of protection under IHL and IRL thus came to be centred on the idea of neutrality, a mirror image of early diplomatic protection, which was implicitly and often explicitly backed by the potential belligerency of the complainant State. The moral landscape of IHL in particular is not one of good and

66, 74; BG Ramcharan, *The Concept and Present Status of the International Protection of Human Rights: Forty Years after the Universal Declaration* (Dordrecht, Netherlands: Martinus Nijhoff Publishers, 1989), 13.

14 Giovanni Distefano, 'The Position of Individuals in Public International Law through the Lens of Diplomatic Protection: The Principle and Its Transfiguration', in Robert Kolb and Georgia Gaggioli (eds), *Research Handbook on Human Rights and Humanitarian Law* (Cheltenham, UK: Edward Elgar Publishing, 2013) 67–70.

15 These included 'the French interventions in Mexico in 1838 and 1861, the intervention of Germany, Great Britain, and Italy in Venezuela in 1902–03, and the American interventions in Santo Domingo in 1904 and in Haiti in 1915': Chittharanjan F Amerasinghe, *Diplomatic Protection* (Oxford: Oxford University Press, 2008) 15.

16 See, for example, Fourth Geneva Convention, n 8, Articles 11, 24, 27, 28, 31, 33, 38, 46, 54, 67, 75, 147.

17 See Fourth Geneva Convention, n 8, Articles 9–12.

18 See Fleck, n 9, 1734–7; 12394–3092.

evil—concepts associated with *jus ad bellum*, the rightness of war—but rather of belligerency and neutrality, of combatants and civilians. By remaining neutral, whether as a neutral nation governed internally by the law of peace[19] or as a civilian, refugee, or soldier *hors de combat* through presenting no reasonable threat, these legal regimes establish protections within the chaos of war. The act of protecting was also clearly connected to remaining neutral. Protecting powers had to be agreed upon by both parties to the conflict and the ICRC and UNHCR have always highlighted the importance of their neutrality in conducting their work.

B. The logic of human rights

Human rights began as a primarily domestic concern, stretching back to Enlightenment philosophers and the American and French revolutions.[20] These ideas articulated a relationship between States and their people, creating obligations on governments to respect and uphold the rights of individuals. International humanitarian law, in contrast, was always international in nature and grew out of a recognition that in times of war these bonds between government and governed—particularly when the government, through its army, entered foreign territory—were strained or broken.

International human rights law took shape with the establishment of the UN, yet despite the atrocities of the Second World War, some of the UN's founding members initially opposed including references to human rights in the UN Charter. Britain, despite a long human rights tradition, worried about the effects of human rights provisions for its numerous colonies; the Soviet Union had the same concerns for its expanding sphere of influence.[21] These concerns reflected a recognition that an international system of human rights logically implied limits to their sovereignty, despite assurance in the Charter that the UN would not interfere in domestic affairs.[22]

While a sharp distinction was drawn between IHRL and IHL for many years,[23] these views began to change in the 1960s, particularly during the conflicts in Nigeria and Vietnam, and the idea of 'human rights in armed conflict' became '"one of the most popular phrases in the United Nations vocabulary" in the beginning of the 1970s'.[24] This popularity arose in part, however, because at the time it was unclear what 'human rights in armed conflict' encompassed,[25] similar to 'the protection of civilians' today. At the same time, IHRL also filled 'gaps' and answered questions regarding protection in wartime. It acknowledged that parties to the conflict may

[19] Neutral States were said to be governed by the 'law of peace', with the protections provided by a functioning peacetime government, rather than the law of war. Ibid., 12400–39, 2315–35.

[20] See Lynne Hunt, *Inventing Human Rights: A History* (Kindle Edition) (New York: WWW Norton and Company, 2007) Chapter 5.

[21] Ibid., 2390–5. [22] Ibid., 2399–404.

[23] Noëlle Quénivet, 'Introduction: The History of the Relationship between International Humanitarian Law and Human Rights Law', in Roberta Arnold and Noëlle Quénivet, *International Humanitarian Law and Human Rights Law: Towards a New Merger in International Law* (Martinus Nijhoff, 2008), 5.

[24] Ibid. [25] Ibid.

still be required to uphold some human rights and provided a deeper and more nuanced jurisprudence on the balance between government interests and individual rights (drawing both on international and domestic human rights law).[26]

The relationship of IHRL to *jus ad bellum*, *jus in bello*, and associated issues of neutrality has been more complicated. Human rights are explicitly mentioned in the UN Charter, and human rights references pervade it 'like a "golden thread"',[27] linking IHRL to the *jus ad bellum*-related powers of the Council.[28] The crime of aggression in the Rome Statute of the International Criminal Court and the duty to prevent genocide in the Genocide Convention similarly seem to imply a link between human rights standards and *jus ad bellum*.[29] Yet the Rome Statute is clear that aggression within international criminal law is separate from *jus ad bellum* and authorized force,[30] and the nature of obligations under the Genocide Convention remain ambiguous.[31] In practice, prominent human rights actors such as Human Rights Watch and Amnesty International have refrained from commenting on the legitimacy of going to war, espousing positions on neutrality and impartiality nearly as strict as humanitarian counterparts.[32]

At the same time, the conceptual foundations of human rights in the domestic sphere, in which courts and police regularly protect individual rights, established expectations that similar enforcement was possible at the international level. As the Cold War drew to a close, these expectations heightened.

III. The Security Council

Alongside the development of protection standards, the advent of the United Nations in 1945 marked a turning point in international enforcement authority.[33] While the IHL regime established standards for the conduct of war (*jus in bello*) and

[26] Ibid., 9; see also Andrew Clapham, Chapter 6 in this volume.

[27] See Scott Sheeran and Catherine Bevilacqua, 'The Security Council and International Human Rights Obligations: Towards a Theory of Constraints and Derogation', in Scott Sheeran and Nigel Rodley (eds), *The Routledge Handbook on International Human Rights Law* (Abingdon, UK: Routledge, 2013) 383–4, quoting John P Humphrey, *No Distant Millennium: The International Law of Human Rights* (UNESCO, 1989).

[28] See William A Schabas, 'The Right to Life', in Andrew Clapham and Paola Gaeta (eds), *The Oxford Handbook of International Law in Armed Conflict* (Oxford: Oxford University Press, 2009) 381–3.

[29] Rome Statute of the International Criminal Court (adopted, entered into force 1 July 2002) 2187 UNTS 90, Article 5; Convention on the Prevention and Punishment of the Crime of Genocide (adopted 9 December 1948, entered into force 12 January 1951) 78 UNTS 277.

[30] Carrie McDougal, *The Crime of Aggression under the Rome Statute of the International Criminal Court* (Cambridge: Cambridge University Press, 2013) 54–6.

[31] See Orna Ben-Naftali, 'The Obligations to Prevent and Punish Genocide', in Paola Gaeta (ed.), *The UN Genocide Convention: A Commentary* (Oxford: Oxford University Press, 2009) 36–40, 56–7; Separate Opinion of Judge ad hoc Lauterpacht, Provisional Measures Order, *Application of the Convention on the Prevention and Punishment of the Crime of Genocide (Bosnia and Herzegovina v Yugoslavia (Serbia and Montenegro))*, 13 September 1993, ICJ Reports (1993) 441.

[32] Schabas, see n 28, 380–1.

[33] The League of Nations had a degree of enforcement authority, though even if it had the support of powerful States, it did not confer the same collective, international enforcement authority that the UN Charter provides. See Dan Sarooshi, *The United Nations and the Development of Collective Security* (Oxford: Clarendon Press, 1999) 28 n 108.

the use of force in armed conflict, and IHRL provided standards for protection in other situations of violence, the establishment of the UN initiated a significant evolution regarding the law of going to war (*jus ad bellum*). The UN Charter effectively outlawed war but also established a Security Council,[34] which was uniquely empowered to authorize Member States to use force and was placed at the apex of a new (and thus far unchanged) legal regime governing the international use of force.[35] This legal regime would play an important role, and the evolution of Security Council action would eventually shape, new understandings of protection.

A. Challenges for traditional concepts of neutrality and impartiality

The UN's system of collective security and the *jus ad bellum*-related powers of the Security Council established a new era in international relations, which differed markedly from the world in which IHL developed. At that time, the use of force by one nation against another required only military strength and national interest, and wars were played out on a map of belligerents and neutral parties.[36] The UN Charter (building on the Covenant of the League of Nations) fundamentally changed this, effectively outlawing war save a handful of exceptions, and establishing the Security Council to direct the nations of the world to act against a threat to international peace and security.[37] The law of neutrality, and arguably its conceptual basis as well, thus does not apply to actions under Chapter VII.[38]

The Security Council did not speak the language of protection until the 1990s. The Council's early history does, however, highlight important historical elements that would come to influence its concept of protection, particularly in peacekeeping. Through peacekeeping, the UN undertook a new form of protection, justifying its action on the grounds of its neutrality and impartiality, drawing on the same moral precepts as IHL. Yet it would also see those principles deeply challenged.

Peacekeeping—the deployment of Member State military personnel and UN civilian staff, including to monitor peace agreements—is not mentioned or described in the UN Charter but was developed ad hoc 'to anticipate and prevent the rival engagement of major powers in areas of local conflict'.[39] The principles of peacekeeping, developed by Secretary-General Dag Hammarskjöld for the UN Emergency Force during the Suez crisis, viewed the legitimacy and success of this new endeavour as rooted in a commitment to act impartially, with the consent of

[34] Christine Gray, *International Law and the Use of Force* (Oxford: Oxford University Press, 2008) 6–29.

[35] Ibid. [36] See Paul Seger, 'The Law of Neutrality', in Clapham and Gaeta, n 28, 261.

[37] Ibid., 261–2.

[38] Ibid., 262. Note that 'neutrality' in this sense is legally distinct from 'non-belligerence' or being 'non-aligned'. The latter terms may be applicable where a State takes no part in an armed conflict authorized under Chapter VII, even though that State would not have the rights and duties under the traditional law of neutrality. Ibid., 266–7. For an alternative but not incompatible reading, see Fleck, n 9, 12462–500.

[39] Mats Berdal, 'The Security Council and Peacekeeping', in Vaughan Lowe, Adam Roberts, Jennifer Welsh, and Dominik Zaum (eds), *The United Nations Security Council and War: The Evolution of Thought and Practice Since 1945* (Oxford: Oxford University Press, 2008), 179.

the parties to the conflict, and with a minimum use of force.[40] Hammarskjöld justified the UN's authority in taking on this role based upon the neutrality and impartiality of the Organization, which created a unique role for it in a divided and decolonizing world.[41]

All of the principles of peacekeeping would be challenged by the UN Operation in the Congo (ONUC) in 1960, a mission that was in many respects a precursor to today's peacekeeping operations mandated to protect civilians. Hammarskjöld described the situation as concerning 'the maintenance of order in the country and the protection of life'[42] and he and his staff sought to stretch the mission's nominally conservative rules of engagement to enable it to protect civilians through the establishment of safe areas and to 'prevent the burning of villages and killing of civilians by force if necessary'.[43] Yet, also similar to many of today's peacekeeping missions, it 'confronted a fragile central state beset by internal division, ethnic tensions and secessionist pressures',[44] with 'no ceasefire line to monitor and no peace agreement ... with armed rebels, ill-disciplined government troops and lawless civilians all posing a threat to lightly armed peacekeepers'.[45]

While the mission tried to maintain its impartiality, both the Congolese government and the Belgian-backed Katangan secessionists soon viewed it with suspicion if not outright hostility. Through a series of resolutions in 1960, the Security Council exercised its *jus ad bellum*-related powers to engage the UN in what is now generally recognized as the first peace enforcement operation.[46] In the sometimes chaotic fighting that followed, more than 120 UN personnel lost their lives.[47] An enduring lesson of ONUC remains that, '[i]nvariably, when the UN uses force it will be seen to be acting partially in favour of one party against another'.[48]

The UN mission in the Congo was an anomaly, however, as Security Council engagement on issues of protection was almost non-existent during the Cold War.[49] As Gregor Schotten and Anke Biehler note, '[t]he Security Council is the only organ of the United Nations which has no explicit authority to deal with human rights. At the time of its creation, human rights were considered strictly internal matters of the state and consequently outside the scope of the Security Council.'[50]

[40] See Alex J Bellamy and Paul Williams, *Understanding Peacekeeping* (Cambridge: Polity Press, 2010) 177–8; see also Anne Orford, *International Authority and the Responsibility to Protect* (Cambridge: Cambridge University Press, 2011) 64–6.

[41] Orford, see n 40, 86–7, 90, 96.

[42] Statement of Mr Dag Hammarskjold, in UNSC (1960) UN Doc S/PV.873, para. 19.

[43] Trevor Findlay, *The Use of Force in UN Peace Operations* (Oxford: Oxford University Press, 2002) 69, citing Operations Directive No 6, reprinted at 412–14.

[44] Berdal, see n 39, 181.

[45] Findlay, see n 43, 56.

[46] UNSC Res 161 (1960) UN Doc S/4741, para. 1, which Findlay describes as 'the first time the Security Council had authorized a military operation under UN command to use force to carry out a Council decision': Findlay, see n 43, 71, and see 72–81. See also UNSC Res 169 (1960) UN Doc S/5002, para. 4, authorizing force to remove foreign mercenaries in the service of the breakaway Katanga province, effectively targeting the military backbone of the secessionist movement.

[47] Findlay, see n 43, 81–2.

[48] Findlay, see n 43, 83; see also Orford, see n 40, 34.

[49] Gregor Schotten and Anke Biehler, 'The Role of the UN Security Council in Implementing International Humanitarian Law and Human Rights Law', in Arnold and Quénivet, see n 23, 312.

[50] Ibid., 310–12.

B. Expanding the concept of threats to international peace and security

The end of the Cold War created new political space for the Council to act. The 'new wars' of this period also brought increased numbers of refugees, a group whose plight was humanitarian in nature and whose cross-border movements established a basis for international concern. In 1991, the Council first recognized a threat to international peace and security due to humanitarian concerns regarding the movement of Kurds out of Iraq.[51] This was followed by the more direct recognition that 'the magnitude of the human tragedy caused by the conflict in Somalia'[52] also constituted a threat. Since the resolutions for Iraq and Somalia, the Security Council has recognized threats to peace and security in humanitarian and human rights situations in numerous instances.[53]

The Council's actions during this period inaugurated a period of unprecedented activity, and marked an important turning point for the practice of protection. In 1993, Francis Deng articulated the concept of 'sovereignty as responsibility',[54] laying out a justification for international intervention if a country failed to protect its people, even if such a situation were limited to internal events. As the post-Cold War world unfolded, and international intervention by the UN became increasingly frequent, the Council continued to identify its motivations for action as 'humanitarian'.[55] By the 1990s, humanitarian organizations worked at the forefront of conflicts in numerous countries and their independence, neutrality, and impartiality—principles carefully developed and applied over decades[56]—provided them with the moral standing that Hammarskjöld found so important for UN intervention.

[51] Ibid., 317, quoting UNSC Res 688 (1991) UN Doc S/RES/688, preambular para. 2.

[52] Schotten and Biehler, see n 49, 317, quoting UNSC Res 794 (1992) UN Doc S/RES/794, preambular para. 2.

[53] See Erika de Wet, *The Chapter VII Powers of the United Nations Security Council* (Oxford: Hart Publishing, 2004) 150–77, as well as UNSC Res 1769 (2007) UN Doc S/RES/1769; UNSC Res 2149 (2014) UN Doc S/RES/1769. As de Wet notes, with the possible exception of Somalia in 1992, all of these situations all had important international dimensions, such as through refugee flows, and thus it is difficult to isolate a 'pure' case of Council concern for violations of human rights or humanitarian law. See de Wet, ibid., 174–6.

[54] Francis M Deng, *Protecting the Dispossessed: A Challenge for the International Community* (Washington, DC: Brookings Institution, 1993) xxix–xxxvi; see also Francis M Deng, Saidikiel Kimaro, Terrence Lyons, Donald Rothchild, and I William Zartman, *Sovereignty as Responsibility: Conflict Management in Africa* (Washington, DC: Brookings Institution, 1996). Note that many scholars had written on sovereignty, challenging conventional notions, since at least the 1980s. See Luke Glanville, 'Sovereignty and Its Antecedents' (2010) 17 Eur J of Intl Relations 233.

[55] See Adam Roberts, 'Humanitarian Issues and Agencies as Triggers for International Military Action', in Simon Chesterman, *Civilians in War* (London: Lynne Rienner Publishers, 2001) 177, 180–6. Roberts notes, at pages 185–6, that humanitarian considerations in these situations, including Bosnia, Rwanda, Haiti, and Sierra Leone, were not always the sole or exclusive reason for action, but also that the lack of international commitment in most of these cases actually argues in favour of an absence of strong competing motives.

[56] David P Forsythe, *The Humanitarians: The International Committee of the Red Cross* (Cambridge: Cambridge University Press, 2005) 157–200.

IV. Humanitarian Assistance and Protection

The prevalence of humanitarian language in Security Council resolutions during the 1990s reflected the growth of humanitarian action globally, particularly on issues associated with the protection of civilians. This humanitarian action would have an important impact on concepts and practices of civilian protection, including the establishment of the most widely agreed definition to date. This definition arose in large part, however, out of struggles that humanitarian neutrality and impartiality faced in a period of increased politicization of humanitarian activities.

The Fourth Geneva Convention not only required conflicting parties to minimize civilian casualties and guarantee the welfare of civilians under occupation and of detainees, but also established the right of access for impartial providers of humanitarian relief.[57] The legal basis for humanitarian assistance has thus been closely linked to the neutrality and impartiality of the deliverers. Note, in this respect, that the 'impartiality' and 'humanitarian' nature described in the Geneva Conventions very much align with modern humanitarians' understanding of the principle of humanitarian neutrality.[58]

Both the ICRC and UNHCR grew from small to large organizations with staff worldwide, in addition to many humanitarian NGOs carrying out relief activities, but often with little experience in legal protection. UNHCR, for example, went from fewer than twenty formal partnerships with NGOs in the 1960s to more than 500 by the mid-2000s, with NGOs taking on increasingly prominent roles in implementing protection programmes and developing protection policy.[59] This led to tension between the protection mandates of ICRC and UNHCR to promote compliance with IHL and IRL, their increasing involvement with the delivery of humanitarian assistance, and an increasingly complex world of internal armed conflicts.[60]

By the 1990s, these tensions risked splitting the humanitarian community. Supporting humanitarian action became the centrepiece for military intervention in Somalia, the former Yugoslavia, the Great Lakes region of Africa, and Iraq, leaving many humanitarians with the impression that their work was being manipulated

[57] Fourth Geneva Convention, see n 8, art. 23, 38.

[58] 'Neutrality' in the Geneva Conventions is a term reserved for actors with international legal personality, such as sovereign States and the ICRC. See Jean S Pictet, *Commentary IV: Geneva Convention Relative to the Protection of Civilians Persons in Time of War* (Geneva: International Committee of the Red Cross, 1958) 97; Denise Plattner, 'ICRC Neutrality and Humanitarian Assistance' (1996) 36 IRRC 161. Yet the practical effect of the ICRC's legal neutrality, abstaining from taking sides in a conflict, comports fully with the neutrality espoused by most humanitarian actors. See and compare Plattner, n 58, and UN Office for the Coordination of Humanitarian Affairs, 'What are Humanitarian Principles' (New York: United Nations, 2012) <docs.unocha.org/sites/dms/Documents/OOM-humanitarianprinciples_eng_June12.pdf>.

[59] Gil Loescher, Alexander Betts, and James Milner, *The United Nations High Commissioner for Refugees: The Politics and Practice of Refugee Protection in the Twenty-first Century* (London: Routledge, 2006) 90.

[60] Forsythe, see 56, 167; Loescher, Betts, and Milner, see n 60, 3–4.

for political ends.[61] One reaction to this has been vocal advocacy to respect humanitarian principles and active distinguishing of humanitarians from political actors.[62] Just as wrenching, however, was the recognition that, in the face of organized violence, such as in Rwanda and Srebrenica, humanitarian assistance did not provide protection in any meaningful sense.[63] This led to an increasing number of humanitarians advocating for a more explicitly political humanitarianism, willing to support military interventions or great power politics where they could reduce civilian suffering.[64]

This knot of challenges led to a series of workshops chaired by the ICRC between 1996 and 2001 to develop a consensus view on protection among humanitarian and human rights actors, including the UN Inter-Agency Standing Committee.[65] The following consensus definition was agreed upon.

> Protection encompasses all activities aimed at ensuring full respect for the rights of the individual in accordance with human rights law, international humanitarian law (which applies in situations of armed conflict) and refugee law. Human rights and humanitarian organisations must conduct these activities in an impartial manner and not on the basis of race, national or ethnic origin, language or gender.[66]

This definition was an important step. First, it privileged legal protection, making the pursuit of respect for 'rights'[67] in international law the purpose of protection activities. Relief assistance, while doubtlessly important, was considered part of protection only where it was intended to promote legal rights.[68] Second, the definition struck a balance between traditional humanitarians and advocates of a more political or human rights-oriented approach, requiring impartiality but making no mention of neutrality, which some organizations view as incompatible with public statements except in extreme cases.[69] It should be noted in this respect that while the above definition is often referred to as a 'humanitarian' one, the UN Office of the High Commissioner for Human Rights took an active part in these

[61] See Adam Roberts, 'Humanitarian Issues and Agencies as Triggers for International Military Action' in Simon Chesterman (ed.) *Civilians in War* (Boulder, USA: Lynne Rienner Publishers, 2001) 180–8; see also David Rieff, *A Bed for the Night: Humanitarianism in Crisis* (New York: Simon and Schuster Paperbacks, 2002).

[62] See, for example, Forsythe, who argues that a 'broad notion of protection counters the notion that other actors [such as military actors] might take over relief in conflicts'. Forsythe, see n 56, 168–9.

[63] See Rieff, n 61, 129–54, 165–79.

[64] Ibid., 149–54; Barnett, see n 62, 157.

[65] Sylvie Giossi Caverzasio (ed.), *Strengthening Protection in War: A Search for Professional Standards* (Geneva: ICRC, 2001) 6–14.

[66] Ibid., 19.

[67] Presumably, the definition references a practical concept of rights, which may include the duties owed by belligerents to protect civilians under IHL, rather than a more developed concept of human rights, which is distinct from the conceptual underpinnings of IHL.

[68] The current ICRC policy on protection, for instance, clearly distinguishes protection and assistance as separate but 'intrinsically linked', designating protection as preventing or putting a stop to violations while excluding 'other activities carried out within a protection framework or those that aim to have an indirect protection impact, particularly assistance activities that seek to alleviate or to overcome the consequences of violations'. ICRC, 'ICRC Protection Policy' (2008) 90 IRRC 751, 752–3.

[69] See James Darcy, 'Human Rights and Humanitarian Action: A Review of the Issues' (London: Overseas Development Institute, 2004) 8–9 <www.odi.org/sites/odi.org.uk/files/odi-assets/publications-opinion-files/2311.pdf>.

consultations and there is no distinct 'human rights definition' for the protection of civilians.[70]

The reformulation of protection in the 2011 SPHERE standards adds the 'do no harm' concept,[71] and a great deal of humanitarian protection work today is viewed as ensuring that humanitarian assistance is delivered in ways that do not create additional risks for the recipients. The 'do no harm' concept grew from recognition that well-meaning humanitarian assistance could leave people vulnerable to the kinds of physical violence against which humanitarians could not protect them. In this respect, it further seeks to overcome the tension between assistance and protection, making clear that assistance should only be undertaken in ways that will not negatively impact recipients' physical safety.

The 2001 definition of protection has been criticized, however, as vague and unhelpful for operational activities.[72] Some commentators argued that 'protection' had become a 'buzzword' in humanitarian circles that placed unachievable responsibilities on humanitarians' shoulders.[73] Others argued that humanitarians would never 'be able to supply the complete protection product: stop[ping] armed actors from harming people',[74] though of course many humanitarians never claimed this.

The ICRC-chaired workshops and the debates that followed remain one of the first and most important sustained attempts to address the concept of protection and the variety of practices that fell under its heading. It is hardly surprising, moreover, that the opinions, experiences, and beliefs of more than fifty organizations with hundreds of years of collective history could not be reconciled on an exceedingly complex topic. Nonetheless, humanitarians' leading role in thinking about the protection of civilians placed them at the forefront when the Security Council turned to address protection more directly.

V. The Evolution of Enforcement

The year 1999 was an important turning point for the protection of civilians. It was the year that the protection of civilians concept, a concept that had been rooted in impartial action among morally equivalent belligerents, and military force became intertwined as never before. This challenged the notion that the protection of civilians was an inherently impartial act, which has had repercussions that are ongoing today.

[70] OHCHR Staff, 'Protection in the Field: Human Rights Perspectives', in BG Ramcharan (ed.), *Human Rights Protection in the Field* (Leiden, the Netherlands: Martinus Nijhoff Publishers, 2006) 121–2.

[71] See The Sphere Project, *Humanitarian Charter and Minimum Standards for Humanitarian Response* (Bourton-on-Dunsmore, UK: Practical Action, 2011).

[72] See Oxfam Great Britain, 'Protection' (*Oxfam GB*, undated) <policy-practice.oxfam.org.uk/our-work/conflict-disasters/protection> (calling the definition 'broad and flawed').

[73] Christian Captier, 'What Does Humanitarian Protection Really Mean?' *Humanitarian Exchange Magazine* (London, March 2003), 15–18.

[74] Marc DuBois, 'Response to Katy Barnett' *Dialogue* (London, 2007) 8.

The evolution in enforcement was presaged by a series of events that generated momentum within the UN. In addition to the ICRC-chaired discussions on protection, in 1998 the General Assembly requested a review of the 1995 fall of Srebrenica and the Secretary-General submitted a report on the protection of refugees, a year later announcing an independent review of UN action during the 1994 Rwandan genocide.[75] The limited mandates of the UN Assistance Mission in Rwanda (UNAMIR) and the UN Protection Force for the Former Yugoslavia (UNPROFOR), both of which had 'humanitarian' aims but could only use force in self-defence, resulted in horrific loss of life on the Organization's watch. Yet the UN continued to face instability in the Balkans, the Great Lakes region of Africa, Sierra Leone, and East Timor. Perhaps most importantly, in March 1999 the North Atlantic Treaty Organization (NATO) began military operations against Serbia without Security Council authorization, embarking on a bold but still controversial approach to intervention.

In this tense atmosphere, the Security Council, under the presidency of Canada, placed the 'protection of civilians in armed conflict' on its agenda in February 1999. The phrase was chosen because it could serve as an 'umbrella for a number of issues of concern to Canada, including the humanitarian impact of economic sanctions, children and armed conflict, peacekeeping mandates, and peacebuilding and conflict prevention'.[76] Canada sought to avoid a 'piecemeal approach' and to 'consolidate the Council's previous work and provide a holistic framework for protection related efforts'.[77] At the same time, the lessons of 1990s UN operations weighed heavily. The Canadian Presidency viewed its work as an 'important departure' from the Council's past resolutions by focusing explicitly on civilian safety and security rather than simply ensuring the delivery of humanitarian assistance.[78]

A. The Security Council framework for the protection of civilians

One of the Security Council's main motivations behind putting the protection of civilians on its agenda was to establish an 'umbrella' or framework for UN protection activities.[79] Beginning in 1999, the Council and the Secretary-General entered into a dialogue through resolutions, presidential statements, and reports, developing a wide-ranging list of issues that fall under the banner of the protection of civilians in armed conflict,[80] even including, initially, humanitarian

[75] See, respectively, UN General Assembly (UNGA) Res 53/35 (1998) UN Doc A/RES/53/35, para. 18; UNSC, 'Report of the Secretary-General on Protection for Humanitarian Assistance to Refugees and Others in Conflict Situations (1998) UN Doc S/1998/883; UNSC (1999) UN Doc S/1999/1257, referencing letter of 18 March 1999, UN Doc S/1999/339.

[76] Elissa Goldberg and Don Hubert, 'The Security Council and the Protection of Civilians' in Robert Grant McRae and Don Hubert (eds), *Human Security and the New Diplomacy: Protecting People, Promoting Peace* (Montreal: McGill-Queen's University Press, 2001) 224.

[77] Ibid., 225. [78] Ibid., 227. [79] Ibid., 224.

[80] As described in the 2001 Secretary-General's report, '"Protection" is a complex and multi-layered process, involving a diversity of entities and approaches . . . Relevant activities may include the delivery of humanitarian assistance; the monitoring and recording of violations of international humanitarian and human rights law, and reporting these violations to those responsible and other decision

intervention.[81] This effort began to establish far more consistency in protection language and more sustained attention to protection issues. Yet despite more than a decade of resolutions and reports, the Council framework has generally avoided substantive discussion of the norms and concepts of protection.

Sustained attention by the Council, supported by the Secretary-General,[82] has resulted in more consistent and more frequent protection language in Security Council resolutions.[83] At the same time, the 'umbrella' of the thematic discussions on civilian protection has done little to advance the pre-existing conceptual debates over protection. Neither the Council nor the Secretary-General has ever advanced a definition or concept of the protection of civilians, preferring to describe protection through a wide range of activities. While Council action has created a much stronger consensus around the idea of protection action, it is difficult to argue that the protection framework has advanced the standards of protection codified in IHL and IHRL, which have evolved independently.

To some extent, this absence of conceptual or definitional focus is not surprising. Many areas of recent action on protection involve geopolitical situations in which great power interests are not at odds. In such situations, decisions to intervene without reference to principles are simple.[84] In situations such as Syria, discussed later in the chapter, the importance of principles, or at least reasonable expectations based on past action, becomes more important.

B. Peacekeeping

The Council's departure from Cold War practice became more evident in the October 1999 Security Council resolution establishing the UN Assistance Mission in Sierra Leone (UNAMSIL).[85] The mission was deployed to fill the vacuum left by a departing multinational force in the midst of a civil war that had resulted in terrible atrocities. It was authorized to use force to protect civilians under imminent threat of physical violence.[86] While prior missions, such as UNPROFOR and the second UN mission in Somalia (UNSOM II), had made attempts at protection, UNAMSIL was the first peacekeeping force the Council explicitly authorized to 'take the necessary action ... within its capabilities and areas of deployment, to

makers; institution building, governance and development programmes; and, ultimately, the deployment of peacekeeping troops.' UNSC, 'Report of the Secretary-General on the Protection of Civilians in Armed Conflict' (2001) UN Doc S/2001/331, para. 6.

81 UNSC, 'Report of the Secretary-General on the Protection of Civilians in Armed Conflict' (1999) UN Doc S/1999/957, para. 67.

82 The Office for the Coordination of Humanitarian Affairs (OCHA), for instance, has regularly compiled an 'Aide-Memoire' for the Security Council, detailing past or potential language on protection issues—language that can be found in numerous Council resolutions on country situations, in thematic topics, or to establish peacekeeping missions. See, for example, UNSC (2014) UN Doc S/PRST/2014/3, Annex; UNSC (2010) UN Doc S/PRST/2010/25, Annex.

83 A Security Council Report found, for instance, that the Council referenced protection in issues in at least 80 per cent of the resolutions where it was applicable.

84 Jaïr Van Der Lin and Xenia Avezov, *The Future Peace Operations Landscape: Voices from Around the Globe* (Stockholm: Stockholm International Peace Research Institute, 2015) 34–5.

85 See UNSC Res 1270 (1999) UN Doc S/RES/1270.

86 UNSC Res 1270 (1999) UN Doc S/RES/1270, para. 14.

afford protection to civilians under imminent threat of physical violence',[87] sanctioning the use of force beyond self-defence or defence of international aid workers.

Despite the lessons of Rwanda and Srebrenica, the UNAMSIL resolution was not a foregone conclusion. The initial draft of the mandate only included traditional, Chapter VI language. Arguing that the situation in Sierra Leone was at least as serious as that in East Timor—for which a draft peacekeeping resolution already envisioned a Chapter VII mandate[88]—Canada lobbied for the new protection mandate,[89] which was immediately recognized as important by many Council Members.[90] In this respect, the UN's willingness to assume expansive administrative powers in East Timor, and on behalf of a departing multinational force, made it easier for Council Members to countenance this new step on protection. The emphasis on a relatively narrow mandate to protect civilians from physical violence, rather than the expansive 'executive' powers of the UN Transitional Administration in East Timor (UNTAET),[91] was likely influenced by the Council debates on the protection of civilians earlier in the year. This choice would have lasting effects. While 'executive' mandates have all but disappeared from discussions of peacekeeping, the protection of civilians mandate has been provided to every armed peacekeeping mission in the past fifteen years, taken almost verbatim from the UNAMSIL mandate.[92]

i. Greater discretion, greater confusion

The Council faced opposition to opining on legal norms regarding protection, focusing instead on the non-legalized concept of physical security.[93] The protection of civilians mandate in peacekeeping is notable for its complete absence of reference to IHL and IHRL. The use of physical violence against civilians can, of course,

[87] UNSC Res 1270 (1999) UN Doc S/RES/1270, para. 14.

[88] Alan Bones, 'Peacekeeping in Sierra Leone', in McRae and Hubert, n 76, 60–1. The resolution providing the UN Transitional Administration in East Timor (UNTAET) with a Chapter VII mandate, which was not passed until after the UNAMSIL mandate, was never particularly controversial because the mission would be replacing an Australian-led multinational force that already had a Chapter VII mandate and had shown the mandate to be important. James Batley, 'From UNAMET to UNTAET: An Australian Perspective', in Nassrine Azimi and Lang Li Lin (eds), *The United Nations Transitional Administration in East Timor (UNTAET): Debriefing and Lessons Learned* (Leiden: Martinus Nijhoff Publishers, 2003) 48–9.

[89] Alan Bones, 'Peacekeeping in Sierra Leone', in McRae and Hubert, see n 76, 60–1.

[90] UNSC (1999) UN Doc S/PV.4504, 10, 15–17.

[91] UNSC Res 1272 (1999) UN Doc S/RES/1272. Under 'executive' mandates such as in East Timor and Kosovo, the UN mission assumed direct administrative powers, such as running ministries and arresting criminals. See Carsten Stahn, 'The United Nations Transitional Administrations in Kosovo and East Timor: A First Look' (2001) 5 Max Planck YB of United Nations L 105.

[92] See and compare, for example, UNSC Res 1270 (1999) UN Doc S/RES/1270, para. 14; UNSC Res 2149 (2149) UN Doc S/RES/2149, para. 30(a)(i); UNSC Res 1925 (2010) UN Doc S/RES/1925, para. 12(a); UNSC Res 1542 (2004) UN Doc S/RES/1542, para. 7(I)(f); UNSC Res 1528 (2004) UN Doc S/RES/1528, para. 6(i); UNSC Res 1701 (2006) UN Doc S/RES/1701, para. 12; UNSC Res 1509 (2003) UN Doc S/RES/1509, para. 3(j); UNSC Res 2100 (2013) UN Doc S/RES/2100, para. 16(c)(i); UNSC Res 2155 (2014) UN Doc S/RES/2155, para. 4(a)(i); UNSC Res 1769 (2007) UN Doc S/RES/1769, para. 15(a)(ii); and UNSC Res 1990 (2011) UN Doc S/RES/1990, para. 3(d).

[93] Goldberg and Hubert, see n 76, 227.

result in violations of international law, but such law permits physical violence against civilians in certain circumstances.[94] The UN Office of Legal Affairs has also interpreted the mandate broadly, using a definition of 'civilian' that applies beyond just armed conflict, and hence is not conscribed by IHL.[95]

De-linking of the protection mandate from IHL and IHRL distinguished the 'direct protection' provided by peacekeepers from the advocacy and assistance undertaken by human rights and humanitarian colleagues. It has also avoided the technical legal discussions that frequently accompany debates regarding international crimes required for action by the International Criminal Court or under RtoP, such as the existence of 'genocidal intent'. This is not to say that protection in peacekeeping does not have important legal dimensions; protection by peacekeepers through the use of force is only possible, of course, both due to and within the powers of the Council, provided by the UN Charter.[96] But the protection of civilians mandate is notable for its absence of legally defined triggers, such as the 'atrocity crimes' of the RtoP doctrine.[97] While the general, de-legalized reference to a 'threat of physical violence' provides peacekeepers with a great deal of discretion in their operations, it also introduced an element of subjectivity to the protection mandate.

The protection of civilians mandate in peacekeeping may have maintained its popularity in great part due to the fact that its brevity permits widely differing interpretations. A 2010 UN study found 'multiple understandings of the concept of "protection of civilians"', which 'reflects the conceptual confusion ... that persists around the subject of protection'.[98] A 2014 UN internal review found that many of those varied understandings continued despite the efforts of the UN Secretariat to provide more concrete guidance.[99] The language of protection may also serve to obscure indecision and disagreement. The Security Council, through its powerful Member States, has regularly deployed relatively inexpensive peacekeepers (from

94 IHL, for instance, provides for a 'combatant's privilege', or the legalization of murder in wartime. Many human rights, on the other hand, may be derogated during wartime, and only governments or government-like entities can violate human rights law. In each case, the less legalized use of 'physical violence' may cast a wider net of such incidents than legal definitions allow.

95 The definition used is: 'Any person who is not or is no longer directly participating in hostilities or other acts of violence shall be considered a civilian, unless he or she is a member of armed forces or groups. In case of doubt whether a person is a civilian, that person shall be considered a civilian.' See UN DPKO and UN DFS, DPKO/DFS Policy: The Protection of Civilians in United Nations Peacekeeping (2015) Ref 2015.07, para. 14.

96 See Scott Sheeran, 'The Use of Force in United Nations Peacekeeping Operations', in Marc Weller, Jake William Rylatt, and Alexia Solomou, *The Oxford Handbook of the Use of Force in International Law* (Oxford: Oxford University Press, 2015) 356–7, 367–9.

97 These are crimes against humanity, genocide, war crimes, and ethnic cleansing. See UNGA (2005) UN Doc A/60/L.1, para. 138–9. 'Atrocity crime' is not a term used by the General Assembly but is common among scholars and practitioners. See UN Office on Genocide Prevention and the Responsibility to Protect, *Framework of Analysis for Atrocity Crimes: A Tool for Prevention* (New York: United Nations, 2014) 1–9.

98 Victoria Holt and Glyn Taylor, with Max Kelly, *Protecting Civilians in the Context of UN Peacekeeping Operations: Successes, Setbacks and Remaining Challenges* (New York: United Nations, 2010) 169–70.

99 UNGA, 'Evaluation of the Implementation and Results of Protection of Civilians Mandates in United Nations Peacekeeping Operations, Report of the Office of Internal Oversight Services' (2014) UN Doc A/68/787, paras 40, 79(a), 85 (OIOS Report).

less powerful and developing countries) to address conflicts far from the powerful members' national interests, and debate continues as to whether increasingly ambitious mandates are being met with sufficient resources.[100] However, ambiguous language can also present obstacles to progress. A lack of clarity on the concept and attached expectations has resulted in almost no instances of force used to protect civilians despite situations that may have called for it.[101]

ii. The principles of peacekeeping and protection

The protection of civilians mandate in peacekeeping has itself been safeguarded by the principles of peacekeeping. These principles—now defined as: (a) the consent of the host State or parties to the conflict; (b) impartiality in execution of the mandate; and (c) the non-use of force except in self-defence, including in defence of the mandate[102]—promote the UN as a third party capable of acting in the best interests of the international community as a whole. They establish a rationale for peacekeepers' special privileges under treaties such as the Convention on the Safety and Security of UN and Associated Personnel (Safety Convention),[103] which provides treatment that is at least rare, if not exceptional, for an armed actor in wartime.[104] The Security Council and the General Assembly have emphasized these principles.[105] The first Council debate on the Protection of Civilians in Armed Conflict also served to motivate work on the Optional Protocol to the Safety Convention, expanding its special protections to cover humanitarian support operations as well as more traditional peace and security work.[106]

[100] See, for example, United Nations, 'Meetings Coverage: Overburdened, Underfunded, Overstretched Peacekeeping Operations Create "Yawning Gap" Between Expectations, Performance, Fourth Committee Told at Close of Debate' (27 October 2010) UN Doc GA/SPD/465; Katharina P Coleman, 'The Political Economy of Peacekeeping: Incentivizing Effective Participation' (New York: International Peace Institute, 2014). See also Bruno Stagno Ugarte, Chapter 13 in this volume.

[101] OIOS Report, see n 99, para. 79.

[102] UN DPKO and UN DFS, *UN Peacekeeping Operations: Principles and Guidelines* (New York: United Nations, 2008) 31–6 (Capstone Doctrine). Note that these differ slightly from the original principles set out by Hammarsklojd.

[103] Convention on the Safety and Security of United Nations and Associated Personnel (adopted 9 December 1994, entered into force 15 January 1999), annexed to UNGA Res 49/59 (1994) UN Doc A/RES/49/59.

[104] See Tristan Ferraro, 'The Applicability and Application of International Humanitarian Law to Multinational Forces' (2013) 95 IRRC 561, 569–72 (noting that, while the Convention on the Safety and Security of UN Personnel may be interpreted as consonant with traditional interpretations of IHL, the plain language of the treaty appears to establish peacekeepers as a privileged class of combatants in non-international armed conflict).

[105] See, for example, UNSC Res 2098 (2013) UN Doc S/RES/2098, preambular para. 2; UNSC Res 2100 (2013) UN Doc S//RES/2100, preambular para. 3; UNSC Res 2185 (2014) UN Doc S/RES/2185, preambular paras 6, 8; UNGA (2014) UN Doc A/68/19, para. 212, endorsed in UNGA Res 68/277 (2014) UN Doc A/RES/68/277, para. 2.

[106] See Optional Protocol to the Convention on the Safety and Security of United Nations and Associated Personnel (adopted 8 December 2005, entered into force 19 August 2010), annexed to UNGA Res 60/42 (2006) UN Doc A/RES/60/42. For the influence of the protection of civilians debates, see Mahnoush H Arsanjani, 'Convention on the Safety and Security of United Nations and Associated Personnel, Optional Protocol to the Convention on the Safety and Security of United Nations and Associated Personnel: Procedural History' (*United Nations Audiovisual Library of International Law*, undated) <legal.un.org/avl/ha/csunap/csunap.html#2>.

Many of those who favour a neutral or strongly impartial role for the UN, including some humanitarians and some UN troop-contributing countries, interpret the protection mandate as consonant with such a neutral role, where UN troops can remain above the fray and intervene only when absolutely necessary.[107] Such an approach may be difficult to square with traditional military doctrine, however, and the emphasis on neutrality and impartiality may have contributed to the reality that UN troops have very rarely used force to defend civilians.[108] A truly impartial stance is also extremely difficult for peacekeepers to maintain in conflict contexts where host governments expect, and often receive, military or logistical support from the UN mission.

In 2013–14 the Council provided some missions, notably in the Democratic Republic of the Congo, with more aggressive mandates to target specific groups. The 2013 mandate for the UN Stabilization Mission in the Democratic Republic of the Congo (MONUSCO) directed peacekeepers to neutralize militia groups,[109] making the mission a party to the conflict,[110] but many other missions also frequently find themselves taking action that may place them on one side or another. The UN Multidimensional Stabilization Mission in the Central African Republic (MINUSCA), for instance, has conducted targeted arrests in accordance with their mandate to employ 'urgent temporary measures' to maintain law and order.[111] The UN Mission in Côte d'Ivoire (UNOCI) also used force against fighters supporting then-President Laurent Gbagbo, who lost an internationally monitored election but refused to step down, resulting in widespread fighting and attacks on civilians.[112] In Côte d'Ivoire, the Council primarily relied on the mission's pre-existing authority to use force to protect civilians, couching its intervention as an impartial act.[113] Yet arguably its resolution 'served mainly as an identification of the main culprit—Laurent Gbagbo',[114] again appearing to place the mission on one side of the conflict.

The UN has defended all of the above peacekeeping missions, however, on the grounds that they abide by the principles of peacekeeping and, therefore, remain

107 See, for example, Aditi Gorur and Michelle Ker, 'New UN Force May Increase Risks for Civilians' (*Stimson Spotlight*, 11 July 2013) <www.stimson.org/spotlight/new-un-force-may-increase-risks-for-civilians>; Laurie Mincieli, 'The UN's Unprecedented Gamble in the Democratic Republic of the Congo' (Ethics and International Affairs, 8 October 2013) <www.ethicsandinternationalaffairs.org/2013/the-uns-unprecedented-gamble-in-the-democratic-republic-of-congo>.

108 Alexander William Beadle, *Finding the 'Utility of Force to Protect'—Towards a Theory on Protection of Civilians* (Kjeller, Norway: Norwegian Defence Research Establishment, 2011).

109 UNSC Res 2098 (2013) UN Doc S/RES/2098, para. 12(b).

110 See Mona Khalil, Chapter 9 in this volume; see also Scott Sheeran and Stephanie Case, *The Intervention Brigade: Legal Issues for the UN in the Democratic Republic of the Congo* (New York: International Peace Institute, 2014).

111 UNSC, 'Report of the Secretary-General on the situation in the Central African Republic' (2015) UN Doc S/2015/227, paras 49–50; 'Leader of Christian Militia "Andillo" Arrested in CAR' (*United Nations Radio*, 19 January 2015). <www.unmultimedia.org/radio/english/2015/01/leader-of-christian-militia-andilo-arrested-in-car/#.VVeB19NViko>.

112 Fabienne Hara and Gilles Yabi, 'Cote d'Ivoire, 2002–2011', in Jane Boulden (ed.), *Conflict in Africa: The United Nations and Regional Organisations* (New York: Palgrave MacMillan, 2013) 166–7.

113 UNSC Res 1975 (2011) UN Doc S/RES/1975, para. 6.

114 Eliav Lieblich, *International Law and Civil Wars: Intervention and Consent* (Abington, UK: Routledge, 2013) 214.

impartial actors, regardless of the strength of their mandate.[115] Yet even missions that place greater emphasis on impartiality face challenges in remaining nonpartisan. The UN missions in Darfur and South Sudan, for instance, have tried to impartially interpose themselves between armed groups and vulnerable groups of internally displaced persons, yet this has frequently drawn the enmity of both parties to the conflict, including host governments, that have obstructed the work of both missions.[116] As in the Congo in 1960, these recent examples continue to challenge the notion that the use of force to protect civilians in active conflicts can be perceived as neutral or impartial where protection activities threaten the strategic position of either party.

C. Protection and intervention

In addition to pushing the protection of civilians agenda in the Security Council, Canada was an important actor in the development of the RtoP doctrine, supporting the establishment of the International Commission on Intervention and State Sovereignty (ICISS), a group of respected policy-makers and academics, in 2000.[117] The Commission's report, titled *Responsibility to Protect*, built on the idea of sovereignty as responsibility, proposing a justification for international intervention in situations of serious human rights violations. The protection of civilians and RtoP share a common history on the Security Council's agenda and a common legal framework in the *jus ad bellum*, IHRL, and IHL regimes.[118]

The NATO 1999 bombing of Yugoslavia without Security Council approval ignited discussion on what would become RtoP.[119] Under the threat of a Russian veto, NATO undertook the operations without Security Council approval. While the action was on its face illegal, it nonetheless drew sympathy and even support from many international lawyers.[120] In this environment, ICISS presented an extensive justification for humanitarian intervention that emphasized the importance of Council approval and set out principles for intervention.[121] Secretary-General Kofi Annan, however, proposed the basic ideas of RtoP two years before the ICISS report under the rubric of the protection of

[115] See, for instance, Capstone Doctrine, n 102, 31–6; UNSC Res 2098 (2013) UN Doc S/RES/2098, preambular para. 2; UNSC Res 2100 (2013) UN Doc S//RES/2100, preambular para. 3; UNSC Res 2185 (2014) UN Doc S/RES/2185, preambular paras 6, 8; UNGA (2014) UN Doc A/68/19, para. 212, endorsed in UNGA Res 68/277 (2014) UN Doc A/RES/68/277, para. 2.

[116] See, for example, UNSC, 'Special Report of the Secretary-General on the African Union-United Nations Hybrid Operation in Darfur' (2015) UN Doc S/2015/163, paras 35–42; UNSC, 'Report of the Secretary-General on South Sudan' (2015) UN Doc S/2015/118, paras 60–3; see also Colum Lynch, 'Now We Will Kill You', *Foreign Policy* (Washington, DC, 8 April 2014) <foreignpolicy.com/2014/04/08/now-we-will-kill-you>.

[117] See International Commission on Intervention and State Sovereignty (ICISS), *Responsibility to Protect: Report of the International Commission on Intervention and State Sovereignty* (Ottawa: International Development Research Centre, 2001).

[118] See Scott Sheeran and Catherine Kent, Chapter 9, in this volume.

[119] Ibid., vii.

[120] See David Wippman, 'Kosovo and the Limits of International Law' (2001) 25 Fordham J Intl L 129, 135–8.

[121] See generally ICISS, n 117.

civilians.[122] In a brief two paragraphs and with measured language, the Secretary-General endorsed intervention '[i]n the face of massive and ongoing abuses', developing criteria that reflected the principles for intervention later adopted by the ICISS.[123]

The RtoP doctrine found official approval in the UN through the General Assembly's 2005 World Summit, which endorsed Council-approved intervention in cases of genocide, war crimes, crimes against humanity, and ethnic cleansing.[124] While an important step, in the absence of finding an international obligation to act, the World Summit did not break new legal ground. The Council had already recognized harm to civilians (encompassing the four RtoP 'atrocity crimes') as a threat to international peace and security. In this respect, RtoP's focus on four 'atrocity crimes' is less significant than it may at first appear, as these specific crimes are neither required to trigger Security Council action, nor are they necessary as a policy justification for intervention. In addition, while the ICSS report set out a series of principles for action to intervene drawn from just war theory—including such key ideas as intervention as a last resort, right intention, and proportional means[125]—these principles were generally left out of official UN statements. The 'responsibility' of RtoP thus continued to provide substantial discretion for Council members and other Member States to ignore violence against civilians or to intervene under its rubric with questionable motives.

At its heart, the RtoP doctrine is not concerned with imposing binding legal obligations upon States, but rather provides 'a detailed argument for the political authority of the international community and for the consolidation and integration of executive rule by international actors'.[126] The UN Secretary-General elaborated a policy framework for the responsibility to protect, linking the responsibility of States for the protection of their populations to the international community's responsibility to support States in those efforts (such as through development or humanitarian assistance, or the consensual deployment of UN peace operations), and, finally, to intervene where the State is manifestly unable or unwilling to fulfil its protection responsibilities.[127] In this respect, RtoP provides a more robust conceptual framework for the wide variety of protection activities collected under the rubric of the protection of civilians in armed conflict.

The most significant distinction between RtoP and the protection of civilians is that the former is a political judgement, subject to non-impartial

122 UNSC, 'Report of the Secretary-General on the Protection of Civilians in Armed Conflict' (1999) UN Doc S/1999/957, para. 67.

123 See and compare ICISS, see n 117, xii–xiii, and UNSC (1999) UN Doc S/1999/957, para. 67, recommendation 40. The influence of this report on the ICISS's work and the responsibility to protect more generally is unclear, but the ICISS authors were clearly aware of the Secretary-General's recommendation. See ICISS, *The Responsibility to Protect: Research, Bibliography and Background* (Ottawa: International Development Research Centre, 2001) 140 n 42.

124 UNGA (2005) UN Doc A/60/L.1, paras 138–9.

125 ICISS, see n 117, xi–xiii.

126 Orford, see n 40, 33.

127 UNGA, 'Implementing the responsibility to protect, Report of the Secretary-General' (2009) UN Doc A/63/677, para. 11.

application,[128] and countenances non-consensual action against a State, which other mechanisms, such as peacekeeping, ostensibly do not permit.[129] The examples from Libya and Syria, however, link the protection of civilians to non-impartial and non-consensual action.

The Security Council's authorization to 'to take all necessary measures ... to protect civilians and civilian populated areas under threat of attack in the Libyan Arab Jamahiriya' marked the first time that the body had voted to explicitly authorize the use of force to protect civilians, in a country with a functioning government that clearly denied consent.[130] The resolution is frequently cited as a landmark instance of Council endorsement and application of the RtoP doctrine, yet it is notable that the resolutions employ protection of civilians language common to peacekeeping mandates. They contain no explicit references to RtoP and there was little mention of it during Council debates.[131] Many commentators have argued that it was also a highly politicized (partial) intervention, where military force was used early rather than as a last resort, and the welfare of civilians took a lower priority than regime change.[132] It is also generally recognized that the political fallout of the Libya intervention has been, in part, a lack of consensus—one might argue a lack of trust—on whether and how to take action to protect civilians in Syria.

An important breakthrough in Council deliberations over the situation in Syria was resolution 2165 (2014). It was the first Security Council authorization of humanitarian assistance to override sovereign consent of a State.[133] While the resolution authorizes 'assistance' rather than 'protection',[134] the Council refers to the protection of civilians generally and UN agencies have supported protection activities under its auspices.[135] This resolution thus created a similar link between humanitarian protection and the kind of non-consensual action associated with the

128 For instance, the Secretary-General has noted that the protection of civilians is a 'legal concept' while the responsibility to protect is a 'political concept', implying an inherent partiality on the part of the latter. See UNSC, 'Report of the Secretary-General on the protection of civilians in armed conflict' (2012) UN Doc S/2012/376, para. 21. As later noted by the Secretary-General, however, the responsibility to protect is also rooted in international law. UNSC, 'Responsibility to Protect: Timely and Decisive Response, Report of the Secretary-General' (2012) UN Doc A/66/874–S/2012/578, para. 9.

129 Capstone Doctrine, see n 102, 19, 31–2.

130 Alex J Bellamy and Paul D Williams, 'The New Politics of Protection? Côte d'Ivoire, Libya and the Responsibility to Protect' (2011) 87 Intl Affairs 825, 825.

131 Justin Morris, 'Libya and Syria: R2P and the Spectre of the Swinging Pendulum' (2013) 89 Intl Affairs 1265, 1272–3.

132 See Ben Kioko and Lydia Wambagu, Chapter 12 in this volume; David Rieff, 'R2P RIP?' *The New York Times* (New York, 7 November 2011) <www.nytimes.com/2011/11/08/opinion/r2p-rip.html?_r=0>.

133 The Council's 1991 resolution 688 authorized a no-fly zone over Northern Iraq on humanitarian grounds, but the Iraqi government signed a memorandum of understanding with the UN on the delivery of humanitarian assistance in that area. See Peter Malanczuk, 'The Kurdish Crisis and Allied Intervention' (1991) 2 EJIL 114.

134 UNSC 1265 (2014) UN Doc S/RES/1265, para. 2.

135 See UNSC (2015) UN Doc S/2015/368, para. 40.

RtoP. While this was an exercise of Council authority justified by Syria's inability or unwillingness to fulfil its responsibility for protection,[136] the resolution references the Council's executive authority under Chapter V rather than its Chapter VII enforcement powers.[137]

Some commentators have sought to distinguish this resolution from the RtoP, citing the purely humanitarian nature of the endeavour.[138] This distinction, however, relies on an assumption that the RtoP is not compatible with the principles and aims of humanitarian action, yet such principles are neither required nor rejected by either RtoP or the protection of civilians. While humanitarians may dislike the idea of placing their activities within the RtoP framework, the humanitarian modes of operation—raising awareness of obligations, support to States, and substitution or direct action where States are unwilling or unable[139]—fit easily within RtoP's framework.

The Libya intervention and the authorization of cross-border aid into Syria remain controversial. Yet taking these cases at face value, as examples of the protection of civilians, implies that consent is not a pre-condition for action under the protection-of-civilians concept. Absent this distinction, the conceptual difference between the protection of civilians, broadly interpreted, and the responsibility to protect shrinks markedly. It is difficult to conceive of action to protect civilians that would not fit neatly within the RtoP framework, and similarly nearly all actions within the RtoP framework can (and have) been labelled 'protection of civilians'.

VI. Conclusion

This chapter has reviewed concepts and practices of the protection of civilians, seeking to draw a narrative without judging these concepts outside of their historical development. The history is a rich one and could be expanded in many directions, but it highlights both the importance of the protection of civilians in current discourse and its continued fragility as a concept.

The history of the protection of civilians brings together numerous themes of contemporary international law and international relations. The term is first found in IHL during the inter-war period, but is built upon humanitarian concepts that stretch back a century earlier. Contemporary with, and even earlier than, the development of IHL, ideas of human rights established relations between States and individuals. The articulation of these relationships, as much as the content of the rights, strongly influenced the development of IHRL and later the protection of civilians.

The early practice of protection at the international level was, almost by necessity, undertaken primarily by neutral and impartial actors such as the ICRC and

[136] UNSC Res 2165 (2014) UN Doc S/RES/2165, preambular paras 4, 5, 12, 15.

[137] Ibid., preambular para. 19.

[138] Emmanuella Chiara Gillard, 'The Law Regulating Cross-border Relief Operations' (2013) 95 IRRC 351, 352.

[139] See and compare ICRC, n 68, 760–1; UNGA (2009) UN Doc A/63/677, para. 11.

UNHCR. International humanitarian law and IRL grew out of State-centric systems of international relations, when neutrality and impartiality were keys to access and persuasion, as they remain in many places. Humanitarians have faced their limits in numerous situations, however, recognizing that assistance may do little to stop violence.

The UN and its collective security agreement created a new mechanism for protection, albeit one that would not be realized for decades. The UN and the Security Council were established as powerful tools from a legal perspective, with the authority to use force, though with an initial expectation that they would not concern themselves with individuals or their rights. But the conscience of this new system grew along with its strength, leading to an era of extraordinary, if not always successful, international efforts to protect civilians.

Some of these efforts have, however, challenged the tradition of neutral and impartial protection. Some examples of the protection of civilians, such as the Force Intervention Brigade in MONUSCO, raise questions about the role that the UN, particularly UN peacekeepers, can and should play in directly engaging an enemy. Others, such as the Libya intervention, raise even more fundamental questions about the potential abuse of the tools of collective security. Given the history of UN operations, however, it is not yet clear whether these examples are a trend or merely, like ONUC, an aberration.

The UN is sometimes analogized to a global government, and the Security Council and its peacekeepers to global police officers, but these remain imperfect analogies that rely on unrealized aspirations. The realities of armed conflict, upon which IHL is based, remain the reality in many parts of the world. It remains important, then, to take seriously the demands of protection in conflict, including the appearance of impartiality. The Libya intervention's likely impact upon the international community's inability to find agreement in responding to the conflict in Syria remains a significant cautionary tale.

Through this history, and particularly in the distinct fields of practice of humanitarians and peacekeepers, different principles, precepts, and definitions have been developed. The focus on legal basis, practical implementation, and some reference to impartial execution are generally common to all. Yet dissatisfaction with current definitions, as written, remains, and the language of protection continues to register confusion among field practitioners. There is no single, authoritative source for understanding the concept of the protection of civilians, but rather a series of related and sometimes unrelated documents that must be interpreted into a whole, as this chapter has tried to do.

There also remains a risk that many actors, including Member States, prefer the language of protection precisely because its content is vague. When 'protection' can encompass everything from responsibility for providing food and shelter to planning a full military campaign, it becomes language that is easily agreed upon. This is notable in the peacekeeping context, where troop-contributing countries and Security Council members appear to interpret the same mandates very differently. The language of protection has facilitated action on numerous occasions and will likely continue to do so, at least in the near future, but language that means everything can also easily mean nothing. In this respect, the protection of civilians remains a fragile concept.

More than twenty-five years have passed since the end of the Cold War and the advent of modern protection through the Council and the transformation of humanitarian protection. This has been an extremely important period of growth, one made possible in many respects by the existence of a single superpower. This era too will close, however, and the advocates of protection would do well to imagine its place in a more multipolar world.

4

Protecting Civilians

Comparing Organizational Approaches

Stian Kjeksrud, Jacob Aasland Ravndal, Andreas Øien Stensland, Cedric de Coning, and Walter Lotze[1]

I. Introduction

Protecting civilians is a key concern for all organizations involved in peace, stabilization, and counter-insurgency operations. Increasingly, civilians are directly targeted in armed conflicts. Perpetrators are both State and non-State armed actors, and their rationales for attacking civilians are diverse.[2] In acts of genocide and ethnic cleansing, attacking civilians is an end in itself.[3] In insurgencies, attacks against civilians are used to influence an opposing party.[4] To spare civilians from physical harm or to obtain their support, interveners now use military force to physically protect vulnerable populations. United Nations (UN) operations in the Central African Republic (CAR), the Democratic Republic of the Congo (DRC), South Sudan, Abyei, and Mali have protection of civilians as their main priority. North Atlantic Treaty Organization (NATO) operations in Libya and Afghanistan both had civilian protection as core rationales. The African Union (AU) operation in Somalia has made systematic efforts to improve its ability to protect, including developing a mission-wide protection strategy.[5] All AU operations subsequent to Somalia have had protection of civilians as a key component of their mandates. The European Union (EU) operation in the Central African Republic in 2014 was concerned with providing physical protection to civilians in Bangui.

[1] This chapter builds directly on Stian Kjeksrud, Jacob Aasland Ravndal, Andreas Øien Stensland, Cedric de Coning, Walter Lotze, and Erin A Weir, *Protection of Civilians in Armed Conflict: Comparing Organisational Approaches* (Kjeller, Norway: Norwegian Defence Research Establishment (FFI), 2011).

[2] Hugo Slim, *Killing Civilians: Method, Madness and Morality in War* (Oxford: Oxford University Press, 2010) 121–213.

[3] Alexander W Beadle, *Protection of Civilians—Military Planning Scenarios and Implications* (Kjeller, Norway: Norwegian Defence Research Establishment (FFI), 2014) 13.

[4] Rupert Smith, *The Utility of Force: The Art of War in the Modern World* (London: Penguin Books, 2006) Introduction.

[5] PD Williams, 'The African Union Mission in Somalia and Civilian Protection Challenges' (2013) 2 Stability: Intl J of Security and Development 39 <www.stabilityjournal.org/article/view/sta.bz/114>.

Although faced with similar challenges, these organizations debate, conceptualize, and solve their military protection tasks differently. This is first and foremost because their rationale for protecting civilians differs. Their military capabilities and use of military force also vary substantially. Their common challenge is that civilian protection operations rely on a different logic than traditional warfare and peacekeeping. Military forces usually operate opposite an enemy who targets and influences their own operations. Protection operations, however, demand that military efforts are based on understanding how and why perpetrators attack *civilians* and what capabilities they need to do so.[6]

While many humanitarian and human rights actors carry out various types of protection activities,[7] this chapter focuses primarily on military efforts to protect. It provides a comparative analysis of four international and regional organizations involved in protecting civilians from physical harm: the UN, NATO, AU, and EU. It addresses three interrelated aspects of each: discourses, concepts, and operational practices. These three aspects also provide the structure of the chapter. The approach is based on an understanding that discourses influence concepts as well as operational practices. In turn, both concepts and discourses are often influenced by protection challenges in actual operations. Although, in reality, this relationship is neither linear nor necessarily sequential, this structure allows for comparisons across organizations. The analysis seeks to provide a comparative review of how different organizations relate to and use military force to protect civilians under threat.

We show how the institutional framework largely decides how military force is used to protect. The UN knows what it takes to protect, but seldom displays the will to apply military force for this purpose. NATO is willing to use force to protect, but is less aware of how it should be done when civilians are directly targeted. The AU has the knowledge, experience, and willingness to apply force to protect, but remains highly dependent on external resources to do so consistently. The EU has both concepts and relevant capabilities, but struggles to deploy when needed. Importantly, despite the unprecedented concern with improving the physical security of civilians under threat, none of the four organizations does so effectively. Understanding the limitations and comparative advantages of each organization is one important step towards more effective protection in the future. This chapter aims to contribute to making that step.

II. Organizational Discourses on the Protection of Civilians

In our everyday language, a discourse is understood as a written or spoken communication or debate. In the social sciences, discourse refers to language as a system of meaning-making. A discourse thus provides a language for speaking about, analysing, and classifying a social phenomenon. In this context, the phenomenon is the

[6] Beadle, see n 3, 14–21.

[7] For further discussion see, for example, Mamiya, Clapham, Williamson, Keating and Bennett Pantuliano and Svoboda, and Grande, in this volume.

protection of civilians from physical harm. The following reviews the discourse on protection within the UN, NATO, AU, and EU along three dimensions: rationale, organizational drivers, and the main tensions and challenges.

A. The UN: Protection as an end in itself

The discourse on the imperative to protect civilians in armed conflicts has evolved over centuries. In the past fifteen years, the issue has received unprecedented attention. This is true in particular in the UN, where the most substantial conceptual and operational developments have taken place. Since 1999, fourteen UN peacekeeping operations have been given protection mandates.[8]

The UN's rationale for being engaged in the protection of civilians is primarily direct. It is an end in itself. First, the UN acknowledges that civilians are the main victims of war. Second, a moral duty at the core of the UN Charter is saving future generations from the 'scourge of war'.[9] Third, an indirect rationale is linked to the legitimacy and survival of the Organization, which is seen to depend on its ability to protect civilians.[10] As such, the discourse often portrays the Organization as the primary norm developer in the international system, where it plays a dominant role in delivering protection services together with key partners.

The primary organizational driver behind the protection of civilians discourse in the UN is norm development within parts of the UN bureaucracy. Historically, the Office for the Coordination of Humanitarian Affairs (OCHA) was the most active promoter in the UN.[11] OCHA took upon itself the responsibility for developing policy and providing information to the UN Security Council through regular

[8] These are the United Nations (UN) Mission in Sierra Leone (UN Security Council Resolution (UNC Res) 1270 (1999) UN Doc S/RES/1270); the UN Mission in the Democratic Republic of the Congo (UNSC Res 1291 (2000) UN Doc S/RES/1291); the UN Mission in Liberia (UNSC Res 1509 (2003) UN Doc S/RES/1509); the UN Operation in Côte d'Ivoire (UNSC Res 1528 (2004) UN Doc S/RES/1528); the UN Mission in the Central African Republic and Chad (UNSC Res 1778 (2007) UN Doc S/RES/1778); the UN Stabilisation Mission in Haiti (UNSC Res 1542 (2004) UN Doc S/RES/1542); the UN Operation in Burundi (UNSC Res 1545 (2004) UN Doc S/RES/1545); the UN Mission in Sudan (UNSC Res 1590 (2005) UN Doc 1590); the UN Interim Force in Lebanon (UNSC Res 1701 (2006) UN Doc S/RES/1701); the African Union/UN Hybrid Operation in Darfur (UNSC Res 1769 (2007) UN Doc S/RES/1769); the UN Mission in South Sudan (UNSC Res 1996 (2011) UN Doc S/RES/1996); the UN Interim Security Force for Abyei (UNSC Res 1990 (2011); the UN Stabilization Mission in the Democratic Republic of the Congo (UNSC Res 1925 (2010) UN Doc S/RES/1925); the UN Multidimensional Integrated Stabilization Operation in Mali (UNSC Res 2100 (2013) UN Doc S/RES/2100; and the UN Multidimensional Integrated Stabilization Operation in the Central African Republic (UNSC Res 2149 (2014) UN Doc S/RES/2149) (Only first UN SC Res mentioned for each mission).

[9] Charter of the United Nations (adopted 26 June 1945, entered into force 24 October 1945) 1 UNTS XVI, Preamble.

[10] Report of the Panel on United Nations Peace Operations, in UN General Assembly (UNGA) and UNSC (2000) UN Doc A/55/305—S/2000/809, paras 49–52 (The Brahimi Report); UN Department of Peacekeeping Operations (DPKO) and UN Department of Field Support (DFS), *A New Partnership Agenda: Charting a New Horizon for UN Peacekeeping* (New York, United Nations, 2009); 'DR Congo: Amid Fresh Violence, "Presence without Action Undermines Our Credibility"—UN Envoy' *United Nations News Centre* (New York, 26 October 2014) <www.un.org/apps/news/story.asp?NewsID=49172#.VE-WEMm5T5M>.

[11] John Harald Sande Lie and Benjamin de Carvalho, *A Culture of Protection? Perspectives of the Protection of Civilians from Sudan* (Oslo: Norwegian Institute of International Affairs, 2008).

Secretary-General's reports and biannual thematic briefings to the Security Council. However, over fifteen years after the first Security Council resolution on the protection of civilians, there is still no unified definition of what it entails within the UN system. Thus, while the rationale for engaging in civilian protection is largely agreed upon by all contributors to the discourse, its implications are contested.

Latterly, the UN Department of Peacekeeping Operations (DPKO) has also been active in developing the protection discourse, mainly due to a shift in focus of the Security Council to the effective implementation of protection activities in peacekeeping operations.[12] DPKO has articulated a 'Capstone Doctrine' on peacekeeping, which contains references to protection activities; a 2015 DPKO-DFS policy on the protection of civilians, incorporating an 'Operational Concept' developed in 2010; guidance on the development of protection of civilians strategies in peacekeeping operations; a resource and capability matrix for protection mandates; training courses for troop contributors; an overview of co-ordination mechanisms; implementing guidelines for military components; and guidelines on deterrence and the use of force.[13] The DPKO-DFS 'Policy on The Protection of Civilians in United Nations Peacekeeping' addresses a range of multidimensional peacekeeping efforts to protect. It organizes the protection of civilians into three tiers of engagement: (1) protection through political process, (2) protection from physical violence, and (3) establishment of a protective environment.[14] This serves as the basis for how protection of civilians is understood in UN peacekeeping operations.

There are several tensions and challenges in the UN approach to the protection of civilians. Perhaps the greatest challenge is the lack of a shared understanding of what the UN can and should be doing to protect civilians.[15] According to an influential

[12] UNGA, 'Report of the Special Committee on Peacekeeping Operations' (2010) UN Doc A/64/19, para. 147.

[13] UN DPKO and UN DFS, *UN Peacekeeping Operations: Principles and Guidelines* (New York: United Nations, 2008) (Capstone Doctrine); UN DPKO and UN DFS, 'Draft DPKO/DFS Operational Concept on the Protection of Civilians in United Nations Peacekeeping Operations' (New York: United Nations, 2010); UN DPKO and UN DFS, 'Framework for Drafting Comprehensive Protection of Civilians (POC) Strategies in United Nations Peacekeeping Operations' (New York: United Nations, undated) <refworld.org/pdfid/523998464.pdf>; UN DPKO and UN DFS, 'Protection of Civilians (POC) Resource and Capability Matrix for Implementation of UN Peacekeeping Missions with POC Mandates' (New York: United Nations, 2012) <pbpu.unlb.org/PBPS/Library/POC%20resource%20and%20capability%20matrix.pdf>; UN DPKO and UN DFS, 'Protection of Civilians, Coordination Mechanisms in UN Peacekeeping Missions: Comparative Study and Toolkit' (New York: United Nations, 2012) <www.peacekeepingbestpractices.unlb.org/pbps/Library/Protection%20of%20Civilians%20Coordination%20Mechanisms%20in%20UN%20Peacekeeping%20Missions,%20DPKO-DFS%20Comparative%20Study%20and%20Toolkit%20%282012%29.pdf>; UN DPKO and UN DFS, 'UN Tactical Level Protection of Civilians Training Modules' (New York: United Nations) <peacekeepingresourcehub.unlb.org/PBPS/Library/UN_TPOC%20_Trg_package.pdf> (UN Tactical Training Modules); UN DPKO and UN DFS, 'Policy on the Protection of Civilians in United Nations Peacekeeping' (on file with author) (UN DPKO and UN DFS Protection of Civilians Policy); UN DPKO and UN DFS, 'Draft DPKO/DFS Operational Concept on the Protection of Civilians in United Nations Peacekeeping Operations' (New York: United Nations, 2010); UN DPKO and DFS, 'Protection of Civilians, Implementing Guidelines for Military Components of United Nations Peacekeeping Operations' (on file with author) (UN DPKO and UN DFS Draft Military Guidelines on the Protection of Civilians).

[14] UN DPKO and UN DFS Protection of Civilians Policy, see n 13.

[15] For further discussion on the diverse concepts of protection, see Haidi Wilmot and Scott Sheeran, 'The Protection of Civilians Mandate in United Nations Peacekeeping Operations: Reconciling Protection Concepts and Practices' (2013) 95 IRRC 517. For further discussion on protection

DPKO/OCHA study from 2009, uncertainty about what 'protection of civilians' means has been a central obstacle to rendering it operationally effective in UN peacekeeping operations.[16] The same issue was encountered in 2013 with the development of the Secretary-General's Human Rights Up Front initiative.[17] There are several reasons for the lack of a unified definition of protection of civilians. Some members of the Security Council fear that a clear definition would prove too binding or undermine State sovereignty and territorial integrity.[18] In addition, diverging organizational interests and operational goals among key UN agencies and departments, as well as the need for political consensus, have prevailed over conceptual clarity.[19]

The most obvious tension is that between the humanitarian and military elements of the UN Organization. However, it is important to highlight that humanitarians also see the importance of physical protection, and the other way around. There are many instances of functional co-operation between humanitarians and military forces, particularly where there is a dire need to co-ordinate protection of civilians efforts, for example within the UN Organization Stabilization Mission in the DRC (MONUSCO).[20] The tension is most often about *how* the two types of actors should co-exist. A recent turn towards more forceful UN operations, however, may cause renewed concern among some humanitarians.[21]

Protection through political process and protection from physical violence (tiers one and two of the DPKO-DFS Protection of Civilians Policy) may at times be contradictory. Support to the political process is not necessarily conducive to the protection of civilians from physical violence and vice versa. For mission leadership, the choice between intervening militarily to achieve short-term physical protection, while at the same time risking severing relations with one of the parties to the conflict, is a difficult one.[22] There is therefore nothing inevitable about the internal coherence of these two tiers.

action by various UN actors, see in this volume Fiona Blythe and Patrick Cammaert, Chapter 14; Michael Keating and Richard Bennett, Chapter 16; Sara Pantuliano and Eva Svoboda, Chapter 17; and Lise Grande, Chapter 18.

16 Victoria K Holt and Glyn Taylor, with Max Kelly, *Protecting Civilians in the Context of UN Peacekeeping Operations* (New York: United Nations, 2009) 4–7.

17 'Rights Up Front' (May 2014) United Nations Secretary-General <www.un.org/sg/rightsupfront/doc/RuFAP-summary-General-Assembly.htm>.

18 Security Council Report, *Protection of Civilians in Armed Conflict* (New York: Security Council Report, 2010) 29.

19 Andreas Stensland and Ole Jacob Sending, *Unpacking the 'Culture of Protection': A Political Economy Analysis of OCHA and the Protection of Civilians* (Oslo: Norsk Utenrikspolitisk Institutt, 2011).

20 Stian Kjeksrud and Jacob Aasland Ravndal, 'Emerging Lessons from the United Nations Mission in the Democratic Republic of Congo: Military Contributions to the Protection of Civilians' (2011) 20 African Security Rev 3.

21 Aurelie Ponthieu, Christoph Vogel, and Katharine Derderian, 'Without Precedent or Prejudice? UNSC Resolution 2098 and Its Potential Implications for Humanitarian Space in Eastern Congo and Beyond' (2014) J of Humanitarian Assistance <sites.tufts.edu/jha/archives/2032>.

22 Victoria K Holt and Tobias C Berkman, *The Impossible Mandate? Military Preparedness, the Responsibility to Protect and Modern Peace Operations* (Washington, DC: The Henry L Stimson Center, 2006).

Finally, the traditional 'UN peacekeeping principles' of 'impartiality', 'consent', and the 'non-use of force'[23] are increasingly being stretched in contemporary UN operations. They no longer match perceptions of what the UN is doing in practice. UN operations now take sides in conflicts, where there is no peace to keep, without the consent of main parties to the conflict, through robust and offensive military operations.[24] As long as protection is the top priority of the UN's most important operations, these tensions will afflict the UN discourse on protection. A main challenge is the divergent views of peacekeeping and protection. On the one hand, some see an increased 'militarization of peacekeeping' as problematic. On the other hand, some observe a major gap in that 'force is almost never used to protect civilians under attack'.[25]

B. NATO: An indirect approach to protection

NATO's dominant rationale for engaging in protection activities is indirect, in the sense that the primary goal for NATO operations has been to counter or support an insurgency. Protection is not seen as an end in itself, as it is in the UN. Operation *Unified Protector* over Libya in 2011, however, brought NATO into the UN discourse on protection through the Responsibility to Protect mandate in UN Security Resolution 1973.[26] Originally, NATO's *raison d'être* was the protection of its Member States and their populations from aggression. In later years, the perception that conflicts beyond NATO's borders could pose a threat to the security of the alliance partners' territory and populations became dominant. NATO is therefore determined to engage to prevent and manage crises, stabilize post-conflict situations, and support reconstruction.[27]

NATO is concerned about the negative effects of collateral damage among civilians during its own operations. Thus, 'protecting the people' became the overarching task of counterinsurgency operations in Afghanistan from 2010.[28] This had to do with trying to persuade the population that the International Security Assistance Force (ISAF) and the Afghan Government deserved their support, an approach influenced by counterinsurgency theory, rather than providing direct physical protection to a population under threat from insurgent violence.[29]

[23] Capstone Doctrine, see n 13, 31–5.

[24] Secretary-General Ban Ki-moon, 'Statement: Remarks at Security Council Open Debate on Trends in United Nations Peacekeeping' (11 June 2014) <www.un.org/sg/statements/index.asp?nid=7769>.

[25] UNGA, 'Report of the Office of Internal Oversight Services on the Evaluation of the Implementation and Results of Protection of Civilians Mandates in United Nations Peacekeeping Operations' (2014) UN Doc A/68/787, para. 79 (OIOS Report).

[26] UNSC Res 1973 (2011) UN Doc S/RES/1973, para. 4.

[27] North Atlantic Treaty Organization (NATO), *Active Engagement, Modern Defence: Strategic Concept for the Defence and Security of the Members of the North Atlantic Treaty Organization* (Brussels: North Atlantic Treaty Organization, 2010), paras 20–1.

[28] Stanley A McChrystal and Michael T Hall, 'ISAF Commander's Counterinsurgency Guidance' (Kabul: International Security Assistance Force, 2009) 1 <www.nato.int/isaf/docu/official_texts/counterinsurgency_guidance.pdf>.

[29] Jim Garamone, 'Gates Stresses Need to Curtail Civilians Casualties', *DoD News* (Washington, DC, 12 June 2009) <www.defense.gov/news/newsarticle.aspx?id=54760>.

Likewise, in 2011, the main concern for NATO in Libya was avoiding causing harm to civilians. According to Lieutenant General Bouchard:

> There had to be a link between every target that was engaged to [the] protection of civilians. From there two questions followed: Is it legal? Is it moral? We went through every one of those steps for every one of those targets. We decided not to act upon a lot of the targets, because a tactical victory can cause strategic defeat. Misratah had . . . zero collateral damage, which is . . . [the] NATO approach.[30]

The primary organizational driver behind the increased concern for civilian protection in NATO operations has been problem-solving strategies developed in response to its struggle to achieve a decisive victory through traditional military means. The US population-centric approach contributed to reduce the violence in Iraq and was adopted by NATO forces in Afghanistan. While the protection of the population now forms a centrepiece of NATO's counter-insurgency thinking, it has not been defined as an operational objective per se.[31] The population-centric approach is framed as a means to achieve a larger end. This indirect, problem-solving focus is key to NATO's approach to protection.

The main tension and challenge in NATO's discourse is the indirect approach to protection combined with the focus on long-term stabilization. In other words, protection of the civilian population is mostly thought of in terms of avoiding collateral damage, while the population's security is envisioned as the strategic, long-term outcome. On the one hand, this provided NATO with leeway to conduct operations that may have had a negative short-term, but a more positive long-term, effect on protection (ref. the tension between tiers one and two in the DPKO-DFS Protection of Civilians Policy). Simultaneously, and as mentioned in the NATO Joint Operational Guidance,[32] it is unlikely that the long-term efforts at creating stability are achievable unless NATO simultaneously seeks to better the security for the civilian population in an active and direct fashion, i.e. more similar to the UN's tier two (protection from physical violence).

C. The AU: Between direct and indirect rationales for protection

For the AU, the dominant rationale for protecting civilians is direct, similar to the UN.[33] The Constitutive Act of the AU promotes both a rights-based understanding of protection and 'the right of the Union to intervene in a Member State pursuant to a decision of the Assembly in respect of

[30] Lieutenant General Charles Bouchard, 'Lessons Learned from Unified Protector—A Commander's Perspective', in *Norsk Luftmakt over Libya—Suksess Uten Innflytelse?*, eds Torgeir E. Sæveraas and Vidar Løw Owesen (Trondheim: Akademika Forlag, 2012) 127–37.

[31] Alexander William Beadle, *Protection of Civilians in Theory: A Comparison of UN and NATO Approaches* (Kjeller: Norwegian Defence Research Establishment (FFI), 2010) 24.

[32] See NATO, 'Bi-SC Joint Operational Guidelines 10/01, Counterinsurgency (COIN)' (Brussels: North Atlantic Treaty Organization, 2010) <www.operacional.pt/docs/NATO%20TT-6185%20Bi-SC%20Counter-Insurgency%20(COIN)%20.pdf>.

[33] Seth Appiah-Mensah and Rachel Eklou-Assogbavi, 'The Protection of Civilians: A Comparison between United Nations and African Union Peace Operations' [2012] Conflict Trends 11–16.

grave circumstances, namely war crimes, genocide, and crimes against humanity'.[34]

The protection of civilians is understood as all the activities undertaken to improve the security of the population and people at risk in the area of operations, and to ensure the full respect for rights recognized under regional instruments as well as international law. Several elements of the AU discourse on the protection of civilians should be noted. It is contended that protection of civilians activities should support the efforts of host nation authorities and enhance their capacity to secure its civilian population. In addition, the AU requires a multidimensional and co-ordinated approach within the mission, with clear and differentiated roles and responsibilities for the military, police, and substantive civilian components.

Mission-specific challenges in Sudan and Somalia and pressure from the UN Security Council have been instrumental drivers for the development of protection of civilians guidelines in the AU. The AU Mission in Sudan (AMIS) had a protection mandate but no strategy was developed to implement it. The Rules of Engagement and use-of-force directives were not shaped accordingly. Nevertheless, despite the absence of concepts and strategies, AMIS did undertake physical protection activities, designed and carried out by the military component of the mission. The AU Mission in Somalia (AMISOM) was long criticized for causing collateral damage. In response, the AU Commission in 2010 developed Draft Guidelines for the Protection of Civilians in AU Peace Support Operations, which are yet to become formally confirmed by the Organization.[35] They provide guidance at the strategic level, and assist in the formulation of guidance at both the operational and the tactical levels. The guidelines are based on a tiered approach to protection, very similar to the UN.

Based on the experience of AMISOM and the growing importance of the protection of civilians agenda in the Organization, the AU Peace and Security Council has, since 2011, held annual open sessions on the protection of civilians. In 2012 the Council decided that all future AU peace support operations must have the protection of civilians as part of the mandate.[36] Based on this decision, a comprehensive Aide Memoire on the Consideration of Issues Pertaining to the Protection of Civilians in Africa was approved by the AU Chairperson in December 2013. This provided an Organization-wide definition of the protection of civilians, and was designed to aid decision-makers in their planning when responding to situations of armed conflict or otherwise where the protection of civilians was of concern.[37]

[34] Constitutive Act of the African Union (adopted 1 July 2000, entered into force on 26 May 2001) OAU Doc CAB/LEG/23.15, para. 4. For further discussion on the broader protection framework in the AU see Kioko and Wambagu in this volume.

[35] African Union, 'Draft Guidelines for the Protection of Civilians in African Union Peace Support Operations' (Addis Ababa: Africa Union, 2012) (AU Draft Protection of Civilians Guidelines) <www.apsta-africa.org/documentation/resources/key%20resources/Draft%20AU%20PoC%20Guidelines%20-%20English.pdf>.

[36] African Union Peace and Security Council, 'Press Statement of the 326th Meeting of the Peace and Security Council' (2012) AU Doc PSC/PR/BR1 (CCCXXVI).

[37] African Union, Aide Memoire for the Consideration of Issues Pertaining to the Protection of Civilians in Africa (African Union, 2014) (on file with author).

Despite this progress at the policy level, inconsistencies at the operational level remain. One main tension in the AU's discourse on the protection of civilians to date has been that despite its direct concern for protection, its missions, specifically AMISOM, were mostly engaged with avoiding causing collateral damage during operations against Al-Shabaab. This was more similar to NATO's indirect approach to protection.[38] Further, AMISOM does not have a specific protection mandate. Instead, peace enforcement or counter-insurgency rationales drove AMISOM operations. As such, AMISOM's efforts to implement specific protection mechanisms, such as an indirect fire policy, led to a significant decline of civilian casualties in AMISOM's areas of operations.[39]

As the nature of the operations against Al-Shabaab in Somalia changed, and as the civilian population became increasingly directly targeted by Al-Shabaab, this approach to protection no longer sufficed. Consequently, the AMISOM mission-wide protection strategy, approved in May 2013, adopted a much broader and proactive approach to protection. The challenge lay then, as it still does today, in the implementation of this strategy, enabling the mission to move from policy to practice. Similar challenges existed in the short-lived AU missions in Mali (AFISMA) and the CAR (MISCA), both of which had mission-wide protection strategies, and neither of which had the resources or the time to implement these. Accordingly, the biggest challenges for the AU at the operational level at this stage remain (a) moving away from a military-centric approach to protection (dominated by the AMISOM counter-insurgency experience), and (b) finding meaningful ways of turning well-intentioned protection strategies into operational reality.

D. The EU: Mismatch between concepts and practice

The EU's rationale for engaging in the protection of civilians is direct. However, with the exception of operation *Artemis* in the DRC in 2003 and the recent deployment to CAR in 2014, the rationale has not often manifested in operations. The *raison d'être* of the EU is based on its ability to protect its own citizens. The Organization's overall discourse on peace and security hinges on its creation as an effort to end the bloody wars between neighbouring European States.[40] The rationale for involving the EU in civilian protection thus also has an indirect aspect. Over the years, those that should be protected have also come to include populations living beyond its borders. With the development of a Common Security and Defence Policy (CSDP), the EU has increased its engagement in crisis management missions and operations, both civil and military. In this regard, the EU often underscores its comparative advantage relating to furthering civil–military co-operation at all levels

[38] See Alexander William Beadle, *Protecting Civilians While Fighting a War in Somalia—Drawing Lessons from Afghanistan* (Oslo: Norwegian Institute of International Affairs (NUPI), 2012) <www.nupi.no/content/download/343390/1176164/file/PB-10-12-Beadle.pdf>; and Walter Lotze and Yvonne Kasumba, 'AMISOM and the Protection of Civilians in Somalia' [2012] Conflict Trends 17–24.

[39] See Lotze and Kasumba, n 38, 18.

[40] 'The history of the European Union' (*Europa.eu*, undated) <europa.eu/about-eu/eu-history/index_en.htm>.

of operations. Recent political statements do also call for a more ambitious approach to responding to military threats, including the establishment of a permanent EU defence force.[41]

In terms of institutional drivers, the EU has had a dual role in developing the discourse. First, the Organization has actively influenced the deliberations of the UN General Assembly and the mandates of the UN Security Council.[42] To this end, the EU has sought to maintain a unified stand within the Security Council, to influence the normative development of the protection of civilians agenda. In the mid-2000s, the two core EU countries with permanency on the Council—France and the UK—pushed to broaden the scope of the protection of civilians concept, by linking it to a more controversial concept—the Responsibility to Protect.[43] However, this approach was met with 'fierce resistance' which effectively put a damper on similar future efforts.[44] Second, the EU has sought to operationalize the concept within its own domain through the structures of the CSDP. The Organisation first developed draft guidelines on protection of civilians in EU-led crisis-management operations in 2003.[45] These were updated in 2010, in consultation with the UN—notably OCHA and DPKO—and the International Committee of the Red Cross (ICRC). The guidelines were based partially on developments in the UN, but tailored specifically to the EU. The revised version was informed by the implementation of protection-of-civilians activities in CSDP missions and operations and by 'best practices' identified by the UN and other relevant organizations.[46] An updated version of these guidelines was expected to be approved by EU Member States at the time of writing.

Similar to the UN and NATO, civil–military co-operation and the balancing of mandated tasks with relevant capabilities are among the key tensions and challenges inherent in the EU's comprehensive approach to the protection of civilians. The EU guidelines adopt the humanitarian definition of protection, encompassing 'all activities aimed at ensuring full respect for the rights of the individual in accordance with international humanitarian, human rights and refugee law'.[47] By so doing, the EU risks complicating the operationalization of the concept in military terms (cf. the UN's challenges). Additionally, it transforms the protection of civilians from a concrete task into an overarching vision that is virtually impossible to achieve, and is not necessarily attuned to the capabilities and political will of the Organization.

[41] Jean-Claude Juncker, 'Opening Statement: A New Start for Europe: My Agenda for Jobs, Growth, Fairness and Democratic Change, Political guidance for the next European Commission' (European Parliament Plenary Session, Strasbourg, Austria, 15 July 2014) 11 <ec.europa.eu/priorities/docs/pg_en.pdf>.

[42] Sarah Brockmeier, Gerrit Kurtz, and Julian Junk, 'Emerging Norm and Rhetorical Tool: Europe and a Responsibility to Protect' (2014) 14 Conflict, Security and Development 429, 430.

[43] Ibid., 440. [44] Ibid.

[45] Council of the European Union, 'Draft Guidelines on the Protection of Civilians in EU-led Crisis Management Operations' (2003) EU Doc 14805/03.

[46] Council of the European Union, 'Draft Guidelines on the Protection of Civilians in CSDP Missions and Operations' (2010) EU Doc 13047/2/10 (EU 2010 Draft Guidelines on the Protection of Civilians Guidelines).

[47] Ibid., 4.

One of the most prominent differences between the EU and the UN relates to the willingness and obligation to use force to protect. The UN has long experienced difficulties in getting Member States to support a more robust approach to peacekeeping, although recent deployments to the DRC, CAR, and Mali seem to point in a new direction. The EU, on the other hand, sees robustness as a precondition for the effective protection of civilian populations from physical threats, and Member States are generally more favourable to this approach.[48]

III. Conceptual Approaches to the Protection of Civilians

This section reviews and compares protection of civilians concepts within the four organizations. Training, planning, and execution of military operations are usually dependent on some form of formal and comprehensive guidance, sometimes based on an overarching doctrine. Each organisation has dealt with this differently. The UN has been highly influential on both the AU and the EU's approaches. NATO has not come far in conceptualizing 'how to protect' but is the leading organization on guiding its forces on 'how not to kill', i.e. how to avoid civilian casualties.[49] The following three questions are addressed for each concept: (a) how is the protection of civilians defined; (b) what tasks are seen as relevant to achieve increased physical protection; and (c) what is the role of the military? The aim is to determine the current status of key concepts within each organization and assess how they guide military protection practitioners.

A. The UN: Leading the way

The UN is at the forefront of developing guidance, strategies, concepts, planning tools, and training modules to advance the Organization's ability to protect civilians. Due to the plethora of different protection of civilians initiatives within the UN, this chapter will review three key documents: (a) the DPKO-DFS Capstone Doctrine; (b) the DPKO-DFS Protection of Civilians Policy; and, (c) the DPKO-DFS Operational Concept on the Protection of Civilians.

The Operational Concept helps clarify why there is no unified definition of protection in the UN. It describes three paradigms of how practitioners view the protection of civilians in UN peacekeeping: (a) protection as encompassing international humanitarian law and human rights law; (b) protection as providing safety from physical harm; and (c) protection as the inherent end result of peacekeeping (and therefore redundant as a distinct mandated task).[50] Instead of trying to reconcile the paradigms, the Operational Concept promotes a three-tier

[48] Council of the European Union, 'Protection of Civilians in EU-led Crisis Management Operations—Recommendations on the Way Forward' (Brussels: Council of the European Union, 2010) 5.

[49] Beadle, see n 31, 24.

[50] Draft DPKO/DFS Operational Concept on the Protection of Civilians in United Nations Peacekeeping Operations, see n 13, para. 10.

framework for conceptualizing the protection of civilians in UN peacekeeping operations: (a) protection through a political process; (b) providing protection from physical violence; and (c) establishing a protective environment. An approach which was subsequently incorporated into the policy.[51]

The Capstone Doctrine, formally titled 'UN Peacekeeping Operations: Principles and Guidelines',[52] is the overarching official guidance for UN peacekeeping operations. However, it does not provide direction on which tasks should be implemented in fulfilment of a protection mandate. It does, however, briefly describe what protection requires from the UN response in general. This involves a comprehensive approach and a need for co-ordination, including with non-UN protection actors, and the need to include protection of civilians concerns in planning and core UN activities.[53] The Operational Concept and subsequent Policy, aim to provide a shared understanding of the implementation of protection mandates, and order the range of mandated tasks into a conceptual framework.[54] They offer two core prescriptions: (a) each operation must develop its own mission-wide strategy to protect civilians; (b) the protection of civilians should be approached in a coherent and comprehensive manner, taking into consideration the three tiers outlined earlier.[55] The Operational Concept and the Policy list a wide range of activities that may be related to the protection of civilians, before describing activities within each of the three tiers. Particularly relevant for military practitioners, they advocate a four-phased approach to physical protection.

With regard to the military role in civilian protection, the Capstone Doctrine states that it does not address any military tactics, techniques, or procedures, which remain the prerogative of individual Member States. It indicates that military force can be used as a last resort, to influence and deter spoilers working against the peace process or seeking to harm civilians. It should, however, be applied only to deter and halt attacks and not to seek spoilers' military defeat.[56] The Operational Concept and the Policy provide a deeper description of the role of the military. The four-phased approach to physical protection is envisaged as: (a) assurance and prevention, (b) pre-emption, (c) response, and (d) consolidation.[57] These phases provide a general idea of how the UN envisions the physical protection tier. However, recent operations in the Eastern DRC have gone significantly beyond what these guidelines prescribe.[58] More detailed guidance on the use of force to protect has recently been

[51] Ibid., para. 14, and UN DPKO and UN DFS Protection of Civilians Policy, see n 13, para 30. [52] Capstone Doctrine, see n 13.

[53] Draft DPKO/DFS Operational Concept on the Protection of Civilians in United Nations Peacekeeping Operations, see n 13, para. 24, and UN DPKO and UN DFS Protection of Civilians Policy, see n 13, para 24 and 26.

[54] Draft DPKO/DFS Operational Concept on the Protection of Civilians in United Nations Peacekeeping Operations, see n 13, 1, and UN DPKO and UN DFS Protection of Civilians Policy, see n 13, para 30.

[55] Ibid. [56] Capstone Doctrine, see n 13, 9.

[57] Draft DPKO/DFS Operational Concept on the Protection of Civilians in United Nations Peacekeeping Operations, 8–9, and UN DPKO and UN DFS Protection of Civilians Policy, see n 13, para 31.

[58] United States Army Peacekeeping and Stability Operations Institute, 'UN Force Intervention Brigade against the M23' [April 2014] Stability Operations Lessons Learned and Information Management System Sampler 9.

promulgated within the UN. Specific guidance for the military components of peacekeeping operations and a scenario-based training package for troop contributors complement the key guidelines.[59]

B. NATO: Counterinsurgency logic

NATO is much less advanced than the UN in terms of conceptualizing its approach to protecting civilians. The main reason is that the protection of civilians has not been seen as an end in itself, and therefore has received less attention. Counterinsurgency doctrines, however, have been concerned with the importance of providing security for populations under threat. Still, the logic of protection in NATO is mostly preoccupied with how to avoid causing collateral damage, i.e. indirect protection. In fact, this may be where the UN has had most impact on NATO's approach to protection, as UNAMA's human rights investigations in Afghanistan have directly influenced how NATO has developed its approach to avoid harming civilians during operations.[60]

Initially, the US Army promoted the population-centric approach in key documents.[61] This was followed by the influential 2006 Counterinsurgency Field Manual (FM 3-24),[62] which essentially broke with the long-standing preoccupation with the decisive use of military force.[63] The FM 3-24 was soon informally adopted as NATO counterinsurgency doctrine.[64] The Organization then released the Joint Operational Guidelines for Counterinsurgency 10/01 in May 2010[65] and the Allied Joint Publication for Counterinsurgency (AJP-3.4.4).[66] It is worth noting that none of the conceptual developments in NATO are dedicated solely to the protection of civilians. Although operation *Unified Protector* over Libya brought protection issues higher on NATO's agenda, it was still largely concerned with how to avoid civilian casualties rather than providing direct protection to populations.[67] NATO is currently developing new doctrine, but it remains unclear whether

[59] UN DPKO and UNDFS Draft Protection of Civilians Policy, see n 13; UN DPKO and UN DFS Draft Military Guidelines on the Protection of Civilians, see n 13; UN DPKO and UN DFS, 'Draft Guidelines on Deterrence and the Use of Force by Military Components of United Nations Peacekeeping Operations' (on file with author); UN Tactical Training Modules, see n 13.

[60] For further discussion on this point, see Keating and Bennett in this volume.

[61] United States Department of the Army, *Counterinsurgency Operations* (Field Manual—Interim 3-07.22) (Washington, DC: United States Department of the Army, 2004) § 3.10–3.14 <fas.org/irp/doddir/army/fmi3-07-22.pdf>.

[62] United States Department of the Army, *Insurgencies and Countering Insurgencies* (Field Manual 3-24, Marine Corps Warfighting Publication 3-33.5) (Washington, DC: United States Department of the Army, 2014) <www.fas.org/irp/doddir/army/fm3-24.pdf>.

[63] Nathaniel C Fick and John A Nagl, 'Counterinsurgency Field Manual: Afghanistan Edition' *Foreign Policy* (Washington, DC, 1 October 2009) <foreignpolicy.com/2009/10/01/counterinsurgency-field-manual-afghanistan-edition>.

[64] Tore Nyhamar, *Counterinsurgency Field Manual 3-24 and operations* (Kjeller, Norway: Norwegian Defence Research Establishment (FFI), 2009) 7.

[65] NATO, see n 32.

[66] NATO, 'Allied Joint Doctrine for Counterinsurgency' (AJP-3.4.4) (Brussels: North Atlantic Treaty Organization, 2011) <info.publicintelligence.net/NATO-Counterinsurgency.pdf>.

[67] Lieutenant General Charles Bouchard, see n 30.

considerations of the direct protection of civilians will be part of the outcome of that process.

C. The AU: Mirroring the UN

The AU has looked to the UN in developing its protection approach. Conceptually, the AU approach has evolved rather quickly, but there are significant gaps in the practical implementation of its protection guidelines.[68] In the AU, 'protection of civilians' is defined as 'all activities undertaken to improve the security of the population and people at risk and to ensure the full respect for rights of groups and the individual recognised under regional instruments . . . and international law, including humanitarian, human rights and refugee law'.[69]

In terms of relevant tasks, the AU also makes use of a tiered approach to protection which combines both short-term and long-term efforts. It comprises four pillars: (a) protection as part of the political process, (b) protection from physical violence, (c) rights-based protection, and (d) the establishment of a protective environment.[70] Protection as part of the political process is deemed key to the success of protection efforts. As such, AU missions are geared to support the host State to ensure the protection of its civilian population. Where protection from physical violence is required, four phases are envisioned. Similar to the UN, they are: (a) prevention, (b) pre-emption, (c) response, and (d) consolidation.[71] The concept of rights-based protection involves the monitoring and reporting of human rights violations, and support to the development of local capacities. Finally, the establishment of a secure environment is a comprehensive and broad tier, which includes peacebuilding measures over the longer term.

The role of the military is mainly linked to providing physical protection. *Prevention* may include discouraging armed groups from planning hostile activities, for example through patrols. *Pre-emption* is seen as measures to preclude or defeat an imminent threat or to gain advantage over a spoiler group before it launches a violent activity, for example the tactical deployment of troops. *Response* is the proportionate use of force to neutralize or render ineffective a spoiler group after the outbreak of violence. *Consolidation* includes activities necessary to manage a post-conflict situation, including denying threatening groups the ability to restore fighting capability.

The AU is still working on providing more specific guidance and tools to improve the protection of civilians in its peace support missions, specifically through the development of guidance for the development of mission-wide protection strategies, training packages, and other guidance aimed at the operational level.[72]

[68] Lotze and Kasumba, see n 38, 18–24.

[69] AU Draft Protection of Civilians Guidelines, see n 35. [70] Ibid., 9. [71] Ibid., 9.

[72] African Union Peace and Security Council, 'Progress Report of the Chairperson of the Commission on the Development of Guidelines for the Protection of Civilians in African Union Peace Support Operations' (2011) AU Doc PSC/PR/2(CCLXXIX) paras 14–23.

D. The EU: A broad approach

The latest EU effort to provide specific guidelines is found in the 2010 Draft Revised Guidelines on the Protection of Civilians in CSDP Missions and Operations.[73] The EU guidelines do not provide an official definition of the protection of civilians, although they are quite specific in describing how the Organization understands the task. They do include an example definition from the UN Organization Mission in the Democratic Republic of the Congo (MONUC), the UN operation in the DRC until 2010, which refers to both physical protection and a rights-based understanding. The EU guidelines state that the concept of the protection of civilians has not been explicitly mentioned in the mandates of CSDP missions or operations.[74]

The guidelines are intended to provide both an assessment of the implementation of protection of civilians activities in CSDP missions and specific guidance. They include commentary on protection activities undertaken by the EU and other actors. The commentary focuses heavily on the UN experience, with several EU missions mentioned, but not thoroughly assessed.[75] The guidance aspect comprises a structured framework for addressing protection of civilians in CSDP operations at all phases, covering: (a) advance planning, (b) operational planning, (c) conduct of operations, and (d) lessons identified.[76]

The EU guidelines list a number of operational tasks: (a) monitoring the implementation of peace agreements and ceasefires; (b) creating conditions conducive to safe, timely, and unimpeded delivery of humanitarian assistance; (c) ensuring freedom of movement and route security (including for refugees/IDPs); (d) public order management; (e) monitoring (including of the human rights situation) and reporting; (f) police and military patrols; (g) mentoring and training local military or police to ensure the protection of civilians; and (h) stabilization of a post-crisis situation through disarmament, demobilization, and reintegration, and, security sector reform.

The guidelines are not specific about the role of the military. When describing the operational planning phase, they refer to the importance of including protection of civilians considerations in the Concept of Operations (CONOPS) and Operations Plan (OPLAN), but do not explain how such issues should be addressed. The guidelines also list several 'operational aspects', including monitoring the implementation of peace agreements and ceasefires, patrols, public order management, and mentoring and training of local security forces. How these aspects specifically work to improve the protection of civilians is not clarified. In the context of the conduct-of-operations phase, the guidelines indicate nothing about the role of the military. They do, however, underline the importance of clarifying the roles and responsibilities among various protection actors, not only between the ICRC, NATO, AU, and the Organization for Security and Cooperation in Europe (OSCE), but also internally within the EU. At the time of writing, the EU was about to release updated guidance on the protection of civilians in EU-led military operations.

[73] EU 2010 Draft Guidelines on the Protection of Civilians Guidelines, see n 46.
[74] Ibid., 4. [75] Ibid., 3. [76] Ibid., 14.

IV. Protection of Civilians in Practice

A. The UN: Seldom using force to protect

In late 2015, the UN had approximately 105,000 uniformed personnel deployed to peacekeeping operations, of which some 90,000 were military troops.[77] They were deployed to sixteen missions, ten of which had a specific mandate to protect civilians, which means a vast majority of UN peacekeepers are mandated to protect. Most acutely, the UN is trying to protect civilians from imminent threats of physical violence in South Sudan, CAR, the DRC, the Abyei region, and Mali. UN military responses in these missions have ranged from offensive military operations against perpetrators of violence towards civilians in support of host-nation security forces, such as through the Force Intervention Brigade in the DRC,[78] to sheltering more than 100,000 internally displaced South Sudanese in UN protection sites.[79] In developing its protection activities the UN has advanced a wide range of innovative civil–military mechanisms to respond to physical protection challenges.[80]

Despite the UN's leading global role in protection efforts, the Organization's own Office of Internal Oversight Services (OIOS), in a 2014 report, stated that in peacekeeping operations 'force is almost never used to protect civilians under attack'.[81] The OIOS evaluation of UN peacekeeping operations' implementation of protection of civilians mandates underlines a major gap in the UN's approach to providing physical protection. Although the discourse and relevant concepts are well developed, UN peacekeeping operations are often not able or willing to utilise military force to protect. The reasons are varied, including:

> different views in the Security Council and among troop-contributing countries . . . a de facto dual line of command involving mission leadership and troop-contributing countries that regulates the use of force by missions . . . [failure to understand] the obligation . . . to act when host Governments are unable or unwilling to . . . protect civilians . . . insufficient resources to respond to force with force; and . . . [concerns] about possible penalties if . . . use of force is judged inappropriate.[82]

The deployment of the Force Intervention Brigade to the Eastern DRC in 2013 moved UN peacekeeping into new territory (possibly temporarily), where force was mandated to be used 'pro-actively' to 'neutralize' named armed groups. During the autumn of 2013, the Force Intervention Brigade was instrumental in joint operations with the national armed forces of the DRC, which defeated the 'M23' rebel

[77] See UN DPKO, 'Monthly Summary of Military and Policy Contribution to United Nations Operations' (*United Nations Peacekeeping*, 2014) <http://www.un.org/en/peacekeeping/documents/Yearly.pdf>.

[78] UNSC Res 2098 (2013).

[79] See, for example, UNSC, 'Report of the Secretary-General on South Sudan' (2014) UN Doc S/2014/537, para. 80; UNSC, 'Report of the Secretary-General on South Sudan' (2014) UN Doc S/2014/158, paras 48–54; UNSC, 'Report of the Secretary-General on the United Nations Organisation Stabilization Mission in the Democratic Republic of the Congo' (2013) S/2013/757, para. 17.

[80] Kjeksrud and Ravndal, see n 20.

[81] OIOS Report, see n 25, para. 79.

[82] Ibid., 2.

group.[83] Ongoing operations against other recalcitrant armed groups have been less decisive. The broader impact of mandating a special brigade to use robust force to protect civilians is yet to be assessed. It raised some difficult international humanitarian law issues, in particular the challenges to the impartial and protected status of UN peacekeepers.[84] Additionally, it could have the counterproductive effect of implying that the robust use of force was not already incorporated in the usual protection mandate.

B. NATO: Collateral damage near zero but still failing to protect

Despite the absence of specific protection of civilians concepts, NATO has conducted a range of relevant activities, in Afghanistan, Kosovo, and Libya. In Afghanistan, NATO made significant efforts to reduce the number of civilian casualties caused by their own forces. At the same time, the total number of civilian deaths significantly increased. According to Beadle:

> Pro-Government forces have reduced the proportion of civilians killed by own actions in Afghanistan from 41 % in 2007 to 11 % in 2013 [. . .]. However, excessive focus on 'how not to kill' civilians will overlook the fact that insurgent violence remains the biggest threat to civilians [. . .] as they are responsible for the vast majority of civilian casualties. For example, even though pro-government forces kill fewer and fewer civilians in Afghanistan, the total number of deaths doubled from 1,523 in 2007 to 3,131 in 2011.[85]

In operation *Unified Protector* in Libya, NATO applied its lessons from Afghanistan and was able to reduce collateral damage to a minimum. Despite the effectiveness of these efforts, a weakness of NATO's approach to protection is that it fails to address the fact that civilians are increasingly directly targeted by armed groups. As civilian casualty figures from Afghanistan clearly show, reducing the number of civilian casualties caused by NATO had no influence on the total number of civilians killed. In fact, in the period in which NATO managed to drastically reduce collateral damage, there was a significant increase in civilian casualties. As winning the trust of the population is a key tenet of counter-insurgency logic, NATO's efforts must also be able to reduce the number of casualties resulting from insurgent violence. This demands a more direct approach to protection along the lines of that conceptualized in UN guidance.

C. The AU: Learning from Somalia, Mali, and the Central African Republic

To date, the AU has conducted six peace support operations: the AU Mission in Burundi (AMIB); AMIS in Sudan; AMISOM in Somalia; the AU Electoral and Security Assistance Mission to the Comoros (MAES); AFISMA in Mali; and

[83] See United States Army Peacekeeping and Stability Operations Institute, see n 58.
[84] Scott Sheeran and Stephanie Case, 'The Intervention Brigade: Legal Issues for the UN in the Democratic Republic of the Congo' (New York: International Peace Institute, 2014).
[85] Beadle, see n 3, 62.

MISCA in the CAR. Of these, AMIS, AFISMA, and MISCA held an explicit protection mandate, while AMISOM, which was the only active AU peace support operation at the time of writing, did not. It had, however, on several occasions been mandated to mainstream protection of civilians considerations into its operations.

While to date three AU missions have had protection of civilians as a part of their mandates, the AU's experience in Somalia has perhaps been the most formative, as it was this experience that triggered the development of the Organization's protection agenda. It is also where efforts to first develop and then implement a protection strategy have been most consistent and advanced. What has become clear to the Organization through these experiences is that a protection rationale similar to that of NATO—which places an emphasis on not harming the civilian population—is insufficient, and that a broader approach to protection, similar to that of the UN, is required. However, it is in the implementation of such a strategy where the AU has fallen short, committing itself to the protection of the civilian population, but, like the UN, not fully able to live up to such expectations. In 2014 the AU launched a lessons-learned project on its protection of civilians experiences, expected to result in the release of a report in 2015. The lessons identified, and the policy implications that derived therefrom, will likely be key to shaping the AU's future role and actions in protecting civilians.

D. The EU: Occasional military protection attempts

The EU has developed an ambitious approach to peace and stabilization operations under the umbrella of the CSDP. EU engagements in CAR, the Balkans, and the DRC over the past decade demonstrate that the Organization is at times able to activate its *military* structure. The ambitious civil–military 'comprehensive approaches' have, however, often been wanting. Operation *Artemis* in the DRC in 2003, when the EU provided much needed military muscle to a UN operation in crisis, demonstrated that the EU was able to respond rapidly to a protection crisis. The 1,000-troop-strong deployment to CAR in 2014 had the protection of civilians as its main task, but this time the EU struggled to secure sufficient troop contributions in time, questioning again the Organization's ability to be a significant player in the field of providing for international peace and security. Conceptually, the EU is leaning towards a comprehensive approach to protection, but in practice the Organization's operations are largely military and have been on the more robust end of the spectrum. It therefore remains somewhat unclear in which direction the EU's protection approach is evolving.

Perhaps the best future role for the EU is in support of the UN—temporarily providing robust forces *in extremis*. Although the EU has managed to fulfil this important role on a few occasions in the past, there have been others where the EU was harshly criticised for not coming to the aid of the UN.[86] There are several

[86] Per Martin Norheim-Martinsen, 'Our Work Here is Done: European Union Peacekeeping in Africa' (2011) 20 African Security Rev 17, 25.

ongoing processes that are intended to improve EU–UN collaboration in this field. Recently, EU Member States agreed on a Plan of Action for how to better support UN peacekeeping operations. For various reasons, the implementation of the Plan of Action has been 'uneven' to date.[87]

V. Comparative Insights on the Protection of Civilians Discourses, Concepts, and Practices

Although the UN has the most developed discourse and specific protection concepts, it is also the organization with the most significant challenges in employing force to protect in practice. NATO—the strongest military organization, with much hard-earned experience from a decade of counter-insurgency operations—has not yet acknowledged the need to develop specific concepts to better protect civilians, and continues to focus on collateral harm reduction. The AU lingers in between, with developed protection concepts, heavily influenced by those of the UN. AU operations in Mali and the CAR have had protection considerations feature more prominently in the mandates of the operations, and on the basis of the lessons learned, the AU has further advanced its protection agenda at the policy level. However, it still lacks the wherewithal to turn rhetoric into reality. The EU has also struggled with manifesting ambitious intentions into actual operations, but has been influential in the UN discourse on protection and the responsibility to protect.

All four organizations recognize a group of people, 'civilians', who are considered external to the conflict and who should be protected from violence. The obligation to avoid harm to this group is placed upon the parties to the conflict, consonant with international humanitarian law. The responsibilities of actively protecting civilians against the threat of violence lies foremost with the relevant government, but the UN, AU, and EU have recognized a broader duty to protect civilians, residing with each of their own organisations. For NATO, such duty has only been once explicitly recognized, during operation *Unified Protector* in Libya. At that time, the Organization drew upon the UN discourse on protection, not its own.

The UN, AU, and EU discourses all link the protection of civilians to their core values—hence, also to their existence as organizations. For NATO this is not explicit. However, by claiming that 'protecting the people is the mission'[88] in Afghanistan, it linked mission accomplishment, and by extension the Organization's fundamental effectiveness, to its ability to protect civilians.

There are important differences in the drivers of the organizational discourses. The NATO discourse is largely driven bottom-up as a problem-solving strategy. In the UN, the drivers of the protection discourse have been diverse, largely due to the political interests involved, the compartmentalized nature of the UN bureaucracy,

[87] Adam C Smith, 'European Military Capabilities and UN Peace Operations: Strengthening the Partnership' (New York: International Peace Institute, 2014).

[88] McChrystal and Hall, see n 28, 1.

and the fact that protection of civilians touches upon central values of the Organization. In the EU, the protection discourse has been driven from the top, by tapping into the UN discourse and engaging on the development of the responsibility to protect. The AU's recent concern for protection leans heavily on the UN's discourse, however, progress has been slow. The Organization's protection discourse has been largely developed and advanced by the AU Commission, and implementation in operations has been driven more by rhetoric than reality. While the various organizational approaches to the protection of civilians from physical harm by military means diverge significantly, this is even more pronounced when the other aspects of protection, those in the humanitarian and human rights spheres, are also considered.

The UN is driving the development of protection guidance, strategies, concepts, planning, and training tools. It has not, however, solved several of the major dilemmas related to implementation of physical protection mandates. Two major remaining challenges are the lack of a more unified understanding of what the protection of civilians entails for the UN as a whole, and the increasing tension between the traditional 'peacekeeping principles' and current peacekeeping practices. Despite inconsistencies in the UN's approach, the Organization has been able to develop conceptual and practical approaches to protection that resonate well with its overall discourse and have proved useful, if not perfect, in practice.

NATO lacks concepts, guidance, and tools that address the protection of civilians in a manner similar to the other organizations. However, NATO counterinsurgency doctrine is highly concerned with providing security to the civilian population. Unlike the UN's direct approach to protection, this doctrine treats protection as a means to an end. Air operations over Libya were largely concerned with the same challenge, and judging from that operation, NATO has indeed become adept at keeping collateral damage to a minimum. Still, as long as NATO continues to see protection mainly within the framework of international humanitarian law, it fails to address situations where a more direct approach to protection is needed.

Conceptually, the AU and the EU are very close to the UN. Still, both have few operations to learn from and are in the early phases of developing specific guidelines. AMISOM's efforts to avoid civilian casualties during operations have been largely successful. However, as its protection of civilians guidelines envision a more direct approach to protection, some tension will persist as long as counterinsurgency concerns dominate its approach. The EU's acknowledgement of the importance of protection of civilians is well evolved, but the Organization has, up until now, not been able to integrate protection of civilians as a specific effort in its mandates. Forthcoming guidelines may relieve some of these tensions.

A comparative analysis of the major organizations involved in protecting civilians is useful for future troop contributors in that it highlights that different organizations treat this task differently for a range of reasons. Consequently, the institutional framework is highly influential on the ways in which the role of military force to protect is conceptualized and implemented in practice. The comparison also shows that despite the unprecedented concern with improving the physical security of those under threat, no organization can claim that it does so effectively. Guidance is therefore still needed on how military force may be used with more utility to protect. Having different approaches to protecting civilians is not necessarily a bad thing. All organizations display comparative advantages. However, it is critical that future roles and responsibilities in providing protection are clarified to avoid overlap within and between organizations.

5

The Evolution of the UN Collective Security System

Haidi Willmot[1]

I. Introduction

In international discourse on the protection of civilians, significant focus is afforded to human rights and humanitarian law frameworks and ideals. Yet, despite the United Nations (UN) collective security system being the constitutional order that fundamentally governs the use of force in the international community, it is seldom mentioned in that context. Nicholas Tsagourias and Nigel White note that:

> With the growth of specific regimes, such as human rights law and international criminal law, it is sometimes easy to forget the essential foundations of peace and security upon which these more elaborate, detailed and rule-of-law oriented orders, are built. Despite its flaws, without collective security and the law that facilitates and regulates it, not only are the basic foundations of peace and security undermined, but it becomes extremely difficult to achieve self-determination, human rights and, ultimately human flourishing.[2]

The UN collective security system is in many ways a realist manifestation of a liberal ideal. The very concept of States co-operating on a collective security project built upon international law and centred around an international institution draws heavily on liberal thinking, yet the 1945 collective security agreement, captured in the UN Charter, evidences realist forces at work. It focuses strongly on the security of States, not individuals, and it centralizes the management of the system in the victors of the Second World War. The system entrenches a balance of power among them through permanent membership and veto power in the Security Council, and in this way also crystallizes power relations between them and the rest of the membership.

Over the past seventy years the UN collective security system has undergone significant evolution, the result of which has been a fundamental change in the *telos* of

[1] Haidi Willmot serves with the United Nations Department of Peacekeeping Operations. The views expressed herein are her personal views and do not necessarily reflect the views of, nor should they be attributed to the United Nations.

[2] Nicholas Tsagourias and Nigel D White, *Collective Security Theory, Law and Practice*, (Cambridge: Cambridge University Press, 2013) 421.

the order. The Security Council is longer just a guardian of Westphalian geopolitical security between sovereign States, but, to some extent, a guardian of the people in whose name the Charter was promulgated. It is expected to arbitrate disagreements not solely *between* Sates, but *within* them as well. One of the key instruments in this transformation has been UN peacekeeping operations. They are the flagship enterprise of the Organization and almost every peace operation deployed since 1999 has been authorized to use force to protect civilians. In recent years civilian protection has become the *raison d'être* of most missions.

This chapter considers the dominant international relations theories and the theoretical foundations of collective security. It examines the UN collective security agreement, as articulated in the UN Charter in 1945, and compares that with the collective security ideal. It then follows the evolution of the UN collective security system over the past seventy years, highlighting significant change in three key aspects: (a) the *mechanism* for determining aggression and deciding response measures; (b) the *determination* of threats to the peace; and (c) the *measures* used to address such threats. The chapter then moves to analyse the meaning and impact of these changes, particularly as they relate to the protection of civilians.

Finally, the chapter finds that the international community now acknowledges civilians as legitimate actors of the UN collective security system. The system recognizes the legitimacy of civilians as a group to be protected irrespective of their polity, but at the same time remains committed to States as the primary security actors and therefore seeks to execute protection within that paradigm. In doing so, it creates two distinct but closely linked communities, both of which civilians are simultaneously members, and that, it is argued, represents a trajectory toward a cosmopolitan idea of the ordering of global society.

II. International Relations Theory

International relations theory not only offers explanatory and predictive tools, but also demands perspective and requires thinking more deeply about the historical, structural, and systemic forces at work beneath political machinations and practical deeds. It allows us to see the overall situation, the path to the present, and the trajectory of the future. Steve Smith notes that theories 'do not simply explain or predict, they tell us what possibilities exist for human action and intervention; they define not merely our explanatory possibilities, but also our ethical and practical horizons'.[3]

Realism and liberalism are the two primary schools of thought within international relations theory. There are many variations within each, and a number of supplementary theoretical approaches that sit alongside these long-standing traditions.

[3] Steve Smith, 'Positivism and Beyond', in Steve Smith, Ken Booth, and Marysia Zalewski (eds), *International Theory: Positivism and Beyond* (Cambridge: Cambridge University Press, 1996) 113.

Realism generally understands international relations as rational, self-interested States, in an ongoing struggle for power and survival in a situation of anarchy.[4] In the absence of an international government, the theory identifies little to curb the pursuit of national interest. Classical realists, including Thomas Hobbes and Hans Morgenthau, emphasize the importance of the ego-centric and base aspects of human nature, which play out in politics and the relations between States. Hobbes' *Leviathan*[5] describes the state of nature as humans beings in constant conflict and competition. This transposes onto the international stage as States being in a constant state of war. Neo-realists, including Kenneth Waltz, focus less on human nature and more on the absence of supranational government, leading to a condition of anarchy in which States seek to balance power to ensure their own security. Neo-realists see anarchy working against co-operation beyond self-interest, but do acknowledge that international law and international institutions can induce, if not compel, co-operation and adherence to some norms. Such co-operation, however, will be thin and serve the interests of the powerful States that create the institutions and laws.

Liberalism generally understands international relations as holding significant potential for co-operation and interdependence among like-minded States, resulting in a peaceful international order.[6] The theory purports that democratic States that internally uphold the rule of law, respect human rights, and trade freely represent the ideal polity for achieving peace and are less likely to go to war with each other. Such domestic ideals can be replicated on the international stage in the form of international law, universal human rights, and global free trade, leading to a more peaceful international order. Liberalism in international relations draws on broader liberal traditions including the Enlightenment thinking of John Locke and Immanuel Kant, and the idealism of Woodrow Wilson, with its deep-seated belief in universal values and the potential for human progress. Neo-liberals, or liberal intuitionalists, such as Robert Keohane and Joseph Nye, acknowledge a level of anarchy but advocate the ability of institutions or regimes to induce co-operation by enhancing trust and predictability in State interactions, utilizing game theory to support their analysis. In their view, institutions allow States to co-operate to address global issues that may not be able to be solved by a single State. They allow States to reconceive their self-interest, and may also play a role in monitoring compliance, enforcement, and sanctioning defectors.

Lying between realism and liberalism is the English School, which understands international relations as a society of States displaying a precarious but high level of co-operation despite the situation of anarchy in which they

[4] For a deeper account of realism see Jack Donnelly, 'Realism', in Scott Surchill, Andrew Linklater, Richard Devetak, Jack Donnelly, Terry Nardin, Matthew Paterson, Christian Reus-Smit, and Jacqui True (eds), *Theories of International Relations* (Fourth Edition) (Hampshire, UK: Palgrave Macmillan, 2009) 31–56.

[5] Thomas Hobbs, *Leviathan: The Matter, Forme and Power of a Common Wealth Ecclesiasticall and Civil* (originally published in England in 1651).

[6] For a deeper account of liberalism see Scott Burchill, 'Liberalism', in Surchill, Linklater, Devetak, Donnelly, Nardin, Paterson, Reus-Smit, and True, n 4, 57–85.

exist.[7] The central proponent of the English School, Hedley Bull, made a distinction between a 'system of states' and a 'society of states', the latter representing a much deeper form of interaction in which a group of States come to share common interests and values and are bound by a common set of rules and institutions. According to the English School, international society, like domestic societies, is geared toward three primary goals: limiting the use of force, ensuring respect for property, and ensuring that agreements are kept. Unlike realists, the English School believes that this can be achieved in the absence of supranational government, placing the emphasis on order over power. Unlike liberalism, the English School considers that order can exist among States with different political cultures and philosophies of government, accepting the prevalence of pluralism in international society.

Sovereign States remain the central unit of analysis of each of these traditions, with little focus afforded to individuals. For realists, the State is the concentration of power and the main actor in a power-based struggle, although realism does rest upon assumptions of human nature and highlights the impact of individual statesmen. Individuals play a somewhat more significant role in the liberal tradition. Moral concern for individuals is built into the focus on human rights, which imposes constraints on sovereignty and is brought into the international forum through international law.

In this context, the violation of State sovereignty for the purpose of protecting civilians can be explained in a number of ways. A realist analysis may purport that States engage in the protection of civilians in other States because it is in their self-interest to do so, part of an ongoing struggle for power and influence in the many forms that might take. Whether the essential purpose is to halt regional instability, overthrow a government, maintain trade, or combat international criminal and terrorist activities, 'protection' is often a self-serving justification for intervention, or an exercise of powerful States imposing their values on weaker ones. To bolster this argument, realists may point to the selectivity of interventions and how this aligns with the national interests of powerful countries. A liberal analysis may accept that the protection of civilians by the international community is an adjustment of the parameters of State sovereignty to protect human rights and facilitate the implementation of international human rights law. They may cite statements of commitment to the civilian protection ideal proffered in UN forums and point to UN peacekeeping deployments into situations in which few of the interveners have a direct national interest. Nevertheless, in both instances the explanations remain focused on States as the primary global actors.

Bull stated that 'if any value attaches to order in world politics, it is order among all mankind which we must treat as being of primary value, not order within the society of States'.[8] Although seemingly at odds with much of his philosophy, the statement goes to the heart of the nature and purpose of international relations. It

[7] For a deeper account of the English School, see Andrew Linklater, 'The English School', in Surchill, Linklater, Devetak, Donnelly, Nardin, Paterson, Reus-Smit, and True, n 4, 86–110.

[8] Hedly Bull, *The Anarchical Society: A Study of Order in World Politics* (London: Macmillan, 1977) 22.

highlights the role of individuals in the international system, echoing cosmopolitan ideas, which separate individuals from the State and identify them as independent and legitimate actors of a global society. The protection of civilians by international actors poses a challenge in respect of locating the individual in an international political setting. While realism and liberalism provide shallow accounts, cosmopolitanism provides a basis to understand the individual both as a political being and as part of a larger political collective.

David Held identifies three broad accounts of cosmopolitanism. First, *classical cosmopolitanism*, drawing on Stoic ideas of the individual inhabiting both 'a local community and a wider community of human ideals, aspirations and argument'.[9] The Stoic concept contends that people are 'in the first instance, human beings living in a world of human beings and only incidentally members of polities'.[10] It emphasizes that each person is a 'citizen of the world' and owes a duty, above all, 'to the worldwide community of human beings'.[11] Second, *Kantian cosmopolitanism*, characterized by the 'cosmopolitan right', in which 'citizenship can become an attribute not just of national communities, but of a universal system of 'cosmo-political' governance in which the freedom of each person underpins the freedom of others'.[12] Third, *contemporary cosmopolitanism*, centring on the principles of egalitarian individualism and recognition, and on the impartial treatment of claims.[13]

In a similar vein, Philip Allott advocates the pursuit of a 'society of societies', in which 'society' is understood as the collective self-constituting of human beings for their survival and prospering.[14] In Allott's reimagined international order, the UN would be an intermediate society, 'intermediate between the self-constituting of all-humanity and more particular levels of social self-constituting, namely, States'.[15] This would be underwritten by a new international legal paradigm in which the global legal system is designed to pursue the common interest of all humanity rather than the aggregated interests of Sates.[16]

The succeeding sections contain an examination of the evolution of the UN collective security system, and in particular the growth in the protection of civilians by the international community. In an effort to probe beneath the politics and practice, to consider the more fundamental implications of certain developments, the analysis is contextualized within ideas drawn from international relations theory.

[9] David Held, *Cosmopolitanism: Ideals and Realities* (Cambridge: Polity Press, 2010) 40.

[10] Brian Barry, 'Statism and Nationalism: A Cosmopolitan Critique', in Ian Shapiro and Leah Brilmayer (eds), *Global Justice* (New York: New York University Press, 1999) 36.

[11] Held, see n 9, 40, quoting Martha C Nussbaum, 'Patriotism and Cosmopolitism', in Joshua Cohen (ed.), *For Love of Country: Debating the Limits of Patriotism* (Boston: Beacon Press, 1996) 4.

[12] Held, see n 9, 43, quoting Immanuel Kant, *Kant's Political Writings* (ed HS Reiss) (Cambridge: Cambridge University Press, 1970) 47–53, 128–30.

[13] See Held, n 9, 46–9.

[14] Philip Allott, *Eunomia: New Order for a New World* (Oxford: Oxford University Press, 2001), Chapter 1.

[15] Philip Allott, *The Health of Nations: Society and Law Beyond the State* (Cambridge: Cambridge University Press, 2002) 347.

[16] Ibid., 315.

This, in turn, allows us to chart the possible evolutionary trajectory and opportunities for the future.

III. Collective Security

Often encapsulated in the phrase *all for one and one for all*, the concept of collective security has defied an authoritative definition.[17] However, it is clear that it rests on two fundamental features: (a) the general prohibition of the use of force among a community of States; and (b) the agreement that the community will come to the aid of any of their number against which force is threatened or used. The essential purpose of collective security is to provide stability among States through organizing a system in which the use of force is regulated, in order to manage and lessen the destructive anarchy of self-help and curb the escalation potential of the security dilemma—an elegant, if less gentle, example of what Martti Koskenniemi refers to as 'the gentle civilizer of nations'.[18]

Other important features of collective security that are variously identified include: the codification of the agreement in an international legal instrument to provide clarity of standards, obligations, and procedure;[19] the institutionalization of the agreement to provide permanency, predictability, and deterrence;[20] and universalism of membership, resulting in a focus on aggression from within the community, in contrast to defensive alliances which tend to focus on external aggression.[21]

According to M.V. Naidu, drawing on the ideas of Inis Claude, one of the most influential thinkers on collective security,[22] an ideal collective security system requires the following:

I Prohibition of arbitrary use of military force.

— The prohibition of force even in self-defence.

II Collective guarantee of security

[17] See MV Naidu, *Collective Security and the United Nations: A Definition of the UN Security System* (London: The Macmillan Press, 1974), Chapter 1; Peter G Danchin, 'Things Fall Apart: The Concept of Collective Security in International Law', in Peter G Danchin and Horst Fisher (eds), *United Nations Reform and the New Collective Security* (Cambridge: Cambridge University Press, 2010); Leon Gordenker and Thomas G Weiss, 'The Collective Security Idea and Changing World Politics', in Thomas G Weiss (ed.), *Collective Security in a Changing World* (Boulder, USA: Lynne Rienner Publishers, 1993); Inis L Claude, *Swords into Plowshares* (New York: Random House, 1959); and Inis L Claude, *Power and International Relations* (New York: Random House, 1962).

[18] Martti Koskenniemi, *The Gentle Civilizer of Nations: The Rise and Fall of International Law, 1870–1960* (Cambridge: Cambridge University Press, 2001).

[19] Charles A Kupchan and Clifford Kupchan, 'The Promise of Collective Security', in [Summer 1995] Intl Security 20, quoted in Danchin, see n 17, 41; and Jost Delbruck, 'Collective Security' in Rudolf Bernhardt (ed.), *Encyclopaedia of Public International Law*, (Amsterdam: Elsevier Science Publishers BV, 1992) 646, quoted in Danchin, n 17, 41.

[20] Naidu, see n 17, and Gordenker and Weiss, see n 17.

[21] Naidu, see n 17, and Gordenker and Weiss, see n 17.

[22] Naidu, see n 16, based on the ideas of Claude (1959 and 1962), see n 17.

All members are bound to provide assistance for preventing and responding to aggression everywhere; no member can remain neutral.

III Collective force as a deterrent/sanction

There must be a demonstrated willingness to use requisite force if and when necessary.

IV Automatism in collective action

A guarantee that aggression against any State will trigger the collective security mechanism.

V Anonymity of aggressor and victim

The system must be impartial, and the response must not discriminate on basis of the identity of the parties involved.

VI Assignability of guilt

There needs to be an agreed definition of aggression, a pre-determined procedure for determining guilt, and an impartial institution entrusted with the responsibility for making such determinations.

VII Permanency and generality of the system

The system needs to be institutionalized and permanently entrenched.

Collective security straddles the disciplines of international law and international relations. One definition suggests that it is an agreement between States to 'abide by certain norms and rules to maintain stability and, when necessary, to band together to stop aggression'.[23] While such a broad understanding may provide the flexibility to accommodate the contemporary security environment, it fails to convey many of the qualities that differentiate collective security from other defensive alliances. Another conception locates collective security somewhere between *balance of power* and *global government*, incorporating elements of both, seeking to manage power relations and create order without government.[24]

Tsagourias and White identify the UN collective security system as a constitutional[25] order:

Collective security is concerned with public order in international relations. It is a construct of states, acting as public bodies representing the peoples of the world, tasked with the delivery of the public goods of peace and security. Collective security is thus a global public order institution. It consists of a constellation of values, principles, rules, actors, instruments and practices within which, and according to which, collective security organs, institutions and

[23] Kupchan and Kupchan, see n 19, 52–3, quoted in Danchin, see n 17, 41.

[24] Danchin, see n 17, 42, quoting Inis Claude, first in 'Comment on "An Autopsy of Collective Security"' 90 Political Science Q 715, and then in 'The Management of Power in the Changing United Nations' 15 Intl Organisation 219–21, 221.

[25] 'Constitutional' in the sense that it sets out the normative and organizational principles for the order and constitutes the basis of authority within the order. See Tsagourias and White, n 1, 32–8, and Nicholas Tsagourias, 'Introduction: Constitutionalism: A Theoretical Roadmap', in Nicholas Tsagourias (ed), *Transnational Constitutionalism: International and European Perspectives* (Cambridge: Cambridge University Press, 2007) 1–2.

actors operate and interact to ensure the ultimate goal of attaining international peace and security is served effectively.[26]

There are many issues that complicate the conception of collective security. One set of issues focuses on realist political concerns, including the very existence of a 'community' of States, power discrepancies of community members, the assumption that members will act against their bilateral or plurilateral alliances, the imperative for community members to become involved in actions in which they do not have any direct national interest, and the unlikely assumption of acceptance of the status quo. Another set of issues focuses on operational concerns such as the process for determining unacceptable threats or uses of force, the need for forceful collective action to be able to overwhelm the strongest member, and the extension of collective action measures beyond the use of force to other coercive measures such as diplomatic and economic sanctions.

The central idea of collective security demonstrates inherent tensions, many of which are reflected in the modern international system. On the one hand it is predicated on sovereign autonomy and protection of the territorial and political integrity of States, and yet it also depends on the creation of a community in which the sovereign prerogative to use force is, at least somewhat, devolved to the group. While it disavows the threat or use of force as a legitimate instrument of statecraft, it critically relies on the threat and use of collective force to guarantee the system. The traditional conception of collective security is based very much on the Westphalian ideal of territorial security against military incursion. However, the conception of international stability, the primary purpose of collective security, may be served by a legitimate interest on the part of the group in the internal security situation of States, particularly where that may have flow-on effects for neighbouring States. This may in turn lead to a much fuller conception of international peace and security that moves beyond the security of States to focus on the security of people.

When the shield of sovereignty is moved aside, further complications are introduced as the concept of security is overlaid with liberal ideals of human rights and democracy. Once it is accepted that the group has a legitimate interest in the internal situation of States, questions are raised as to whether the territorial integrity of a State should be protected against the exercising of self-determination of a group of individuals, whether the political integrity of a non-democratic State should be protected, and whether individuals against whom human rights abuses are being carried out are legitimate subjects of protection by the group. Each of these issues has provided normative and practical challenges for the UN collective security system.

IV. The UN Collective Security System

The UN sits at the heart of the only universal collective security system. It is the principal collective security institution, with wide-ranging competence and

[26] Tsagourias and White, see n 2, 411.

powers.[27] The UN Charter in effect created a community of States, and is primarily a collective security agreement, although it also incorporates the promotion of human rights and economic and social development among the purposes of the Organization.[28]

The Charter sets up a collective security system whereby States are generally prohibited from threatening or using force against other States (Article 2(4)) except in self-defence (Article 51). It bestows upon the Security Council the primary responsibility for the maintenance of international peace and security (Article 24(1)), empowering the Council to determine the existence of threats to the peace, breaches of the peace, or acts of aggression, and to decide measures to respond to such threats (Article 39), including the use of force (Article 42). The Charter commits all members to carry out the decisions of the Security Council (Article 2 (5)), including through the provision of standing military forces (Articles 43 and 45).

While the collective security system agreed in 1945 at the United Nations Conference on International Organization (San Francisco Conference)[29] was a vast improvement on the League of Nations arrangements,[30] the UN version falls far short of an ideal collective security system. It was, in effect, a balance between liberalism and realism. The ideals of collective security were traded off against the power realities of the moment. Consequently, the need for universalism trumped ideals of automatism and anonymity. The Great Powers framed the agreement to include for themselves permanent membership and the power of veto in the centralized managing body—the Security Council. With the introduction of this aspect, the system would never be non-discriminatory, as the Great Powers would presumably not allow action against themselves or their close allies. With the process of determination of aggression lying with the Council, a collective reaction would never be automatic.[31] This situation caused Inis Claude to proclaim that the UN Charter is 'a curious amalgam of collective security, dominant in ideological terms, and balance of power, dominant in practical application'.[32]

Like many subsequent UN agreements, consensus on the Charter was reached through the application of power in negotiations and ambiguity of text that could be open to the varying interpretation of its parties. The Charter contains no definition of 'aggression' despite the requests for inclusion of such by a number of smaller States at the San Francisco Conference.[33] Nor does it contain any detail on the concept of 'self-defence', a situation that has been taken advantage of by States

[27] For a thorough examination of the UN collective security system see Tsagourias and White, n 2, 91–114.

[28] Charter of the United Nations Charter (adopted 26 June 1945, entered into force 24 October 1945) 1 UNTS XVI, Article 1 (UN Charter).

[29] The United Nations Conference on International Organization was held from 25 April 1945 to 26 June 1945 in San Francisco, USA.

[30] For further discussion and comparison see Tsagourias and White, n 2, 12–18.

[31] Naidu, see n 17, based on the ideas of Claude (1959 and 1962), see n 17.

[32] Claude (1961), see n 17, 229.

[33] Bruno Simma, *The Charter of the United Nations: A Commentary* (Second Edition) (New York: Oxford University Press, 2002) 703. States were concerned both about the determination of the need for action being selective, based on Great Power preferences, and about the potential reach of the Council's enforcement powers.

justifying an otherwise illegal use of force as 'pre-emptive' or 'preventive' self-defence.[34] Critically, the Charter is not clear about the powers of the Council to address situations regarding the use of force *within* States.

The UN collective security system has been heavily criticized, predominantly for its selectivity in application.[35] The shortfalls identified above, which render the UN regime far from the classical ideal, are viewed by some as such fundamental failings that they result not in a collective security system at all, but in a 'selective security' system or simply a mechanism for maintaining the existing entrenchment of power.[36] However, at its essence, the system fulfils the two fundamental features of collective security: it proscribes force among the community of States and provides for a collective response when force is threatened or used against one of the community. As well as offending notions of equality and justice, the use of the veto by the permanent members of the Security Council does profoundly undermine the ideal of automatism. Nevertheless, most States comply with the regime most of the time, and when they do not, often attempt to justify their actions in the context of the regime. The Security Council frequently deals with threats to international peace and security that lie well beyond the national interests of the permanent members and transcend their power concerns. While deep imperfections of the design and implementation of the UN Charter are evident, they do not so fundamentally undermine the foundational principles of the regime that it is no longer properly considered a collective security system—just an imperfect one.

The establishment of a collective security regime, built upon international law and an international institution, is very much a liberal project. However, the UN collective security system resulted in a realist manifestation of the liberal ideal. The need to ensure that the Great Powers were part of the regime resulted in the entrenchment of power among them and the selective and uneven application of the system. Although deeply flawed, the UN collective security regime remains the constitutional order for global security, setting the parameters (principles, rules, actors, instruments, and practices) according to which the international community seeks to attain international peace and security.

[34] The US and UK justified their invasion of Afghanistan on the grounds of pre-emptive self-defence under Article 51 of the Charter. See United Nations Security Council (UNSC), 'Letter dated 7 October 2001 from the Permanent Representative of the United States of America to the United Nations addressed to the President of the Security Council' (2001) UN Doc S/2001/946; UNSC, 'Letter dated 7 October 2001 from the Charge d'affaires a.i. of the Permanent Mission of the United Kingdom of Great Britain and Northern Ireland addressed to the President of the Security Council' (2001) UN Doc S/2001/947; see also Mary Ellen O'Connell, 'The Myth of Preemptive Self-Defence', *American Society of International Law Task Force Papers* (Washington, DC: American Society of International Law, 2002) <www.asil.org/taskforce/oconnell.pdf>.

[35] See Adam Roberts and Dominik Zaum, *Selective Security: War and the United Nations Security Council since 1945* (Oxford: Routledge, 2008); Danchin and Fischer, see n 17; Gary Wilson, *The United Nations and Collective Security* (Milton Park, UK: Routledge, 2014).

[36] Roberts and Zaum, see n 35, 19. The authors go on to acknowledge that the selectivity of the UN system provides a basis for realistic and constructive international debate about the Coucil's role, at page 77.

V. Evolution of the UN Collective Security System

Fortunately the UN Charter has proved to be a flexible instrument, as the collective security arrangements envisaged in 1945, in particular the provision of a standing military force, failed to come into existence. Seventy years of interpretation and evolution have resulted in a version of the collective security system which, while not true to the vision of the Charter and although maintaining some of the failings of the original agreement, more closely reflects the totality of the constitutional purposes of the Organization, and is more appropriate to the contemporary security environment.

The founders of the UN realized that an organization based so firmly on the political exigencies of the post-Second World War environment may require adjustment over time. Consequently Article 109 of the Charter provided for a major constitutional review conference within ten years of coming into force, if not before. Such a conference never took place.[37] The founders were correct; adjustment was required for the UN to remain relevant in the constantly changing international political and security environment. This adjustment occurred, however, in the terms of Donald Puchala and Raymond Hopkins, as a process of evolution rather than revolution.[38] Evolution of the UN collective security system occurred not through a constitutional conference, or (for the most part) by major declaration, but incrementally, through practice.

The evolution of the system has occurred essentially on three fronts: (a) the *mechanism* for determining aggression and deciding response measures; (b) the *determination* of threats to the peace; and (c) the *measures* used to address such threats and the management of those measures.

The primary catalysts for the evolution of the UN collective security system centred on changes in the international political and security environment as well as shifts in the values of UN Member States. These included:

- The Cold War and the resulting paralysis of the Security Council, as well as the need for the Organization to take what measures it could to avoid superpower confrontation.
- The decolonization movement, the accompanying rise in conflicts of independence, and the eventual increase in the number of States.
- The end of the Cold War and the advance of liberalism.
- The failure of the UN to protect civilians against mass violence in Rwanda and the former Yugoslavia, and growing global concern about the plight of civilians in conflict situations.

[37] For further discussion see Stephen Schlesinger, 'Can the United Nations Reform', *World Policy Journal* (New York, Fall 1997).

[38] Donald J Puchala and Raymond F Hopkins, 'International Regimes: Lessons from Inductive Analysis', in Stephen D Krasner (ed.), *International Regimes* (Ithaca, USA: Cornell University Press, 1983).

- The major terrorist attack against the US in 2001 and the resulting rise in US unilateralism.

These drivers manifested in three imperatives for the UN: (a) the need to ensure the ongoing relevance of the Organization as a security actor during the Cold War, and subsequently amid deepening regionalism and in the face of US unilateralism; (b) the need to address the growing instances of civil wars and/or internal conflicts; and (c) the promotion of liberal ideals of democracy, human rights, and international law.

A. Mechanism for determining aggression and deciding response measures

At the 1944 Washington Conversations on International Peace and Security Organization (Dumbarton Oaks Conference),[39] the United States, the United Kingdom, China, and the Soviet Union agreed to create a collective security system that would have a strong central management body, in contrast to the failed decentralized system of the League of Nations. The proposal met with acceptance at the 1945 San Francisco Conference and the result was the UN collective security system, which had at its core a Security Council with wide and binding powers.

While Council members have carefully guarded their role in determining acts of aggression and deciding response measures, two significant adjustments have occurred. Both took place during the Cold War when the Council was often in a state of paralysis, with the United States and the Soviet Union unable to agree on many issues. Both adjustments were related to the deployment of a UN force in response to the invasion of South Korea by the Democratic People's Republic of Korea.

Article 27(3) of the Charter requires that Council decisions on substantive matters are made by a special majority of the Council 'including the concurring votes of the permanent members'. However, this requirement for positive consensus among the permanent members was altered early in the UN's history. The decisions to deploy a UN force in defence of South Korea were made in the absence of, and therefore without the concurring vote of, the Soviet Union.[40] In order to grease the mechanics of the Council and allow permanent members to take a principled position without obstructing Council action, a practice has developed over time whereby decisions on substantive matters may be made with a special majority of the Council and permanent member concurrence, even if a permanent member is absent or abstains.[41]

Potentially a more powerful development was the *Uniting for Peace* resolution, which calls for the General Assembly to consider threats to the peace and make

[39] The Washington Conversations on International Peace and Security Organization were held from 21 August to 7 October 1944 in Dumbarton Oaks, a residence in Washington, DC.

[40] See UNSC Resolution (Res) 82 (1950) UN Doc S/RES/82; UNSC Res 83 (1950) UN Doc S/RES/83; UNSC Res 84 (1950) UN Doc S/RES/84; and UNSC Res 85 (1950) UN Doc S/RES/85. For discussion on why the Russian delegation absented itself, see Tsagourias and White, n 2, 108.

[41] Simma, see n 33, 493.

recommendations for collective measures when the Security Council fails to exercise its responsibilities for the maintenance of international peace and security because of a lack of unanimity.[42] Although the Security Council holds the 'primary responsibility for the maintenance of international peace and security',[43] the General Assembly is empowered to 'make recommendations to the Members of the United Nations or to the Security Council' on any matters within the scope of the Charter, except 'matters relative to the maintenance of international peace and security which are being dealt with by the Security Council'.[44] The *Uniting for Peace* resolution allowed for the contemporaneous consideration of such issues in both organs, fundamentally altering the collective security system.[45] A proposal for such a mechanism had been put forward by Mexico and refused at the San Francisco Conference.[46]

Although the legitimacy of the resolution was contested at the time, the International Court of Justice, in the *Certain Expenses* advisory opinion, upheld the legality of the resolution, and did not rule out the General Assembly recommending coercive action to address a threat to the peace.[47] However, the legality of the General Assembly recommending the use of force, and thus creating a third exception to the general prohibition, continues to be questioned.[48]

Originally introduced to circumvent Soviet vetoes of the Korea campaign, the *Uniting for Peace* resolution has been used to convene ten Emergency Special Sessions of the General Assembly. It has been used to authorize two peacekeeping operations: the first UN Emergency Force deployed in response to the 1956 Suez crisis (UNEF I)[49] and the 1960 UN Operation in the Congo (ONUC).[50] However, it has been argued that these did not technically constitute 'coercive measures' as they were not 'enforcement actions', given that they were mandated with the consent of the respective host authorities.[51]

[42] UN General Assembly Resolution (UNGA Res) 377 A(V) (1950) UN Doc A/RES/377 A(V), para. 1.

[43] UN Charter, see n 28, Article 24(1).

[44] UN Charter, see n 28, Articles 10, 12.

[45] UNGA Res 377 A(V) (1950) UN Doc A/RES/377A(V), § A, para. 1, reads (emphasis added): *The General Assembly* . . . *Resolves* that if the Security Council, because of lack of unanimity of the permanent members, fails to exercise its primary responsibility for the maintenance of international peace and security in any case where there appears to be a threat to the peace, breach of the peace, or act of aggression, the General Assembly shall consider the matter immediately with a view to making appropriate recommendations to Members for collective measures, *including in the case of a breach of the peace or act of aggression the use of armed force when necessary*, to maintain or restore international peace and security. If not in session at the time, the General Assembly may meet in emergency special session within twenty-four hours of the request therefore. Such emergency special session shall be called if requested by the Security Council on the vote of any seven [now nine] members, or by a majority of the Members of the United Nations.'

[46] Simma, see n 33, 703.

[47] *Certain Expenses of the United Nations* (Advisory Opinion) [1962] ICJ Rep 151.

[48] Larry D Johnson, *'Uniting for Peace': Does It Still Serve Any Useful Purpose?* (AJIL Unbound, 15 July 2014) <www.asil.org/blogs/%E2%80%9Cuniting-peace%E2%80%9D-does-it-still-serve-any-useful-purpose>; see also Tsagourias and White, n 2, 108–13.

[49] UNGA Res 998(ES-I) (1956) UN Doc A/RES/998(ES-I).

[50] UNGA Res 1474 (ES-IV) (1960) UN Doc A/RES/1474(ES-IV).

[51] Johnson, see n 48, but compare the views of Tsagourias and White, see n 2, 111.

The Security Council's inability to make real progress on the Syrian conflict since 2011 would seem an opportune situation for the General Assembly to take up its residual responsibility for the maintenance of international peace and security. The General Assembly did pass a resolution that condemned the Council's failure to be more active on Syria.[52] However, there was no attempt made to use the *Uniting for Peace* resolution to recommend coercive action. While the likelihood of gaining the required two-thirds majority to pass such a resolution was in question,[53] so too was the appetite of any Member States to take action recommended. With the General Assembly's failure to invoke the resolution to precipitate UN action in a situation as dire as that presented in Syria, questions have been raised about its utility and continued viability.[54]

The developments in the mechanisms to determine acts of aggression and decide response measures were significant in the evolution of the UN collective security system. The move from the requirement of positive to negative consensus of the permanent members of the Security Council provided a lower threshold for unity, creating greater scope for action by allowing political dissension to be noted without obstructing decisions. The expansion of the General Assembly's secondary role for the maintenance of international peace and security provided a potential safeguard against Security Council inaction and selectivity. However, that potential remains mostly unfulfilled.

B. Determination of threats to the peace

Article 39 of the Charter empowers the Security Council to 'determine the existence of any threat to the peace, breach of the peace, or act of aggression'. The Great Powers were not willing to be bound by a restrictive interpretation of this authority. At the San Francisco conference a proposal from Bolivia to define 'aggression' was rejected.[55] However, it is clear that the original objectives of the 1945 agreement were focused on the use of force between States, and the Council was not intended to concern itself with purely internal situations.[56]

Article 2(4) states that 'All Members shall refrain in their international relations from the threat or use of force against the territorial integrity or political independence of any State, or in any other manner inconsistent with the Purposes of the United Nations'. Article 2(7) states that 'Nothing contained in the present Charter shall authorise the United Nations to intervene in matters which are essentially within the domestic jurisdiction of any State [. . .]; but this principle shall not prejudice the application of enforcement measures under Chapter VII.'

These articles support the proposition that the Charter was intended to govern the use of force *between* States. Bruno Simma indicates that 'the task of the [Secu-

[52] UNGA Res 66/253 (2012) UN Doc A/RES/66/253, preambular para. 16.

[53] Jérémie Labbé, *1950s UN Resolution Could Break Security Council Deadlock on Syria* (International Peace Institute Global Observatory, 27 September 2013) <theglobalobservatory.org/2013/09/overcoming-the-un-security-councils-deadlock-syria-and-the-uniting-for-peace-resolution>.

[54] Ibid. [55] Simma, see n 33, 719.

[56] Ibid., 720; and Inger Österdahl, *Threat to the Peace: The Interpretation by the Security Council of Article 39 of the UN Charter* (Uppsala: Iustus Förlag, 1998), 11–12.

rity Council] was originally identified mainly, though not exclusively, with the prevention of inter-State war, and thus corresponds with the fact that Article 2(4) prohibits the use of force only between, not within States'.[57] However, the fact that Article 2(7) provides an explicit exception to the blanket protection of sovereignty over internal matters and Article (4) links the use of force with the purposes of the UN, which include co-operation on humanitarian problems and the promotion of human rights, leaves room for interpretation.

In response to the growing incidence of internal conflicts, partly due to the decolonization process and partly due to Cold War proxy clashes, Security Council practice quickly developed in the direction of determining threats to the peace in internal conflicts, even when those conflicts did not have significant international impacts. As early as 1948 the Council determined the Israel–Palestine conflict as a threat to the peace,[58] as it did the Indonesian conflict[59] and the conflict in the Congo.[60] With the surge in Security Council activity that followed the end of the Cold War, this practice was reinforced and threats to the peace were determined in internal conflicts in countries including Yugoslavia,[61] Somalia,[62] Liberia,[63] Angola,[64] Rwanda,[65] Burundi,[66] Zaïre,[67] Albania,[68] the Central African Republic,[69] Sierra Leone,[70] East Timor,[71] Democratic Republic of the Congo,[72] Côte d'Ivoire,[73] Sudan,[74] South Sudan,[75] Libya,[76] and Mali.[77] Accordingly, Simma states that 'it seems by now widely accepted that extreme violence within a State can give rise to Chapter VII enforcement action'.[78]

Internal conflicts are often characterized by massive human rights violations and breaches of humanitarian law; it is therefore not surprising that a correlative interpretative development occurred with respect to the determination of violations of human rights and humanitarian law as threats to the peace.[79] Although the Council initially declined to determine the violation of human rights as a threat to international peace and security,[80] its determination of the situation in Rhodesia as

[57] Simma, see n 33, 720.
[58] UNSC Res 54 (1948) UN Doc S/RES/54.
[59] UNSC (1948) UN Doc S/PV.392.
[60] UNSC (1961) UN Doc S/RES/161.
[61] UNSC (1991) UN Doc S/RES/713.
[62] UNSC (1992) UN Doc S/RES/733.
[63] UNSC (1993) UN Doc S/RES/788.
[64] UNSC (1993) UN Doc S/RES/864.
[65] UNSC (1994) UN Doc S/RES/918.
[66] UNSC (1996) UN Doc S/RES/1072.
[67] UNSC (1996) UN Doc S/RES/1078.
[68] UNSC (1997) UN Doc S/RES/1101.
[69] UNSC (1997) UN Doc S/RES/1125.
[70] UNSC (1997) UN Doc S/RES/1123.
[71] UNSC (1999) UN Doc S/RES/1264.
[72] UNSC (2000) UN Doc S/RES/1291.
[73] UNSC (2004) UN Doc S/RES/1528.
[74] UNSC (2005) UN Doc S/RES/1590.
[75] UNSC (2011) UN Doc S/RES/1996.
[76] UNSC (2011) UN Doc S/RES/1973.
[77] UNSC (2012) UN Doc S/RES/2056.
[78] Simma, see n 33, 723.
[79] Simma, see n 33, 724–5; and Österdahl, see n 56, 33–5.
[80] See UNSC, 'Report of the Sub-Committee on the Spanish Question' (1946) UN Doc S/75.

a threat to the peace[81] opened the path for later determinations. In the wake of American ascendance and as the ideology of liberalism prevailed at the end of the Cold War, the position of the Council, and its willingness to act in defence of human rights and humanitarian law, became clearer. This was evident in the determination of threats to the peace on the basis of human rights violations and dire humanitarian situations particularly in northern Iraq,[82] Somalia,[83] Rwanda,[84] and the Darfur region of Sudan.[85] While human rights violations and the humanitarian situation were explicitly elements of the Council determination of threat in other instances,[86] the four cases just highlighted were the clearest examples in which human rights violations and the humanitarian situation were the primary bases for the determination of the threat, whether or not they would have regional implications.

There has been some practice that also indicates a willingness on the part of the Council to determine a threat to the peace due to the violation of democratic principles.[87] In particular, the Council determined that the failure to restore democratically elected governments in Haiti and Sierra Leone constituted threats to the peace.[88] The Council has also determined insufficient action by States to combat terrorism as threats to the peace,[89] as occurred in the cases of Libya,[90] Sudan,[91] and Afghanistan.[92] How expansive the concept of threats to the peace is, whether it would stretch to security threats associated with environmental and disease-related problems, remains an issue of contention.[93]

The expansion of the concept of threats to and breaches of the peace is remarkable in that it demonstrates a fundamental change in the *telos* of the UN collective security system. The system has evolved from one concerned primarily, if not exclusively, with the security of States to one concerned also with the security of individuals and the protection of human rights.

[81] UNSC Res 217 (1965) UN Doc S/RES/217.
[82] UNSC Res 668 (1991) UN Doc S/RES/688.
[83] UNSC Res 794 (1992) UN Doc S/RES/794.
[84] UNSC Res 929 (1994) UN Doc S/RES/929.
[85] UNSC Res 1706 (2006) UN Doc S/RES/1706.
[86] Such as in Sierra Leone (UNSC Res 1270 (1999) UN Doc S/RES/1270), Democratic Republic of the Congo (UNSC Res 1291 (2000) UN Doc S/RES/1291), Liberia (UNSC Res 1509 (2003) UN Doc S/RES/1509), Côte d'Ivoire (UNSC Res 1528 (2004) UN Doc S/RES/1528), Haiti (UNSC Res 1542 (2004) UN Doc S/RES/1542), Burundi (UNSC Res 1545 (2004) UN Doc S/RES/1545), Sudan (UNSC Res 1590 (2005) UN Doc S/RES/1590), Lebanon (UNSC Res 1701 (2006) UN Doc S/RES/1701), Chad and Central African Republic (UNSC Res 2009 (2009) UN Doc S/RES/1861), Abyei (UNSC Res 1990 (2011) UN Doc S/RES/1990), Libya (UNSC Res 1973 (2011) UN Doc S/RES/1973), Mali (UNSC Res 2100 (2013) UN Doc S/RES/2100), Central African Republic (UNSC Res 2149 (2014) UN Doc S/RES/2149), and South Sudan (UNSC Res 2155 (2014) UN Doc S/RES/2155).
[87] Simma, see n 33, 725; and Österdahl see n 56, 33–5.
[88] Haiti (UNSC Res 841 (1993) UN Doc S/RES/841), and Sierra Leone (UNSC Res 1132 (1997) UN Doc S/RES/1132).
[89] Simma, see n 33, 725–6.
[90] UNSC Res 731 (1992) UN Doc S/RES/731.
[91] UNSC Res 1054 (1996) UN Doc S/RES/1054.
[92] UNSC Res 1267 (1999) UN Doc S/RES/1267.
[93] See Joachim Wolf, 'Responses to Non-military Threats: Environment, Disease and Technology', in Danchin and Fisher, n 17.

C. Measures to respond to threats to the peace, breaches of the peace, and acts of aggression

Once a threat to or breach of the peace has been determined, Article 39 of the Charter empowers the Council to 'decide what measures shall be taken in accordance with Articles 41 [non-coercive] and 42 [coercive], to maintain or restore international peace and security'. As originally envisaged in the Charter, the collective security system was designed to be underwritten by a standing military capacity ready to enforce Security Council decisions. However, when this failed to come into being, the Council undertook significant innovation in developing alternate measures. Two key military initiatives were adopted: (a) the authorization of single States or coalitions of States to undertake coercive action, and (b) the deployment of UN peacekeeping operations. Other significant, non-coercive, innovations included the development of special political missions[94] and the establishment of international criminal tribunals for the former Yugoslavia[95] and Rwanda,[96] for the purpose of prosecuting serious crimes committed during the respective conflicts.

On numerous occasions the Security Council has authorized single States or coalitions of States to undertake coercive action.[97] However, this has proven controversial, being viewed as a delegation (in some cases improper) or 'sub-contracting' the Chapter VII responsibilities of the Security Council.[98] Once authorization has been provided, the Security Council has had little visibility and influence over the execution of the measures, and some have argued the need for greater UN oversight of such activities.[99] There have also been many examples of regional arrangements undertaking enforcement action with the authorization of the Council.[100]

[94] See UNGA, 'United Nations Political Missions: Report of the Secretary-General' (2013) A/68/223, and subsequently A/69/325 (2014). See also Alischa Kugel, *No Helmets, Just Suits: Political Missions as an Instrument of the UN Security Council for Civilian Conflict Management* (Berlin: Friedrich-Ebert-Stiftung, 2011) <library.fes.de/pdf-files/iez/07899.pdf>.

[95] UNSC Res 827 (1993) UN Doc S/RES/827.

[96] UNSC Res 955 (1994) UN Doc S/RES/955.

[97] US-led United Task Force (UNITAF) in Somalia (UNSC Res 794 (1992) UN Doc S/RES/794); French-led 'Operation Turquoise' in Rwanda (UNSC Res 929 (1994) UN Doc S/RES/929); US-led multinational forces 'Operation Uphold Democracy' in Haiti (UNSC Res 940 (1994) UN Doc S/RES/940); Italian-led 'Operation Alba' in Albania (UNSC Res 1101 (1997) UN Doc S/RES/1101); Australian-led International Force for East Timor (INTERFET) in East Timor (UNSC Res 1264 (1999) UN Doc S/RES/1264); International Security Assistance Force (ISAF) in Afghanistan (UNSC Res 1386 (2001) UN Doc S/RES/1386); French-led 'Operation Licorne' in Côte d'Ivoire (UNSC Res 1464 (2003) UN Doc S/RES/1464 and UNSC Res 1528 (2004) UN Doc S/RES/1528); US-led Multi-National Force-Iraq (MNF-I) in Iraq (UNSC Res 1483 (2003) UN Doc S/RES/1483); Australian-led International Stabilization Force (ISF) in East Timor (UNSC Res 1690 (2006) UN Doc S/RES/1690); French 'Operation Serval' in Mali (UNSC Res 2085 (2012) UN Doc S/RES/2085); and French 'Operation Sangaris' in the Central African Republic (UNSC Res 2127 (2013) UN Doc S/RES/2127).

[98] For further discussion see Danesh Sarooshi, *The United Nations and the Development of Collective Security: The Delegation by the UN Security Council of Its Chapter VII Powers* (Oxford: Oxford University Press, 2000).

[99] Tsagourias and White, see n 2, 274–7; and Wilson, see n 35, 158–78.

[100] For example, NATO in the former Yugoslavia in the 1990s and Libya in 2011; ECOWAS in Côte d'Ivoire in 2002, the AU in Burundi in 2003, Sudan in 2004, Somalia in 2007 and the Central African Republic in 2013; and the EU in the Democratic Republic of the Congo in 2003.

Although such action is provided for under Chapter VIII of the Charter, the substantial use of regional arrangements to address threats to international peace and security, including outside their geographic regions, has raised questions about whether the UN's place in the international security order is being challenged by regional organizations and deepening regionalism.[101]

UN peacekeeping operations are today the flagship activity of the Organization and perhaps the most innovative evolution in the UN collective security system. Mandated by the Security Council, they comprise troops, police, and civilians who are under the command and control of the UN, and are managed by the UN Departments of Peacekeeping Operations (DPKO) and Field Support (DFS). Military and police personnel are voluntarily contributed by UN Member States, who are reimbursed for their activities through the UN budget, met by assessed contributions of all UN members.[102] Although peacekeeping operations are often authorized by the Security Council to use force to implement their mandate, because they are generally deployed with the consent of the host State, they do not represent a coercive action *against* a State.

The traditional principles of peacekeeping are: (a) consent to the deployment by the parties to the conflict; (b) impartiality in mandate implementation; and (c) non-use of force, except in self-defence and in defence of the mandate.[103] However, the continued relevance of those principles is questionable given that the primary mandated purpose of most modern missions is to protect civilians, for which the use of force is specifically authorized. This presupposes the absence of consent on the part of at least one of the parties to the conflict. In implementing the mandate impartiality can often be undermined, particularly where the UN force is mandated to support the government uphold its civilian protection responsibilities.

The UN peacekeeping instrument has remained relevant and valuable through its dynamic evolution and remarkable flexibility to address the requirements of the changing security environment.[104] This has been characterized by six key trends:

1. Deployment of operations into internal as well as inter-State conflict situations;
2. Deployment of operations to respond to humanitarian crises and gross violations of human rights;
3. Deployment of operations in partnership with other security actors, such as regional organizations;

101 See discussion in Tsagourias and White, n 2, 115–37.

102 For further information see the UN Department of Peacekeeping Operations (DPKO) website: <www.un.org/en/peacekeeping/operations/peacekeeping.shtml>.

103 UN DPKO, *United Nations Peacekeeping Operations: Principles and Guidelines* (Capstone Doctrine) (New York: United Nations, 2008) 26 <www.peacekeepingbestpractices.unlb.org/Pbps/Library/Capstone_Doctrine_ENG.pdf>.

104 For detail on the history of peacekeeping see Alex J Bellamy, Paul Williams, and Stuart Griffin, *Understanding Peacekeeping* (second edition) (Cambridge: Polity Press, 2010); William J Durch (ed.), *The Evolution of UN Peacekeeping* (New York: St Martin's Press, 1993); William J Durch (ed.), *UN Peacekeeping, American Policy and the Uncivil Wars of the 1990s* (New York: St Martin's Press, 1996); and William J Durch (ed.), *Twenty-First-Century Peace Operations* (Washington DC: United States Institute of Peace and The Henry L Stimson Center, 2006).

4. Inclusion of early peacebuilding activities in mission mandates;
5. Inclusion of robust peace enforcement activities in mission mandates;
6. Inclusion of civilian protection activities in mission mandates.

The evolution of UN peacekeeping has not been without challenge and controversy. But the thing that most threatened the credibility of the instrument was the failure to protect civilians during the 1994 Rwandan genocide and the 1995 Srebrenica massacre. While the international community grappled with the humanitarian intervention concept and the Responsibility to Protect doctrine, from 1999, UN peacekeeping missions began to be mandated to use force to protect civilians under imminent threat of physical violence.

The development of new measures to respond to international peace and security has resulted in a dilution of the power of the Security Council. In the absence of a standing military force to carry out its decisions, the Council is reliant upon other Member States and regional organizations. Often this dynamic results in members approving initiatives that originate outside the Council, and over which they have little oversight of the practical implementation.[105] In the case of peacekeeping missions, the intent of the Council is shaped by the preferences of the broader Membership, since the Council is dependent upon them to voluntarily contribute troops and police to carry out the mandate and to finance the mission.[106]

VI. The Protection of Civilians

Internal conflicts are now far more prevalent than conflicts between States, and in them civilians are increasingly at risk of violence.[107] While the UN collective security system has evolved to address such conflicts and considerations, the change in values which has been reflected in these developments is, as yet, unmatched by legal and practical commitment.

[105] For example, the African Union Mission in Somalia (AMISOM) grew out of the Intergovernmental Authority on Development (IGAD) Peace Support Mission in Somalia (IGASOM), which was approved by the African Union in September 2006 and by the UN Security Council three months later. The 2011 NATO intervention in Libya was precipitated by calls from the Arab League, NATO, and the EU. The deployment of MINUSMA in Mali, in 2013, was preceded by the deployment of the AU mission, AFISMA, approved by the Security Council, and the French 'Operation Serval' upon request of the Malian Government. The 2013 deployment of the MONUSCO Force Intervention Brigade was initially conceived by the International Conference on the Great Lakes Region (ICGLR) and the Southern African Development Community.

[106] For information on contributions to UN peacekeeping see <www.un.org/en/peacekeeping/resources/statistics/contributors.shtml>; and for information on funding UN peacekeeping see <www.un.org/en/peacekeeping/operations/financing.shtml>.

[107] See UN Secretary-General's Reports on the Protection of Civilians in Armed Conflict: UNSC (1999) UN Doc S/1999/957; UNSC (2001) UN Doc S/2001/331; UNSC (2002) UN Doc S/2002/1300; UNSC (2004) UN Doc S/2004/431; UNSC (2005) UN Doc S/2005/740; UNSC (2007) UN Doc S/2007/643; UNSC (2009) UN Doc S/2009/277; UNSC (2010) UN Doc S/2010/579; UNSC (2012) UN Doc S/2012/376; and UNSC (2013) UN Doc S/2013/689.

A. Development of the protection of civilians peacekeeping mandate

Drawing on the work of the International Commission on Intervention and State Sovereignty (ICISS), and their advocacy of the Responsibility to Protect doctrine,[108] at the 2005 World Summit, the General Assembly declared that the 'international community' was 'prepared to take collective action ... through the Security Council, in accordance with the Charter, including Chapter VII ... should peaceful means be inadequate and national authorities are manifestly failing to protect their populations from genocide, war crimes, ethnic cleansing and crimes against humanity'.[109] However, the Security Council never accepted an *obligation* to act to protect civilians. Even when the Council authorized the military intervention to protect civilians in Libya in 2011, it specifically avoided language confirming an *obligation* to protect, instead highlighting its traditional responsibility for the maintenance of international peace and security.[110]

Tsagourias and White argue that a strong argument can be made that

> the UN ought to act to prevent genocide, crimes against humanity and other egregious violations of human rights, either because there is a duty on states and therefore on other actors, possessing rights and duties to act within their legal competence to prevent such violations of international law, or simply because such actions inherently undermine peace and security in that they are antithetical to global order as well as being international crimes.[111]

They question whether, in the absence of the Security Council assuming this responsibility (including through the threat or casting of veto), other collective security organs (in particular, the UN General Assembly) or institutions (such as regional organizations) should have the legitimate and lawful competence to fulfil the international community's responsibility to protect civilians.[112] They conclude that unaddressed violations of peremptory norms may be causing a realignment of the rules on the use of force, such that where the Security Council fails to take action to uphold basic principles of international law, then authority to do so passes to the General Assembly[113] and may also pass to regional organizations.[114]

While the Security Council has failed to exhibit a commitment to the Responsibility to Protect doctrine, the provision of protection mandates to UN peacekeeping operations demonstrates a constant, if less ambitious, commitment to civilian protection. Early Council efforts elaborated a somewhat ambiguous, indirect or vicarious concept of protection: 'protection *through* the provision of humanitarian assistance', 'protection *through* the promotion of human rights', and 'protection *through* the defence of territory' (i.e. 'safe areas').[115] In all instances there was a process or an additional link between the action authorized by the Council and the

[108] See *The Responsibility to Protect: Report of the International Commission on Intervention and State Sovereignty* (Ottawa: International Development Research Centre, 2001) <responsibilitytoprotect.org/ICISS%20Report.pdf>.

[109] UNGA, 'World Summit Outcome Document' (2005) UN Doc A/RES/60/1, para. 139.

[110] See UNSC Res 1973 (2011) UN Doc S/RES/1973.

[111] Tsagourias and White, see n 2, 98. [112] Ibid., 100. [113] Ibid., 100–14.

[114] Ibid., 137.

[115] For example, UNPROFOR in the former Yugoslavia (UNSC Res 743 (1992) UN Doc S/RES/743, UNSC Res (1992) UN Doc S/RES/758, UNSC Res 776 (1992) UN Doc S/RES/776) and

protection of civilians. When the Council began authorizing the use of force for the physical protection of civilians, it moved a step beyond earlier protection efforts. The distinction lay in the directness of the activity and the authorization of the use of force beyond passive defence. The protection mandate implied the use of offensive force (when necessary) in order to actively protect individuals from violence. Protection was no longer to occur as the outcome of some other activity, the intervening elements disappeared, and a direct link was created between the international community (through the Council) and the people to whom protection was to be afforded. The protection of civilians was no longer about promoting human rights within the political system, nor demilitarizing and defending territory (ideas intimately associated with the State): it was about the direct physical protection of people. In some cases the protection of civilians against government elements was explicitly authorized,[116] and in other cases generally implied into the mandate.[117]

In 1999, the Security Council mandated the UN Mission in Sierra Leone (UNAMSIL) to 'take the necessary action [. . .] within its capabilities and areas of deployment, to afford protection to civilians under imminent threat of physical violence, taking into account the responsibilities of the Government of Sierra Leone'.[118] The language used in the UNAMSIL mandate resolution set a precedent that has been employed in almost all subsequent peacekeeping missions.[119] The Council has also authorized a number of non-UN peacekeeping operations with the same civilian protection functions.[120]

UNSOM I and II in Somalia (UNSC Res 775 (1992) UN Doc S/RES/775, and UNSC res 814 (1993) UN Doc S/RES/814).

116 See, for example, MONUC (UNSC Res 1856 (2008) UN Doc S/RES/1856, para. (3)(a)), which authorizes the mission to use force to protect civilians against violence 'emanating from any of the parties engaged in the conflict'; and UNMISS (UNSC res 2155 (2014) UN Doc S/RES/2155, para. (4)(a)(i)), which authorizes the mission to use force to protect civilians 'irrespective of the source of such violence'.

117 See Mona Khalil, Chapter 9, in this volume.

118 UNSC Res 1270 (1999) UN Doc S/RES/1270, para. 14.

119 MONUC (Democratic Republic of the Congo) protection-of-civilians language was added to the mandate on 24 February 2000, UNSC Res 1291 (2000) UN Doc S/RES/1291, para. 8; UNMIL (Liberia) UNSC Res 1509 (2003) S/RES/1509, para. 3(j); UNOCI (Côte d'Ivoire) UNSC Res 1528 (2004) UN Doc S/RES/1528, para. 6(i); MINUSTAH (Haiti) UNSC Res (2004) UN Doc S/RES/1542, para. 7(I)(f); ONUB (Burundi) UNSC Res 1545 (2004) UN Doc S/RES/1545, para. 5; UNMIS (Sudan) UNSC Res 1590 (2005) UN Doc S/RES/1590, para. 16(i); UNIFIL (Lebanon) protection-of-civilians language was added to the mandate on 11 August 2006, UNSC Res 1701 (2006) UN Doc S/RES/1701, para. 12; UNAMID (Sudan (Darfur) protection of civilians language was in the original mandate, UNSC Res 1769 (2007) UN Doc S/RES/1769, para. 15(a)(2); MINURCAT (Chad and Central African Republic) protection-of-civilians language was added to the mandate on 14 January 2009, UNSC Res 1861 (2009) UN Doc S/RES/1861, para. 7(a)(i); MONUSCO (Democratic Republic of the Congo) protection of civilians language was in the original mandate, UNSC Res 1925 (2010) UN Doc S/RES/1925, paras 11, 12(a); UNISFA (Abyei) UNSC Res 1990 (2011) UN Doc S/RES/1990, para. 3(d); UNMISS (South Sudan) UNSC Res 1996 (2011) UN Doc S/RES/1996, para. 3(b); MINUMSA (Mali) UNSC Res 2100 (2013) UN Doc S/RES/2100, para. 16(c)(i); and MINUSCA (Central African Republic) UNSC Res 2149 (2014) UN Doc S/RES/2149, para. 30(a)(i). The exceptions were the UN missions in East Timor (UNTAET, UNMISET, UNMIT); Ethiopia and Eritrea (UNMEE), and Syria (UNSMIS).

120 These include the Interim Emergency Multinational Force (IEMF), 'Operation Artemis', in the Democratic Republic of the Congo (UNSC Res 1484 (2003) UN Doc S/RES/1484); French-led forces, 'Operation Licorne', in Côte d'Ivoire (UNSC Res 1464 (2003) UN Doc S/RES/1464 and

The debate which occurred in advance of the adoption of the UNAMSIL mandate is revealing as to the intentions of the Security Council. The Argentinean delegation made the following statement:

> We believe that the protection of civilians under Chapter VII is a pertinent development in the context of the mandate of a peacekeeping operation. This draft resolution is significant in that it introduces a new, fundamental political, legal and moral dimension. This bears on the credibility of the Security Council and shows that the Council has learned from its own experience and that it will not remain indifferent to indiscriminate attacks against the civilian population. At the same time, we are realistic. The objective to be fulfilled must be consonant with the means provided. For that reason, we agree with the limits that operative paragraph 14 of the draft resolution sets on UNAMSIL's actions. It establishes an objective limit, the competence the Council wishes to give UNAMSIL, a geographic limit—UNAMSIL's area of deployment—and a functional limit.[121]

However, from 2002 Council engagement on the issue lost its dynamism, and focus on the protection of civilians by UN peacekeepers waned. In part this was undoubtedly due to the strained Council dynamics following the 2003 US-led invasion of Iraq.[122] However, there were other factors that contributed to the hiatus in the advancement of the protection of civilians peacekeeping mandate. These included: (a) missions' inability to implement protection mandates in a meaningful way;[123] (b) the Office for the Coordination of Humanitarian Affairs (OCHA) leadership on protection issues in the Council, resulting in the agenda focusing on humanitarian priorities rather than peacekeeping issues; (c) the focus of the Council turning towards the protection of specific at-risk groups such as women and children;[124] and (d) consideration of civilian protection issues moving from the Council forum to the broader UN membership and focusing on the overarching normative dilemmas associated with 'humanitarian intervention' and the Responsibility to Protect,[125] holding back progress on the less controversial protection of civilians in UN peacekeeping operations.

UNSC Res 1528 (2004) UN Doc S/RES/1528); ECOWAS in Côte d'Ivoire (ECOMICI) (UNSc Res 1464 (2003) UN Doc S/RES/1464); AU in Darfur (AMIS) (UNSC Res 1574 (2004) UN Doc S/RES/1574); EUFOR RD Congo in the Democratic Republic of the Congo (UNSC Res 1671 (2006) UN Doc S/RES/1671); EU operation in Chad (EUFOR) (UNSC Res 1778 (2007) UN Doc S/RES/1778); French 'Operation Serval' in Mali (UNSC Res 2085 (2012) UN Doc S/RES/2085); and French 'Operation Sangaris' in the Central African Republic (UNSC Res 2127 (2013) UN Doc S/RES/2127).

121 UNSC (1999) UN Doc S/PV.4054, 16.

122 Security Council Report, *Cross-Cutting Report 2008 No.2: Protection of Civilians* (New York: Security Council Report, 2008) 8.

123 In Sierra Leone, UNAMSIL struggled to protect its own personnel, let alone civilians, when hundreds of UN peacekeepers were taken hostage early in the deployment. It took the deployment of British troops under Operation Palliser to restore order. Similarly, in Côte d'Ivoire, French led forces deployed under Operation Licorne shouldered the burden of civilian protection. In the Democratic Republic of the Congo, the failure of UN forces to protect civilians in Bunia caused some focus to be returned to the issue, but again the response was the deployment of an EU force under Operation Artemis.

124 See for example, UNSC Res 1325 (2000) UN Doc S/RES/1325 and UNSC Res 1612 (2005) UN Doc S/RES/1612.

125 See in particular, UNGA, 'Report of the UN Secretary-General: We the Peoples: The Role of the United Nations in the 21st Century' (2000) UN Doc A/54/2000, para. 217; International

It was not until 2007, following the significant failures of UN peacekeeping missions to protect civilians particularly in the Democratic Republic of the Congo,[126] that focus returned to the protection of civilians in the peacekeeping context. In response to such failures, the Security Council began to explicitly prioritize protection efforts in several UN peacekeeping missions.[127]

Complementary to the focus on the protection of civilians in country specific situations, the Council also progressed the issue through a thematic agenda item. In 1999 the Council held the first open debate on the protection of civilians,[128] beginning a cycle of thematic activity comprising biannual open debates. Since 1999 the Secretary-General has delivered ten reports on the protection of civilians in armed conflict,[129] and the Council has issued six thematic resolutions.[130] While the thematic debates covered several elements related to protection, the physical protection element grew in prominence, and the Council devoted more attention to protection mandates in peacekeeping operations. In 2009 the Council adopted Resolution 1894 stating:

> [The Council] [*r*]*eaffirms* its practice of ensuring that mandates of UN peacekeeping and other relevant missions include, where appropriate and on a case-by-case basis, provisions regarding the protection of civilians, *stresses* that mandated protection activities must be given priority in decisions about the use of available capacity and resources, including information and intelligence resources, in the implementation of mandates; and *recognizes*, that the protection of civilians when and as mandated requires a coordinated response from all relevant mission components.[131]

Commission on Intervention and State Sovereignty, *The Responsibility to Protect* (IDRC Books, Ottawa, 2001); and UNGA (2005) UN Doc A/60/L.1, paras 138–9.

126 See for example Human Rights Watch, *Killings in Kiwanja: The UN's Inability to Protect Civilians* (New York: Human Rights Watch, 2008) <www.hrw.org/reports/2008/12/12/killings-kiwanja>; Human Rights Watch, *Abandoning Abyei: Destruction and Displacement* (New York: Human Rights Watch, 2008) <www.hrw.org/reports/2008/07/21/abandoning-abyei-0>; The Darfur Consortium, *Putting People First: The Protection Challenge Facing UNAMID in Darfur* (Kampala: The Darfur Consortium, 2008) <www.darfurconsortium.org/darfur_consortium_actions/reports/2008/Putting_People_First_UNAMID_report.pdf>.

127 Darfur (UNAMID) (UNSC Res 1769 (2007) UN Doc S/RES/1769, para. 15(a)(ii); UNSC Res 2003 (2011) UN Doc S/RES/2003, para. 3(a)); the Democratic Republic of the Congo (MONUC) (UNSC Res (2008) UN Doc S/RES/1856, paras 3 and 6; see also, UNSC (2008) UN Doc S/PV.6055, 2–3; Chad and the Central African Republic (MINURCAT) (UNSC Res 1778 (2007) UN Doc S/RES/1778); and more recently South Sudan (UNMISS) (UNSC Res 2057 (2012) UN Doc S/RES/2057); Liberia (UNMIL) (UNSC Res 2066 (2012) UN Doc S/RES/2066); Mali (MINUSMA) (UNSC 2164 (2014) UN Doc S/RES/2164); and the Central African Republic (MINUSCA) (UNSC res 2149 (2014) UN Doc S/RES/2149).

128 UNSC (1999) UN Doc S/PRST/1999/6.

129 UNSC (1999) UN Doc S/1999/957; UNSC (2001) UN Doc S/2001/331; UNSC (2002) UN Doc S/2002/1300; UNSC (2004) UN Doc S/2004/431; UNSC (2005) UN Doc S/2005/740; UNSC (2007) UN Doc S/2007/643; UNSC (2009) UN Doc S/2009/277; UNSC (2010) UN Doc S/2010/579; UNSC (2012) UN Doc S/2012/376; and UNSC (2013) UN Doc S/2013/689.

130 UNSC Res (1999) UN Doc S/RES/1265; UNSC Res 1296 (2000) S/RES/1296; UNSC Res 1674 (2006) UN Doc S/RES/1674; UNSC Res 1738 (2006) UN Doc S/RES/1738; UNSC Res 1894 (2009) UN Doc S/RES/1894; and UNSC Res 2175 (2014) UN Doc S/RES/2175.

131 UNSC Res 1894 (2009) UN Doc S/REF/1894.

B. Implementation of the protection of civilians mandate

UN DPKO and DFS have undertaken work to provide operational guidance to missions on the implementation of protection of civilians mandates.[132] However, a level of ambiguity remains, particularly regarding the pro-active or pre-emptive use of force authorized, and the discretionary/obligatory nature of the mandate.[133]

The implementation of the mandate in peacekeeping operations has constantly proven challenging. Practically, it raises the expectations of local populations, which UN peacekeepers are often unable to meet, including due to a lack of resources and capabilities—most notably force enablers, such as helicopters.[134] The use of force to protect civilians potentially puts peacekeepers at higher risk of injury or fatality—risks that troop-contributing countries may not be willing to take.[135] The mandate also carries with it certain political challenges. Missions are often mandated to assist the forces of the host government to execute their civilian protection responsibilities. Where the government forces are a party to the conflict (as is often the case), this may compromise the impartiality of the UN force supporting them. It may also have flow-on effects for the political engagement of the mission with the host government. Conversely, protection of civilians by the UN against violence perpetrated by host government, or government-backed, forces may result in the withdrawal of host State consent for the mission to remain in the country or obstruction of the mission's activities.[136]

132 UN DPKO and UN Department of Field Support (DFS), *Policy, The Protection of Civilians in United Nations Peacekeeping* (New York: United Nations, 1 June 2017) <http://www.ccopab.eb.mil.br/biblioteca/documentos/150323%20POC%20policy%20final.pdf>; UN DPKO and UN DFS, *Framework for Drafting Comprehensive Protection of Civilians (POC) Strategies in United Nations Peacekeeping Operations* (New York: United Nations, Undated) <refworld.org/pdfid/523998464.pdf>; UN DPKO and UN DFS, *Protection of Civilians Resource and Capability Matrix for Implementation of UN Peacekeeping Missions with POC Mandates* (New York: United Nations, 2012) <pbpu.unlb.org/PBPS/Library/POC%20resource%20and%20capability%20matrix.pdf>; UN DPKO and UN DFS, *Protection of Civilians, Coordination Mechanisms in UN Peacekeeping Missions: Comparative Study and Tookit* (New York: United Nations, 2012) <www.peacekeepingbestpractices.unlb.org/pbps/Library/Protection%20of%20Civilians%20Coordination%20Mechanisms%20in%20UN%20Peacekeeping%20Missions,%20DPKO-DFS%20Comparative%20Study%20and%20Toolkit%20%282012%29.pdf>; UN DPKO and UN DFS, *UN Tactical Level Protection of Civilians Training Modules* (New York: United Nations) <peacekeepingresourcehub.unlb.org/PBPS/Library/UN_TPOC%20_Trg_package.pdf> (UN Tactical Training Modules); UN DPKO and UN DFS, *Policy on the Protection of Civilians in United Nations Peacekeeping* (UN DPKO and UN DFS Protection of Civilians Policy) (on file with author); UN DPKO and DFS, *Protection of Civilians, Implementing Guidelines for Military Components of United Nations Peacekeeping Operations* (on file with author); UN DPKO and UN DFS, *Draft Military Guidelines on the Protection of Civilians* (on file with author).

133 For further discussion see Mona Khalil, Chapter 9, in this volume.

134 See Victoria Holt and Glyn Taylor, *Protecting Civilians in the Context of UN Peacekeeping Operations: Successes, Setbacks and Remaining Challenges* (New York: United Nations, 2009), and *Assessment of Helicopter Force Generation Challenges for United Nations Peacekeeping Operations*, Study, Workshop, and Consultations Report prepared by the Center on International Cooperation in partnership with the United States Global Peace Operations Initiative (December 2011) <usun.state.gov/documents/organization/179150.pdf>.

135 For further discussion see Haidi Willmot, Scott Sheeran, and Lisa Sharland, *Safety and Security in UN Peace Operations: Meeting the Challenges of Operating in Complex and Diverse Threat environments* (International Peace Institute, 14 July 2015) <http://www.ipinst.org/2015/07/safety-and-security-challenges-in-un-peace-operations>.

136 For an illustration of these dilemmas faced by the UN in South Sudan, see Aditi Gorur, 'In South Sudan, U.N. Peacekeepers' Biggest Challenge: Staying Neutral', *World Politics Rev* (25

In addition to the practical and political issues, the protection of civilians presents a number of legal challenges. In the pursuit of the protection of civilians, a mission may be mandated to offensively target a particular party to the conflict. In MONUSCO, both the UN's support for military operations of national Congolese forces and the mission's Force Intervention Brigade being mandated to 'neutralize' specific armed groups in the east of the Democratic Republic of the Congo[137] reinforced the International Committee of the Red Cross's view that the UN military forces had lost the protection of international humanitarian law.[138] The consequence of this is that the UN military forces in the Democratic Republic of the Congo are now legally considered a 'legitimate target', having become a 'party to the conflict'.[139] This is the case for the entire UN military presence, whether Force Intervention Brigade or regular MONUSCO contingent.

A 2014 report by the UN Office of Internal Oversight Services, Evaluation of the Implementation and Results of Protection of Civilians Mandates in United Nations Peacekeeping Operations, found that the implementation of protection mandates had improved, but stated the following:

> [T]he evaluation noted a persistent pattern of peacekeeping operations not intervening with force when civilians are under attack. The use of force is legally authorized and consistent with the intent of the Security Council and the expectations of civilians, but appears to have been routinely avoided as an option by peacekeeping operations. The reasons include different views in the Security Council and among troop-contributing countries and, importantly, a de facto dual line of command involving mission leadership and troop-contributing countries that regulates the use of force by missions. In addition, the obligation of missions to act when host Governments are unable or unwilling to discharge their primary responsibility to protect civilians is not well understood; missions perceive themselves as having insufficient resources to respond to force with force; and contingent members themselves are concerned about possible penalties if their use of force is judged inappropriate. Partly as a result, and despite major commitments by the United Nations and troop- and police-contributing countries, civilians continue to suffer violence and displacement in many countries where United Nations missions hold protection of civilians mandates.[140]

Despite the numerous implementation challenges, the Security Council continues to mandate the protection of civilians. Currently, over 90 per cent of UN peacekeepers serve in missions with protection of civilians mandates,[141] and it has been

November 2014) <www.worldpoliticsreview.com/articles/14525/in-south-sudan-u-n-peacekeepers-biggest-challenge-staying-neutral>.

137 UNSC Res 2098 (2013) UN Doc S/RES/2098.

138 For further discussion see Scott Sheeran and Stephanie Case, *The Intervention Brigade: Legal Issues for the UN in the Democratic Republic of the Congo* (New York: International Peace Institute, 2014) <www.ipinst.org/wp-content/uploads/publications/ipi_e_pub_legal_issues_drc_brigade.pdf>.

139 Secretary-General's Bulletin on Observance by United Nations forces of international humanitarian law (1999) UN Doc ST/SGB/1999/13.

140 UNGA (2014) UN Doc A/68/787.

141 As of November 2015, there were ten UN peacekeeping missions with POC mandates: UNIFIL, UNMIL, UNOCI, MINUSTAH, UNAMID, MONUSCO, UNISFA, UNMISS, MINUSMA, and MINUSCA. For data see United Nations Peacekeeping Operations Fact Sheet, 30 September 2015, available at: <http://www.un.org/en/peacekeeping/documents/bnote0915.pdf>.

identified as the primary function of the UN's largest missions, in Darfur (UNAMID), Democratic Republic of the Congo (MONUSCO), South Sudan (UNMISS), Mali (MINUMSA), and the Central African Republic (MINUSCA).[142]

C. Impact of the protection of civilians mandate

The trajectory of the protection of civilians in UN peacekeeping operations is not only indicative of the Security Council's approach to the issue. Because UN peacekeeping operations are a voluntary enterprise and require the involvement of all Member States, the strong focus on protection mandates reflects a consensus of the whole membership, even if this has, at times, been reluctant.[143] The General Assembly Special Committee on Peacekeeping Operations (C-34) has recognized the importance of the protection of civilians mandate in successive reports of its regular sessions.[144] The Administrative and Budgetary (Fifth) Committee, at which all UN Member States are represented, has continued to finance peacekeeping operations, the primary purpose of which is civilian protection.[145] And, critically, a spectrum of Member States have continued to contribute national military and police personnel to UN peacekeeping operations with protection of civilians mandates.[146] All of which evidences an active acceptance of the protection mandate across the Organisation.

While the stated political commitment to the protection of civilians by UN peacekeepers is broad across the UN membership, in practice it remains relatively shallow. Those who are mandating such missions are, on the whole, reluctant to contribute troops of their own.[147] The Administrative and Budgetary (Fifth) Committee does not provide missions with sufficient resources to robustly execute the mandate.[148] And those who contribute troops generally seem to prefer a less ambitious reading of the mandate that does not

[142] See UN Security Council Resolutions authorizing UNAMID, UNSC Res 2003 (2011) S/RES/2003; MONUSCO, UNSC Res 2098 (2013) UN Doc S/RES/2098; UNMISS, UNSC Res 2155 (2014) UN Doc S/RES/2155; MINUSMA, UNSC Res 2164 (2014) UN Doc S/RES/2164; and MINUSCA, UNSC Res 2149 (2014) UN Doc S/RES/2149.

[143] The author was part of the Australian delegation to the General Assembly Special Committee on Peacekeeping Operations 2007–9, and was involved in negotiations on protection-of-civilians issues. During these negotiations, a number of Member States were extremely reluctant to recognize the protection of civilians as a legitimate, let alone important, element of UN peace operations. Over time, acceptance of the mandate grew among the membership.

[144] See UNGA, *Annual Reports of the Special Committee on Peacekeeping Operations*, UN Docs A/63/19 (2009), A/64/19 (2010), A/65/19 (2011), and A/66/19 (2012) (no report was agreed in 2013), A/68/19 (2014).

[145] See the following for information on the financing of peace operations and resolutions relating to mission budgets: <www.un.org/en/peacekeeping/operations/financing.shtml>; and <www.un.org/en/ga/fifth/69/resdec69.shtml>.

[146] See the following for a breakdown of military and police contributions: <www.un.org/en/peacekeeping/resources/statistics/contributors.shtml>.

[147] For data and analysis see the International Peace Institute's Providing for Peacekeeping Project at <www.providingforpeacekeeping.org>.

[148] UNGA (2014) UN Doc A/68/787, paras 15–17.

require their troops to proactively use force and put their lives at risk.[149]

Despite the ever present challenges, the protection of civilians by UN peacekeeping operations has engendered far more support among the UN membership than the Responsibility to Protect doctrine. Well beyond a rhetorical commitment, it is employed in practice on a daily basis. The primary difference between the two concepts is that the protection of civilians in peacekeeping operations takes place with the consent of the host State, while the Responsibility to Protect doctrine allows for non-consensual intervention.[150] However, consent to the deployment of a UN peacekeeping operation may not necessarily be willingly given but instead may be politically or diplomatically coerced: it may be a condition of a peace agreement, a necessity to ensure the flow of aid, or assessed by the State as a politically expedient means of avoiding more forceful intervention; it may also be given and then withdrawn. The consent issue is not as determinative as it may initially appear—host State consent is more accurately viewed as a spectrum. While UN peacekeeping operations are not deployed into the most dangerous theatres where they have to fight their way in against government forces, they are regularly deployed into volatile conflict situations where civilians face extreme violence, and they are expected to protect them, including against government-supported elements. The power and impact of the protection of civilians mandate should not, therefore, be underestimated. It is not an easy win for the Council, or used only in easy situations. It is often the only option remaining to the Council where Member States do not see sufficient national interest to deploy unilaterally or in coalitions.

The protection of civilians mandate has been both reflective of the changing *telos* of the UN collective security system and a key driver of it. The proliferation, prominence, and acceptance of the mandate across the Membership evidences the recognition of civilians as legitimate actors of the collective security system, separate from their polity. However, the mandate has proven more palatable than the Responsibility to Protect doctrine, in part because it is premised on a level of Member State consent and thereby maintains the primacy of State actors in the international security system.

VII. Conclusion

The foregoing analysis demonstrates the evolution of the UN collective security system on three fronts: (a) an extension of the mechanisms for determining threats to the peace and deciding response measures; (b) an expansion of the concept of threats to the peace to include aggression within States, massive human rights abuses, and grave humanitarian situations; and (c) in the absence of a standing

[149] Ibid. However, see also Kigali Principles on the Protection of Civilians, as issued from the International Conference on the Protection of Civilians held in Rwanda (1 June 2015) <http://www.african-defense.com/?p=2705>

[150] For further discussion, see Scott Sheeran and Catherine Kent, Chapter 2, in this volume.

military force to implement Security Council decisions, a reliance upon Member States volunteering to use force either through contributing military personnel to peacekeeping operations under UN command or by taking part in unilateral, multilateral, or regional operations authorized by the UN.

The impact of these changes is significant. Together they dilute the authority of the Security Council, subtly changing the power dynamics, and render the system concerned with human security as much as State security. While the Security Council maintains primacy over the management of the system and the veto remains a powerful tool, the secondary role of the General Assembly for the maintenance of international peace and security, and the the residual role of the international community more generally, have resulted in a slight, and at this stage mostly potential, but legitimate and lawful, diffusion of power. The absence of a standing military capacity to implement Security Council decisions, and the resulting structure whereby the realization of the Security Council's intent is heavily shaped by the agreement of Member States to willingly finance and populate an operation, results in a practical diffusion of power. Finally, the overwhelming focus on internal conflicts wherein civilians are at risk has altered the concept of international peace and security to include a strong human security element.

The impact of such fundamental changes in the values, instruments, and processes of the global constitutional order for the provision of security raises a number of pertinent questions. Are the changes reflective of a broader evolution in international relations? Is the evolution of the collective security system reflective of the international community transcending the paradigm of the State? If so, what does that augur for our ethical and practical horizons?

There are, undeniably, deep failings in the ability of the UN collective security system to protect civilians. The unequal and outdated balance of power remains entrenched, and results in action being taken in some situations and not others. In the absence of an automatic enforcement mechanism, the system is dependent on the preferences of Member States, which politicizes and slows the response time, and often results in a delegation of the Council's responsibilities. The implementation of civilian protection mandates, in both UN peacekeeping operations and other authorized missions, is often gravely inadequate. While a civilian protection norm has taken hold and does traverse international and national spheres, it does not have the character of a universal law. However, compared to when the system was created in 1945, there is a strong focus on the protection of civilians. UN peacekeeping operations are frequently deployed with civilian protection mandates. It has become the primary purpose and *raison d'être* of many missions. Seventy years on, the Organization is actively engaged in protecting civilians on a daily basis.

The recognition of civilians as a discrete group and legitimate actors of the collective security system, does, in effect, recognize a society of individuals that transcends the State, while at the same time continuing to recognize the legitimacy of the State. The idea that the collective security order can both recognize the legitimacy of civilians as a group to be protected irrespective of their polity and recognize that States remain the primary security actors and therefore seek to execute civilian protection within that paradigm is consistent with the idea of a 'society of societies'. It represents a trajectory toward a cosmopolitan idea of the ordering of society, creating two distinct but closely linked communities, both of which civilians are simultaneously members. In this way, ideas inherent in cosmopolitanism may be helpful for understanding the evolution of the system, and its possible trajectory.

While the current system falls well short of the cosmopolitan ideal, the collective security system has internalized the idea of 'we the people,' in the name of whom the Charter was promulgated, and recognizes actors and obligations that transcend the State. It is evident that there are forces at play reflecting the dual communities of Stoic concern. Despite retaining significant flaws, the UN collective security system has undergone a remarkable evolution. It now sits precariously on a cosmopolitan trajectory, with significant potential to support human flourishing.

PART II

LEGAL FRAMEWORK

6

Protection of Civilians under International Human Rights Law

Andrew Clapham

I. Introduction

The protection of civilians is central to a series of United Nations (UN) Security Council debates and resolutions.[1] More significantly, it has become an organizational principle for UN peacekeeping operations.[2] As of 31 August 2015, the UN had 106,245 uniformed personnel and 16,79161 civilian personnel (30 June 2015) involved in peacekeeping operations. Out of a total of sixteen peacekeeping operations, ten are specifically mandated to use force for the protection of civilians. The vast majority of UN personnel serve in operations with protection of civilians mandates.[3] Despite the Security Council authorizations and the vast numbers of personnel involved, there is nevertheless still considerable resistance, both to the use of force by peacekeepers and to the inclusion of a human rights perspective in the UN's field work in general.[4]

The reticence to use force can be summarized as stemming from: ambiguity in the Security Council mandates; lack of clarity in the rules of engagement; troops following advice from capitals; a perception that the mandate only allows for joint work with the government authorities; and fear of being accused of excessive use of force, leading to allegations of war crimes or human rights violations. These points

1 See, for example, United Nations Security Council Resolution (UNSC Res) 1265 (1999) UN Doc S/RES/1265; UNSC Res 1296 (2000) UN Doc S/RES/1296; UNSC Res 1674 (2006) UN Doc S/RES/1674; UNSC Res 1738 (2006) UN Doc S/RES/1738; UNSC Res (2008) UN Doc S/RES/1836; UNSC Res (2011) UN Doc S/RES/2016.

2 For the history of this development see Haidi Willmot and Ralph Mamiya, 'Mandated to Protect: Security Council Practice on the Protection of Civilians', in Marc Weller and Alexia Solomou (eds), *The Oxford Handbook on the Use of Force in International Law* (Oxford: Oxford University Press, forthcoming); see also Haidi Willmot and Scott Sheeran, 'The Protection of Civilians Mandate in UN Peacekeeping Operations: Reconciling Protection Concepts and Practices' (2014) 95 IRRC 517.

3 At the end of 2013, 97 per cent of uniformed UN personnel and 95 per cent of civilian personnel came from operations mandated to protect civilians. See UN General Assembly (UNGA), 'Report of the Office of Internal Oversight Services, Evaluation of the implementation and results of protection of civilian mandates in United Nations peacekeeping operations' (2014) UN Doc A/68/787, para. 5 (OIOS Report).

4 For further discussion on the UN's human rights fieldwork, see Michael Keating and Richard Bennett, Chapter 16 in this volume.

emerge in stark form in the recent criticism of UN peacekeeping operations by the UN's own Office of Internal Oversight Services (OIOS).[5]

The particular resistance to including a human rights perspective, human rights advisers and experts, or even human rights law can be explained as follows. There is a conviction that raising human rights issues will hinder humanitarian access and lead to a deterioration of the UN's relationship with the host government. The UN's Member States more generally are cautious about allowing human rights questions to be mixed up with mandates authorized by the Security Council for fear of generating an expectation that human rights violations will be met with mandatory sanctions or the use of force. They fear that cherished State sovereignty could be overridden by the use of Chapter VII measures under the UN Charter. In turn, those States hosting peacekeeping or humanitarian operations become defensive and intimidating when accused of violating human rights. A host State always retains the power to expel, without giving any reason, any UN personnel with which it becomes annoyed. Many have in this way been declared *persona non grata* and expelled. Taking a human rights approach does not always therefore recommend itself to UN personnel on the ground or their superiors back in UN headquarters. This is compounded by the UN hierarchy failing to support expelled personnel in terms of their careers. Lastly, we have to admit that we may be faced with considerable ignorance or prejudice among diplomats and members of the UN Secretariat concerning what are 'human rights' and what are the obligations that surround them. This chapter is aimed at making a contribution to a better understanding of what constitutes human rights obligations.

The role of international human rights law in this context is not as obvious as one might think. First, human rights law does not normally distinguish between civilians and others as does, for example, international humanitarian law.[6] Human rights law protects individual human beings because their inherent dignity deserves respect. It does not usually exclude combatants, fighters, or civilians who directly participate in hostilities from its protective reach, nor does it simply abandon them to other branches of law such as the law of armed conflict. Second, there may be debates as to whether certain human rights obligations apply to a State and its troops when they are operating outside of their own territory (extraterritorially). Third, there is considerable confusion and controversy over whether armed non-State actors owe human rights obligations to those who find themselves under their control. Fourth, there is the related problem of the international legal responsibility and accountability of the UN itself for human rights violations. Fifth, in the wake of the UN's failure to avert the Rwanda genocide, protect the population of Srebrenica, or address the human rights violations in Sri Lanka, there is a realization that human rights warnings should not be brushed under the carpet, and yet there is apprehension about what the duties are of those who become aware of human rights atrocities. This is manifested in the enduring references to the concept of the international community's 'responsibility to protect' and the Human Rights Up

[5] UNGA, see n 3, 2, 7, 13, 15.

[6] See Jean-Marie Henckaerts and Louise Doswald-Beck, *Customary International Humanitarian Law, Volume 1: Rules* (Cambridge: Cambridge University Press, 2005), Rules 1–14.

Front strategy of the Secretariat. Let us now consider each of these issues in more detail.

II. The Relevance of International Human Rights Law for the Protection of Civilians

International human rights law applies to every individual, while some categories of persons benefit from special protections under particular human rights treaties, namely the internally displaced, persons with disabilities, migrant workers, children, and women.[7] In rare situations, some human rights, such as rights to political participation in elections, may be limited by nationality. And in times of emergency, some limited restrictions may be imposed on certain rights, or perhaps even on foreigners, where this is strictly required by the exigencies of the situation. In such 'states of emergency', the restrictions will be publicly declared and notified to the UN or the relevant regional organization.[8] Much is made in the literature of how human rights may be derogated from in times of emergency, but in practice the key rights related to the protection of civilians are non-derogable.[9] In any event, the relevance of any such derogation may be minimal in the context of UN peacekeeping, as explained by an expert in the field: 'No derogation may be declared on behalf of international organisations, which are not parties to human rights treaties, but

[7] See, for example, African Union Convention for the Protection and Assistance of Internally Displaced Persons in Africa (adopted 22 October 2009, entered into force 6 December 2012) 52 ILM 397; Convention on the Rights of Persons with Disabilities (adopted 13 December 2006, entered into force 30 March 2007), in UNGA Res 61/106 (2007) UN Doc A/61/106, Annex I; International Convention on the Protection of the Rights of All Migrant Workers and Members of Their Families (adopted 18 December 1990, entered into force 1 July 2003) 2220 UNTS 3; African Charter on the Rights and Welfare of the Child (adopted 11 July 1990, entered into force 29 November 1999) OAU Doc CAB/LEG/24.9/49; UN Convention on the Rights of the Child (adopted 20 November 1989, entered into force 2 September 1990) 1577 UNTS 3; Optional protocol to the Convention on the Rights of the Child on the involvement of children in armed conflict (adopted 20 May 2000, entered into force 12 February 2002) 2173 UNTS 222; Inter-American Convention on the Prevention, Punishment and Eradication of Violence against Women (adopted 9 June 1994, entered into force 5 March 1995) 33 ILM 1534; Council of Europe Convention on Preventing and Combating Violence against Women and Domestic Violence (adopted 11 May 2011, entered into force 1 August 2014) CETS No 210; African Union Protocol to the African Charter on Human and People's Rights on the Rights of Women in Africa (signed 11 July 2003, entered into force 5 November 2005) <www.au.int/en/treaties>; Convention on the Elimination of All Forms of Discrimination against Women (adopted 18 December 1979, entered into force 3 September 1981) 1249 UNTS 13.

[8] In practice, the scope for States to make these derogations is very limited according to human rights jurisprudence. The African Charter on Human and Peoples' Rights does not make provision for such derogations in times of emergency. For an overview, see Walter Kälin and Jörg Künzli, *The Law of International Human Rights Protection* (Oxford: Oxford University Press, 2009), 143–8; Scott Sheeran, 'Reconceptualizing States of Emergency under International Human Rights Law: Theory, Legal Doctrine and Politics' (2013) 34 Mich J Intl L 101–68.

[9] Under the International Covenant on Civil and Political Rights (1966), in Article 4, the following rights cannot be derogated from: the right to life; the prohibition on torture and cruel, inhuman or degrading treatment and punishment; the prohibition on slavery; the right not to be imprisoned for non-fulfilment for a contractual obligation; the prohibition on retrospective application of criminal law; the right to recognition as a legal person; and the right to freedom of thought, conscience, and religion. See further Susan Marks and Andrew Clapham, *International Human Rights Lexicon* (Oxford: Oxford University Press, 2005) 350–8.

which nevertheless are bound by custom and policy to comply with human rights standards in their operations.'[10]

Some relevant phenomena are additionally covered by specific human rights treaties. This is the case for torture and enforced disappearances, and violations of these obligations can be considered offences which can lead to individual criminal prosecutions in national jurisdictions.[11] Lastly, we should mention that the basic human rights catalogue is to be found in what is sometimes known as the International Bill of Rights: the 1948 Universal Declaration of Human Rights (UDHR), the 1966 International Covenant on Economic Social and Cultural Rights (ICESCR), and the 1966 International Covenant on Civil and Political Rights (ICCPR). Most of the rights in the UDHR reflect customary international law obligations and so there is no question of needing to determine whether the host State or the States comprising the contributing troops are parties to human rights treaties before raising basic questions of human rights.[12] As we shall see, however, the legal obligations of the relevant entities (which may or may not be able to join these treaties) are actually less relevant than the political commitment to human rights more generally.

An assumption in the context of the UN peacekeeping 'protection of civilians' mandates may be that human rights relate to the right to life and physical integrity, with a special emphasis on protection from sexual violence and violations committed against children. Consider the Security Council's mandate for the UN Multidimensional Integrated Stabilization Mission in the Central African Republic (MINUSCA) created in 2014, in which the Council authorized the 'Protection of Civilians' and the 'Promotion and Protection of Human Rights' as separate 'priority tasks' for the mission:

Protection of Civilians;

(i) To protect, without prejudice to the primary responsibility of the Central African Republic's authorities, the civilian population from threat of physical violence, within its capabilities and areas of deployment, including through active patrolling;

(ii) To provide specific protection for women and children affected by armed conflict, including through the deployment of Child Protection Advisers and Women Protection Advisers.[13]

[10] Dieter Fleck, 'The Law Applicable to Peace Operations', in Andrew Clapham and Paola Gaeta (eds), *The Oxford Handbook of International Law in Armed Conflict* (Oxford: Oxford University Press, 2014) 206, 234–5. For a different view, see Scott Sheeran and Catherine Bevilacqua, 'The UN Security Council and International Human Rights Obligations: Towards a Theory of Constraints and Derogation', in Scott Sheeran and Nigel Rodley (eds), *The Routledge Handbook on International Human Rights Law* (Abingdon, UK: Routledge, 2013) 396–402.

[11] See, for example, the UN Convention against Torture and Other Cruel, Inhuman or Degrading Treatment or Punishment (adopted 10 December 1984, entered into force 26 June 1987) 1465 UNTS 85, Article 13; the International Convention for the Protection of All Persons from Enforced Disappearance (adopted 20 December 2006, entered into force 23 December 2010), Article 11; the Inter-American Convention to Prevent and Punish Torture (adopted 9 December 1985, entered into force 28 February 1987) OAS Treaty Series No 67, Article 3; and Inter-American Convention on the Forced Disappearance of Persons (adopted 9 June 1994, entered into force 28 March 1996) Article IV.

[12] Hurst Hannum, 'The Status of the Universal Declaration of Human Rights in National and International Law' (1996) 25 Ga J Intl Comp L 287–397.

[13] UNSC Res 2149 (2014) UN Doc S/RES/2149, para. 30(a).

But the mandate gives equal priority to the promotion and protection of human rights more generally. Another 'priority task' is:

Promotion and protection of human rights;

(i) To monitor, help investigate and report publicly and to the Security Council on violations of international humanitarian law and on abuses and violations of human rights committed throughout the Central African Republic, in particular by different armed groups, including the former Séléka and the anti-Balaka, and to contribute to efforts to identify and prosecute perpetrators, and to prevent such violations and abuses, including through the deployment of human rights observers;
(ii) To monitor, help investigate and report specifically on violations and abuses committed against children as well as violations committed against women, including all forms of sexual violence in armed conflict, and to contribute to efforts to identify and prosecute perpetrators, and to prevent such violations and abuses;
(iii) To support the International Commission of Inquiry and the implementation of its recommendations;
(iv) To assist the Central African Republic authorities in the effort to protect and promote human rights.[14]

We see that the Security Council mandates protection, in a broad sense, and is less interested in defining exactly which human rights treaties are applicable and to whom. The issue is first a question of protection of the civilian population, whether or not this actually involves rights and duties under human rights law, and second of the protection and promotion of human rights more generally, again more or less irrespective of the international legal obligations that may or may not apply. The idea that the operation would look beyond the applicable treaties is supported by the use of the expression 'violations and abuses' which, for the avoidance of doubt, may extend the scope of human rights beyond the strict legal obligations that attach to States Parties through the human rights treaties they have ratified.[15]

What then is the role of human rights law as such? And why is there a need for human rights expertise? The answers to these questions in part explain why there is a disconnect between the Security Council's apparent enthusiasm to grant a mandate to promote human rights to its peacekeeping operations and the reluctance in the UN to incorporate human rights officers into the policy, planning, and political meetings. International human rights law allows one to go beyond a commitment to physical protection and to remind governments, armed groups, and individuals concerned that they are breaking international law and that there can be accountability for their actions before a court of law. It is precisely this challenge which can threaten not only international reputations and individual liberty, but also the very

[14] Ibid., para. 30(e).

[15] While some authors reserve the notion of human rights abuses for armed non-State actors and violations for States, one cannot necessarily derive any legal significance from such labelling. See generally David Weissbrodt, 'Non-State Entities and Human Rights within the Context of the Nation-State in the 21st Century', in Monique Castermans, Fried van Hoof, and Jacqueline Smith (eds), *The Role of the Nation-State in the 21st Century* (Dordrecht: Kluwer, 1998) 175–95; Nigel Rodley, 'Non-state Actors and Human Rights', in Sheeran and Rodley, see n 10, 523–44; Andrew Clapham (ed.), *Human Rights and Non-State Actors* (Cheltenham: Edward Elgar, 2013). See also Office for the High Commissioner of Human Rights (OHCHR), *Training Manual on Human Rights Monitoring: Professional Training Series No. 7* (Geneva: United Nations, 2001) 10, 336–43.

legitimacy of the actors with which the UN is engaging. The movement to end impunity for gross human rights violations reminds the various actors that there can now be very concrete consequences which flow from being accused of violating human rights. Nowhere is this more apparent than with regard to the work of the International Criminal Court (ICC). The ICC has jurisdiction over genocide and war crimes. In addition, where certain human rights violations are committed as part of a widespread or systematic attack directed against any civilian population, they may amount to crimes against humanity falling within the jurisdiction of the ICC or any State with jurisdiction.[16] Conceptually, these crimes were at one point referred to by the UN's International Law Commission in its Draft Code of Crimes Against the Peace and Security of Mankind as 'systematic or mass violations of human rights'.[17]

While there may be multiple obstacles to prosecution at the ICC or in national courts, raising the spectre of conduct amounting to an international crime can trigger strong reactions as there is a perception in some conflict zones that atrocities will be eventually punished, especially where the UN is present and able to bear witness. In this regard, the UN OIOS quotes a member of local civil society as saying:

> Our own government is scared to commit human rights violations in the presence of the United Nations. The armed groups are scared of the international criminal tribunals. Everyone knows that people who commit massacres and genocides will be captured and sent to justice.[18]

Specialist knowledge is required to understand and explain the elements of these crimes, the possibilities for courts to exercise jurisdiction, and the modes of secondary liability for assisting in the commission of such crimes.

But human rights law is potentially much more useful in providing a framework for accountability and the rule of law beyond the international criminal arena. While mass violations of human rights may amount to crimes which can be prosecuted under the ICC Statute, the route to proper protection of the civilian population lies more with early preventive action through the creation of a legal order that complies with human rights, allows for human rights complaints, and fosters a culture of respect for human rights across the population. It is perhaps here that UN human rights officers have most to offer. The UN Office of the High Commissioner for Human Rights (OHCHR) now has considerable experience in developing human rights programmes in the field; programmes which lay the foundations for the rule of law and do much more than highlight what norms have been

[16] See Rodney Dixon and Christopher K. Hall, 'Article 7', in Otto Triffterer (ed.), *Commentary on the Rome Statute of the International Criminal Court* (Baden-Baden, Denmark: Nomos, 2008) 159–273.

[17] Draft Code of Crimes against the Peace and Security of Mankind, adopted by the International Law Commission, in UNGA, 'Report of the International Law Commission on the Work of its Forty-third Session' (1991) UN Doc A/46/10, 96; for the history of the development of this category of crimes into what eventually became the catalogue of crimes against humanity listed in the ICC Statute see Roger S Clark, 'History of Efforts to Codify Crimes Against Humanity: From the Charter of Nuremberg to the Statute of Rome', in Leila Nadya Sadat (ed.), *Forging a Convention for Crimes Against Humanity* (Cambridge: Cambridge University Press, 2011) 8–27.

[18] OIOS Report, see n 3, para. 72.

violated. As far back as 2006, OHCHR staff saw their approach as broader than simply saving the lives of civilians:

From OHCHR's point of view human rights protection is a wider concept including not only civilians but all individuals in time of peace and war. OHCHR emphasises, as well, obligations of promotion, alongside protection. OHCHR's approach to protection is based on the provisions of international human rights law, international humanitarian law, international criminal law, and international refugee law. Our approach is informed by the full range of internationally agreed human rights standards, as well as the Vienna Declaration [and] the mandate of the High Commissioner for Human Rights.[19]

This holistic approach not only allows for structural work on the rule of law but also seeks to provide the framework that resolves tensions before they blow up into armed conflicts or even atrocity crimes.[20] This means working on human rights issues with multiple actors, the police, the judiciary, lawyers, the military, parliamentarians, civil society, the business sector, journalists, and in some cases the armed groups themselves.[21]

III. The Extraterritorial Effect of International Human Rights Law

While the government of the host State will be unlikely to object to assertions that they are bound by international human rights law (of course allegations of violations will nevertheless provoke arguments about the facts), the government of any State whose troops have been sent abroad may contest the *extraterritorial* application of human rights law that would bind them when acting at home in their own territory. This is a complex and developing area of the law, and for present purposes it suffices to state that human rights treaties will often be applicable, either when States are in control of territory and exercising a public function, or when their personnel bring individuals within their jurisdiction through an exercise of their authority. While the United States and Israel have rejected such extraterritorial application of the ICCPR, the International Court of Justice (ICJ) and the UN Human Rights Committee have consistently held that this treaty is applicable even when troops are operating abroad, either as an occupation force or as part of a peace operation.[22] The UN Human Rights Committee's General Comment on the scope of the ICCPR is clear:

19 See OHCHR Staff, 'Protection in the Field: Human Rights Perspectives', in BG Ramcharan (ed.), *Human Rights Protection in the Field* (Leiden: Martinus Nijhoff, 2006) 119, 121; see also Ben Majekodunmi, 'United Nations Human Rights Field Officers', in Yael Danieli (ed.), *Sharing the Front Line and the Back Hills* (New York: Baywood, 2002) 137–48; William G. O'Neill, 'Enhancing UN Human Rights Work on the Ground', in Felice D Gaer and Christen L Broecker (eds), *The United Nations High Commissioner for Human Rights: Conscience of the World* (Leiden: Nijhoff, 2014) 175–96; and Sima Samar, 'The Role of the High Commissioner in Protecting and Promoting Human Rights in Afghanistan and Sudan', in Gaer and Broecker, ibid., 312–29.

20 See for example the series of nine booklets, OHCHR, *Rule of Law Tools for Post Conflict States* (Geneva: United Nations, 2009) <www.ohchr.org/EN/PublicationsResources/Pages/Methodological Materials3.aspx>.

21 On this last point see Frederick Rawski, 'Engaging with Armed Groups: A Human Rights Field Perspective from Nepal' (2009) 6 Intl Org L Rev 601–26.

22 Human Rights Committee, 'General Comment 31, Nature of the General Legal Obligation on States Parties to the Covenant' (2004) UN Doc CCPR/C/21/Rev.1/Add.13. para. 10 (General

States Parties are required by article 2, paragraph 1, to respect and to ensure the Covenant rights to all persons who may be within their territory and to all persons subject to their jurisdiction. This means that a State Party must respect and ensure the rights laid down in the Covenant to anyone within the power or effective control of that State Party, even if not situated within the territory of the State Party . . . This principle also applies to those within the power or effective control of the forces of a State Party acting outside its territory, regardless of the circumstances in which such power or effective control was obtained, such as forces constituting a national contingent of a State Party assigned to an *international peace-keeping* or *peace-enforcement operation*.[23]

Although the law relating to the scope of a State's extraterritorial obligations under the various treaties can be quite complex,[24] this factor should not be allowed to obfuscate the fact that all States are in any event bound by the general body of customary international law, something that has been explicitly recognized with regard to the protection of civilians by a recent US Army training manual. According to the *Operational Law Handbook* of the International and Operational Law Department of the Judge Advocate General's Legal Centre and School of the US Army:

For official U.S. personnel (i.e., 'State actors' in the language of IHRL [international human rights law]) dealing with civilians outside the territory of the United States, it is CIL [customary international law] that establishes the human rights considered fundamental, and therefore obligatory. Unfortunately, however, there exists no authoritative source that articulates which human rights the United States considers to be CIL.[25]

We could suggest that relevant human rights applicable by virtue of customary international law include the right to life and the right not to be subjected to torture or enforced disappearances. Of course, understanding the scope of these rights again requires a degree of expertise: the exact parameters of when lethal force can be used, what constitutes self-defence, or the point at which a detention becomes an enforced disappearance will be based on case law and the practice of the relevant UN bodies. What is not fair, however, is to suggest that human rights

Comment 31); most recently see Human Rights Committee, 'Concluding Observations on the fourth periodic review of the United States of America' (2014) UN Doc CCPR/C/USA/CO/4, para. 4.

23 General Comment 31, see n 22, para. 10 (emphasis added).

24 For a detailed discussion of extraterritoriality with regard to this treaty and other human rights treaties see Wouter Vandenhole, 'Extraterritorial Human Rights Obligations: Taking Stock, Looking Forward' (2013) 5 Eur J Hum Rts 804–35; K. da Costa, *The Extraterritorial Application of Selected Human Rights Treaties* (Leiden: Brill, 2012); Marko Milanovic, *Extraterritorial Application of Human Rights Treaties: Law Principles, Policy* (Oxford: Oxford University Press, 2011); Mark Gibney and Sigrun Skogly (eds), *Universal Human Rights and Extraterritorial Obligations* (Philadelphia, USA: University Pennsylvania Press, 2010); for the particular issues arising in peace operations see Terry D Gill and Dieter Fleck (eds), *The Handbook of the International Law of Military Operations* (Oxford: Oxford University Press, 2010), Chapters 4, 24, 25.

25 See Chapter 3 of the Handbook, 'International Human Rights Law', at 45. Note that the preface States that the *Handbook* 'is not intended to represent official U.S. policy regarding the binding application of varied sources of law'. Maj Andrew Gillman and Maj Williams Johnson (eds), *Operational Law Handbook* (Charlottesville, USA: US Army, 2012), ii, 45. See also Kenneth Watkin, who notes that: 'even if it were determined that a human rights system of accountability did not apply as a matter of law to occupied territory, it would ordinarily be logical as a matter of policy to apply human rights norms to an occupier's policing function.' Kenneth Watkin, 'Controlling the Use of Force: A Role for Human Rights Norms in Contemporary Armed Conflict' (2004) 98 AJIL 1, 27.

determinations are simply 'aspirations', 'political', or 'subjective'. The law is as concrete as the law of the sea or international investment law, and is just as subject to adjudication in national and international courts.[26] Part of the explanation as to why human rights officers are seen as bringing in unwelcome politicization is that human rights law is confused with human rights politics at the UN Human Rights Council or in foreign affairs. States are notoriously selective in choosing which States to criticize for human rights violations; human rights are therefore seen as something politicized and riddled with double standards.[27]

IV. The International Human Rights Obligations of Armed Non-State Actors

We have mentioned several times the perceived disadvantages of the UN highlighting human rights violations by a government. The UN's own internal review panel into UN action in Sri Lanka in 2007–9, however, highlights at multiple points that various UN reports and a Human Rights Council resolution found it easier to report on violations by the armed rebel group, the Liberation Tigers of Tamil Eelam (LTTE), than on the violations being committed by the government of Sri Lanka.[28] Such selectivity has been criticized, not only as a failure to fulfil the UN's mandate but also because it presents a misleading picture to policy-makers seeking to prevent further harm to civilians and hold all parties to account. In most situations where UN peacekeepers are mandated to protect civilians, there will be threats from armed non-State actors, as well as from the agents of the State. There is, however, some confusion concerning the legal rationale for reporting on violations committed by armed groups. The following section addresses some of the recent developments.

Although armed non-State actors are not party to the human rights treaties, it is increasingly recognized that these groups have human rights obligations[29] and that a UN peacekeeping mandate involving the protection of civilians must extend to reporting on violations committed by such groups. This reporting may eventually lead to individual criminal accountability either at the national level or in an

[26] For books dealing with the case-law, see: Nihal Jayawickrama, *The Judicial Application of Human Rights Law: National Regional and International Jurisprudence* (Cambridge: Cambridge University Press, 2002); Kälin and Künzli, see n 8; Daniel Moeckli, Sangeeta Shah, and Sandesh Sivakumaran (eds), *International Human Rights Law* (Oxford: Oxford University Press, 2014).

[27] For a detailed discussion of the arguments surrounding when international obligations attach to the UN or a regional organization, rather than to the State contributing troops, see Mona Khalil, Chapter 9 and Siobhán Wills, Chapter 10, in this volume. For some of the human rights case law concerning the attribution of acts to troop contributing countries, see also Kjetil Mujezinović Larsen, *The Human Rights Treaty Obligations of Peacekeepers* (Cambridge: Cambridge University Press, 2012).

[28] *Report of the Secretary-General's Internal Review Panel on United Nations action in Sri Lanka* (November 2012) para. 25, Annex III paras 105, 127, 137, 141, 155, Annex V para. 17 (Sri Lanka Internal Review Panel) <www.un.org/News/dh/infocus/Sri_Lanka/The_Internal_Review_Panel_report_on_Sri_Lanka.pdf>.

[29] See, for example, Rodley, 'Non-State Actors and Human Rights', n 15, and compare Andrew Clapham, 'Focusing on Armed Non-State Actors', in Clapham and Gaeta (eds), see n 10.

international tribunal. Stepping back a moment, and putting aside the framing of the legal obligations, it ought to be obvious that it would be untenable for the UN or even a non-governmental organization (NGO) to claim it was unable to report on violence by the armed opposition because this fell outside the meaning of human rights.[30] The UN and civil society have increasingly met this challenge by reporting on violations and abuses by non-State actors. In recent times, UN missions have started to develop their legal reasoning. Consider the following two UN reports, the first from Afghanistan and the second from South Sudan.

In 2012 the UN Assistance Mission in Afghanistan (UNAMA) and OHCHR produced a report entitled *Afghanistan: Annual Report on Protection of Civilians in Armed Conflict 2011*. It contained the following explanation for their reporting on the Taliban:

> While non-State actors in Afghanistan, including non-State armed groups, cannot formally become parties to international human rights treaties, international human rights law increasingly recognises that where non-State actors, such as the Taliban, exercise *de facto* control over territory, they are bound by international human rights obligations.[31]

In the context of South Sudan, the United Nations Mission in the Republic of South Sudan (UNMISS) went further in their 2014 report entitled *Conflict in South Sudan: A Human Rights Report*:

> The most basic human rights obligations, in particular those emanating from peremptory international law (*ius cogens*) bind both the State and armed opposition groups in times of peace and during armed conflict. In particular, international human rights law requires States, armed groups and others to respect the prohibitions of extrajudicial killing, maiming, torture, cruel inhuman or degrading treatment or punishment, enforced disappearance, rape, other conflict related sexual violence, sexual and other forms of slavery, the recruitment and use of children in hostilities, arbitrary detention as well as any violations that amount to war crimes, crimes against humanity, or genocide.[32]

Both reports were produced by UN field operations in fulfilling a human rights function. Other UN entities with a broader mandate covering the identification of individual perpetrators—such as the UN Commissions of Inquiry on Darfur, Libya, and Syria[33]—have sought to systematically identify violations committed by armed groups together with the relevant individual criminal responsibility for members of those same armed groups.

While the importance of impartiality has already been stressed, it bears noting that the obligations on the State will be greater than the obligations on the armed

[30] Ravi Nair, 'Confronting the Violence Committee by Armed Opposition Groups' (1998) 1 Yale Hum Rts Dev L J 1.

[31] UN Assistance Mission in Afghanistan and UN Office of the High Commissioner for Human Rights, *Afghanistan Annual Report on Protection of Civilians in Armed Conflict 2011* (Kabul: United Nations, 2012) iv, <unama.unmissions.org/Portals/UNAMA/Documents/UNAMA%20POC%202011%20Report_Final_Feb%202012.pdf>.

[32] UN Mission in South Sudan, *Conflict in South Sudan: A Human Rights Report* (United Nations, 2014) para. 18, <https://unmiss.unmissions.org/Portals/unmiss/Human%20Rights%20Reports/UNMISS%20Conflict%20in%20South%20Sudan%20-%20A%20Human%20Rights%20Report.pdf>.

[33] For a discussion, see Clapham, n 29.

group. The State will inevitably be party to several human rights treaties with their detailed provisions, and the positive obligations on the State to protect everyone from private violence, and to take steps to fulfil their obligations and provide remedies, will certainly extend beyond what is expected of the armed group. Furthermore, the UN and NGOs have developed alternative techniques for engaging with such groups—one cannot use the same methods as one would with a Member State of the UN.[34]

We have already mentioned that individuals belonging to such groups could find themselves prosecuted for international crimes either in the ICC or before a national jurisdiction. In closing this section we should also explain that the Security Council has developed procedures for monitoring violations of children by armed non-State actors. Reports by the UN Secretary-General to the Security Council on certain country situations now list the non-State actors concerned and whether or not they are involved in any of six categories of extrajudicial crimes:

1. Killing or maiming of children;
2. recruiting or using child soldiers;
3. attacks against schools or hospitals;
4. rape or other grave sexual violence against children;
5. abduction of children;
6. denial of humanitarian access for children.

The UN Secretary-General's initial report explains that these violations are based on international norms, and commitments that have been made by the parties to the conflict, as well as national laws and peace agreements.[35] Subsequent reports on various country situations have detailed the 'grave violations of children's rights' committed by the non-state actors concerned. These reports dedicate as much, if not more, space to the violations committed by the non-State actors as they do to addressing the States concerned. Although the focus started with recruitment, the Security Council has now requested the Secretary-General to include in his reports 'those parties to armed conflict that engage, in contravention of applicable international law, in patterns of killing and maiming of children and/or rape and other sexual violence against children, in situations of armed conflict'.[36]

[34] See OHCHR, *Training Manual on Human Rights Monitoring: Professional Training Series No. 7* (Geneva: United Nations, 2001), 336–7; and see generally UNICEF, 'Programme Guidance Note on Engaging with Non-State Entities in Humanitarian Action' (New York: United Nations, 2011); Gerard McHugh and Manuel Bessler, *Humanitarian Negotiations with Armed Groups* (New York: United Nations, 2006); Pascal Bongard and Jonathan Somer, 'Monitoring Armed Non-state Actor Compliance with Humanitarian Norms: A Look at International Mechanisms and the Geneva Call *Deed of Commitment*' (2011) 93 IRRC 673; Annyssa Bellal and Stuart Casey-Maslen, *Rules of Engagement: Promoting the Protection of Civilians through Dialogue with Armed Non-State Actors* (Geneva: Geneva Academy of International Humanitarian Law and Human Rights, 2011); Marina Mattirolo and Stuart Casey-Maslen, with Alice Priddy, *Reactions to Norms Armed Groups and the Protection of Civilians* (Geneva: Geneva Academy of International Humanitarian Law and Human Rights, 2014).

[35] UNGA and UNSC, 'Report of the Secretary-General, Children and Armed Conflict' (2005) UN Doc A/59/695—S/2005/72, paras 70–3.

[36] UNSC Res 1882 (2009) UN Doc S/RES/1882, para. 3.

The Security Council's addressing vis-à-vis the non-State actor works not only through naming and shaming, but also by encouraging the non-State actor to submit an 'action plan'; under this scheme the group can eventually be removed from the list of violators. The Security Council also has in mind that it could adopt

> country-specific resolutions, targeted and graduated measures, such as, *inter alia*, a ban on the export and supply of small arms and light weapons and of other military equipment and on military assistance, against parties to situations of armed conflict which are on the Security Council's agenda and are in violation of applicable international law relating to the rights and protection of children in armed conflict.[37]

While such activity has proven to have some effect on the ground in some conflicts, the limited scope of this work and the periodicity of the reporting cycle led to criticism from the UN's internal review panel on UN action in Sri Lanka. That report concluded that the monitoring and reporting mechanism established in the context of Security Council Resolution 1612, concerning use and requirement of child soldiers, was hampered by the limited focus on the six violations, by the informal nature of the notes prepared, by tardy reporting with regard to the actual conflict, by underestimates of the killings on the ground, and by a failure to attribute any of the casualties to shelling by the government.[38] We are faced here with a real challenge. On the one hand, a peacekeeping operation charged with protecting civilians and promoting human rights may be able to challenge the behaviour of the host government and hold them to account using the traditional human rights machinery, and yet there may be a deference to the host State for fear of upsetting a UN Member State and the host of the operation. On the other hand, the same operation may distort the picture by enthusiastically reporting on violations committed by the opposition armed group, and in this situation the legal framework and mechanisms for accountability are underdeveloped. The first steps taken by the Security Council represent a welcome development, but any UN operation needs to be aware of the challenge presented by trying to protect civilians from armed groups.

V. The International Human Rights Obligations of United Nations Peacekeepers

Much has been written in order to explain why international human rights obligations are binding on the UN as a matter of international law.[39] This is not the place to rehearse those theories as the strict legal accountability of the UN is not, for the

[37] UNSC Res 1612 (2005) UN Doc S/RES/1612, para. 9; for a site with the relevant documents produced by the Security Council's Working group on Children in Armed Conflict, see <www.un.org/sc/committees/WGCAAC/Table%20of%20WG%20documents.html>.

[38] Sri Lanka Internal Review Panel, see n 28, Annex III para. 127, Annex V paras 18, 113–4.

[39] See, for example, Larsen, n 27; Guglielmo Verdirame, *The UN and Human Rights: Who Guards the Guardians?* (Cambridge: Cambridge University Press, 2011); Siobhán Wills, *Protecting Civilians: The Obligations of Peacekeepers* (Oxford: Oxford University Press, 2009), chapter 3; Marten Zwanenburg, *Accountability of Peace Support Operations* (Leiden: Nijhoff, 2005); Frédeéric Mégret and

moment, actually of much practical relevance insofar as claims brought in national fora are likely to be met by UN assertions of immunity.[40] Moreover, the European Court of Human Rights has rejected the claim that such a denial of access to the courts represents a violation of human rights by the Member State concerned; upholding the UN's immunity from suit is considered a proportionate restriction on an individual's right to remedy.[41]

What is relevant is the fact that the Security Council, in authorizing a mandate, will demand that this be carried out in accordance with international human rights law. For example the resolution on peacekeeping in the Central African Republic includes the following paragraph where the Council emphasized:

> [T]he need for MISCA [the African Union force], EUFOR RCA [the European Union force] and the French forces operating in the CAR [Central African Republic], while carrying out their mandate, to act in full respect of the sovereignty, territorial integrity and unity of CAR and in full compliance with applicable international humanitarian law, human rights law and refugee law and recalls the importance of training in this regard.[42]

The same resolution '[r]equests MINUSCA to ensure that any support provided to non-United Nations security forces is provided in strict compliance with the Human Rights Due Diligence Policy on United Nations support to non-United Nations security forces (HRDDP)'.[43] While one could construct a complicated explanation of what sort of activity by the UN would lead to complicity in violations of human rights by those that the UN assists, this is again not strictly necessary for day-to-day policy-making as the UN has developed its own due diligence policy in this context. It states that the support given by UN entities to non-UN security forces must be consistent with the Organization's purposes and principles under the UN Charter and with its obligations 'under international law to respect, promote and encourage respect for international humanitarian law, human rights and refugee law'.[44] There is a further, third, obligation to 'intercede with the relevant authorities' where there are substantial grounds to believe that the recipient of UN support is committing 'grave violations' of human rights.[45] What constitute 'grave violations' is answered for the purposes of the policy as including:

Florian Hoffman, 'The UN as Human Rights Violator? Some Reflections on the United Nations Changing Human Rights Responsibilities' (2003) 25 Hum Rts Q 314.

[40] For the developments concerning Haiti see The Associated Press, 'Haitians File Suit against UN over Cholera Epidemic' *Al Jazeera America* (New York, 12 March 2014) <america.aljazeera.com/articles/2014/3/12/haitians-sue-un-overcholeraepidemic.html>.

[41] *Stichting Mothers of Srebrinica and others v the Netherlands* Application No 65542/12 (ECtHR, 11 June 2013), para. 169; with regard to holding the Netherlands accountable rather than the UN, see Siobhán Wills, Chapter 10 of this volume, discussing *Mothers of Srebrenica v. The Netherlands and the United Nations*, Case No C/09/295247 / HA ZA 07-2973 (District Court of the Hague, the Netherlands, Judgment of 16 July 2014). See also André Nollkaemper, 'Dual Attribution: Liability of the Netherlands for Conduct of Dutchbat in Srebrenica' (2011) 9 JICJ 1143.

[42] UNSC Res 2149 (2014) UN Doc S/RES/2149, para. 42.

[43] Ibid., para. 39.

[44] 'Human Rights Due Diligence Policy on United Nations Support to non-United Nations Security Forces', in UNGA and UNSC (2013) UN Doc A/67/775–S/2013/110, Annex para. 1 (UN Human Rights Due Diligence Policy); see also Scott Sheeran, 'A Constitutional Moment? United Nations Peacekeeping in the Democratic Republic of Congo' (2011) 8 Intl Org L Rev 55.

[45] UN Human Rights Due Diligence Policy, see n 44, para. 1, 12.

'[C]rimes against humanity', as defined in the Rome Statute of the International Criminal Court, or 'gross violations' of human rights, including summary executions and extrajudicial killings, acts of torture, enforced disappearances, enslavement, rape and sexual violence of a comparable serious nature.[46]

This leaves us the question: what else is included in the applicable human rights law for a UN peacekeeping operation mandated to protect civilians? It would be tempting to limit ourselves to the sorts of customary obligations that we saw listed by the UN in the context of holding armed groups accountable in contexts such as South Sudan or Syria. But this would be too narrow; the UN is often faced with playing the role of public authority and fulfilling functions more related to law enforcement and local government than fighting a civil war. Issues will arise with regard to policing peaceful protest, determining the suitability of certain media broadcasts, detaining those accused of crimes, and, of course, the use of force as law enforcement officials or in self-defence.

In one operation, the UN Mission in Kosovo (UNMIK), the UN promulgated rules stating that the operation was bound by human rights and provided a procedure for human rights complaints.[47] Situations such as Kosovo and East Timor have reminded the UN that its human rights obligations may go beyond the prohibitions against torture and ill-treatment and arbitrary killing. One is perhaps just as likely to come across questions related to freedom of expression and non-discrimination. When it comes to issues of the use of force and detention, perhaps the best guidelines are those found in UN instruments such as the Basic Principles on the Use of Force and Firearms (1990),[48] the Code of Conduct for Law Enforcement Officials (1979),[49] and the Body of Principles for the Protection of All Persons under Any Form of Detention (1988).[50] These are not treaties, and so no issues arise as to whether a contributing State, the host State, or the UN itself is a party. The principles on detention are designed to cover 'all persons under any form of detention' and the use-of-force provisions apply to law enforcement officials even 'in a state of war'[51] or 'public emergency'.[52] These standards are important as they apply whether or not there is an armed conflict and can be used as global standards rather than resorting to treaties that do not go into the requisite detail.

46 Ibid., para. 12(a)(i).

47 Christine Chinkin, 'Sources', in Moeckli, Shah, and Sivakumaran, see n 26, 90; see United Nations Mission in Kosovo (UNMIK), 'Regulation on the Authority of the Interim Administration in Kosovo' (1999) UN Doc UNMIK/REG/1999/1, § 2 <www.unmikonline.org/regulations/1999/reg01-99.htm>; UNMIL, 'Regulation No 2006/12 on the establishment of the Human Rights Advisory Panel' (2006) UN Doc UNMIK/REG/2006/12, Annex A, 31.

48 Basic Principles on the Use of Force and Firearms by Law Enforcement Officials (adopted by the Eighth United Nations Congress on the Prevention of Crime and the Treatment of Offenders, Havana, Cuba, 27 August to 7 September 1990), reproduced in OHCHR, *Human Rights a Compilation of Instruments* (Volume 1) (New York: United Nations, 2002) 351 (Basic Principles on the Use of Force and Firearms).

49 UNGA, 'Code of Conduct for Law Enforcement Officials' (1979) UN Doc A/RES/34/179 (Code of Conduct for Law Enforcement Officials).

50 UNGA, 'Body of Principles for the Protection of All Persons under Any Form of Detention' (1988) UN Doc A/43/173.

51 See Code of Conduct for Law Enforcement Officials, n 49, Article 5.

52 Basic Principles on the Use of Force and Firearms, see n 48, principle 8.

The *Handbook of the International Law of Military Operations* explains that where peace enforcement operations do not reach the level of armed conflict, whether international or non-international, personnel must adhere to law enforcement principles, and that 'the use of force provisions under human rights law are based on the requirements necessary for law enforcement, essentially the minimum force required to counter the threat posed'.[53] The Handbook refers to the UN Basic Principles on the Use of Force and Firearms at this point. Because peacekeepers are often faced with threats of violence to civilians outside the context of an armed conflict, it is worth us going into a little more detail as to what should be expected of them and the UN. Principles 4 and 9 are particularly apposite in this context:

> 4. Law enforcement officials, in carrying out their duty, shall, as far as possible, apply non-violent means before resorting to the use of force and firearms. They may use force and firearms only if other means remain ineffective or without any promise of achieving the intended result.
>
> . . .
>
> 9. Law enforcement officials shall not use firearms against persons except in self-defence or defence of others against the imminent threat of death or serious injury, to prevent the perpetration of a particularly serious crime involving grave threat to life, to arrest a person presenting such a danger and resisting their authority, or to prevent his or her escape, and only when less extreme means are insufficient to achieve these objectives. In any event, intentional lethal use of firearms may only be made when strictly unavoidable in order to protect life.[54]

These principles address the use of firearms in particular. The more general question of the use of force is dealt with in the Code of Conduct for Law Enforcement Officials and its official commentary:

> 3. Law enforcement officials may use force only when strictly necessary and to the extent required for the performance of their duty.
>
> Commentary:
>
> (a) This provision emphasises that the use of force by law enforcement officials should be exceptional; while it implies that law enforcement officials may be authorised to use force as is reasonably necessary under the circumstances for the prevention of crime or in effecting or assisting in the lawful arrest of offenders or suspected offenders, no force going beyond that may be used.[55]

The point at which law enforcement-type activity turns into combat and yet remains covered by human rights law concerning the right to life remains a difficult issue which may depend on the degree of control exercised by the UN over the territory or persons concerned, and whether those targeted are clearly fighters posing an imminent danger in a situation where arrest is not practicable.[56]

[53] Charles HB Garraway, 'Applicability and Application of International Humanitarian Law to Enforcement and Peace Enforcement Operations', in Gill and Fleck, see n 24, 129.

[54] Basic Principles on the Use of Force and Firearms by Law Enforcement Officials, see n 48, paras 4, 9.

[55] Code of Conduct for Law Enforcement Officials, see n 49, para. 3.

[56] OHCHR, *International Legal Protection of Human Rights in Armed Conflict* (New York and Geneva: United Nations, 2011) 67–8.

Today it seems axiomatic that UN peacekeepers must respect human rights. While there may be arguments as to the legal basis for this assumption, the Security Council's inclusion of a demand that forces act in full compliance with applicable human rights law means that it is clear that peacekeeping forces have some human rights obligations. The UN's own human rights standards on the use of force and firearms are particularly pertinent in this context. Other standards related to detention may also be important when one considers that human rights law demands that lethal force has to be avoided where it is possible to detain the persons concerned. Perhaps the focus should now shift from thinking about the legal reasoning that determines the applicability of various human rights norms to thinking about the sort of appropriate training that is given to the forces that are deployed to protect civilians.

VI. 'Responsibility to Protect' and 'Human Rights Up Front'

The commitment to a 'responsibility to protect' can be traced back to the sense that more should have been done to protect those in Rwanda and Srebrenica from genocide and crimes against humanity. For a while there was, within the International Commission on Intervention and State Sovereignty, a sense that one could fashion a new right to humanitarian intervention where the Security Council was failing to live up to its responsibilities. The eventual Outcome Document adopted by the General Assembly at the 2005 Summit, however, failed to leave much room for legitimizing any such unauthorized military intervention.[57] Instead the focus has shifted to reminding States and the UN that, in addition to the obligations on States not to engage in genocide, war crimes, crimes against humanity, or ethnic cleansing, there are expectations that all States will work to prevent such atrocities and that there should be a readiness, if need be, to use force under a Security Council mandate.[58] To the extent that human rights violations rise to the level of these atrocities, violations of international human rights law are part of the picture. It is sometimes assumed that these sorts of atrocities trigger legal obligations on other non-affected States to act. To some extent this may now be true. The international legal obligation to act, however, is more properly traced to the work of the International Law Commission (ILC) and their 2001 Articles on State Responsibility.

Article 41, paragraph 2 of the ILC's 2001 Draft Articles on the Responsibility of States for Internationally Wrongful Acts (DARSIWA) prohibits States from rendering aid or assistance in maintaining situations created by a serious breach of a peremptory norm of international law.[59] Article 40(2) defines a serious breach as one that 'involves a gross or systematic failure by the responsible State to fulfill the

[57] For more detail see Andrew Clapham, 'Responsibility to Protect: "Some Sort of Commitment"', in Vincent Chetail (ed.), *Conflits, sécurité et cooperation/ Conflicts, security and cooperation: Liber Amicorum Victor—Yves Ghebali* (Brussels: Bruylant, 2007) 169–92.

[58] See Scott Sheeran and Catherine Kent, Chapter 2 in this volume.

[59] See Draft Articles on the Responsibility of States for Internationally Wrongful Acts (DARSIWA), in UNGA, 'Report of the International Law Commission' (2001) UN Doc A/56/10, 85.

obligations'. Although no list of peremptory norms has been established, the ILC's commentaries do provide the following indication: 'Those peremptory norms that are clearly accepted and recognised include the prohibitions of aggression, genocide, slavery, racial discrimination, crimes against humanity, torture, and the right to self-determination.'[60] Other examples included in commentaries are 'the slave trade ... and apartheid ... the prohibition against torture as defined in article 1 of the Convention against Torture and Other Cruel, Inhuman or Degrading Treatment or Punishment ... the basic rules of international humanitarian law applicable in armed conflict'.[61] This list is carefully described as exemplary rather than definitive. The UN Human Rights Committee has described as peremptory norms Articles 6 and 7 of the ICCPR (prohibitions on arbitrary deprivation of life and torture or cruel, inhuman or degrading treatment or punishment). The Committee also refers to further examples such as 'taking hostages, by imposing collective punishments, through arbitrary deprivations of liberty or by deviating from fundamental principles of fair trial, including the presumption of innocence.'[62]

We can conclude that, faced with serious breaches of these types of international human rights obligations, States, and the UN itself, will be under an international legal obligation to halt any assistance which might maintain the situation. This will be so irrespective of whether these human rights violations are seen in the political arena as reaching the level of atrocity which is covered by the notion of the responsibility to protect. There is no doubt that, when they do amount to the violations covered by the responsibility to protect, then there is a legal obligation (reflected in the DARSIWA) on all States and international organizations to 'cooperate to bring to an end through lawful means' any serious breach of a peremptory norm.[63]

The Human Rights Up Front initiative of the UN Secretariat is again a response to a tragic failure to protect people from widespread human rights violations. The UN's Internal Review into UN action in Sri Lanka in 2007–9 detailed the steps along the way where the UN chose to ignore, exclude, and override human rights concerns from its activity and policy in Sri Lanka. Raising human rights issues with the government was seen as threatening continued co-operation and jeopardizing humanitarian assistance. Even after there was no further prospect of delivering assistance, raising human rights was seen as controversial, confrontational, and counterproductive. This amounted to a failure to protect. In the words of the report:

> In fact, with its multiplicity of mandates and areas of expertise, the UN possessed the capabilities to simultaneously strive for humanitarian access while also robustly condemning the perpetrators of killings of civilians. It should have been able to push further for respect for

[60] Ibid., Commentary to Article 26, para. 5.

[61] Ibid., Commentary to Article 40, paras 3–5.

[62] Human Rights Committee, General Comment 29, States of Emergency (article 4) (2001) UN Doc CCPR/C/21/Rev.1/Add.11.

[63] See DARSIWA, n 59, art 41(1). With regard to breaches committed by an international organization, see the Draft articles on the responsibility of international organizations, in UNGA, 'Report of the International Law Commission' (2011) UN Doc A/66/10, Article 42(1).

international norms in the delivery of assistance to IDPs [internally displaced persons] and avoid accusations of complicity in the detention of IDPs.[64]

The UN Secretariat's resulting Human Rights Up Front initiative consists of six actions:

Action 1: Integrating human rights into the lifeblood of the UN so all staff understand their own and the Organization's human rights obligations.

Action 2: Providing Member States with candid information with respect to peoples at risk of, or subject to, serious violations of human rights or humanitarian law.

Action 3: Ensuring coherent strategies of action on the ground and leveraging the UN System's capacities to respond in a concerted manner.

Action 4: Clarifying and streamlining procedures at Headquarters to enhance communication with the field and facilitate early, coordinated action.

Action 5: Strengthening the UN's human rights capacity, particularly through better coordination of its human rights entities.

Action 6: Developing a common UN system for information management on serious violations of human rights and humanitarian law.[65]

It is worth highlighting two points. First, there is an explicit mention of the UN's own human rights obligations and that each individual staff member should consider themselves bound by human rights obligations. Second, the scope of human rights in this context is not limited to the atrocities which are central to the 'responsibility to protect' idea. Nor is it limited to the obligations binding on States due to their treaty commitments. The vision encompasses the whole range of human rights as reflected in the UDHR of 1948. The UN's summary of the initiative states: 'The success of *Rights Up Front* depends on leadership at every level—to show the courage to speak up for the values in the Charter and the Universal Declaration of Human Rights.'[66]

VII. Final Remarks

It has been a long struggle to have human rights taken seriously in peacekeeping operations. This is for multiple reasons: first, human rights complaints disrupt and sour the relationship between the UN and its Member States; second, because peacekeeping involves the deployment of military personnel, it is assumed that the relevant legal framework is the law of war; third, the advent of international criminal law means that allegations of human rights violations can be seen as the first

[64] 'Report of the Secretary-General's Internal Review Panel on United Nations Action in Sri Lanka', November 2012, para. 75.

[65] 'Rights Up Front' (May 2014) United Nations Secretary-General <www.un.org/sg/rightsupfront/doc/RuFAP-summary-General-Assembly.shtml>.

[66] Ibid.

steps towards individual prosecutions; and fourth, human rights are seen as selective politicized foreign policy tools mired in controversy and ideology.

The failure of the UN to protect civilians in situations such as Sri Lanka and the creation of new explicit mandates for the protection of civilians have forced a reflection on what it means for the UN to respect and protect human rights as part of a peacekeeping operation. This chapter has sought to show that human rights exist as a matter of law; that the laws of war apply to fighting wars, but outside that context, and even in emergency situations, the detailed standards for behaviour of those carrying out law enforcement and detention are found in the UN's own universal standards related to the use of force and covering all forms of detention; and lastly, that we are all obliged to prevent and work together lawfully to halt any violations of human rights wherever they may be occurring. All these conclusions apply whether the UN is specifically charged with protecting civilians or has some other mission; but the case for applying them becomes all the more important when the UN has set out to protect civilians. The credibility of any such operation will be dependent on respect for human rights.

7

Protection of Civilians under International Humanitarian Law

Jamie A Williamson[1]

I. Introduction

The year 2014 marked the 150th anniversary of the adoption of the 1864 Geneva Convention for the Amelioration of the Wounded in Armies in the Field,[2] the first in a series of international humanitarian law (IHL) treaties seeking to regulate and limit the conduct of warfare, with the most recent being the 2005 Additional Protocol III to the 1949 Geneva Conventions, which created an additional emblem to the Red Cross and Red Crescent.[3] Although the IHL treaties of the nineteenth century referred only marginally to civilians, the twentieth century, marked by the ever-changing nature of conflicts and its increasing toll on civilians, saw the protection of civilians take a more central role in IHL.[4] The adoption of the Fourth Geneva Convention of 1949, seventy-five years after the 1864 Convention, specifically addressed the protection of civilians in times of war. The path to the adoption of the 1949 Convention was not an easy one, but with it, through perseverance and diplomacy, the humanitarian ideal of ensuring the protection of civilians was finally enshrined in a legal instrument.[5]

[1] Jamie A Williamson is the Head of Unit of the International Committee of the Red Cross (ICRC) Unit on Relations with Arms Carriers and Security Forces. The views expressed in this paper are the author's alone and do not necessarily represent those of the ICRC.

[2] Convention for the Amelioration of the Condition of the Wounded in Armies in the Field, (adopted 22 August 1864, in force from 22 June 1865 to 16 August 1966) 11 LNTS 440.

[3] Protocol Additional to the Geneva Conventions of 12 August 1949, and relating to the Adoption of an Additional Distinctive Emblem (Protocol III) (adopted 8 December 2005, entered into force 14 January 2007) 45 ILM 558.

[4] As then President Max Huber stated, 'War, as it becomes more and more total, annuls the differences which formerly existed between armies and civilian populations in regard to exposure to injury and danger.' Statement of Max Huber, quoted in Jean S Pictet (ed), Oscar M Uhler, and Henri Coursier, with Frédéric Siordet, Claude Pilloud, Roger Boppe, René-Jean Wilhelm, and Jean-Pierre Schoenholzer, *The Geneva Conventions of 12 August 1949: Commentary: IV, Geneva Convention Relative to the Protection of Civilian Persons in Time of War* (translated by Ronald Griffin and CW Dumbleton) (Geneva: ICRC, 1958) 5 (ICRC Commentary to the Fourth Geneva Convention).

[5] Ibid., 3–9.

The initial IHL treaties mentioned civilians only in a cursory manner. In all ten articles of the 1864 Convention,[6] the protection of civilians was only specifically addressed once, in Article 5. The 1864 Convention primarily sought to provide protections to medical personnel and facilities, evacuation parties, and the wounded, in times of armed conflict. The distinctive Red Cross became the emblematic symbol of protection under which this activity was carried out. The reference to civilians in Article 5 was to protect those deemed to be 'inhabitants of the country who bring help to the wounded'. Because they were taking care of the wounded they were to be respected, allowed to remain free, and 'exempted from billeting and from a portion of such war contributions as may be levied'.[7] The modalities of implementation of the Convention were simply left to the 'Commanders-in-Chief of the belligerent armies following the instructions of their respective Governments and in accordance with the general principles set forth in [the] Convention'.[8]

Over time, States endeavoured to develop greater protections for civilians in armed conflicts. The 1899 Regulations concerning the Laws and Customs of War on Land, which were annexed to the 1899 Hague Convention with respect to the Laws and Customs of War on Land, introduced a number of provisions to protect civilians from attack.[9] They prohibited the attack or bombardment of towns, villages, habitations, or buildings that were not defended.[10] The Regulations required parties to an armed conflict to take the necessary steps to spare civilian objects such as hospitals, places of worship, and cultural property during attacks.[11] Similar obligations were articulated in the 1907 Hague Convention concerning the Bombardment by Naval Forces in Times of War.[12] Likewise, the 1907 Hague Convention on the Laws and Customs of War on Land provided for some protections to be accorded to civilians in occupied territories.[13]

[6] Convention for the Amelioration of the Condition of the Wounded in Armies in the Field, see n 2, which was agreed to by sixteen States during a diplomatic conference held in Switzerland on 22 August 1864. For more on the creation of the International Committee of the Red Cross and the 1864 diplomatic conference see François Bugnion, 'Birth of an Idea: The Founding of the International Committee of the Red Cross and of the International Red Cross and Red Crescent Movement: From Solferino to the Original Geneva Convention (1859–1864)' (2012) 94 IRRC 1299.

[7] Convention for the Amelioration of the Condition of the Wounded in Armies in the Field, see n 2, Article 5. Fifty-seven States became party to the 1864 Convention. The Convention was replaced by subsequent Geneva Conventions and stopped being applicable in 1966. See ICRC, 'Convention for the Amelioration of the Condition of the Wounded in Armies in the Field, 22 August 1864' (*Treaties and States Parties to such Treaties*, undated) <www.icrc.org/ihl/INTRO/120?OpenDocument>.

[8] See Convention for the Amelioration of the Condition of the Wounded in Armies in the Field, n 2, Article 8.

[9] Regulations respecting the Laws and Customs of War on Land, annexed to the Hague Convention (II) with Respect to the Laws and Customs of War on Land (adopted 29 July 1899, entered into force 4 September 1900) 32 Stat 1803, 1 Bevans 247, 26 Martens Nouveau Recueil (ser 2) 949, 187 Consol TS 429.

[10] Ibid., Article 25. [11] Ibid., Article 27.

[12] Convention (IX) concerning Bombardment by Naval Forces in Time of War (adopted 18 October 1907, entered into force 26 January 1910) 205 Consol TS 345, 3 Martens Nouveau Recueil (ser 3) 604.

[13] Regulations respecting the Laws and Customs of War on Land, annexed to Convention (IV) respecting the Laws and Customs of War on Land (adopted 18 October 1907, entered into force 26 January 1910) 205 Consol TS 277, 3 Martens Nouveau Recueil (ser 3) 461, Articles 42–56.

However, despite their progressive nature, these treaties were only patchwork attempts at filling the legal gaps in the protection of civilians in times of armed conflict. The efforts of the International Committee of the Red Cross (ICRC) to reinforce then existing international law to regulate the internment of civilians, a large-scale practice witnessed during the First World War (1914–18), met with no success at the 1929 Diplomatic Conference.[14] States found the timing inappropriate, many considering that initiatives of the sort could betray the cause of peace.[15] The ICRC persevered undeterred, and facilitated the preliminary approval of draft text at a 1934 International Red Cross Conference.[16] Unfortunately, with the outbreak of the Second World War, the diplomatic conference scheduled by the Swiss Government in 1939 to consider the text was not convened. It took another ten years for States to adopt the Fourth Geneva Convention on the Protection of Civilians in Time of War.[17]

In many ways, the 1949 Fourth Geneva Convention was borne out of the death and suffering deliberately inflicted upon civilians during the Second World War. This carnage drove the international community to question the validity, both morally and as a military strategy, of waging an unrestricted 'total war'.[18] It also led to the recognition that steps had to be taken to minimize the harm caused to civilians during hostilities, and highlighted anew the worrying gaps in IHL concerning the protection of civilians.[19]

The 1949 Fourth Geneva Convention thus represents an incredible feat of drafting and political consensus, with its 159 articles and three annexes. A total of seventeen States signed the final text of the Convention on 12 August 1949, at the end of the Diplomatic Conference of Geneva, which had lasted the best part of four months.

To date, 196 States have become party to the Fourth Geneva Convention, which, supplemented by the Additional Protocols I and II of 1977, represents the IHL linchpin for the protection of civilians in international, as well as non-international, armed conflicts. Moreover, the near universal ratification of the Convention reflects the commitment of the international community to the idea that even war has its limits, and that the suffering of civilians must be kept to a minimum during hostilities.

[14] The Diplomatic Conference of 1929 was convened by the Swiss Federal Council for the purpose of revising the Geneva Convention of 1906 and adopting a new convention in relation to the treatment of prisoners of war. The Conference, at which forty-seven governments were represented, lasted from 1 to 27 July 1929. The Final Act has no force of law. See ICRC, 'Final Act of the Diplomatic Conference. Geneva, 27 July 1929' (*Treaties and parties to such treaties*, undated) <www.icrc.org/ihl/INTRO/295?OpenDocument>.

[15] See ICRC Commentary to the Fourth Geneva Convention, n 4, 4.

[16] Ibid.

[17] Geneva Convention relative to the Protection of Civilian Persons in Time of War (adopted 12 August 1949, entered into force 21 October 1950) 75 UNTS 287 (Fourth Geneva Convention).

[18] Total war is broadly defined as 'military conflict in which the contenders are willing to make any sacrifice in lives and other resources to obtain a complete victory, as distinguished from limited war'. See 'Total War', *Encyclopedia Britannica* (Online, undated) <www.britannica.com/EBchecked/topic/600428/total-war>, and specifically Carl von Clausewitz, *On War* (translated by Michael Eliot Howard and Peter Paret) (Princeton, USA: Princeton University Press, 1989, original 1832).

[19] For further reading see Laurie Blank and Gregory Noone, *International Law and Armed Conflict: Fundamental Principles and Contemporary Challenges in the Law of War* (New York: Wolters Kluwer, 2013) 57–82.

Yet, more than sixty-five years after the adoption of the Fourth Geneva Convention, the number of civilian casualties remains alarmingly high in many armed conflicts, and too often belligerents seem to act with utter disregard for the protection of civilians, with many of the most egregious attacks against civilians committed by non-State actors.[20] As reflected in the various United Nations (UN) Secretary-General's reports on the protection of civilians, this trend has given rise to much concern within the international community.[21]

This chapter will consider the extent to which this worrying development can be apportioned to any conceptual limitations of IHL as a body of law to protect civilians, or whether it simply reflects the challenges posed by the complex dynamics of many contemporary armed conflicts. As the chapter will argue, improving compliance with IHL and the protection of civilians clearly requires more integrated efforts by the international community, not only to prevent harm from occurring, but also to address the root causes of today's humanitarian challenges.

II. The International Humanitarian Law Framework

The concept of 'protection of civilians', as used in the lexicon of IHL, carries a meaning distinct to that afforded to it in the realm of peacekeeping operations, and as understood within the thematic priorities of the UN Security Council, discussed in more detail in other chapters in this volume.[22] Under IHL, the protection of civilians essentially encompasses all those obligations seeking to minimize harm to civilians by limiting the means and methods of warfare of the parties to the conflict. In other words, restrictions are placed on the actions of the parties to limit the effect of hostilities. There are also a number of positive obligations, notably with regard to ensuring humanitarian access and delivery of humanitarian aid.

The Fourth Geneva Convention and relevant parts of the Additional Protocols offer a rich tapestry of nearly 200 articles, many of which have crystallized into customary international law. Together they provide a multilayered framework for the protection of civilians, in a very practical and nearly exhaustive manner.

The pragmatic nature of IHL is most evident in the fact that it seeks, at all times, to balance military necessity and humanitarian considerations.[23] While reconciling

[20] See, among many sources, Tara Cooper, Sebastian Merz, and Mila Shah, *A More Violent World? Globalized Trends in Organized Violence* (Berlin: Berghof Foundation, 2011) < http://www.berghof-foundation.org/de/publikationen/category/handbook-1/>; Kristine Eck and Lisa Hultman, 'One-Sided Violence against Civilians in War: Insights from New Fatality Data' (2007) 44 J of Peace Research 223.

[21] As reiterated by the UN Secretary-General: 'Nonetheless, further efforts to strengthen the protection of civilians remain crucial. While the last 10 years have seen peace come to some of the world's major conflicts, others have continued to smolder and burn and new ones have broken out. Common to old and new ones alike are persistent and sometimes appalling levels of human suffering owing to the fundamental failure of parties to conflict to fully respect and ensure respect for their obligations to protect civilians. Actions on the ground have not yet matched the progress in words and the development of international norms and standards': UN Security Council (UNSC), 'Report of the Secretary-General on the Protection of Civilians in Armed Conflict' (2009) UN Doc S/2009/277, para. 4.

[22] See also Haidi Willmot and Scott Sheeran, 'The Protection of Civilians Mandate in UN Peacekeeping Operations: Reconciling Protection Concepts and Practices' (2013) 95 IRRC 517.

[23] As stated in the Lieber Code, '[m]ilitary necessity, as understood by modern civilized nations, consists in the necessity of those measures which are indispensable for securing the ends of the war, and

these is difficult and sometimes appears impossible, with much being left to the discretion of the parties to the conflict, it is the very existence of this finely tuned balancing act that adds to its credibility among belligerents.[24]

Unfortunately, under IHL a certain level of harm to civilians can be deemed acceptable as long as the belligerents have, at a minimum, fully complied with the three key principles regulating the conduct of hostilities, namely 'distinction', 'proportionality', and 'precaution', before and during an attack.[25] While a civilian is not to be directly targeted, as long as an attack is not deemed indiscriminate, incidental harm to civilians ('collateral damage') is acceptable if it is not excessive in relation to the anticipated concrete and direct military advantage. Similarly, a building which appears to the general observer to be a civilian object may be a legitimate military target if it, by its 'nature, location, purpose or use makes an effective contribution to military action and whose total or partial destruction, capture or neutralization, *in the circumstances ruling at the time*, offers a definite military advantage'.[26] As such, even if commanders cause civilian casualties during an attack, they will not necessarily be liable for any wrongdoing under IHL if they can show that they took all feasible precautions in the planning and launching of the attack, and exercised constant care to spare the civilian population throughout the hostilities.[27]

Analogous issues, requiring subjective determination of the balance of military necessity and humanitarian considerations, can be found in other areas of IHL that touch upon the protection and well-being of civilians. For instance, although parties to the conflict must allow and facilitate the rapid and unimpeded passage of humanitarian relief for civilians, by invoking military necessity they can exercise a level of control and subject humanitarian passage to their consent.[28]

which are lawful according to the modern law and usages of war'. United States, 'General Orders No. 100, Adjutant General's Office, 1863' (Washington, DC: US Government Printing Office, 1898) <www.icrc.org/ihl/INTRO/110> (the Lieber Code), Article 14. As a more recent authority notes, '[t]he principle of humanity provides the foundation for both the prohibition against subjecting an opponent to superfluous injury (injury or suffering which goes beyond that which is necessary to bring about the opponent's prompt submission) and the obligation to treat humanely those who are no longer or never were participants in armed hostilities'. Geoffrey S Corn, Victor Hansen, M Christopher Jenks, Richard Jackson, Eric Talbot Jensen, and James A Shoettler, *The Law of Armed Conflict: An Operational Approach* (New York: Wolters Kluwer Law and Business, 2012) 118.

[24] By their very nature, the fundamental principles of precaution, distinction, and proportionality leave room for interpretation. IHL effectively places much of the responsibility on the commanders in theatre to ensure their faithful application, based on the circumstances prevailing at the time. See Jean-Marie Henckaerts, 'Study on Customary International Humanitarian Law: A Contribution to the Understanding and Respect for the Rule of Law in Armed Conflict' (2005) 87 IRRC 175, 198–200, Rules 6–24 (ICRC Customary Law Study). See also Jamie A Williamson, 'Humanity in War: Leading by Example; The Role of the Commander in Modern Warfare', in Carroll Connelly and Paolo Tripoli (eds), *Aspect of Leadership, Ethics, Law, and Spirituality* (Quantico, USA: Marine Corps University Press, 2012).

[25] See ICRC Customary Law Study, n 24, Rules 6–24.

[26] Protocol Additional to the Geneva Conventions of 12 August 1949, and relating the Protection of Victims of International Armed Conflicts (adopted 8 June 1977, entered into force 7 December 1978) 1125 UNTS 3, Article 52 (Additional Protocol I) (emphasis added).

[27] Ibid., Article 57; ICRC Customary Law Study, see n 24, Rule 15.

[28] Additional Protocol I, see n 26, Article 70; Protocol Additional to the Geneva Conventions of 12 August 1949, and relating the Protection of Victims of Non-International Armed Conflicts (adopted 8 June 1977, entered into force 7 December 1978) 1125 UNTS 609, Article 18 (Additional Protocol II); ICRC Customary Law Study, see n 24, Rule 55. It should be noted that these issues were extensively

Thus, while IHL provides a solid and extensive legal framework for protecting civilians in conflict, the protection it affords is inherently qualified, as IHL recognizes that civilian death in the course of armed conflict may be unavoidable: 'Mankind has sought to limit the effect of conflict on combatants and non-combatants and has come to regard war not as a state of anarchy justifying infliction of unlimited suffering, but as an unfortunate reality which must be regulated by *some* rule of law.'[29]

Mitigation of such harm requires IHL theory to be turned into practice, its abstract rules translated into operational reality and effective compliance. Training, dissemination, and integration of IHL into military doctrine are essential activities, without which the Geneva Conventions and their Protocols would remain empty shells. They are developed to ensure that if and when those bearing arms are involved in hostilities, it becomes a natural reflex to respect IHL, which has been ingrained into their mindset. In essence, the aim is to have IHL principles form part of the fighter's DNA, a sense acquired before deployment and engagement in hostilities. Once hostilities begin, both access to the fighting forces and the space provided for IHL training shrink as operational and in-theatre priorities take precedence. Processes must then be devised by the belligerents, with an onus on the commanders to lead by example, to ensure that relevant IHL norms are fully incorporated in the planning of any operation and integrated into rules of engagement, tactical directives, and codes of conduct, so that IHL is better respected during each engagement. In addition, mechanisms to allow for effective 'after action review' have proven valuable, in particular for operations that have resulted in civilians being wounded or killed.

III. Implementing International Humanitarian Law—Developing an Operational Dialogue

The ICRC, the custodian of IHL, has found that if the protection of civilians in conflict situations is to be improved, a dialogue has to be developed between it and the various arms carriers, be they regular armed forces or non-State armed groups. ICRC contact and interaction with the relevant actors is essential to enable access to civilians and others not taking part in the hostilities, and to remind the parties of their obligations under IHL.[30]

debated before the United Nations Security Council in 2014, in particular in this context of cross-border humanitarian assistance. See UNSC (2014) UN Doc S/PV.7216.

[29] Judge Advocate General's Legal Center and School, *Law of Armed Conflict Deskbook* (Charlottesville, USA: United States Army, 2013) 8. Emphasis added.

[30] Examples given by the ICRC at the Follow-up to the 28th International Conference of the Red Cross and Red Crescent include dialogue with the Israel Defence Forces in 2006 to gain better access to southern Lebanon, and dissemination sessions with the armed forces of Côte d'Ivoire and Democratic Republic of Congo during 2004–7. See ICRC, 'Follow-up to the 28th Conference of the Red Cross and Red Crescent' (Online, undated) <www.icrc.org/applic/p128e.nsf/va_IBP/56D4654FE7911101C12573360056B520?openDocument&section=IBP>.

At the time of the adoption of the 1949 Geneva Conventions, when armed conflicts were mainly international, the process of mapping the belligerents and understanding their motivations was a somewhat easier affair than in present-day armed conflicts, which are for the most part non-international phenomena.[31] Today, in addition to members of the regular armed forces, other arms carriers who might have an impact on the well-being of civilians include non-State armed groups, the police and security forces, international peacekeepers, personnel of private military contractors, and even mercenaries. Given the dynamics of many contemporary armed conflicts, with fluctuations in violence and a changing mix of actors with varying incentives, it can be arduous to make sense of complex and hostile situations. Nonetheless, identifying and engaging with all the arms carriers, from the outbreak of hostilities and as they unfold, is vital for effectively encouraging compliance with the law.

One of the priorities of the ICRC is to open channels of communication with operations staff (for instance the J-3 in NATO and the US Military) at the level of the command centres at headquarters and in theatre, in any conflict situation. Such a dialogue will also be initiated with the Force Commanders and Police Commissioners of UN peacekeeping operations, and, where relevant, with the Heads of Mission. Thus, at the beginning of any conflict, the ICRC takes steps to engage in dialogue with those involved in the conflict and, when appropriate, will submit a confidential memorandum to the respective command structures. In this memorandum, the ICRC will explain, based on the factual situation, whether it views the conflict as international or non-international in nature, and recall the applicable law.[32] In addition to reminding parties of the relevant legal framework and of their responsibilities, this confidential memorandum is an important step towards a continuous operational dialogue on all matters related to the conduct of hostilities, security and access, the provision of humanitarian assistance, detention visits, and evacuation. In relation to peacekeepers, at all times obligated to respect IHL, the specific legal framework governing their actions will very much depend on the nature of their mandate and whether in effect they become party to the conflict by virtue of their actions.[33]

Practice has shown that the very initiation of such a dialogue can in itself be a fraught exercise—especially in certain non-international armed conflicts, where

[31] See for example discussion in Halvard Buhag, Scott Gates, Håvard Hege, and Håvard Strand, 'Global Trends in Armed Conflict' (Oslo: Norwegian Ministry of Foreign Affairs, 2007) 3 <www.hbuhaug.com/wp-content/uploads/2014/02/Global-Trends_final.pdf>.

[32] In situations of international armed conflicts, the parties are therefore reminded, at a minimum, of their responsibilities under the relevant provisions of the four Geneva Conventions, and, if ratified by the concerned State, of Additional Protocol I as well. Where appropriate, customary IHL and international human rights are also cited. In non-international armed conflicts, Common Article 3 to the 1949 Geneva Conventions, Additional Protocol II (where applicable), customary law, and international human rights law are referenced.

[33] See Secretary-General's Bulletin, 'Observance by United Nations Forces of International Humanitarian Law' (January 13, 20161999) UN Doc ST/SGB/1999/13; Tristan Ferraro, 'The Applicability and Application of International Humanitarian Law to Multinational Forces' (2013) 95 IRRC 561; Scott Sheeran and Stephanie Case, 'The Intervention Brigade: Legal Issues for the UN in the Democratic Republic of Congo' (New York: International Peace Institute, 2014).

State authorities may be unwilling to recognize that they are involved in an armed conflict and that IHL applies, arguing instead that they are dealing with an internal security matter, such as countering terrorism, in a law enforcement paradigm, although involving military personnel. In such circumstances, the State authorities will seek to fall back on international human rights law and its derogations, as well as domestic law, to determine the legal framework governing the use of force and detention by its law enforcement agencies, which may include the military.[34]

While there may be testing moments in developing a substantive confidential dialogue with States, which can at times be a time-consuming process requiring tact, diplomacy, and patience, such dialogue should be easier than interacting with non-State actors. As a party to the 1949 Geneva Conventions, each State has committed to respect and ensure the respect of IHL, and, despite possible disagreement as to the interpretation or applicability of the law and facts on the ground, will expect to be contacted by the ICRC if they become involved in a conflict. Moreover, to the extent that the concerned State party has fulfilled its obligations to train its armed forces and integrate IHL into military doctrine, manuals, and rules of engagement, it should be familiar with the workings of IHL.[35] As such, prior to the start of hostilities, the military should already be familiar with the working modalities and role of the ICRC, as well as with the basic tenets of IHL. As a consequence, it should be more open to dialogue.[36]

By contrast, developing a similar discourse and encouraging a level of acceptance of IHL and the work of the ICRC with non-State armed groups can be more problematic. As parties to an armed conflict, non-State actors, like the regular armed forces of States, are bound to respect IHL.[37] However, unlike State actors who

[34] It should be recalled that concepts of proportionality and necessity in law enforcement paradigms have a different meaning to the same terms when used in armed conflict situations where IHL is applicable. See ICRC, *To Serve and to Protect: Human Rights and Humanitarian Law for Police and Security Forces* (Geneva: ICRC, 2014); ICRC, *Handbook on International Rules Governing Military Operations* (Geneva: ICRC, 2014). On the interplay between IHL and human rights law, see ICRC, '31st International Conference of the Red Cross and Red Crescent: International Humanitarian Law and the Challenges of contemporary armed conflicts' Ref No 31IC/11/5.1.2 (Geneva: ICRC, 2011) <www.icrc.org/eng/resources/documents/report/31-international-conference-ihl-challenges-report-2011-10-31.htm>.

[35] See ICRC Customary Law Study, n 24, Rule 42, which stipulates that 'States and parties to the conflict must provide instruction in international humanitarian law to their armed forces'. This reflects articles 47, 48, 127, and 144 of the four Geneva Conventions, respectively, and article 83 of Additional Protocol I. See Geneva Convention for the Amelioration of the Condition of the Wounded and Sick in Armed Forces in the Field (adopted 12 August 1949, entered into force 21 October 1950) 75 UNTS 31, Article 47 (First Geneva Convention); Geneva Convention for the Amelioration of the Condition of Wounded, Sick and Shipwrecked Members of Armed Forces at Sea (adopted 12 August 1949, entered into force 21 October 1950) 75 UNTS 85, Article 48 (Second Geneva Convention); Geneva Convention relative to the Treatment of Prisoners of War (adopted 12 August 1949, entered into force 21 October 1950) 75 UNTS 135, Article 124 (Third Geneva Convention); Fourth Geneva Convention, see n 17, Article 144. The ICRC also provides IHL training to State armed forces globally; thus they would also be familiar with the work and mandate of the ICRC. For an overview of ICRC activities with armed forces see ICRC, *Dialogue with Weapon Bearers* (Online, undated) <www.icrc.org/en/what-we-do/building-respect-ihl/dialogue-weapon-bearers>.

[36] For more on how the ICRC works in the field see for instance Alain Aeschlimann, 'Protection of Detainees: ICRC Action behind Bars' (2005) 87 IRRC 83.

[37] The obligations laid out in Common Article 3 and Additional Protocol II as they relate to the protection of civilians, and as supplemented by the rules of customary international humanitarian law

should already be versed in the basics of IHL prior to going into combat, non-State actors may be wholly unaware of their obligations, and may have never been exposed to either the Geneva Conventions or the ICRC. In addition, the starting point for any dialogue with non-State actors cannot simply be a reference to the State's treaty obligations, especially in cases where they reject the legitimacy of State authorities and feel that they are not bound by international legal obligations to which the government has subscribed. The ICRC and other humanitarian actors can thus face significant challenges engaging with armed non-State actors, particularly those motivated by radical ideology or irrational beliefs.

To complicate matters further, in some contexts, States may be reluctant to allow humanitarian agencies, such as the ICRC, to interact with non-State armed groups operating on their territory, for fear that such interaction may strengthen the formal standing of the group. States often hold the concern that any form of discourse with non-State actors could bring the latter undue legitimacy. During the drafting of Common Article 3 to the 1949 Geneva Conventions, States expressed their fears that the extension of IHL to cases of internal armed conflicts would confer belligerent status, and consequently increased authority, upon the adverse party. As a result, the final text of Common Article 3 specifies that the application of its provisions 'shall not affect the legal status of the Parties to the armed conflict'. Had this clause not been included, Common Article 3 would not have been adopted.[38] More recently, the UN Secretary-General has reaffirmed that engagement with non-State actors 'does not constitute political recognition. This is vital, as concerns over the political recognition and "legitimacy" that engagement is perceived to confer have prevented some States from permitting such engagement'.[39]

Despite these challenges, given that most present-day armed conflicts are non-international and that non-State groups are responsible for much, although not all, of the harm caused to civilians, interacting with and influencing the behaviour of these groups remains imperative in order to encourage implementation of IHL and, through doing so, to alleviate the suffering of civilians trapped in conflicts. This requires mapping the myriad armed groups operating in various contexts, taking into account the historical, socio-political, and economic indices of the environment in which they operate and their varying and evolving motivations, diversity of structures, and levels of organization. Much effort is also devoted to acquiring the trust of the groups, at all times maintaining a truly impartial and neutral stance in

deemed to be applicable in non-international armed conflicts. See *Case concerning military and paramilitary activities in and against Nicaragua* (Nicaragua v United States of America) (Merits) [1986] ICJ Rep 14, para. 218; see also Daragh Murray, 'How International Humanitarian Law Treaties Bind Non-State Armed Groups' (2014) J of Conflict and Security L 101, 1–31; Marco Sassòli and Yuval Shany, 'Should the Obligations of States and Armed Groups under International Humanitarian Law Really Be Equal?' (2011) 92 IRRC 425.

[38] Jean S Pictet, with Frédéric Siordet, Claude Pilloud, Jean-Pierre Schoenholzer, René-Jean Wilhelm, and Oscar M Uhler, *The Geneva Conventions of 12 August 1949: Commentary: I, Geneva Convention for the Amelioration of the Condition of the Wounded and Sick in Armed Forces in the Field* (translated from the French) (Geneva: ICRC, 1952) 38–49 (ICRC Commentary to the First Geneva Convention).

[39] See UNSC, 'Report of the Secretary-General on the Protection of Civilians in Armed Conflict' (2012) UN Doc S/2012/376, para. 44.

interactions with their members, even where their motivations and *raison d'être* may appear abhorrent.[40] Failure to engage with non-State armed groups can only be detrimental to the protection of civilians and to compliance with IHL.

IV. Improving Compliance with International Humanitarian Law

The ICRC engaging with parties to a conflict is a crucial step in persuading them to respect IHL. It would be naïve, though, to suggest that this alone will succeed in guaranteeing no harm will come to the civilian population. Recourse to other measures, notably those undertaken by the UN Security Council, is clearly necessary to protect civilian populations.[41] There is undoubtedly an essential role for peacekeeping operations. Yet history has shown that unless properly equipped, trained, and operating under a clear and unambiguous mandate, even the best-intentioned peacekeepers may face an uphill struggle to guarantee the safety of civilians.[42] The recent trend of empowering peacekeeping operations with more forceful mandates, based on a more interventionist model, may be a step in the right direction. The use of force against insurgents can arguably create the space necessary for peacebuilding. But it is still too soon to conclude whether this is the best approach to countering the threat of harm to civilians.[43] That being said, even if not quantifiable, the IHL prevention and peacekeeping protection models have, without doubt, succeeded in lessening the effect of hostilities on civilians in many conflicts over the years. The question remains, then: given the fact that in contemporary armed conflicts civilian casualties are still relatively high, are there any other measures that could improve compliance with IHL and ultimately the protection of civilians?

[40] Ibid.

[41] For an overview of these developments, see Office for the Coordination of Humanitarian Affairs, *Security Council Norms and Practice on the Protection of Civilians in Armed Conflict: Analysis of Normative Developments in Security Council Resolutions 2009–2013* (New York: United Nations, 2014).

[42] See UN General Assembly (UNGA) and UNSC, 'Report of the Panel on United Nations Peace Operations' (2000) UN Doc A/55/305—S/2000/809, viii (Brahimi Report).

[43] See, for instance, UNSC, 'Report of the Secretary-General on the United Nations Organization Stabilization Mission in the Democratic Republic of the Congo' (2014) UN Doc S/2014/957, para. 30: 'The performance and effect of some MONUSCO contingents has drawn much criticism, especially from national interlocutors. MONUSCO's deployment is mainly static and passive. Neither the Force Intervention Brigade nor the framework brigades were found to operate at the optimum level. Many framework brigades were described as not having conducted patrols to the most vulnerable areas on several occasions, while limiting their patrolling activities to daylight hours only. There were reports of certain contingents being reluctant to engage militarily against armed groups despite orders from the MONUSCO leadership to do so.' Also, on 31 October 2014, in appointing a High-Level Independent Panel on Peace Operations, the UN Secretary-General recognized that '[t]he world is changing and UN peace operations must change with it if they are to remain an indispensable and effective tool in promoting international peace and security . . . We must take stock of evolving expectations and consider how the Organization can most effectively advance peace, assist countries caught in conflict and ensure that our peacekeeping operations and special political missions remain strong and effective in a changing global context.' See United Nations, 'Press Release: Secretary-General appoints High-Level Panel on Peace Operations' (31 October 2014) UN Doc SG/SM/16301-SG/A/1521-PKO/451.

Assuredly, there should be some form of criminal accountability for the perpetrators of mass atrocities. Unfortunately, effective war crimes trials at the domestic level have been few and far between, be it for legal, political, or other reasons.[44] The international community has sought to address some of the gaps resulting from deficiencies of domestic judicial mechanisms through the creation of the International Criminal Court and ad hoc UN tribunals, including the international criminal tribunals for the former Yugoslavia and Rwanda, and hybrid courts such as the Special Court for Sierra Leone and the Extraordinary Chambers in the Courts of Cambodia. However, with their limited jurisdiction and structural capacities, there is only so much that international and hybrid tribunals can achieve to close the impunity gap and deter future offenders.[45] International tribunals are only able to try a small number of those allegedly responsible for war crimes, crimes against humanity, or genocide, in relatively few contexts. The cases usually only concern those who bear the greatest responsibility for the crimes committed in the conflict—mostly leaders, or persons who have committed a high number of atrocities.[46] Recent setbacks in relation to alleged offenders in conflicts in Darfur and Kenya have also shown the limits of the current system of international justice in the face of political realities.[47] Given the substantial limitations, it is unrealistic to expect the current system to result in a vast improvement in the protection of civilians through the deterrent effect of international courts alone.

Understandably, the lack of truly effective mechanisms to compel the parties to armed conflicts to respect IHL and to protect civilians is today a grave concern for the international community. The creation of the High-Level Independent Panel on Peace Operations by the UN Secretary-General in October 2014 underscored the intent of the UN to try to improve the ability of peacekeeping operations to protect civilians in contemporary armed conflicts. Similarly, States party to the Geneva Conventions have agreed that improving compliance with IHL is a priority issue. Indeed, even though IHL provides a robust, wide-ranging, and detailed legal framework to facilitate the protection of civilians in armed conflicts, there is no

[44] See Joanne Foakes, 'Immunity for International Crimes? Developments in the Law on Prosecuting Heads of State in Foreign Courts' (London: Chatham House, 2011) <www.chathamhouse.org/sites/files/chathamhouse/public/Research/International%20Law/bp1111_foakes.pdf>; Eve La Haye, *War Crimes in Internal Armed Conflicts* (Cambridge: Cambridge University Press, 2008) 383. Note also statement of UN Secretary-General on the lack of domestic accountability: 'Fundamental to enhancing compliance is the need to enhance accountability for violations of international humanitarian and human rights law, both for parties to conflict and individual perpetrators. As noted in my previous report, in many conflicts it is to a large degree the absence of accountability, and, worse still, the lack in many instances of any expectation thereof, that allow violations to thrive.' UNSC, 'Report of the Secretary-General on the Protection of Civilians in Armed Conflict' (2010) UN Doc S/2010/579, para. 82.

[45] See Cécile Aptel, 'Prosecutorial Discretion at the ICC and Victims' Right to Remedy, Narrowing the Impunity Gap' (2012) 10 J of Intl Criminal Justice 1357.

[46] Lilian A Barria and Steven D Roper, 'How Effective are International Criminal Tribunals? An Analysis of the ICTY and ICTR' (2005) 9 Intl J of Human Rights 349; Robert Cryer, *Prosecuting International Crimes: Selectivity and the International Criminal Law Regime* (Cambridge: Cambridge University Press, 2005).

[47] 'First Kenya, Now Sudan', *The Economist* (London, 20 December 2014) <www.economist.com/news/middle-east-and-africa/21636780-international-criminal-court-takes-another-bad-knock-first-kenya-now-sudan>.

enforcement mechanism with the power to truly halt violations in conflicts. This is 'one of the main weaknesses of current international humanitarian law'.[48]

A review of the Geneva Conventions and their Protocols reveals that unlike many international human rights conventions, there is no provision for the creation of a strong monitoring body or complaints procedures, be it for States or individuals.[49] Attempts have been made to include within the Geneva Conventions and their Protocols varying forms of mechanisms to oversee, or at least assist with, IHL compliance. However, for a number of reasons, they have never been fully utilized. These include the system of Protecting Powers in international armed conflicts provided for in the Geneva Conventions,[50] whereby each State party to the conflict could designate, with the agreement of the other side, a neutral State to safeguard its humanitarian interests. Protecting Powers have rarely been called upon to act.[51] Similarly, Enquiry Procedures, applicable only in international armed conflicts and originally envisaged in Article 30 of the 1929 Geneva Convention for the Amelioration of the Condition of the Wounded and Sick in Armed Forces in the Field and included in the four Geneva Conventions of 1949, have never been fully initiated. As with the Protecting Powers mechanisms, the institution of an enquiry into alleged violations of IHL is at the request and upon the agreement of the interested States.[52]

The International Humanitarian Fact-Finding Commission established in Article 90 of Additional Protocol I, composed of fifteen members of high moral standing and acknowledged impartiality, is competent to enquire into any facts alleged to be grave breaches and other serious violations of the Geneva Conventions and Additional Protocol I. However, it can only act where a State has made a declaration to that effect in relation to another State party accepting the same obligation, or on an ad hoc basis, again subject to the consent of all the parties involved. The Commission can also offer its good offices to facilitate the restoration of an

[48] ICRC, '31st International Conference of the Red Cross and Red Crescent: Strengthening Legal Protection for Victims of Armed Conflicts' (Geneva: ICRC, 2011) 13.

[49] For instance, such as the monitoring bodies created by the Conventions on Torture and Child Rights. See UN Convention against Torture and Other Cruel, Inhuman or Degrading Treatment or Punishment (adopted 10 December 1984, entered into force 26 June 1987) 1465 UNTS 85, Articles 17–24, and its Optional Protocol (adopted 18 December 2002, entered into force 22 June 2006) 2375 UNTS 237; UN Convention on the Rights of the Child (adopted 20 November 1989, entered into force 2 September 1990) 1577 UNTS 3, Articles 43–5; Optional protocol to the Convention on the Rights of the Child on the involvement of children in armed conflict (adopted 20 May 2000, entered into force 12 February 2002) 2173 UNTS 222, Article 8.

[50] See First Geneva Convention, n 35, Article 8; Second Geneva Convention, n 35, Article 8; Third Geneva Convention, n 35, Article 8; Fourth Geneva Convention, n 17, Article 9.

[51] The last reported use of the Protecting Power occurred during the 1982 conflict between the United Kingdom and Argentina. See Claude Pilloud, Jean de Preux, Yves Sandoz, Bruno Zimmerman, Philippe Eberlin, Hans-Peter Gasser, Claude D Wenger, and Sylvie-S Junod, with the collaboration of Jean Pictet, *Commentary to the Additional Protocols of 8 June 1977 to the Geneva Conventions of 12 August 1949* (Geneva: ICRC/Martinus Nijhoff Publishers, 1987) 77 n 2; 'Working Group Meeting on Strengthening Compliance with IHL: Background Document' (Geneva, 2012) 4, <www.icrc.org/eng/assets/files/2013/2012-11-strenghtening-ihl-and-chairs-conclusions-meeting-states-november-2012.pdf>.

[52] See First Geneva Convention, n 35, Article 52; Second Geneva Convention, n 35, Article 53; Third Geneva Convention, n 35, Article 132; Fourth Geneva Convention, n 17, Article 149.

'attitude of respect' for the Conventions and Additional Protocol I.[53] Besides the demonstrated lack of institutional support by States for these mechanisms, their respective mandates are limited to acting in situations of international armed conflicts, effectively rendering them of questionable utility in the majority of today's conflicts, which are non-international.

Under Common Article 3 and Additional Protocol II, parties to the conflict are encouraged to 'bring into force, by special agreements, all or part' of the Conventions. While not compliance mechanisms per se, the fact that non-State armed groups decide to make 'Deeds of Commitment' or 'Declarations to respect the principles of International Humanitarian Law' is a positive step towards improving the protection of civilians, in that the non-State actors have voluntarily committed to respect fundamental IHL principles and may, as a result, also be more open to a constructive operational dialogue with the ICRC and other humanitarian actors. If their words of commitment to respect IHL are translated into practice, there is an increased chance of civilians being protected, and also of essential humanitarian assistance and aid being effectively distributed in the territories that the groups control.[54]

As a consequence of the palpable compliance gap within IHL, the 31st International Conference of the Red Cross and Red Crescent held in Geneva in 2011 invited the ICRC, in co-operation with States, to identify and propose a range of options and recommendations to 'enhance and ensure the effectiveness of mechanisms of compliance with international humanitarian law'.[55] While there are still many uncertainties regarding the creation and structure of a compliance mechanism, the outcomes of the numerous inter-State meetings and consultations hosted by the ICRC and the Swiss government since 2011 are indicative of the inherent complexity in defining a mechanism able to successfully enhance compliance with IHL.[56] Although the various proposals under consideration have given rise to divergent views on key issues, States have agreed that any compliance system must be

[53] In October 2015, the International Humanitarian Fact-Finding Commission was contacted by Médecins Sans Frontières (MSF) in relation to the airstrikes against the MSF hospital in Kunduz, Afghanistan, of 3 October 2015. On its own initiative, the IHFFC also proposed its services to the governments of the United States of America and Afghanistan through identical letters dated 7 October 2015. For more on the activities of the International Humanitarian Fact-Finding Commission see *International Humanitarian Fact-Finding Commission* <www.ihffc.org/index.asp?Language=EN& page=home>.

[54] See for instance Churchill Ewumbue-Monono, 'Respect for International Humanitarian Law by Armed Non-state Actors in Africa' (2006) 88 IRRC 864.

[55] Resolution 1 on Strengthening legal protection for victims of armed conflicts, adopted at the 31st International Conference of the Red Cross and Red Crescent, Geneva, Switzerland, 28 November–1 December 2011, 2 < www.icrc.org/eng/resources/documents/resolution/31-international-conference-resolution-1-2011.htm>.

[56] A number of proposals are being considered, including: (a) periodic reporting, to allow for self-assessment and exchanges among States on their practical experiences in IHL implementation, (b) thematic discussions on, inter alia, States' legal and policy positions on current and emerging IHL, (c) fact-finding, with a possible role for the International Humanitarian Fact Finding Commission, and (d) a Meeting of State Parties to allow for a regular dialogue amongst States on IHL. See 'Background Document, Fourth Meeting of States on Strengthening Compliance with International Humanitarian Law (IHL)' (ICRC, March 2015) and 'Concluding Report Strengthening Compliance with International Humanitarian Law' (ICRC, June 2015) <www.icrc.org/eng/what-we-do/other-activities/development-ihl/strengthening-legal-protection-compliance.htm>.

devoid of politicization, be State-driven and consensus-based, and not duplicate other compliance systems (such as the Universal Periodic Review or the Human Rights Special Procedures). Further debates on the way forward were tabled at the December 2015 32nd International Conference in Geneva.[57]

Periodic reports, thematic discussions, and fact-finding may all benefit the medium- to long-term compliance efforts and go some way to strengthening the protection of civilians. Arguably, though, the litmus test will be whether States can agree on a compliance mechanism that will have the actual ability and power to halt violations of IHL against the civilian population as and when they are occurring, or to act as an early warning mechanism to prevent violations from arising. It may be easier said than done, given the nature of many contemporary armed conflicts, involving numerous non-State armed groups that may not be part, formally or informally, of such an agreement.

V. The Challenge of Protecting Civilians in Modern Conflicts

From the adoption of the 1864 Convention until late in the twentieth century, conflicts were generally either inter-State or driven by the desires of non-State actors to overthrow and replace the sitting government or to annex territory. The parties to a conflict were identifiable, and a dialogue could generally be established. Moreover, determining when the 'active hostilities' had ceased, giving way to peace—as fragile as it may have been—was often less complex than today. The mechanisms for dealing with these conflicts evolved within, and without necessarily challenging, the Westphalian system.[58]

Today's conflicts, for the most part non-international, have lost the sense of predictability found in more 'conventional' warfare. Instead, there is increasing polarization and radicalization, with oftentimes morally disengaged fighters dehumanizing the victims, as illustrated, for instance, by the many reported atrocities being committed in Iraq by the Islamic State of Iraq and al-Sham (ISIS). The majority of today's more violent situations implicate non-State actors, whether fighting against other such organized armed groups or against State apparatus. The motivations of these actors are in many instances driven by radical ideology, often with religious and ethnic underpinnings.[59]

57 'Working Group Meeting on Strengthening Compliance with IHL: Background Document', see n 51, 24–5.

58 See for instance the World Bank, *World Development Report 2011: Conflict, Security, and Development* (Washington, DC: World Bank, 2011) 2: 'Global systems in the 20th century were designed to address interstate tensions and one-off episodes of civil war. War between nation-states and civil war have a given logic and sequence. The actors, sovereign states or clearly defined rebel movements, are known. If a dispute escalates and full-scale hostilities ensue, an eventual end to hostilities (either through victory and defeat or through a negotiated settlement) is followed by a short "post-conflict" phase leading back to peace. The global system is largely built around this paradigm of conflict, with clear roles for national and international actors.'

59 As the UN's Syria Commission of Inquiry noted in 2013: 'Despite efforts to limit the extremists' influence in opposition circles, the radicalization of anti-government fighters continued. Alongside a

In these modern conflicts, most non-State belligerents reject outright any system built around State authority and sovereignty. Many also operate transnationally, oblivious to limitations imposed by borders. Their aim is not to overthrow a government in order to simply replace it. Instead, it is in large part the desire to impose their ideology and values that drives their belligerency. The situations with Boko Haram in Nigeria,[60] ISIS in Iraq and Syria,[61] Séléka and the Christian militias in the Central African Republic,[62] and Al-Shabaab in Kenya and Somalia[63] are just some examples of an array of non-international conflicts and violent situations increasingly driven by radical ideology, fomented by extremism.[64]

One of the most evident consequences of the radicalization of these conflicts is the increased impact on civilians. In the case of all of the situations referred to, there are countless public reports of vicious attacks against civilians.[65] In many cases, the 'enemy' is no longer considered just the other armed party to the conflict, but all individuals, including civilians, who do not share certain beliefs or traditions, by virtue of their membership of different ethnic, tribal, or religious groups. As noted by a number of UN commissions of inquiry, this is a very dangerous development, and is one of the greatest challenges to ensuring the protection of civilians.[66] In these conflicts, civilian deaths may not simply be a matter of collateral damage or

growing number of foreign fighters, the discipline and operational abilities of radical fighters, combined with better access to reliable sponsors, allowed them to outmatch the fractious moderate groups. The most radical, such as Jabhat Al-Nusra and the Islamic State of Iraq and Al-Sham (ISIS), developed their own strongholds in the north. ISIS subsumed the Islamic State of Iraq, a group which, with Al-Nusra, is on the sanctions list maintained by the Security Council Committee pursuant to resolution 1267 (1999).' UNGA, 'Report of the Independent International Commission of Inquiry on the Syrian Arab Republic' (2013) UN Doc A/HRC/24/46, para. 33.

60 For discussion, see Jacob Zenn, 'Northern Nigeria's Boko Haram: The Prize in Al-Qaeda's Africa Strategy' (Washington, DC: Jamestown Foundation, 2012).

61 For discussion see Tom Landsford (ed.), *Political Handbook of the World 2014* (Los Angeles, USA: CQ Press, 2014) 678–9.

62 For more information, see Human Rights Watch, *'They Came to Kill': Escalating Atrocities in the Central African Republic* (New York: Human Rights Watch, 2013).

63 For discussion, see StigJarle Hansen, *Al-Shabaab in Somalia: The History and Ideology of a Militant Islamist Group, 2005–2012* (Oxford: Oxford University Press, 2013).

64 Ibid., 57–8.

65 See, for instance, Stuart-Casey Maslin, *The War Report: Armed Conflict in 2013* (Oxford: Oxford University Press, 2013) 173–8 (on Boko Haram), 188–90 (on Somalia); Landsford, see n 61, 678–9; Human Rights Watch, see n 62; Hansen, see n 63.

66 See for instance UN Human Rights Council, 'Oral Update of the Independent International Commission of Inquiry on the Syrian Arab Republic' (2014) UN Doc A/HRC/26/CRP.2, para. 65: 'The most dangerous aspect of these developments has been the rise of the sectarian threat, a direct consequence of the dominance of extremist groups like ISIS. Growing numbers of radical fighters are targeting not only Sunni communities under their control but also minority communities including the Shia, Alawites, Christians, Armenians, Druze and Kurds.' See also UNSC, 'Report of the Secretary-General on the Central African Republic Submitted Pursuant to Paragraph 48 of Security Council Resolution 2127 (2013)' (2014) UN Doc S/2014/142, para. 3: 'The attacks by anti-balaka elements against ex-Séléka forces on 5 December in Bangui and Bossangoa, which involved heavy weapons, led to a reversal in the conflict dynamic and a significant deterioration in the security situation and sparked a cycle of reprisals among civilians and clashes between anti-balaka and ex-Séléka forces throughout the country. These developments have led to a grave deterioration in the human rights situation, resulting in a serious protection crisis, with civilians being targeted by all armed groups and by civilians on the basis of their religious affiliation.' Moreover, the negative impact on the civilian population does not end with the hostilities, but can lead to major internal and cross-border displacement. The United Nations High Commission for Refugees (UNHCR) noted that in 2013 alone there were '2.2 million

even the result of military strategy, but rather may become the fundamental objective of armed actors. Engaging with these groups, let alone having them sign deeds of commitment or encouraging them to issue unilateral declarations to respect IHL, is challenging.

Indeed, where extremism permeates the motivations and actions of non-State armed groups, resulting in a denial of universal human dignity and rejection of State sovereignty, persuading the offending armed groups to comply with IHL seems to be an insurmountable challenge. Yet, without rising to it, civilians will continue to bear the brunt of the suffering. It is therefore essential, as advocated by the UN and humanitarian actors, such as the ICRC and Geneva Call,[67] to continue working in a comprehensive manner to better understand the motivations, incentives, and networks of these more radical armed groups, and to devise effective approaches to influence their behaviour.[68]

VI. Conclusion

International humanitarian law has proven to be a practical, durable, and adaptable framework to provide passive protection to civilians in the midst of conflict, placing limits on the actions of the parties involved. Understandably, in recent times there has been some questioning of the relevance of 'Geneva law', viewed by some as ill suited and insufficiently refined to address today's conflicts.[69] Certainly, some of the law may still require clarification. It is also apparent that there is a need to establish an enforceable compliance mechanism, to effectively prevent IHL violations.

Contemporary conflicts are giving rise to an array of new humanitarian problems, which, arguably, cannot be addressed only by the restraints imposed by IHL. Improved peacekeeping and peace-making capabilities are needed if the protection of civilians is to become not an illusory goal, but rather a fundamental and credible concept driving the UN. A holistic and comprehensive approach must therefore be

Syrian refugees . . . and hundreds of thousands fled their country across Africa, from the Central African Republic, the Democratic Republic of the Congo, South Sudan, Sudan, and Mali': UNHCR, *Global Trends Report 2013: War's Human Cost* (Geneva: UNHCR 2014) 11. A natural consequence of mass population movement is the instability it causes to neighbouring countries, and, as underscored by the ICRC, continuing insecurity for many of those displaced: 'displacement and migration continued to have traumatic consequences for men, women and children. Millions of IDPs in the Central African Republic (hereafter CAR), Colombia, Somalia, Syria and elsewhere suffered multiple displacements, loss of property and livelihoods, physical and sexual abuse and other adversities.' See ICRC, *2013 Annual Report of the International Committee of the Red Cross* (Volume 1) (Geneva: ICRC, 2014) 90 <www.icrc.org/eng/assets/files/annual-report/icrc-annual-report-2013.pdf>.

67 Geneva Call is a neutral and impartial non-governmental organization dedicated to promoting respect by armed non-State actors for international humanitarian norms in armed conflict and other situations of violence, in particular those related to the protection of civilians. See Geneva Call <www.genevacall.org>.

68 See UNSC, 'Report of the Secretary-General on the Protection of Civilians in Armed Conflict' (2010) UN Doc S/2010/579, paras 52–7.

69 For discussion see Sandesh Sivakumaran, 'Re-envisaging the International Law of Internal Armed Conflict' (2011) 22 EJIL 1.

maintained if the level of harm befalling civilians in today's conflicts is to be curbed. Indeed, as the various UN thematic reports on the protection of civilians and related ICRC statements have highlighted over the years, the effective protection of civilians is a multifaceted endeavour with a variety of components. These include the strengthening of legal norms, improved training of armed actors, developing substantive operational dialogue with the parties to the conflict, and ending impunity. In addition, improving the plight of refugees and internally displaced persons, ensuring humanitarian access and the safety of humanitarian actors, and reducing the availability of illicit small arms and light weapons, must be fully factored into protection of civilians efforts.[70]

Finally, in light of the prevalence of non-international armed conflicts, it is imperative to find the means and mechanisms to develop a sense of ownership of IHL by all non-State actors, irrespective of their motivations and beliefs. To this end, a broader approach is required, identifying the trends that are giving rise to humanitarian concerns and tailoring integrated responses to the threats, so that all armed actors assume their responsibilities vis-à-vis the protection of civilians.

[70] See on this, 'Aide-Mémoire for the Consideration of Issues Pertaining to the Protection of Civilians in Armed Conflict', annexed to UNSC (2014) UN Doc S/PRST/2014/3.

8

Displacement and the Protection of Civilians under International Refugee Law

Erin Mooney

I. Introduction

The tragedy of civilians fleeing in search of safety has been a corollary of armed conflict since time immemorial. Currently, nearly 60 million people are displaced as a result of conflict, generalized violence, or persecution. The 59.5 million people displaced at the end of 2014 marks the highest global figure for such displacement since the Second World War.[1] In 2014 alone, conflict and violence forced a record-breaking 13.9 million individuals to flee their homes, an average of 42,250 persons a day, half of them chidren.[2] Of those forced to flee in 2014, 2.9 million persons found refuge in another country, marking the highest level of new refugees in a single year since 1994, when the Rwandan genocide and ongoing conflict in the former Yugoslavia, in particular, caused mass exoduses. However, both in 2014 and for more than two decades now, the vast majority of people forced to flee remain within their own country. The 11 million new 'internally displaced persons' (IDPs) in 2014 represented the highest ever annual figure on record for new internal displacement.[3]

Conflict and its concomitant dangers for civilians inevitably compel people to flee. One possible exception arises in siege warfare, which effectively prevents civilians from leaving their community in search of safety and assistance elsewhere. Generally, conflicts engender mass population displacement. Yet, displacement is not simply a side-effect of violence; in many cases, displacement is deliberate and a central aim, for instance, as part of a war strategy of ethnic cleansing.[4] Whatever

[1] United Nations High Commissioner for Refugees (UNHCR), *World at War: Global Trends 2014* (Geneva: UNHCR, 2015), 2 <www.unhcr.org/ 556725e69.html#_ga=1.19795000.1018826459.1408318260> These figures do not include the many millions more people displaced by other causes, including natural disasters and development projects.

[2] Ibid., 3.

[3] Internal Displacement Monitoring Centre (IDMC) and the Norwegian Refugee Council, 'Global Overview 2014: People Displaced Internally by Conflict and Violence' (Geneva, May 2014) <www.internal-displacement.org/publications/2015/global-overview-2015-people-internally-displaced-by-conflict-and-violence>.

[4] The term 'ethnic cleansing' entered the international lexicon during the wars in the former Yugoslavia in the early 1990s to describe the 'elimination by the ethnic group exercising control over a given territory of members of other ethnic groups. A wide variety of methods are used to accomplish this end, including . . . transfer or relocation of populations by force.' UN General Assembly (UNGA) and UN Security Council (UNSC), 'Report on the Situation of Human Rights in the Territory of the

its cause, displacement inherently exposes civilians to particular vulnerabilities and risks.

Whether and where displaced persons succeed in finding temporary refuge and safety is by no means assured. For those who seek and gain asylum in another country, protection comes in the form of international refugee law and the well-established international protection regime for refugees. As of end-2014, some 19.5 million persons in the world are legally recognized refugees; an additional 1.8 million persons are asylum-seekers pending decisions of their refugee status.[5] However, as noted above, this external, cross-border, dimension of displacement is only one part of the story. Nearly twice as many people— some 38.2 million persons as of end-2014—have been forced from their homes by violence but are still in their own country. These IDPs often remain caught in the midst of armed conflict, alongside other civilians, and typically continue to be at serious risk.

Epitomizing these global displacement trends is the ongoing conflict in Syria, which began in March 2011. Traditionally a country of asylum for refugees, the situation in Syria now represents the largest displacement crisis in the world. As of the November 2015, nearly 11.9 million people—amounting to half of the country's entire population—had been displaced by the conflict: 4.29 million as refugees to other countries and 7.6 million, as IDPs inside Syria.[6] Conflict in this one country has displaced more civilians than the First World War, and in less time.[7] New displacements are ongoing: on average, every minute in 2013, one family fled; this amounts to 9,500 people a day, at least half of them children.[8] Amid ongoing conflict and ever-shifting frontlines, most IDPs find themselves uprooted multiple times.

Inside Syria, some 4.5 million civilians in need of protection and assistance in Novmeber 2015, including many IDPs, are in areas classified by the United Nations as 'hard-to-reach' for humanitarian actors due to insecurity and obstructions to humanitarian access by parties to the conflict. Some 393,700 civilians are besieged, and thereby completely cut off from humanitarian assistance as well as unable to flee; this includes some 181,200 people besieged by government forces, 200,000 besieged by Islamic State in Syria and the Levant (ISIL), and

Former Yugoslavia' (1992) UN Doc A/47/666—S/24809, para. 9. Though the label was new, the phenomenon is not; indeed, it dates back to ancient times. See Andrew Bell-Fialkoff, *Ethnic Cleansing* (New York: St Martin's Griffin, 1999)); Norman M Naimark, *Fires of Hatred: Ethnic Cleansing in the Twentieth-Century* (Cambridge, USA: Harvard University Press, 2001); Alfred M de Zayas, *A Terrible Revenge: The Ethnic Cleansing of the East European Germans* (New York: Palgrave Macmillan, 2006); Ilan Pappe, *The Ethnic Cleansing of Palestine* (London: Oneworld, 2006).

[5] UNHCR, see n 1, 2.

[6] Syria Regional Refugee Response, <http://data.unhcr.org/syrianrefugees/regional.php>, figures as of 14 November 2015.

[7] The First World War displaced an estimated ten million civilians. Hugo Slim, Chapter 1 in this volume, citing Geoffrey Best, *War and Law Since 1945* (Oxford: Oxford University Press, 1994).

[8] IDMC, *Global Overview 2014: People Internally Displaced by Conflict and Violence* (Geneva: Norwegian Refugee Council, 2014) 10; Guillaume Charon, 'Blog Post: With One Family Displaced Every 60 Seconds in Syria, There's No More Time for Diplomatic Delay' (*IDMC*, 14 March 2014) <www.internal-displacement.org/blog/2014/with-1-family-displaced-every-60-seconds-in-syria-theres-no-more-time-for-diplomatic-delay>.

some 12,500 persons besieged by other non-state armed groups.[9] These besieged communities are out of the reach—often for years—of the United Nations (UN) and other international humanitarian actors due to insecurity or other impediments imposed by warring parties.[10] Meanwhile, neighbouring countries are making it increasingly difficult for civilians to flee Syria in search of protection and assistance elsewhere; deportations of asylum-seekers back into Syria are on the rise.[11]

Faced with these realities, what protection does international law offer civilians, whether in Syria or elsewhere, in situations of forced displacement? To answer this question, this chapter begins by situating the protection of displaced persons in the broader challenge of protecting civilians in conflict situations, including identifying the place that displacement occupies in the 'protection of civilians' agenda in the UN Security Council. The second section examines the protection that international law affords civilians who are at risk of, or who are actually experiencing, displacement in situations of armed conflict. This analysis focuses on three particular elements: (a) protection against the act of forced displacement; (b) protection when displacement does occur, examining separately the different legal contexts of cross-border and internal displacement; and (c) safe and sustainable solutions to displacement. The analysis not only considers existing legal standards in the abstract, but also endeavours, if only cursorily, to relate these norms to contemporary conflicts and actual situations of displacement. After all, whether and to what extent international law responds to the real-life protection concerns of refugees and IDPs is the only true measure of its adequacy to protect the millions of civilians forcibly uprooted by war.

II. Displacement and the Protection of Civilians

'The first casualty of war is not usually truth, as the proverb would have it, but space.'[12] So asserts Hugo Slim, who explains: 'one of the most persistent and profound effects of war on civilians is often a dramatic change in their normal patterns of space and movement.'[13] Displacement is among the most evident and devastating manifestations of this 'spatial suffering', constituting one of seven spheres of civilian suffering in armed conflict that he has delineated.[14] Moreover, displacement typically also exposes civilians to the six other spheres of suffering in

[9] United Nations, Statement of the Under-Secretary-General for Humanitarian Affairs and Emergency Relief Coordinator, Mr Stephen O'Brien, Statement to the UN Security Council on Syria, 16 November 2015.

[10] Ibid.

[11] See generally Norwegian Refugee Council and International Rescue Committee, *No Escape: Civilians in Syria Struggle to Find Safety Across Borders* (New York: Norwegian Refugee Council and International Rescue Committee, 2014) <www.rescue.org/sites/default/files/resource-file/No%20Escape%20Syria%20report%20IRC%20final%20Nov2014.pdf>; Human Rights Watch, *Not Welcome: Jordan's Treatment of Palestinians Escaping Syria* (New York: Human Rights Watch, 2014) <www.hrw.org/reports/2014/08/07/not-welcome-0>.

[12] Slim, Chapter 1 in this volume. [13] Ibid.

[14] Hugo Slim, *Killing Civilians: Method, Madness and Morality in War* (London: Hurst, 2007) 30–120, see especially 72–90.

Slim's typology, namely killing, rape, impoverishment, famine, disease, and distress. Although less immediately evident than physical abuse, the social and economic dislocation that displacement entails is particularly destructive. According to Slim, 'in poorer societies where people routinely live much closer to subsistence, people tend to suffer and die more often from a damaging spiral of movement and impoverishment than they do from shrapnel, bullet or blade'.[15] Analyses of the impact of conflict on civilians that measure merely the number of deaths simply do not capture this reality and can lead to a gross underestimation of civilian suffering in war.[16] Indeed, a survey conducted by the International Committee of the Red Cross (ICRC) across eight war zones around the world found that displacement is one of civilians' three greatest fears, along with losing a loved one and economic hardship. In some contexts, fear of becoming displaced even outranks the fear of physical injury and of sexual violence.[17]

Displacement inherently exposes affected civilians to a range of specific protection risks and vulnerabilities. Forced from their homes, compelled to abandon most of their belongings, cut off from their usual livelihood, and detached from their community, displaced persons suddenly find themselves stripped of their normal sources of security and habitual means of survival. In the chaos of flight, families often become separated, thereby disintegrating the most fundamental unit of protection, with especially serious consequences for children, older persons, and persons with disabilities. Compounding their plight, displaced persons are frequently stigmatized and viewed with suspicion, even hostility, in the very communities where they seek safety. Many remain at risk of ongoing acts of violence, including sexual and gender-based violence, and abuses including arbitrary arrest and forced military recruitment. Often, displaced persons live under constant threat of eviction and even of forcible return to places where their lives would be endangered. Moreover, these and other vulnerabilities associated with displacement are protracted. More than 80 per cent of refugee crises last for ten years or more; 40 per cent last twenty years or more. Situations of internal displacement, meanwhile, persist on average duration of displacement for twenty-three years.[18] The protracted nature of displacement, whether for refugees or IDPs, underscores both the necessity and the challenges of securing safe and sustainable solutions to displacement.

The plight of displaced persons remaining inside their own country—who constitute two-thirds of the world's displaced—is particularly precarious.[19] Often,

[15] Slim, Chapter 1 in this volume.

[16] Human Security Report Project, *Human Security Report 2013: The Decline in Global Violence: Evidence, Explanation, and Contestation* (Vancouver, Human Security Press, 2014) 37, 44–6; Human Security Report Project, *Human Security Report 2009/2010. The Causes of Peace and the Shrinking Costs of War* (New York: Oxford University Press, 2011) 105–9.

[17] International Committee of the Red Cross (ICRC) and Ipsos, *Our World: Views from the Democratic Republic of the Congo. Opinion Survey, 2009* (Geneva: Ipsos and ICRC, 2009) 16; ICRC and Ipsos, *Our World: Views from Afghanistan. Opinion Survey, 2009* (Geneva: Ipsos and ICRC, 2009) 17.

[18] Nicholas Crawford, John Cosgrave, Simone Haysom, and Nadine Walicki, *Protracted Displacement: Uncertain Paths to Self-Reliance in Exile* (Overseas Development Institute, September 2015), 12 <http://www.odi.org/sites/odi.org.uk/files/odi-assets/publications-opinion-files/9851.pdf>.

[19] See generally Erin Mooney, 'The Concept of Internal Displacement and the Case for Internally Displaced Persons as a Category of Concern' (2005) 24 Refugee Survey Q 9; Francis M Deng and

IDPs remain trapped in areas of armed conflict, with all of the attendant risks. Millions are out of reach of humanitarian assistance due to insecurity or other obstructions to humanitarian access. Of course, it is the government who bears the primary responsibility for protecting and assisting IDPs and all other persons under its territorial control. Yet, governments often lack the capacity and sometimes political will to fulfil this responsibility. Compounding the plight of IDPs, and in contrast to refugees, when their own government fails them, there is no established international regime to which IDPs can turn to ensure their protection and welfare. The consequences of this double standard can be dramatic, even deadly. IDPs have experienced some of the highest rates of mortality and malnutrition recorded in humanitarian emergencies, in large part because they were not provided key elements of humanitarian assistance routinely provided to refugees.[20] Whereas international responsibility for ensuring protection and assistance for refugees falls to the UN High Commissioner for Refugees (UNHCR) or, in the case of Palestinian refugees, to the UN Relief and Works Agency (UNRWA), IDPs, as UN Secretary-General Kofi Annan noted in 2005, 'often fall into the cracks between different humanitarian bodies'.[21]

That the situation of refugees and IDPs in armed conflict requires specific attention has been evident from the outset of the UN Security Council's consideration of the protection of civilians. In 1991, the Security Council recognized the link between civilian displacement and the maintenance of international peace and security in Resolution 688, which condemned attacks on Iraqi Kurds and was motivated in part by concerns over refugee flows into neighbouring countries.[22] Following a comprehensive review of UN support to displaced persons and returnees, in 1992 the UN Secretary-General appointed a Representative on Internally Displaced Persons,[23] with a broad mandate and reporting responsibilities both to the UN Commission on Human Rights (as of 2010, the Human Rights Council) and

Roberta Cohen, *Masses in Flight: The Global Crisis of Internal Displacement* (Washington, DC: Brookings Institution, 1998); Francis M Deng and Roberta Cohen, *The Forsaken People: Case Studies of the Internally Displaced* (Washington, DC: Brookings Institution, 1998).

[20] Peter Salama, Paul Spiegel, and Richard Brennan, 'No Less Vulnerable: The Internally Displaced in Humanitarian Emergencies' (2001) 357 The Lancet 1430, 1430–1. A major factor leading to these high mortality rates has been that IDPs often lack access to vaccination for entirely preventable diseases such as measles, whereas they note that '[m]ajor outbreaks of vaccine-preventable diseases such as measles have been uncommon in refugee camps since the late 1980s' owing to the high priority placed on vaccination campaigns in refugee camps. A study in 2003 by Médecins Sans Frontières (MSF) found IDPs in northern Uganda suffered mortality rights five to ten times higher than expected in Uganda, owing to the rate of violence as well as measles outbreaks due to lack of vaccination. N Nathan, M Tatay, P Piola, S Lake, and V Brown, 'High Mortality in Displaced Populations of Northern Uganda' (2004) 363 The Lancet 1402.

[21] UNGA, 'In Larger Freedom: Toward Development, Security and Human Rights for All, Report of the Secretary-General' (2005) UN Doc A/59/2005, para. 210.

[22] UNSC Res 688 (1991) UN Doc S/RES/688, para. 1; Gregor Schotten and Anke Biehler, 'The Role of the UN Security Council in Implementing International Humanitarian Law and Human Rights Law', in Roberta Arnold and Noëlle Quénivet, *International Humanitarian Law and Human Rights Law: Towards a New Merger in International Law* (Martinus Nijhoff, 2008) 317.

[23] This occurred following a request of the UN Commission on Human Rights. See UN Commission on Human Rights (CHR) Resolution (Res) 1991/25 (1991) UN Doc E/CN.4/RES/1991/25; CHR Res 1992/73 (1992) UN Doc E/CN.4/RES/1992/73.

to the UN General Assembly.[24] In 1993, the Security Council expressed concern regarding 'the incidence of humanitarian crises, including mass displacement of population, becoming or aggravating threats to international peace and security'.[25] The Council proceeded to recognize the plight of refugees and IDPs as a threat to international peace and security in numerous contexts throughout the decade, including in northern Iraq, the former Yugoslavia, Rwanda, and Somalia.

In 1997, in what may be considered the precursor to the protection of civilians eventually becoming a standing Council agenda item,[26] the UN Security Council held a thematic debate on 'protection for humanitarian assistance to refugees and others in conflict situations'. Recognizing that 'massive displacement of civilian populations in conflict situations may pose a serious challenge to international peace and security', the Council expressed 'grave concern at the recent increase in attacks or use of force in conflict situations against refugees and other civilians, in violation of the relevant rules of international law', condemned such acts, called for strict compliance with the relevant laws, and called upon all parties to conflicts 'to ensure the safety of refugees, displaced persons and other civilians, and guarantee the unimpeded and safe access of United Nations and other personnel to those in need'.[27] The following year, after considering two Secretary-General's reports on the issue,[28] the Council restated that the provision of security to refugees 'can contribute to the maintenance of international peace and security'[29] and recognized a particular lack of protection for IDPs in Africa.[30] These various initiatives drawing attention to the specific protection concerns of refugees and IDPs and to the implications of displacement for international peace and security suggest that the issue of displaced persons was an influential factor in protection of civilians concerns featuring in the UN Security Council's agenda from the outset.[31]

On 12 February 1999, the Security Council, under the presidency of Canada, held its first thematic debate devoted to the protection of civilians. Refugees and internally displaced persons were cited as specific groups of concern.[32] The Secretary-General's first report on the protection of civilians also gave significant

[24] CHR Res 1992/73 (1992) UN Doc E/CN.4/RES/1992/73.

[25] UNSC (1993) UN Doc S/25344.

[26] Bryan Deschamp, *Victims of Violence: A Review of the Protection of Civilians Concept and its Relevance to UNHCR's Mandate* (Geneva: UNHCR, 2010) para. 26; Security Council Report, 'Cross-Cutting Report No 2: Protection of Civilians' (New York: Security Council Report, 2008) 6.

[27] UNSC (1997) UN Doc S/PRST/1997/34.

[28] UNSC, 'Report of the Secretary-General on the Protection for Humanitarian Assistance to Refugees and Others in Conflict Situations' (1998) UN Doc S/1998/883; UNGA and UNSC, 'Causes of Conflict and the Promotion of Durable Peace and Sustainable Development in Africa, Report of the Secretary-General' (1998) UN Doc A/52/871—S/1998/318.

[29] UNSC Res 1208 (1998) UN Doc S/RES/1208, preambular para. 3.

[30] UNSC Statement by the President (2000) UN Doc S/PRST/2000/1.

[31] See, for example, UNSC Res 688 (1991) UN Doc S/RES/688, which was the first time that the Security Council recognized a threat to international peace and security on the grounds of human suffering—in this case, of displaced Kurds.

[32] UNSC Statement of the President (1996) UN Doc S/PRST/1999/6. For an insider's account of the outcome, including regarding issues of displacement, see Elissa Golberg and Don Hubert, 'The Security Council and the Protection of Civilians', in Rob McRae and Don Hubert (eds), *Human Security and the New Diplomacy: Protecting People, Promoting Peace* (Montreal: McGill-Queen's University Press, 2001) 226.

attention to forced displacement, highlighting the importance of adherence to international humanitarian, refugee, and human rights law, as well as the Guiding Principles on Internal Displacement.[33] In response to the report, the Council specifically requested the Secretary-General to bring to its attention situations where refugees and IDPs' vulnerability may constitute a threat to international peace and security,[34] and also requested an aide-memoire providing guidance on measures to protect civilians.[35] The resulting Aide-Memoire on the Protection of Civilians in Armed Conflict, which continues to be regularly updated, is 'a practical tool that provides the basis for improved analysis and diagnosis of key protection issues',[36] in which issues of displacement feature prominently.[37]

In May 2014, the Security Council held its first meeting devoted to discussing the protection of IDPs and its own role in this regard.[38] Although informal, the meeting sought to identify ways to address the protection of IDPs more consistently and effectively through the Security Council's work.[39] At the meeting, the UN Special Rapporteur on the Human Rights of Internally Displaced Persons[40] commended the Council's integration of protection measures for IDPs and refugees in its resolution, adopted just days before, bolstering the protection of civilians mandate and capacity of the UN Mission in South Sudan (UNMISS).[41]

As South Sudan rapidly descended into civil war in December 2013, tens of thousands of civilians, the majority of whom were targeted because of their ethnicity or political affiliation, sought refuge with the UN mission, which established 'protection of civilians sites' within their bases. Security Council Resolution 2155 authorized UNMISS to protect civilians, 'with particular attention to displaced

[33] UNSC, 'Report of the Secretary-General on the Protection of Civilians in Armed Conflict' (1999) UN Doc S/1999/957, paras 11–15, 18, 24, 35, 36, 39, 57, 61, 63, 64, 71.

[34] UNSC Resolution (Res) 1296 (2000) UN Doc S/RES/1296, para. 14.

[35] UNSC, 'Letter dated 21 June 2001 from the President of the Security Council addressed to the Secretary-General' (2001) UN Doc S/2001/614.

[36] UNSC Statement of the President (2014) UN Doc S/PRST/2014/3. For all of the issues covered in the Aide-Memoire, an addendum provides the Council with suggested language, mostly based on previous Council resolutions, to utilize in future Council resolutions so as to more systematically and effectively address key issues in the protection of civilians, including displacement.

[37] See Aide-Memoire on the Protection of Civilians in Armed Conflict, annexed to UNSC (2014) UN Doc S/PRST/2014/3, § B, F, addendum.

[38] The meeting was convened in 'Arria-formula', meaning an informal and confidential exchange of views among Council members and invited experts from international organizations and non-governmental organizations (NGOs), for which no official meeting report is published. See UNSC, 'Background Note on the "Arria-Formula" Meetings of the Security Council Members' in UNSC, *Working Methods Handbook* (New York: United Nations, 2011) <www.un.org/en/sc/about/methods/bgarriaformula.shtml>.

[39] 'Security Council Meeting in Arria Formula on Protection of Internally Displaced Persons: Challenges and the Role of the Security Council' <www.ohchr.org/Documents/HRBodies/SP/ArriaFormula_SC_on_protection_of_IDPs.pdf>.

[40] In 2010, the UN Human Rights Council reformulated the long-standing mandate, since 1992, of a Representative of the Secretary-General on the Human Rights of Internally Displaced Persons to be a Special Rapporteur on the Human Rights of Internally Displaced Persons. UN Human Rights Council (HRC) Res 14/6 (2010) UN Doc A/HRC/14/6.

[41] 'Security Council Meeting in Arria Formula on Protection of Internally Displaced Persons: Challenges and the Role of the Security Council' (No attribution, undated) <www.ohchr.org/Documents/HRBodies/SP/ArriaFormula_SC_on_protection_of_IDPs.pdf>.

civilians, including those in protection sites and refugee camps'; 'to monitor, investigate, verify, and report publicly and regularly on abuses and violations of human rights and violations of international humanitarian law'; to contribute to the creation of the conditions for the 'full, safe and unhindered access of relief personnel to all those in need in South Sudan and timely delivery of humanitarian assistance, in particular to internally displaced persons and refugees'; and 'to foster a secure environment for the eventual safe and voluntary return of IDPs and refugees'.

The UNMISS mandate is only the most prominent example of recent Security Council action to address threats to displaced persons.[42] Issues of displacement have featured in numerous peacekeeping mandates, including regarding physical protection for IDP camps by the African Union–United Nations Hybrid Operation in Darfur (UNAMID)[43] and the provision of a secure environment to enable the durable return of displaced persons in a contested area of Sudan by the UN Interim Security Force for Abyei (UNISFA).[44] The Council also emphasized displacement due to ethnic and religious violence as a key factor of instability in the Central African Republic, where refugees and displaced persons were cited as specific groups to be protected from physical violence by the UN mission (MINUSCA).[45]

Concerns regarding displacement have consistently been a part of and, to a certain extent, also have influenced broader consideration of the protection of civilians in armed conflict. The UN Security Council has recognized the particular vulnerabilities of displaced persons in times of conflict, and that such displacement may constitute a threat to international peace and security. Increasingly, refugees and IDPs constitute a focus of this broader protection agenda.

III. The International Legal Framework

In thematic resolutions on the protection of civilians and in country-specific resolutions, the UN Security Council regularly reaffirms the obligation of all parties involved in an armed conflict to comply with international humanitarian law as well as with the rules and principles of international human rights law and refugee

[42] For example, regarding the UN Mission in the Central African Republic and Chad, see UNSC Res 1861 (2009) UN Doc S/RES/1861, para. 7(a)(i); regarding the UN Stabilization Mission in the Democratic Republic of the Congo, see UNSC Res 2098 (2014) S/RES/2098, paras 12(a), 13, and UNSC Res 2053 (2012) UN Doc S/RES/2053, para. 20; regarding the UN Mission in Liberia, see UNSC Res 2116 (2013) UN Doc S/RES/2116, para. 13. This is in addition to Council mandates to co-ordinate with humanitarians to create an environment conducive to return and to facilitate return movements.

[43] UNSC Res 2113 (2013) UN Doc S/RES/2113, para. 4(a); and see UNSC Res 1769 (2007) UN Doc S/RES/1769, para. 1, referencing UNSC, 'Report of the Secretary-General and the Chairperson of the African Union Commission on the Hybrid Operation in Darfur' (2007) UN Doc S/2007/307/Rev.1, para. 55(b)(1).

[44] UNSC Res 1990 (2011) UN Doc S/RES/1990, preambular paras 9, 12, and operational paras 3(d), 3(e) (recognizing that nearly all civilians in the Abyei area after May 2011 were returning displaced persons or seasonal migrants).

[45] UNSC Res 2149 (2014) UN Doc S/RES/2149, preambular para. 16, operational paras 28(a), 45.

law.[46] In some cases it 'demands' that parties comply strictly with their obligations under those bodies of law.[47] Collectively, the three bodies of law offer civilians extensive protection in situations of displacement. Indeed, the breadth and depth of the international legal framework that can be mobilized for protection in situations of displacement during times of war is such that a compilation and analysis of all of the norms goes beyond the scope of this chapter, but can be found elsewhere.[48] The following analysis covers three key dimensions: (a) the act of displacement; (b) protection of displaced persons, separately examining protection for refugees and IDPs; and (c) solutions to displacement.

A. The act of displacement

Despite much evidence to the contrary, it is not a foregone conclusion that the occurrence of armed conflict in itself compels people to flee. International humanitarian law, in particular its core principle of distinction between civilian and military targets, provides a framework for avoiding this outcome. In the words of one ICRC official:

> [D]uring armed conflict, the civilian population is entitled to an immunity intended to shield it as much as possible from the effects of war. Even in time of war, civilians should be able to lead as normal a life as possible. In particular, they should be able to remain in their homes; this is a basic objective of international humanitarian law.[49]

Indeed, at the January 2014 Security Council open debate on the protection of civilians, the ICRC stated: 'One of the most widespread and daunting humanitarian problems arising from violations of [international humanitarian law]—at least in terms of numbers—is that of internal displacement.'[50] The ICRC routinely emphasizes that respect for international humanitarian law (particularly the provisions prohibiting attacks on civilians and civilian property, indiscriminate attacks, starving civilians as a method of warfare, destroying objects indispensable to their survival, and carrying out reprisals against civilians and civilian property) would prevent most forced displacement.[51] In addition, international human rights law

[46] See, for example, UNSC Res 1894 (2009) UN Doc S/RES/1894, para. 1; UNSC Res 2175 (2014) UN Doc S/RES/2175, para. 1; UNSC Res 2165 (2014) UN Doc S/RES/1265, para. 1, 8; UNSC Res 2155 (2014) UN Doc S/RES/2155, paras 17–18.

[47] See, for example, UNSC Statement of the President (2014) UN Doc S/PRST/2014/3.

[48] See, in particular, Mélanie Jacques, *Armed Conflict and Displacement: The Protection of Refugees and Displaced Persons under International Humanitarian Law* (Cambridge: Cambridge University Press, 2012); Walter Kälin, *Guiding Principles on Internal Displacement: Annotations* (Washington, DC: American Society of International Law and the Brookings Institution, 2008); Guy S Goodwin-Gill, *The Refugee in International Law* (Oxford: Oxford University Press, 1996); James C Hathaway, *The Law of Refugee Status* (London: Butterworths, 1991).

[49] Jean-Philippe Lavoyer, 'Refugees and Internally Displaced Persons: International Humanitarian Law and the Role of the ICRC' (1995) 35 IRRC 162, 170.

[50] Statement by Mr Yves Daccord, in UNSC (2014) UN Doc S/PV.7109, 9.

[51] See, for example, Jakob Kellenberger, 'The ICRC's Response to Internal Displacement: Strengths, Challenges and Constraints' (2009) 91 IRRC 475, 476 and 482; Lavoyer, see n 49, 170; Statement by Yves Daccord, see n 50, 8–9.

continues to apply, in large measure, during conflict.[52] Respect for the rights to life and physical integrity—to freedom of movement, choice of residence, and protection of property, for instance—would go a long way to obviating the need for many civilians to flee. Based on these two bodies of law, the UN Guiding Principles on Internal Displacement state: 'All authorities and international actors shall respect and ensure respect for their obligations under international law, including human rights and humanitarian law, in all circumstances, so as to prevent and avoid the conditions that might lead to displacement of persons.'[53]

Forcible displacement of civilians is generally prohibited under international humanitarian law. The prohibition of the deportation or transfer of civilians during times of war dates back to the Lieber Code of 1863, which was written and issued by the United States Army during the American Civil War. In Article 23 it prescribes that: 'Private citizens are no longer [to be] murdered, enslaved, *or carried off to distant parts*.'[54] Although binding only on armed forces of the United States, the Lieber Code is generally considered to have reflected international laws and customs of war at the time, and to represent the first codification of the laws of war. Further, it 'served as a model and source of inspiration' for the efforts subsequently taken at the international level to codify the law and customs of war, resulting in the adoption of the Hague Conventions on land warfare of 1899 and 1907.[55] It is therefore perhaps surprising that the Hague Conventions make no mention of a prohibition of deportation or transfer of civilians, as had been articulated in the Lieber Code.[56] Jean Pictet, however, argues that it was not an oversight, but rather that the drafters of the Hague Conventions deemed it unnecessary to restate the prohibition, as 'the practice of deporting persons was regarded at the beginning of [the twentieth century] as having fallen into abeyance'.[57]

The Second World War made tragically clear that mass deportations were not confined to the annals of history, and underscored the need for an explicit

[52] See, for example, GIAD Draper, 'The Relationship between the Human Rights Regime and the Laws of Armed Conflict' (1971) 1 Israel YB on Human Rights 205, 208; Louise Doswald-Beck and Sylvain Vite´, 'International Humanitarian Law and Human Rights Law,' (1993) 33 IRRC 94; René Provost, *International Human Rights and Humanitarian Law*, (Cambridge: Cambridge University Press, 2002); Hans-Joachim Heintze, 'On the Relationship between Human Rights Law Protection and International Humanitarian Law' (2004) 86 IRRC 789. See also Andrew Clapham, Chapter 6 in this volume.

[53] Guiding Principles on Internal Displacement, in CHR, 'Report of the Representative of the Secretary-General, Mr Francis M Deng, Submitted pursuant to Commission resolution 1997/39' (1998) UN Doc E/CN.4/1998/53/Add.2, addendum, Principle 5.

[54] United States, 'General Orders No. 100, Adjutant General's Office, 1863' (Washington: US Government Printing Office, 1898) <www.icrc.org/ihl/INTRO/110> (the Lieber Code). Emphasis added.

[55] Frits Kalshoven, *Constraints on the Waging of War* (Geneva: ICRC, 1991) 12.

[56] A persuasive argument has been put forth that implicit protection against the deportation of civilians nonetheless can be found in the provisions of the Hague Regulations relating to the responsibilities of an occupying power. See Jacques, n 48, 23, citing M Sherif Bassiouni, *Crimes against Humanity* (Cambridge: Cambridge University Press, 1999) 302; Henckaerts, 'Deportation and Transfer of Civilians' (1993–1994) 26 Vanderbilt J Transnatl L 469, 481; Alfred de Zayas, 'Mass Population Transfers' (1975) Harvard L J 207, 212.

[57] Jean S Pictet, *The Geneva Conventions of 12 August 1949: Commentary* (Volume IV) (Geneva: ICRC, 1958) 279.

prohibition of the practice. The Charter of the International Military Tribunal established at Nuremberg to prosecute major war crimes committed by the European Axis Powers pronounced that 'deportation to slave labour or for any other purpose of civilian population of or in occupied territory constitutes a war crime'.[58] Further, the Nuremberg Charter classified 'deportation and other inhumane acts committed against any civilian population before or during the war' as crimes against humanity.[59] Consistent with pre-existing standards and with the relevant, albeit implicit, provisions of the Hague Regulations, the Nuremberg Charter (and jurisprudence of the Tribunal as well as other case law relating to the Second World War) made clear that the deportation of civilians from occupied territories constituted a violation of customary international law.[60]

A general prohibition of forcible transfer or deportation of civilians from occupied territories in international armed conflict is set forth in Article 49 of the Fourth Geneva Convention of 1949.[61] An Occupying Power may undertake the total or partial evacuation of population from a given area only if it is necessary for the security of the population or imperative military reasons. Even then, a number of guarantees must be met by the Occupying Power in order for such evacuations to be lawful. These safeguards include ensuring 'satisfactory conditions of hygiene, health, safety and nutrition', 'proper accommodation', and that members of the same family are not separated. Moreover, '[p]ersons thus evacuated shall be transferred back to their homes as soon as hostilities in the area in question have ceased'. Further, the Occupying Power may 'not deport or transfer parts of its own civilian population into the territory it occupies'.[62] Unlawful deportation or transfer of populations in violation of Article 49 constitutes a breach of the Fourth Geneva Convention and its Additional Protocol I.[63] Under the Rome Statute of the International Criminal Court, deportation or transfer by the Occupying Power of all or parts of the population of the occupied territory, within or outside the occupied territory, constitutes an international war crime.[64] These international norms, as well as State practice, confirm the following as a rule of customary international law: 'Parties to an international armed conflict may not deport or forcibly transfer the

58 Agreement for the establishment of an International Military Tribunal for the prosecution and punishment of the major war criminals of the European Axis (8 August 1945) 82 UNTS 279, articles 6(b), 6(c).

59 Ibid.

60 Jacques, note 48, 23, citing Theodore Meron, 'Deportation of Civilians as a War Crime', in Donna Gomien (ed.), *Broadening the Frontiers of Human Rights: Essays in Honor of Asbjørn Eide* (Oslo: Scandavia University Press, 1993), and de Zayas, see n 56; Jean-Marie Henckaerts and Louise Doswald-Beck, *Customary International Humanitarian Law: Volume I: Rules* (Cambridge: Cambridge University Press, 2009) 458, n 8.

61 Geneva Convention relative to the Protection of Civilian Persons in Time of War (adopted 12 August 1949, entered into force 21 October 1950) 75 UNTS 287 (Fourth Geneva Convention).

62 Ibid., Article 49.

63 Ibid., Article 147; Protocol Additional to the Geneva Conventions of 12 August 1949, and Relating to the Protection of Victims of International Armed Conflicts (adopted 8 June 1977, entered into force 7 December 1978) 1125 UNTS 3, Article 85(4)(a) (Additional Protocol I).

64 Rome Statute of the International Criminal Court (adopted 17 July 1998, entered into force 1 July 2002) 2187 UNTS 90, Article 8(2)(b)(viii).

civilian population of an occupied territory, in whole or in part, unless the security of civilians involved or imperative military reasons so demand.'[65]

In non-international armed conflicts, the prohibition is broader as it is not limited to population transfers taking place on occupied territory. Entitled 'Prohibition of forced movement of civilians', Article 17, paragraph 1 of Additional Protocol II to the Geneva Conventions prohibits military commanders from ordering the displacement of a civilian population, unless the security of the civilians involved or imperative military reasons demand it. As in international armed conflict, the prohibition of displacement is not absolute. The official commentary on the Protocols explains: 'It is self-evident that a displacement designed to prevent the population from being exposed to grave danger cannot be expressly prohibited.'[66] In fact, in accordance with the principle of distinction between civilians and combatants, as well as the prohibition on the use of human shields, parties to an armed conflict, whether international or non-international in nature, have a duty in territory under their control to remove civilians, to the extent feasible, from the vicinity of military objectives. This responsibility is a rule of customary international law.[67]

As for displacement for military necessity, the criterion of 'imperative military reasons' is intended to set a high bar for what is lawful, and the ICRC emphasizes the need for careful scrutiny of each potential case.[68] Certain scenarios unequivocally are non permissible. The ICRC explains: 'Clearly, imperative military reasons cannot be justified by political motives. For example, it would be prohibited to move a population in order to exercise more effective control over a dissident ethnic group.'[69] Forced displacement for ethnic cleansing, which aims to change the demographic composition of a territory, is prohibited prima facie.[70] In addition, as stated earlier, it is a rule of customary international law that 'States may not deport or transfer parts of their own civilian population into a territory they occupy'.[71] While the prohibition on forced displacement is not absolute, the burden is on the warring party to demonstrate that the displacement is both justified and absolutely necessary. As with international armed conflict, if displacement in non-international armed conflict is found to be both justified and absolutely necessary then 'all possible measures must be taken in order that the civilians concerned are received under satisfactory conditions of shelter, hygiene, health, safety and nutrition and that members of the same family are not separated'.[72] This is a rule of customary international law, applicable in both international and non-international armed conflict.[73]

[65] Henckaerts and Louise Doswald-Beck, see n 59, 457, Rule 129.A.

[66] Yves Sandoz, Christophe Swinarski, and Bruno Zimmermann (eds), *Commentary on the Additional Protocols of 8 June 1977 to the Geneva Conventions of 12 August 1949* (Geneva: ICRC and Martinus Njihoff Publishers, 1987) 1472.

[67] Henckaerts and Doswald-Beck, see n 59, 74–6, Rule 24.

[68] Sandoz, Swinarski, and Zimmermann, see n 66, 1472–3.

[69] Ibid.

[70] Henckaerts and Doswald-Beck, see n 59, 461–2.

[71] Ibid., 462, Rule 130.

[72] Ibid., 463, Rule 131.

[73] Ibid.; Fourth Geneva Convention, see n 611, Article 49, para. 3; Protocol Additional to the Geneva Conventions of 12 August 1949, and Relating to the Protection of Victims of Non-International Armed Conflicts (adopted 8 June 1977, entered into force 7 December 1978) 1125 UNTS 609, art 17(1), 4(3)(b) (Additional Protocol II).

In the context of non-international armed conflicts, Additional Protocol II, Article 17(2) provides: 'Civilians shall not be compelled to leave their own territory for reasons connected with the conflict.'[74] This prohibition of deportations is absolute. However, the wording is potentially ambiguous in two respects. First, what constitutes 'their own territory' is left rather unclear. It may refer to the country as a whole, the tribal territory of the civilian group, their personal estate, or possibly the territory under the control of armed forces.[75] According to the ICRC, from the perspective of the drafters 'it is clear that there was never any doubt in anyone's mind that the phrase was intended to refer to the whole of the territory of a country'.[76]

Omission of the adjective 'national', when referring to 'their own territory', is significant nonetheless. In the view of the ICRC: 'In fact, this formula appears to be better suited to all the possible cases which might arise in a situation covered by Protocol II, and to take into account, in particular, situations where the insurgent party is in control of an extensive part of the territory.'[77] According to this authoritative interpretation of Article 17(2), the prohibition it contains relating to non-international armed conflict is thus akin to the prohibition of forced displacement from occupied territory in international armed conflict that is provided under Article 49(1) of the Fourth Geneva Convention. Effectively, this means that not only governments but also insurgents have an obligation not to compel civilians to leave the territory under their control.[78] The prohibition of deportations in internal armed conflict articulated in Article 17(2) of Protocol II, like Article 49(1) of the Geneva Conventions on which it is based, is absolute and permits no exception, whether for the security of civilians or imperative military reasons. However, in internal armed conflict, the prohibition only applies to deportations ordered 'for reasons connected with the conflict'. This qualification was added 'so as not to interfere with judicial systems that use exile as a penalty or with normal extradition proceedings'.[79] Thus, whereas deportation following a judicial conviction and with no relation to the conflict 'remains within the realm of a state's exclusive jurisdiction on domestic matters', if the deportation ordered is in any way connected with the conflict, it constitutes a forced movement prohibited by Article 17.[80]

Under the Rome Statute of the International Criminal Court, in non-international armed conflicts 'ordering the displacement of the civilian population for reasons related to the conflict, unless the security of the civilians or imperative military reasons so demand' constitutes a war crime.[81] In addition, the Rome Statute adopts, from the Statutes of the International Criminal Tribunals of the former

[74] Additional Protocol II, see n 733, Article 17(2).

[75] Jacques, see n 48, 63, citing Karen Hulme, 'Armed Conflict and the Displaced' (2005) 17 Intl J Refugee L 97, 103.

[76] Sandoz, Swinarski, and Zimmermann, see n 66, 1474.

[77] Ibid.

[78] Jacques, see n 48, 63–4.

[79] Jacques, see n 48, 65, citing Michael Bothe, Karl Josef Partsch, and Waldemar A Solf (eds), *New Rules for Victims of Armed Conflicts* (Leiden: Martinus Nijhoff Publishers, 1982); and see *Official Record of the Diplomatic Conference on the Reaffirmation and Development of International Humanitarian Law Applicable in Armed Conflicts* (Volume XV) (Bern: Federal Political Department, 1978) 295, CDDH/215/Rev.1, para. 150.

[80] Jacques, see n 48, 65.

[81] Rome Statute of the International Criminal Court, see n 644, art 8(2)(e)(viii).

Yugoslavia and Rwanda, the provision that the deportation or transfer of the civilian population constitutes a crime against humanity.[82]

The combined effect of the above-mentioned norms and State practice have converged to constitute as a rule of customary international law: 'Parties to a non-international armed conflict may not order the displacement of the civilian population, in whole or in part, for reasons related to the conflict, unless the security of the civilians involved or imperative military reasons so demand.'[83] Thus, both in international and in non-international armed conflict, the caveated prohibition of ordering the displacement of civilians is a customary norm.

Given that displacement is only lawful in armed conflict in exceptional and heavily proscribed circumstances, and that international human rights norms generally protect freedom of movement and choice of residence, it has been possible to articulate a general prohibition of arbitrary displacement. Principle 6 of the UN Guiding Principles on Internal Displacement affirms: 'Every human being shall have the right to be protected against being arbitrarily displaced from his or her home or place of habitual residence.'[84] The parameters of 'arbitrary' displacement have been defined as including: displacement in situations of armed conflict; displacement in any circumstances when it is based on policies of apartheid, ethnic cleansing, or similar practices aimed at or resulting in altering the ethnic, religious, or racial composition of the affected population; and displacement used as collective punishment.[85] Another limit on non-arbitrary displacement is that it 'shall last no longer than required by the circumstances'.[86]

Moreover, the Guiding Principles require that prior to any decision requiring the displacement of persons, the authorities concerned must meet a number of guarantees, including ensuring that all feasible alternatives have been explored to avoid displacement and, should no alternatives exist, ensuring that all measures are taken to minimize displacement and its adverse effects.[87] Those undertaking the displacement are obliged to ensure, to the greatest practicable extent, 'satisfactory conditions of safety, nutrition, health and hygiene, property accommodation, and that members of the same family are not separated'.[88] If a decision for displacement is effected outside of the emergency stages of armed conflict, a number of additional guarantees must be met.[89] In all circumstances, displacement 'shall not be carried out in a manner that violates the rights to life, dignity, liberty and security of those

[82] Ibid., Article 7(1)(d); Statute of the International Tribunal for the Prosecution of Persons Responsible for Serious Violations of International Humanitarian Law in the Territory of the Former Yugoslavia since 1991, Article 5(d), annexed to UNSC, 'Report of the Secretary-General Pursuant to Paragraph 2 of Security Council Resolution 808' (1993) UN Doc S/25704, adopted in UNSC Res 827 (1993) UN Doc S/RES/827; Statute of the International Tribunal for Rwanda, Article 3(d), annexed to UNSC Res 955 (1994) UN Doc S/RES/955.

[83] Henckaerts and Doswald-Beck, see n 59, 457, Rule 129.B.

[84] Guiding Principles on Internal Displacement, see n 53. On the background and status of the Guiding Principles, see section II of this chapter.

[85] Guiding Principles on Internal Displacement, see n 53, Principle 6(2)(a), (b), and (e). Principle 6 also defines displacement that is arbitrary in the context of natural disasters and in large-scale development projects.

[86] Ibid., Principle 6(3).

[87] Ibid., Principle 7(1).

[88] Ibid., Principle 7(2).

[89] Ibid., Principle 7(3).

affected'.[90] Further, States have 'a particular obligation to protect against the displacement of indigenous peoples, minorities, peasants, pastoralists and other groups with a special dependency on and attachment to their lands'.[91]

The situation in Syria illustrates the relevance of these norms to contemporary armed conflicts. Among the violations of international law documented by the UN Commission of Inquiry is 'arbitrary and forcible displacement', caused both by government forces and non-State armed groups. More specifically, the Commission reports that the 'Government's aerial bombardments and shelling of civilian-inhabited areas have caused extensive arbitrary displacement' and that '[b]y causing such large-scale displacement, the Government has failed in its obligations under international human rights law to protect civilians'.[92] The Government has also 'failed to comply with its duties under customary international law to take all possible measures to provide displaced civilians with shelter, hygiene, health care, safety and nutrition and to ensure that family members are not separated'.[93] Meanwhile, the orders issued by the non-State armed group, Islamic State of Iraq and al-Sham (ISIS), for all Kurdish residents to leave several areas under its control 'cannot be justified on the grounds either of the security of the civilians involved or of military necessity'.[94] To the contrary, the Commission has determined that they constitute 'a widespread and systematic attack against the Kurdish civilian population' amounting to 'the crime against humanity of forcible displacement' and 'to the war crime of displacing civilians'.[95]

The findings of the UN Commission of Inquiry have been presented to and discussed with the UN Security Council.[96] Absent 'strict compliance' by parties to the conflict with these norms, the Council has indicated its readiness to '[c]ondemn and call for the immediate cessation of displacement in violation of international humanitarian law and international human rights law' and to 'consider applying targeted and graduated measures against parties to armed conflict who commit violations of applicable international law related to forced displacement'. In Resolution 2170 (2014), principally concerned with the 'terrorist actions of ISIS', the Council expressed further concern regarding displacement, stressing that those

[90] Ibid., Principle 7(2). [91] Ibid., Principle 9.

[92] UNGA, 'Report of the Independent Commission of Inquiry on the Syrian Arab Republic' (2014) UN Doc A/HRC/25/65, para. 144 (Seventh Report of the Syria COI).

[93] UNGA, 'Report of the Independent Commission of Inquiry on the Syrian Arab Republic' (2014) UN Doc A/HRC/27/60, para. 132 (Eighth Report of the Syria COI).

[94] Ibid., para. 135.

[95] Ibid., para. 135; Independent International Commission of Inquiry on the Syrian Arab Republic, 'Report of the Independent International Commission of Inquiry on the Syrian Arab Republic, Rule of Terror: Living under ISIS in Syria' (United Nations, 14 November 2014) paras 28–9, 77 <www.ohchr.org/Documents/HRBodies/HRCouncil/CoISyria/HRC_CRP_ISIS_14Nov2014.pdf>.

[96] For example, on 21 June 2013 and 25 July 2014, the commission briefed Council Members through Arria-formula meetings; thus no official verbatim records are published. For a recording of the two proceedings see, respectively, 'Syria Commission of Inquiry presents latest report to Security Council' *United Nations Radio* (New York, 21 June 2013) <www.unmultimedia.org/radio/english/2013/06/syria-commission-of-inquiry-presents-latest-report-to-security-council/>; and 'Syria Arria' *United Nations Audiovisual Library* (New York, 25 July 2014) <www.unmultimedia.org/avlibrary/asset/1142/1142297/>.

responsible for violations of international human rights, refugee, and humanitarian law in Syria or Iraq must be held accountable.[97]

The protection provided by international law for displaced persons begins as a preventive measure, prohibiting the vast majority of forms of intentional displacement during conflict. Much of the law is rooted in well-established, although not always observed, rules of international humanitarian law, which are buttressed by international human rights law and international criminal law. The breadth and depth of these preventive obligations has resulted in the articulation of a principle of customary international law prohibiting forced displacement of civilians in armed conflict absent military imperatives or reasons of civilian safety, as well as a general principle prohibiting arbitrary displacement, whether during armed conflict or not, in the Guiding Principles on Internal Displacement.

B. Protection of displaced persons

Notwithstanding the prohibition of arbitrary displacement, if and when displacement does occur, displaced persons require protection and assistance. The concept of asylum—providing safe sanctuary to strangers in danger—dates back to ancient times and is found, in one form or another, in various historical texts and in all of the world's major religions.[98] In modern international law, the applicable norms vary depending on whether the situation concerns refugees who, by definition, are outside of their country or IDPs who, by contrast, remain in their own country. A summary of the key legal norms for each of these two situations follows.

i. Protection of refugees

Under the Universal Declaration on Human Rights, everyone has the right to seek, and to enjoy in other countries, asylum from persecution.[99] This right remains intact in times of conflict. The corresponding obligations of States towards refugees and asylum-seekers are set out in international refugee law, the core texts of which are the 1951 Convention on the Status of Refugees and its 1967 Protocol. These legal instruments were developed in order to resolve the residual refugee crisis in Europe caused by the Second World War. Indeed, the Refugee Convention originally limited the protection it offered to persons who had fled 'as a result of events occurring before 1 January 1951', and in particular owing to 'events occurring in Europe'.[100] The temporal restriction was removed by the 1967 Protocol relating to

[97] UNSC Res 2170 (2014) UN Doc S/RES/2170.

[98] UNHCR, *The State of the World's Refugees: The Challenge of Protection* (New York: Penguin Books, 1993) 33; UNHCR, 'Welcoming the Stranger: Affirmations for Faith Leaders' (Geneva: UNHCR, 2012) <www.unhcr.org/51b6de419.html>.

[99] Universal Declaration of Human Rights (UDHR) Article 14, which also specifies: 'This right may not be invoked in the case of prosecutions genuinely arising from non-political crimes or from acts contrary to the purposes and principles of the United Nations.' UNGA Res 217(III), 'A Universal Declaration of Human Rights' (1948) UN Doc A/810, 71.

[100] Convention relating to the Status of Refugees (adopted 28 July 1951, entered into force 22 April 1954) 189 UNTS 137 (1951 Refugee Convention). Article 1A, paragraph 2 of the Convention limits

the Status of Refugees,[101] and the geographic limitation has also effectively disappeared.[102]

Article 1 of the 1951 Convention on the Status of Refugees defines a refugee as follows:

> Any person who ... owing to a well-founded fear of being persecuted for reasons of race, religion, nationality, membership of a particular social group or political opinion, is outside the country of his nationality, and is unable to, or owing to such fear, is unwilling to avail himself of the protection of that country.

Regional protection instruments, specifically in Africa[103] and in Latin America,[104] have broadened the definition to include people fleeing events that seriously disrupt public order, including armed conflicts. However, under international law, namely the 1951 Convention and 1967 Protocol, persons compelled to leave their country of origin as a result of an armed conflict are normally not eligible for refugee status on that basis alone: the determining factor is a well-founded fear of persecution based on one of the five enumerated grounds.[105] Any person who has committed, or strongly appears to have committed, a war crime, crime against humanity, or crime against peace, or a serious non-political crime outside of the country of refuge prior to her or his admission to that country as a refugee, or is guilty of acts contrary to the purposes and principles of the UN, is automatically ineligible for refugee status.[106]

When recognized refugees or asylum-seekers find themselves in a country involved in an armed conflict, international humanitarian law also applies. Provided the displaced persons do not become combatants, they are protected like other civilians. In addition, refugees enjoy specific protection under international humanitarian law, in recognition of the fact that they no longer enjoy the protection of their national government. In particular, the Fourth Geneva Convention provides that refugees must not be treated as enemy aliens solely on the basis of their nationality.[107] Additional Protocol I to the Geneva Conventions extends the prohibition of adverse distinction to all persons who, before the beginning of the

the scope of the Convention to persons who fled 'as a result of events occurring before 1 January 1951' and States had the option, according to article 1B, paragraph 1(a), to interpret this provision as 'events occurring in Europe before 1 January 1951.'

[101] Protocol relating to the Status of Refugees (adopted 31 January 1967, entered into force 4 October 1967) 606 UNTS 267, Article I(2).

[102] In April 2015, only four States retained the geographical limitation: Congo, Madagascar, Monaco and Turkey. See UNHCR, 'States Parties to the 1951 Convention relating to the status of Refugees and the 1967 Protocol' (UNHCR, 2015) <www.unhcr.org/3b73b0d63.html>.

[103] Convention Governing the Specific Aspects of Refugee Problems in Africa (adopted 10 September 1969, entered into force 20 June 1974) 1001 UNTS 45.

[104] Cartagena Declaration on Refugees (published 22 November 1984) OAS Doc OEA/Ser.L/V/II.66/doc.10, rev. 1, 190–3.

[105] UNHCR, *Handbook on Procedures and Criteria for Determining Refugee Status Under the 1951 Convention and the 1967 Protocol Relating to the Status of Refugees* (Geneva: UNHCR, 2011) para. 164; Hathaway, see n 48, 93. See and compare, James Cantor and Jean-Francois Durieux (eds), *Refuge from Inhumanity? War Refugees and International Humanitarian Law* (Leiden: Brill, 2014).

[106] 1951 Refugee Convention, see n 100, Article 1.F.

[107] Fourth Geneva Convention, see n 611, Article 44; Additional Protocol I, see n 633, Article 73.

hostilities, were regarded as refugees or stateless persons under relevant international or national instruments, and designates them as protected persons under the Fourth Geneva Convention.[108]

There are also explicit references to refugees who are under the control of a party to the conflict, which may exist in three situations.[109] The first scenario arises when nationals of a State with which the receiving country is at war have been admitted as refugees, either prior to or during the conflict. These refugees are to be protected as aliens on the territory of the receiving State and not treated as enemy aliens exclusively because of their nationality.[110]

The second scenario arises when nationals of a neutral country have been admitted as refugees to the territory of a party to a conflict, either before or during the war. Even if their home country, because of its neutrality, maintains no diplomatic relations with the State party to the armed conflict, Additional Protocol I extends to them the protections of the Fourth Geneva Convention.[111]

In the third scenario, the refugees flee to a State with which their own country is, or eventually becomes, at war and then, as a result of their own country occupying all or part of the territory of the receiving State, the refugees fall back under the control of their country of origin. In such instance, the Occupying Power is prohibited from arresting, prosecuting, or convicting the refugees, or from deporting them from the occupied territory except under specific circumstances.[112]

In addition to the provisions explicitly addressing refugees, international humanitarian law also contains other important guarantees relevant to their situation. The Fourth Geneva Convention stipulates that '[i]n no circumstances shall a protected person be transferred to a country where he or she may have reason to fear persecution for his or her political opinions or religious beliefs'.[113] This prohibition evokes and reinforces the principle of *non-refoulement*, which is the cornerstone principle of international refugee law.[114] Also of relevance to many refugees and displaced persons, parties to an international armed conflict are obliged to facilitate the making of enquiries for the purpose of enabling families dispersed by the war to renew contact with one another. The parties to conflict are to facilitate in every possible way the reunion of dispersed families, including by enabling the work of organisations with specific expertise in family tracing.[115]

Additionally, in times of war, refugees continue to benefit from the aspects of refugee law that have passed into customary international law. Of chief importance is the principle of *non-refoulement*, which prohibits the expulsion or return of a

[108] Additional Protocol I, see n 633, Article 73.

[109] For a more detailed analysis, see Jacques, n 48, 159–84; Walter Kälin, 'Flight in Times of War' (2001) 83 IRRC 629–50; see also Lavoyer, n 49.

[110] Fourth Geneva Convention, see n 611, Articles 35–46.

[111] Fourth Geneva Convention, see n 611, Article 4, para. 2. Kälin, see n 109, 632, citing Additional Protocol I, see n 613, Article 73.

[112] Namely, 'for offences committed after the outbreak of hostilities, or for offences under common law committed after the outbreak of hostilities, or for offences under common law committed before the outbreak of hostilities which, according to the law of the occupied State, would have justified extradition in time of peace'. Fourth Geneva Convention, see n 611, Article 70, para. 2.

[113] Ibid., Article 45. [114] 1951 Refugee Convention, see n 100, Article 33.

[115] Fourth Geneva Convention, see n 611, Article 26; Additional Protocol I, see n 613, Article 74.

refugee to territories where his or her life or freedom would be threatened on account of his or her race, nationality, membership of a particular social group, or political opinion.[116] Respect for the principle of *non-refoulement* not only entails refraining from returning a refugee to a country where his or her life or safety would be at risk; it also prohibits rejection and turning away an asylum-seeker at the border if a real risk exists that they would face violations of fundamental human rights, in particular the rights to life or physical integrity, upon their return.[117] The principle of *non-refoulement* is a norm of customary international law, binding on all States.[118]

The Refugee Convention continues to apply in times of war.[119] While it does allow that 'in time of war or other grave and exceptional circumstances' a State Party may take 'measures which it considers to be essential to [its] national security', such measures must be provisional and limited to what is necessary.[120] Refugee law was not designed to address the special circumstances that exist during armed conflict and has certain weaknesses in this respect, including a lack of non-derogable protections for refugees.[121] However, the limitations of the Convention are largely offset by the protections for civilians, including refugees, provided for in international humanitarian law.[122] As such, refugee law and international humanitarian law offer highly complementary protection to refugees who find themselves in armed conflict situations.[123]

It is therefore surprising that, according to a former UNHCR official, in practice 'one senses [. . .] a certain reluctance on the part of UNHCR to invoke the provisions of the Geneva Conventions and their Additional Protocols in the protection of refugees'.[124] Among the possible explanations offered is that humanitarian law unhelpfully limits the protection concept to only those refugees caught in armed conflict.[125] However, even then, the number of refugees is significant, counting several millions and currently including Syrian refugees caught up in conflict zones

[116] 1951 Refugee Convention, see n 100, Article 33.

[117] Goodwin-Gill, see n 48, 121–24. The principle of *non-refoulement* is also found in the Convention against Torture, respect for which is monitored by the Committee against Torture. See, for example, UNGA, 'Report of the Committee against Torture' (2014) UN Doc A/69/44, para. 22; Convention against Torture and Other Cruel, Inhuman, or Degrading Treatment or Punishment (adopted 10 December 1984, entered into force 26 June 1987), in UNGA Res 39/46 (1984) UN Doc A/RES/39/46.

[118] See Jean Allen, 'Insisting on the *Jus Cogens* Nature of *Non-Refoulement*', in Joanne van Selm, Khoti Kamanga, John Morrison, Aninia Nadig, Sanja Špoljar-Vržina, and Loes van Willigen, *The Refugee Convention at Fifty: A View from Forced Migration Studies* (Oxford: Lexington Books, 2003) 84–6; and see Elihu Lauterpacht and Daniel Bethlehem, 'The Scope and Content of the Principle of *non-refoulement*: Opinion', in Erika Feller, Volker Türk, and Frances Nicholson, *Refugee Protection in International Law: UNHCR's Global Consultations on International Protection* (Cambridge: Cambridge University Press, 2003) 149–64. But see and compare James C Hathaway, *The Rights of Refugees under International Law* (Cambridge: Cambridge University Press, 2005) 364–8.

[119] Atle Grahl-Madsen, *Commentary on the Refugee Convention 1951* (Geneva: UNHCR, 1963) 42.

[120] 1951 Refugee Convention, see n 100, Article 9.

[121] Stéphane Jacquemet, 'The Cross-fertilization of International Humanitarian Law and International Refugee Law' (2001) 83 IRRC 651, 654.

[122] Ibid. [123] Ibid.

[124] Deschamp, see n 26, paras 14, 88. [125] Ibid., para. 15.

in Iraq and Yemen, Iraqi refugees in Syria, Somali refugees in Yemen, and Chadian refugees in the Central African Republic. It has also been suggested that the apparent 'ambivalence' and even 'reticence on the part of UNHCR vis-à-vis the [protection of civilians] concept in discharging its refugee mandate' also 'derives, in part, from the importance the concept in question has come to assume in the mandates of UN peacekeeping missions, especially integrated missions [and] the perception that [the protection of civilians] is an OCHA-owned [UN Office for the Coordination of Humanitarian Affairs] concept'.[126] Yet, considering the particularly vulnerable situation of refugees caught in conflict situations, any and all international norms that can enhance their protection should be mobilized.

ii. Protection of internally displaced persons

Pursuant to the basic precepts of international law, the fact that IDPs remain within the territorial jurisdiction of their own country means that they continue to enjoy its protection, at least in principle. It is for this reason that IDPs, unlike refugees, do not acquire a specific status under international law. In all situations, IDPs continue to enjoy the rights inherent to all human beings, as codified in international human rights law, and their governments are obliged to protect those rights. In situations of armed conflict, international humanitarian law also comes into effect. IDPs, provided they are non-combatants, are entitled to the full array of guarantees afforded to all other civilians.

The fact that IDPs enjoy the same entitlements under international humanitarian law as other civilian victims in conflict has led some observers to question the need to focus specific attention on their plight in armed conflict.[127] Similarly, in the international human rights law framework, James Hathaway asks: 'Why should they be treated as a category of concern distinguished from other internal victims of human rights violations who have not been displaced?'[128] However, the reality is that not all IDPs are displaced by violations of human rights or armed conflict that reach the threshold to engage those bodies of law: some may be displaced, for

[126] Ibid., para. 88.

[127] See Lavoyer, n 49; Françoise Bouchet-Saulnier and Anastasia M Warpinski, 'Using the Law of War to Protect the Displaced', *MSF Activity Report, 2000–2001* (Paris: Médecins Sans Frontières, 2001). See also Marguerite Contat-Hickel, 'Protection of Internally Displaced Persons affected by Armed Conflict: Concept and Challenges' (2001) 83 IRRC 699; ICRC, *Internal Displacement in Armed Conflict: Facing Up to the Challenges* (Geneva: ICRC, 2009) 6–7.

[128] James Hathaway, 'Forced Migration Studies: Could We Agree Just to "Date"?' (2007) 20 J of Refugee Studies 349, 360. See also Sarah Collinson, James Darcy, Nicholas Waddell, and Anna Schmidt (eds), *Realising Protection: The Uncertain Benefits of Civilian, Refugee and IDP Status*, (London: Overseas Development Institute, 2009); John Cosgrave, *Synthesis of Findings on ECHO's Policy of Treating Affected Populations Without Regard to Pre-Conceived Categories, Specifically IDPs, Refugees, and Returnees, and Local Population, based on Reviews in Sudan, Angola and Afghanistan* (Brussels: European Community Humanitarian Aid Office, 2004) <ec.europa.eu/echo/files/evaluation/2003/idp_synthesis_report.pdf>; John Borton, Margie Buchanan Smith, and Ralf Otto, 'Learning from Evaluations of Support to Internally Displaced Persons: IDP Synthesis Report: Final Report' (Ohain, Belgium: Channel Research, 2005) <ec.europa.eu/echo/files/evaluation/watsan2005/annex_files/ECHO/ECHO16%20-%20IDP%20Synthesis%20Final%20Report%20090105.doc>.

example, by natural disasters, or violence not reaching the threshold of armed conflict. More fundamentally, the fact is that displacement, whatever its cause, inevitably creates specific needs. Displaced persons, by definition, have lost their habitual place of residence and have an immediate need for alternative shelter in a safe location. A strong body of empirical evidence reveals that they are at heightened risk for a range of vulnerabilities and abuses.[129] Furthermore, and unique compared with other civilians caught in armed conflict, IDPs require a solution to their state of displacement.[130]

Significantly, the ICRC now explicitly recognizes that the vulnerability of civilians is exacerbated if they are displaced. While IDPs may have the same need for legal protection as other civilians during conflict, 'it goes without saying that, deprived of shelter and their habitual sources of food, water, medicine and money, they have different, and often more urgent material needs'.[131] At the policy level, the ICRC has confirmed that the particular needs of displaced persons are systematically taken into account in its vulnerability assessments.[132]

Unlike the case of refugees, there exists no international convention articulating the rights of IDPs and the responsibilities of States towards them. In 1992, the UN Representative of the Secretary-General on IDPs was requested by the UN Commission on Human Rights to study the extent to which international law met the needs of IDPs. After several years of research by a group of international legal experts, the result was a comprehensive two-part Compilation and Analysis of Legal Norms pertaining to IDPs, which reviewed international human rights law, international humanitarian law, and international refugee law.[133] While the study reached the conclusion that there were 'only minor gaps' in the protection coverage provided to IDPs, it stressed the complexity of applying the provisions in situations of displacement. The UN Commission on Human Rights and the General Assembly welcomed the report and requested the development of 'an appropriate normative framework' to enhance the protection of IDPs.[134] The framework was developed by the UN Representative for IDPs and a group of independent experts,

[129] Erin Mooney, 'The Concept of Internal Displacement and the Case for Internally Displaced Persons as a Category of Concern' (2005) 24 Refugee Survey Q 9; Francis M Deng and Roberta Cohen, *Masses in Flight: The Global Crisis of Internal Displacement* (Washington, DC: Brookings Institution, 1998); Francis M Deng and Roberta Cohen, *The Forsaken People: Case Studies of the Internally Displaced* (Washington, DC: Brookings Institution, 1998).

[130] Walter Kälin, 'Walter Kälin on the Outlook for IDPs' (2011) 37 Forced Migration Rev 43, 43–4.

[131] Jean-Daniel Tauxe, 'We Should Have Access to Displaced Civilians', *International Herald Tribune* (Paris, 1 March 2009) 10. At the time of writing this article, the author was the Director of Operations for the ICRC.

[132] Françoise Krill, 'The ICRC's Policy on Refugees and Internally Displaced Civilians' (2001) 83 IRRC 607, 610.

[133] CHR, 'Report of the Representative of the Secretary-General, Mr Francis Deng, submitted pursuant to Commission on Human Rights resolution 1993/95' (1995) UN Doc E/CN.4/1995/50/Add.3; and CHR, 'Report of the Representative of the Secretary-General, Mr Francis M. Deng, Submitted pursuant to Commission on Human Rights resolution 1995/57: Compilation and analysis of legal norms' (1996) UN Doc E/CN.4/1996/52/Add.2.

[134] CHR Res 1997/39 (1997) UN Doc E/CN.4/RES/1997/39; UNGA Res 52/130 (1998) UN Doc A/RES/52/130.

taking the form of the Guiding Principles on Internal Displacement, which were submitted to the Commission in 1998.[135]

The Guiding Principles bring together and compress into one short document the protection derived from a panoply of relevant international norms, which otherwise are dispersed and diffused across a wide range of different legal instruments and therefore not easily accessible. The thirty principles consolidate the key guarantees and rights relevant to all phases of internal displacement: protection from arbitrary displacement; protection and assistance during displacement; and protection during IDPs' return or resettlement and reintegration.[136] The Principles define IDPs as follows:

> Persons or groups of persons who have been forced or obliged to flee or to leave their homes or places of habitual residence, in particular as a result of, or in order to avoid the effects of armed conflict, situations of generalized violence, violations of human rights or natural or human-made disasters, and who have not crossed an internationally recognized State border.[137]

This definition has two core elements: (a) the coercive or otherwise involuntary nature of the individual's movement and (b) the fact that such movement takes place within national borders. It is essential to understand that the definition of IDPs provided in the Principles is a descriptive definition, not a legal definition; it does not connote or confer upon IDPs a specific legal status in the same way that recognition of a person as a 'refugee' does. This is not necessary for IDPs, the main drafter of the Principles explained, because whereas refugees, who by definition have lost the protection of their own country and, being outside their own State, require a special status under international law, 'the rights and guarantees to which IDPs are entitled stem from the fact that they are human beings and citizens or habitual residents of a particular state'.[138] Indeed, Guiding Principle 1 affirms: 'IDPs shall enjoy, in full equality, the same rights and freedoms under international and domestic law as do other persons in their country. They shall not be discriminated against in the enjoyment of any rights and freedoms on the ground that they are internally displaced.' And while States have 'the primary duty and responsibility to provide protection and humanitarian assistance to IDPs within their jurisdiction' (Principle 3), the Principles are to be 'observed by all authorities, groups and persons' (Principle 2), by which is understood to include non-State armed groups.[139] The Introduction to the Principles indicates that their purpose is to provide guidance not only to States, but also to 'all other authorities, groups and persons' and to inter-governmental and non-governmental organizations.

The main sections of the Principles set out the rights of IDPs and the responsibilities of States and other actors towards them in all phases of displacement. Principles 5–9 address the issue of protection from displacement.[140] Especially noteworthy is Principle 6 which, based on relevant provisions of international

[135] Guiding Principles on Internal Displacement, see n 53. [136] Ibid.

[137] Ibid., Introduction: Scope and Purpose, para. 2. [138] Kälin, see n 48, 2.

[139] Participation by the author of this chapter in the final drafting meetings and consultations permits this observation. The fact that the Principles are based inter alia on international humanitarian law further underscores their applicability to non-state armed groups. See also Kälin, n 48.

[140] Guiding Principles on Internal Displacement, see n 53, Principles 5–9.

humanitarian law and human rights guarantees, recognizes the right of every persons not to be arbitrarily displaced. Principles 10–23, constituting the largest section of the document, cover a wide range of rights, for instance the rights to life; to physical, mental, and moral integrity; to freedom of movement; to an adequate standard of living; to family life; to education; and to political participation.[141] In each case, the Principle specifies the relevance of these general guarantees to the specific needs and concerns of IDPs. For example, Principle 12 reaffirms the right of every human being to liberty and then specifies that 'to give effect to this right' for IDPs, they shall not be interned in or confined to a camp, shall be protected from discriminatory arrest and detention as a result of their displacement, and shall not be taken hostage.[142] Principle 15 inter alia affirms that IDPs, like all persons, have the right to seek asylum in another country, that is, to become a refugee. Moreover, evoking the principle of *non-refoulement* from international refugee law, Principle 15 also recognizes that IDPs have the 'right to be protected against forcible return to or resettlement in any place where their life, safety, liberty and/or health would be at risk'.[143] Principles 24–27 address the issue of humanitarian assistance to IDPs, reaffirming international norms regarding humanitarian access. The final section of the document addresses solutions to displacement.

Although the Guiding Principles on Internal Displacement do not constitute a binding instrument as such, they do reflect and are consistent with international human rights and international humanitarian law, which *is* binding. The legal basis of each of the Principles is set out in detail in their Annotations.[144] The legal basis is also evident in the Principles themselves, which are modelled on, and in several cases restate verbatim, key passages from international human rights law and international humanitarian law.[145]

The purpose of the Guiding Principles is not to replace the guarantees in these two bodies of international law but rather to facilitate their application in situations of displacement. The Principles strive to do so, their main drafter Walter Kalin explains, 'by synthesizing the many applicable norms of international human rights and humanitarian law into clear principles, and by highlighting those more concrete aspects of human rights and humanitarian law guarantees that are of special significance for the displaced'.[146] Basing the normative framework applicable in situations of displacement on hard law was a deliberate and conscious decision of the drafters.[147]

Indeed, the fact that the Guiding Principles are based on hard law is a key reason why the Principles have gained considerable international standing in a relatively short period of time.[148] The ICRC contributed to the development of the Principles and supports their dissemination and use.[149] In 2005, the 196 Heads of

[141] Ibid., Principles 10–23. [142] Ibid., Principles 12.

[143] Ibid., Principle 15. [144] See Kälin, n 48.

[145] For examples, see Erin Mooney, 'Principles of Protection for Internally Displaced Persons' (2001) 38 Intl Migration 81, 86.

[146] Kälin, see n 109, 646. [147] Ibid., 647. [148] Ibid.

[149] For a personal account of the main ICRC representative in this process, see Lavoyer, n 49; Kellenberger, n 511; Cordula Dorege, 'Developments in the Legal Protection of IDPs' [December 2008] Forced Migration Rev 8. See also Krill, n 132, 620.

State assembled at the World Summit recognised the Guiding Principles 'as an important international framework for the protection of internally displaced persons'.[150] More than twenty-three States to date have adopted domestic legislation or national policies explicitly referring to and based on the Principles.[151] Also particularly noteworthy is the fact that in 2009 the African Union adopted the first-ever international legal instrument specifically concerning IDPs, the Convention for Protection and Assistance to Internally Displaced Persons in Africa. The 'Kampala Convention', named for the city of its adoption, makes explicit mention of the Guiding Principles, which heavily informed the drafting process.[152]

The real 'protection gap' for IDPs is not a lacuna of international standards but rather, as the UN Security Council observed in 2000, one of 'inadequate implementation of existing international norms for IDPs' protection'.[153] This still rings true years later. Certainly, the disregard by parties to armed conflict of many of their obligations to protect civilians remains a significant challenge. This problem, however, is exacerbated in some cases by passivity on the part of international organizations which, as the Guiding Principles emphasize, also have responsibilities when providing humanitarian assistance to 'give due regard to the protection needs and human rights of internally displaced persons and take appropriate measures in this regard'.[154] In this connection, the report of an official review of UN action in Sri Lanka in the closing months of the conflict in 2009 makes for sobering reading. Among the many identified examples that culminated in what the report characterized as a 'systemic failure' of protection on the part of the UN was that the UN 'should have been able to push further for respect for international norms in the delivery of assistance to IDPs and avoid accusations of complicity in the detention of IDPs'.[155]

C. Solutions to displacement

A distinguishing feature of protection in the context of refugees and IDPs is the need to find solutions to the situation that inherently exposes them to vulnerabilities, namely being uprooted from their place of habitual residence.

International human rights law recognizes that everyone has the right to freedom of movement, including the right to return to one's country and the freedom to choose one's residence.[156] The Fourth Geneva Convention provides that in

[150] UNGA Res 60/1, '2005 World Summit Outcome' (2005) UN Doc A/RES/60/1, para. 132.

[151] See Brookings-LSE Project on Internal Displacement, *IDPs Laws and Policies Index* (Washington, DC: Brookings Institution, Online, undated) <www.brookings.edu/about/projects/idp/resources/idp policies index>.

[152] African Union Convention for the Protection and Assistance of Internally Displaced Persons (adopted 22 October 2009, entered into force 6 December 2012) <au.int/en/content/african-union-convention-protection-and-assistance-internally-displaced-persons-africa>.

[153] UNSC (2000) UN Doc PRST/2000/1.

[154] Guiding Principles on Internal Displacement, see n 53, Principle 27.

[155] *Report of the Secretary-General's Internal Review Panel on UN Action in Sri Lanka* (United Nations, 2012) para. 77; see also paras 37 and 164 <www.un.org/News/dh/infocus/Sri_Lanka/The_Internal_Review_Panel_report_on_Sri_Lanka.pdf>.

[156] Universal Declaration of Human Rights, see n 99, Article 12.

international armed conflict, persons who have been evacuated must be transferred back to their homes as soon as hostilities in the area have ceased.[157] Indeed, unjustifiable delay in the repatriation of civilians uprooted by international armed conflict constitutes a grave breach of Additional Protocol I.[158] As for IDPs, the Guiding Principles on Internal Displacement emphasize that 'displacement shall last no longer than required by the circumstances'.[159] The UN Security Council, General Assembly, Commission on Human Rights, and its successor the Human Rights Council have repeatedly emphasized, both generally and in resolutions regarding specific country situations, 'the right of refugees and displaced persons to voluntary return in safety and dignity to their homes', and this right is also recognized in several peace agreements and other agreements regarding refugees and displaced persons.[160] It is now a well-established norm of customary international law, applicable both in international and non-international armed conflicts, that 'Displaced persons have the right to voluntarily return in safety to their homes or places of habitual residence as soon as the reasons for their displacement cease to exist'.[161]

The Guiding Principles on Internal Displacement further elaborate key normative elements of solutions for IDPs. 'Competent authorities', which include not only States but also non-State armed groups, have the responsibility to establish conditions, as well as provide the means, allowing IDPs 'to return voluntarily, in safety and with dignity, to their homes or places of habitual residence, or to resettle voluntarily in another part of the country'.[162] Thus, in addition to the solution of return, IDPs also have the option to resettle elsewhere in the country, including to integrate into the locality where they lived while displaced. Whichever solution IDPs choose, the authorities are to facilitate their reintegration.[163] These three possible solutions for IDPs are akin to the right of refugees to choose among three solutions: return to their home country once it is possible to re-avail themselves of its protection; re-establish themselves through local integration in the country of asylum; or, through resettlement, establish themselves in another country.[164] The Principles proscribe that IDPs should participate in the planning and management of their return or resettlement and reintegration.[165] Wherever IDPs choose to re-establish themselves, they must not be discriminated against as a result of having been displaced, they must have equal access to public services, and they must have the opportunity to participate fully and equally in public affairs.[166] The authorities

[157] Fourth Geneva Convention, see n 611, Article 49(2).
[158] Additional Protocol I, see n 633, Article 85(4)(b).
[159] Guiding Principles on Internal Displacement, see n 53, Principle 6.
[160] For key such examples see Kälin, n 48, 125–30; Henckaerts and Doswald Beck, see n 59, 469.
[161] This right to return applies to those who have been displaced on account of the conflict and not to non-nationals who have been lawfully expelled. See Henckaerts and Doswald-Beck, n 59, Rule 132, 468–72.
[162] Guiding Principles on Internal Displacement, see n 53, Principle 28. [163] Ibid.
[164] UNHCR Executive Committee Conclusion No 75 (XLV), 'Internally Displaced Persons' (1993), in UNHCR, *A Thematic Compilation of Executive Committee Decisions* (Geneva: UNHCR, 2014) 85.
[165] Guiding Principles on Internal Displacement, see n 53, Principle 28.
[166] Ibid., Principle 29(1).

also have the responsibility to assist IDPs to recover, to the extent possible, the property and possessions that they left behind or were dispossessed of upon displacement. If restitution is not possible, the authorities are to assist IDPs to obtain appropriate compensation or other just reparation.[167] All authorities concerned are to facilitate rapid and unimpeded access for international humanitarian organizations and others, and to assist IDPs in their return or resettlement and reintegration.[168] As a rule of customary international law, 'The property rights of displaced persons must be respected'.[169]

The Security Council, in its Aide-Memoire on the Protection of Civilians, reaffirms and calls for 'strict compliance' by parties to armed conflict, with all applicable standards of international law relevant to securing durable solutions to displacement. As for its own role, the Council indicates its readiness, when faced with any given conflict situation causing displacement, to consider mandating UN peacekeeping and other relevant missions to contribute to creation of security conditions conducive to voluntary, safe, dignified, and sustainable returns. This may include mobilization of police patrols in areas of return; ensuring the protection of returning refugees and IDPs; preventing the illegal appropriation and confiscation of land and property belonging to refugees and IDPs; and supporting domestic mechanisms for addressing housing, land, and property claims.[170]

In 2008, the Representative of the Secretary-General on Internally Displaced Persons emphasized that finding durable solutions to displacement was 'an essential dimension of peacebuilding'. He stated:

> Resolving internal displacement—and preventing future displacement—is inextricably linked to achieving lasting peace. On one hand, unresolved problems of displacement may cause instability and thus threaten peacebuilding efforts. On the other hand, durable solutions, particularly return, cannot be achieved for internally displaced persons as long as there is a lack of security; property is not returned and conditions for sustainable solutions are not in place.[171]

IV. Conclusion

Displacement is an almost inevitable feature of armed conflict and displaced persons typically comprise a disproportionate number of civilians affected by armed

167 Ibid., Principle 29(2).
168 Ibid., Principle 30.
169 Rule 133. Henckaerts and Doswald-Beck, see n 59, 472–4.
170 See, for example, UNSC Res 2165 (2014) UN Doc S/RES/2165, preambular para. 7; UNSC Res 2100 (2013) UN Doc S/RES/2100, para. 16(e); UNSC Res 1925 (2010) UN Doc S/RES/1925, para. 12(g); UNSC Res 2098 (2013) S/RES/2098, para. 12(a); UNSC Res 2096 (2013) UN Doc S/RES/2096, para. 7(d); UNSC Res 1769 (2007) UN Doc S/RES/1769, para. 1; UNSC Res 1509 (2003) UN Doc S/RES/1509, para. 3(l); UNSC Res 1996 (2011) UN Doc S/RES/1996, para. 3(b)(v).
171 Walter Kälin, *Durable Solutions for Internally Displaced Persons: An Essential Dimension of Peacebuilding*, Brookings Institute, 13 March 2008, http://www.brookings.edu/research/papers/2008/03/13-peacebuilding-kalin. At the time of writing, the author was the Representative of the Secretary-General on the Human Rights of Internally Displaced Persons and Co-Director, Brookings-LSE Project on Internal Displacement.

conflict. An examination of the protection of civilians in any given conflict situation therefore would be incomplete without considering the possibility, the plight, and the specific protection concerns of civilians forced to flee. Indeed, concern regarding the growing global displacement crisis and the particular vulnerabilities of displaced persons helped to propel the issue of protection of civilians onto the agenda of UN Security Council in 1999. In addition to featuring prominently in the Council's now regular deliberations on the protection of civilians, displacement also receives attention in other thematic debates of the Council, in particular on women, peace, and security, and on children in armed conflict. Most importantly, in its consideration of specific crises, the Council now customarily calls upon parties to conflict to fulfil their obligations under international humanitarian law, international human rights law, and international refugee law, and urges parties to conflict to pay specific attention to addressing the differential protection and assistance issues facing refugees and IDPs.

International law, in particular international humanitarian law, international human rights law, and international refugee law, offers significant and specific protection to civilians in situations of displacement during armed conflict. International humanitarian law explicitly prohibits ordering the displacement of people unless this is absolutely necessary for imperative military reasons or for the protection of the affected civilians themselves. Moreover, compliance with the more extensive set of rules of international humanitarian law regarding the protection of civilians, as well as respect for international human rights law, would inevitably result in far fewer people being compelled to flee. In the event that displacement does occur, international human rights law, international humanitarian law, and international refugee law offer complementary and, collectively, comprehensive protection.

The lack of protection experienced by many displaced persons today owes to the inadequacy not of international legal norms but of their implementation. This observation is not novel, nor perhaps is it surprising. What is new and somewhat encouraging in recent years is the growing readiness on the part of the UN Security Council to call attention to the specific protection concerns of IDPs and refugees, to advocate respect for the international norms for their protection, and, most significantly, to adopt specific measures aiming to enhance the protection of IDPs and refugees in practice. Promising in this regard is the robust protection-of-civilians mandate, including specific measures to enhance the protection of refugees and IDPs, that the UN Security Council authorized for the UN Mission in South Sudan in 2014. At the same time, realities in South Sudan and other contemporary conflicts lay bare that much more needs to be done to effectively protect civilians in armed conflicts, including all those forced to flee.

The UN Secretary-General's 'Human Rights Up Front' initiative, launched in late 2013, underscores that when governments fail to protect their populations, the UN 'must do everything it can to meet its responsibilities'.[172] To this end, a global

[172] 'Rights Up Front' (May 2014) United Nations Secretary-General <www.un.org/sg/rightsupfront/doc/RuFAP-summary-General-Assembly.htm>.

action plan is being implemented by the UN Secretariat.[173] At the core of this initiative is the notion that protection is a collective responsibility. In this connection, at a 2014 meeting of the Security Council on the protection of civilians, the Under-Secretary-General for Humanitarian Affairs emphasized:

> Parties to conflict must be pressed to do more to comply with their legal obligations and ensure accountability whenever such obligations are violated. But the responsibility does not lie solely with the parties themselves. This Council and the international community must take steps to tackle the impunity that continues to fuel many conflicts [. . .]. There is nothing that emboldens violators more than knowing that they will not be brought to account for their crimes.[174]

This statement brings to mind the Council's indication of its readiness, in any given situation, to '[c]onsider applying targeted and graduated measures against parties to armed conflict who commit violations of applicable international law related to forced displacement'.[175] Indeed, more systematic Security Council action that goes beyond statements of condemnation of violations to concretely promote and support respect for international humanitarian law, international human rights law, and international refugee law is needed to enhance protection for civilians, including for the millions forced into displacement.

173 See Michael Keating and Richard Bennett, Chapter 16 in this volume.

174 Statement of Ms Kyung-wha Kang on behalf of Ms Valerie Amos, in UNSC (2015) UN Doc S/PV.7374, 4.

175 See Aide-Memoire on the Protection of Civilians in Armed Conflict, in UNSC Statement of the President (2010) UN Doc S/PRST/2010/25, annex.

9

Legal Aspects of the Use of Force by United Nations Peacekeepers for the Protection of Civilians

Mona Ali Khalil[1]

I. Introduction

To the same degree that the United Nations (UN) was built on the ashes and rubble of the First and Second World Wars, the protection of civilians mandate in UN peacekeeping was borne out of the lost lives and failed UN mandates in Srebrenica and Rwanda.

By prohibiting the use of force, except in self-defence and as authorized by the Security Council in the exercise of its primary responsibility to maintain international peace and security, the founding members of the UN promised, in the preamble of the UN Charter, to 'save succeeding generations from the scourge of war, which twice in our lifetime has brought untold sorrow to mankind'. By mandating UN peacekeepers to protect civilians from physical violence and by authorizing them to use all necessary means to do so, the Security Council equally sent a message that never again would UN forces stand helplessly by while civilians were being massacred in their areas of deployment.

More than fifteen years after the UN Mission in Sierra Leone (UNAMSIL) was authorized in 1999 to take all necessary actions to protect civilians from the imminent threat of physical violence, the UN Office of Internal Oversight Services (OIOS) recently concluded that 'civilians continue to suffer violence and displacement in many countries where United Nations missions hold [protection of civilians] mandates'.[2] The OIOS evaluation found that 'although peacekeeping missions have successfully prevented and mitigated harm to civilians while deployed over huge territories and facing asymmetrical threats with limited resources, the chain linking the intent of the Security Council to the actions of the

[1] Mona Ali Khalil is a Senior Legal Officer on special leave from the Office of the Legal Counsel, Office of Legal Affairs of the United Nations. The views expressed herein are her personal views and do not necessarily reflect the views of the Office of the Legal Counsel or of the United Nations.

[2] United Nations General Assembly (UNGA), 'Report of the Office of Internal Oversight Services, Evaluation of the Implementation and Results of Protection of Civilians Mandates in United Nations Peacekeeping Operations' (2014) UN Doc A/68/787, 2 (OIOS Report).

Secretariat, troop- and police-contributing countries and peacekeeping missions themselves remains broken in relation to the use of force'.[3]

In its report, OIOS noted that 'in only a minority of incidents reported in Secretary-General's reports involving direct attacks on civilians, including very serious incidents, was any immediate response reported by missions'.[4] OIOS also noted that 'where mission personnel (including uniformed personnel) actually were on site at the time of an attack or threatened attack against civilians, force was almost never used'.[5]

In this chapter, we seek to examine the legal aspects of the evolution and *raison d'être* of the protection of civilians mandate and to elaborate the legal framework governing the use of force by UN peacekeepers to protect civilians from the imminent threat of physical violence. We shall also inquire whether the apparent reluctance to use force to implement the protection of civilians mandate can be attributed, in whole or in part, to the legal framework or to misunderstandings relating to or arising therefrom. In particular, we will examine whether confusion regarding the meaning and scope of the legal terminology, concerns regarding the consent of the host State, lack of clarity around the roles and responsibilities of mission leadership, the potential for criminal accountability and/or becoming a party to the conflict, the duality of contingent and mission command structures, and the basic principles of peacekeeping have had an inhibiting effect on UN peacekeepers using force beyond self-defence and for the protection of civilians.

A. The tragic lessons learned in Srebrenica and Rwanda

The legacy of the failures of the UN in Srebrenica and Rwanda is primarily the recognition of the inadequate mandates and insufficient resources provided to UN peacekeeping forces that are expected to keep a peace that is either absent or elusive, in the midst of ongoing armed conflict.

In his report pursuant to General Assembly Resolution 53/35, the then Secretary-General concluded that '[t]he cardinal lesson of Srebrenica is that a deliberate and systematic attempt to terrorize, expel or murder an entire people must be met decisively with all necessary means'.[6] He further observed that '[w]hen the international community makes a solemn promise to safeguard and protect

[3] Ibid.

[4] Ibid., para. 18. In paragraph 19, the Office of Internal Oversight Services (OIOS) reports that '[o]f the 507 incidents involving civilians reported in Secretary-General's reports from 2010 to 2013, only 101, or 20 per cent, were reported to have attracted an immediate mission response. Conversely, missions did not report responding to 406 (80 per cent) of incidents where civilians were attacked. The rate of reported response varied across missions, reflecting the seriousness of incidents and the availability of early warning, the accessibility of incident sites and other factors.'

[5] Ibid., para. 22. OIOS goes on in this paragraph to note that '[r]esponses included supporting local security forces, securing areas and facilities, evacuating or escorting civilians to safety, sheltering them on United Nations premises, creating security conditions conducive to the provision of humanitarian assistance and launching human rights investigations. Parallel approaches included political intervention at the national, regional and/or local levels.'

[6] UNGA, 'Report of the Secretary-General pursuant to General Assembly resolution 53/35: The Fall of Srebrenica' (1999) UN Doc A/54/549, para. 502.

innocent civilians from massacre then it must be willing to back its promise with the necessary means'.[7]

Building on the conclusions of the Secretary-General's report on the fall of Srebrenica, the UN's Independent Inquiry into the actions of the UN during the 1994 genocide in Rwanda found that '[f]aced in Rwanda with the risk of genocide, and later the systematic implementation of a genocide, the United Nations had a duty to act which transcended the basic principles of peacekeeping. In effect, there can be no neutrality in the face of genocide, no impartiality in the face of an effort to exterminate part of a population.'[8]

Beyond the obvious gaps in mandates and resources, which have continued to narrow over the years, both the above-mentioned reports of the Secretary-General and of the Independent Inquiry pointed to other problems in the implementation of the mandates by the respective missions and their troop-contributing countries, including in particular, the lack of unified command of, and operational control over, military contingents.[9] As discussed later in the chapter, these and other issues confronting peacekeeping missions continue to impede the efficient and effective implementation of protection of civilians mandates today.

B. The *raison d'être* of robust peacekeeping

By virtue of its second mandate, the UN Operation in the Congo (ONUC) was the first peacekeeping operation to receive explicit authorization to use force beyond self-defence. By its Resolutions 161A (1961) and 169 (1961), respectively, the Security Council explicitly authorized the use of force, as a last resort, to prevent the occurrence of civil war in the Congo and to ensure the apprehension, detention pending legal action, and deportation of all foreign fighters not under UN command, and mercenaries, and to prevent their return.[10] ONUC was also arguably the first UN peacekeeping operation to engage in protection of civilians activities, albeit without an explicit mandate to do so. In his statement after the adoption of Resolution 161A on 21 February 1961, the Secretary-General stated that 'I feel entitled to use those operative paragraphs with the full moral value which they have in our efforts in the Congo' and 'finally, as a matter of course, the standing instructions, to the United Nations authorities in the Congo to take all possible measures to prevent occurrences of outrages will be reaffirmed and even, if possible, strengthened'.[11]

[7] Ibid., para. 504.

[8] UN Security Council (UNSC), 'Report of the Independent Inquiry into the Actions of the UN during the 1994 Genocide in Rwanda' (1999) UN Doc S/1999/1257, 50.

[9] Ibid.; see also UNGA, 'Report of the Secretary-General pursuant to General Assembly resolution 53/35: The fall of Srebrenica' (1999) A/54/549, para. 471.

[10] UNSC Resolution (Res) 161 (1961) UN Doc S/RES/161, and UNSC Res 169 (1961) UN Doc S/RES/169.

[11] Statement of Secretary-General Dag Hammarskjold, 'Statement in the Security Council after the adoption of the Afro-Asian Resolution' (21 February 1960), in Andrew J Cordier and Wilder Foote (eds), *Public Papers of the Secretaries-General of the United Nations: Volume 5, 1960–1961* (New York: Columbia University Press, 1975) 359–60. The Secretary-General's statement in this connection must be read in the context of his statement of 9 September 1960 where, after describing the terrible events

Nonetheless, the first explicit protection of civilians mandate was not introduced until forty years later. In operative paragraph 14 of its Resolution 1270 (1999), the Security Council, acting under Chapter VII of the UN Charter, decided that UNAMSIL 'may take the necessary action ... within its capabilities and areas of deployment, to afford protection to civilians under imminent threat of physical violence, taking into account the responsibilities of the Government of Sierra Leone'.[12]

In operative paragraph 13 of its Resolution 1296 (2000), the Security Council affirmed 'its intention to ensure, where appropriate and feasible, that peacekeeping missions are given suitable mandates and adequate resources to protect civilians under imminent threat of physical danger'.[13] Since the first protection of civilians mandate was entrusted to UNAMSIL in 1999, the Security Council has consistently authorized protection of civilians mandates for UN peacekeeping missions. There are currently ten active UN peacekeeping missions with protection of civilians mandates, in situations as varied as the Central African Republic, Côte d'Ivoire, Democratic Republic of the Congo, Haiti, Lebanon, Liberia, Mali, South Sudan, and Sudan.[14] With the exception of the UN Interim Force in Lebanon (UNIFIL),[15] each has explicit Chapter VII authority to use force, up to and including deadly force, for the protection of civilians against physical violence.[16]

in the Kasai region, which he characterized as a 'flagrant violation of elementary human rights and have the characteristics of the crime of genocide', the Secretary-General asked: '[s]hould it be supposed that the duty of the United Nations to observe strict neutrality in the domestic conflicts and to assist the Central Government means that the United Nations cannot take action in such cases?'. Statement of Secretary-General Dag Hammarskjold, 'Opening Statement in the Security Council' (9 September 1960), in Cordier and Wilder, ibid., 167.

12 UNSC Res 1270 (1999) UN Doc S/RES/1270 (1999) para. 14.

13 UNSC Res 1296 (2000) UN Doc S/RES/1296 (2000) para. 13.

14 UNSC Res 2149 (2149) UN Doc S/RES/2149; UNSC Res 1925 (2010) UN Doc S/RES/1925; UNSC Res 1542 (2004) UN Doc S/RES/1542; UNSC Res 1528 (2004) UN Doc S/RES/1528; UNSC Res 1701 (2006) UN Doc S/RES/1701; UNSC Res 1509 (2003) UN Doc S/RES/1509; UNSC Res 2100 (2013) UN Doc S/RES/2100; UNSC Res 2155 (2014) UN Doc S/RES/2155; UNSC Res 1769 (2007) UN Doc S/RES/1769; and UNSC Res 1990 (2011) UN Doc S/RES/1990.

15 Although Chapter VII is not explicitly invoked, Security Council resolution 1701 nonetheless authorizes UNIFIL to '[t]ake all necessary action in areas of deployment of its forces and as it deems within its capabilities, to ensure its area of operations is not utilised for hostile activities of any kind ... and without prejudice to the responsibility of the Government of Lebanon, *to protect civilians under imminent threat of physical violence*' (emphasis added). UNSC Res 1701 (2006) UN Doc S/RES/1701, para. 12.

16 Peacekeeping missions without protection of civilians mandates are the traditional peacekeeping missions monitoring armistice or ceasefire lines, as follows: the UN Truce Supervision Organization (UNTSO), the UN Disengagement Observer Force (UNDOF), and the UN Military Observer Group in India and Pakistan (UNMOGIP). While UNIFIL, the UN Peacekeeping Force in Cyprus (UNFICYP), and the UN Mission for the Referendum in Western Sahara (MINURSO) also have mandates involving ceasefire or demarcation lines, and while their mandates also involve monitoring and reporting on violations by both State and non-State actors, only UNIFIL has a protection of civilians mandate. See UNSC Res 1701 (2006) UN Doc S/RES/1701, para. 12. While the UN Stabilization Mission in Haiti (MINUSTAH) has a protection-of-civilians mandate, there is no current armed conflict in Haiti. UNSC Res 1542 (2004) UN Doc S/RES/1542, para. 7.I(f). Neither the UN Mission in Kosovo (UNMIK) nor the UN Mission in Afghanistan (UNAMA) have the authority to use force to protect civilians.

II. The Legal Framework for the Use of Force by UN Peacekeepers to Protect Civilians

The use of force by UN peacekeepers is governed by the Charter of the UN, the relevant Security Council resolutions establishing the mission-specific mandate and authority to use force, and the mission-specific rules of engagement (ROE), which are themselves governed by the UN Charter, the mission mandate, and customary international law, including international humanitarian law, to the extent that it is applicable.

In accordance with the Secretary-General's Bulletin on 'Observance by United Nations forces of international humanitarian law' (ST/SGB/1999/13), 'the fundamental principles and rules of international humanitarian law set out in the present bulletin are applicable to UN forces when in situations of armed conflict they are actively engaged therein as combatants, to the extent and for the duration of their engagement'.[17] More generally, and as a matter of established UN policy and practice, peacekeepers are bound by the obligation to respect international humanitarian law, international human rights law, and refugee law, to the extent that they are applicable, in order not to become abusers or perpetrators of violations against the very people they are meant to protect.

The ROE of any UN peacekeeping operation that has been accorded the authority to use all necessary means to protect civilians explicitly enshrine the authority to use force, up to and including deadly force, to protect civilians under imminent threat of physical violence.[18] While there is no lack of mandate or authority in this regard, commanders and contingents alike have often failed to understand the full extent of their rights and obligations, and/or failed to exercise their prerogatives and duties in respect of the use of force, in order to protect civilians.[19] Such failure may, at least in part, be attributable to the following legal considerations.

A. Confusion regarding legal terminology

The now standard formulation for the authority to use force reads as follows: the Security Council '[a]uthorizes [the peacekeeping mission concerned] to use all necessary means, within the limits of its capabilities and areas of deployment, to protect civilians under [imminent] threat of physical violence, without prejudice to the responsibility of the host Government'.[20] Several of these words and phrases have

[17] Secretary-General's Bulletin, 'Observance by United Nations Forces of International Humanitarian Law', UN Doc ST/SGB/1999/13 (1999) § 1.1. In their annual meetings, the UN and the International Committee of the Red Cross have explored the nuances between their respective positions on the extent of the applicability of international humanitarian law to UN forces and the interpretation and implementation of ST/SGB/1999/13, including in respect of the geographic and temporal scope of international humanitarian law if, when, and under what circumstances it is applicable.

[18] The specific authorizations to use force are set out in numbered rules in Annex A of the mission-specific rules of engagement (ROE).

[19] See OIOS Report, n 2, para. 70.

[20] In its most recent resolutions on the UN Stabilization Mission in the Democratic Republic of the Congo (MONUSCO), the UN Multidimensional Integrated Stabilization Mission in the Central

been the subject of differing interpretations and applications in the field. A concerted effort has been made by the UN Department of Peacekeeping Operations (DPKO) and the UN Department of Field Support (DFS), in consultation with the UN Office of Legal Affairs (OLA) and others, to elaborate the necessary guidance to UN Force Commanders, contingent commanders, and military contingents, as well as to the civilian leadership of peacekeeping missions.[21]

Nonetheless, even among Member States and UN officials, there remains a certain degree of confusion between, and possible conflation of, three related but distinct protection concepts: the responsibility to protect, the protected status of civilians under international humanitarian law, and the protection of civilians mandate. The responsibility to protect consists of three pillars which can be briefly summarized as follows: (a) each individual State has the responsibility to protect its populations from genocide, war crimes, ethnic cleansing, and crimes against humanity, including the incitement of these acts; (b) the international community should, as appropriate, help States to exercise this responsibility; and finally, (c) the international community has the responsibility to take measures, both peaceful but if necessary also under Chapter VII, to prevent such crimes and to help to protect such populations from genocide, war crimes, ethnic cleansing, and crimes against humanity.[22] In contrast, international humanitarian law accords protected status to civilians, and preserves the distinction between civilians and parties to the conflict, by prohibiting the intentional targeting of civilians and requiring the use of the minimum necessary and proportionate force to achieve an authorized objective against a legitimate military target while avoiding or at least minimizing civilian casualties and damage to civilian property. Finally, the mandate to protect civilians in UN peacekeeping is a whole-of-mission activity pursued through a range of measures and activities by the civilian, police, and military components of a peacekeeping mission, which includes but is in no way limited to the use of force, up to and including the use of deadly force, by the military component to protect civilians under imminent threat of physical violence.[23] While the responsibility to protect is limited to genocide, war crimes, ethnic cleansing, and crimes against humanity, the mandate to protect civilians covers physical violence in general. While the protected

African Republic (MINUSCA), and the UN Mission in South Sudan (UNMISS), the Security Council has referred only to the 'threat of physical violence'. See UNSC Res 2147 (2014) UN Doc S/RES/2147, para. 4(a)(i); UNSC Res 2149 (2014) UN Doc S/RES/2149, para. 30(a)(i); UNSC Res 2155 (2014) UN Doc S/RES/2155, para. 4(a)(i). However, in its latest resolution on the UN Multidimensional Integrated Stabilization Mission in Mali (MINUSMA), also from 2014, the Security Council still refers to 'imminent threat of physical violence'. See UNSC Res 2164 (2014) UN Doc S/RES/2164, para. 13(a)(ii).

[21] See, for example, UNGA, 'Report of the Special Committee on Peacekeeping Operations, 2011 Substantive Session' (2011) UN Doc A/65/19, para. 180; and UNGA, 'Report of the Special Committee on Peacekeeping Operations, 2012 Substantive Session' (2012) UN Doc A/66/19, paras 191–205.

[22] UNGA Res 60/1, 'World Summit Outcome Document' (2005) UN Doc A/RES/60/1, paras 138–139; UNGA, 'Report of the Secretary-General, Implementing the Responsibility to Protect' (2009) UN Doc A/63/677.

[23] It should also be made clear that the term 'protection' has a broader meaning under international human rights law than in the peacekeeping context. The protection of civilians mandate focuses on protection only from 'physical violence' and the threat thereof (i.e. a threat to kill, torture, beat, or rape).

status of civilians under international humanitarian law prohibits the intentional targeting of civilians and requires measures to avoid or minimize collateral damage, the protection of civilians mandate involves the authority and responsibility to use all necessary means to protect civilians.

As such, it is necessary to distinguish between the negative obligation to avoid harming civilians under international humanitarian law and the affirmative mandate to protect civilians from harm under the protection of civilians mandate. UN forces are authorized to use force against an individual or group if they commit or threaten to commit physical violence against civilians or against other persons under the protection of the peacekeeping operation or if there is reasonable belief, as demonstrated by intent and capacity, that they are preparing to commit such physical violence against civilians.

Distinctions between the long-standing reference to 'imminent threat' and more recent references to 'threat' alone, while apparently intended to remove some of the confusion, may actually create even greater interpretive confusion by creating two separate standards within the mandates and practice of UN peacekeeping operations. The UN Secretariat never understood the term 'imminent' as requiring actual or guaranteed attacks on civilians to trigger the mandate. Both the comprehensive and mission-specific protection of civilians strategies seek to enhance the protection-of-civilians mandate by clarifying the right and duty of UN forces to prevent, pre-empt, deter, or respond to threats of physical violence against civilians. Under these strategies and in accordance with the ROE, all that is required is a reasonable belief that a potential aggressor has the intent and capacity to inflict physical violence.[24] While UN guidance has consistently maintained that a threat of physical violence against civilians is imminent from the time it is identified until such time that the mission can determine that the threat no longer exists, such guidance is not found in the UN ROE and the Annexes of those rules do not contain a specific definition of 'imminent threat'.

Finally, in accordance with the terms of the mandate, a peacekeeping operation authorized to protect civilians may only act within its capabilities and areas of deployment. It is important to recall, however, that protection of civilians is a priority mandate and that, as explicitly confirmed in Security Council Resolution 1894 (2009), 'mandated protection activities must be given priority in decisions about the use of available capacity and resources'.[25] As such, the proviso 'within its capabilities and areas of deployment' is intended to recognize the constraints on the ability of the peacekeeping mission to project its presence and power throughout the entire territory of a host country, especially if there is an ongoing armed conflict;

[24] The standard definition of 'hostile intent' in Annex B of the UN Rules of Engagement (ROE) defines the term to mean a 'threat of imminent and direct use of force, which is demonstrated through an action or behaviour which appears to be preparatory to a hostile act. Only a reasonable belief in the hostile intent is required, before the use of force is authorised. Whether or not hostile intent is being demonstrated must be judged by the on-scene commander, on the basis of one or a combination of the following factors: (a) the capability and preparedness of the threat; (b) the available evidence which indicates an intention to attack and (c) historical precedent within the Mission's Area of Responsibility'.

[25] UNSC Res 1894 (2009) UN Doc S/RES/1894, para. 19.

the proviso is not intended to excuse unwilling or complacent military contingents from the duty to take all necessary action and to use all necessary means to prevent, pre-empt, deter, or respond to imminent threats from physical violence against civilians. It appears, however, that some contingents remain on their bases or in the immediate vicinity thereof, fearing, or failing to deploy to, where the danger is.[26]

B. Undue reliance on the primary responsibility of the host State

Pursuant to the relevant Security Council resolutions, the protection of civilians mandate is without prejudice to the responsibility of the host State. By reaffirming the primary responsibility of the government and/or authorities of the host State to protect its civilian population, the Security Council intends to confirm that the protection of civilians mandate does not relieve the government and/or authorities of the host State of its ultimate responsibility for the well-being and security of persons on its territory, and that the mandate and authority accorded to the peacekeeping operation in no way diminishes that responsibility. The protection of civilians mandate allows the peacekeeping operation to assist the host State to fulfil that responsibility, to act independently when the host State is unable or unwilling, and even to take action against elements of the State's armed forces in the event that they themselves pose a threat of physical violence against civilians.[27]

C. Misunderstanding of the respective roles of the Special Representative of the Secretary-General and the Force Commander

Pursuant to the UN ROE, the Force Commander has ultimate responsibility for their enforcement.[28] It is thus the Force Commander's authority and his or her responsibility to order the necessary use of force to fulfil the protection of civilians mandate. While co-ordination between the Force Commander and the Special Representative of the Secretary-General (SRSG), as the Head of Mission, is both advisable and desirable, and while the military component should, whenever possible, co-ordinate with the other components of the peacekeeping mission, the decision whether to use force, and at what level and intensity, rests with the Force Commander and the other commanders under his or her command subject to the mandate and the ROE.[29]

[26] See discussion in part III.B of this chapter.

[27] The UN Secretariat has consistently maintained that the protection of civilians mandate applies 'irrespective of the source of the threat', that is, including the use of force against elements of State forces where and when they pose a threat of physical violence to civilians. The first explicit reference to this understanding of the protection of civilians mandate appeared recently in operative paragraph 4(a) of Security Council resolution 2155 (2014), which mandates UNMISS to protect civilians under threat of physical violence 'irrespective of the source of such violence'.

[28] The UN ROE consistently provide that '[t]he implementation of these ROE is a command responsibility ... The Force Commander is ultimately responsible for the enforcement of these ROE.'

[29] UN ROE.

While military contingents in UN peacekeeping operations continue to be subject to their national legal systems, including the exclusive criminal jurisdiction thereof, many contingents, including their contingent commanders, do not fully accept, or act under, the unified command or operational control of the Force Commander of the UN operation.[30] The resulting dual lines of authority undermine the authority of the Force Commander, the responsiveness of national contingents to his or her orders, and ultimately the efficiency and effectiveness of the military component.

'National caveats' or restrictions imposed by the troop-contributing countries limiting the use of force by their national contingents and/or constraining their deployment in certain situations further impede consistent interpretation of mandates and uniform application of the ROE. They also threaten to undermine cohesion among the military contingents, which are intended to act as a single unified force under UN command.

It is also a matter of concern that, too often, Force Commanders have in the past and continue to defer to their respective SRSG and/or wait for direct instructions from UN Headquarters, DPKO, or its Office of Military Affairs before taking the necessary measures to pre-empt, prevent, deter, or respond to attacks or threats of physical violence against civilians.[31] Undue reliance on the primary responsibility of the host State, as discussed earlier in the chapter, or on the consent of the host State, as discussed later, also leads some Force Commanders and SRSGs to mistakenly believe that such civilian protection activities must be requested or approved by the government of the host State.[32]

D. Complacency regarding the legal consequences of failure to fulfil the mandate

The protection of civilians concept, as articulated by DPKO and DFS, makes it abundantly clear that the protection of civilians from physical violence consists of several phases—namely, prevention, pre-emption, response, and consolidation—and explicitly notes that these phases do not necessarily occur in sequential order, as a mission may have to respond to rapidly unfolding circumstances.[33] As such, it is not intended that peacekeepers will be merely reactive or responsive; rather, they are expected to be constantly working to analyse threats of physical violence in order to take proactive measures to prevent and mitigate harm to civilians.

The failure to use authorized force may thus amount to a failure to fulfil the protection of civilians mandate. As the Force Commander has ultimate responsibility for the enforcement of the ROE,[34] he or she is ultimately accountable

[30] OIOS Report, see n 4, paras 35–9.

[31] OIOS Report, see n 4, para. 42. [32] Ibid., paras 40–1.

[33] UN Department of Peacekeeping Operations (DPKO) and UN Department of Field Support (DFS), 'Draft DPKO/DFS Operational Concept on the Protection of Civilians in United Nations Peacekeeping Operations' (New York: United Nations, 2010).

[34] See n 28.

for both acts of commission and acts of omission when it comes to the use of force by military contingents under the mandate and the ROE. Military contingents are also accountable for any failure to obey the Force Commander's (or other commanders') lawful orders, which are those orders which are consistent with the mandate and the ROE as well as with customary international law, including international humanitarian law where applicable.[35]

While great deference is owed to the judgement of the commander on the ground, it is understood that inaction or failure to use authorized force is often a function of perceived risk of escalation and/or of potential criminal accountability. It should equally be understood, however, as has consistently been maintained by the DPKO Office of Military Affairs and the OLA Office of the Legal Counsel, that failure to use authorized force can also lead to escalation by virtue of the consequent perception that the UN force is unwilling or unable to act, thereby increasing its vulnerability and undermining its credibility.[36] Such perceptions undermine the deterrent capacity and invite further attacks both against the UN peacekeeping mission and its personnel, as well as against civilians and other persons under the protection of the operation concerned.

The recent deployment of unarmed unmanned aerial systems to the UN Stabilization Mission in the Democratic Republic of the Congo (MONUSCO) and their more recent deployment to the UN Multidimensional Integrated Stabilization Mission in Mali (MINUSMA) are both intended to enhance situational awareness, thereby enabling those missions to strengthen their deterrent posture and ability to take preventative actions.[37] It is expected that such missions will be in a better position to protect themselves, protect civilians, and monitor and deter

[35] UN mission-specific ROE consistently provide that military personnel 'are required to comply with International Law, including the Law of Armed Conflict, and to apply the ROE in accordance with those laws'. The UN Secretariat is of the view that '[m]ilitary personnel placed by Member States under United Nations command, although remaining in their national service are, for the duration of their assignment to the force, considered international personnel under the authority of the United Nations and subject to the instructions of the Force Commander . . . [and] bound to discharge their functions with the interest of the United Nations only in view'. See International Law Commission, 'In Responsibility of International Organizations: Comments and Observations Received from International Organizations' (2004) UN Doc A/CN.4/545, 28. Also, the Secretary-General's Bulletin on International Humanitarian Law provides that '[t]he present provisions do not constitute an exhaustive list of principles and rules of international humanitarian law binding upon military personnel, and do not prejudice the application thereof, nor do they replace the national laws by which military personnel remain bound throughout the operation'. Secretary-General's Bulletin, see n 17, § 2.

[36] The DPKO Office of Military Affairs and the Office of Legal Affairs, Office of Legal Counsel have consistently included this message in the orientation briefings provided to incoming Force Commanders and in the Annual Meetings of the Heads of Military Components.

[37] In his letter dated 27 December 2012 (S/2013/43), the Secretary-General informed the President of the Security Council of his intention, for example, to deploy unmanned aerial systems to enhance situational awareness and permit timely decision-making, including to improve the ability of MONUSCO to protect civilians and to monitor and report on flows of arms and related materiel across the borders of eastern Democratic Republic of the Congo. In his letter dated 22 January 2013, the President of the Security Council informed the Secretary-General that his letter had been brought to the attention of the members of the Security Council and that they took note of the intention expressed therein. In his letter, the President also stated that '[t]he members of the Security Council also note[d] that the trial use in this operation in the Democratic Republic of the Congo of "external imagery/electronic equipment and associated analysis capabilities, notably surveillance capability such as that provided by unmanned aerial systems", is in line with the Secretariat's intention to use assets to enhance

movements of armed groups and weapons. The advantages of having early warning of emerging threats against civilians provided by the analysis of the data collected by the unmanned aerial systems arguably provides greater opportunity to take all necessary actions and to use all necessary means within the missions' capabilities, to deploy proactively to pre-empt, prevent, and deter such threats from materializing or at least to be in a better position to efficiently and effectively respond to them, if and when they occur. Failure to act under these circumstances is harder to justify, and may very well expose the peacekeeping missions concerned to a greater degree of scrutiny of the reasonableness of their actions, or lack thereof, to protect civilians in fulfilment of their protection of civilians mandate.

E. Inhibition to use force arising from fear of criminal accountability or loss of protected status

National contingents and their commanders have time and again confessed serious concern about the prospect of facing courts martial under their respective national systems or, worse yet, being brought to international justice, in particular before the International Criminal Court.[38] Soldiers and commanders alike seem to underestimate the full scope of their authority to use force legally under their mandates and mission-specific ROE, including under international humanitarian law, where it is applicable. They also seem unnecessarily concerned with prosecution in or by the host State in light of the exclusive criminal jurisdiction enjoyed by their respective troop-contributing countries under the mission-specific Status of Force Agreement (SOFA)[39] and under the relevant troop-contributing country's Memorandum of Understanding.[40]

Despite dedicated training by national authorities, the International Committee of the Red Cross, and of course the UN, national contingents and their commanders remain insufficiently familiar with, and therefore consequently reluctant to exercise, the extent of their authority to use force not only to protect civilians against

situational awareness, if available, on a case-by-case basis and without prejudice to the ongoing consideration by relevant United Nations bodies of legal, financial and technical implications of the use of unmanned aerial systems'. UNSC (2013) UN Doc S/2013/44.

[38] OIOS Report, see n 2, para. 50. These concerns are likely to increase in light of the Dutch Court Judgment of 16 July 2014 in the 'Mothers of Srebrenica' case. See *Mothers of Srebrenica v The Netherlands and the United Nations*, Case No C/09/295247 / HA ZA 07-2973 (District Court of the Hague, the Netherlands, Judgment of 16 July 2014).

[39] Pursuant to para. 47(b) of the Model Status of Forces Agreement (SOFA) for Peacekeeping Operations, '[m]ilitary members of the military component of the United Nations peace-keeping operation shall be subject to the exclusive jurisdiction of their respective participating States in respect of any criminal acts which may be committed by them in [host country/territory]'. Draft Model Status of Forces Agreement between the United Nations and Host Countries, in UNGA (1990) UN Doc A/45/594, Annex, para. 60 (UN Model SOFA).

[40] Under 7.22 of the Model Memorandum of Understanding, '[m]ilitary members and any civilian members subject to national military law of the national contingent provided by the Government are subject to the Government's exclusive jurisdiction in respect of any crimes or offences that might be committed by them'. See Model Memorandum of Understanding, revised in UNGA, 'Report of the Special Committee on Peacekeeping Operations and its Working Group on the 2007 resumed session' (2007) UN Doc A/61/19 (Part III) Annex, Article 7, para. 1.

physical violence but even in anticipatory self-defence.[41] Greater familiarity with the mission-specific mandate and ROE prior to arrival at the mission area and regular implementation of periodic training in accordance with the mission-specific ROE would contribute to a better understanding of the protection of civilians mandate, the corresponding authority to use force in fulfilment thereof, and the legal immunities and protections they enjoy when deployed in a UN peacekeeping mission under the model SOFA and the mission-specific SOFA, including, in particular, the exclusive criminal jurisdiction of their respective troop-contributing countries and the criminalization of attacks against UN peacekeepers.[42]

Many contingents and their national governments are also concerned about losing the protected status they presumptively enjoy under international humanitarian law. The continued provision of briefings and training by DPKO and OLA should enhance their understanding of when, under international humanitarian law, and/or under the long-standing Secretary-General's Bulletin on the applicability of international humanitarian law, UN peacekeeping forces may be deemed to become parties to an armed conflict.

While, in theory, any military component of any peacekeeping mission may in the course of defending itself become engaged in sustained or intensive armed hostilities within a non-international armed conflict and thereby become a party to the conflict, the likelihood of that eventuality is, in practice, increased where peacekeepers are deployed in operating environments where such armed conflicts are ongoing, such as in the Democratic Republic of the Congo, and possibly also in Mali or the Central African Republic. The eventuality is nearly inevitable where the mandate itself, by its explicit terms, places UN forces in hostile opposition with

[41] OIOS Report, see n 2, 2. It is also worth noting that mission-specific UN ROE consistently provide for 'anticipatory' or 'pre-emptive' self-defence against an anticipated attack provided that 'there is credible evidence or information that justifies a reasonable belief that hostile units or persons are about to launch an immediate attack'.

[42] Pursuant to paragraph 45 of the Model SOFA, host governments undertake an obligation to 'ensure the prosecution of persons subject to its criminal jurisdiction who are accused of acts in relation to the United Nations peace-keeping operation or its members which, if committed in relation to the forces of the Government, would have rendered such acts liable to prosecution'. Model SOFA, see n 39, para. 45. Pursuant to the Convention on the Safety of United Nations and Associated Personnel of 1994 (the Convention), the relevant provisions of which are now consistently reflected in mission-specific SOFAs provides that States parties are, inter alia, required to make certain crimes against UN and associated personnel punishable by appropriate penalties, to establish their jurisdiction over such crimes and to prosecute or extradite the alleged offenders. See Convention on the Safety of United Nations and Associated Personnel (adopted 9 December 1994, entered into force 15 January 1999) 2051 UNTS 363. In accordance with Security Council Resolution 1502 (2003) and the General Assembly's annual resolutions, since 2002, on 'Safety and security of humanitarian personnel and protection of United Nations personnel', the Secretary-General has, in recent years, routinely sought, and almost without exception obtained, the inclusion of the key provisions of the Convention (as enumerated in those resolutions), as well as the above-mentioned clause from the Model SOFA, within mission-specific SOFAs negotiated with host States. Finally, in accordance with the Rome Statute of the International Criminal Court, the definition of 'war crimes' in Article 8 includes 'intentionally directing attacks against personnel, installations, material, units or vehicles involved in a humanitarian assistance or peacekeeping mission in accordance with the Charter of the United Nations, as long as they are entitled to the protection given to civilians or civilian objects under the international law of armed conflict'. See Rome Statute of the International Criminal Court (adopted 17 July 1998, entered into force 1 July 2002) 2187 UNTS 3, Article 8.

named actors. This we have seen with MONUSCO, in the Democratic Republic of the Congo, which is mandated to undertake enforcement actions against armed groups, including but not limited to the explicit authorization given to its Force Intervention Brigade to conduct targeted offensive operations against the M23,[43] as well as its support to and joint operations with the armed forces of the Democratic Republic of Congo (FARDC).[44]

The protection of civilians mandates of the other peacekeeping missions should not, however, be viewed through the prism of MONUSCO's unique and explicit mandate to conduct targeted offensive operations.[45] There is no such presumptive trigger of applicability of international humanitarian law with respect to the other protection of civilians-mandated peacekeeping missions. The determination in respect of these other UN peacekeeping missions cannot be made based solely on the protection of civilians mandate, but rather must rely on the nature, intensity, and duration of actual military actions taken by the UN forces in response to actions taken by other armed actors or in support of government or other armed forces, in light of the situation in the operating environment. The high-threat operating environment facing MINUSMA in northern Mali and the UN Multidimensional Integrated Stabilization Mission in the Central African Republic (MINUSCA), as well as their co-operation with their host governments and the African Union and French forces operating in the countries (who themselves are parties to the conflicts), may increase the likelihood of those missions also potentially becoming party to the armed conflicts in the respective countries. These eventualities and emerging realities need to be addressed with greater clarity and transparency and with a view to achieving greater understanding and consistency.[46]

The need for clarity and consistency is all the more pronounced in the face of the continuing penalization of attacks on MONUSCO peacekeepers under the Chapter VII Security Council sanctions regime in the Democratic Republic of the Congo, even when such attacks may be lawful under international humanitarian law. Under international law, the Security Council is within its prerogative to continue to impose sanctions in respect of attacks against MONUSCO peacekeepers, even if such attacks are otherwise legal under international humanitarian law, in the same way as States may criminalize attacks by armed groups on their own armed forces not as 'war crimes' under international humanitarian law but as ordinary crimes under their national laws. When it penalizes such attacks under the relevant sanctions regime, without clarifying its intentions vis-á-vis the status of such attacks under international humanitarian law, the Security Council risks greater confusion about the applicability of international humanitarian law to UN forces.

[43] The 'March 23 Movement', also known as the Congolese Revolutionary Army.

[44] The acronym derives from the French 'Forces Armées de la République Démocratique du Congo'.

[45] UNSC Res 2098 (2013) UN Doc S/RES/2098, para. 12(b).

[46] See also Mona Khalil, 'Peacekeeping Missions as Parties to Conflicts' (2014) *Professionals in Humanitarian Assistance and Protection* <phap.org/thematic-notes/2014/february/humanitarian-law-policy-2014-peacekeeping-missions-parties-conflicts>; and Mona Khalil, Remarks during the Panel on Peace Forces at War, 2014 Session of the American Society of International Law, 10 April 2014 (on file with author).

Troop-contributing countries and their contingents deserve greater clarity as to whether and on what basis attacks on UN peacekeepers are legally punishable.

F. Unwillingness to use force due to perceived contravention of the basic principles of peacekeeping

Major troop-contributing countries' reference to the traditional or basic principles of UN peacekeeping—namely, consent, impartiality, and the use of force except in self-defence[47]—often interferes with their ability and/or willingness to use force in a manner consistent with the evolving nature of peacekeeping and the principles which have evolved with it. The impact of the evolution of peacekeeping and the tensions with its basic principles are discussed in more detail in the next section.

III. The Use of Force and the Basic Principles of Peacekeeping

UN peacekeeping missions continue to deploy with the consent of the host State and, despite having authorization to use force for the protection of civilians against threats of physical violence, continue to use force in actual terms, primarily in self-defence.[48]

The major troop-contributing countries and their contingents have, however, voiced concerns that the increasingly robust tasks with which UN peacekeepers are being mandated, and the increasingly volatile operating environments to which they are being deployed, are threatening to undermine the basic principles of peacekeeping to which they wish to adhere.

While it is true that the evolving nature of mandates and operating environments has had a tangible impact on the basic principles of UN peacekeeping, it is also true that the interpretation and application of these principles have evolved, to varying degrees, in a similar and corresponding manner. While the General Assembly, through its Special Committee on Peacekeeping Operations (the C-34), and the Security Council have continued to reaffirm the basic principles of peacekeeping,[49] they have not codified the corresponding evolution in the understanding of those principles. In this, they have sent mixed messages both to the ranks of UN peacekeepers and to the local populations in the host countries in which they serve.

A. Consent of the host State

While host State consent continues to be the primary distinction between UN peacekeeping and peace enforcement,[50] the Security Council has increasingly

[47] See, for instance, UN DPKO and UN DFS, *UN Peacekeeping Operations: Principles and Guidelines* (New York: United Nations, 2008) (Capstone Doctrine).

[48] OIOS Report, see n 2, paras 13–28.

[49] See, for example, UNGA 'Report of the Special Committee on Peacekeeping Operations, 2012 Substantive Session' (2012) UN Doc A/66/19; UNGA, 'Report of the Special Committee on Peacekeeping Operations, 2010 Substantive Session' (2010) UN Doc A/64/19; UNSC Res 2100 (2013) UN Doc S/RES/2100; UNSC Res 2149 (2014) UN Doc S/RES/2149.

[50] Capstone Doctrine, see n 48.

resorted to explicit references to Chapter VII of the UN Charter in resolutions establishing peacekeeping missions and their mandates.[51] While the Security Council must refer to Chapter VII for purposes of authorizing a peacekeeping mission to use force beyond self-defence, there is no legal requirement that the mandate as a whole be so authorized. By making explicit reference to Chapter VII in the chapeau of an establishing resolution, the Security Council creates the misleading impression that the mandate is an enforcement action and obfuscates the fact that the peacekeeping mission and its mandate are being established with the consent of the government and, as is often the case, pursuant to its request.

On a practical level, the consent of the host State to the presence of a UN peacekeeping mission in its territory implies its government's willingness to co-operate with the mission and is essential to the mission's ability to carry out its mandated activities. Since 1999, the Security Council has consistently adopted resolutions, invoking Chapter VII of the UN Charter, authorizing UN peacekeeping missions to use force beyond the inherent right of self-defence in order to achieve certain objectives of the mission, including the protection of civilians under imminent threat of physical violence. While the once clear legal distinction between the primarily defensive use of force in UN peacekeeping and the Chapter VII authority to use force in enforcement operations was long ago 'blurred', the Security Council has, nonetheless, rightly maintained the requirement of host State consent for the establishment and extension of the mandate of peacekeeping missions, notwithstanding their authorization to use 'all necessary means' to achieve that mandate.

Host State consent can manifest implicitly or explicitly, by virtue of the terms of a peace or ceasefire agreement or by a government's confirmation in writing to the Secretary-General or the Security Council either requesting or supporting the establishment of a mission and its intended mandate.[52] Once the Security Council has explicitly defined the period of the mandate of a peacekeeping mission, however, the host State, pursuant to Article 25 of the UN Charter, is not legally in a position to effectively withdraw its consent prior to the expiration of that period. The government of the host country is presumptively obliged to accept and respect the decision of the Security Council once it has been taken, whether the decision was originally taken with the host State's explicit consent or implicit consent. Thus, to avoid a breach of its obligations under the UN Charter, a host State's withdrawal of its consent can legally only effectively occur at the end of an authorized mandate period whereupon, unless a binding Chapter VII obligation is imposed on it by the

[51] Security Council Report, 'In Hindsight: Chapter VII' (*Security Council Report Monthly Forecast*, 30 September 2013) <securitycouncilreport.org/monthly-forecast/2013-10/in_hindsight_chapter_vii.php>.

[52] By way of example, please see UNSC Res 1769 (2007) UN Doc S/RES/1769, preambular para. 6, commending 'the agreement of Sudan that the Hybrid operation shall be deployed in Darfur'; UNSC Res (2013) UN Doc S/RES/2100, taking note of the letter, dated 25 March 2013, preambular para. 18, addressed to the Secretary-General by the transitional authorities of Mali, which 'requests the deployment of a [UN] operation to stabilize and restore authority and the sovereignty of the Malian State throughout its national territory'; and UNSC Res 2149 (2014) UN Doc S/RES/2149, preambular para. 34, taking note of the letter from the Minister for Foreign Affairs of the Central African Republic dated 27 January 2014 requesting 'the deployment of a UN peacekeeping operation to stabilize the country and address the civilian aspects of the crisis'.

Security Council, the government of the host State has the sovereign right to withhold its consent to any further extension of the mandate of the mission concerned. In that event, the host State remains, in accordance with the mission-specific SOFA, under an international legal obligation to allow the peacekeeping mission to remain in its territory for the period reasonably required to withdraw the final elements of the mission and to liquidate its activities.[53]

Based on the foregoing, there is no legal basis to question the continuing relevance of the consent of the host State prior to the establishment of a peacekeeping mandate and deployment of a peacekeeping mission on that State's territory. Once given, however, the host State's consent may not legally be withdrawn, as discussed earlier, until the mandate period in question has expired unless otherwise decided by the Security Council.

B. Impartiality

The peacekeeping missions with protection of civilians mandates that are operating in countries where there is an ongoing, non-international armed conflict between the host country government and armed opposition forces or other armed groups are vulnerable to challenges regarding their presumed impartiality. Military contingents under unified UN command and operational control are currently deployed in countries where there was armed conflict—the UN Stabilization Mission in Haiti (MINUSTAH), the UN Mission in Liberia (UNMIL), the UN Operation in Côte d'Ivoire (UNOCI), and UNIFIL in Lebanon—or where there still is armed conflict—MONUSCO in the Democratic Republic of the Congo, MINUSMA in Mali, MINUSCA in the Central African Republic, the UN-African Union Mission in Darfur (UNAMID), the UN Mission in South Sudan (UNMISS), and the UN Interim Security Force in Abyei (UNISFA).

The mandate of UN peacekeeping missions to support the host government, and the need to sustain the consent and co-operation of the host government, in order to carry out extended mandates often has political and practical implications for the actual or perceived impartiality of the peacekeeping mission and its personnel. The protection of civilians mandate, however, requires UN peacekeepers to protect civilians from physical violence regardless of the source of that threat.[54] The protection of civilians mandate therefore includes, where necessary, the use of force by UN peacekeepers, up to and including deadly force, against elements of government forces, where such elements are themselves engaged in, or pose an imminent threat of, physical violence against civilians.[55] As a matter of policy, the protection of civilians framework and the mission-specific protection of civilians strategies uphold these principles and confirm the impartiality of the UN forces. As a matter

[53] See Draft Model Status of Forces Agreement between the United Nations and Host Countries, in UNGA (1990) UN Doc A/45/594, Annex, para. 60.

[54] UN DPKO and UN DFS, 'Framework for Drafting Comprehensive Protection of Civilians (POC) Strategies in United Nations Peacekeeping Operations' (New York: United Nations, Undated), para. 5 <refworld.org/pdfid/523998464.pdf>.

[55] Ibid.

of practice, however, the perceived weakness of the UN forces in the face of clear violations by the host governments, as we have seen most visibly in Sudan and in South Sudan,[56] calls into question the impartiality and even the credibility of the UN peacekeeping missions concerned.

According to the OIOS Evaluation, '[s]ome missions, including UNAMID and UNMISS, convinced of their weakness, appear to have ruled out the use of force as a realistic option'.[57] UNMISS is further cited as having a 'pattern of non-intervention' and as being 'less than effective during the November–December 2012 crisis that resulted in more than 600 civilian deaths'.[58] While UNMISS must be applauded for saving nearly 100,000 civilians from the ongoing violence in South Sudan, it has done so by 'opening its gates' and establishing 'protection of civilians sites' within five of its own bases on UNMISS premises. In its most recent resolution on South Sudan, the Security Council has recognized the protection of civilians sites and mandated UNMISS to 'maintain public safety and security within and of UNMISS protection of civilians sites';[59] it has nonetheless also continued to insist on UNMISS' mandate to protect civilians from physical violence and to deter violence against them through proactive deployment and active patrolling.[60]

The reluctance of UN military personnel to use force against government forces to protect civilians, whether for political or military reasons, has clearly added to perceptions (whether rightly or wrongly) that they are not impartial actors.

C. Use of force primarily in self-defence

As mentioned, there are currently ten protection of civilians-mandated UN peacekeeping missions, and, with the exception of UNIFIL in Lebanon, each has explicit Chapter VII authority to use force, up to and including deadly force, for the protection of civilians against physical violence. To the extent that these missions have, to varying degrees, been reluctant to use force, even in anticipatory self-defence as discussed earlier, it comes as no surprise that the OIOS evaluation concluded that they have failed to translate their legal authority to use force to protect civilians with proactive or effective implementation on the ground.

Any assessment of the effectiveness of UN peacekeeping forces in fulfilling their protection of civilians mandate must, in accordance with the specific terms of that protection of civilians mandate, take into account the limited capabilities of the missions concerned and their inability to project their force beyond their areas of deployment. While the Security Council does not expect, and the levels of troops authorized in its relevant resolutions do not allow, UN forces to prevent or even to respond to every attack on civilians everywhere within the territory of the host State, the Security Council, at a minimum, expects UN forces to act in the face of large-scale and/or systematic attacks against civilians.

[56] OIOS Report, see n 2, para. 45. [57] Ibid. [58] Ibid., para. 70.
[59] UNSC Res 2155 (2014) UN Doc S/RES/2155, para. 4. [60] Ibid.

The inherent right of self-defence remains the primary instance for the use of force by UN peacekeepers, and the use of force also remains a last resort in the broad range of legal means available to UN peacekeepers to fulfil their Security Council-authorized protection of civilians mandate. In implementation of that mandate, however, UN forces have not only the right but also the duty, under Chapter VII of the UN Charter, to use force, up to and including deadly force, where and when necessary and appropriate to pre-empt, prevent, deter, and/or respond to targeted or systematic attacks on civilians within the limits of their capabilities and areas of deployment.

IV. Conclusions

The legal framework embodied by the UN Charter, the relevant Security Council resolutions, the mission-specific ROE, and the mission-specific SOFA is broad enough and deep enough to place the protection of civilians mandate and the authority to use all necessary means, up to and including deadly force, on solid legal ground. Nonetheless, confusion regarding the meaning and scope of the legal terminology, concerns regarding the consent of the host State, lack of clarity around the roles and responsibilities of mission leadership, the potential for criminal accountability and/or becoming a party to the conflict, the duality of contingent and mission-command structures, and the basic principles of peacekeeping appear to have an inhibiting effect on the use of force by UN peacekeepers beyond self-defence and for the protection of civilians.

More than fifteen years after the first explicit protection of civilians mandate was authorized by the Security Council, however, controversy continues to plague the concept of 'robust' peacekeeping. Questions linger regarding the consensual nature of UN peacekeeping missions established by resolutions adopted under Chapter VII. The support that UN peacekeepers are mandated to provide to host governments calls into question their impartiality in operating environments defined by ongoing armed conflicts, and where the ability of the mission to interpose itself politically between the government and the other parties to such conflicts hangs in the balance. Where and when such support involves military assistance, concerns regarding impartiality fall in the wake of the spectre of the mission itself becoming a party to the conflict. Where the protection-of-civilians mandate places UN peacekeepers in the position of having to use force against elements of the host government's forces, the underlying consent is difficult to sustain over extended mandates and the viability of the mission, which is ultimately dependent upon the government's co-operation, is at stake. The debate over whether peacekeeping has crossed over to peace enforcement, when force is used beyond self-defence, inhibits contingents from exercising the full authority accorded to them and from fulfilling the mandates entrusted to them. While the willingness of troop-contributing countries to put their troops in harm's way in the service of peace is noble, it cannot be taken for granted where and when such peace is absent or elusive.

To the extent that the use of force remains a last resort, its place in the UN's contribution to the protection of civilians should not be overstated. It is nonetheless a right afforded to, and a duty expected from, UN peacekeepers, and it is therefore not only appropriate but necessary to assess the effectiveness with which it is exercised in the fulfilment of the protection of civilians mandate.

10

International Responsibility for Ensuring the Protection of Civilians

Siobhán Wills

I. Introduction

This chapter will examine whether under international law the United Nations (UN) or its Member States have a legal obligation to protect civilians from deliberately inflicted violence by third parties (in certain circumstances); and, if so, the implications of those obligations for UN missions.[1] The chapter will focus primarily on the protection obligations of UN Security Council-mandated missions, particularly those with a specific protection mandate, since these have been the primary drivers of the protection of civilians doctrine.[2]

Since 1999 most UN peacekeeping missions have been explicitly mandated to provide protection, whether as a subsidiary function of the mission or as its *raison d'être*. As of August 2015 ten UN peacekeeping operations have mandates to 'protect civilians under imminent threat of physical violence'[3] and to also undertake other protection measures. These missions account for more than 90 per cent of peacekeepers currently deployed.[4] Nevertheless, analysing whether protection of civilians and the closely aligned doctrine of the responsibility to protect give rise to positive legal obligations to protect civilians is complex. Norms of civilian protection have developed in an ad hoc manner through a combination of legal and

[1] The author would like to thank colleagues at the Transitional Justice Institute, Ulster University, in particular Rory O'Connell, for their helpful comments.

[2] There is now a whole body of standard-setting material presented under the banner of the protection of civilians (PoC), much of it using the acronym PoC, which, due to the morally charged expectations that underpin it, could best be described as 'PoC doctrine'.

[3] Field Mission Mandate Table, 1 August 2015, Security Council and Charter Research Branch, Security Council Affairs Division, Department of Political Affairs, United Nations;United Nations Security Council (UNSC), 'Annex to the letter dated 3 February 2014 from the Permanent Representative of Lithuania to the United Nations addressed to the Secretary-General, Concept note for the Security Council open debate to be held on 12 February 2014 on Protection of civilians in armed conflict: effective implementation of protection of civilians mandates in United Nations peacekeeping operations' (2014) UN Doc S/2014/74.

[4] As of November 2015 there were 123,036 uniformed and civilian personnel in the sixteen UN peacekeeping missions deployed, of which 116,182 were in the ten missions that have a protection of civilians mandate. Uniformed numbers represent Security Council-authorized ceilings as of 31 August 2015; civilian numbers represent General Assembly-approved mission staffing budgets as of 30 June 2015.

political enterprises that have been driven by a range of actors, each of which may share a partial common goal but have different primary or subsidiary aims and objectives. Consequently, although mandates authorize protection activities there is little established guidance as to what a force is expected to do, and even less as to what it is obliged to do, to carry out its mandated protection activities.[5]

This chapter argues that there are legal obligations to protect—derived largely from international human rights law (IHRL), international humanitarian law (IHL), and the Draft Articles on the Responsibilities of International Organizations—that are binding on UN missions. These obligations are comparatively weak because they depend on a narrow intersection of developing (or debatable) law, practice, and circumstance; but nevertheless they have important operational implications for UN missions, that have not been discussed elsewhere to any significant degree.

UN missions, as traditionally conceived, were thought of as having predominantly negative legal obligations, essentially to do no harm.[6] A mission that has largely negative legal obligations retains considerable flexibility within the confines of its mandate as to how that mandate should be implemented, and also as to how decisions relating to the mandate are made, documented, and communicated. A legal obligation to protect is a positive legal obligation: it cannot be achieved simply by refraining from action. It follows that if today's missions have a legal obligation to protect people in the areas in which they are deployed, they have positive legal obligations. With positive legal obligations come procedural obligations, and with procedural obligations come the obligation to carry out the procedures unless there is a good reason why this is not possible.

The existence of a protection of civilians mandate gives rise to the presumption that the mission is aware that civilians are at risk. In order to fulfil a positive obligation to protect, in a situation where it is known that that attacks on civilians are likely, the mission must assess the probability, seriousness, and location of likely attacks; draw up plans to counter the risks to civilians that it has concluded are likely; document those plans; and pass that information up the chain of command to a level of seniority that can take responsibility for approving the effectiveness of the plans in light of the scale of likely harm. The need for proactive planning in order to protect is recognized by the UN Department of Peacekeeping (DPKO). In its Civil Affairs Handbook of 2012 it states that missions with protection of

[5] The most detailed guidance currently available is to be found in Victoria Holt and Glenn Taylor, with Max Kelly, *Protecting Civilians in the Context Of UN Peacekeeping Operations* (New York: United Nations, 2009).

[6] A peacekeeping force was initially expected to achieve its goals 'not through military combat but by the simple fact of its presence'. Ramesh Thakur, *United Nations Peacekeeping In Lebanon: United Nations Authority and Multinational Force* (Boulder, USA: Westview Press, 1987) 57. The UN's 'Ten Rules: Code of Personal Conduct for Blue Helmets' reflects an approach focused on negative rather than positive obligations. Examples of the ten rules include 'displaying the highest integrity and impartiality', 'respect[ing] the law of the land of the host country, their local culture, traditions, customs and practices', and 'respect[ing] and regard[ing] the human rights of all'. See United Nations, 'Ten Rules: Code of Personal Conduct for Blue Helmets' (New York: United Nations, 1998) <www.un.org/en/peacekeeping/documents/ten_in.pdf>, recognized in UNSC Statement of the President (1998) UN Doc S/PRST/1998/28, 2.

civilians mandates 'are required to conduct a detailed analysis of risks facing civilians in the area of operations and to devise a comprehensive protection of civilians strategy that articulates the mission's approach towards addressing the priority protection of civilians risks that it has identified'.[7] Drawing up protection plans pursuant to an obligation to protect implies an obligation to carry out those plans unless unable to do so, or unless to do so would cause other serious harm that had not been foreseen (or the scale of which had not been foreseen) at the time the plan was initially drafted.

II. Responsibility for Complicity in Attacks on Civilians

Missions are frequently deployed for durations spanning many years, and inevitably their presence deeply infiltrates the structures of the societies that they are deployed to protect. Local elites often become adept at exploiting the presence of the UN to further their own ambitions. The UN may then find itself not only failing to protect civilians but inadvertently aiding the commission of human rights violations or war crimes against them, a problem that became particularly troublesome for the UN Mission in the Democratic Republic of the Congo (MONUC, now succeeded by MONUSCO). MONUC was severely criticized for working alongside the Forces Armées de la République Démocratique du Congo (FARDC), which has had known war criminals serving in its ranks,[8] including some that have been indicted by the International Criminal Court.[9] At least in relation to this specific case, the UN has recognized that it may have legal obligations in relation to serious violations of IHL and IHRL by third parties. In 2009 the Under-Secretary-General for Legal Affairs and UN Legal Counsel, Patricia O'Brien, stated in a note to the Under-Secretary-General for Peacekeeping Operations, Alain Le Roy, that:

> MONUC may not lawfully provide logistics or 'service' support to any FARDC operation if it has reason to believe that the FARDC units involved are in violation of any of those bodies of law [IHL, IHRL and international refugee law] . . . this follows from the Organization's obligations under customary international law and from the Charter to uphold, promote and encourage respect for human rights, international humanitarian law and refugee law.[10]

Moreover:

> If MONUC has reason to believe that FARDC units involved in an operation are violating one or other of these bodies of law, and if, despite MONUC's intercession with FARDC and

[7] UN Department of Peacekeeping Operations (DPKO) and Department of Field Support (DFS), *Civil Affairs Handbook* (New York: United Nations, 2012) 53–4.

[8] Pursuant to a 2009 amnesty pact agreed between President Kabila of the Democratic Republic of the Congo (DRC) and President Kagame of Rwanda. See International Crisis Group, *Congo: No Stability in Kivu Despite Rapprochment with Rwanda* (Brussels: International Crisis Group, 2010) 9–10.

[9] Former general of the Congrès National pour la Défense du Peuple, Bosco Ntaganda, became a commander of the armed forces of the DRC, despite his indictment by the International Criminal Court for war crimes. Ibid., 1.

[10] Patricia O'Brien, 'Note of 12 October 2009 to Alain Le Roy', cited in Vladyslav Lanovoy, 'Complicity in an Internationally Wrongful Act' (Amsterdam: University of Amsterdam, 2014) 19 <www.sharesproject.nl/wp-content/uploads/2014/03/SHARES-RP-38-final.pdf>.

with the Government of the DRC, MONUC has reason to believe that such violations are being committed, then MONUC may not lawfully continue to support that operation, but must cease its operation completely.[11]

Ms O'Brien did not state whether the UN or troop-contributing States could be held legally responsible if they were to unlawfully provide support to a FARDC operation, in the manner just described. Nor did she indicate what criteria should be used to measure whether 'MONUC has reason to believe that FARDC units involved in an operation are violating one or other of these bodies of law' or what entity might have authority to determine whether MONUC was acting unlawfully. What is clear, however, is that she considered that the UN has positive 'obligations under customary international law' and has positive obligations derived 'from the Charter', that require it 'to uphold, promote and encourage respect for human rights, international humanitarian law and refugee law'.[12] In her view, these obligations were sufficiently compelling as to require MONUC to cease its operation completely rather than support a force that is violating IHL, IHRL, or international refugee law.[13]

Ms O'Brien's statement is cited in the commentary to Article 14 of the Draft Articles on the Responsibilities of International Organisations (DARIO) as an example of the kind of situation in which an international organization might be held responsible for giving aid or assistance in the commission of an internationally wrongful act.[14] The commentary notes that Article 14 'only introduces a few changes in relation to Article 16 on the responsibility of States for internationally wrongful acts' and that under the comparable provisions regarding State responsibility, the relevant State organ must have 'intended, by the aid or assistance given, to facilitate the occurrence of the wrongful conduct' and the aid or assistance must have contributed 'significantly' to the commission of the act.[15] MONUC never intended to facilitate the occurrence of a wrongful act, but the commentary to the DARIO does not address this point. However the text of Article 14 does not mention intention; it merely states that to be held responsible under the article, the organization must be providing assistance 'with knowledge of the circumstances of the internationally wrongful act'.[16] Scott Sheeran has suggested that:

the ambiguity may be best resolved by the plain meaning and purpose of the rule. While in the commentaries the words 'deliberate' and 'intention' are used almost interchangeably, this is inconsistent with the plain meaning of 'knowledge of the circumstances' contained in both versions of the article. 'Knowledge' is a broader category than 'intent' . . . knowledge

[11] Ibid. [12] Ibid.

[13] In November 2009 the UN did withdraw its support from a unit of the Congolese army, a decision that 'represents a constitutional moment for the United Nations' and confirms 'that the Secretary-General is normatively constrained under the Charter, including by the Organization's obligations, when implementing the decisions of the Security Council'. Scott Sheeran, 'A Constitutional Moment? United Nations Peacekeeping in the Democratic Republic of Congo' (2011) 8 Intl Org L Rev 55, 55.

[14] Draft Articles on the Responsibility of International Organizations, with Commentaries, in UNGA (2011) UN Doc A/66/10, 52-170, 103–4 (Draft Articles on the Responsibility of International Organizations).

[15] Ibid. [16] Ibid.

would appear to be a sounder basis for international responsibility, rather than a need to demonstrate intent to assist the internationally wrongful act.[17]

Articles 42(1) of the DARIO, which provides that 'States and international organizations shall cooperate to bring to an end through lawful means any serious breach' of a peremptory norm, and 42(2) of the DARIO, which provides that '[n]o State or international organization shall recognize as lawful a situation created by a serious breach' of a peremptory norm 'nor render aid or assistance in maintaining that situation',[18] may also be relevant to UN missions, especially those that are assisting governments that have a poor human rights record to restore stability following armed conflict or serious internal political violence. An example might be if a State to which the UN mission is giving post-conflict support had previously obtained its position, or secured its position against insurgent threats, through serious breaches of peremptory norms such as large-scale violations of the right to life and the right not to be tortured. If the violations continue in the post-conflict period because the government continues to torture and kill persons who were detained during the conflict, and the UN provides substantial military support to the government to enable it to retain power and secure it against further insurgency, the UN could possibly be responsible under Article 42 of the DARIO, as well as Article 14, for rendering assistance in maintaining a situation created, in part, by serious breaches of peremptory norms.

III. The View that a Security Council Mandate to Protect Creates an Independent Legal Obligation

It is sometimes argued that a Security Council mandate to protect civilians under threat of imminent attack itself creates a legal obligation to protect them, to the extent that the force is capable of doing so.[19] One possible basis for holding this view would be to argue that an explicit mandate to protect civilians from imminent violence constitutes a unilateral declaration creating a legal obligation.[20] However, the majority view is that mandates provide an authorization to act but do not, in themselves, create any legal obligation to do so.[21] In 2014 the District Court of the Hague, in *Mothers of Srebrenica v The Netherlands*, held that '[w]hilst UNPROFOR's mandate is indeed regarded as a decision by an international law

[17] Sheeran, see n 13, 76.

[18] Draft Articles on the Responsibility of International Organizations, see n 14, 62, Article 42.

[19] Discussed in Kjetil Mujezinović Larsen, *The Human Rights Treaty Obligations of Peacekeepers* (Cambridge: Cambridge University Press, 2012) 392; Mona Khalil, Chapter 9 in this volume.

[20] The International Court of Justice (ICJ) has stated that 'when it is the intention of the State making the declaration that it should become bound according to its terms, that intention confers on the declaration the character of a legal undertaking, the State being thenceforth legally required to follow a course of conduct consistent with the declaration', in *Nuclear Tests Case (Australia and New Zealand v France)* [1974] ICJ Rep 253, 457, para. 43.

[21] Larsen, see n 19, 392; Haidi Willmot and Scott Sheeran, 'The Protection of Civilians Mandate in UN Peacekeeping Operations: Reconciling Protection Concepts and Practices' (2014) 95 IRRC 517–38.

organisation it only has a powers-creating character and does not call to life any obligations Claimants can enforce at a court of law'.[22] The European Court of Human Rights in the *Al Jedda* case noted that resolution 1546 (which welcomed the willingness of the multinational force to continue efforts to contribute to the maintenance of security and stability in Iraq) 'appears to leave the choice of the means to achieve' the mission's objectives 'to the Member States within the Multi-National Force', and concluded that the effect of mandates drafted in this way is to authorise rather than oblige action on the part of the mission.[23]

As Michael Woods noted more than ten years ago, Security Council resolutions 'are frequently not clear, simple, concise or unambiguous. They are often drafted by non-lawyers, in haste, under considerable political pressure, and with a view to securing unanimity within the Council.'[24]

Woods' point remains true, with the added complication that drafters of resolutions have found it convenient to keep reusing phrases from previous resolutions (that have passed muster with other Security Council members without causing too much controversy), which creates the impression that these phrases have developed a core meaning; in practice, however, subtle changes in language are used to facilitate very different interpretations of apparently similar mandates. This is particularly true of protection of civilians language (which for the past decade has become increasingly routinely incorporated into mandates), because delegates are less likely to object to a mandate authorizing the protection of civilians (obviously a desirable goal) than to one authorizing more overtly political changes within a Member State (changes that may indeed enhance the prospect of successful protection of vulnerable civilians).

For example, in 2011, Security Council resolution 1973 authorized certain Member States acting through the North Atlantic Treaty Organization (NATO) 'to take all necessary measures ... to protect civilians and civilian populated areas under threat of attack in the Libyan Arab Jamahiriya, including Benghazi'.[25] This language is similar to the protection of civilians phrases routinely used in peacekeeping mandates, but slightly expanded to include 'civilian populated areas', an expansion that had major implications. As Nils Blokker has observed, whatever the intentions of the Security Council might have been in adopting resolution 1973, '[i]n practice' it was 'used to support the opposition in its successful fight for regime change'.[26] In resolution 1975 on Côte d'Ivoire, adopted two weeks after resolution

[22] District Court of the Hague, *Mothers of Srebrenica v The Netherlands and the United Nations*, Judgment of 16 July 2014, Case No C/09/295247 / HA ZA 07-2973, para. 4.149

[23] *Al-Jedda v The United Kingdom* Application 27021/08 (ECtHR, 2011) para. 105. The Court also stated, at para. 105, that '[i]n the light of the United Nations' important role in promoting and encouraging respect for human rights, it is to be expected that clear and explicit language would be used were the Security Council to intend States to take particular measures which would conflict with their obligations under international human rights law'.

[24] Michael C Wood, 'The Interpretation of Security Council Resolutions' (1998) 2 Max Planck YB UN L 73, 73.

[25] UNSC Res 1973 (2011) UN Doc S/RES/1973.

[26] Niels Blocker, 'Security Council Authorizations to Use Force: Recent Developments' in *The Oxford Handbook of the Use of Force in International Law*, Chapter 9, edited by M Weller and A Solomou (Oxford: Oxford University Press, forthcoming 2015).

1973, the Security Council mandated the peacekeeping operation, the UN Operation in Côte d'Ivoire (UNOCI), to use all necessary means to protect civilians under imminent threat of physical violence, within its capabilities and its areas of deployment,[27] language that is routinely used in peacekeeping mandates. However, in this case the resolution indicated that the phrase was to be construed as 'including to prevent the use of heavy weapons against the civilian population',[28] which effectively, albeit controversially, allowed for much greater intervention by the UN mission in the conflict.[29]

UNOCI, working alongside French troops, was instrumental in assisting Alessane Ouatarra's forces to remove Laurent Gbagbo from power in order to prevent a return to civil war, and with it a likely return to human rights abuses on a large scale. The Ivorian Independent Electoral Commission had declared that Outarra had won the presidential election and therefore was the legitimate president, a declaration reiterated by the UN Secretary-General, Ban Ki-moon, but the Constitutional Council of Cote d'Ivoire had confirmed Gbagbo as the winner of the presidential election, prompting controversy as to the authority of the Secretary-General to make such pronouncements on an apparently internal matter. UNOCI's intervention was based on the need to protect civilians rather than the election results per se. Gbagbo's appalling human rights record was not in doubt;[30] however, Outarra's human rights record was also poor. Notably, throughout 2011, after Gbagbo had been arrested and later sent to the Hague following UNOCI's assistance in his removal, 'former rebels loyal to Ouattara' were 'still committing abuses such as executions and torture' without any response from UNOCI.[31] Martin Kouakou Fofié, one of the commanders promoted by Outarra in 2011, was placed on the UN Security Council sanctions list in 2006 for a catalogue of serious human rights violations,[32] after French peacekeepers found nearly one hundred bodies with their hands tied behind their backs that had been executed by forces under Fofié's command.[33] Despite UN DPKO's first-hand knowledge of the 'particularly appalling' conduct of this commander '[e]ven by the former rebel army's standards',[34] in its 2012 World report on Côte d'Ivoire, Amnesty International concluded that '[i]nternational actors that had rightfully taken a hardline stance against the Gbagbo camp's abuses during the conflict—including the United Nations, the

[27] UNSC Res 1975 (2011) UN Doc S/RES/1975, para. 6.

[28] Ibid.

[29] For overviews of the mission, see UNSC, 'Thirty-fourth Progress Report of the Secretary-General on the UN Operation in Côte d'Ivoire' (2014) UN Doc S/2014/342; and UNSC, 'Thirty-first Progress Report of the Secretary-General on the UN Operation in Côte d'Ivoire' (2012) UN Doc S/2012/964.

[30] John James, 'Gbagbo Transfer to The Hague Shocks Supporters', *BBC News* (London, 30 November 2011) <www.bbc.co.uk/news/mobile/world-africa-15962777>.

[31] Aaron Gray-Block, 'Gbagbo, Ouattara Forces Engaged in War Crimes: ICC', *Reuters* (London, 23 June 2011) <www.reuters.com/article/2011/06/23/us-ivorycoast-icc-idUSTRE75M76620110623>.

[32] Forces under his command engaged in recruitment of child soldiers, abductions, imposition of forced labour, sexual abuse of women, arbitrary arrests, and extra-judicial killings: Human Rights Watch, 'News Release: Côte d'Ivoire: Military Promotions Mock Abuse Victims' (New York, 5 Aug 2011).

[33] Ibid. [34] Ibid.

European Union, France, and the United States—appeared less willing to publicly pressure Ouattara's government on the same issues and on the importance of impartial accountability'.[35] There may be legitimate reasons for States to condemn one president's poor human rights record and not that of his successor, but UNOCI had a strong protection of civilians mandate. UN peacekeeping missions are expected to carry out their mandates impartially.[36] In May 2011, Amnesty International reported that that when challenged on the mission's failure to protect civilians as provided for in its mandate, UNOCI officials responded that 'it is the duty of the state to protect civilians',[37] which suggests that they did not think that the Security Council mandate created a legal obligation to protect where the State was failing to do so.[38] Arguably, UNOCI's failure to respond to serious violations of peremptory norms by Outarra's forces, despite having a protection of civilians mandate, was a breach of the UN's obligations under the DARIO to take steps to bring violations of peremptory norms to an end through lawful means, as discussed in Section II of this chapter.

Under Security Council resolution 1894 (2009), 'mandated protection activities must be given priority in decisions about the use of available capacity and resources';[39] therefore, as Mona Khalil observes elsewhere in this volume, the almost routine proviso limiting a mission's protection obligations to what is 'within its capabilities and areas of deployment' is 'not intended to excuse unwilling or complacent military contingents' from 'the duty to take all necessary action and to use all necessary means to prevent, pre-empt, deter or respond to imminent threats from physical violence against civilians'.[40] Nevertheless, the varied way in which mandates are interpreted, and the opacity of some of the terms frequently used in them, suggests that most political actors do not regard peacekeeping mandates as legally binding in any meaningful sense: if they did, there might be pressure to nail down the meaning of them. This rarely happens, partly because securing agreement to Security Council resolutions is often achieved by deliberately drafting them in such a way as to allow for different interpretations.[41]

[35] Human Rights Watch, *World Report 2012* (New York: Human Rights Watch, 2012) 97–103.

[36] Report of the Panel on United Nations Peace Operations, in UNSC and UNGA (2000) UN Doc A/55/305–S/2000/809, para. 50 (Brahimi Report).

[37] Amnesty International, 'Press Release: Côte d'Ivoire: Both Sides Responsible for War Crimes and Crimes against Humanity' (London, 25 May 2011) <www.amnesty.org/en/news-and-updates/report/c%C3%B4te-divoire-both-sides-responsible-war-crimes-and-crimes-against-humanity-2>.

[38] A 2013 report in Africa Review states that the UN sanctions experts committee found that Fofié's rise to power under Outarra enabled him to extend his 'warlord-style predatory economic activities' to 'the entire Ivorian territory' and that he was using his 'military-economic network' to plunder the country's exports of cocoa, cashew nuts and other resources to the tune of millions of dollars: AFP, 'Côte d'Ivoire 'Warlord' Commanders Plunder Cocoa Exports: UN', *Africa Review* (Nairobi, 29 April 2013) <www.africareview.com/News/Cote-dIvoire-warlord-commanders-plunder-cocoa-exports-UN-/-/979180/1761296/-/14ckv74z/-/index.html>.

[39] UNSC Res 1894 (2009) UN Doc S/RES/1894, paragraph 19.

[40] See Mona Khalil, Chapter 9 in this volume.

[41] Occasionally provisions are included whose purpose is to narrow the range of possible actions that might be taken to further the aims of the resolution; for example, the provisions in resolution 1973 'excluding a foreign occupation force of any form on any part of Libyan territory'. UNSC Res 1973 (2011) UN Doc S/RES 1973, para. 4.

However, it may be worth noting that some provisions in peacekeeping mandates do imply that at least those particular paragraphs are intended to be obligatory.[42] For example, under resolution 1996 of 2011, the UN Mission in South Sudan (UNMISS) was mandated to support the government of South Sudan through, inter alia:

> monitoring, investigating, verifying, and reporting *regularly* on human rights and potential threats against the civilian population as well as actual and potential violations of international humanitarian and human rights law, working as appropriate with the Office of the High Commissioner for Human Rights, bringing these to the attention of the authorities as necessary, and *immediately* reporting gross violations of human rights to the UN Security Council.[43]

Under resolution 2155 of May 2014 UNMISS is additionally authorized 'to use all necessary means' to, inter alia:

> monitor, investigate, verify and report *specifically* and publicly on violations and abuses committed against children and women, including all forms of sexual and gender-based violence in armed conflict by accelerating the implementation of monitoring, analysis and reporting arrangements on conflict-related sexual violence and by strengthening the monitoring and reporting mechanism for grave violations against children.[44]

A mandate to report is one thing, but a mandate to report *regularly* or *immediately* or *specifically* imports something beyond authorization. It makes no sense to interpret 'report immediately' as purely powers-creating except in a context where, absent the authorization, the addressee is prohibited from reporting immediately, which is unlikely to be the case for peacekeeping missions. Arguably, the addition of qualifying factors as to the timing and nature of the mandated task (in this case reporting) suggests that those paragraphs at least are intended to be obligatory: otherwise the qualifying phrases in those paragraphs would have to be treated as redundant.[45]

UNMISS takes its reporting duties seriously. The reason it does so, and the reason for the inclusion of detailed reporting requirements in UNMISS mandates since 2011, is largely because of credible allegations that the South Sudanese government has committed very serious violations of human rights (and continues to do so).[46] UNMISS was initially mandated inter alia to provide support to the South Sudanese government, but its mandate was revised in 2014 to focus on protection because of the government's continued poor human rights record. The specific reporting requirements in the UNMISS mandates quoted above were intended to

[42] UNSC Res 2164 (2014) UN Doc S/RES 2164, para. 13.

[43] UNSC Res 1996 (2011) UN Doc S/RES 1996, para. 3(b)(iii), emphasis added.

[44] UNSC Res 2155 (2014) UN Doc S/RES 2155, para. 4(b)(ii), emphasis added.

[45] Under Article 25 of the UN Charter, 'the Members of the United Nations agree to accept and carry out the decisions of the Security Council in accordance with the present Charter'. But peacekeeping missions are generally UN-commanded and therefore if there are provisions in the mandate that are legally binding, it will normally be the UN itself that is responsible for carrying them out (see section VI on accountability).

[46] Human Rights Watch, *South Sudan's New War: Abuses by Government and Opposition Forces* (New York: Human Rights Watch, 2014).

protect civilians, but it is likely that they were also intended to minimize the risk of a repeat of the problems that MONUC faced in the Democratic Republic of the Congo (DRC). The UN's Human Rights Due Diligence Policy on UN Support to Non-UN Security Forces, adopted following criticism of MONUC, requires that the UN must put in place 'procedures for monitoring the recipient entity's compliance with international humanitarian, human rights and refugee law' and that if 'despite intercession by the United Nations entity concerned' the recipient entity does commit grave violations, then 'the United Nations entity must suspend or withdraw support from the recipient'.[47]

However, at this point in time, the view that a Chapter VII mandate is obligatory in its entirety remains a minority one. Therefore if the UN does have an obligation to protect, the mandate is unlikely to be the primary source of that obligation. If the UN's obligation to protect exists independently of any resolution it adopts, the absence of a mandate authorizing the protection of civilians from violence does not absolve the UN from an obligation to do so. The Brahimi Report of 2000 stated that 'United Nations peacekeepers—troops or police—who witness violence against civilians should be presumed to be authorized to stop it, within their means, in support of basic United Nations principles'.[48] If this is the case, the authority to protect civilians is afforded all peacekeeping missions, and therefore all missions have a lawful means of protecting civilians (provided applicable rules of IHRL and IHL on use of force are respected) regardless of any objections from host States.

IV. Obligations of United Nations Missions to Protect Civilians under International Human Rights Law

Other than the mandate itself, the most likely sources of a legal obligation to protect are IHRL, the customary law element of which is embedded in the Charter as a foundational principle,[49] and customary IHL. The aspects of IHRL and IHL that are most relevant to the protection of civilians from physical violence concern the right to life in IHRL, the principles of distinction and proportionality in IHL, and the prohibition on torture and ill-treatment in both IHL and IHRL.[50] However, there is no evidence that the UN, in adopting protection of civilians mandates, regards itself as fulfilling IHRL or IHL obligations directly; rather, it seems to see itself as fulfilling part of a more general commitment to human security in line with

[47] United Nations Human Rights Due Diligence Policy on UN Support to Non-UN Security Forces, in UNGA and UNSC (2013) UN Doc A/67/775–S/2013/110, Annex, paras 2, 27 (UN Human Rights Due Diligence Policy).

[48] Brahimi Report, see n 36, x.

[49] As reflected in its Preamble and article 2.3 in particular.

[50] See Peter Maurer, 'War, Protection and the Law: the ICRC's Approach to International Humanitarian Law' (Statement at the 2nd Foreign & Commonwealth Annual Lecture on International Law, London, 19 May 2014) <www.icrc.org/eng/resources/documents/statement/05-23-war-protection-and-the-law-icrc-approach-fco-2nd-international-law-lecture-19-may-2014.htm>; see also Tom Hadden and Colin Harvey, 'The Law of Internal Crisis and Conflict' (1999) 81 IRRC 119.

the broad spirit of the principles of the Charter and the Universal Declaration of Human Rights. As the High Level Panel on Threats, Challenges and Change reported in 2004:

> history teaches us all too clearly that it cannot be assumed that every State will always be able, or willing, to meet its responsibilities to protect its own people and avoid harming its neighbours. And in those circumstances, the principles of collective security mean that some portion of those responsibilities should be taken up by the international community, acting in accordance with the Charter of the United Nations and the Universal Declaration of Human Rights, to help build the necessary capacity or supply the necessary protection, as the case may be.[51]

One reason for the focus on security is because the maintenance of international peace and security is the primary function of the UN, and it is the basis on which the Security Council may utilize Chapter VII of the Charter. Security Council resolution 1894 on Protection of Civilians in Armed Conflict notes that:

> the deliberate targeting of civilians as such and other protected persons, and the commission of systematic, flagrant and widespread violations of applicable international humanitarian and human rights law in situations of armed conflict may constitute a threat to international peace and security, and reaffirms in this regard its readiness to consider such situations and, where necessary, to adopt appropriate steps.[52]

A. Protection obligations of the United Nations under international human rights law

The UN is not a party to any IHRL treaties. However, it is bound by peremptory norms, by its Charter, and by its own human rights undertakings as reflected in its resolution and bulletins. Arguably, it is also bound by core human rights principles promulgated through the human rights regime it has created.[53] The Human Rights Due Diligence Policy on UN Support to Non-UN Security Forces,[54] adopted in 2013 in response to the controversy over MONUC (discussed earlier), asserts that the UN has 'obligations under international law to respect, promote and encourage respect for international humanitarian, human rights and refugee law',[55] but it does not assert that the UN has positive human rights obligations that are directly derived from IHRL. The Aide-Memoire to the Secretary-General's Human Rights

[51] Report of the High Level Panel on Threats, Challenges and Change, 'A More Secure World: Our Shared Responsibility', in UNGA (2004) UN Doc A/59/565, Annex, para. 29.

[52] UNSC Res 1894 (2009) UN Doc S/RES/1894, para. 19.

[53] Marten Zwanenburg, 'United Nations and International Humanitarian Law', in *Max Planck Encyclopedia of Public International Law* (Oxford University Press, online edition, 2013) 6 <www.mpepil.com>; Jordan J Paust, 'The UN is Bound by Human Rights: Understanding the Full Reach of Human Rights, Remedies and Nonimmunity' (2010) 51 Harvard Intl L J Online <www.law.harvard.edu/studorgs/ilj>.

[54] UN Human Rights Due Diligence Policy, see n 47. The UN Human Rights Due Diligence Policy was adopted in 2013 in response to, among other things, criticisms of the UN Mission in the Congo for working alongside the Congolese armed forces despite their poor human rights record. See Carla Ferstman, 'Clean Hands in Peacekeeping: The U.N. Needs to Do More' (*The Olive Branch*, 13 May 2013) <www.usip.org/olivebranch/clean-hands-in-peacekeeping-the-un-needs-do-more>.

[55] UN Human Rights Due Diligence Policy, see n 47, Annex, para. 1.

Up Front Plan of Action, adopted in 2013 in response to criticism of the UN's failure to protect civilians during the war in Sri Lanka,[56] states that '[p]rotecting human rights is a core purpose of the United Nations and defines our identity as an organization'[57] and that the UN will 'put the imperative to protect people, wherever they may be, at the heart of UN strategies and operational activities'.[58] Moreover, it goes on to state that '[w]e will integrate human rights into the life-cycle of all staff ... so that all staff understand what the UN's commitment to human rights means for their department, agency, fund or programme and for them personally'.[59]

While the Human Rights Up Front initiative 'is designed primarily for settings where the UN does not have a political or peacekeeping mission ... its spirit can and should also be applied to "mission settings"'.[60] For many years the UN took a similar approach to the applicability of IHL to its missions, committing only to upholding the 'spirit' of IHL, but it later replaced references to 'spirit' in relevant bulletins with 'rules'.[61] It should be noted that over the past decade the UN has promoted the concept of 'integration' as a core aspect of its approach to its engagement in countries emerging from conflict. The 'main purpose of integration is to maximize the collective and individual impact of all the various UN efforts in support of peace consolidation'.[62] In complex humanitarian crises a peacekeeping mission, a special political mission, and a UN Country Team may all be deployed alongside each other.[63] While the Human Rights Up Front Action Plan is not intended to be formally applicable in such situations, its effectiveness depends on being integrated into the UN's entire approach. To hold UN Country Teams to different human rights standards depending on whether or not they are working alongside a military or political mission would undermine both the goal of integration and the effectiveness of the Human Rights Up Front Action Plan.

However, despite the stated intention to mainstream awareness of the UN's human rights responsibilities throughout all its activities, the Human Rights Up

[56] 'Rights Up Front' (May 2014) United Nations Secretary-General, <https://undg.org/home/guidance-policies/country-programming-principles/human-rights/rights-up-front-initiative/>.

[57] Aide-Mémoire to the Rights Up Front Plan of Action, on file with author.

[58] Ibid.

[59] Ibid. Admittedly the reference to 'the life-cycle of all staff' is odd and might be off-putting to anyone considering a career in the UN.

[60] 'Rights Up Front', see n 56, 3.

[61] Model agreement between the United Nations and Member States contributing personnel and equipment to United Nations peacekeeping operations, in UNGA (1991) UN Doc A/46/185 (Model SOFA), para. 28, reprinted in Adam Roberts and Richard Guelff (eds), *Documents on the Laws of War* (Oxford: Oxford University Press, 2000) 625, 723; Daphna Shraga, (then Senior Legal Officer, Office of the Legal Counsel, Office of Legal Affairs, UN), 'UN Peacekeeping Operations: Applicability of International Humanitarian Law and Responsibility for Operations-Related Damage' (2000) 94 AJIL 406, 406. From 1993, Status of Forces Agreements between the UN and host States included the obligation to respect the 'principles and spirit' of the laws of armed conflict but by the end of the twentieth century, 'spirit' had been replaced by 'rules'. See PC Szasz, 'UN Forces and International Humanitarian Law' in LC Green and Michael N Schmitt (eds), *International Law across the Spectrum of Conflict, Essays in Honour of Professor LC Green on the Occasion of His Eightieth Birthday* (Newport, USA: US Naval War College, 2000) 507, 516.

[62] UN DPKO and DFS, see n 7, 17–18.

[63] Ibid.

Front Plan is cautious as to the source and scope of those responsibilities. The Aide-Mémoire to the Human Rights Up Front Action Plan notes that

> Member States have mandated the Secretary-General and the UN system, through the Charter and successive General Assembly resolutions, to use our moral authority, diplomatic creativity and operational reach to help them meet the standards so powerfully expressed in the Universal Declaration of Human Rights, and to hold them accountable for doing so.[64]

It also notes as additional justification, presumably in light of the UN's role in eliminating 'the scourge of war',[65] that '[p]rotecting human rights helps prevent conflict'.[66]

Nevertheless, while the exact scope of the UN's IHRL obligations remains a matter of debate and the UN Human Rights Up Front Plan is noncommittal as to their source, few commentators would dispute that at a minimum the UN has an obligation not to violate peremptory norms.[67] The reference to UN operations in the commentary to Article 14 of the DARIO implies as much: it would be very odd if the UN was legally precluded from assisting a State in violating peremptory norms but could do so itself. While there is no consensus on the full content of peremptory norms, there is a strong view that 'killings which are committed outside the judicial process and which cannot be considered lawful under the law of armed conflict' violate peremptory norms protecting the right to life.[68] The prohibition on torture is also widely regarded as peremptory.[69]

In its General Comment 29, the Human Rights Committee asserted that the proclamation of certain provisions of the Covenant as being of a non-derogable nature 'is to be seen partly as recognition of the peremptory nature' of these rights.[70] The right to life and the prohibition on torture and inhumane treatment (the rights that are most relevant to protection of civilians from violence) are non-derogable under the International Covenant on Civil and Political Rights, the European Convention on Human Rights and Fundamental Freedoms, and the

[64] Aide-Mémoire to the Human Rights Up Front Plan of Action, see n 57.

[65] Charter of the United Nations Charter (adopted 26 June 1945, entered into force 24 October 1945) 1 UNTS XVI, Preamble.

[66] Aide-Mémoire to the Human Rights Up Front Plan of Action, see n 57.

[67] Larsen, see n 19, 323–33; see generally Paust, n 53.

[68] Lauri Hanikainen, *Peremptory Norms (Jus Cogens) in International Law: Historical Development, Criteria, Present Status* (Helsinki: Finnish Lawyers' Publishing Company, 1988) 516–17. The Inter-American Commission on Human Rights has stated that the right to life is part of jus cogens, see *Victims of the tugboat '13 de Marzo' v Cuba*, Report No. 47/96 (IACHR, 1996), para. 79. See also Jordan Paust, 'The Right to Life in Human Rights Law and the Law of War' (2002) 65 Saskatchewan L Rev 412, 412–13; Larsen, see n 19, 323–33

[69] Erika de Wet, 'The Prohibition of Torture as an International Norm of Jus Cogens and its Implications for National and International Law' (2004) 15 EJIL 97, 97–100.

[70] 'Furthermore, the category of peremptory norms extends beyond the list of non-derogable provisions . . . States parties may in no circumstances invoke article 4 of the Covenant as justification for acting in violation of humanitarian law or peremptory norms of international law, for instance by taking hostages, by imposing collective punishments, through arbitrary deprivations of liberty or by deviating from fundamental principles of fair trial, including the presumption of innocence.' Human Rights Committee, 'General Comment 29, States of Emergency (article 4)' (2001) UN Doc CCPR/C/21/Rev.1/Add.11, Annex VI, para. 11 (General Comment 29).

American Convention on Human Rights.[71] Upholding these rights entails both direct and indirect responsibilities, usually referred to as negative and positive obligations in the European human rights system and as obligations to respect, protect, and fulfil in the UN system. The positive obligation to protect the right to life is engaged where a State has failed to take measures to prevent a death from occurring, including systems of implementation, or has failed to carry out an effective investigation or to provide an effective remedy.[72] This includes a duty to take care in the planning and conduct of security operations so as to protect as far as possible the right to life.[73] However, it is questionable whether the entirety of the obligations entailed in upholding non-derogable rights is peremptory. Torturing people or subjecting them to inhumane treatment or carrying out extra-judicial killing clearly violates peremptory norms, but it is not clear that the obligation to secure the right to life, or to secure the right not to be tortured, against threats from third parties, is also a peremptory norm.

The title of the UN's Human Rights Up Front intiative, with its strong emphasis on rights (rather than something like 'Protection Our Priority', with an emphasis on protection), along with the UN's Human Rights Up Front commitment to 'integrate human rights into the life-cycle of all staff', could be interpreted as an acknowledgment that the UN has positive obligations to fulfil at least some 'rights' of the people it serves, in particular to protect them from serious violations of human rights.[74] However, even if the UN's formal human rights obligations do not extend beyond compliance with peremptory norms, and even if peremptory human rights norms do not encompass positive obligations per se, under the DARIO, 'States and international organizations shall cooperate to bring to an end through lawful means any serious breach' of a peremptory norm.[75] A Chapter VII protection of civilians mandate is evidence of co-operation amongst Member States, acting through the UN, to find a lawful means of bringing to an end the murder and inhumane treatment of civilians. This is so even if the mandate also serves other purposes (as it invariably does), especially given that Security Council resolution 1894 of 2009 requires that mandated protection activities be given priority in decisions about the use of available capacity and resources.[76] Article 42 of the DARIO clearly intends that, having co-operated in finding a lawful means of

[71] International Covenant on Civil and Political Rights (adopted 16 December 1966, entered into force 23 March 1976) 999 UNTS 171, Article 4; Convention for the Protection of Human Rights and Fundamental Freedoms (adopted 4 November 1950, entry into force 3 September 1953) 213 UNTS 222, Article 15; American Convention on Human Rights (adopted 22 January 1969, entered into force 18 July 1978) 1144 UNTS 123, Article 27 (2); see also General Comment 29, see n 70. The African Charter on Human and Peoples' Rights does not have a derogation clause.

[72] *Velasquez-Rodriguez v Honduras*, Inter-American Ct Hum Rts (IACHR) Series C, Case 4 (1988).

[73] *McCann* et al. *v The United Kingdom* Application 1998/91 (1995) ECtHR; *Jordan v The United Kingdom* Application 24746/94 (2001) ECtHR; *Neira Alegría* et al. *v Peru*, IAHCR Series C No. 20 (1995) 3; *Camargo (on behalf of Suarez de Guerrero) v Colombia*, Human Rights Committee, Communication No. 45/197 (1982) UN Doc Supp No 40 (A/37/40) 137.

[74] The Human Rights Up Front plan also commits to protecting people from violations of international humanitarian law (IHL), but traditionally IHL has been conceived more in terms of obligations than as rights, though in practice the distinction may be quite fine.

[75] Draft Articles on the Responsibility of International Organizations, see n 14, Article 42.

[76] UNSC Res 1894 (2009) UN Doc S/RES/1894, para. 19.

ending specified violations of peremptory norms, States and international organizations must act on it, unless precluded from doing so by changes in circumstances that would render the proposed action more harmful than beneficial.

B. Protection obligations of troop-contributing States

In recent years, a number of courts have taken the position that a State's human rights obligations may apply outside its territory where it maintains 'effective control' over territory or persons.[77] In such circumstances the human rights violations of a UN peacekeeping force may be attributable to the troop-contributing State, and possibly to both the UN and the contributing State. In the view of the United States, IHL operates during armed conflict and IHRL does not,[78] except to the extent that '[w]here the LOAC [Law of Armed Conflict] is silent or its guidance inadequate, specific provisions of applicable human rights law may supplement the LOAC'.[79] However, the International Court of Justice,[80] the European Court of Human Rights,[81] the International Committee of the Red Cross (ICRC),[82] and many international legal scholars maintain that IHL and IHRL may both apply in situations of armed conflict.[83]

The Human Rights Committee has stated that State parties 'must respect and ensure the rights laid down in the Covenant to anyone within the power or effective control of that State Party ... regardless of the circumstances in which such power or effective control was obtained, such as forces constituting a national contingent of a State Party assigned to an international peace-keeping or

[77] Oona Hathaway, Philip Levitz, Elizabeth Nielsen, Aileen Nowlan, William Perdue, Chelsea Purvis, Sara Solow, and Julia Spiegel, 'Human Rights Abroad: When Do Human Rights Treaty Obligations Apply Extraterritorially?' (New Haven: Yale University, 2011) <www.law.yale.edu/documents/pdf/cglc/Hathaway_HumanRightsAbroad.pdf>.

[78] William Johnson (ed.), *Operational Law Handbook, 2013* (Charlottesville, USA: The Judge Advocate General's Legal Center and School, 2013) 46–7.

[79] Ibid., 47. The United States also does not accept that the ICCPR applies extra-territorially, citing the text of the ICCPR and the *travaux preparatoires*. However, the United States *Army Operational Law Handbook* does acknowledge the potential extra-territorial applicability of customary human rights law. See Johnson, n 78, 48; Noam Lubell, *Extraterritorial Use of Force against Non-State Actors* (Oxford: Oxford University Press, 2011) 232–5.

[80] The ICJ has stated that in armed conflict 'both branches of international law, namely international human rights law and international humanitarian law, would have to be taken into consideration' and that 'international human rights instruments are applicable "in respect of acts done by a State in the exercise of its jurisdiction outside its own territory, particularly in occupied territories"'. *Case Concerning Armed Activities on the Territory of the Congo (DRC v Uganda)* (Judgment) [2005] ICJ Rep 168, para. 216.

[81] As of September 2014, 'the European Court of Human Rights has delivered more than 230 judgments finding violations of the Convention in connection with the armed conflict in the Chechen Republic of the Russian Federation'. European Court of Human Rights Press Unit, 'Fact Sheet—Armed Conflicts' (*European Court of Human Rights*, November 2014) 7 <www.echr.coe.int/Documents/FS_Armed_conflicts_ENG.pdf>.

[82] Jean-Marie Henckaerts and Louise Doswald-Beck, *Customary International Humanitarian Law* (Volume 1) (Cambridge: Cambridge University Press, 2005) 299–305.

[83] *Legality of the Threat or Use of Nuclear Weapons* (Advisory Opinion) [1996] ICJ Rep 226, para. 25.

peace-enforcement operation'.[84] The United States does not accept this interpretation of the ICCPR, arguing that the text of the Convention itself, supported by the *travaux preparatoires*, implies that it is not intended to apply extra-territorially.[85] However, the International Court of Justice rejects this view.[86] Most human rights treaties, other than the African Charter on Human and Peoples' Rights, provide for derogation in times of emergency (though derogation is not possible in respect of inter alia violations of the right to life and the right not to be tortured), an option that States involved in armed conflicts outside their own territory have never taken up, which might suggest that their governments do not think IHRL conventions are applicable in these circumstances. In 2011 the European Court of Human Rights held in *Al-Jedda*,[87] a case dealing with the obligations of UK forces in Iraq, that 'whenever the State through its agents exercises control and authority over an individual, and thus jurisdiction, the State is under an obligation under Article 1 to secure to that individual the rights and freedoms under Section 1 of the Convention that are relevant to the situation of that individual. In this sense, therefore, the Convention rights can be divided and tailored'.[88]

To date the European Court of Human Rights has not heard any cases concerning UN peacekeeping missions. In the *Behrami* and *Saramati* cases (which concerned claims against the NATO-led Kosovo Force), the European Court of Human Rights stated that it lacked jurisdiction to review missions undertaken pursuant to Security Council decisions because, inter alia, the 'Convention cannot be interpreted in a manner which would subject the acts and omissions of Contracting Parties which are covered by UNSC Resolutions and occur prior to or in the course of such missions, to the scrutiny of the Court'. To do so 'would be to interfere with the fulfilment of the UN's key mission in this field ... [and] with the effective conduct of its operations'.[89] However, the extent to which positive obligations under the European Convention on Human Rights are applicable to States contributing troops to a UN mission has been argued before the Dutch courts in a number of cases.

In 2013, in the joined *Nuhanovic* and *Mustafic* cases,[90] concerning events in Srebrenica, the Dutch Supreme Court held that since the Bosnian Serb army respected the Dutch battalion's authority over its own compound, 'Dutchbat ... was actually able to ensure compliance with the human rights enshrined in Articles 2 and 3 ECHR [European Convention on Human Rights] and Articles 6 and 7 ICCPR

[84] Human Rights Committee, 'General Comment 31, Nature of the General Legal Obligation on States Parties to the Covenant' (2004) UN Doc CCPR/C/21/Rev.1/Add.13, para. 10.

[85] Human Rights Committee, 'Concluding Observations on the Fourth Periodic Review of the United States of America' (2014) UN Doc CCPR/C/USA/CO/4, para. 4.

[86] *Legal Consequences of the Construction of a Wall in Occupied Palestinian Territory* (Advisory Opinion) [2004] ICJ Rep 136, paras 105–7.

[87] *Al-Jedda v The United Kingdom* Application 27021/08, (ECtHR, 7 July 2011); *Al-Skeini and Others v The United Kingdom* Application 55721/07 (ECtHR, 7 July 2011).

[88] *Al-Skeini*, see n 87, para. 137.

[89] *Behrami and Behrami v France and Saramati v France, Germany and Norway* Application nos. 71412/01 and 78166/01 (ECtHR, 2 May 2007), para. 149.

[90] *The State of the Netherlands v Mustafic* 12/03329 (Supreme Court of the Netherlands, 2013) and *The State of the Netherlands v Nuhanovic* 12/03324 (Supreme Court of the Netherlands, 2013).

[International Covenant on Civil and Political Rights]'[91] within the compound, noting that in order for the Netherlands to be held responsible for violations of IHRL 'it is not necessary for the State to have countermanded the command structure of the United Nations by giving instructions to Dutchbat or to have exercised operation command independently'.[92] The Court also stated that a judgment against the Netherlands did not preclude the possibility that the UN might also have responsibilities under human rights law in relation to the same situation, though for jurisdictional reasons these could not be determined before the Dutch courts.[93]

In the *Mothers of Srebrenica* case, the District Court in The Hague found that the Netherlands was not liable for the deaths of the approximately 7,000 massacre victims that were not forcibly evacuated from the Dutch compound but were killed after fleeing to the woods, but it was responsible for failing to protect the people that were within the Dutchbat compound after 11 July, since at that time 'the compound was a fenced-off area in which Dutchbat had the say and over which the UN after the fall of Srebrenica exercised almost no actual say any more'.[94] However, the failure of Dutchbat to sound the general alarm about the flight of the male refugees on 11 July, despite the fact that 'they were aware of the real risk these men were running', is 'not attributable to the State'. The Netherlands was only responsible for matters within its effective control, and the Court concluded that the matters that were within the mission's effective control at that time related only to providing humanitarian assistance and the evacuation of the refugees.[95] Sounding the alarm was presumably the UN's responsibility alone. This may seem like sophistry. Evidence suggests that the massacre came as no surprise to either the UN or Dutchbat. Corwin, the chief UN political officer in Bosnia, noted in his diary on 12 July 1995, just days before the massacre, that:

> Not a single one of us believes that the Moslem population of Srebrenica will be safe. The pattern is all too familiar, and it is a pattern used by Croats and Moslems as well. The draft-age men will be separated from their families, then tortured, imprisoned, executed. Women will be raped. Mass graves will be hurriedly dug to hide the evidence.[96]

This may explain the Dutch court's finding that failure to sound the general alarm, despite awareness of the refugees' likely fate, was not imputable to the Netherlands. The UN was formally in command and therefore prima facie responsible for the

[91] These articles deal with the right to life and the right not to be subjected to torture or inhumane treatment.

[92] *The State of the Netherlands v Mustafic*, see n 90, paras 3.11.3, 3.17.3.

[93] Ibid., paras 3.11.3, 3.17.3.

[94] *Mothers of Srebrenica v The Netherlands*, The Hague District Court C-09/295247/HA ZA 07-2973, 2014, para. 4.160. The Court stated 'in order to accept *effective control* there would be no requirement for the State in giving instructions to Dutchbat to have broken the structure of the chain of command at the UN or exercised independent operational authority to give orders. It comes down to the actual say over specific actions whereby all of the actual circumstances and the particular context of the case must be examined' (para. 4.46). The Court explicitly left open the possibility that the Netherlands and the UN might both be responsible.

[95] Ibid., paras 4.109–4.110.

[96] Phillip Corwin, *Dubious Mandate: A Memoir of the UN in Bosnia, Summer 1995* (Durham, USA: Duke University Press, 1999) 212.

acts and omissions of its force. The UN had declared Srebrenica a safe area. The UN was aware that a massacre (and mass rape and torture) of civilians was likely.

V. Obligations of United Nations Peacekeeping Missions to Protect Civilians under International Humanitarian Law

The core provisions of common Article 3 (e.g. those prohibiting murder of all kinds, torture and inhumane treatment, and the taking of hostages) are peremptory norms. As noted earlier, under Article 42 of the DARIO, States and international organizations must 'cooperate to bring to an end through lawful means any serious breach' of a peremptory norm.[97] A Chapter VII protection-of-civilians mandate may provide a lawful means of bringing to an end such breaches. Obligations under common Article 1 of the Geneva Conventions, and also under the laws of occupation if they are applicable, may add further weight to this argument.

A. The law of occupation

Prima facie, 'any actual control by one State over the territory of another State brings with it the duty to respect some or all of the laws of occupation'.[98] In the *Israeli Wall* opinion[99] and in the *Case Concerning Armed Activities on the Territory of the Congo*,[100] the International Court of Justice treated the status of occupation as in itself triggering obligations under the human rights laws to which the occupant is party, as well as the IHL obligations of Geneva Convention IV. In the *Case Concerning Armed Activities on the Territory of the Congo*, the International Court of Justice found by sixteen votes to one that Uganda (which it had determined was an occupying power) had violated obligations under both IHRL and IHL, on the grounds that Ugandan forces had failed to take action to put an end to violence that had resulted in some 100,000 deaths and the displacement of some 500,000 people. The Court noted that the Uganda People's Defence Force 'stood by during the killings and failed to protect the civilians'.[101]

The UN has never suggested that the law of occupation might apply to its operations, the argument against being that since a UN force acts pursuant to the mandate conferred upon it by the UN Security Council, occupation does not represent the source of authority in the mission's area of operation.[102] The Secretary-General's Bulletin on Observance by United Nations forces of International

[97] Draft Articles on the Responsibility of International Organizations, see n 14, Article 42.

[98] Adam Roberts, 'What is a Military Occupation?' (1984) 55 British YB Intl L 249, 250.

[99] *Legal Consequences of the Construction of a Wall in Occupied Palestinian Territory*, see n 86, paras 11–114.

[100] *Case Concerning Armed Activities on the Territory of the Congo (DRC v Uganda)*, see n 80, paras 178–9.

[101] Ibid., para. 345.

[102] Zwanenburg 'rejects this view, because it is in contradiction with the fundamental distinction between *ius ad bellum* and *ius in bello*'. Martin Zwanenburg, 'United Nations and International

Humanitarian Law makes no reference to occupation.[103] It is unlikely that occupation law would be considered applicable to forces deployed with the consent of the host State government, notwithstanding that, as both Simon Chesterman and Steven Ratner note, even where missions have the consent of the government, 'they often lack the consent of the population'.[104] However, some participants in the ICRC's 2012 study on occupation stated that occupation law 'could become the legal framework of reference especially when the UN operation contained an element of enforcement in its mandate and found itself having to run the entire territory in which it was deployed or parts of it'.[105] The majority of the participants in the ICRC's study 'believed that occupation law could apply de jure to UN administrations',[106] and that to exclude the applicability of occupation law 'consent to the UN administration must be given by the legitimate sovereign—and not by any other entity exerting effective control over the territory concerned, in particular the occupier—in order to thwart the de jure applicability of occupation law'.[107] In their view, '[t]he fact that it was the UN administering a territory would not alter the rules of the game'.[108] Other participants noted that 'the existence of a Security Council resolution validating the UN administration would not exclude the relevance and application of occupation law, in particular because Security Council resolutions establishing a UN administration usually did not include a detailed description of the applicable legal regime'.[109]

UN peacekeeping missions, although they may have extensive administrative responsibilities, generally do not constitute UN administrations as such. However, if it is the case that the fact of UN involvement does not 'alter the rules of the game', then the criteria is not the formal existence of an administration per se but whether the mission is exercising sufficient authority and control over territory to trigger the applicability of the laws of occupation (and that the host State government, if there is one, is not in a position to govern). One example where this arose was in Somalia in the early 1990s, where there was no State capable of giving consent to the deployment of a mission. The legal advisor to the Australian forces in UNITAF (Unified Task Force, a US-led mission authorized under Chapter VII of the UN Charter) considered that the laws of occupation applied to that mission de jure because UNITAF was the sole organized entity capable of exercising authority in the areas it occupied; the United States disagreed with this approach on the grounds that the mission was primarily humanitarian.[110]

Humanitarian Law', in *Max Planck Encyclopedia of Public International Law* (Oxford University Press, online edition, available at <www.mpepil.com>) 6; para. 21.

[103] Secretary-GeneralSecretary-General's Bulletin, 'Observance by United Nations Forces of International Humanitarian Law' (1999) UN Doc ST/SGB/1999/13.

[104] Steven Ratner, 'Foreign Occupation and International Territorial Administration: The Challenges of Convergence' (2005) 16 EJIL 695, 698; Simon Chesterman, *You, the People: The United Nations, Territorial Administration, and State-Building* (Oxford: Oxford University Press, 2004) 152, 239.

[105] Tristan Ferraro (ed.), *Meeting Report: Occupation and other Forms of Administration of Foreign Territory* (Geneva: International Committee of the Red Cross (ICRC), 2004) 79.

[106] Ibid., 79. [107] Ibid., 81.

[108] Ibid., 79. [109] Ibid., 82.

[110] The United States noted its 'concern over the responsibilities that might flow from acknowledging the application of the law in the context of the extremely minimalist approach dictating

B. Common Article 1

Outside of occupation the most significant provision of IHL that could be construed as obliging a UN mission to take action to protect civilians from serious abuses of human rights is Article 1, common to the four Geneva Conventions, by which the High Contracting Parties undertake to 'respect and ensure respect' for the provisions of the Conventions 'in all circumstances'.[111] All troop-contributing States are parties, but the UN is not and cannot become so since it is not a State. Unlike many IHRL conventions, the Geneva Conventions were not drafted under the auspices of the UN.

For many years the UN did not acknowledge that IHL applied formally to its forces, although it did require its forces to comply with the 'spirit' of them.[112] However, in 1999 the Secretary-General promulgated his Bulletin on Observance by United Nations forces of International Humanitarian Law, which states that the 'fundamental principles and rules of international humanitarian law set out in the present bulletin are applicable to United Nations forces when in situations of armed conflict they are actively engaged therein as combatants, to the extent and for the duration of their engagement'.[113] The Bulletin makes no specific reference to common Article 1. It is focused on the obligations of UN forces rather than on the UN as an organization, whereas Article 1 is primarily directed at the parties to the Conventions rather than their armed forces.[114] However, the UN has long held that peacekeepers, even if they are not engaged as combatants, are obliged to uphold the principles and rules of IHL.[115] The International Court of Justice has stated that, in the terms of Article 1 of the Geneva Conventions, to 'respect' the Conventions, and even to 'ensure respect' for them 'in all circumstances', is an obligation that

the shape of the mission'. Michael J Kelly, *Restoring and Maintaining Order in Complex Peace Operations* (The Hague: Kluwer, 1999) 17.

111 See Geneva Convention Relative to the Protection of Civilian Persons in Time of War (Fourth Geneva Convention) (adopted 12 August 1949, entered into force 21 October 1950) 75 UNTS 287, para. 1; and compare Protocol Additional to the Geneva Conventions of 12 August 1949, and relating to the Protection of Victims of International Armed Conflicts (Protocol I) (adopted 8 June 1977, entered into force 7 December 1978) 1125 UNTS 609, Article 1.

112 Model SOFA, see n 61, para. 28.

113 Secretary-General's Bulletin on Observance by UN Forces of International Humanitarian Law (1999) UN Doc ST/SGB/1999/13, para. 1. See also the resolution of the Institut de Droit International, applicable to 'internal armed conflicts in which peacekeeping forces intervene' among others, which states that 'all parties to armed conflicts in which non-State entities are parties, irrespective of their legal status, as well as the United Nations, and competent regional and other international organizations have the obligation to respect international humanitarian law as well as fundamental human rights'. Institute de Droit International, Resolution on 'The Application of International Humanitarian Law and Fundamental Human Rights in Armed Conflicts in which non-State Actors Are Parties' (Fourteenth Commission) (Berlin, 25 August 1999), paras I, II.

114 Since IHL is binding on individuals as well as States, Article 1 must also bind troops, though exactly what it means for troops is not clear. Siobhán Wills, *Protecting Civilians: The Obligations of Peacekeepers* (Oxford: Oxford University Press, 2009) 107.

115 Status of Forces Agreements between the UN and host States now generally include the obligation to respect the 'principles and rules' of the laws of armed conflict. See Paul C Szasz, 'UN Forces and International Humanitarian Law', in Michael N Schmitt (ed.), *International Law across the Spectrum of Conflict, Essays in Honour of Professor LC Green on the Occasion of His Eightieth Birthday* (Newport, USA: US Naval War College, 2000) 507, 516.

'does not derive only from the Conventions themselves, but from the general principles of humanitarian law to which the Conventions merely give specific expression'.[116] Laurence Boisson de Chazournes and Luigi Condorelli argue that Article 1 is a foundational principle that derives from general principles of humanitarian law and

> belongs to a select group of norms and principles held by the international community to be of cardinal importance for the promotion of 'elementary considerations of humanity'. Such norms play what may be termed a 'constitutional role' in a system of collective security where humanitarian values have become a reason for the adoption of a large number of measures.[117]

Thus, arguably, although the Geneva Conventions were intended to be applicable to States involved in international armed conflicts, the Article 1 obligation may also be applicable in situations of non-international armed conflict on the basis of the customary law status of the principles to which Article 1 merely gives expression (a view supported by the ICRC's research into State practice with regard to the status of the Article 1 obligation under customary IHL),[118] and may also be applicable to UN missions.

It is unlikely that the drafters of Article 1 envisaged that it encompassed obligations beyond ensuring that a State's own forces and civilian personnel complied with the conventions. Nevertheless the International Court of Justice, the ICRC, the Tehran Conference on Human Rights, and IHL and IHRL commentators have all affirmed that, whatever the original drafters might have intended, the provision now carries an obligation to 'ensure respect' by all States (since the four Geneva Conventions are universally ratified).[119] The preamble to resolution XXIII adopted at the Tehran Conference on Human Rights, 1968, asserts that 'States parties to the Red Cross Geneva Conventions sometimes fail to appreciate their responsibility to take steps to ensure respect of these humanitarian rules in all circumstances by other States, even if they are not themselves directly involved in the conflict'. In 1990 the Security Council adopted resolution 681 calling on the parties to the Geneva Conventions, pursuant to their obligations under common Article 1, 'to ensure respect' by Israel for its obligations under the Fourth Convention in relation to the Occupied Palestinian Territories.[120] In 2001 a conference of parties to the conventions

[116] *Military and Paramilitary Activities in and against Nicaragua (Nicaragua v United States of America)* (Judgment) [1986] ICJ Rep 14, para. 220.

[117] Laurence Boisson de Chazournes and Luigi Condorelli, 'Common Article 1 of the Geneva Conventions Revisited: Protecting Collective Interests' (2000) 82 IRRC 67, 85–6.

[118] Henckaerts and Doswald-Beck, see n 82, Rule 144.

[119] The International Conference on Human Rights Resolution XXIII, 'Human Rights in Armed Conflicts' (adopted 12 May 1968, Tehran) <www.icrc.org/applic/ihl/ihl.nsf/INTRO/430?OpenDocument>; *Legal Consequences of The Construction of A Wall In The Occupied Palestinian Territory*, see n 86, para. 158. As Carlo Focarelli notes in 'Common Article 1 of the 1949 Geneva Conventions: A Soap Bubble?' (2010) 21 EJIL 125, 127: 'under Article 1 contracting states have also undertaken to adopt all measures necessary to ensure respect for the Conventions against other contracting states which fail to comply with them. The latter no doubt reflects the prevailing view today.'

[120] Israel rejects the contention that the convention is applicable to those territories on the basis that any occupation there is not an occupation of territory belonging to a High Contracting party to the Geneva Conventions.

published a declaration, also directed towards Israel's responsibilities in the Occupied Palestinian Territories, in which they 'encourage[d] the initiatives by State Parties, both individually and collectively, according to Article I of the Convention and aimed at ensuring respect for the Convention, and they underline[d] the need for the parties, to follow up on the implementation of the present Declaration'.[121] In 2004 the International Court of Justice, in its Advisory Opinion concerning the *Legal Consequences of the Construction of a Wall in the Occupied Palestinian Territory*, affirmed that Article 1 entails third party obligations, stating that 'it follows from that provision that every State party to that Convention, whether or not it is a party to a specific conflict, is under an obligation to ensure that the requirements of the instruments in question are complied with'.[122]

The heavy focus on Israel in these resolutions and declarations might be seen by some as bias, which might undermine their perceived validity despite their being made by reputable bodies such as the International Court of Justice. However, not all of the assertions on the broad scope of Article 1 concern Israel. In 2001, the ICRC cited common Article 1 in its 'position statement' on humanitarian intervention in which it argued that '[u]nder Article 1 common to the Geneva Conventions, there is an individual and collective obligation to "respect and ensure respect" for international humanitarian law. If grave violations of that law are committed, the States are obliged to take action jointly or separately, in co-operation with the United Nations and in accordance with the UN Charter.'[123] But 'the question of what measures are to be taken by the States and United Nations in order to put an end to those breaches is not dealt with by humanitarian law but by the UN Charter'. [124] The usefulness of this argument is undermined by the fact that IHL and the Charter are two different bodies of law that are arguably impossible to knit together into any kind of coherent whole, since the former is intended to regulate the *ius in bello* and to apply without moral or political distinction to all parties to a conflict, whereas the latter is primarily designed to regulate the *ius ad bellum* and to facilitate political decision-making in order to maintain international peace and security and further the Security Council's view of an optimum international order (especially as viewed by the permanent five).

The ICRC textbook for teaching IHL, *How Does Law Protect in War*, asserts that 'it is clear that all States can—and therefore must—react to breaches of IHL by retortion measures that do not violate its international obligations'.[125] However, '[c]onsidering the number of States addressed by Article 1, and the number of cases to which it applies, we can say that it is the most frequently violated provision of IHL'.[126] If this is true, it raises questions as to the validity of the claims that the

[121] Three States declined to take part in the conference, among them the United States and Israel.
[122] *Legal Consequences of The Construction of A Wall In The Occupied Palestinian Territory*, see n 86, para. 158.
[123] Anne Ryniker, 'The ICRC's Position on Humanitarian Intervention' (2001) 83 IRRC 482, 530.
[124] Ibid.
[125] Marco Sassoli and Antoine A Bouvier, *How Does Law Protect in War* (Volume 1) (Geneva: ICRC, 2006) 284.
[126] Ibid.

broad interpretation of common Article 1 (i.e. that it encompasses third party obligations) constitutes customary law, since customary law is based on State practice. Arguably, widespread violations of the prohibition on torture present a similar challenge to its customary law nature; but this can be countered by the argument that States invariably deny that they torture. An argument of that nature would be difficult to apply to a positive obligation such as the Article 1 obligation to ensure respect. However, rule 144 of the ICRC's Study on Customary International Humanitarian Law asserts that under customary law, 'States ... must exert their influence, to the degree possible, to stop violations of international humanitarian law'.

The ICRC's analysis of Rule 144 asserts that it 'involves obligations beyond those of the parties to the conflict', citing inter alia the International Court of Justice Advisory Opinion concerning the *Legal Consequences of the Construction of a Wall in the Occupied Palestinian Territory* and the Declaration by the Parties to the Geneva Conventions on the Obligations of Israel under the Fourth Convention in 2000 (both discussed earlier in this section) as well as resolutions by the UN General Assembly, the Council of Europe, NATO, the Organisation of African Unity, and the Organization of American States; military manuals of a number of States; and Article 16 of the 2001 International Law Commission's Draft Articles on State Responsibility.[127] But the study adds the caveat that

> it should be noted that neither the intention of the drafters of common Article 1 of the Geneva Conventions, nor practice since then, justifies the obligation to ensure respect for international humanitarian law being used as the sole basis for resort to the use of force. It is therefore expected that measures aimed at ensuring respect, beyond those decided by the UN Security Council, be peaceful ones.[128]

Yves Sandoz, a member of the ICRC, in an interview with Frits Kalshoven suggested that, notwithstanding the scale of academic debate and rhetoric on third party obligations under Article 1, it merely creates the rather modest obligation 'for governments to consider seriously whether there is something that they might do in respect of the situation'.[129] Such an obligation would be difficult to enforce given its intangible nature, but could be harnessed to ensure that, at the very least, the issue is debated.

If the broad interpretation of the scope of Article 1 that has been asserted by the International Court of Justice, the General Assembly, the ICRC, and academics is accepted, the entirety of the common Article 1 obligation (respect and *ensure* respect) is formally binding on a State whether or not it is a party to a conflict. If this is the case, the fact that peacekeeping forces are generally not party to a conflict would not in itself exculpate the State that has deployed the force from an obligation to ensure that the belligerents respect IHL. The extent of the obligation to

[127] ICRC, 'Rule 144. Ensuring Respect for International Humanitarian Law Erga Omnes' (*Customary International Humanitarian Law Database*, 2015) <www.icrc.org/customary-ihl/eng/docs/v1_rul_rule144>.

[128] Ibid.

[129] Frits Kalshoven, 'The Undertaking to Respect and Ensure Respect in All Circumstances: From Tiny Seed to Ripening Fruit' (1999) 2 YB Intl Humanitarian L 61.

'ensure respect' under common Article 1 must surely be linked to the contracting party's ability to effect the belligerents' conduct, which would be greater for a State that has forces deployed in the conflict zone than for one that doesn't, particularly if deployed under a mandate that authorizes protection. Certainly the International Court of Justice, in interpreting the scope of the obligation to prevent genocide under Article 1 of the 1948 Convention on the Prevention and Punishment of the Crime of Genocide, held that the obligation of State parties is 'to employ all means reasonably available to them so as to prevent genocide as far as possible'.[130] A similar logic would surely apply to the High Contracting Parties' obligations to 'ensure respect' for the Geneva Conventions.

VI. Accountability

Under the law of State responsibility, States may be held responsible for wrongful acts that are imputable to them. Similarly, international organizations are responsible for internationally wrongful acts imputable to them. An internationally wrongful act of an organization or of a State occurs when conduct consisting of an act or omission is attributable to the international organization or State under international law and constitutes a breach of an international obligation of that international organization or State.[131] The DARIO deal fairly briefly with allocation of responsibilities between two or more entities. Three situations are addressed: (a) attribution of conduct of an organ or agent that is placed at the disposal of another international organization to the organization that exercises effective control over the conduct; (b) giving aid or assistance to another State or international organization in the commission of an internationally wrongful act; and (c) exercising direction and control in the exercise of an internationally wrongful act by another State or international organization.[132]

The UN and a regional organization may have interlinked responsibilities in the same situation but are likely to be operating interdependently rather than the regional organization placing itself at the disposal of the UN, though its activities may be mandated under the same Security Council resolution as the UN mission.[133] The UN and all of its Member States are bound by the UN Charter.

[130] *Application of the Convention on the Prevention and Punishment of the Crime of Genocide (Bosnia and Herzegovina v Serbia and Montenegro)* (Judgment) [2007] ICJ Rep 43, para. 430.

[131] Draft Articles on the Responsibility of States for Internationally Wrongful Acts, in UNGA (2001) UN Doc A/56/10, 68, Article 2; Draft Articles on the Responsibility of International Organizations, see n 14, Article 4.

[132] Draft Articles on the Responsibility of International Organizations, see n 14, arts 7, 14, 15.

[133] Article 54 of the UN Charter requires regional organizations to keep the Security Council fully informed of the activities they undertake for the maintenance of international peace and security though these tend to be brief factual accounts. The briefness of Article 54 reports may be due in part to internal requirements of regional organizations, which may require that reports to the Security Council be adopted by consensus. See Mauricio Artiñano, 'Peace Operations Partnerships: The UN Security Council and (Sub-)Regional Organizations' (Berlin: Center for International Peace Operations, 2012) <www.zif-berlin.org/fileadmin/uploads/analyse/dokumente/veroeffentlichungen/ZIF_Policy_Briefing_Mauricio_Artinano_Mar_2012_ENG.pdf>.

Regional organizations are not directly bound by the Charter except through customary law. Customary international law is applicable to international organizations, including the UN, and to troop-contributing States, but may apply differently to organizations than it would to a State, especially since customary law is premised on State practice.[134]

Traditionally, the UN has taken the view that authorized multinational operations are outsourced operations over which the Security Council exercises only limited control, and therefore responsibility normally lies with the States conducting the mission.[135] The Secretary-General's report A/51/389 of September 1996 states that in the absence of formal arrangements between the UN and the State or States providing troops to the multinational mission, liability must 'be determined in each and every case according to the degree of effective control exercised by either party in the conduct of the operation'.[136]

By contrast, 'as a subsidiary organ of the United Nations, an act of a peacekeeping force is, in principle, imputable to the Organization, and if committed in violation of an international obligation entails the international responsibility of the Organization and its liability in compensation'.[137] The 'fact that any such act may have been performed by members of a national military contingent forming part of the peacekeeping operation does not affect the international responsibility of the United Nations vis-à-vis third States or individuals'.[138] However, attribution of conduct is not always clear-cut. Troop-contributing States place their forces under the command of the UN via agreements that confer on the Secretary-General authority over the deployment, conduct, and direction of their personnel; but the States still retain control over some matters, in particular criminal jurisdiction and disciplinary authority. Thus '[n]ational contingents taking part in international operations ... occupy a dual legal position and act in a dual role: in an international capacity as part of the institutional structure of the international organisation conducting the operation, and in a national capacity as an organ of their sending State'.[139] As the Special Rapporteur on the Responsibility of International

[134] Moritz Moelle, 'Cooperation of International Organisations in Peacekeeping Operations and Issues of International Responsibility' (Unpublished thesis) (Universities of Geneva and Leiden, 2014).

[135] See Blokker, n 26.

[136] UNGA, 'Report of the Secretary-General, Financing of the United Nations Protection Force, the United Nations Confidence Restoration Operation in Croatia, the United Nations Preventive Deployment Force and the United Nations Peace Force Headquarters' (1996) UN Doc A/51/389, para. 18.

[137] International Law Commission, 'Responsibility of International Organizations' (2004) UN Doc A/CN.4/545, 28. The Secretary-General's report A/51/389 of September 1996 on third-party liability of the UN states that '[i]n recognition of its international responsibility for the activities of its forces, the United Nations has, since the inception of peacekeeping operations, assumed its liability for damage caused by members of its forces in the performance of their duties'. UNGA, see n 136, para. 7. See also Dan Sarooshi, *The United Nations and the Development of Collective Security: The Delegation by the UN Security Council of its Chapter VII Powers* (Oxford: Clarendon Press, 1999).

[138] Hans Corell, United Nations Legal Counsel, Memorandum to the Director of the Codification Division, Václav Mikulka, 3 February 2004, para. 7, cited in Giorgio Gaja, 'Second Report on Responsibility of International Organizations' (2004) UN Doc A/CN.4/541, para. 36.

[139] Aurel Sari, 'Jurisdiction and International Responsibility in Peace Support Operations: The *Behrami* and *Saramati* Case' (2012) 8 Hum Rts L Rev Intl Org L Rev 151, 161.

Organizations for the International Law Commission, Giorgio Gaja, noted in a 2004 report, '[w]hile it is understandable that, for the sake of efficiency of military operations, the United Nations insists on claiming exclusive command and control over peacekeeping forces, attribution of conduct should also in this regard be based on a factual criterion'.[140] Nevertheless, prima facie acts and omissions of a UN-commanded peacekeeping force are imputable to the UN.[141]

The extensive immunity of UN missions from legal claims is set out in the Convention on the Privileges and Immunity of the United Nations,[142] and affirmed in the International Court of Justice's *Mazuli* and *Cumaraswamy* Advisory Opinions[143] and in the Model Status of Forces Agreement for Peacekeeping Operations.[144] Paragraph 51 of the Model Status of Forces Agreement for Peacekeeping Operations states that the UN will 'settle by means of a standing claims commission claims resulting from damage caused by members of the force in the performance of their official duties and which for reasons of immunity of the Organization and its Members could not have been submitted to local courts'.[145] General Assembly resolution 52/247 of 1998 provides that if damage is caused by gross negligence or wilful misconduct on the part of the UN, it will pay full compensation.[146]

In 2000, London-based lawyer Geoffrey Robinson and former South Australian State-prosecutor Michael Hourigan planned to sue the UN for alleged complicity in the Rwandan genocide, acting for two Rwandan women whose families were among the victims.[147] However they were unable to get over the hurdle of UN immunity. Kofi Annan, who was Secretary-General at the time, argued that not only did the UN have nothing to answer for, but also, 'if we allowed our peacekeepers to be brought to courts and tried over matters like this, that would be the end of

140 Gaja, see n 138, para. 41.

141 For discussion of attribution of responsibility to international organizations see Pierre Klein, 'The Attribution of Acts to International Organizations', in James Crawford, Alain Pellet, and Simon Olleson (eds), *The Law of International Responsibility* (Oxford: Oxford University Press, 2010) 306–14.

142 Convention on the Privileges and Immunities of the United Nations (adopted 13 February 1946, entry into force 17 September 1946) 1 UNTS 15.

143 See, respectively, *Applicability of Article VI, Section 22, of the Convention on the Privileges and Immunities of the United Nations* (Advisory Opinion) [1989] ICJ Rep 177, paras 40–52; and *Difference Relating to Immunity from Legal Process of a Special Rapporteur of the Commission on Human Rights* (Advisory Opinion) [1999] ICJ Rep 62, paras 38–56. In the latter opinion ([1999] ICJ Rep 62, para. 50) the Court stated that the Secretary-General, as the chief administrative officer of the UN, had the primary responsibility and authority to assess whether its agents, including experts on mission, acted within the scope of their functions and, where he so concludes, to protect these agents by asserting their immunity.

144 Model SOFA, see n 61, para. 6.

145 Ibid.

146 The UN retains the right to request reimbursement from the staff member, the member of a contingent, or her troop or police-contributing State: UNGA Res 52/247 (1998) UN Doc A/RES/52/247, para. 6, endorsing UNGA (1997) UN Doc A/51/903, para. 14.

147 Mark Riley, 'UN To Seek Immunity on Rwanda', *Sydney Herald* (Sydney, 14 January 2000) <www.globalpolicy.org/security/issues/rwanda/suit.htm>. The women claimed that the UN soldiers who were assigned to protect them either ran away or handed their families over to the Hutu militia to be killed. One of them said that the UN soldiers who were supposed to protect her and her family were drinking and socializing with the Hutus while she and her children were being tortured.

peacekeeping'.[148] The reasonableness of this approach has recently come under strain in the wake of the UN's alleged negligence in causing the outbreak of cholera in Haiti in 2011, and its subsequent denial of responsibility and covering up of evidence.[149] Three lawsuits were filed against the UN in the District Courts of New York in 2013 and 2014 in the wake of a number of highly critical NGO reports on the conduct of the UN Mission in Haiti (MINUSTAH).[150] While the applicants are unlikely to be successful in their efforts to overcome UN immunity on this occasion, they have garnered considerable academic and political support.[151] The fact that Secretary-General Ban Ki-moon was reportedly personally served with papers in June 2014 is a landmark development.[152]

Given the UN's general immunity to legal proceedings to date, it is important that the Organization establishes mechanisms that promote accountability beyond legal and claims processes, which it is already beginning to do through, inter alia, its Human Rights Due Diligence Policy regarding support to human rights violators and the Human Rights Up Front plan to integrate commitment to human rights protection throughout all of the UN's activities. As noted, the UN DPKO Civil Affairs Handbook states that missions with protection of civilians mandates 'are required to conduct a detailed analysis of risks facing civilians in the area of operations and to devise a comprehensive protection of civilians strategy that articulates the mission's approach towards addressing the priority protection of civilians risks that it has identified'.[153] Devising a protection of civilians strategy is not fulfilment of a protection obligation; to fulfil the obligation, the mission must implement the strategy that it has devised or show good reason why it cannot. In order to devise and implement a protection of civilians strategy, the mission must, at a minimum, monitor threats to civilians, document its responses to those threats, and report them up the chain of command. A failure to monitor threats, and to document and report up the chain of command the mission's planned responses to them, would reduce the mission's protective actions to the level of ad hoc (essentially dependent on the best efforts of the individual commander and her/his advisors at the time). Ad hoc responses are not sufficient to meet a positive obligation to protect in situations where civilians are known to be at risk.

[148] Ibid.

[149] Armin Rosen, 'How the U.N. Caused Haiti's Cholera Crisis—and Won't Be Held Responsible', *The Atlantic* (Boston, USA, 26 February 2013) <www.theatlantic.com>

[150] *D Georges v United Nations* et al., US (2013); *Jean-Robert* et al. *v United Nations*, US (2014); *LaVenture* et al. *v United Nations*, US (2014)

[151] For example, see *Delma Georges* et al. *v United Nations* (Brief) No 1:13-cv-07146 (JPO) 'Brief of Amici Curiae Fanm Ayisyen Nan Miyami, Inc. and the Haitian Lawyers Association in support of plaintiffs' motion for affirmation that service has been made on defendants' (United States Court, Southern District of New York, 2014) <www.ijdh.org/wp-content/uploads/2011/11/DE-19-1-Proposed-Amicus-Brief.pdf>.

[152] Rick Gladstone, 'U.N. Chief Served Papers in Suit by Haitian Victims, Lawyers Say', *The New York Times* (New York, 20 June 2014) <www.nytimes.com/2014/06/21/world/americas/un-chief-served-papers-in-suit-by-haitian-cholera-victims-lawyers-say.html?_r=0>.

[153] UN Department of Peacekeeping Operations and UN Department of Field Support, *Civil Affairs Handbook* (New York: United Nations, 2012).

If the UN Assistance Mission for Rwanda (UNAMIR) had been obliged to plan a response to protect the civilians sheltering in its base at Kicukiro; and had been obliged to document and sign those plans; and had been obliged to report them up the chain of command, the massacre in 1994 of 2,000 Rwandans might have been avoided. The presence of the refugees, and the crowds waiting outside for days with machetes in hand,[154] would have had to have been reported as soon as the situation arose, along with the mission's plan in response and the mission's reasons for concluding that its proposed plan was the most effective means available to protect those civilians. The scale of the genocide at Srebrenica might also have been mitigated by a requirement to draw up protection plans in response to the risk of massacre and ensure that those plans were acted on, and the steps taken to do so reported up the chain of command.

VII. Conclusion

The Brahimi Report, reviewing peacekeeping doctrine and practice in response to protection failures of the 1990s, concluded that impartiality for peacekeeping missions must 'mean adherence to the principles of the Charter and to the objectives of a mandate that is rooted in those Charter principles', not neutrality, noting that 'in some cases, local parties consist not of moral equals but of obvious aggressors and victims'.[155] This is true; but equally, it has too often been the case that civilians are attacked by everybody, including the government (or local political figures favoured by the government), that the mission is supporting.

The prohibitions on violating the right to life and the right not to be subjected to torture or inhumane treatment are recognized as peremptory norms: however, the obligation to secure those rights may not be. Despite significant changes in the nature of peacekeeping and in the scope of mandates, formally a mandate still has a 'powers-creating character'[156] rather than an obligations-creating character (though there may be some sections in the resolution that detail specific requirements that read as obligations, for example requirements to report to certain named authorities at specific times on specific matters). But the combination of legal obligations to protect derived from IHRL and IHL, together with articles 14, 41, and 42 of the DARIO, may render the protection of civilians element of a Security Council mandate de facto something very close to an obligation. However, the UN's obligation to protect people from attacks that violate peremptory norms, since it is not derived directly from protection of civilians mandates but from a broader range of sources, may apply regardless of whether or not a protection of civilians-mandated mission is deployed in the area.

Under Article 42 of the DARIO, both States and international organizations are required to 'cooperate to bring to an end through lawful means any serious breach'

[154] Romeo Dallaire, *Shake Hands with the Devil* (London: Arrow Press, 2004) 290.

[155] Brahimi Report, see n 36, para. 50.

[156] *Mothers of Srebrenica v The Netherlands* (Judgment) Case No C-09/295247/HA ZA 07-2973 (The Hague District Court, 2014), para. 4.149.

of a peremptory norm.[157] Violations of the right to life and the right not to be tortured or subjected to inhumane treatment, and violations of common Article 3 of the Geneva Conventions, committed on a large scale or frequently, would presumably be considered serious breaches of peremptory norms. A Chapter VII mandate authorizing protection may provide a peacekeeping mission with a lawful means to bring them to an end. In light of the role of the Security Council, a protection of civilians mandate adopted under Chapter VII could be construed as one means (possibly the primary means) by which States and the UN have chosen to 'co-operate to bring to an end through lawful means' serious breaches of peremptory norms. If so, the mission surely has an obligation under Article 42 of DARIO to carry out at least the protection of civilians aspect of its mandate, if it is capable of doing so while also taking into account its responsibilities towards other civilians and UN personnel. In addition, the UN, in its Human Rights Up Front Action Plan as well as in the Human Rights Due Diligence Policy on UN Support to Non-UN Security Forces, asserts that it has obligations in relation to IHRL and that these include positive obligations to protect civilians from serious violations of human rights and humanitarian law.

Mandates that authorize 'all necessary measures' to carry out protection rarely specify what is necessary, since the most effective response to any given threat cannot be predicted in advance of the threat arising. Protection can take many forms, including interposition of troops between attackers and victims, clearing mines, providing water (for example if wells have been poisoned), providing escorts to vulnerable people, allowing potential victims to shelter in a UN base, and communication of information. Protection of civilians obligations are often linked, at least in the media, to an expectation that troops should use force against perpetrators of attacks on civilians, in order to prevent the attacks from continuing. However, the use of force is merely an option authorized under the mandate: an option (whether it is use of force or anything less) cannot be the essence of an obligation, merely one means of fulfilling it and one that may not always be available even to a Chapter VII protection of civilians-mandated mission. Member States contributing military personnel to a Chapter VII-mandated mission do so voluntarily and may place caveats on the applicability of some of the mission's Rules of Engagement (including those governing when force may be used) for various reasons, for example in order to comply with their own domestic law or to prevent their forces from becoming involved in an armed conflict.

Attempting to use force to protect all civilians from all attacks may impair the ability of the mission to effectively provide protection where it is most acutely needed, taking into account the whole pattern of threats against all the civilians at risk, likely chains of events, and the capabilities of the mission, including the commander's protection obligations towards her/his own troops. Hence the obligation to protect cannot be an absolute one even where the mission has the means to stop a foreseeable attack and has a mandate that authorizes 'all necessary means' or 'all necessary measures'.

[157] Draft Articles on the Responsibility of International Organizations, see n 14, Article 42.

This is not so radically different from the protection obligations of States towards potential victims of violence within their country: these are also not absolute. In *Mahmout Kaya v Turkey*, the European Court of Human Rights, citing its decision in *Osman v United Kingdom*, stated that '[f]or a positive obligation to arise, it must be established that the authorities knew or ought to have known at the time of the existence of a real and immediate risk to the life of an identified individual or individuals' and that 'they failed to take measures within the scope of their powers which, judged reasonably, might have been expected to avoid that risk'.[158] Baroness Hale, in an appeal decision before the UK House of Lords,[159] stated that 'as a general principle, a police officer is not entitled to stand by and let one person kill or seriously ill-treat another, when he has the means of preventing it, just because he fears the wider consequences of doing so. He has to step in, come what may.'[160] But she went on to say that the situation may not always be 'as straightforward as that'.[161] She did not think that it had been demonstrated that, had the police acted differently, the victim's experience would have been any better, and the difficulties and dangers to the police 'in doing what it is now suggested should have been done cannot be ignored'.[162]

This chapter argues that prima facie UN missions cannot stand by and let one or more persons kill or seriously ill-treat civilians if they have the means to stop it, especially if they have a Chapter VII mandate authorizing the mission to protect civilians from violence. Under Security Council resolution 1894 of 2009, the Council stresses that a UN mission's 'mandated protection activities must be given priority in decisions about the use of available capacity and resources including information and intelligence resources, in the implementation of mandates; and recognizes, that the protection of civilians when and as mandated requires a coordinated response from all relevant mission components'.[163] However, in an armed conflict the situation may not always be 'as straightforward as that', to use Baroness Hale's phrase.

In the view of this author, the scale of attacks against vulnerable people, and the degree of force permissible in response, is likely to be higher in an armed conflict situation than in a domestic law enforcement one; but equally, the flexibility given to military commanders as to how and when to protect civilians is likely to be broader in an armed conflict situation than in a domestic law enforcement one, since the risks of triggering an escalation in violence are likely to be higher in wartime. However, in the event of a protection of civilians-mandated mission's

158 *Mahmout Kaya v Turkey*, 22535/93 [2000] ECHR 129 (28 March 2000), para. 86; *Osman v United Kingdom*, 23452/94 [1998] ECHR 101 (28 October 1998), para. 116.

159 *PF and EF* v *United Kingdom* (Application no. 28326/09) [2010] ECHR 2015. The case considered whether the police in Belfast had done enough to protect the children of Holy Cross Catholic school from loyalists 'throwing bricks, rubbish, balloons filled with urine and dog excrement, firecrackers and, on one occasion, an explosive device at those making the journey to and from the school; shouting death threats, sectarian abuse and obscenities of a sexual nature; displaying explicit pornographic material; accusing priests on the school's Board of Governors of being paedophiles; spitting at the children and their parents; wearing masks; and using whistles, sirens, horns and other instruments to create an intimidating atmosphere'. Ibid., para. 15.

160 Ibid., 31. 161 Ibid. 162 Ibid.

163 UNSC Res 1894 (2009) UN Doc S/RES/1894, para. 19.

failure to protect, it will not be enough for the UN to say after the event that it tried; it must be able to prove it by producing the documents or other evidence (signed and dated) demonstrating its plan of action and the efforts made to implement it. A positive obligation to protect cannot be effectively carried out ad hoc. Therefore, if there is a legally binding obligation to protect, and arguably there is at least in relation to violations of peremptory norms, it should shape the way the mandate is carried out both at the macro level (e.g. initial assessment of risks and operational planning in light of them) and at the micro-level (e.g. documenting and reporting of protection plans and of the steps taken to implement them at local level), and the continuous updating of protection plans in light of the continuous assessment of risks, assessed at both local and general level.

PART III

POLITICS AND PRACTICE

11

The United Nations and the Protection of Civilians

Jean-Marie Guéhenno[1]

I. Introduction

The protection of civilians is one of the most prominent issues of international relations and is at the core of much of the United Nations' (UN) work on international peace and security. The UN Security Council holds regular debates on the topic, it has been the subject of a number of thematic Council resolutions, and more than 90 per cent of UN peacekeepers deployed today are mandated to protect civilians. The UN Secretariat reports to the Security Council annually on the protection of civilians, covering a range of aspects including the use of force by peacekeepers, humanitarian issues, criminal accountability for gross violations of international humanitarian and human rights law, and the development of the Responsibility to Protect doctrine. The General Assembly Special Committee on Peacekeeping Operations has also taken up the subject at its annual sessions.

This chapter examines how the UN has responded to the changing nature of conflict, tracing the development of the civilian protection concept from its humanitarian roots and questioning whether the UN, comprising a collection of politically motivated actors, has effectively used the range of tools at its disposal to protect civilians in conflict. In this context, it questions the role that the UN, the international community, individual States, and civilian populations can and should play in the protection of civilians. While considering a range of tools available to the Council, the chapter focuses mainly on peacekeeping operations, acknowledging that other aspects of protection are analysed elsewhere in this volume.[2]

The UN has crafted an extremely broad definition of the protection of civilians.[3] Navigating between the aspirations of the UN Charter and the realities of politics and resources, the definition includes both the concept of physical protection

[1] The author would like to thank Jikita de Schot for her assistance preparing this chapter.

[2] See, in this volume, Sara Pantuliano and Eva Svoboda, Chapter 17, and Lise Grande, Chapter 18.

[3] See Ralph Mamiya, Chapter 3 in this volume.

through the use of force and the concept of building the capacity of States to protect their own civilians. Unfortunately, the UN's efforts both to provide physical protection and to build State capacity have real limitations.

Central to these limitations is the shallow political consensus at the UN when dealing with protection issues. Despite frequent lofty rhetoric, the political will to 'persuade' States to protect their own civilian populations is often absent, or dependent on strategic alliances. While Member States profess the importance of the role of the UN, many are unwilling to provide the resources—personnel, material, and financial—to enable UN peacekeepers to effectively protect civilians. Indeed, the increasing priority given to the protection of civilians in UN fora may not evidence the international community's commitment to a more comprehensive view of human security. Rather, it may simply reflect recourse to a concept adopted from humanitarian law, used to mask continuing political divisions. For the protection of civilians to truly serve people on the ground and be more than a temporary response to an emergency, it needs to go beyond the superficial and address what constitutes the creation of a lasting protective environment. The key to protection may ultimately lie in empowering communities.

II. UN Concept of the 'Protection of Civilians'

The concept of the protection of civilians, derived from international humanitarian law, developed first as a reaction to the civilian casualties of conventional wars, and later as a response to the changing nature of conflict and its impact on civilians. Twenty-five years since the end of the Cold War, it is now possible to draw some lessons from the experience of the UN in protecting civilians.

The UN, and its Security Council, only gradually became aware that they would not be faithful to the spirit of the UN Charter if they did not put the safeguarding of civilian lives at the centre of their concerns. The first post-Cold War decade was marked by the Rwandan genocide[4] and by the killings of the Yugoslav wars,[5] and in particular the Srebrenica massacre, in which 7,000 Bosniacs lost their lives despite being in a 'safe area' established by a resolution of the Security Council.[6] At the strategic level in Rwanda, and at the tactical level in Srebrenica, the 'international community' massively failed the 'people of the UN'.

[4] Between April and June 1994, an estimated 800,000 Tutsi and moderate Hutu were killed in the Rwandan genocide. See Philip Gourevitch, *We Wish to Inform You that Tomorrow We Will Be Killed with Our Families: Stories from Rwanda* (New York: Picador, 1998) 3.

[5] Ethnic conflicts fought from 1991 to 1999 in the territory of the former Yugoslavia resulted in approximately 140,000 deaths. See International Center for Transitional Justice, 'Transitional Justice in the Former Yugoslavia' (International Center for Transitional Justice, 2009) 1 <www.ictj.org/sites/default/files/ICTJ-FormerYugoslavia-Justice-Facts-2009-English.pdf>.

[6] Heather McRobie, 'Bosnia: Remembering the Srebrenica Massacre', *Aljazeera* (Doha, 15 July 2014) <www.aljazeera.com/indepth/features/2014/07/bosnia-remembering-srebrenica-massacre-201471583512715776.html>.

The reports that were commissioned by the Secretary-General of the UN on Rwanda[7] and Srebrenica[8] in 1999, and on peacekeeping[9] in 2000, were a response to those failures. The reports contributed to a change in the posture of the UN, which has put an increasing emphasis on the protection of civilians in peacekeeping operations, to the point that it has been identified as the priority task in some of the most recent resolutions of the Security Council.[10]

Beginning in 1999, the same year as the reports on Rwanda and Srebrenica, the UN Secretary-General and the Security Council began a regular cycle of reporting and a series of debates on the protection of civilians in armed conflict, resulting in a number of resolutions.[11] Neither the Secretary-General nor the Security Council has offered a definition of the protection of civilians. However, the regular thematic reports of the Secretary-General and the resolutions of the Security Council cover wide-ranging topics, including: civilian casualties, refugees, and internally displaced persons in ongoing conflicts; the protection responsibilities of Member States; compliance with international humanitarian and human rights law; accountability mechanisms; humanitarian access; and the protection of civilians by UN peacekeeping missions. Every year since 1999, the Council has met, issued statements, or passed resolutions dealing with the protection of civilians in armed conflict.[12]

While one can only applaud an increased focus on the people on behalf of whom the UN was founded, there is a need to evaluate the adequacy of the resources that

[7] See United Nations Security Council (UNSC), 'Report of the Independent Inquiry into the Actions of the UN During the 1994 Genocide in Rwanda' (1999) UN Doc S/1999/1257.

[8] See United Nations General Assembly (UNGA), 'Report of the Secretary-General Pursuant to General Assembly Resolution 53/35: The Fall of Srebrenica' (1999) UN Doc A/54/549.

[9] See UNGA and UNSC, 'Report of the Panel on UN Peace Operations' (2000) UN Doc A/55/305–S/2000/809.

[10] UNSC Resolution (Res) 2155 (2014) UN Doc S/RES/2155, para. 5: '*Emphasizes* that protection of civilians, as described in paragraph 4(a), must be given priority in decisions about the use of available capacity and resources within the Mission'; UNSC Res 2147 (2014) UN Doc S/RES/2147, para. 3: '. . . *decides* that future reconfigurations of MONUSCO and its mandate should be determined on the basis of the evolution of the situation on the ground and . . . in line with the three priorities of protection of civilians, stabilisation and support to the implementation of the PSC framework, as set out in the mission concept'; UNSC Res 1894 (2009) UN Doc S/RES/1894, para. 19: '*Reaffirms* its practice of ensuring that mandates of UN peacekeeping and other relevant missions include . . . provisions regarding the protection of civilians, *stresses* that mandated protection activities must be given priority in decisions about the use of available capacity and resources, including information and intelligence resources, in the implementation of mandates.'

[11] See, e.g., UNSC Res 1265 (1999) UN Doc S/RES/1265; UNSC, 'Report of the Secretary-General on the Protection of Civilians in Armed Conflict' (1999) UN Doc S/1999/957.

[12] See, e.g., UNSC Res 1265 (1999) UN Doc S/RES/1265; UNSC Res 1296 (2000) UN Doc S/RES/1296; UNSC, '4312th Meeting' (2001) UN Doc S/PV.4312; UNSC Statement of the President (2002) UN Doc S/PRST/2002/6; UNSC Statement by the President (2003) UN Doc S/PRST/2003/27; UNSC Statement of the President (2004) UN Doc S/PRST/2004/26; UNSC Statement of the President (2005) UN Doc S/PRST/2005/25 (2005); UNSC Res 1674 (2006) UN Doc S/RES/1674 (2006); UNSC, '5703rd Meeting' (2007) UN Doc S/PV.5703; UNSC Statement of the President (2008) UN Doc S/PRST/2008/18; UNSC Res 1894 (2009) UN Doc S/RES/1894; UNSC Statement of the President (2010) UN Doc S/PRST/2010/25; UNSC, '6650th Meeting' (2011) UN Doc S/PV.6650; UNSC, '6790th Meeting' (2012) UN Doc S/PV.6790; UNSC Statement of the President (2013) UN Doc S/PRST/2013/2 (2013); UNSC Statement of the President (2014) UN Doc S/PRST/2014/3.

the UN can mobilize compared to the goals it sets for itself, and the conceptual framework that informs its actions. Are the concepts of 'protection of civilians' and of 'protected persons' borrowed from international humanitarian law applicable to a political organization like the UN?

III. Responding to the Changing Nature of Conflict

The first question that needs to be addressed is the changing nature of conflict and the resulting implications for the protection of civilians in contemporary warfare. The former deputy North Atlantic Treaty Organization (NATO) Supreme Allied Commander Europe (SACEUR), British General Rupert Smith, has described the new wars as 'wars amongst the people'.[13] In some respects, there is more continuity than generally acknowledged between the new and the old wars. The 'total wars' of the twentieth century exacted a heavy toll on civilians: the need to destroy the industrial support system of the war machine led to massive bombings that killed many, and many of the indiscriminate weapons decried today were developed during 'traditional' wars.[14] As for the new wars, whether one considers gangs in a Haitian slum, militias in a Congolese village, or Taliban in an Afghan valley, the distinction between combatants and civilians is increasingly difficult to make. The same persons can be civilians by day and combatants by night. Their tactics are deployed in the midst of a civilian population, wittingly or unwittingly. Whether gangs or militias try to protect themselves by using human shields or are just inexorably mixed with the civilian population, the context of warfare changes significantly.

This evolution in tactics reflects a more fundamental change in strategy. Traditional wars were characterized by the confrontation of professional armies. If the army of an adversary was defeated, one could take control of the State and political apparatus it was defending. It was assumed that there was a functioning State system, which the victor would take control of. Most of today's wars are different. There is no assumption of a functioning State, let alone an effective chain of command that would allow a central authority to assert its control over the civilian population or territory. On the contrary, the strategic goal is resources and the civilian population, so a bottom-up approach replaces a top-down strategy. Taking direct control of a civilian population is at once a tactic and a strategy. The means used to achieve such control range from outright terror and intimidation to the delivery of services and creation of parallel State structures, which can be combined in varying degrees.[15] The implications for the civilian population are dire. Compared to traditional combat, the risk to civilians is now heightened, as fighting takes

[13] Rupert Smith, *The Utility of Force: The Art of War in the Modern World* (London: Penguin Books, 2005) xiii.

[14] Eric Hobsbawm, *The Age of Extremes* (London: Abacus, 1994) 21–54.

[15] Examples of groups who primarily use terror and intimidation include Al-Shabaab in Somalia and the Islamic State of Iraq and Levant (although it has provided limited services in some locations), with groups at the other end of the spectrum such as Hezbollah in Lebanon, which acts like a parallel

place in populated areas, and in many situations, civilians are not collateral victims, but have become the primary targets of warfare.

At the same time, other trends have been working in the opposite direction: methods of warfare are being developed that are more individualized. The progress of technology has led to the development of 'smart weapons' such as laser-guided bombs and drones that are increasingly precise and can, in principle, discriminate between civilian and military targets.[16] This technological evolution is part of a broader trend that points to what one could call an 'individualization' of warfare, in evidence in counter-terrorism operations.[17] This evolution in warfare has its counterpart in diplomacy, as economic sanctions also become more individualized (see further discussion later in this chapter).

No objective appreciation of the combined impact of these opposite trends can be made without a careful monitoring of their actual impact on the protection of civilians. In recent years, a more systematic effort of monitoring civilian casualties and understanding how they occur has been instigated. Organizations as diverse as the International Security Assistance Force (ISAF) in Afghanistan and the African Union Mission to Somalia (AMISOM) have begun to put in place effective monitoring systems of civilian casualties, and the UN Department of Peacekeeping Operations (DPKO) is considering introducing similar tracking cells.[18] Understanding how the new ways of war affect civilian lives is a pre-condition to developing an adequate response that will minimize civilian casualties. Independent non-governmental organizations such as the Centre for Civilians in Conflict have pushed that agenda, helping to develop effective monitoring and adequate training.[19] The involvement of independent organizations is particularly useful to build trust with civilian populations and confidence in the figures released. Systems and procedures that better connect armed forces and the civilian population can ensure, at a minimum, that those forces that are deployed to protect civilians will do no harm. Even irregular forces may, in some circumstances, adjust their posture and tactics if they become convinced that the targeting of civilians will not further their political goals.[20]

State with health, education, and security services. See and compare Anniseh Van Engeland, 'Hezbollah: From a Terrorist Group to a Political Party—Social Work as a Key to Politics', in Annisseh Van Engeland and Rachael M Rudolph (eds) *From Terrorism to Politics* (Hampshire, UK: Ashgate Publishing, 2008) 29–50, and Melissa Simpson, 'An Islamic Solution to State Failure in Somalia?', in John Davis (ed.), *Terrorism in Africa: The Evolving Front in the War on Terror* (Plymouth, UK: Lexington Books, 2010) 9–24.

[16] For discussion, see Sarah Kreps and John Kaag, 'The Use of Unmanned Aerial Vehicles in Contemporary Conflict: A Legal and Ethical Analysis' (2012) 44 Polity 260.

[17] For more discussion, see Gabriella Blum, 'The Individualization of War: From War to Policing in the Regulation of Armed Conflicts', in Austin Sarat, Lawrence Douglas, and Martha Merrill Umphrey (eds), *Law and War* (Stanford, USA: Stanford University Press, 2013) 48–83.

[18] Oxfam, 'The Role of UN Peacekeeping Missions in the Protection of Civilians' (Oxford: Oxfam, 2012), 5 <www.oxfam.org/sites/www.oxfam.org/files/hpn-role-un-peacekeeping-missions-protection-civilians-170712-en.pdf>.

[19] See its work and reports at Center for Civilians in Conflict: <www.civiliansinconflict.org>.

[20] Stuart Casey Maslin, 'Rebels With a Cause? The Role of Non-state Armed Actors in the Protection of Civilians', *Humanitarian Exchange* (London, July 2013) 6; Oliver Kaplan, 'Nudging Armed

IV. Protecting Civilians through Force

Improvements in the processes governing military operations may minimize the potential harm such operations can cause, but they leave open the question of the positive contribution that military forces can make to protecting civilians. There is a vast gap between the avoidance of collateral harm to civilians and actively operating to protect them. In the immediate aftermath of the failures of the 1990s, the Brahimi Report underscored that the notion that peacekeepers could witness civilians being massacred while they had the capability to stop the violence was morally abhorrent and strategically inept.[21]

A. Elements of effective UN peacekeeping

In order for a peacekeeping mission to retain the required credibility, it must have the confidence of the population, which is in large part dependent on its ability and perceived willingness to actively protect civilians. These considerations led to the insertion in Security Council resolutions of a sentence that mandates the peacekeeping force (with minor variations in language), acting under Chapter VII of the UN Charter, 'to protect civilians under imminent threat of physical violence and prevent attacks against civilians, within its capability and areas of deployment, without prejudice to the responsibility of the Government of the [host country]'.[22] At the request of troop contributors, and so as not to set up UN peacekeepers for failure, the language of UN resolutions includes some precautions. The reference to the government of the host country is an important reminder that the UN does not exempt the host country of its primary responsibility and only has a subsidiary role. The references to 'areas of deployment', 'capabilities', and 'imminent threat' make it clear that the UN cannot be expected to protect all people, at all times, in all locations.[23]

Despite these legal precautions, once a peacekeeping mission has been deployed in a country, expectations are created among the local population and within the international community, regardless of whether the peacekeepers are equipped and resourced for the task.[24] Such was the case in Ituri—a district in North-eastern Congo—where the UN Organization Mission in the Democratic Republic of the

Groups: How Civilians Transmit Norms of Protection' (2013) 3 Stability: Intl J Security Development 62, available at <http://www.stabilityjournal.org/article/view/sta.cw/165>.

21 Report of the Panel on United Nations Peace Operations, in UNGA and UNSC (2000) UN Doc A/55/305—S/2000/809, para. 50 (The Brahimi Report).

22 Language used is a reflection of that in most recent peacekeeping mandates. See, for example, UNSC Res 1996 (2011) UN Doc S/RES/1996, para. 3(b)(iv); UNSC Res 1769 (2007) UN Doc S/RES/1769, para. 15(a)(ii); UNSC Res 1270 (1999) UN Doc S/RES/1270, para. 14.

23 See Mona Khalil, Chapter 9 in this volume.

24 United Nations, 'Meetings Coverage: Overburdened, Underfunded, Overstretched Peacekeeping Operations Create "Yawning Gap" Between Expectations, Performance, Fourth Committee Told At Close Of Debate' (New York, 27 October 2010) UN Doc GA/SPD/465 <www.un.org/News/Press/docs/2010/gaspd465.doc.htm>.

Congo (MONUC) deployed armed peacekeepers after a 2003 outbreak of violence.[25] Despite lacking the troop strength and equipment to effectively protect civilians, the mere presence of peacekeepers led civilians to congregate near the airstrip and UN compound of Bunia. The peacekeeping mission was in the unenviable situation of being accused of criminal neglect if it had not deployed troops to Ituri, and of criminal incompetence if the violence had escalated. It was eventually saved by the deployment of a French-led European multinational force that stabilized the situation in the summer of 2003.[26]

This example illustrates a weakness of the UN in all situations where it is mandated to protect civilians. Nowhere is the ratio of UN troops to the population to be protected close to what would be needed to provide effective protection. According to the US manual on counter-insurgency,[27] twenty soldiers are required to protect 1,000 people. A less ambitious ratio would be that of police officers to populations found in major cities, although situations in which peacekeepers deploy are obviously more volatile and more logistically challenging, including because the population is often dispersed over vast areas with poor infrastructure. In New York City, 35,000 police officers provide for the security of eight million people (a ratio of 4.34 police officers for 1,000 people). Even if this more favourable ratio were applied to the eastern regions of the Democratic Republic of the Congo (DRC), with a population of 14.5 million, the number of peacekeepers deployed would need to more than double the mission's authorized troop strength. Whether one looks at Darfur (18,211 uniformed personnel), South Sudan (8,975 uniformed personnel), Liberia (6,094 uniformed personnel), or the Central African Republic (11,820 uniformed personnel),[28] UN deployments never reach a level that would allow for a 'saturation' of the area of operation[29] and effective blanket protection.[30]

UN peacekeeping missions and DPKO are aware of these limitations, and take available measures to compensate. Missions adapt their posture, emphasizing deterrence, prevention, and sometimes pre-emption over reaction; they try to make the most judicious use of their limited assets; they do what they can to increase their

[25] Human Rights Watch, *Democratic Republic of the Congo, Ituri: Covered in Blood, Ethnically Targeted Violence in Northeastern DR Congo* (New York: Human Rights Watch, 2003) 2.

[26] 'DRC: EU Calls Artemis Operation "a Big Success"', *Integrated Regional Information Networks* (Nairobi, 17 September 2003) <www.irinnews.org/report/46206/drc-eu-calls-artemis-operation-a-big-success>.

[27] The key hypothesis of the manual is that an insurgency wins by intimidating/terrorizing the civilian population, which therefore needs to be protected if the insurgency is to be defeated. This may be a questionable assumption, but it does not invalidate the work done to identify what is the right number of troops to provide effective protection to civilians. The United States Army and Marine Corps, *The U.S. Army/Marine Corps Counter Insurgency Field Manual* (Chicago, USA: University of Chicago Press, 2007) § 3–91.

[28] UN Department of Peacekeeping Operations (DPKO), *UN Peacekeeping Fact Sheet* (United Nations, updated 31 October 2014) <www.un.org/en/peacekeeping/resources/statistics/factsheet.shtml>.

[29] An exception is south Lebanon, but UNIFIL does not have a traditional protection-of-civilians mandate.

[30] Paul D Williams, 'Enhancing Civilians Protection in Peace Operations: Lessons from Africa' (Washington, DC: National Defense University Press, 2010) 27–9.

mobility; they trade quantity for quality; and they boost their capacities by combining forces with a multinational or national force under separate command, or with the forces of the host country. Over the past fifteen years, the UN has tested—in various combinations, with various degrees of success—all of these measures.[31]

B. Pre-emption and prevention in UN peacekeeping

Pre-emption is a better option than mere protection, but was, for a long time, difficult to reconcile with a cardinal principle of peacekeeping, which restricts the use of force to self-defence.[32] The need to allow scope for pre-emption was acknowledged in the Brahimi Report, which noted that UN forces should be able to 'silence a source of deadly fire that is directed at United Nations troops or at the people they are charged to protect' and UN forces need not 'cede the initiative to their attackers'.[33]

For civilians in need of protection, the use of force only in self-defence would result in the intolerable situation that a dangerous militia posing a direct threat to a village nearby would not be challenged before it launched an attack. Since 2000, good UN force commanders with competent troops have, in several cases, managed to overcome the potential limitation. In the DRC, General Cammaert, who was in charge of an Eastern Division in 2005, launched a series of cordon and search operations which, in effect, led to the disarmament of militias.[34] General Santos Cruz, who was until recently the force commander in DRC, launched similar operations against armed gangs in Port-au-Prince, Haiti.[35] These were not traditional offensive operations, since the targets had been warned and were given the opportunity to voluntarily disarm, but they went far beyond what peacekeeping forces were used to, and represented a significant change of posture.

Prevention does not necessarily require the proactive use of force, but like deterrence it works only if the force has sufficient visibility and, more importantly, sufficient capacity to escalate, so that spoilers are not tempted to test the force's resolve. Establishing and maintaining a robust peacekeeping posture requires commitment and resources from the UN and troop contributors. However, many traditional troop contributors do not want to put their troops at risk to proactively protect

[31] See generally Victoria Holt and Glyn Taylor, with Max Kelly, *Protecting Civilians in the Context of UN Peacekeeping Operations* (New York: United Nations, 2009) 246–84, 301–9, 324–31, 353–62; J Arthur Boutellis, 'From Crisis to Reform: Peacekeeping Strategies for the Protection of Civilians in the Democratic Republic of the Congo' (September 2013) 2 Stability: Intl J Security Development 48.

[32] The original UN peacekeeping principle, which states that force should only be used in 'self-defence', was expanded to include 'self-defence and defence of the mandate'; the meaning of the latter, however, has not been authoritatively interpreted. See Scott Sheeran, 'The Use of Force in United Nations Peacekeeping', in Marc Weller and Alexia Solomou (eds), *The Oxford Handbook on the Use of Force in International Law* (Oxford: Oxford University Press, 2015).

[33] The Brahimi Report, see n 21, para. 49. Please also see the observations of Fiona Blythe and Patrick Cammaert on the use of force to protect civilians in Chapter 14 in this volume.

[34] See Jim Terrie, 'The Use of Force in UN Peacekeeping: The Experience of MONUC' (2009) 18 African Security RPv 21.

[35] 'Haiti: UN Peacekeepers Launch Large-scale Operation against Criminal Gangs', *UN News Centre* (New York, 9 February 2007) <www.un.org/apps/news/story.asp?NewsID=21515#.U-_h6sWSwdU>.

civilians, such as through night patrols and mobile operating bases.[36] At the same time, Member States that push for a more robust posture are generally unwilling to put their own troops at risk. As a result, in most missions, the quick reaction force is weak or nonexistent, and the deterrent capability of the UN lacks credibility.[37] UN peacekeeping operations have no other option than to try to establish their credibility in the heat of action, when they confront actual threats to civilians, making the best use of their limited assets.

A judicious and effective use of limited assets requires sophisticated command based on good intelligence and situational awareness.[38] A UN mission can bolster its credibility and effectiveness if it knows when and where to be prepared to fight. A decisive action in the early days of a deployment can send a message of strength that will provide some measure of protection to civilians. But a miscalculation leading to a failure—even limited failure—will project an image of weakness from which it will be hard for the mission to recover. Unfortunately, in the leadership of a UN peacekeeping mission, it is rare to find the combination of an experienced military commander who has been trained for such situations—which differ from traditional conflict situations taught in war colleges—and an experienced political leader who understands the political use of force. While the creation of Joint Mission Analysis Centres (JMACs)[39] has strengthened the capacity of peacekeeping missions to understand the tactical and strategic context in which they operate, more remains to be done to provide the mission leadership with a sound base of information on which to make decisions.[40]

Mobility is vital for missions deployed across vast areas of operation, in which it is impossible to have a permanent widespread presence. The rapid deployment of reinforcements can prevent a situation from further deteriorating, or can contain it. Unfortunately, military helicopters are the asset most needed for tactical mobility, and they are in short supply.[41] It is remarkable that in 2014 the UN was not able to find the planned number of military helicopters in several missions, despite widespread recognition among Member States of the importance of mobility assets for the effective protection of civilians.[42]

[36] UNGA, 'Report of the Office of Internal Oversight Services, Evaluation of the Implementation and Results of Protection of Civilians Mandates in United Nations peacekeeping operations' (2014) UN Doc A/68/787, paras 45–9 (OIOS Report).

[37] Ibid.

[38] See importance of situational awareness in UN DPKO and UN Department of Field Support (DFS), *UN Infantry Battalion Manual, Volume II* (New York: United Nations, 2012).

[39] The JMAC is responsible for producing all-source integrated analysis to assess threats to the mandate and assist with planning and decision-making. For further information, see Philip Shetler-Jones, 'Intelligence in Integrated UN Peacekeeping Missions: The Joint Mission Analysis Centre' (2008) 15 Intl Peacekeeping 517.

[40] See Ralph Mamiya and Haidi Willmot, 'Early Warning, the Protection of Civilians and United Nations Peacekeeping Operations' (2013) 22 African Security Rev 68.

[41] Colum Lynch, 'India's Withdrawal of Helicopters from Congo Points to Wider Trend', *The Washington Post* (Washington, DC, 14 June 2011) <www.washingtonpost.com/national/national-security/indias-withdrawal-of-helicopters-from-congo-points-to-wider-trend/2011/06/10/AGH5loUH_story.html>.

[42] United Nations, 'Meetings Coverage: Security Council Issues Presidential Statement Reaffirming Commitment To Protection Of Civilians In Armed Conflict' (New York, 12 February 2014) UN Doc SC/11274 <www.un.org/News/Press/docs/2014/sc11274.doc.htm>.

The difficulty of securing key assets is reflective of the broader problem that the UN confronts when attempting to generate troops from developed countries.[43] The bulk of peacekeeping troops are currently provided by developing countries.[44] Many of them provide valuable experience of complex peacekeeping environments that troops from developed countries often do not have. However, the best equipped armies of the world, which combine robust training with mobility and firepower, unsurprisingly are to be found in the wealthiest nations, from which the personnel contributions to peacekeeping under the UN flag remain minimal.[45]

The consequence is that sometimes under-equipped and insufficiently trained forces are sent to the most dangerous places, where they provide inadequate protection and are themselves exposed to excessive levels of risk. The poorly resourced African Union Mission in Somalia (AMISOM), for example, has suffered the highest ratio of casualties of any recent peace operation, as several hundred peacekeepers have lost their lives in challenging combat situations.[46]

C. Partnership arrangements

As Member States are unwilling to contribute forces in numbers that would allow the UN to provide an adequate level of protection, the UN has increasingly sought partners to boost missions' capacities. Such partnership arrangements are often preferred by NATO countries, which would rather operate outside the UN chain of command[47] even when they are deployed in a theatre where the UN is present.

[43] See generally Katarina Coleman, 'The Political Economy of Peacekeeping: Incentivizing Effective Participation' (New York: International Peace Institute, 2014) <www.ipinst.org/media/pdf/publications/ipi_political_economy.pdf>; Adam C Smith and Arthur Boutellis, 'Rethinking Force Generation: Filling the Capacity Gaps in UN Peacekeeping' (New York: International Peace Institute, 2013) <www.ipinst.org/media/pdf/publications/ipi_rpt_rethinking_force_gen.pdf>.

[44] The top contributors to UN missions as at 31 October 2014 are Bangladesh (8,758 personnel), Pakistan (8,247), India (7,886), and Ethiopia (7,827). See UN Department of Peacekeeping Operations (UN DPKO), 'Ranking of Military and Police Contributions to UN Operations' (New York, 31 October 2014) 2–3 <www.un.org/en/peacekeeping/contributors/2014/oct14_2.pdf>.

[45] For example, as at 31 October 2014, the UK provided 291 personnel, the USA 132, Canada 88, and Australia 44. Ibid., 2–3.

[46] The total number of uniformed personnel is 22,000. A spokesman for the African Union Mission in Somalia (AMISOM) has refuted the number of 3,000 casualties mentioned by a senior UN official (or the figure of 2,700 Ugandan losses mentioned by a Kenyan minister), stating that fewer than 500 were killed. Yet even if the casualties are in the hundreds rather than the thousands, this would still qualify AMISOM as the mission with the highest rate of casualties. See African Union Mission in Somalia, 'Frequently Asked Questions' (African Union Mission in Somalia, undated) <http://amisom-au.org/frequently-asked-questions>; United Nations, 'Press Conference by Deputy Secretary General Jan Eliasson at United Nations Headquarters' (New York, 9 May 2013) UN Doc DSG/SM/668 <www.un.org/press/en/2013/dsgsm668.doc.htm>; Jason Straziuso, 'Kenyan Official: 2,700 Ugandans Dead in Somalia' *Associated Press* (New York, 31 October 2012) <news.yahoo.com/kenyan-official-2-700-ugandans-dead-somalia-140340249.html>; Abdi Moalim, 'AMISOM Spokesman Refutes Casualty Numbers, Outlines Long Term Plan' *Sabahionline.com* (online, 22 May 2013) <sabahionline.com/en_GB/articles/hoa/articles/features/2013/05/22/feature-01>.

[47] The reluctance of countries of the North Atlantic Treaty Organization (NATO) to deploy under UN command is generally explained by their lack of confidence in the UN chain of command, based on their experience of the UN Protection Force in Yugoslavia. Although NATO countries had a dominant role at all levels of the chain of command, and the political divisions among Western countries

The previously mentioned European Union (EU) mission in Ituri in 2003[48] undoubtedly contributed to the protection of civilians in Eastern DRC, as did the EU mission deployed during the first presidential election in the same country in 2006.[49] Although its actual operational capacity was minute, it was perceived as a strong force, and probably contributed to relatively peaceful elections.[50] It is more difficult to assess the impact of the French forces deployed in Côte d'Ivoire,[51] Mali,[52] and the Central African Republic[53] on the protection of civilians. In Côte d'Ivoire, the presence of a French contingent working alongside UN peacekeepers throughout the protracted crisis that started in 2004 and found a provisional end when President Gbagbo was transferred to the International Criminal Court (ICC) in 2011 was certainly a factor in preventing the conflict from escalating to a level of violence that could have spiralled out of control. The fact that the mission could call on the French forces gave it a valuable escalation capacity that may well have had a deterrent effect.

While the protection of civilians was a consideration when France deployed its forces, it was only one aspect of broader national considerations that motivated its involvement. Because national interests play such a prominent role in deciding whether to commit resources, the UN cannot rely fully on such partnerships to augment its limited civilian protection capabilities. In some instances, it may be the case that a State's interests, such as a counter-terrorism agenda, run counter to an effective protection of civilians strategy; for example, the rejection of any engagement with groups designated as terrorist organizations, whether in Gaza or Somalia, may harm the civilian population.[54]

The limited support to peacekeeping provided by developed countries since the end of the Yugoslav wars has led the UN to increasingly leverage regional resources, engaging States with national interests in the mission and allowing the UN to recruit troops that have a greater tolerance for risk and casualties. In Mali and the Central African Republic, regional countries have provided a significant

were the main source of problems, this is not yet acknowledged, in spite of significant improvements in the UN, and the mixed record of the NATO chain of command in Afghanistan.

[48] Operation Artemis. See UNSC Res 1484 (2003) UN Doc S/RES/1484.

[49] European Union, 'EU Missions in the Democratic Republic of the Congo' (Europa.eu, last updated 11 September 2008) <europa.eu/legislation_summaries/foreign_and_security_policy/cfsp_and_esdp_implementation/ps0005_en.htm>.

[50] See Catherine Gegout, 'Causes and Consequences of the EU's Military Intervention in the Democratic Republic of the Congo: A Realist Explanation' (2005) 10 Eur Foreign Affairs Rev 427, 435. The aftermath of elections was not so peaceful, as artillery was used in Kinshasa against Jean-Pierre Bemba, the defeated challenger of President Kabila, but by then Operation Artemis had departed. See ibid. and compare with Mike Pflanz, 'EU Troops Fly into Chaos of Kinshasa', *The Telegraph* (London, 23 August 2006) <http://www.telegraph.co.uk/news/1527048/EU-troops-fly-into-chaos-of-Kinshasa.html>.

[51] Operation Licorne. See UNSC Res 1528 (2004) UN Doc S/RES/1528, paras 16–17.

[52] Operation Serval was launched in 2013 to oust Islamist militants in northern Mali. UNSC Res 2085 (2013) UN Doc S/RES/2085, paras 13–16.

[53] Operation Sangaris. UNSC Res 2127 (2013) UN Doc S/RES/2127, paras 49–50.

[54] See Sara Pantuliano and Eva Svaboda, 'Humanitarian Protection—Moving Beyond the Tried and Tested', Chapter 17 in this volume. See also Ashley Jackson and Eleanor Davey, *From the Spanish Civil War to Afghanistan* (London: Overseas Development Institute, 2014).

contribution, even when they were perceived to harbour a direct interest in the conflict.[55] In the DRC, the UN Intervention Brigade, mandated to tackle armed groups that exploit Eastern DRC's porous borders,[56] is commanded by a Tanzanian general and includes troops from Tanzania and South Africa, two countries that have strong interests in the DRC. The international presence in Somalia goes even further in combining a UN political role with regional engagement through an African Union (AU) military mission. Most countries engaged in AMISOM[57] have direct interests in Somalia, and some, including Ethiopia and Kenya, are neighbours. While these examples show that regional partners can provide engagement options, such partnerships risk diverging significantly from a key principle of peacekeeping: impartiality.[58] There is also a risk of the conflict regionalizing.[59] The impact of such direct regional engagement on the protection of civilians needs to be assessed on a case-by-case basis but it will depend in part on how the intervening countries reconcile their protection of civilians tasks with their other military objectives.

Another option for the UN to bolster its ratio is to join efforts with one of the most directly interested parties—the forces of the host country. That is what the UN has done in the DRC, with mixed results.[60] Its experience there, in which the UN supported a national army implicated in human rights abuses, led to the development of the UN Human Rights Due Diligence Policy, now applicable to all UN operations, whether peacekeeping missions or development agencies.[61] While this policy provides an important framework, it is fraught with moral dilemmas. By supporting poorly commanded troops, the UN could become complicit in war crimes; but not supporting them can push the troops to exploit the civilian population to an even greater degree, as they have no effective oversight, discipline, or logistical support. Politically, the association of the UN with the military of a

[55] For instance, Chad was slated to provide a significant contribution to the mission in the Central African Republic, although eventually that failed to come to fruition after serious accusations of partiality and human rights violations. See John Irish, 'Chad to Withdraw Troops from AU Mission in Central African Republic', *Reuters* (London, 3 April 2014) <www.reuters.com/article/2014/04/03/us-centralafrica-idUSBREA320YT20140403>.

[56] For more information on armed groups see International Crisis Group, *Eastern Congo: Why Stabilisation Failed* (Brussels: International Crisis Group, 2012); International Crisis Group, *The ADF-NALU's Lost Rebellion* (Brussels: International Crisis Group, 2012).

[57] The countries taking part in AMISOM are Burundi, Djibouti, Ethiopia, Kenya, Sierra Leone, Uganda, Ghana, and Nigeria. See Communiqué of the Peace and Security Council of the African Union CDLXII (2014) AU Doc PSC/PR/Comm. (CDLXII), para. 8.

[58] The 'Capstone Doctrine' distinguishes impartiality from neutrality by declaring that peacekeepers should be impartial but not neutral in the implementation of their mandate. See UN DPKO and UN Department of Field Support (DFS), *United Nations Peacekeeping Operations Principles and Guidelines* (New York: United Nations, 2008) 33–4 (The Capstone Doctrine).

[59] An example is the increasing terrorist activity generated by Al-Shabaab in Kenya. See International Crisis Group, *Kenya: Al-Shabaab—Closer to Home* (Brussels: International Crisis Group, 2014).

[60] Kimia II, Amani Leo, and Rudia II were among the operations that received significant logistical support from MONUC. For a strong criticism of this approach, see Human Rights Watch, 'Press Release: Surge in Army Atrocities: UN Peacekeeping Force Knowingly Supports Abusive Military Operations' (New York, 2 November 2009) <www.hrw.org/news/2009/11/02/eastern-dr-congo-surge-army-atrocities>.

[61] See Human Rights Due Diligence Policy on United Nations Support to Non-United Nations Security Forces, annexed to UNGA and UNSC (2013) UN Doc A/67/775–S/2013/110.

country that is still in the process of reconciliation raises some difficult questions, including issues of impartiality and whether the UN is assisting in consolidating the power of one group over others without creating a lasting institutional base for peace.

Such questions highlight the flawed nature of relying exclusively on the use of force to protect civilians. While increasingly ambitious peacekeeping mandates are difficult, if not impossible, to fulfil with limited material resources, the use of force alone will never be sufficient to ensure the protection of civilians. At worst, the use of force may deprive the UN of its capacity to broker a peace agreement in an impartial way. At best, the use of force can help create conditions for peace, but it cannot in and of itself achieve such an ambitious goal. Acknowledging such limitations has led UN Member States and the Secretariat to consider other non-military instruments.

V. Alternatives to Force: Tools for the Maintenance of International Peace and Security

In his November 2013 report on the protection of civilians, the Secretary-General reminded the Security Council that it has several tools at its disposal, beyond the use of force, to put pressure on parties to a conflict: 'targeted measures, fact-finding missions, commissions of inquiry, referrals to the International Criminal Court'.[62] The UN has also strengthened its political and mediation activities by deploying non-military special political missions in places such as Afghanistan, Libya, Iraq, and Somalia.[63] Other pacific measures include UN Special Envoys[64] and a stand-by team of mediation experts, deployable at short notice to prevent and resolve conflict.[65] On occasion, the Security Council has employed multiple tools at one time: for instance, after militia attacked the Congolese regional capital of Goma in 2012, with alleged support from a neighbouring country, a UN Special Envoy was deployed to lead regional discussions while peacekeepers addressed issues of physical protection in the DRC.[66]

In the peacekeeping context, DPKO and the Department of Field Support (DFS) have developed a broad and more sustainable policy and operational concept for the protection of civilians by peacekeeping operations, incorporating three pillars: 'protection through political process; providing protection from physical

[62] UNSC, 'Report of the Secretary-General on the Protection of Civilians in Armed Conflict' (2013) UN Doc S/2013/689, para. 5.

[63] UNGA, 'Report of the Secretary-General on Overall Policy Matters Pertaining to Special Political Missions' (2013) UN Doc A/68/223, paras 20–8.

[64] Ibid., para. 19.

[65] See UN Department of Political Affairs, 'Factsheet: Standby Team of Mediation Experts' (New York: United Nations, 2014) <http://peacemaker.un.org/sites/peacemaker.un.org/files/SBT-FactSheet-2014_0.pdf>.

[66] 'DR Congo: UN Envoy Welcomes End of M23 Rebellion, Commitment to Peace Talks', *UN News Centre* (New York, 5 November 2013) <www.un.org/apps/news/story.asp?NewsID=46423#.VCAvZytdXmU>.

violence; and, establishing a protective environment'.[67] This broader approach raises two related sets of questions: (a) What leverage, if any, does the international community have in consolidating peace in a fractured society? (b) What are the foundations of a peaceful environment in which civilians feel protected?

The past fifteen years have seen a qualitative change in the use of new instruments for the maintenance of international peace and security by the international community, but it is still too early to assess their full impact on the protection of civilians. A common characteristic is greater emphasis on individual accountability, whether it is achieved through sanctions targeting designated individuals,[68] through international justice,[69] or through fact-finding missions that document harm to civilians and investigate responsibility.[70]

However, the effectiveness of such measures is hampered by a lack of political consensus, challenging in the process the notion of an emerging international community or global society. On a number of occasions, the Security Council has been incapable of reaching agreement on issues relevant to the protection of civilians, its incapacity to deal with the Syrian crisis being the most egregious example from recent history.[71] Paradoxically, the Council acted decisively in response to conflict in Libya in early 2011, authorizing 'all necessary measures . . . to protect civilians and civilian populated areas under threat of attack'.[72] Here, the protection of civilians language from the consensual peacekeeping environment was co-opted into a responsibility to protect operation in a non-consensual environment. The use of protection language, which already had wide acceptance through its frequent use, probably signals an efficient way to deal with political division within the Council, rather than a genuinely progressive approach to human security.

Security Council paralysis affects not only the people living the conflict, as no collective enforcement action is authorized, but also the overall authority and credibility of the Security Council and the broader UN. Even in those situations where the Council has been able to reach agreement, detractors highlight its inconsistency in determining which situations to address and how to address them, questioning the Council's impartiality and accusing it of double standards.[73] This dynamic is of fundamental importance, as a true international community exists only when most of its members adhere to its fundamental values.

[67] UN DPKO and UN DFS, DPKO/DFS Policy: The Protection of Civilians in United Nations Peacekeeping (New York: United Nations 2015) Ref 2015.07, UN DPKO and UN DFS, 'Draft DPKO/DFS Operational Concept on the Protection of Civilians in United Nations Peacekeeping Operations' (New York: United Nations, 2010).

[68] Sanctions include those against individuals from Guinea-Bissau, the Central African Republic, and Iraq and Syria. See UNSC Res 2048 (2012) UN Doc S/RES/2048, paras 4, 6; UNSC Res 2134 (2014) UN Doc S/RES/2134, paras 30, 32; UNSC Res 2161 (2014) UN Doc S/RES/2161, paras 18–21.

[69] Such as international criminal tribunals or the International Criminal Court.

[70] Examples include fact-finding missions on the conflicts in Gaza and Syria. See UNGA, 'Resolution Adopted by the Human Rights Council' (2009) UN Doc A/HRC/RES/S-91, para. 14; UNGA, 'Resolution Adopted by the Human Rights Council' (2011) UN Doc A/HRC/RES/S-16/1, para. 7.

[71] See, for example, Somini Sengupta, 'In Dealings on Syria, the Security Council Exposes its Failings', *The New York Times* (New York, 9 May 2014) A12.

[72] UNSC Res 1973 (2011) UN Doc S/RES/1973, para. 4.

[73] See Adam Roberts and Dominik Zaum, *Selective Security: War and the United Nations Security Council Since 1945* (London: The International Institute for Strategic Studies, 2008).

The impact of sanctions, international justice, or fact-finding missions can also be limited by potential perpetrators' cost–benefit analysis.[74] In many cases, the odds that they will suffer personal consequences are low, and their motivations—political, religious, ethnic—will easily override other considerations, especially when they can claim that a so-called international community is biased and inconsistent. That does not mean that these non-military tools should be dismissed, but, as with the use of force, their efficacy in protecting civilians should be weighed against potential negative collateral effects on civilian populations. Comprehensive sanctions regimes have the capacity to harm civilians, for instance, as evidenced in Iraq in the 1990s. It is estimated that the US and UN sanctions cost Iraq 48 per cent of its GDP,[75] resulting in increased mortality rates and reduced incomes among the civilian population.[76] Similarly, there is an ongoing debate regarding the impact of international criminal justice campaigns in contexts where peace negotiations are in process.[77] The 2008 ICC indictment of Sudanese President Omar al-Bashir highlighted this issue.[78]

In the long term, the development of international norms of behaviour, even if they are systematically violated, may herald transformations that have little impact on the protection of civilians today but will contribute to positive change decades from now, just as the development of international humanitarian law, which started in the nineteenth century, eventually had a positive impact on the behaviour of regular armies. Such a conclusion justifies continued efforts to develop and strengthen international norms for the future of civilian protection, but it is a very unsatisfactory answer to the threats that affect civilians today.

In the end, outsiders to a conflict that victimizes civilians cannot protect them in a lasting and sustained way. This may be the main flaw of the protection of civilians concept. The wording assumes that a third party will come and 'protect', which is indeed what should happen in emergencies, but cannot be a lasting response. Civilians are not to be protected; they are to be empowered. Civilians will continue to feel under threat as long as they see people with guns—including the security forces of their own country—as a threat rather than a reassurance.[79] Civilians can be said to be protected when they can be confident that there is a body of law that makes the government trustworthy, the security forces predictable and accountable,

74 For commentary on the rationale behind actors' behaviour including utilization of the game theory, see Kenneth W Abbott, 'Modern International Relations Theory: A Prospectus for International Lawyers' (1989) 14 Yale J Intl L 335; Annette Freyberg-Inan, *What Moves Man: The Realist Theory of International Relations and Its Judgement of Human Nature* (Albany, USA: State University of New York Press, 2004) Chapter 3.

75 Lance Davis and Stanley Engerman, 'History Lessons: Sanctions—Neither War nor Peace' (2003) 17 J Economic Perspectives 187, 193.

76 Ibid.; Gary Clyde Hufbauer, Jeffrey J Schott, and Kimberley Ann Elliott, *Economic Sanctions Reconsidered: History and Current Policy* (Washington, DC: Institute for International Economics, 1990) 84–90, 283–98; Dursun Peksen, 'Better or Worse? The Effect of Economic Sanctions on Human Rights' (2009) 46 J Peace Research 59.

77 International Crisis Group, *Justice in Conflict? The International Criminal Court and Peace Processes in Africa* (Brussels: International Crisis Group, 2007).

78 Simon Robinson, 'Choosing Justice over Peace in Darfur', *Time Magazine* (New York, 14 June 2008) <content.time.com/time/world/article/0,8599,1822529,00.html>.

79 For further discussion see Lise Grande, Chapter 18 in this volume.

non-government militia deactivated and brought to justice, and a working judicial system in place.

How can the UN, as an outsider, contribute to such a process, when it needs to be nationally owned? The two pillars identified by DPKO and DFS—'protection through a political process' and 'protection through the creation of a protective environment'—provide tentative answers to that question. Protection through a political process is the most important, and a condition for the creation of a protective environment. Building a State when the basic political foundations of a political community have not been laid down is unlikely to work.

In that context, the UN experience of State-building in South Sudan should provide some important lessons for an effective strategy to ensure lasting civilian protection. Encouraged by influential Member States whose overly optimistic view of the new State of South Sudan was influenced by their sympathy for the struggle against Sudan,[80] the UN focused its post-independence efforts on building the capacities of the State of South Sudan, assuming that its political foundation had already been secured.[81] Yet divisions within South Sudan ran deep and there was no genuine agreement among major stakeholders on the dispensation of power. The last report released by the UN before South Sudan slipped into major violence at the end of 2013 tellingly referred to the reshuffle of the cabinet in mid-July[82] as a 'positive sign', which justified 'cautious optimism'.[83] This assessment reflected the priority given by the mission to 'service delivery' and 'performance', two important components of the legitimacy of any government, but irrelevant if the basic political compact is not secure. In South Sudan, there could not be a protective environment resulting from a well-functioning State because protection through a political process had not been achieved. The UN mission had been active in defusing a number of peripheral conflicts, but had neglected the central conflict over power that was brewing in Juba.[84] In the end, the only option left to the mission was physical protection—a task that it performed remarkably well considering its limited resources, taking care of thousands of civilians seeking refuge in UN compounds.[85]

80 The US and Norway are examples of this.

81 Programmes were put in place to train the police, build the judiciary, and more generally help the government of South Sudan consolidate its authority. For further discussion of capacity building in South Sudan, see Lise Grande, Chapter 18 in this volume.

82 President Salva Kiir dismissed vice president Riek Machar, an action that was a sign of the deepening divisions in the top leadership and a trigger for the violence that occurred later in the year. See Carol Berger, 'Old Emnities in the Newest Nation: Behind the Fighting in South Sudan', *The New Yorker* (New York, 23 January 2014) <www.newyorker.com/news/news-desk/old-enmities-in-the-newest-nation-behind-the-fighting-in-south-sudan>.

83 UNSC, 'Report of the Secretary-General on South Sudan' (2013) UN Doc S/2013/65, para. 79.

84 Simon Tisdall, 'South Sudan President Sacks Cabinet in Power Struggle', *The Guardian* (London, 24 July 2013) <www.theguardian.com/world/2013/jul/24/south-sudan-salva-kiir-sacks-cabinet>; Carl Odera, 'Leaders' Personal Power Struggle Destroying South Sudan: U.N. Rights Chief', *Reuters* (London, 30 April 2014) <www.reuters.com/article/2014/04/30/us-southsudan-unrest-idUSBREA3T0DL20140430>.

85 Steps taken by the mission included building 'protection of civilians' sites to relieve congestion at UN bases already sheltering displaced persons, screening of those entering and exiting sites, weapons searches, patrols, guarding perimeter fences, and the building of fences and ditches. See Damian Lilly, 'Protection of Civilians Sites: A New Type of Displacement Settlement?' *Humanitarian Exchange* (London, September 2014) 31–3.

VI. Conclusion

The emphasis placed by the international community on the protection of civilians in conflict has rightly made the safeguarding of civilian lives a priority of the UN. It came as a reaction to the failures of the 1990s, and the initial focus was on the physical protection of civilians. At its core, physical protection is a moral obligation; the failure of peacekeepers to protect civilians when they have the capability to do so is a moral failure. In that limited sense, the protection of civilians is a self-evident imperative that does not warrant a long discussion. But the difficulties start when the use of force has a greater ambition than the tactical protection of civilians in imminent danger. There are political implications to a more systematic use of force by peacekeepers, whether it empowers a questionable government or prevents a mission from acting as a broker in a peace process. It is, however, notable that the Security Council usually avoids addressing such political dilemmas.

In the DRC, a potentially decisive role of the Intervention Brigade could have given the UN mission real leverage for improved governance by the Congolese authorities—the only way to eventually create a 'protective environment'—but the government's strengthened position has actually made it more confident and less open to reforms. In such a case, the immediate success achieved in the realms of physical protection can eventually undermine the longer-term goal of creating a protective environment.

If the protection of civilians is to be more than a temporary response to an emergency, it needs to address the foundations of what constitutes a 'protective environment'; that is, the consolidation of a State, the legitimacy of which is founded not only on the services it delivers, but on the political trust it inspires. What is required for the implementation of such an ambitious agenda may be even more difficult to mobilize than the capacities required to provide physical protection through military deployments. Military battalions and civilian capacities are generally in short supply, but the political support of Member States, when the UN needs to effectively challenge governments that abuse their power, is often even harder to obtain.

The UN thus finds itself caught between two equally unappealing definitions of the 'protection of civilians'. A narrow definition that focuses on physical protection exposes its operational limitations and, paradoxically, may make it more difficult to press a government to address underlying political and governance issues. A broader definition that includes support to a political process and the creation of a protective environment brings back familiar political dilemmas, but hides them behind a façade of capacity and State-building. Member States remain reluctant to openly support a UN engagement that might be seen by the host government as a challenge to its sovereignty; they would much rather encourage the UN to support, through technical co-operation, the consolidation of the superstructure of the State, even if its political foundations remain shaky.

The absolute priority given in some recent UN mandates to the protection of civilians is therefore not a sign that the international community has come closer to a comprehensive view of human security. On the contrary, it may reflect the increasing difficulty that a divided Security Council has in addressing political issues. By borrowing from international humanitarian law the concept of protection, it can achieve a superficial unanimity that may be more a diversion than a step forward.

12
The African Union and the Protection of Civilians

Ben Kioko and Lydia Wambugu[1]

I. Introduction

The African Union (AU) has taken an increasingly important role in protecting civilians in conflict situations. It has placed the protection of civilians as a central strategic priority of its agenda, in part as a reaction to the widespread and, in some instances, systematic gross violations of international human rights law (IHRL) and serious violations of international humanitarian law (IHL) in several of its Member States. The AU has also developed guidelines for the protection of civilians that comprehensively address all aspects of peace support operations, including confidence-building measures among the population, provision of security to civilians and businesses, and humanitarian aid. While this framework is relatively new and still in a nascent stage of implementation, it is being utilized in the AU Mission in Somalia (AMISOM), where it has shown great promise and been well received by the Somali citizenry. However, many challenges remain, not least a lack of political will among AU Member States and difficulties ensuring adequate resources for effective implementation. In addition, while the AU has put in place a normative framework and mechanisms that could support efforts towards effective civilian protection, they have not worked as a coherent whole and require better co-ordination to enhance effectiveness and delivery.

This chapter seeks to examine the legal and political aspects of recent developments in African conflicts, regional responses, and future challenges. It provides an overview of the AU framework for the protection of civilians, based on an examination of relevant AU organs and actual regional responses. It also addresses the intervention in Libya in 2011 and concludes with reflections on how the AU framework for the protection of civilians may be effectively operationalized. The chapter proceeds from the assumption that the protection of civilians is achieved through the legal protection of human rights and the implementation of IHL. Nonetheless, it should be acknowledged that there are other factors at play including, inter alia, *enforcement actions* by peacekeeping operations, the delivery of humanitarian aid,

[1] The views expressed in this chapter are those of the authors and do not necessarily represent the views of the institutions with which the authors are affiliated.

and the development of national security sectors, as demonstrated by AMISOM in Somalia.

II. The African Union Framework for the Protection of Civilians

Protection against violations of IHRL and IHL is not only a matter of great importance but also a right that civilians are entitled to expect under international law. The process of negotiating a treaty to replace the Charter of the Organization of African Unity (OAU) of 1963 presented an opportunity to rethink and re-engineer the norms, values, and standards at the core of inter-State relations within Africa. It allowed for reflection on the atrocities and gross violations of human rights across the continent, ranging from Uganda in the 1970s[2] to the Central African Republic in the 1980s,[3] Mozambique in the 1980s[4] to Sierra Leone in the 1990s,[5] as well as the genocide in Rwanda in 1994.[6] Despite the OAU's attempts to address the challenges of governance and human rights violations, the lack of democratic rule, and the prevalence of impunity on the continent, it was heavily criticized for having failed in all of these areas.

The legitimacy of collective intervention in circumstances of genocide, war crimes, and crimes against humanity was first enshrined by the AU in the year 2000, in its founding document, the Constitutive Act, which embodies principles that address the shortcomings of the OAU, most notably in the area of international crimes, human rights, the rule of law, and democratic values.[7] The adoption of the Constitutive Act was preceded by a number of declarations, decisions, and treaties relating to human rights, peace and security, and good governance.[8] As

[2] See Daniel Chirot, *Modern Tyrants: The Power and Prevalence of Evil in Our Age* (Princeton, USA: Princeton University Press, 1996) 375.

[3] Ibid.

[4] See generally Hilary Andersson, *Mozambique: A War against the People* (New York: St Martin's Press 1992).

[5] Ibrahim Abdullah, 'Bush Path to Destruction: The Origin and Character of the Revolutionary United Front/Sierra Leone' (1998) 36 J Modern African Studies 203, 203–35; Yusuf Bangura, 'The Political and Cultural Dynamics of the Sierra Leone War', in Ibrahim Abdullah (ed.), *Between Democracy and Terror: the Sierra Leone Civil War* (Pretoria: UNISA Press, 2004).

[6] See generally Gerard Prunier, *The Rwanda Crisis: History of a Genocide* (New York: Columbia University Press, 1995).

[7] Constitutive Act of the African Union (adopted 1 July 2000, entered into force on 26 May 2001) OAU Doc CAB/LEG/23.15. Article 4 (h), (m), and 4(o) of the African Union (AU) Constitutive Act lists among its founding principles: (h) The right of the AU to intervene in a member State in grave circumstances such as genocide, war crimes and crimes against humanity; (m) Respect for democratic principles, human rights, the rule of law and good governance; and (o) Respect for the sanctity of human life, condemnation and rejection of impunity and political assassination, acts of terrorism and subversive activities.

[8] It should be recalled that the Organisation of African Unity (OAU)/AU had previously adopted a number of legal instruments aimed at deepening and consolidating democracy and respect for human rights on the continent, including the Solemn Declaration of the Conference on Security, Stability, Cooperation and Development (2000) OAU Doc AHG/Decl.4 (XXXVI); the Memorandum of Understanding on Security, Stability, Development and Cooperation in Africa (2002) AU Doc OAU/CIVIL SOCIETY.3 (II); the various instruments adopted within the framework of the New Economic Partnership for Africa's Development (NEPAD), including the African Peer Review Mechanism (see

such, the framework for the protection of civilians in Africa is underpinned by a body of mechanisms and legal instruments, including: (a) the Constitutive Act of the AU; (b) the African Peace and Security Architecture, described later in the chapter; (c) the African human rights system, centred on the African Charter on Human and Peoples' Rights and comprising more than twenty-five legal instruments;[9] and (d) the African Governance Architecture, established to serve as a co-ordination framework among AU bodies (and subsequently with other African organizations), and designed to complement the African Peace and Security Architecture.[10] The common thread that runs through these instruments, with differing emphasis and nuances, is that Africa needed to look within itself to find home-grown solutions to the many challenges confronting the continent. In this regard, there is a need to address the internal issues that negatively impact on socio-economic development such as conflict, human rights violations, and democracy and governance deficits.

Article 4(h) of the Constitutive Act empowers the Union to intervene militarily in a Member State, pursuant to a decision of the Assembly of Heads of State and Government, in grave circumstances such as where war crimes, genocide, and crimes against humanity are occurring.[11] In addition, a Member State is entitled to request intervention in order to restore peace and security under Article 4(j). Member States are required, under Article 4(o), to respect democratic principles, human rights, rule of law, and good governance, and to ensure respect for the sanctity of human life and condemn and reject impunity, political assassination, acts of terrorism, and subversive activities. Further, in accordance with Article 7 of the 2002 Protocol relating to the Peace and Security Council of the AU, the Council can recommend to the Assembly, pursuant to Article 4(h) of the Constitutive Act, intervention in a Member State in grave circumstances such as war crimes, genocide, and crimes against humanity, as defined in relevant conventions and instruments.[12] According to Article 4(h) of the Constitutive Act, where diplomacy and other peaceful means have failed, the AU may use force to protect populations at risk of mass atrocities. It should be noted that since resort to Article 4(h) requires coercive

'About the APRM' (*African Peer Review Mechanism*, undated) <aprm-au.org/about-aprm>); as well as the Declaration on the Principles Governing Democratic Elections in Africa (2002) AU Doc AHG/Decl. 1 (XXXVIII).

[9] Others include the OAU/AU Convention Governing the Specific Aspects of Refugee Problems in Africa of 1969 (adopted 10 September 1969, entered into force 20 June 1974) 1001 UNTS 45; the African Union Convention for the Protection and Assistance of Internally Displaced Persons in Africa (Kampala Convention) (adopted 22 October 2009, entered into force 6 December 2012) 52 IM 397; the African Charter on the Rights and Welfare of the Child (adopted 11 July 1990, entered into force 29 November 1999) OAU Doc CAB/LEG/24.9/49; the African Union Protocol to the African Charter on Human and Peoples' Rights on the Rights of Women in Africa (signed 11 July 2003, entered into force 5 November 2005) AU Doc CAB/LEG/66.6, reprinted in (2001) 1 African Hum Rts L J 40; the Protocol Relating to the Establishment of the Peace and Security Council of the African Union (signed 9 July 2002, entered into force 26 December 2003) <www.au.int/en/treaties>; and the Constitutive Act of the African Union, see n 7.

[10] George Mukundi Wachira, 'Consolidating the African Governance Architecture' (Johannesburg: South African Institute of International Affairs, 2014) <www.saiia.org.za/policy-briefings/consolidating-the-african-governance-architecture>.

[11] Constitutive Act of the African Union, see n 7, Article 4(h).

[12] Protocol Relating to the Establishment of the Peace and Security Council of the African Union, see n 9, Article 7(1)(e), 7(1)(f).

measures, in particular the use of military force, a decision of the Assembly is required.[13]

Since the adoption of the Constitutive Act, no intervention by the Union has been undertaken under the provisions of Articles 4(h) and (j), nor has any specific reference been made to these provisions in the mandating decisions setting up AU peace support missions.[14] This has been so even though there have been references in the mandating decisions to the need to protect civilians, such as in Darfur[15] and Somalia.[16] The AU has also not adopted any implementing guidelines detailing how these provisions would be applied, leaving a number of procedural issues unresolved, including who in the Union has standing to suggest the need for intervention. The Rules of Procedure of the Assembly of the AU stipulate that 'the Assembly shall decide on intervention in a Member State in respect of grave circumstances, namely: war crimes, genocide and crimes against humanity',[17] and may also do so 'at the request of that Member State in order to restore peace and security'.[18] However, neither of these instruments provide any guidance on the factors that may be considered in application of this provision.

The African Peace and Security Architecture was designed to provide the AU with the necessary tools for conflict prevention, early warning, promoting democratic practices, intervention, humanitarian action, and disaster management.[19] It is based largely on the Protocol relating to the Peace and Security Council of the AU and envisages a number of co-ordinated activities between the Council and the

[13] Ben Kioko, 'The Right of Intervention under the African Union's Constitutive Act: From Non-interference to Non-indifference' (2003) 85 IRRC 807, 812.

[14] Perhaps the reason for this is to avoid attracting unnecessary debates on whether Article 4(h) was applicable or not. AU peace support missions since 2003 include the African Union Mission in Burundi (AMIB) (African Union Central Organ for Conflict Prevention, Management and Resolution at the Ambassadorial Level Communiqué (Comm) XCI (2003) AU Doc Central Organ/MEC/AMB/Comm. (XCI)); the African Union Mission in Sudan (AMIS) (African Union Peace and Security Council (AUPSC) Comm XVII (2004) AU Doc PSC/PR/Comm.(XVII)); the Africa Union Mission in Somalia (AUPSC Comm LXIX (2007) AU Doc PSC/PR/Comm(LXIX)); the African Union Electoral Assistance Mission to the Comoros (AUPSC Comm XLVII (2006) AU Doc PSC/PR/Comm.1(XLVII)); and the African-led International Support Mission to the Central African Republic (AUPSC Comm CCCXLI (2012) AU Doc PSC/PR/COMM.2(CCCXLI)). The African Union also co-leads the AU–UN Hybrid Operation in Darfur (AUPSC Comm LXXIX (2007) AU Doc PSC/PR/Comm(LXXIX), United Nations Security Council (UNSC) Resolution (Res) 1769 (2007) UN Doc S/RES/1769).

[15] AUPSC Comm XVII (2004) AU Doc PSC/PR/Comm. (XVII), para. 6, which requires AMIS to 'protect civilians whom it encounters under imminent threat and in the immediate vicinity, within resources and capability, it being understood that the protection of the civilian population is the responsibility of the [Government of Sudan]'.

[16] AUPSC Comm CXC (2009) AU Doc PSC/PR/Comm. (CXC), paras Comm 3, 5; UNSC Res 2010 (2011) UN Doc S/RES/2010, paras 5, 6, 16, 22.

[17] Assembly of the African Union, Rules of Procedure of the Assembly of the Union (2002) AU Doc ASS/AU/2(I)—a, Rule 13(3)(f) (Rules of Procedure of the Assembly of the Union).

[18] Ibid., Rule 4(1)(f).

[19] African Union, *Moving Africa Forward: African Peace and Security Architecture, 2010 Assessment Study* (Addis Ababa: African Union, 2010) (adopted by the Third Meeting of the Chief Executives and Senior Officials of the African Union, Regional Economic Communities and Regional Mechanisms for Conflict Prevention, Management and Resolution, 4–10 November 2010, Zanzibar, Tanzania), para. 46.

Regional Economic Communities, as well as with other critical actors on the continent. Its key components, in the context of the protection of civilians, are: (a) the Peace and Security Council; (b) the AU Commission; (c) the Continental Early Warning System; (d) the African Standby Force; (e) the Panel of the Wise; and (f) the Peace Fund. The vertical co-ordination between the Council and the Regional Economic Communities through the Continental Early Warning System and the African Standby Force is fairly well developed and has worked well, perhaps due to the fact that there are clear timelines for implementation.[20] Nonetheless, the horizontal co-ordination that was envisaged between the various components of the African Peace and Security Architecture, in terms of information exchange, has achieved limited success due to lack of effective co-ordination and communication.[21]

The African Standby Force has the capacity to protect populations at risks of mass atrocities and to deter potential perpetrators of mass atrocities. Article 13 3(f) of the Protocol relating to the Peace and Security Council of the AU[22] provides that the functions of the African Standby Force, which constitute its *raison d'être* as an organ of the African Peace and Security Architecture, include providing humanitarian assistance to alleviate the suffering of civilian populations in conflict areas and supporting efforts to address major natural disasters.

Guidelines for the protection of civilians in AU peace support operations were developed between 2009 and 2012.[23] They provide guidance on missions' obligations regarding the civilian population, highlighting the need to ensure respect for IHL and integrate key humanitarian rules and principles into the mission operational orders, procedures, and training.[24] The experience of implementing the protection of civilians guidelines in Somalia has shown that while military operations are important, the confidence-building measures that accompany the provision of humanitarian aid, medical care, educational facilities, and security for business activities enhance prospects for long-term stability and socio-economic recovery. However, obtaining the requisite capacity to deal with issues such as child protection and gender-based violence remains challenging. In Mali and the Central African Republic, while AU missions did not have protection of civilians mandates in the same way as the UN, both played important protection roles before the arrival of UN peacekeepers.[25]

[20] Ibid., para. 3. [21] Ibid., para. 5.

[22] Protocol Relating to the Establishment of the Peace and Security Council of the African Union, see n 9, Article 13(3)(f).

[23] African Union, 'Draft Guidelines for the Protection of Civilians in African Union Peace Support Operations' (Addis Ababa: Africa Union, 2012) <www.apsta- africa.org/documentation/resources/key%20resources/Draft%20AU%20PoC%20Guidelines%20-%20English.pdf>. See also AUPSC, 'Progress Report of the Chairperson of the Commission on the Development of Guidelines for the Protection of Civilians in African Union Peace Support Operations' (2011) AU Doc PSC/PR/2(CCLXXIX) and <www.operationspaix.net/DATA/DOCUMENTTEXTE/8763.pdf>.

[24] Ibid., para. 22.

[25] For further discussion on the protection of civilians in AU peace support operations see Stian Kjeksrud, Jacob Aasland Ravndal, Andreas Øien Stensland, Cedric de Coning, and Walter Lotze, Chapter 4, in this volume.

III. African Union Organs and Regional Responses

This section discusses the leverage achieved by the combined capacities of the AU's constituent organs as required by the Protocol relating to the Peace and Security Council of the AU, in terms of regional responses. It considers how these have enhanced or have the potential to enable the AU to meet its responsibility under the Constitutive Act and other relevant instruments and, in doing so, to centralize the protection of civilians on the AU's agenda by identifying and responding to situations in which people are at risk of or subject to serious violations of IHRL and IHL. An examination of the various AU mechanisms indicates, unfortunately, that they have not been co-ordinated effectively towards addressing emerging issues in peace and security, including the protection of civilians. As already indicated, the only existing effective co-ordination among AU organs has been in the area of the African Governance Architecture, and perhaps only there because the African Charter on Democracy, Elections and Governance[26] prescribes such co-ordination.

A. African Union Peace and Security Council

The AU Peace and Security Council is the central pillar of the African Peace and Security Architecture, and is the standing decision-making organ for the prevention, management, and resolution of conflicts.[27] It is a collective security and early warning arrangement intended to facilitate timely and efficient response to conflict and crisis situations in Africa, and to promote peace, security, and stability, in order to guarantee the protection and preservation of life and property.

The Council is key to the work of the AU in ensuring peace and stability, and in particular the protection of civilians on the continent. In exercise of its mandate, the Council is entitled to request the assistance and support of other AU organs as well as the regional mechanisms, including, for example, requesting studies from the AU Commission on International Law or an expert or advisory opinion from the judicial organs of the Union. In December 2013, responding to reports of serious violations in South Sudan, the Council mandated the establishment of a commission of inquiry.[28] The Commission of Inquiry, chaired by former President Olesegun Obasanjo of Nigeria, observed the devastation of the armed conflict, confirmed that there were violations of IHRL and IHL, investigated mass graves,

[26] African Charter on Democracy, Elections and Governance, <http://www.au.int/en/sites/default/files/AFRICAN_CHARTER_ON_DEMOCRACY_ELECTIONS_AND_GOVERNANCE.pdf>.

[27] See Articles 2 and 7 of the PSC Protocol at <http://www.au.int/en/sites/default/files/Protocol_peace_and_security.pdf>.

[28] See AUPSC Comm CDXI (2013) AU Doc PSC/AHG/COMM.1(CDXI), para. 8, where the Peace and Security Council requested 'the Chairperson of the African Union Commission (AUC) in consultation with the Chairperson of the African Commission on Human and Peoples' Rights (ACHPR) and other relevant AU structures to urgently establish a Commission to investigate the human rights violations and other abuses committed during the armed conflict in South Sudan and make recommendations on the best ways and means to ensure accountability, reconciliation and healing among all South Sudanese communities'.

and noted that it had encountered many individuals who alleged having suffered or witnessed crimes, including sexual and gender-based violence.[29] In January 2015, the Commission submitted its report to the AU Peace and Security Council.[30] The report presented findings on human rights violations and other abuses committed during the armed conflict in South Sudan and made recommendations on ways and means to ensure accountability, reconciliation, and healing among South Sudanese communities, as requested in the relevant Assembly decision. It identified State and non-State actors considered to bear criminal accountability for the crimes that took place and which were considered to amount to international crimes.[31] The Peace and Security Council took note of the report and deferred its consideration to a future date[32]—a decision subsequently endorsed by the Assembly.[33] The Report of the Commission of Inquiry on South Sudan (AUCISS) was finally released on 27 October 2015 by the Chairperson of the African Union Commission following a decision by the Peace and Security Council (PSC) at its 547th meeting at Heads of State and government level. The AUCISS recommended the establishment of 'an Africa-led, Africa-owned, Africa-resourced legal mechanism under the aegis of the African Union supported by the international community, particularly the United Nations to bring those with the greatest responsibility at the highest level to account'.[34]

Since the Commission made the assessment of the impact of the conflict on civilians central to its work, it is hoped that the recommendations in the report will inform AU work elsewhere, and that the protection of civilians will be highlighted when the report is finally considered and acted upon.

B. Assembly of Heads of State and Government

The Assembly is the supreme organ of the AU, comprising representatives of all Member States. While the fifteen-member Peace and Security Council holds

[29] See Assembly of the African Union, 'Interim Report of the African Union Commission of Inquiry on South Sudan (CISS)' (2014) AU Doc Assembly/AU/19(XXIII).

[30] See <http://peaceau.org/en/article/communique-of-the-484th-meeting-of-the-psc-on-the-situation-in-south-sudan>.

[31] In May 2014, for example, the Commission of Inquiry stated that it was 'leaning towards the creation of a hybrid court along the lines of the Extraordinary African Chambers in Senegal (Hissène Habré Tribunal), to be established jointly by the AU UN, should evidence disclose commission of international crimes'. See <http://www.au.int/en/content/commission-inquiry-south-sudan-undertakes-consultations-nairobi>. In addition, the Chair, in his address to the UN Human Rights Council in September 2014, stated: 'There was no doubt that gross violations of human rights were being committed, and that no political leader in South Sudan could claim innocence.' See <http://www.ohchr.org/EN/NewsEvents/Pages/DisplayNews.aspx?NewsID=15098&LangID=E#sthash.llPhp0AE.dpuf>.

[32] Communiqué of the 484th Meeting of the PSC on the Situation in South Sudan; see <http://allafrica.com/stories/201501310485.html>

[33] Assembly/AU/Dec.559 (XXIV) Decision on the Report of the Peace and Security Council on its Activities and the State of Peace and Security in Africa (Doc. Assembly/AU/7(XXIV). For further reading see <http://summits.au.int/en/sites/default/files/Assembly%20AU%20Dec%20546%20-%20568%20(XXIV)%20_E.pdf>

[34] See more on the Press Release of the Chairperson at <http://www.peaceau.org/en/article/abc>, and the Report at <http://www.peaceau.org/en/article/abc#sthash.SIDBw7Sl.dpuf>, page 300, para. 1148.

primary responsibility for the promotion of peace, security, and stability in Africa, and for the deployment of peacekeeping and intervention forces,[35] importantly, the Assembly retains the power to direct the Council on the management of conflicts, war, acts of terrorism, and emergency situations and decide on intervention in a Member State.[36] In reality, the Council makes decisions in between sessions of the Assembly, which are acted upon immediately and subsequently reported to the Assembly for endorsement. Whenever the Assembly is in session, the Council, as the specialized organ of the AU, meets first and adopts decisions that are then reported to the Assembly. It is the Assembly that is mandated to make decisions relating to intervention under Article 4(h) of the Constitutive Act.

C. Pan-African Parliament

The Pan-African Parliament was established by Article 17 of the Constitutive Act, as one of the nine organs provided for in the Treaty Establishing the African Economic Community adopted in Abuja in 1991.[37] Its creation was informed by a vision to provide a common platform for African peoples and their grass-roots organizations to be more involved in discussions and decision-making on the problems and challenges facing the continent. It is intended to encourage good governance, human rights, democracy, transparency, and accountability in Member States and to promote peace, security, and stability.[38] The Parliament has, through its committees and in plenary, held debates on peace and security issues and undertaken missions to conflict areas such as Darfur, Somalia, and the Central African Republic.[39]

D. African Court on Human and Peoples' Rights

The African Court on Human and Peoples' Rights, as presently constituted, has jurisdiction over violations of the African Charter on Human and Peoples' Rights and other human rights instruments ratified by African States.[40] While in theory

[35] Protocol Relating to the Establishment of the Peace and Security Council of the African Union, see Article 6(a) and (d).

[36] Constitutive Act of the African Union, see n 8, Article 4(h) and (j), and Article 9(g).

[37] AU Constitutive Act, see n 8, Article 17; Treaty Establishing the African Economic Community (adopted 3 June 1991, entered into force 12 May 1994) 30 ILM 1241, Article 7(1)(c).

[38] The ultimate aim of the Pan-African Parliament is to evolve into an institution with full legislative powers, whose members are elected by universal adult suffrage. See Protocol to the Treaty Establishing the African Economic Community Relating to the Pan African Parliament (adopted 2 March 2001, adopted 14 December 2003) AU Doc CM/2198(LXXIII), Article 2(3).

[39] For example, the Pan-African Parliament (PAP) Committee on Cooperation, International Relations and Conflict Resolution has undertaken peace missions to conflict areas including Darfur, Sudan. The PAP has also held plenary debates on conflict situations on the continent including Darfur, Somalia, Central African Republic, and Mali. See AFP, 'Pan-African Team Heads to Darfur', *Aljazeera* (Doha, 30 September 2004) <www.aljazeera.com/archive/2004/09/20084101095775317.html>; Pan-African Parliament, 'Press Release, PAP Debates Peace and Security in Africa' (Johannesburg, 16 October 2012) <www.pan-africanparliament.org>.

[40] 'The African Court In Brief' (*African Court on Human and Peoples' Rights*, undated) <www.african-court.org/en/index.php/about-the-court/brief-history>.

the decisions of the Court are binding, the machinery for execution of its judgments and orders largely relies on the Executive Council of the AU[41] and the system has not yet been fully tested in a situation where a State has been unwilling to implement the Court's decision.[42] The only case in which the Court has addressed the protection of civilians relates to Libya, discussed in greater detail in section IV.

In the coming years, the Court is likely to be seized with matters falling under the provisions of the 2009 AU Convention for the Protection and Assistance of Internally Displaced Persons in Africa (Kampala Convention). These may include matters relating to interpretation and application of the Kampala Convention, which in the view of the authors is both a human rights convention as well as a humanitarian law instrument.[43] Presently, the reach of the Court is limited by the fact that only twenty-eight States have ratified the Protocol establishing the African Court on Human and Peoples' Rights and only seven have filed the necessary declaration under Article 34(6) of the Protocol accepting the jurisdiction of the Court to receive cases directly from individuals and non-governmental organizations. Thus, interpretation and implementation of the Kampala Convention is presently limited to cases concerning the twenty-eight States that have ratified the Protocol and to individuals and NGOs from the seven States that have filed the requisite declaration.

In 2008, the AU adopted a protocol agreeing to merge the African Court on Human and Peoples' Rights and the not-yet-existent African Court of Justice. In 2014, the Union agreed that the merged court, the African Court of Justice and Human Rights,[44] would have international criminal jurisdiction. However, the expanded Court will only come into existence once the statute has received fifteen ratifications, which may take a number of years given the average time it takes for an AU legal instrument to enter into force.[45] The crimes over which the Court

[41] The Executive Council is composed of Ministers of Foreign Affairs, as per Article 10 of the Constitutive Act, and it is mandated under Article 30 of the Protocol to ensure execution of the court's judgments. See Protocol to the African Charter of Human and Peoples' Rights on the Establishment of the African Court on Human and Peoples' Rights (adopted 10 June 1998, entered into force 24 January 2004) OAU Doc OAU/LEG/EXP/AFCHPR/PROT (III), Article 30; see also Ben Kioko, 'The African Union and implementation of Decisions of the African Court on Human and Peoples' Rights' (2005) 15 Interights Bulletin 7.

[42] At the time of writing, the Court has not been able to establish that its order in the matter of *African Commission vs. Libya*, App No 002/2013 (ACtHPR, 2013), directing access by Seif El Islam to family and a lawyer and or doctor of his choice, has been implemented. See Assembly of the African Union, 'Executive Council Decision on the 2013 Activity Report of the African Court on Human and Peoples' Rights' (2014) AU Doc EX.CL/Dec.806 (XXIV), para. 1.

[43] The Kampala Convention, as the only legally binding instrument for the prevention and protection of internal displacement and assistance to internally displaced persons, provides for the rights of internally displaced persons (IDPs) and the obligations of States to protect and assist them. See and compare Articles 6, 7, and 9, which are strongly influenced by international humanitarian law, with Articles 11–13, which have a strong influence from international human rights law, and with Articles 2–4, which explicitly reference both legal regimes. See Kampala Convention, see n 9, Article 2–4, 6, 7, 9, 11–13.

[44] Protocol on Amendments to the Protocol on the Statute of the African Court of Justice and Human Rights (signed 27 June 2014, not yet in force) <www.au.int/en/treaties>.

[45] African Union instruments take on average about five years to enter into force, particularly for those where the number of ratifications required is fifteen signatories from Member States. The major examples of treaties that came into force much earlier than that are the Constitutive Act of the African Union, see n 8, which came into force in about one year, and the Protocol to the African Charter on

would have jurisdiction include genocide; crimes against humanity; war crimes; unconstitutional change of government; piracy; terrorism; mercenarism; corruption; money laundering; trafficking in persons, drugs, and hazardous wastes; illicit exploitation of natural resources; and the crime of aggression. While the Prosecutor may decide to initiate investigations on any matter in exercise of his *proprio motu* powers in respect of the above crimes, a situation in which one or more of the crimes appears to have been committed may also be referred to the Prosecutor by a State party, the Assembly, or the Council.[46] The Draft Statute of the African Court of Justice and Human Rights also introduces corporate responsibility, which is new to international criminal tribunals around the world.[47] The proposed Court's development of jurisprudence regarding protecting IHRL and IHL, particularly in respect of crimes that have never been litigated before an international tribunal, will be of interest.

E. African Commission on Human and Peoples' Rights

The African Commission on Human and Peoples' Rights is mandated to promote and protect human rights and has the power to interpret its own mandate, allowing it considerable flexibility, including to undertake advocacy campaigns. The Commission is empowered by Article 61 of the African Charter on Human and Peoples' Rights to draw inspiration from outside sources,[48] which in effect allows it to apply IHL. It is also specifically allowed to bring cases to the African Court on Human and Peoples' Rights against State parties in relation to situations constituting mass atrocities.[49] The Commission has referred one case relating to the protection of civilians to the Court in exercise of this mandate.[50] It has among its mechanisms a Special Rapporteur on Refugees, Asylum Seekers, Migrants and Internally

Human and Peoples' Rights on the Rights of Women in Africa, see n 10, which took about two years to come into force. For both of them there were major advocacy and mobilizing forces that ensured early entry into force. See African Union, 'OAU/AU Treaties, Conventions, Protocols, and Charters', <www.au.int/en/treaties>. For a comprehensive assessment of the processes and patterns of ratification of OAU/AU instruments, see Tiyanjana Maluwa, 'Ratification of African Union Treaties by Member States: Law, Policy and Practice' (2009) 13 Melbourne J Intl L 1.

[46] Protocol on Amendments to the Protocol on the Statute of the African Court of Justice and Human Rights, see n 42, Article 46(F).

[47] Ibid., Article 46(C).

[48] Article 61 of the African Charter on Human and Peoples' Rights provides that 'The Commission shall also take into consideration, as subsidiary measures to determine the principles of law, other general or special international conventions, laying down rules expressly recognised by Member States of the Organization of African Unity, African practices consistent with international norms on Human and Peoples' Rights, customs generally accepted as law, general principles of law recognised by African States as well as legal precedents and doctrine.' African (Banjul) Charter on Human and Peoples' Rights (adopted 27 June 1981, entered into force 21 October 1986) 21 ILM 58, Article 61.

[49] Rule 118 (3) of the African Court on Human and Peoples' Rights, Rules of Court (adopted 2 June 2010, entered into force 2 June 2010) < http://www.african-court.org/en/images/documents/Court/Interim%20Rules%20of%20Court/Final_Rules_of_Court_for_Publication_after_Harmonization_-_Final__English_7_sept_1_.pdf >.

[50] See *African Commission on Human and Peoples' Rights v The Great Socialist Libyan Arab Jamahiriya* [2011] AHRLR 175 (AfCtHPR, 2011); but also see African Commission on Human and Peoples' Rights v The Republic of Kenya, App No 006/2012 (ACtHPR, 2012).

Displaced Persons, who has focused on protection of these categories of civilians affected by conflict on the continent.[51]

F. African Union Commission on International Law

The AU Commission on International Law is established as an independent advisory organ of the Union in accordance with Article 5(2) of the Constitutive Act. Its purposes include: (a) undertaking activities relating to codification and the progressive development of international law on the African continent; (b) conducting studies on legal matters of interest to the Union and its Member States; and (c) encouraging the teaching, study, publication, and dissemination of literature on international law with a view to promoting acceptance of and respect for the principles of international law, and the peaceful resolution of conflicts. The Commission on International Law has undertaken a number of research studies, including the preparation of a draft model national law for implementation of the Kampala Convention, which would be useful to Member States in the process of domesticating and implementing the Convention at the national level.[52]

G. African Committee of Experts on the Rights and Welfare of the Child

The African Committee of Experts on the Rights and Welfare of the Child is a treaty organ established under the 1989 African Charter on the Rights and Welfare of the Child, with a mandate to protect the rights of children.[53] Under the Charter, State parties undertake the following: (a) to respect and ensure respect for rules of international humanitarian law applicable in armed conflicts which affect the child; (b) to ensure that no child takes a direct part in hostilities; (c) to refrain from recruiting any child; and (d) to protect the civilian population in armed conflicts and ensure the protection and care of children who are affected by armed conflicts or in situations of internal armed conflicts, tension, and strife.[54] The Committee of Experts may undertake missions, comment on the reports of AU Member States, and access the African Commission on Human Rights. The African Court on Human and Peoples' Rights has recently decided that the Committee of Experts' access is limited to advisory opinions and does not include bringing substantive matters before

[51] See African Commission on Human and Peoples' Rights, 'Final Communiqué of the 54th Ordinary Session' (Banjul, 2013) paras 28(v), 32(iii) <www.achpr.org/files/sessions/54th/info/communique54/achpr54_fincom_2013_eng.pdf>; see also 'Special Rapporteur on Refugees, Asylum Seekers, Migrants and Internally Displaced Persons' (*African Commission on Human and Peoples' Rights*, undated) <www.achpr.org/mechanisms/refugees-and-internally-displaced-persons>.

[52] For further reading see AUCIL Yearbook 2013, 64–5, paragraphs 42–8, reference AUCIL/Legal/Rpt (V) for discussions on the Draft Model Law.

[53] African Charter on the Rights and Welfare of the Child, see n 10, Article 32.

[54] See Lydia Wambugu and Getachew Adem, *Rights of Children in Conflict: An Evaluation of Japanese Official Development Assistance in Acholiland Northern Uganda* (Pretoria: Institute for Security Studies, 2008) 16.

the Court.[55] However, the Court recommended that necessary action be taken by the competent organs of the AU to ensure that the Committee has unfettered access to the Court in order to ensure effective protection of the rights and welfare of children.

H. Economic, Social and Cultural Council

The Economic, Social and Cultural Council is a representative organ for civil society in the AU. Its mandate includes the following: (a) carrying out studies and submitting recommendations, as appropriate; (b) contributing to the promotion of human rights, the rule of law, good governance, democratic principles, gender equality, and child rights; and (c) fostering and consolidating partnerships between the Union and civil society organizations through effective public enlightenment, mobilization, and feedback on the activities of the Union.[56] However, the Economic, Social and Cultural Council has failed to be the mobilizing force that was intended.[57] Moreover, although it does have *locus standi* to request advisory opinions before the African Court on Human and Peoples' Rights, which can be utilized for the purposes of advocacy to enforce IHRL and IHL and to protect civilians, it has not yet exercised its rights under this framework.

IV. The Libyan Conflict: Political Developments and the Protection of Civilians

From the perspective of the protection of civilians, the Libyan intervention in 2011 presented an interesting case that raised many issues. Most prominently, it highlighted the all-embracing question of what the concept of the protection of civilians really means—whether there is a common understanding of its scope, and what may legitimately be done by interveners seeking to protect.

The crisis in Libya, an AU member, began on 15 February 2011 when the Libyan government armed forces violently suppressed peaceful protests by Libyan citizens demanding political reforms.[58] On 23 February 2011, the AU Peace and Security Council 'expressed deep concern with the situation in Libya, and strongly condemned the indiscriminate and excessive use of force and lethal weapons against peaceful protestors in violation of human rights and international humanitarian

[55] The protocol establishing the Court grants direct access to the African Commission but does not make reference to the African Committee of Experts on the Rights and Welfare of the Child. See Protocol to the African Charter of Human and Peoples' Rights on the Establishment of the African Court on Human and Peoples' Rights (2008), see n 39, Article 5.

[56] Constitutive Act of the African Union, see n 8, Article 22. See also the Statutes of Economic, Social, and Cultural Council (adopted by the Assembly of the African Union on 8 July 2004) AU Doc Assembly/AU/Dec.48(III) Rev.1 <pages.au.int/sites/default/files/ECOSOCC%20Statutes.pdf>.

[57] Mohammed Sameh Amr, 'The Economic, Social, and Cultural Council of the African Union', in Abdulqawi A Yusuf and Fatsah Ouguergouz (eds), *The African Union: Legal and Institutional Framework: A Manual on the Pan-African Organization* (Leiden, the Netherlands: Martinus Nijhoff Publishers, 2012) 182.

[58] David Cutler, 'Timeline: Libya's Uprising against Muammar Gaddafi', *Reuters* (London, 22 July 2011) <http://www.reuters.com/article/2011/08/22/us-libya-events-idUSTRE77K2QH20110822>.

law involving the loss of human life and the destruction of property'.[59] It also underscored that 'the aspirations of the people of Libya for democracy, political reform, justice, and socio-economic development are legitimate, while stressing the need to preserve the territorial integrity and unity of Libya'.[60] Shortly after, the Arab League Secretary-General issued a statement calling for the 'imposition of a no-fly zone on Libyan military aviation' and for the establishment of 'safe areas in places exposed to shelling' as precautionary measures that allowed the protection of the Libyan people and foreign nationals residing in the Libyan Arab Jamahiriya.[61]

In dealing with an urgent application filed by the African Commission on Human and Peoples' Rights,[62] the African Court on Human and Peoples' Rights decided that the situation in Libya was of 'extreme gravity and urgency posing a risk of irreparable harm'.[63] The Court unanimously ordered provisional measures, and called on Libya to immediately 'refrain from any action that would result in loss of life or violation of physical integrity of persons, which could be a breach of the provisions of the African Charter or of other international human rights instruments to which Libya is a party'.[64] Responding to the Court on 9 April 2011, the Libyan government denied the claims and expressed its willingness to subject itself to criminal investigations by the Court if deemed necessary.[65]

The United Nations (UN) Security Council adopted resolution 1970 on 26 February 2011, denouncing the 'gross and systematic violations of human rights, including the repression of peaceful demonstrators', noting that the attacks may have amounted to crimes against humanity and referring the situation to the Prosecutor of the International Criminal Court.[66] In March 2011, the UN Security Council adopted resolution 1973, authorizing Member States 'to take all necessary measures, to protect civilians and civilian populated areas under threat of attack in the Libyan Arab Jamahiriya, including Benghazi, while excluding a foreign occupation force of any form on any part of Libyan territory'.[67] It also imposed a 'no-fly

[59] AUPSC Comm CCLXI (2011) AU Doc PSC/PR/COMM (CCLXI), para. 17(a).

[60] See the AUPSC Comm CCLXI (2011) AU Doc PSC/PR/COMM (CCLXI), paras 17(a), 17(b), 17(d). The Peace and Security Council called on the Libyan authorities to ensure the protection and security of the citizens of Libya, as well as the delivery and provision of humanitarian assistance to the injured and other persons in need.

[61] On 21 February 2011, prior to the PSC statement, the Arab League Secretary-General, Amr Moussa, called for an end to violence in Libya, asserting that the demands of the Arab people for change were legitimate and that the Arab League had suspended Libya. See 'Arab League to Reject Intervention in Libya', *Reuters* (London, 2 March 2011) <http://af.reuters.com/article/libyaNews/idAFLDE7210EO20110302>. This position was supported by the Council of the League of Arab States Meeting at the Ministerial Level. See UNSC, 'Letter dated 14 March 2011 from the Permanent Observer of the League of Arab States to the United Nations addressed to the President of the Security Council' (2011) UN Doc S/2011/137, Annex.

[62] *African Commission on Human and Peoples' Rights v The Great Socialist Libyan Arab Jamahiriya* [2011] AHRLR 175 (AfCtHPR, 2011).

[63] Ibid., para. 22. [64] Ibid., para. 25(1).

[65] See Dan Juma, 'Provisional Measures under the African Human Rights System: The African Court's Order Against Libya' (2012) 30 Wisconsin J Intl L 344, 371.

[66] United Nations, 'Meetings Coverage: In Swift, Decisive Action, Security Council Imposes Tough Measures on Libyan Regime, Adopting Resolution 1970 in Wake of Crackdown on Protesters' (26 February 2011) UN Doc SC/10187/Rev.1.

[67] UNSC Res 1973 (2011) UN Doc S/RES/1973.

zone' in response to threats of attacks against the civilian population and the failure of the Libyan authorities to heed the demand under resolution 1970 to end violence against civilians, and out of concern that the Libyan authorities had used threatening statements designed to incite massacre of the people of Benghazi.[68]

In implementation of resolution 1973, the North Atlantic Treaty Organization (NATO) intervened militarily, relying on air power rather than deploying ground troops. It targeted government installations, such as air defences and troop concentrations, and carried out airstrikes that supported the opposition militias.[69] At the time that resolution 1973 was adopted and the bombing immediately commenced, the AU High-Level Ad Hoc Committee on Libya, meeting at the level of Heads of State and Government, was concluding its meeting in Nouakchott, Mauritania, and was scheduled to travel to Tripoli and Benghazi to meet the parties to the conflict and deliver the AU's five-point mediation plan.[70] However, the Committee was forced to cancel the trip when the UN Secretariat indicated that no exemption to the no-fly ban had been secured, even though the authorizing resolution had also encouraged the AU Committee to promote dialogue between the parties.[71] At the time that the bombing of Libya's air defences started, Libya had already announced a ceasefire. One cannot know for certain whether Libya would have observed its own ceasefire or not, but what is known is that no attempt was made to test this.

There is no consensus on the number of casualties arising from the NATO operations in Libya; however, it has been argued by the AU, among others, that the case for intervention was weak, that threats to civilians were exaggerated and manipulated in order to ensure adoption of UN Security Council resolution 1973, and that the intervention resulted in the loss of more lives than it saved and undermined the possibility of a peaceful resolution through dialogue.[72] While one might accept that civilians must be protected at all costs, it is difficult to believe that the UN Security Council, in authorizing 'all necessary measures', intended to exclude diplomatic and political means for resolving the conflict. Nor could it have logically intended that military advisers and lethal and non-lethal weapons could be supplied to one

[68] 'Gaddafi Tells Benghazi His Army Is Coming Tonight', *Reuters* (London, 17 March 2011) <uk.reuters.com/article/2011/03/17/libya-gaddafi-address-idUKLDE72G2E920110317>; see also David Kirkpatrick and K Fahim, 'Qaddafi Warns of Assault on Benghazi as U.N. Vote Nears', *New York Times* (New York, 17 March 2011) <www.nytimes.com/2011/03/18/world/africa/18libya.html?pagewanted=all>.

[69] See Etienne Durand, 'The French Perspective', in Torgeir E. Sæveraas and Vidar Løw Owesen (eds), *Norsk luftmakt over Libya—suksess uten innflytelse?* (Trondheim, Norway: Akademika forlag, 2012) 80; Amnesty International, 'Libya: The Forgotten Victims of NATO Strikes' (London: Amnesty International, 2012) 5–6; see also Tineke Strik, 'Lives Lost in the Mediterranean Sea: Who is Responsible?' (Strasbourg, France: Council of Europe, 2012) paras 14, 125–9, 133–6. <assembly.coe.int/CommitteeDocs/2012/20120329_mig_RPT.EN.pdf>.

[70] See Anyway Sithole, 'The African Union Peace and Security Mechanism's Crawl from Design to Reality: Was the Libyan Crisis a Depiction of Severe Limitations?' (2011) 12 African J Conflict Resolution 111, 116–18; see also African Union, 'Statement of the Chairperson of the African Union Commission, Dr Jean Ping, at the Meeting of the International Contact Group on Libya' (Rome, 5 May 2011) www.au.int/en/sites/default/files/Final%20version.%20AU%20speech.%20Rome.%2005.05.2011%5D.pdf.

[71] Ibid.

[72] See Jean Ping, *Eclipse Sur l'Afrique: Fallait-il tuer Kadhafi?* (Paris: Michelon Editions, 2014).

side of the armed conflict or that the oil wealth of that country could be used to benefit some parts of the population and not others.

The AU, and others, expressed concern about the measures taken and the methods used by NATO to achieve the ends of resolutions 1970 and 1973. The AU Commission on International Law questioned whether the intervention complied with international law in a variety of ways, including the degree of force used, the provision of military and political support to one side, and whether it respected Libya's sovereignty as required by the resolutions.[73] Further concerns with the implementation of resolution 1973 were raised by a cross-section of African society as demonstrated in an open letter entitled 'Libya, Africa and the new world order', signed by over 200 'ordinary citizens' of Africa, including former President of South Africa Thabo Mbeki, academics, and members of civil society.[74] In addition, South Africa, at the time a member of the Security Council that voted in favour of resolution 1973, later became one of the harshest critics of the operations undertaken under the auspices thereof.[75] The immediate former Chairperson of the AU Commission, Jean Ping, has argued that 'the intervention of the great powers led to the destabilisation of the Sahel region, the looting of the vast arms depots of the "Guide of the Revolution", an explosion in all kinds of trafficking and the spread of the Jihadi peril from the Mediterranean to the Horn of Africa'.[76]

In the view of the authors, UN Security Council resolutions 1970 and 1973 did not authorize the litany of actions that were undertaken in Libya in the name of protecting civilians. In undertaking protection missions, account should always be taken of the likely consequences and possible adverse impacts that might result, such as those that have been witnessed in Libya, and indeed the region, since the intervention. The bombing of civilian infrastructure in Libya and arming and resourcing one party to a conflict went beyond the overall objectives of the protective mission. In addition, the military actions taken should not have eclipsed the political and diplomatic initiatives, as this was the only way in which sustainable peace and stability could have been achieved. As it was, a number of political

[73] African Union Commission on International Law, 'Report of the AU Commission on International Law (AUCIL) on Certain Aspects of the Situation in Libya: Scope, Legal Implications and Obligations of Member States of the United Nations, including African Union States, Arising from United Nations Security Council resolutions 1970 and 1973' (12 May 2011) 2nd Extraordinary Session (on file with author).

[74] See 'Libya, Africa and the New World Order: An Open Letter—To the People of Africa and the World from Concerned Africans', in Horace Campbell, *Global NATO and the Catastrophic Failure in Libya: Lessons for Africa in the Forging of African Unity* (New York: Monthly Review Press, 2013), Annex 1.

[75] See 'Zuma Lashes Nato for "Abusing" UN Resolutions on Libya', *Mail and Guardian* (Johannesburg, South Africa, 14 June 2011) <mg.co.za/article/2011-06-14-zuma-lashes-nato-for-abusing-un-resolutions-on-libya>; Nick Meo, 'Libya: Jacob Zuma Accuses Nato of Not Sticking to UN Resolution', *The Telegraph* (London, 14 June 2011) <http://www.telegraph.co.uk/news/worldnews/africaandindianocean/libya/8575984/Libya-Jacob-Zuma-accuses-Nato-of-not-sticking-to-UN-resolution.html>; 'Jacob Zuma Criticizes Military Action in Libya', *BBC News* (London, 18 July 2011) <www.bbc.com/news/uk-politics-14180863>.

[76] Marc Miramon, 'Jean Ping: "Western Countries Didn't Let the African Union Play a Role": Marc de Miramon interviews Jean Ping, former chair of the African Union's Commission' *L'Humanité* (Paris, 14 June 2014) www.humaniteinenglish.com/spip.php?article2486.

initiatives supported by some key Libyan political actors had to be called off due to the bombings in that country.[77]

The perception of the military intervention in Libya could have been different, and perhaps positive, if it had brought about expansion of the democratic space, and peace and stability in the country. However, this was not the case and now Libya has degenerated into chaos. Additionally, neighbouring countries in the Sahel region have been adversely impacted by the trafficking of arms in the region, originating from huge stockpiles of weapons that Gaddafi had established.[78] While many African States had previously strongly supported efforts aimed at intervention to protect civilians, even the continent's strongest supporters have had their belief in the internationalization of intervention shaken by the manner in which the resolutions to intervene in Libya were implemented.[79]

It is still too early to know the full impact that the intervention in Libya may have on future efforts aimed at protecting civilians, but what seems evident is that African States may be cautious of external intervention in an African country in the future.[80] Nevertheless, when the situations in Mali and the Central African Republic escalated, African countries accepted the respective French interventions in order to stop the Islamists from advancing further in Mali and to halt the killings of civilians in the Central African Republic. The AU has always avoided taking a position on situations outside of the continent, although African Member States of the UN may of course take national positions on global issues, such as Russia's annexation of Crimea. Yet the chaos resulting from the Libya intervention, which has spilled over into the Sahel, may make it extremely difficult to build consensus on future missions aimed at protecting civilians in Africa. It has also brought to light the need for consensus on general principles governing how future protection missions should be carried out.

V. Conclusion

The AU is unique among international organizations in recognizing and supporting a right to intervention to stop mass violations of IHRL and IHL. This is a noble part of the AU's history, one that has been informed by many tragedies across the continent. Yet situations such as the 2011 intervention in Libya have placed this idea under threat. Preserving the possibility of international action for the protection of civilians may thus require a deeper reflection on the actions that may be taken to protect them.

[77] Ibid.

[78] UNSC, 'Report of the Assessment Mission on the Impact of the Libya Crisis on the Sahel Region, 7 to 23 December 2011' (2012) UN Doc S/2012/42, paras 4, 15–17, 32–62.

[79] For example, South Africa, a proponent of intervention in many African conflicts, initially voted for the UN Resolution that authorized the Libyan no-fly zone but heavily criticized the implementation of the resolution. See 'Zuma Lashes Nato for "Abusing" UN Resolutions on Libya', n 69; 'Libya: Jacob Zuma Accuses Nato of Not Sticking to UN Resolution', n 69; Jacob Zuma Criticizes Military Action in Libya', n 74.

[80] See Miramon, n 76.

A good starting point would be an inquiry, undertaken by the UN, the AU, or an independent commission, into whether the actions taken by States pursuant to UN Security Council resolutions 1970 and 1973, which authorized the protection of civilians and enforcement of sanctions regimes in Libya, were implemented in accordance with the UN Charter and international law, in particular IHRL and IHL. In this context, it would be useful if definitions of 'all necessary measures' and 'civilian populated areas under threat of attack' were produced. Such an initiative would go some way to reassuring African States that their concerns regarding how the Libyan intervention was carried out would be addressed at the level of the UN Security Council in building consensus for mandating future missions aimed at protecting civilians. At the level of the AU, while the Libyan case may not greatly impact the implementation of Article 4(h) of the Constitutive Act, it ought to inspire the development of guidelines and practices that could be replicated elsewhere.

International or regional intervention for the protection of civilians would be more likely to be embraced by African States if the duties and responsibilities of intervening States were more clearly articulated. Representatives of Brazil have raised this idea in the UN under the rubric of 'Responsibility while Protecting' (completing the 'Responsibility to Protect'),[81] but the AU could develop doctrine of its own. Indeed, because the AU has, in many respects, better defined standards with regard to intervention, it is in a good position to address some of the complex issues involved. While examining the impact of the intervention in Libya is important, the AU would need to move beyond criticism and reservations to develop constructive and concrete proposals on the safeguards to govern future missions for consideration within the framework of the UN. In doing so, such proposals could preserve what might be an important tool in the future.

Perhaps the most effective measure for ensuring civilian protection on the continent would be for the AU to operationalize its unique normative framework for intervention so that it becomes a living instrument for protecting civilians and arresting violations of IHRL, IHL, and refugee law in Africa. Drawing from the successes and challenges in Somalia, where a variety of non-military activities have been shown to be as important as the military operations, the AU's non-military civilian protection efforts also need to be strengthened through additional financial and human resources. Such a process would allow the AU the opportunity to learn from the successes and challenges faced by the UN, which has had more experience dealing with protection of civilians in multidimensional peace operations. It would also allow for a review and improvement of co-ordination among the various AU organs, including to ensure that the protection of civilians is given requisite attention. Turning AU policy into regional practice could have very real benefits for the safety of civilians in Africa.

[81] See UN General Assembly and UNSC, 'Letter Dated 9 November 2011 from the Permanent Representative of Brazil to the United Nations Addressed to the Secretary-General' (2011) UN Doc A/66/551–S/2011/701.

13

Security Council Diplomacy on the Protection of Civilians

A Convoluted History

Bruno Stagno Ugarte

'*. . . never send to know for whom the bell tolls; it tolls for thee.*'

John Donne, Meditation XVII,
Devotions upon Emergent Occasions (1624)

I. Introduction

While low clouds loomed over the United Nations (UN) Headquarters during the grey morning of 22 May 2014, China and Russia cast their fourth joint veto of a Security Council draft resolution addressing the dire situation in Syria. Unlike the previous three vetoes, however, the draft killed that morning was about prosecution of crimes committed against civilians. It was a balanced text, referring both sides of the conflict to the International Criminal Court for prosecution. Yet the inability of the Security Council to abide by its previous pronouncements and commitments regarding the protection of civilians in Syria[1] and beyond[2] was a tragic reminder that, notwithstanding heightened and more sustained attention to civilian casualties, political considerations continued to trump moral or legal obligations. The protection of civilians in situations being dealt with by the Council is still subject to case-by-case consideration, and thereby a political perspective, not a moral or legal imperative. Although a great deal has changed for the better since the dismal failures of the Council in Rwanda in 1994 and Srebrenica in 1995, not to mention others, in the end, the politics within the Council frequently derail the best intentions, preparations, and obligations to reduce harm to civilians.

[1] United Nations Security Council (UNSC) Resolution (Res) 2139 (2014) UN Doc S/RES/2139; UNSC Res 2165 (2014) UN Doc S/RES/2165.

[2] In addition to country-specific resolutions, the Security Council has adopted the following thematic resolutions on the protection of civilians, including the protection of children. See UNSC Res 1265 (1999) UN Doc S/RES/1265; UNSC Res 1296 (2000) UN Doc S/RES/1296; UNSC Res 1674 (2006) UN Doc S/RES/1674; UNSC Res 1738 (2006) UN Doc S/RES/1738; UNSC Res 1894 (2009) UN Doc S/RES/1894; UNSC Res 2068 (2012) UN Doc S/RES/2068; UNSC Res 2106 (2013) UN Doc S/RES/2106; UNSC Res 2122 (2013) UN Doc S/RES/2122.

Less than a week later, on 27 May 2014, the Security Council adopted Resolution 2155 on South Sudan, which, although seemingly a positive contribution to the protection of civilians overall, contained a dangerous precedent that undercuts the more robust protection of civilians mandate given to the UN Mission in South Sudan (UNMISS): 'to deter violence against civilians [. . .] in areas at high risk of conflict including, as appropriate, schools, places of worship, hospitals, and the oil installations.'[3] In adding oil installations to the list, the Council was placing a strategic economic asset on par with a select subset of civilian facilities. As Council members were perfectly aware that the 8,975 total uniformed personnel then deployed to South Sudan were incapable of providing adequate protection to civilians, adding oil installations was a conscious yet dangerous distraction of already scarce mission capacities and resources. This operational decision, based on political imperatives to please one permanent member (China), speaks to another source of concern: the belittling of the imminent threat to civilians.

This chapter will summarily track the practice of the Security Council, and some of its members, in addressing the protection of civilians. Since the first consideration of the issue, to the inception of the protection of civilians agenda, to highlights in the enforcement (successful and unsuccessful) or abandonment of previously stated commitments, the chapter will present the 'inside story' of protection of civilians diplomacy within the Council. As the Council is not a world unto itself, but needs other Member States (including host States and troop-contributing countries), the UN Secretariat, and regional and sub-regional organizations to implement its decisions, the chapter will also briefly examine Council interaction with these and other stakeholders. It will go on to draw conclusions about the benefits and limitations of Council engagement on protection issues given its composition and function as prescribed by the UN Charter as well as its working methods, highlighting the fundamental importance of political will and the role of non-permanent Council members.

II. An Abbreviated History: From Rwanda (1994) to Syria (2014)

Since 1951, when it reaffirmed the authority of the UN Mixed Armistice Commission to make 'all necessary arrangements for the restoration and protection of civilian life' as per the terms of the 1949 General Armistice Agreement between Israel and Syria,[4] the Security Council has developed a remarkable array of tools to protect civilians. From merely highlighting breaches of international humanitarian law or international human rights law or calling on perpetrators to cease such breaches to actually threatening or authorizing counter-measures, including deploying a visiting mission or a commission of investigation, establishing or else referring the violations to a criminal court, imposing sanctions, mandating a peacekeeping

[3] UNSC Res 2155 (2014) UN Doc S/RES/2155, para. 4(a)(ii).

[4] See UNSC Res 93 (1951) UN Doc S/RES/93 (adopted 10–0–1 with the Soviet Union abstaining).

operation, and authorizing humanitarian assistance or military intervention, the Council does not suffer from a lack of tools.

Despite a convoluted history with the protection of civilians, the Security Council has made protection a core mandate of the maintenance of international peace and security.[5] Concern for the protection of civilians, however, came only after a series of humiliating and humbling failures by the Council, including most prominently the 1992–5 ethnic cleansing in Bosnia and Herzegovina[6] and the 1994 genocide in Rwanda.[7] Unlike previous situations blemished with mass atrocities, including Biafra (1967–70), Bangladesh (1971), Burundi (1972), Kampuchea (1975–9), or Ethiopia (1977–8), the Council was already seized of and had peacekeeping forces deployed in both Bosnia and Herzegovina and Rwanda when the mass killings began. Unlike the previous situations, where the 'pretence that they were not impacting international peace and security was an exercise in sophistry'[8] to justify the unassailability of national sovereignty, the Council had already crossed that rubicon in regards to Bosnia and Herzegovina and Rwanda. Nonetheless, the Council failed to protect civilians due to tragic political, moral, and operational miscalculations as well as financial considerations, all of which are arguably best exemplified by Rwanda due to the exponentially higher death toll.

As confirmed by the recently and selectively declassified and carefully redacted documents released by some Security Council members regarding the situation in Rwanda, politically, the Council was 'in the "unenviable position" of not wanting to make statements on the one hand which it could not follow up on, or of hand wringing concern without action on the other'.[9] According to these documents, although no Council member was guiltless, it would seem that the United States was widely seen as the party most responsible for delaying Council action.[10] Two weeks before the genocide, the United States had fully withdrawn from Somalia after losing its resolve in the aftermath of the 3–4 October 1993 Battle of Mogadishu, negatively impacting its political, financial, and operational support for

[5] For a more detailed history of Council action on protection of civilians see Rosa Brooks, 'Civilians and Armed Conflict', in Jared A Genser and Bruno Stagno-Ugarte (eds), *The United Nations Security Council in the Age of Human Rights* (Cambridge: Cambridge University Press, 2014) 35–67.

[6] See UNSC, 'Final report of the Commission of Experts Established Pursuant to Security Council Resolution 780 (1992)' (1994) UN Doc S/1994/674.

[7] See UNSC, 'Report of the Independent Inquiry into the Actions of the United Nations during the 1994 Genocide in Rwanda' (1999) UN Doc S/1999/1257.

[8] Bruno Stagno-Ugarte and Jared A. Genser, 'Evolution of the Security Council's Engagement on Human Rights', in Genser and Stagno-Ugarte, see n 5, 27.

[9] Permanent Mission of New Zealand to the UN, Declassified cable CO4362/NYK (25 April 1994) 3, in National Security Archive, *Inside the UN Security Council: April–July 1994* (Washington, DC: National Security Archive, George Washington University).

[10] At the 17 June informal consultations, United States Deputy Ambassador Karl F. Inderfurth stated that 'delay, which you all criticized the US for, is now the responsibility of others'. Permanent Mission of New Zealand to the UN, Declassified cable CO4641/NYK (17 June 1994) 4, in National Security Archive, see n 9. Also see Permanent Mission of New Zealand to the UN, Declassified cable CO4656/NYK (22 June 1994) 3, in National Security Archive, see n 9: 'Probably the best case for the intervention was made by the United States, though Mrs [Madeleine K] Albright's words comment [sic] that the nature of the humanitarian crisis demanded a swift response from the international community came oddly from the representative of the country most responsible for the delay in Council action in Rwanda.'

humanitarian operations and UN peacekeeping operations in Africa, if not more generally.[11] That mindset explains why the United States thought it was worth'taking the lead in the Security Council to authorize the evacuation of the bulk of UNAMIR [UN Assistance Mission for Rwanda], while leaving behind a skeletal staff'.[12] In addition, the parties in Rwanda, both the government—a sitting Council member at the time—and the opposition Rwandan Patriotic Front, were quick to appreciate that 'Council members were generally beguiled by the outcome'[13] of the Arusha Peace Agreement of 4 August 1993. Both were adept at playing with the ignorance and indifference of the Council in regard to Rwanda to their respective benefit, with the government having the added benefit of full access to Council proceedings. Tellingly, however, the extent to which its presence could be a source of obstruction only came to the fore as of 29 April, when there was a first reference to its 'becoming a problem'.[14]

Beyond Rwanda and the United States, the Department of Peacekeeping Operations of the UN Secretariat, under the responsibility of then Under-Secretary-General Kofi Annan, also played an infamous role. It not only adhered to a restrictive interpretation of the UNAMIR mandate, disallowing it to conduct an offensive operation to seize an arms cache that may have confirmed warnings of the genocidal plans, but also suppressed from Council members key insights into the coming genocide given to UNAMIR by an anonymous informant.[15]

In the absence of a united political front and a concerted effort to support the additional troops and assets requested by the UNAMIR Force Commander, Lt. Gen. Roméo Dallaire, the Council went from considering a reduction of UNAMIR to 'a paper operation authorized by resolution, but with no presence on the ground',[16] to downsizing it from 2,558 to 270 personnel two weeks into the genocide,[17] to having 'two operations with different command structures and authorities operating in parallel'[18] following its authorization for France to deploy *Opération Turquoise.*[19] Financially, the cost of having a larger UN presence in Rwanda[20] was avoided by deferring to France despite serious apprehensions by

[11] As the genocide began, the White House was putting the finishing touches to a 'new peacekeeping policy'. See Office of the White House Press Secretary, 'Statement of the Press Secretary:President Clinton Signs New Peacekeeping Policy' (Washington, DC, 5 May 1994) <fas.org/irp/offdocs/pdd25.htm>.

[12] Permanent Mission of the United States to the UN, Declassified cable 01503 (12 April 1994) 2, in National Security Archive, see n 9. 'UNAMIR' refers to the United Nations Assistance Mission in Rwanda.

[13] Colin Keating, 'Rwanda: An Insider's Account', in David M Malone (ed.), *The UN Security Council: From the Cold War to the 21st Century* (Boulder, USA: Lynne Rienner, 2004) 501.

[14] Permanent Mission of the United Kingdom to the UN, Declassified cable 1559 (30 April 1994) 2, in National Security Archive, see n 9.

[15] Roméo A. Dallaire and Krystal Carrier, 'Rwanda', in Genser and Stagno-Ugarte, see n 5, 281–2.

[16] Permanent Mission of the United Kingdom to the UN, Declassified cable 1306 (13 April 1994) 4, in National Security Archive, see n 9.

[17] UNSC Res 912 (1994) UN Doc S/RES/912, para. 8.

[18] New Zealand Declassified cable CO4656/NYK, see n 10.

[19] UNSC Res 929 (1994) UN Doc S/RES/929, paras 2–3.

[20] Embassy of New Zealand in Washington, DC, Declassified cable CO2734/WSH (4 April 1994) 2, in National Security Archives, see n 9: ' . . . financial considerations also play a part [in] the US position'.

many as to the purported humanitarian purpose of *Opération Turquoise*.[21] Morally, while most members sought to maintain a façade of concern regarding the unfolding events, many were transacting for other interests: France to save the remains of the Habyarimana regime in Rwanda, Russia for Georgia,[22] and the United States and the United Kingdom mainly concerned for, and interested in, Bosnia and Herzegovina. As poignantly noted by an unprecedented multinational review effort conducted in 1996, the genocide 'occurred in a period when the United Nations was acting in an expansive yet highly selective fashion, reflecting a structural mismatch between the responsibilities of international institutions and interests of states'.[23] Tellingly, however, not one of these other interests could redeem the Council, with *Opération Turquoise* being faulted by many as too close to the *génocidaires*, the Srebrenica massacre yet to happen despite undivided attention being paid to Bosnia and Herzegovina by the United Kingdom and the United States in particular, and Russia gaining an important foothold in Georgia.

The remaining Council members either failed to make a principled stance or only did so in half-measures, unanimously voting for the downsizing of UNAMIR and, in the case of some, abstaining with regards to *Opération Turquoise*. Nigeria is an interesting case, as it was the first to mention the possibility of declaring a 'safe area', at least around Kigali airport, where 'UNAMIR could concentrate its forces'.[24] Less than two weeks into the genocide, some Council members were already aware that comparisons between the scant attention being paid to Rwanda in contrast to the 'activism and absorption' with the situation in Bosnia and Herzegovina—where safe havens would be later established—would be 'very difficult [. . .] for the Africans'.[25] Yet, notwithstanding the contrasts, and its strong reservations regarding both Resolutions 912 and 929,[26] Nigeria largely failed in providing an adequate narrative to cast the indifference of the Council in a negative

[21] New Zealand Declassified cable CO4641/NYK, see n 10, 3, 5: '[US] concerned about the possible "perception" that [France] will be entering Rwanda in order to assist the "government"' and 'Others have recalled to us the closeness of links between France and the late Habirimana regime'. Also includes a reference to China poignantly questioning France on its relationship with the government during the 21 June 1994 meeting between the five permanent members. Gérard Prunier, 'Operation Turquoise: A Humanitarian Escape', in Howard Adelman and Astri Suhrke (eds), *The Path of a Genocide* (New Brunswick, USA: Transaction, 1999).

[22] New Zealand Declassified cable CO4641/NYK, see n 10, 3: 'For the Russians it is possible that they may see a linkage between the French request for Council approval of their proposal and the Russian proposal for Georgia, making it difficult for them to oppose.'

[23] John R Eriksson, Tor Sellstro¨m, Howard Adelman, Astri Suhrke, Bruce Jones, John Borton, Krishna Kumar, and the Joint Evaluation of Emergency Assistance to Rwanda, *The International Response to Conflict and Genocide: Lessons from the Rwanda Experience* (Copenhagen: Steering Committee of the Joint Evaluation of Emergency Assistance to Rwanda, 1996) 22.

[24] United Kingdom cable 1306, see n 16, 3. Later on Argentina and Spain likewise considered safe areas. See Permanent Mission of the United Kingdom to the UN, Declassified cable 1481 (26 April 1994) 3, in Nations Security Archives, see n 9.

[25] Permanent Mission of New Zealand to the UN, Declassified cable CO4348 (20 April 1994) 1, in Nations Security Archives, see n 9. When the Council adopted resolution 912 on 21 April, 1994, it practically did so as 'an intermission in the lengthy debate on Bosnia that had been taking place throughout the day'. See Ibrahim Gambari, 'Rwanda: An African Perspective', in Malone, see n 13, 516.

[26] Gambari, see n 25, 516, 518.

light. This may have been a result of the self-described 'cooperative' approach taken by Nigeria 'to try to decongest' the Council of issues in Africa.[27] Probably the most far-sighted at the time was Spain, which cautioned that it 'was quite easy to wind an operation down but not so easy to expand it again'[28] and early on raised the idea of a commission of inquiry and the establishment of an ad hoc international criminal tribunal.[29] Both were to become realities, albeit belatedly, thereby depriving these measures of any deterrent effect while the genocide was ongoing. New Zealand, which had the dubious honour of presiding over the Council in April 1994, was moved by the right intentions but ultimately privately conceded 'that it was becoming increasingly difficult to explain credibly why in the face of the most horrific killings the Council could remain formally silent'.[30] To their credit, the Czech Republic and Spain, supported by New Zealand, were the most keen to characterize the situation in Rwanda as genocide and to place primary responsibility on the government in Rwanda, yet were resisted by the 'non-aligned' members (Oman, Pakistan, and Rwanda) and China,[31] as well as the United Kingdom and the United States.[32] Interestingly, neither the declassified record nor the accounts by insiders provide any truly redeeming insights into Argentina or Brazil.[33]

Following Rwanda and Srebrenica, the Security Council drastically curtailed its peacekeeping presence, reducing the number of peacekeepers on the ground worldwide from 69,961 in 1993 to only 14,879 in 1997, thereby compounding its failure to protect civilians. Arguably the one redeeming element of Council activity on Bosnia and Herzegovina was the establishment of the International Criminal Tribunal for the former Yugoslavia (ICTY),[34] which in fact pre-dated the worst violence (Srebrenica), yet ultimately did not deter the ethnic cleansing from continuing. In the case of Rwanda, the International Criminal Tribunal on Rwanda (ICTR)[35] was not about prevention or protection, but about accountability, as the genocide was over by the time the ICTR was established. Both are interesting creations based on an expansive interpretation of the powers granted to the Council in Article 29 of the UN Charter, allowing for the establishment of ad hoc tribunals as subsidiary bodies of the Council whose statutes were granted primacy over the national jurisdiction and legislation of the concerned States. Yet it is disheartening to see that the Council was willing to go to these lengths to prosecute the alleged perpetrators of mass atrocities, but unwilling to be as creative or normative in protecting civilians upon the first signs of violence.

Without it being destined to be a threshold year, 1999 proved to be a game-changer of sorts. To start with, the decision by the North Atlantic Treaty

[27] Ibid., 513. [28] New Zealand Declassified cable CO4348, see n 25, 4.

[29] New Zealand Declassified cable CO4362/NYK, see n 9, 3.

[30] New Zealand Declassified cable CO4348/NYK, see n 25, 2.

[31] United Kingdom Declassified cable 1559, see n 14, 1.

[32] Keating, see n 13, 508, and Gambari, see n 25, 519.

[33] 'I knew I could only really rely on four colleagues in the Council, the ambassadors of the Czech Republic, Spain, Nigeria and Djibouti. They indicated that they would support a strategy to preserve the UN presence in Rwanda to provide protection to civilians.' Keating, see n 13, 507.

[34] See UNSC Res 827 (1993) UN Doc S/RES/827.

[35] See UNSC Res 955 (1994) UN Doc S/RES/955.

Organization (NATO) to initiate *Operation Allied Force* against the Federal Republic of Yugoslavia in the war over Kosovo, without authorization from the Security Council, 'highlighted a triple policy dilemma—that is, a threefold protection gap—of complicity, paralysis or illegality'.[36] In addition, 1999 also saw the publication of two damning UN reports on the paralysis of the Council in addressing the situations in Rwanda and Srebrenica.[37] Although Resolution 1261 (1998)[38] on the protection of children in armed conflict had already provided a point of inflection, it was Resolution 1265 (1999)[39] on the protection of civilians in armed conflict and Resolution 1270 (1999),[40] which mandated the UN Mission in Sierra Leone (UNAMSIL) to 'take the necessary action ... within its capabilities and areas of deployment, to afford protection to civilians under imminent threat of physical violence', that brought protection of civilians to the fore. In rather quick succession, non-permanent members led the charge: Portugal, a non-permanent member elected for the 1997–8 term, convened the first debate/briefing on children; Canada, elected for the 1999–2000 term, first introduced a presidential statement[41] and then drafted Resolution 1265 on the protection of civilians in armed conflict; and Bangladesh, elected for the 2000–1 term, introduced the next thematic subset in the protection of civilians series—women, peace, and security. Continuing the trend, Norway, elected for the 2001–2 term, led on the development of an *aide mémoire* on protection of civilians as a practical tool to assist the Council in analysing and diagnosing protection issues.[42] Interestingly, although the permanent members acquiesced to, and at times supported, the addition of these thematic issues to the agenda of the Council, none were in the lead.[43]

While the Security Council had used a wide array of terms to characterize the deliberate targeting of civilians, Resolutions 1265 and 1270 allowed the protection of civilians to become a term of standard usage. However, its very ambiguity has allowed Council members and others to remain relatively comfortable with its usage. Adding to the ambiguity—and the comfort of those that are dead set against further fine-tuning of the concept—are the many different approaches and usages that different departments within the UN have made of the term, notwithstanding useful guidance issued by the Departments of Peacekeeping Operations and Field

[36] Ramesh Thakur, 'Foreword', in Angus Francis, Vesselin Popovski, and Charles Sampford (eds), *Norms of Protection: Responsibility to Protect, Protection of Civilians and their Interaction* (New York: United Nations University Press, 2012) xii.

[37] UNSC, 'Report of the Independent Inquiry into the Actions of the United Nations during the 1994 Genocide in Rwanda' (1999) UN Doc S/1999/1257; UN General Assembly (UNGA), 'Report of the Secretary-General pursuant to General Assembly Resolution 53/35: The Fall of Srebrenica' (1999) UN Doc A/54/549.

[38] UNSC Res 1261 (1999) UN Doc S/RES/1261.

[39] UNSC Res 1265 (1999) UN Doc S/RES/1265.

[40] UNSC Res 1270 (1999) UN Doc S/RES/1270.

[41] UNSC Statement of the President (1999) UN Doc S/PRST/1999/6.

[42] UNSC Statement of the President (2002) UN Doc S/PRST/2002/6.

[43] France later actively chaired the Working Group on Children and Armed Conflict established by Resolution 1612 (2005), and the United Kingdom has chaired the Informal Working Group on Protection of Civilians in Armed Conflict established by Resolution 1265 (1999).

Support.[44] Yet even such efforts, including the operational concept on the protection of civilians for UN peacekeeping missions, fall short of a definition. The emergence of, and at times conflation with, the concept of the Responsibility to Protect has further muddled a common understanding, with Resolution 1970 on Libya being a prime example.[45]

Since 1999, the Security Council has made protection of civilians a core mandate of no less than sixteen peacekeeping operations.[46] Yet the embryonic language used in Resolution 1270 remains the template for all UN missions with mandates for the protection of civilians,[47] notwithstanding the changes that have intervened in the nature of conflict since. Without a doubt, conflicts are having an increasing toll on civilian populations, with crimes and abuses being committed by an increasing variety of actors, leading Secretary-General Ban Ki-moon to correctly warn that 'the current state of protection of civilians leaves little room for optimism'.[48] As conflict has changed, and with it its impact on civilian populations, it is to be expected that the strategies and responses of the Council with regard to the protection of civilians would adapt accordingly. Since 2008, multidimensional missions, with strong political mandates and robust military tasks, have become quite prevalent.[49] The climax of this trend, to date, has been the robust peace enforcement mandate granted to the intervention brigade embedded within the UN Multidimensional Stabilization Operation in the Democratic Republic of the Congo (MONUSCO), tasked with 'neutralizing armed groups' and 'reducing the threat posed by armed groups to state authority and civilian security',[50] with both the UN

[44] UN Department of Peacekeeping Operations and UN Department of Field Support, *Draft Operational Concept on the Protection of Civilians in United Nations Peacekeeping Operations* (New York: United Nations, 2010).

[45] See UNSC Res 1970 (2011) UN Doc S/RES/1970.

[46] The UN Mission in Sierra Leone (UNSC res 1270 (1999) UN Doc S/RES/1270), the UN Mission in the Democratic Republic of Congo (UNSC Res (2000) UN Doc S/RES/1291), later the UN Stabilization Mission in the Democratic Republic of Congo (UNSC Res 1565 (2004) UN Doc S/RES/1565), the UN Mission in Liberia (UNSC Res 1509 (2003) UN Doc S/RES/1509), the UN Operation in Côte d'Ivoire (UNSC Res 1528 (2004) UN Doc S/RES/1528), the UN Stabilization Mission in Haiti (UNSC Res 1542 (2004) UN Doc S/RES/1542), the UN Operation in Burundi (UNSC Res 1545 (2004) UN Doc S/RES/1545), the UN Mission in Sudan (UNSC Res 1590 (2005) UN Doc S/RES/1590), the UN Interim Force in Lebanon (UNSC Res 1701 (2006) UN Doc S/RES/1701), the African Union–UN Hybrid Operation in Darfur (UNSC Res 1769 (2007) UN Doc S/RES/1769), the UN Mission in the Central African Republic and Chad (UNSC Res 1778 (2007) UN Doc S/RES/1778), and the UN Multidimensional Integrated Stabilization Mission in the Central African Republic (UNSC Res 2127 (2013) UN Doc S/RES/2127), the UN Mission in South Sudan (UNSC Res 1996 (2011) UN Doc S/RES/1996), the UN Interim Security Force for Abyei (UNSC Res 1990 (2011) UN Doc S/RES/1990), the UN Multidimensional Integrated Stabilization Mission in Mali (UNSC Res 2100 (2013) UN Doc S/RES/2100), and the UN Assistance Mission in Afghanistan (UNAMA, UNSC Res 2145 (2014) UN Doc S/RES/2145; UNAMA is a political mission without the authorization to use force to protect civilians, but civilian protection nonetheless remains prominent in its mandates.

[47] UNGA, 'Report of the Office of Internal Oversight Services, Review of the Reporting by United Nations Peacekeeping Missions on the Protection of Civilians' (2013) UN Doc A/67/795, para. 11.

[48] UNSC, 'Report on the Protection of Civilians in Armed Conflict' (2013) UN Doc S/2013/689, para. 8.

[49] See Michiel Hofman, 'The Evolution from Integrated Missions to "Peace Keepers on Steroids": How Aid by Force Erodes Humanitarian Access' (2014) 6 Global Responsibility to Protect 246.

[50] UNSC Res 2098 (2013) UN Doc S/RES/2098, para. 9.

Multidimensional Stabilization Operations in Mali (MINUSMA) and the Central African Republic (MINUSCA) continuing the trend.

The re-emergence of robust peacekeeping is not entirely surprising, as the concerns associated with maintaining or imposing the peace where there is in effect no peace to keep (yet) pale in comparison to those associated with the failure to act. As noted by a keen analyst of the Security Council,

> the three peace operations in which troops under UN command engaged in the use of force on a significant scale—Congo from 1960–1963, Somalia in 1993, and Bosnia and Herzegovina from 1994–1995—were traumatic experiences for the organization. The controversies to which these operations gave rise were surpassed only by two occasions on which force was not used at all: in Rwanda and Srebrenica.[51]

Yet before embarking anew on robust peacekeeping, the Security Council had to internalize, in addition to the reports on Rwanda and Srebrenica,[52] the 1995 Supplement to the Agenda for Peace presented by Secretary-General Boutros Boutros-Ghali,[53] the 2000 Brahimi Report,[54] and, most importantly, the 2008 Capstone Doctrine.[55] The Capstone Doctrine, a peacekeeping policy document produced by the UN Departments of Peacekeeping Operations and Field Support, attempted to articulate a distinction between robust peacekeeping and peace enforcement, stating that whereas the former employs force 'at the tactical level with the authorization of the Security Council and the host nation and/or the main parties to the conflict', the latter 'does not require consent of the main parties and may involve the use of force at the strategic or international level'.[56] In exploring the parameters of peacekeeping, the Council has experimented with hybrid missions and different, more or less generous logistical and financial support packages to Council-mandated non-UN missions in various settings. Yet despite their nature, from the UN–AU Hybrid Mission in Darfur (UNAMID)[57] to the African-led International Support Missions in Mali (MISMA/AFISMA)[58] and the Central African Republic (MISCA/AFISM-CAR)[59] and their respective UN successors MINUSMA[60] and MINUSCA,[61] virtually all missions have had significant protection of civilians mandates.[62]

[51] Simon Chesterman, 'The Use of Force in UN Peace Operations' (New York: United Nations, 2005) <www.peacekeepingbestpractices.unlb.org/PBPS/Library/Chesterman%20External%20Paper%20(31-08-2004).pdf>.

[52] See UNSC, n 6; UNSC, see n 7.

[53] UNGA, 'An Agenda for Peace: Preventive Diplomacy and Related Matters' (1992) UN Doc A/RES/47/120A.

[54] UNGA and UNSC, 'Report of the Panel on United Nations Peace Operations' (2000) UN Doc A/55/305—S/2000/809.

[55] UN Department of Peacekeeping Operations and UN Department of Field Support, *United Nations Peacekeeping Operations: Principles and Guidelines* (New York: United Nations, 2008).

[56] Ibid., 34.

[57] See UNSC Res 1769 (2007) UN Doc S/RES/1769, para. 15(a)(ii).

[58] See UNSC Res 2085 (2012) UN Doc S/RES/2085, paras 9(b), 9(e), 17, 18.

[59] See UNSC Res 2127 (2013) UN Doc S/RES/2127, para. 28(i).

[60] See UNSC Res 2100 (2013) UN Doc S/RES/2100, paras 16(c), 16(e), 26.

[61] See UNSC Res 2149 (2014) UN Doc S/RES/2149, paras 28(a), 28(c).

[62] The AU Mission in Somalia (AMISOM) does not have protection of civilians as part of its mandate. See Security Council Report, *Cross-Cutting Report on the Protection of Civilians* (New York: Security Council Report, 2013) 11.

The shift to multidimensional missions with robust protection mandates, notwithstanding some case-specific limitations, seems to have delivered in terms of relative effectiveness, according to the findings of a recent study on compliance with Security Council prescriptions by parties to internal conflicts. As noted in the study, 'demands made in the presence of a peacekeeping operation with a multidimensional mandate [. . .] are associated with higher odds of compliance'.[63] In contrast, demands made in the presence of a traditional peacekeeping operation, even alongside a sanctions regime, 'tend to be associated with lower odds of compliance'.[64] According to the same study, while adherence to Council demands to change 'military or humanitarian conduct was lower, on average, than compliance with other demands',[65] the worst option is probably inaction.

Whatever the faults that critics could raise regarding the sixteen UN peacekeeping operations mandated by the Security Council at the time of writing, the most flagrant recent failure of the Council is without any doubt Syria. To date, after more than four years of internecine conflict aggravated by a series of State and non-State actors, and with more than 220,000 civilians killed, the Council has failed to determine that the situation in Syria constitutes a threat to peace.[66] The vetoes cast by Russia—with China joining out of solidarity, albeit not having any strategic stake in the situation—have drastically reduced the margins for action within the Council to adequately address the dire situation in Syria. Notwithstanding these reduced margins, however, Russia and the United States were able to arrive at a compromise in jointly negotiating Resolution 2118, which solely addressed the issue of chemical weapons in Syria. With France and the United Kingdom likewise primarily concerned with the chemical weapons stockpile, the Council adopted as an outcome what was in essence a bilateral agreement between Russia and the United States. Although Resolution 2118 would eventually lead to the destruction of the entire declared chemical weapons stockpile in Syria—not a minor undertaking—it came at a high price: the murderous Bashar al-Assad regime became an indispensable partner in the orderly destruction of the stockpile. While the 'P3' (the United States, United Kingdom, and France, three traditionally aligned permanent members of the Security Council) maintained the pretence on the political front that they would no longer recognize the regime as a legitimate authority, on the chemical weapons front they had to recognize the regime and oversee, as permanent members of the Council, the work of the UN Organization for the Prohibition of Chemical Weapons Joint Mission in Syria. It was two elected members, Australia and Luxembourg, which took the lead on the humanitarian front. Although the chemical weapons were responsible for a small fraction of the total death toll at the

[63] Christoph Mikulaschek and Chris Perry, 'When Do Civil-War Parties Heed the UN? Findings from the IPI Security Council Compliance Database' (New York: International Peace Institute, 2013) 1 <www.ipinst.org/publication/policy-papers/detail/418-when-do-civil-war-parties-heed-the-un-findings-from-the-ipi-security-council-compliance-database.html>.

[64] Ibid. [65] Ibid.

[66] Resolution 2118 determined only 'that the use of chemical weapons in the Syrian Arab Republic constitutes a threat to international peace and security', not the wider conflict. See UNSC Res 2118 (2013) S/RES/2118, preambular para.

time,[67] with the al-Assad regime being a partner in the weapons destruction exercise, all other issues were subordinated. It was only due to the insistence of Australia and Luxembourg that the issue of humanitarian access was not entirely abandoned. Despite strong resistance from the five permanent members of the Council (P5),[68] both countries were able to 'seize the pen' and take leadership on producing a presidential statement.[69] After scoring a first success, they teamed up with incoming Council member Jordan (as of 1 January 2014) to draft and fight for what would become Resolution 2139.[70] Yet it was only once Syria had destroyed or surrendered its declared chemical weapons that the P5 were willing to take an unprecedented step encroaching on national sovereignty: the authorization in Resolution 2165 to provide humanitarian assistance across border and conflict lines without host State consent.[71]

While Resolution 2165 reportedly allowed for improved access to besieged and affected civilian populations, the Council's attention to the ravages caused by the ongoing civil war in Syria was almost immediately distracted by the threat posed by the expansion and consolidation of the Islamic State of Iraq and al-Sham (ISIS) in Iraq and Syria. At the time of writing, despite vehement denials, most Council members were resigning themselves to having to deal privately with the al-Assad regime in order to fight ISIS. Once again, the plight of ordinary civilians had fallen by the wayside beside more existential threats with potential implications for national security among the P5.

III. Tools for the Protection of Civilians

The Security Council has many tools available to become seized of a situation of concern that is likely to harm civilians. Not only does the UN Charter provide for a quite complete toolkit, but it also allows the Council to be creative and expansive in deploying or employing new tools. Articles 29 and 30, in particular, allow the Council to create whatever subsidiary bodies it needs to perform effectively and to provide for and amend, as necessary, its own rules of procedure. In this sense, since 1999, the Council has created a number of working groups the mandates of which are directly or closely aligned with the protection of civilians.[72] Due to the distinction Article 27 of the Charter makes between procedural and non-procedural matters, the threshold for adoption of novel procedural avenues is lower than that of

[67] 'Syria Chemical Attack: What We Know', *BBC News* (London, 24 September 2013) <www.bbc.co.uk/news/world-middle-east-23927399>.

[68] China, France, Russia, the United Kingdom, and the United States.

[69] UNSC Statement of the President (2013) UN Doc S/PRST/2013/5.

[70] UNSC Statement of the President (2014) UN Doc 2139, S/RES/2139.

[71] See UNSC Res 2165 (2014) S/RES/2165, para. 2.

[72] At a minimum, in addition to the Informal Working Group on the Protection of Civilians in Armed Conflict, the Working Group on Children and Armed Conflict and the Ad Hoc Working Group on Conflict Prevention and Resolution in Africa address issues that are closely related to the protection of civilians. See Security Council Report, 'Security Council Subsidiary Bodies: An Overview' (New York: Security Council Report, 2013) <www.securitycouncilreport.org/about-the-un-security-council.php>.

substantive issues, requiring any nine affirmative votes and therefore not being subject to the veto. In this regard, one of the more interesting innovations, the 'Arria formula', was developed by another non-permanent member, Venezuela, in an effort to get credible information on the situation in Bosnia and Herzegovina using an informal meeting format.[73] The first Arria meeting is largely credited as a game-changer that brought an eyewitness account of the atrocities being committed in Bosnia and Herzegovina to the attention of Council members. Yet the fate of the 'Arria formula' has since been mixed; it fell into disuse for long stretches of time, but has recently made a significant comeback.[74] Informal interactive dialogues, another informal meeting format, also provide Council members with an alternative to the overly scripted formal meetings of the Council and the increasingly scripted 'pre-runs' in the informal consultations. Yet caution is required, as at times these informal formats are used to cover for the absence of formal Council action, as best exemplified by the informal interactive dialogues on the situation in Sri Lanka.[75] At the time, three elected Council members, Austria, Costa Rica, and Mexico, insisted that the Council become seized of the disproportionate and indiscriminate final military offensive by the government against the Liberation Tigers of Tamil Elaam, during which a reported 90,000 civilians were killed. Although their joint efforts were unsuccessful, the Council did hold three dialogues on Sri Lanka, albeit with no formal outcome.[76]

Security Council visiting missions can be an effective tool for protecting civilians if they are deployed urgently and are unequivocally mandated to deliver stern messages of potential consequences to the parties on the ground. The 8–12 September 1999 visiting mission to Timor-Leste is considered to be a best practice, as it deployed within days and delivered strong words of caution to Indonesia regarding its non-observance of the results of the independence referendum.[77] More recently, although described by some Council members as an 'emergency visit',[78] the 12 August 2014 Council visiting mission to South Sudan came almost nine months after the 15 December 2013 coup/self-coup that started the civil war in that nascent country recently midwifed by the Council. Although stern messages were delivered, the absence of credible Council implementation of its own threats regarding neighbouring Sudan in regard to the situation in Darfur, where the Council-mandated sanctions regime has remained effectively dormant, probably blunted the

73 An Arria meeting is an informal, off-the-record, private gathering of Council members, called for by one or more Council members, with persons or organizations that the organizers believe can provide beneficial insights on an issue of concern that may or may not be on the formal Council agenda.

74 Security Council Report, *Special Research Report: Security Council Working Methods—A Tale of Two Councils?* (New York: Security Council Report, 2014) 22–33.

75 UN Secretariat, *Report of the Secretary-General's Internal Review Panel on United Nations Action in Sri Lanka* (New York: United Nations, 2012) 14 <www.un.org/News/dh/infocus/Sri_Lanka/The_Internal_Review_Panel_report_on_Sri_Lanka.pdf>.

76 Security Council Report, see n 73, 33–4.

77 Ibid., 40–1; José Ramos Horta and Benedict Rogers, 'Timor-Leste', in Genser and Stagno-Ugarte, see n 5, 327.

78 Security Council Report, 'Dispatches from the Field: Council Meetings in South Sudan' (*What's in Blue*, 13 August 2014) <www.whatsinblue.org/2014/08/dispatches-from-the-field-council-meetings-in-south-sudan.php>.

deterrent effect of those messages and the potential consequences. Failure by the Council to abide by its own threats in one case can have a deleterious effect on threats elsewhere, as parties on the ground hedge on the unlikelihood that the Council will proceed from word to deed to protect civilians.

As early as 1985, on the fortieth anniversary of the founding of the UN, Secretary-General Javier Pérez de Cuellar highlighted that as 'crises have frequently been brought before the Council too late for preventive action, it would seem to follow that the Council might well establish a procedure to keep the world under continuing survey in order to detect nascent causes of tension'.[79] Notwithstanding its missing early warnings in Rwanda and elsewhere, the Council has been quite reluctant to survey the horizon, despite the efforts of the United Kingdom to install periodic 'horizon-scanning' briefings.[80] Credit is also due to then Department of Political Affairs Under-Secretary-General B Lynn Pascoe for implementing such briefings, although the United States never supported the practice and quietly lobbied for their discontinuance. Judging by the reluctance shown by Under-Secretary-General Jeffrey Feltman in continuing with the practice—which, it should be noted, is in line with the prerogatives of the Secretary-General under Article 99 of the UN Charter and the imperatives outlined in the Human Rights Up Front strategy launched by the Secretary-General on 17 December 2013—the United States has successfully undermined one of the few early warning tools available to the Council. While it is true that other avenues are available, including raising issues of concern under 'any other business' in informal consultations, Council members are generally reluctant to do so as to avoid incurring the wrath of the concerned State(s).

Yet the availability and multiplicity of tools available to the Security Council is not the real issue, as the Council has been creative and expansive when the interests of the permanent members have aligned. The real issue is the alignment or misalignment of interests within the Council, and the opportunities and avenues for political compromise they make either possible or impossible. In general, the protection of civilians, beyond Council rhetoric, is not an issue that in and of itself aligns the interests of the permanent members. Two other security threats have priority and have traditionally aligned the permanent members: countering international terrorism and the proliferation of weapons of mass destruction.

Without belittling the threat of nuclear weapons, the likelihood of nuclear retaliation or mutually assured destruction has ensured that the first and last time these inherently disproportionate and indiscriminate weapons were used, including on civilians, was in Hiroshima and Nagasaki in 1945. Since then, millions of civilians have died due to conventional and small weapons, yet the Council has sought to limit the proliferation of nuclear weapons while failing to abide by its UN Charter responsibility to regulate armaments in general. The inaction of the Council in bringing Article 26 to life is quite revealing, yet partly explained by the 'coincidence' that the five permanent members are the top arms producing–exporting

[79] UNSC (1985) UN Doc S/PV.2608, para. 15.
[80] Security Council Report, see n 73, 6–7, 19–22.

States. As noted earlier on other issues, it was once again an elected Council member, Costa Rica, which in 2008–9 first attempted to revive Article 26, albeit with limited success.[81]

Despite the undisputable impact of conventional and small weapons on civilians, to date the Security Council has been loath to impose targeted sanctions on parties violating the arms embargoes in place. In fact, its first ever standalone resolution on small arms was only adopted on 26 September 2013, at the behest of Australia.[82] In contrast, at the time of writing, the Council had two sanctions regimes in place (1718 on Democratic People's Republic of Korea and 1737 on Iran) to constrain a Member State from either consolidating or acquiring a nuclear State status and a separate committee to constrain non-State actors from acquiring nuclear weapons (1540 Committee). No less than ninety-eight entities and fifty-five individuals were subject to proliferation-related targeted sanctions.[83]

Similarly, while not seeking to belittle the threat of international terrorism, the total casualty toll attributable to terrorism pales in comparison to the mass killings attributable to war crimes, genocides, or ethnic cleansings. Yet, at the time of writing, the Security Council had two counter-terrorism sanctions regimes (1278/1989 on Al-Qaida and 1988 on the Taliban) in addition to a separate subsidiary body (1373 on the Counter-Terrorism Committee) with an adjunct directorate (Counter-Terrorism Executive Directorate). No less than 80 entities and 393 individuals were subject to terrorism-related targeted sanctions as of 12 November 2015.[84]

Regarding the protection of civilians, despite having progressively added a number of designation criteria for targeted sanctions under a number of sanctions committees, only twelve entities (6.3 per cent of the 190 in total targeted by the Council) and eighty-eight individuals (16.4 per cent of the 536 in total targeted by the Council) were listed as of 12 November 2015.[85] There is therefore a stark disproportionality between the substantial efforts of the Council to use sanctions to counter international terrorism and nuclear proliferation, despite them being responsible for fewer civilian casualties, and its more limited efforts to constrain the myriad spoilers that trouble the peace or perpetrators of crimes against civilians (not terrorism-related), despite them being responsible for most civilian casualties.

In addition, whereas the Security Council has expansively interpreted its powers under the UN Charter, legislating and imposing binding obligations on all Member States without distinction to counter international terrorism (Resolutions 1257 and 1373) and the proliferation of weapons of mass destruction (Resolution 1540), it has been loath to do likewise to promote or enshrine international human rights

81 UNSC Statement of the President (2008) UN Doc S/PRST/2008/43.

82 UNSC Res 2117 (2013) UN Doc S/RES/2117.

83 See UNSC, 'Consolidated United Nations Security Council Sanctions List' (12 November 2015) <www.un.org/sc/committees/consolidated.pdf>.

84 Ibid.

85 Ibid. The 1518 Iraq Sanctions Committee list is not included in these totals due to the methodological difficulties in determining whether its 86 individuals and 208 entities were designated under non-proliferation, counterterrorism, or civilian protection criteria, due to the shifting narratives provided by the occupying powers.

and humanitarian law. Its unwillingness to advance human rights law and humanitarian law in general—beyond a country-specific context—is in line with its own belated acceptance of key instruments such as the Universal Declaration of Human Rights of 1948 or the 1949 Geneva Conventions. Surprisingly, the Council first referenced these instruments in 1963 and 1967, respectively, whereas the General Assembly had already done so decades earlier. This legal–temporal divide casts a long shadow over the alleged commitment by the Council to the protection of civilians.

IV. Conclusion

As this chapter has highlighted, it is often the elected members that have taken the most progressive initiatives and stances regarding the protection of civilians, with permanent members adhering to the issue in alignment with their specific interests rather than in a principled manner. While there have certainly been many exceptions to both patterns, the answer may not lie in Security Council reform. After all, most of the claimants to permanent seats have not distinguished themselves as proactive defenders of the protection of civilians. Brazil did not do so in Rwanda, and was hard pressed to move beyond calls for dialogue in Syria when the al-Assad regime was slaughtering civilians. India and South Africa toed similar lines regarding Syria in 2011–12, with India also weighing in on the Council to pre-empt it becoming seized of the situation in Sri Lanka in 2008–9. Even the 'Responsibility while Protecting' initiative launched by Brazil was, in the end, not about protecting civilians, but about scoring points with the global South at the expense of the NATO operation in Libya authorized by the Council in Resolution 1973. The abject silence Brazil has kept following the stealth occupation of the Crimea peninsula by Russia and its ongoing aggression against eastern Ukraine has revealed the political bias. Germany, likewise, abstained on Resolution 1973, considered by many to be *the* landmark responsibility to protect resolution, yet soon thereafter seemed to regret its alignment with the BRICS (Brazil, Russia, India, China, and South Africa) instead of its European Union–NATO partners.

In addition, some of the permanent members have at times led novel initiatives that have had an important angle for the protection of civilians. Probably the most revolutionary, in that it operationalized the otherwise abstruse Article 11 of the UN Charter, was the 'Uniting for Peace' initiative led by the United States in 1950.[86] First implemented to sidestep the veto of the Soviet Union regarding the Korean War, this resolution has established a process that has been used to address a number of situations where civilians were at risk: the Middle East (1967), Bangladesh (1971), and Afghanistan (1980). Nevertheless, at present all permanent members, first and foremost the United States, are against a revival of Uniting for Peace, which they collectively see as a threat to the primacy of the Security Council within the

[86] UNGA Res 377 (V) (1950) UN Doc A/RES/377(V).

UN system.[87] As mentioned earlier, the ad hoc international tribunals (ICTY, ICTR) and special tribunals established by the Council, initially at the behest of the United States, could be considered tools of deterrence against further crimes against civilians. More recently, in line with a recommendation included in one of the reports that fed into the 2005 World Summit Outcome Document, France has proposed a 'code of conduct' to rein in the veto in situations of mass atrocity crimes.[88] Notwithstanding its own unwillingness to date to drop the caveat providing for the veto if it is in the national interest, France has yet to be joined by the other permanent members. Instead of reacting and limiting its responses to the baseline requirements of international humanitarian law at best, the Security Council could explore whether effective protection may require mitigating the effects of conflict above and beyond international human rights and humanitarian law. Although States are not keen to see the Council acquiring a normative role, which is seen as an invasion of the prerogatives of the General Assembly under Article 10, the Council has nonetheless been creating legal obligations that apply *erga omnes* in countering nuclear proliferation and international terrorism.

There is no single and simple fix to the Security Council's wavering commitment to the protection of civilians. Each case is different, not only with respect to the actors involved, the interests concerned, and the internal and/or external impacts and dynamics, but also in terms of its actual or potential harm to civilians. Yet the Council mainly reemploys what is known as 'previously agreed language', that is, descriptions and prescriptions that have previously been agreed to in other settings, in an effort to expedite and facilitate the internal negotiation process. Of late, the Council has also postponed taking action with decisions (resolutions or presidential statements), opting instead for non-binding press statements whose effect on the parties concerned is negligible at best. This was most evidently the case with the recent situation in the Central African Republic, where the emergence of the *Séléka* was addressed through nine press statements between 19 December 2012 and 29 August 2013.[89]

[87] Security Council Report, see n 73, 69.

[88] See United Nations, 'Meetings Coverage: Calling for Security Council Reform, General Assembly President Proposes Advisory Group to Move Process Forward' (7 November 2013) UN Doc GA/11450 <www.un.org/News/Press/docs/2013/ga11450.doc.htm>.

[89] See UNSC, 'Press Release: Security Council Press Statement on Central African Republic' (19 December 2012) UN Doc SC/10867; UNSC, 'Press Release: Security Council Statement on Central Africa Republic' (27 December 2012) UN Doc SC/10874-AFR/2496; UNSC, 'Press Release: Security Council Statement on Central Africa Republic' (4 January 2013) UN Doc SC/10877-AFR/2501; UNSC, 'Press Release: Security Council Statement on Central Africa Republic' (11 January 2013) UN Doc SC/10880-AFR/2503; UNSC, 'Press Release: Security Council Statement on Central Africa Republic' (20 March 2013) UN Doc SC/10948-AFR/2582; UNSC, 'Press Release: Security Council Statement on Central Africa Republic' (22 March 2013) UN Doc SC/10955-AFR/2583; UNSC, 'Press Release: Security Council Statement on Central Africa Republic' (25 March 2013) UN Doc SC/10960-AFR/2586; UNSC, 'Press Release: Security Council Statement on Central Africa Republic' (29 April 2013) UN Doc SC/10993-AFR/2608; UNSC, 'Press Release: Security Council Statement on Central Africa Republic' (29 August 2013) UN Doc SC/11093-AFR/2678.

Political will is the irreplaceable element. For an effective protection of civilians mandate, political will must be shown by Council members, both in the appropriate formulation and implementation of its decisions; by troop-contributing countries in deploying troops that are committed to protecting and enforcing the mandate despite the risks involved; and by the UN Secretariat, both at headquarters and at the mission level, in ensuring that UN system-wide action is coherent and in line with the principles and purposes of the Charter. All three are crucial, because parties to a conflict often prove to be unwilling partners and thereby exploit any hesitation or lack of co-ordination among the former. But in the end, within the Security Council—which proudly claims its primary responsibility for the maintenance of international peace and security—the duty and responsibility to protect civilians from harm ultimately depends on its members. Lord Caradon already recognized this as early as 1970, poignantly stating that 'there is nothing fundamentally wrong with the United Nations, except its members'.[90] In this regard, elections of non-permanent members to the Security Council should not be taken lightly, as the composition of the Council can make a significant difference for better or worse.

[90] J Martin Rochester, *Waiting for the Millennium: The United Nations and the Future of World Order* (Columbia, USA: University of South Carolina Press, 1993) 109.

14

Using Force to Protect Civilians in United Nations Peacekeeping Operations

Fiona Blyth and Patrick Cammaert[1]

Force alone cannot create peace; it can only create the space in which peace may be built.[2]

I. Introduction

Drafted in the wake of two world wars, the United Nations (UN) Charter commits parties to using peaceful means to address threats to international peace and security. Should such means fail, however, Chapter VII of the Charter makes provision for the Security Council to take 'necessary' action, including the use of force, to restore and maintain international peace and security.[3] The Council has exercised its power to authorize military action through two primary means: the use of force by single States or coalitions of States (including regional bodies) and, most often, the deployment of UN peacekeeping operations.

There is no explicit reference to peacekeeping in the Charter: the concept has evolved in response to world events since its drafting. Consequently, the purpose, function, and appropriate parameters of UN peacekeeping have been the subject of continued debate within the UN. The extent to which peacekeeping operations should use force has been an issue of particular contention. As the protection of civilians has become a central function of UN peacekeeping, the use of force to protect has become a pressing issue. While the Charter remains the touchstone of the normative framework for the use of force, more recent pronouncements have shaped the landscape of peacekeeping.[4]

[1] Fiona Blyth is a member of the Permanent Mission of the United Kingdom and Northern Ireland to the United Nations (UN). This chapter is written in her personal capacity and the views presented herein do not necessarily reflect the views of the Government of the United Kingdom and Northern Ireland. Maj Gen (rtd) Patrick Cammaert is a former UN Military Adviser and former General Officer Commanding the Eastern Division of the UN Mission in the Democratic Republic of the Congo (MONUC).

[2] UN General Assembly (UNGA) and United Nations Security Council (UNSC), 'Report of the Panel on United Nations Peace Operations' (2000) UN Doc A/55/305—S/2000/809, viii (Brahimi Report).

[3] UN Charter, Chapter VII, Article 42.

[4] See for example, 2005 World Summit Outcome, A/RES/60/1, 24 October 2005, para. 77 and 79 'we are determined to take effective collective measures for the prevention and removal of threats to the

Peacekeeping operations are often deployed into theatres where there is no peace to keep. In many instances the environment is volatile, with ongoing conflict among armed groups. UN peacekeepers are often mandated to assist local security forces in confronting armed rebel groups, which are increasingly inclined to target the UN. Tragically, civilians have always been victims of armed conflicts, and those theatres into which the UN has deployed have been no exception. Providing physical protection to the civilian population was implicit in the mandate of several early UN peacekeeping operations. However, the scale of atrocities committed in Bosnia, Somalia, and Rwanda in the 1990s, all in close proximity to international troops, necessitated explicit direction to UN peacekeepers to prioritize the protection of civilians.[5] Ten of the current UN peacekeeping operations have an explicit protection mandate,[6] with the UN Organisation Stabilization Mission in the Democratic Republic of the Congo (MONUSCO) and the UN Mission in South Sudan (UNMISS) having demonstrated how force can be used to provide security through offensive and defensive military operations.[7]

The protection of civilians peacekeeping mandate has multiple components, but the most fundamental is the physical protection of people. However, the extent to which the UN should deploy military force, to deflect violence, provide a shield, and ensure physical protection, is contested. In the view of some Member States, the use of force by UN peacekeepers should be limited to self-defence; defence of mission personnel, premises, and equipment; and, only in the event of an attack, the defence of civilians seeking refuge. Others are of the view that increasingly complex operating environments and fragile peace agreements require the UN to use greater and more frequent military force to prevent and deter violence against civilians. All agree that the primary responsibility for protecting civilians lies with the host State and that force should only be used as a last resort. However, agreement on the extent of that use of force remains elusive and the expectations of the protection of civilians mandate unclear. As a result the mandates are 'interpreted' rather than universally implemented, and the degree to which force is used often depends

peace and for the suppression of acts of aggression or other breaches of the peace . . . We further reaffirm the authority of the Security Council to mandate coercive action to maintain and restore international peace and security.'

[5] See Haidi Willmot and Ralph Mamiya, 'Mandated to Protect: Security Council Practice on the Responsibility to Protect', in Marc Weller and Alexia Solomou (eds), *Oxford Handbook on the Use of Force in International Law* (Oxford: Oxford University Press, 2015) 382.

[6] These are: the UN Mission in Liberia (UNSC Res 1509 (2003) UN Doc S/RES/1509); the UN Operation in Côte d'Ivoire (ONUCI) (UNSC Res 1528 (2004) UN Doc S/RES/1528); the UN Stabilization Mission in Haiti (UNSC Res 1542 (2004) UN Doc S/RES/1542); the UN Interim Force in Lebanon (UNSC Res 1701 (2006) UN Doc S/RES/1701); the African Union/UN Hybrid Operation in Darfur (UNSC Res 1769 (2007) UN Doc S/RES/1769); the UN Mission in South Sudan (UNSC Res 1996 (2011) UN Doc S/RES/1996); the UN Stabilization Mission in the Democratic Republic of the Congo (UNSC Res 1925 (2010) UN Doc S/RES/1925); the UN Multidimensional Integrated Stabilization Operation in Mali (UNSC Res 2100 (2013) UN Doc S/RES/2100; the UN Multidimensional Integrated Stabilization Operation in the Central African Republic (UNSC Res 2149 (2014) UN Doc S/RES/2149).

[7] See UNSC, 'Report of the Secretary-General on the United Nations Organization Stabilization Mission in the Democratic Republic of the Congo' (2013) UN Doc S/2013/757, paras 17–28; UNSC, 'Report of the Secretary-General on South Sudan' (2014) UN Doc S/2014/158, paras 26, 35–7, 44–54.

on the risk appetite of contingent commanders and their capitals, the capability and resources of the troops, and the personality and vision of the mission Force Commander. In reality, force is rarely used in UN peacekeeping missions.

This chapter will examine the framework under which force is authorized to protect civilians, the role that force can play in the protection of civilian populations, and the challenges facing the UN when deploying forces with protection mandates. Using examples drawn from the authors' operational experience, the chapter argues that for force to be effectively employed, troops must be well trained and equipped, supported by adequate assets, and led by visionary and proactive commanders at all levels. To allow adequate resources to be mobilized, there must be political cohesion at the strategic level among Member States and with the Secretariat with a focus on effects-based force generation. The chapter also considers a number of political challenges, including differing interpretations by troop contributors of protection of civilians mandates, a lack of political will to implement such mandates to their fullest extent, and the need to hold troop contributors accountable for mandate implementation. Above all, it is argued that there must be a political peace process in place, without which the impact of any military operations will be transitory.

II. The Use of Force

Unlike national militaries or the militias that seek to undermine them, UN peacekeeping forces do not seek to battle an enemy or use overwhelming force to hold ground or gain tactical advantage. Peacekeepers are authorized to use force to deter spoilers and to create the environment for a political peace process to be implemented. This is evident in the simple numbers of UN troops deployed into theatres of conflict. Even in the largest peacekeeping operations, the relatively small number of UN troops could not engage in large-scale ground operations. Peacekeepers are not occupying forces and require the consent of the host government and/or the consent of the main parties in the conflict. Force is intended to be used as a last resort and UN troops are generally seeking not the military defeat of armed groups, but to deter them from undermining a peace process or harming civilians.[8] In 2012, a spokesperson for MONUSCO stated: 'Our mandate is the protection of civilians. It's not fighting armed groups, unless they're threatening the population.'[9]

The term 'force' or 'military force' covers a spectrum of operational activities. Offensive operations are those actions intended to 'seek to seize, retain, and exploit the initiative',[10] and are pre-emptive military operations such as conducting a

[8] UN Department of Peacekeeping Operations (DPKO) and UN Department of Field Support (DFS), *UN Peacekeeping Operations: Principles and Guidelines* (New York: United Nations, 2008) 35 (Capstone Doctrine).

[9] Robyn Dixon, 'UN Force in Congo, MONUSCO, Criticized as Ineffective', *Los Angeles Times* (Los Angeles, USA, 22 December 2012) <articles.latimes.com/2012/dec/22/world/la-fg-un-congo-20121223>.

[10] United States Army, Unified Land Operations (Army Doctrine Publication FM 3-0) (Washington, DC: Department of the Army, 2011), para. 1.

search, seizing weapons, detaining spoilers, or attacking groups preparing to attack civilians before they start their operations. Defensive operations include area security; checkpoints; monitoring and reporting on ceasefires; and using military measures such as static observation posts, patrols, and over-flights to report on the progress of peace agreement implementation and reinforce buffer zones.[11] Force can also be used to protect civilians indirectly through troops providing security for convoys and humanitarian access to civilians at risk.[12] The standard UN Rules of Engagement (ROE) for peacekeeping operations mandated under Ch VII of the Charter authorize the use of force for self-defence and 'beyond self-defence', effectively allowing offensive operations for certain purposes, typically to protect civilians.

Operationalizing the use of force to protect civilians in UN peacekeeping missions is the responsibility of the Secretary-General, acting through the Department of Peacekeeping Operations (DPKO), since its creation in 1992.[13] While the Secretary-General exercises UN operational authority on behalf of the Security Council, the civilian backgrounds and appetites of individual Secretaries-General to act as military commanders mean that historically they have had little operational engagement, although on occasion, distinct operations have necessitated their specific authorization.[14]

DPKO, in co-ordination with the Department of Field Support (DFS) and the Office of Legal Affairs, conclude between the UN and the host State a Status of Forces or Status of Mission Agreement (SOFA or SOMA), which articulates inter alia the host State's agreement to the use of force by UN troops in its territory. DPKO and DFS also produce a military Concept of Operations (CONOPS), a detailed breakdown of the mission's mandate, allocating areas of responsibility and tasks to the military component and setting out timelines and end states. These are complemented by the ROE, which set out the legal parameters for the use of force and are intended to be mission-wide and applied uniformly.[15] Member States contributing troops to a peacekeeping operation do so under this overarching framework; however, some include operational caveats within the Memorandum of Understanding between the UN and the contributing State. Such caveats, particularly when they limit the use of force, can, in effect, undermine the CONOPS, ROE, and the authority of the Force Commander, resulting in confusion and substandard performance.

[11] Capstone Doctrine, see n 8, 20.

[12] See, for example, UNSC Resolution (Res) 1894 (2009) UN Doc S/RES/1894, para. 15(b), which requires peacekeepers 'to assist in creating conditions conducive to safe, timely and unimpeded humanitarian assistance'.

[13] See DPKO and DFS, *Policy: Authority, Command and Control in United Nations Peacekeeping Operations* (Ref 2008.4) (New York: United Nations, 2008), paras 7, 17–19.

[14] On 5 December 1961, the Secretary-General's authority was sought in advance to use military measures to restore freedom of movement in Katanga, Democratic Republic of the Congo (DRC). Secretary-General U Thant authorized 'all counter-action—ground and aerial—deemed necessary'. Trevor Findlay, *The Use of Force in UN Peace Operations* (Oxford: Oxford University Press, 2002) 78. Secretary-General Ban Ki-moon was also directly involved in authorizing specific activities of the UN mission during the 2010–11 Ivorian crisis.

[15] Capstone Doctrine, see n 8, 35.

While the Force Commander has operational control of the peacekeeping force, each national contingent has a commander who is often directed by the instructions of their capital. If the risk appetite of the UN Force Commander is greater than that of a contingent's capital, inevitable tensions arise within the force. In some cases UN orders are directly undermined by national dictates, particularly when the orders of a Force Commander will only be carried out by a national contingent following political clearance from their capital. This is particularly problematic when proactive operations are planned where offensive force might be required.

III. Role of the Use of Force

A report issued by the UN Office of Internal Oversight Services (OIOS) in March 2014 noted: 'peacekeeping is one of the most important tools used by the international community to protect civilians and probably the only area in which organizational performance can literally mean the difference between life and death for a civilian in a conflict zone'.[16]

UN authorization of the use of force can be used to demonstrate the international community's commitment to addressing a particular threat to international peace and security. In 1999, the Sierra Leonean delegation told the Security Council: 'we believe that it [the protection mandate] sends a clear message to any potential violator of human rights on a mass scale; the international community will not turn a blind eye if and when innocent civilians are under threat of physical violence.'[17] In addition, the deployment of a Security Council-mandated peacekeeping mission in the early days of a fragile peace agreement can ensure momentum, signal international resolve, and, if necessary, help ensure compliance.[18]

The mere presence of military troops, and a 'show of force' in areas of fragile peace, can be effective in deterring potential spoilers and building confidence among the local population.[19] In 2003, higher visibility of UN patrols in the North Kivu area of eastern Democratic Republic of the Congo (DRC) improved civilian security to such an extent that thousands of internally displaced persons (IDPs) were able to return home, having been forced out of their villages by rebel violence earlier that year.[20]

[16] UNGA, 'Report of the Office of Internal Oversight Services on the evaluation of the implementation and results of Protection of Civilians mandates in United Nations peacekeeping operations' (2014) UN Doc A/68/787, para. 3 (OIOS Report).

[17] UNSC (1999) UN Doc S/PV.4054, 6.

[18] For example, the United Nations Operation in Côte d'Ivoire (ONUCI) was originally authorized in 2004 with the primary objective of facilitating the implementation of the peace agreement to end the Ivorian civil war signed in January 2003. UNSC Res 1528 (2004) UN Doc S/RES/1528, paras 6 (a), 6(b), 6(c).

[19] In 1994 the Security Council authorized a peacekeeping mission to Haiti to facilitate the prompt return of the legitimate Haitian authorities, maintain a secure and stable environment in the country, and promote the rule of law. UNSC Res 940 (1994) UN Doc S/RES/940, paras 9–10.

[20] Lawrence Smith, 'MONUC's Military Involvement in the Eastern Congo', in Mark Malan and Jão Gomes Porto (eds), *The Challenges of Peace Implementation: The UN Mission in the Democratic Republic of the Congo* (Pretoria: Institute for Security Studies, 2004) 242–3.

In many theatres of operation, presence alone is not a sufficient deterrent. As missions deploy to more complex and dangerous environments, military tasks have increasingly incorporated proactive operations, requiring them to seek out and act on reports of forthcoming attacks on civilian targets. Early warning mechanisms, cordon and search operations, and rapid response have been used to enable troops to respond to credible threats of violence.[21] When the Security Council renewed the mandate of the African Union/United Nations Hybrid Operation in Darfur (UNAMID) in 2011, it provided additional guidance to the mission on the protection of civilians, including tasking 'proactive deployment and patrols in areas at high risk of conflict, securing IDP camps and adjacent areas, and implementation of a mission-wide early-warning strategy and capacity'.[22]

Since 2008, peacekeeping mission mandates have included stronger language, prioritizing the protection of civilians and highlighting the use of force to do so. Yet, despite strong mandates, the OIOS report found that there was a 'persistent pattern of peacekeepers not intervening with force when civilians were under attack'.[23] The report highlighted that 'peacekeeping missions with protection of civilians mandates focus on prevention and mitigation activities and force is almost never used to protect civilians under attack'.[24] It concluded that the chain of intent from the Security Council to those on the ground in peacekeeping operations remains 'broken',[25] so civilians continue to suffer displacement and violence. The following examination of practical and political challenges explains why this is still the case.

IV. Practical Challenges

A. Who needs protection, and from whom?

When mandating peacekeepers to 'protect civilians', the Security Council rarely provides guidance on who is to be protected and from whom—fundamental issues that are not without complexity.[26] On the ground, peacekeepers sometimes find it difficult to identify who may be a potential attacker and who may be at risk in rapidly changing situations.[27] Defining the population to protect is vital considering missions' limited resources. The Security Council has identified groups particularly vulnerable to violence or harm—notably women, who may be subject to sexual violence—and DPKO has developed comprehensive mission strategies to identify which communities should be the focus of protection efforts. In resolution 1794

[21] See generally Haidi Willmot and Ralph Mamiya, 'Early Warning, the Protection of Civilians and United Nations Peacekeeping Operations' (2013) 22 African Security Rev 68.

[22] UNSC Res 2003 (2011) UN Doc S/RES/2003, para. 3(a).

[23] OIOS Report, see n 16, § B.

[24] Ibid., para. 79.

[25] Ibid. This conclusion was first reached in Victoria Holt and Glyn Taylor with Max Kelly, *Protecting Civilians in the Context of UN Peacekeeping Operations: Successes, Setbacks and Remaining Challenges* (New York: United Nations, 2010) 5–9.

[26] See Ralph Mamiya, Chapter 3 in this volume.

[27] See Hugo Slim, Chapter 1 in this volume.

(2007), the Council mandated the UN Organization Mission in the DRC (MONUC) 'to strengthen prevention, protection and response to sexual violence',[28] and in an open debate in 2008, speakers noted the particular threats against women in areas of instability or conflict. They identified that these threats were not being countered in a systematic or persistent manner, and noted that often mandates to address the threat of sexual violence were vague. The debate resulted in the adoption of a strong resolution on the issue,[29] but women remain particularly at risk of rape being used as a tactic of war. The Council has also recognized that children, people with disabilities, and older people are also particularly vulnerable to violence in armed conflicts,[30] but safeguarding these individuals on the ground is problematic.

Traditional peacekeeping operations had easily identifiable opposition forces, with relatively clearly defined paramilitary or militant groups who threatened the peace. In most of today's peacekeeping environments, opposition forces are harder to identify, as they blend into the civilian population, at times are civilians, and use communities as a shield. This presents difficulties for peacekeepers who then require detailed local knowledge to identify potential attackers. When force is used, there are heightened risks of civilian casualties if spoilers are misidentified or if, due to proximity, civilians are caught in the crossfire. In 2006, MONUC faced such challenges dealing with the forces of Laurent Nkunda, and in 2013 its successor, MONUSCO, had similar issues addressing the M23.[31]

This continuing challenge was recently highlighted during an open debate of the Security Council in 2014, in which the Indian delegation made reference to an incident on 19 December 2013 in which approximately 2,000 armed youth attacked an UNMISS base in Akobo, South Sudan, where protection was being provided to Dinka refugees:

> The 40 Indian peacekeepers were heavily outnumbered. They had superior fire power and a robust mandate which would have allowed them to use force, not just in self-defence, but also in defence of the mission. Had they opened fire, hundreds of lives would have been lost. Would those lives have been civilian or combatant? And the troops who availed their superior firepower, would they have been peacekeepers or war makers?[32]

In the same debate, the Pakistani delegation argued that while peacekeepers should not be 'passive bystanders', nor should they become parties to the conflict. In the view of the Pakistani delegation, comprehensive patrolling and effective demobilization, disarmament, and reintegration practices alone could create a credible deterrent, and obviate the need to use offensive force.[33]

[28] UNSC Res 1794 (2007) UN Doc S/RES/1794, para. 18.

[29] UNSC Res 1820 (2008) UN Doc S/RES/1820.

[30] UNSC Res 1894 (2009) UN Doc S/RES/1894.

[31] The 'March 23 Movement', an armed rebel group in the DRC.

[32] Statement by Ambassador Asoke Kumar Mukerji, Permanent Representative of India to the UN at the Security Council Open Debate on 'Protection of Civilians in Armed Conflict: Effective Implementation of Protection of Civilians Mandates in UN Peacekeeping Operations', 12 February 2014.

[33] Statement by Masood Khan, in UNSC (2014) UN Doc S/PV.7109, 47.

As one of the UN's largest troop contributors, the position of Pakistan in this debate is important. However there is evidence that an aggressive show and, when needed, use of force by the UN can reduce the threat of rebel groups, at least for a limited time. For example, between 2005 and 2007, MONUC Eastern Division offensive operations were a successful deterrent against rebel forces in the Ituri district. They also proved effective in North and South Kivu provinces against the Democratic Forces for the Liberation of Rwanda (FDLR), the Interahamwe, the Lord's Resistance Army, and the Allied Democratic Forces–National Army for the Liberation of Uganda (ADF–NALU). The shift in approach from 'reaction' to 'pursuit' successfully deterred spoilers from engaging in conflict and nudged them towards the political process, which enabled the DRC's first legitimate government to take office in January 2007.[34]

As conflicts shift from opposing militias and rebel groups to asymmetric and terrorist threats, as currently seen in Mali, civilian environments increasingly become conflict zones as homes, schools, and hospitals are targeted. In instances where a UN peacekeeping operation has been deployed before a peace agreement has been concluded, peacekeepers have found themselves ahead of the political process and exposed to significant asymmetric threats as a result. This was particularly evident in Mali in 2013–14, when negotiations between the government and armed groups on territorial control of the north of the country were ongoing. The security vacuum created by the lack of political agreement produced the conditions for insurgent groups to operate and attack peacekeeping troops. Between 1 July 2013 and 7 October 2014, thirty-one peacekeepers were killed and ninety-one wounded in extremist attacks against the mission.[35]

Areas of high threat to peacekeepers are very different operating environments to theatres where a peace agreement is in place and observed, and to those where armed groups target each other and the local population. Each environment requires a different composition of the peacekeeping force. To be effective, such forces need to be specifically tailored to address the situation through particular military activities. However, the fundamental overarching objective of protecting the civilian population remains the same.

B. Regional support

The MONUSCO Force Intervention Brigade was authorized by the Security Council in March 2013 to conduct pre-emptive and aggressive operations against the rebel armed groups in eastern DRC.[36] Although mandated by the Security Council, the roots of the initiative lay in the region. In July 2012, the International Conference on the Great Lakes Region sought to address what they perceived as the

[34] Maj Gen (ret) Patrick Cammaert and Fiona Blyth, 'Issue Brief, The UN Intervention Brigade in the Democratic Republic of the Congo' (New York: International Peace Institute, 2014) 8 <www.ipinst.org/publication/all-publications/detail/403-the-un-intervention-brigade-in-the-democratic-republic-of-the-congo-.html>.

[35] 'Mali: Ban Voices "Outrage" as UN Peacekeeper Killed in Second Deadly Attack this Month', *UN News Centre* (New York, 8 October 2014).

[36] UNSC Res 2089 (2013) UN Doc S/RES/2089.

twin failures of the government of the DRC and MONUSCO, namely the continued instability in eastern DRC, which presented a threat to regional peace and security. They agreed to deploy a neutral intervention force of approximately 3,500 soldiers (mostly from the Southern African Development Community), to conduct offensive operations to protect civilians and neutralize and disarm rebel groups. The cost and lack of deployment experience hampered regional implementation of the plan, but it coincided with a UN desire to take proactive steps following the fall of Goma in November 2012.[37]

The political support from the region for a robust force was a critical factor in the creation of the Force Intervention Brigade. The same regional consensus was important in the forward-leaning mandate for the UN Multidimensional Integrated Stabilization Mission in Mali (MINUSMA), which was mandated to take over from the African-led International Support Mission to Mali (AFISMA) and assume some of the tasks of the French *Opération Serval*.[38] The regional threat posed by the infiltration of international terrorist groups into the ungoverned territory of northern Mali meant that neighbouring States were willing to let first regional and subsequently international troops take 'active steps' to tackle the armed groups.

C. Rapid deployment

The standing military force envisaged in the UN Charter[39] failed to come into existence, and the UN has no rapidly deployable reserve troops under its authority. Force generation is therefore dependent on UN Member States committing troops for each peacekeeping operation, on a case-by-case basis. Troops for UN peacekeeping operations are drawn from a wide geographic spread of nations, and the level of troop capability, training, and resources varies among contributing countries. Therefore, once the UN has secured agreement to deploy troops on a particular peacekeeping mission, ensuring those troops are of an acceptable standard is a lengthy element of mission planning.

The delay of military deployment to areas of crisis has hampered UN peacekeepers' ability to protect civilians. Research has shown a correlation between rapid deployment and a decrease in attacks against civilians.[40] If peacekeepers are deployed in the early stages of a conflict, there is a greater chance of protecting civilians than if they are deployed once things have escalated. Mobilizing forces quickly, however, remains a major challenge for the UN. The slow pace of troop generation for operations in Mali and the Central African Republic (CAR) in 2014

37 Cammaert and Blyth, see n 34.

38 See UNSC Res 2100 (2013) UN Doc S/RES/2100, paras 7, 18.

39 Charter of the United Nations Charter (adopted 26 June 1945, entered into force 24 October 1945) 1 UNTS XVI, Chapter VII, Articles 43–9.

40 Ford Institute for Human Security, Protecting Civilians; Key Determinants in the Effectiveness of a Peacekeeping Force (Pittsburgh: University of Pittsburgh, 2009) 12 <fordinstitute.pitt.edu/Portals/3/Pub_PDF/Protecting_Civilians_Final_Report.pdf>.

demonstrated the ongoing difficulties of deploying appropriately trained troops and equipment in a timely manner.[41]

Efforts have been made to develop a UN force reserve. In the mid-1990s, the Netherlands, Canada, and Denmark instigated related initiatives. The UN Standing High Readiness Brigade (SHIRBRIG) proposed by Secretary-General Boutros-Ghali in 1995 was briefly activated, and in 2007 the General Assembly Special Committee on Peacekeeping Operations considered options for an Enhanced Rapidly Deployable Capacity (ERDC).[42] The primary reasons why the initiatives were unsuccessful concerned the cost of keeping troops on standby, the delays associated with securing national political approval to deploy troops, and the difficulties associated with moving deployed troops between missions. While the UN has not been able to establish a standby force, the African Union has taken steps to establish a regional rapid response force, with international support.[43]

A rapidly deployable force, able to respond to imminent danger to civilian populations, would be a step change for peacekeeping operations and would undoubtedly save lives. However, until such initiative is achieved, enhancing the UN force generation process to get troops on the ground swiftly is necessary to retain the Organization's credibility and effectively use force to protect civilians.

D. Troop professionalism and troop levels

The effective use of force requires troops with a high level of professionalism, who are well trained and resourced. Currently most UN troops are contributed by countries in South Asia, Africa, and South America, from which some very capable contingents operate under a UN flag.[44] When peacekeeping was first conceived, Western countries were the main contributors; however, those States have rarely contributed military contingents to modern peacekeeping.[45] Irrespective of nationality, inclusion of troops from modern and well-equipped militaries is important to drive up the overall standard of UN peacekeeping and encourage less professional providers to improve their offering in order to be included in the operation.

[41] 'France Criticizes Slow Deployment of Peacekeepers in Mali', *Reuters* (London, 27 October 2014) <reuters.com/article/2014/10/27/us-mali-france-idUSKBN0IG1O920141027>; Samuel Oakford, 'Peacekeepers Greenlighted for CAR, but Mission Will Take Months', *Inter Press Service News Agency* (10 April 2014) <ipsnews.net/2014/04/peacekeepers-greenlighted-car-mission-will-take-months>.

[42] H Peter Langille, 'Options for Rapid Deployment of UN Standing Forces', in Oliver Ramsbotham and Tom Woodhouse (eds), *Peacekeeping and Conflict Resolution* (London: F Cass, 2010) 224.

[43] Reuters, 'African Leaders Create a Rapid Reaction Force', *New York Times* (New York, 28 May 2013) <www.nytimes.com/2013/05/28/world/africa/leaders-create-a-rapid-reaction-force.html>; Pamela Dockins, 'Obama Announces Rapid Response Peacekeeping Plan', *Voice of America* (Washington, DC, 7 August 2014) <www.voanews.com/content/obama-announces-rapid-response-peacekeeping-plan/1973380.html>.

[44] See UN DPKO and UN DFS, UN Peacekeeping Fact Sheet Ranking of Military and Police Contributions to UN Operations, 31 December 2014 <http://www.un.org/en/peacekeeping/contributors/2014/dec14_2.pdf>.

[45] See Alex J Bellamy and Paul D Williams, 'Broadening the Base of United Nations Troop- and Police-Contributing Countries' (New York: International Peace Institute, 2012).

Research indicates that the international composition of peacekeeping forces can impact the level of protection afforded to civilians.[46] Ideally UN peacekeeping missions should include troops from the region, with local knowledge, cultural awareness, and language skills, but these need to be complemented by troops from outside the region, who can check political bias and partiality, as well as troops with a high level of training and operational experience. Incorporating in a peacekeeping force troops from countries neighbouring the host State needs to be addressed with care. The vested interest of such countries may provide a positive incentive for active engagement, but it may also play a negative role, as was experienced in the UN deployment to CAR in 2014.[47]

Troop levels also determine how effectively force can be used to protect civilians. In 2014, the Special Representative of the Secretary-General (SRSG) Kobler, the head of MONUSCO, observed that the Force Intervention Brigade had only 3,000 troops, while in Afghanistan the United States had 150,000 soldiers and considerable financial resources.[48] As the area of the DRC is approximate to that of Western Europe, the ability of 3,000 troops to project force to provide protection to civilians is limited. A study by the Ford Institute found that missions deployed to countries where the ratios of displaced populations per peacekeeper were relatively small were far better able to protect civilians.[49] Similarly, in the cases of the DRC and Sudan, the simple size of a force is irrelevant if consideration of the density of the force compared to the geographic size of the zone of conflict is neglected. In the African conflicts studied, where the ratio of square kilometres per peacekeeper was relatively small, the force was better able to protect civilians and prevent attacks on camps. Therefore, large conflict zones require proportionately sized forces, not simply larger ones.[50]

One of the primary challenges for any troop-contributing country is that their capital must be willing to accept the risks that come with operational deployments. Lieutenant-General Emmanuel Erskine, the head of the UN Interim Force in Lebanon (UNIFIL) in the late 1970s, believed that one of the constraining factors in UN operations in Southern Lebanon at the time was troop-contributing countries' fear of casualties:

> It was my strong and unshakable feeling that TCCs [troop-contributing countries] would be prepared to accommodate a few casualties in the cause of UNIFIL troops defending their mandate, themselves and UN/contingent property, but that casualties outside this spectrum of operational activities could provoke national political difficulties and serve as a catalyst for

46 Ford Institute for Human Security, see n 40, 11–13.

47 Somini Sengupta and Alan Cowell, 'Chad, Amid Criticism, Will Pull Troops From Force in Central Africa', *New York Times* (New York, 3 April 2014) <www.nytimes.com/2014/04/04/world/africa/as-leaders-meet-report-describes-chaos-in-central-african-republic.html?_r=0>.

48 James Verini, 'Should the United Nations Wage War to Keep Peace?' *National Geographic* (Washington, DC, 27 March 2014) <news.nationalgeographic.com/news/2014/03/140327-congo-genocide-united-nations-peacekeepers-m23-kobler-intervention-brigade>.

49 Ford Institute for Human Security, see n 40, 10–13.

50 Ibid., 19.

the collapse of the mission. There was no way TCCs would be prepared to receive sealed coffins from Naqoura at their respective international airports on a daily basis.[51]

That fear of casualties is still very much present. When addressing the Security Council in June 2014, the Permanent Representative of the Hashemite Kingdom of Jordan, HRH Prince Zeid Ra'ad Zeid Al Hussein, said: 'Fewer countries than was the case twenty years ago, will accept casualties when there is no direct national interest at stake for that contributor.'[52]

E. Resources

In order to effectively use force to implement their mandate, UN peacekeepers must have the necessary resources to do so, yet they are progressively being asked to do more with less. The frustration felt by commanders constrained in the execution of their mandate by a lack of resources was candidly expressed by Lieutenant General Francis Briquemont, a Belgian commander of UN troops in Bosnia in 1993: 'I don't read the Security Council resolutions anymore because they don't help me... There is a fantastic gap between the resolutions of the Security Council, the will to execute those resolutions and the means available to commanders in the field.'[53] General Martin Agwai, the first Force Commander in UNAMID, said repeatedly in interviews that he was given 'a mission impossible' due to the lack of vital resources such as utility helicopters.[54] In a 2000 statement, Secretary-General Annan referred to Rwanda and the former Yugoslavia where 'we learned, the hard way, that lightly armed troops in white vehicles and blue helmets are not the solution to every conflict. Sometimes peace has to made—or enforced—before it can be kept.'[55]

The UN has incurred reputational damage when the demands placed on a military contingent have outweighed the resources allocated to it. In 2000, the Panel on United Nations Peacekeeping noted the following in their report (the Brahimi Report): 'If an operation is given a mandate to protect civilians ... it must also be given the specific resources needed to carry out that mandate.'[56] Nearly ten years later, the Security Council stressed 'that mandated protection activities must be given priority in decisions about the use of available capacity and resources, including information and intelligence resources, in the implementation of mandates'.[57] However, such recognition has not resulted in a noticeable change. The fault lies

[51] EA Erskine, *Mission with UNIFIL: An African Soldier's Reflections* (New York: St Martin's Press, 1989) 114–15.

[52] Statement by Zeid Ra'ad Zeid Al Hussein, in UNSC (2014) UN Doc S/PV.7196, 17.

[53] 'U.N. Bosnia Commander Wants More Troops, Fewer Resolutions', *New York Times* (New York, 31 December 1993) <nytimes.com/1993/12/31/world/un-bosnia-commander-wants-more-troops-fewer-resolutions.html>.

[54] Andrew Geoghegan, 'The General's Dilemma' (*ABC News Foreign Correspondent*, 28 October 2008) <www.abc.net.au/foreign/content/oldcontent/s2463805.htm>.

[55] 'Fifty years of United Nations peacekeeping has helped pave the road to peace, Secretary-General tells special commemorative meeting of Assembly' [Press statement] (6 October 1998) Ref SG/SM/6732.

[56] Brahimi Report, see n 2, para. 63.

[57] UNSC Res 1894 (2009) UN Doc S/RES/1894, para. 19.

not only with ambitious mandates provided by the Council but also with troop-contributing countries. Despite the responsibility upon troop-contributing countries to deploy serviceable equipment, vehicles, weapons, and ammunition,[58] contingents often arrive in theatre with glaring deficiencies.[59] This could be improved by greater emphasis being placed on the effect a contingent is required to achieve on the ground, rather than the Secretariat specifying equipment they must bring. If properly implemented, such approach would contract contingents to be resourced to carry out the task assigned and ultimately make units more flexible and effective.

F. Mobility

As attacks on civilian populations typically occur in isolated locations, rapid reaction and resource mobility are critical for effectively countering them. Many missions operate in locations with limited infrastructure and difficult terrain, constrained by rainy seasons or lack of paved roads. Air assets not only provide mobility but can also add to situational awareness and force protection, making both utility and attack helicopters valuable commodities. The UN's Special Report on UNAMID found that '[the mission's] effectiveness is seriously constrained by access restrictions, mobility constraints and shortfalls in the operational capabilities of several troop and police contingents', further noting that nearly half of all protection incidents occurred more than 100 km from the nearest UNAMID base.[60]

G. Training

Civilian protection requires soldiers to approach situations and exercise judgement in a different way from their national war-fighting role. Tactical decisions made by individual peacekeepers or units can save or forfeit lives and have strategic consequences. Many UN protection failures could have been averted with comprehensive training.

There is a continuing lack of knowledge at all levels of command regarding the mission mandate and the rights and obligations to use of force to protect civilians.[61] Scenario-based training is a particularly important element of raising troops' ability to protect civilians. Peacekeepers need practical instruction on the prevention of violence against civilians—including sexual violence—as well as basic understanding of human rights and humanitarian law obligations. Scarred by the

[58] Manual on Policies and Procedures Concerning the Reimbursement and Control of Contingent-Owned Equipment of Troop/Police Contributors Participating in Peacekeeping Missions (COE Manual), in UNGA (2011) UN Doc A/C.5/66/8, chapter 1, paras 12–13; chapter 3, para. 11.

[59] Alex J Bellamy and Paul D Williams, *Understanding Peacekeeping* (Cambridge: Polity Press, 2010) 63–5.

[60] UNSC, 'Special Report of the Secretary-General on the Review of the African Union–United Nations Hybrid Operation in Darfur' (2014) UN Doc S/2014/138, paras 14, 34, and 35.

[61] Based on the authors' visits and lectures to numerous peacekeeping missions and peacekeeping training centres over the past five years.

mistakes of the past, the Security Council adopted resolution 1894 (2009), which requested the development of an operational concept, mission-wide planning, and training on the protection of civilians.[62] A tactical training manual to be released by DPKO is a welcome development.[63] While the UN Secretariat may develop training modules and make them mandatory, national armies retain the responsibility for training their soldiers.

H. Leadership

In multidimensional peacekeeping operations, the senior leadership typically comprises the Head of Mission or SRSG, supported by one or two Deputy SRSGs (one responsible for the mission's political engagement and the other for the UN's humanitarian and development activity in the area); the Head of the Military Component (the Force Commander); the Head of the Police Component; and the Director of Mission Support.

The success and failure of the protection of civilians by UN peacekeeping missions has often been dependent on the vision of the Force Commander and the mission leadership in interpreting the mission mandate.[64] If the Force Commander and his subordinates are conservative in their reading of the mandate phrase 'all necessary means to protect civilians', whether due to national restrictions, experience, or personality, then the use of force will be limited and the adverse may also apply. The extent to which these variables impact operational and tactical decision-making should not be underestimated. For civilian lives to be protected by the use of force, commanders must be prepared to make judgements based on local knowledge and a clear understanding of the mission's mandate and ROE.[65] The effective execution of command responsibilities would be facilitated by the UN limiting national caveats and holding troop-contributing countries accountable for mandate implementation.[66]

In a 2014 Security Council debate on the protection of civilians in armed conflict, the Jordanian delegation suggested that the Secretariat should establish a UN field commanders' academy to instil young commanders with 'the sort of leadership that could be required of them'.[67] The Permanent Representative indicated that 'with the right commanders ... we can better ensure UN peacekeeping will

[62] UNSC Res 1894 (2009) UN Doc S/RES/1894.

[63] Statement of Ioannis Vrailas, in UNSC (2014) UN Doc S/PV.7109, 46.

[64] In a multidimensional peacekeeping operation, the senior leadership typically comprises the Head of Mission or SRSG (SRSG), supported by one or two Deputy SRSGs, one responsible for the mission's political engagement and the other for the UN's humanitarian and development activity in the area, as well as the Head of the Military Component (Force Commander), the Head of the Police Component, and the Director of Mission Support (DMS).

[65] Julie Reynaert, *MONUC/MONUSCO and Civilian Protection in the Kivus* (Antwerp: International Peace Information Service, February 2011) 16–17 <www.ipisresearch.be/publications_detail.php?id=327>.

[66] For further discussion on the accountability of troop-contributing countries, see the chapters by Mona Khalil, Chapter 9, and Siobhán Wills, Chapter 10, in this volume.

[67] Statement by Zeid Ra'ad Zeid Al Hussein, in UNSC (2014) UN Doc S/PV.7196, 18.

remain the flagship activity of this organization'.[68] Since 2011, newly appointed Heads of Military Components have undertaken an intensive orientation course, during which they are mentored by a former Force Commander on the challenges of command in modern peacekeeping operations.[69] Establishing an institution stretching across the levels of command, as suggested, could ensure a consistent level of training and universal doctrine, leading to more homogenous forces capable of greater interoperability.

I. Intelligence

The use of force to protect civilians requires, in the first instance, credible and timely intelligence to ensure early warning of forthcoming attacks. Missions have introduced a range of information-gathering techniques that vary from the low-tech Community Alert Networks (CAN) to the high-tech use of aerial surveillance vehicles. In the DRC, MONUSCO has provided mobile phones on closed networks to community focal points to create a direct, 24-hours-a-day link to Community Liaison Assistants or MONUSCO commanders for the purpose of relaying information in case of an outbreak of violence.[70] Linking the mission to more than 225 communities, the mobile network facilitates communication between the Force and the local population and authorities.[71] The deployment of unarmed aerial surveillance vehicles in the DRC has also improved situational awareness. Such surveillance capabilities enable information to be gathered on cross-border smuggling, trafficking, and the movement of internally displaced persons and armed groups. In Mali, the Dutch contribution to MINUSMA has included surveillance equipment and an analysis cell.[72]

Member States have been reluctant, however, to supply UN missions with high-quality information and intelligence capabilities. Even the term 'intelligence' is often avoided in UN peacekeeping fora, although it is less sensitive than was the case fifteen years ago. As Victoria Holt and Glyn Taylor highlighted, the UN identified 'the need for better information and intelligence, specifically in relation to the protection of civilians yet . . . most missions do not have sufficient capacity to collect and analyse the information'.[73] Joint Mission Analysis Centres (JMACs) and equivalents, which are integrated information assessment hubs, are important for

[68] Ibid.

[69] Statement of Under-Secretary-General for Peacekeeping Operations, Hervé Ladsous, to the Fourth Committee of the General Assembly (New York, 1 November 2013) <www.un.org/en/peacekeeping/articles/4thc_dpkousg_01112012.pdf>.

[70] Willmot and Mamiya, see n 21, 72.

[71] UNSC, 'Report of the Secretary-General on the United Nations Organization Stabilization Mission in the Democratic Republic of the Congo' (2013) UN Doc S/2013/288, para. 22.

[72] See Colum Lynch, 'The Dutch Double Down in Mali', *Foreign Policy* (Washington, DC, 1 December 2013) <foreignpolicy.com/2013/12/01/dutch-double-down-in-mali/#sthash.MpyuQo0F.dpbs>; David Lewis, 'Dutch Special Forces in Mali Tackle Changing Threat—Minister', *Reuters* (London, 9 July 2014) <uk.reuters.com/article/2014/07/09/uk-mali-security-dutch-idUKKBN0FE1YS20140709>.

[73] Holt and Taylor with Kelly, see n 25, 9.

the collection, analysis, and dissemination of intelligence within the mission. However, information security is also a real challenge for missions composed of soldiers and civilians from dozens of nations who may have a variety of motivations for releasing information to other organizations, the media, or governments.

J. Host State co-operation

The deployment of a peacekeeping mission to protect civilians is often a result of the national government being unable or unwilling to fulfil its responsibilities to protect its population.[74] Peacekeeping mandates therefore often include an imperative to build the capacity of host State security forces.[75] Building host State security force capacity aims to transfer responsibility for security from the mission to the government once stability returns, but capable host State troops can also act as force multipliers for the mission's troops. Equally, a lack of host State capability can undermine mission efforts, as MONUSCO discovered when 7,000 Congolese army soldiers fled Goma, abandoning it to the rebel M23 group, in November 2012.[76] As discussed further in Chapter 18, building host State protection capacities can be challenging.[77]

Maintaining a workable relationship with the host State has also been difficult for a number of peacekeeping operations. In Darfur, poor relations have limited the peacekeeping mission's ability to operate.[78] The Sudanese government has hampered operations by limiting the mission's freedom of movement, denying visas, refusing troops from particular countries, and failing to authorize flight clearance for aircraft. As in other operational theatres, the host government is a party in the conflict and a potential spoiler of the peace process.[79] Many of the gravest attacks against the civilian population were conducted by Sudanese firepower and aircraft, yet the mission leadership's decision to appease the host government in order to avoid further restrictions on operations has meant that atrocities have gone unreported to the Security Council and the civilian population remains unprotected.[80]

K. Peace process

The use of force must be accompanied by a credible and comprehensive peace process, addressing the root causes of conflict to prevent renewed instability.

[74] UNGA, 'Report of the Secretary-General, implementing the Responsibility to Protect' (2009) UN Doc A/63/677, paras 40–3.

[75] UNSC Res 1996 (2011) UN Doc S/RES/1996 (2011), paras 3 (a), (b)(iv), (c); UNSC Res 2098 (2013) UN Doc S/RES/2098, paras 10, 11 (b), 14 (a), 15 (c), 15 (d), 20.

[76] Nick Long, 'UN Defends Performance in Eastern DRC', *Voice of America* (Washington, DC, 22 November 2012) <m.voanews.com/a/1550868.html>.

[77] See Lise Grande, Chapter 18 in this volume.

[78] Colum Lynch, 'Special Report into the Darfur Genocide, Part I: They Just Stood Watching', *Foreign Policy* (Washington, DC, 7 April 2014) <foreignpolicy.com/articles/2014/04/07/special_report_darfur_united_nations_peacekeeping_investigation>.

[79] Government-backed militias in Darfur continue to displace and massacre civilians. See UNSC, 'Report of the Secretary-General on the African Union–United Nations Hybrid Operation in Darfur' (2014) UN Doc S/2014/279, paras 7–14.

[80] Colum Lynch, 'Special Report into the Darfur Genocide, Part III: A Mission that Was Set Up to Fail', *Foreign Policy* (Washington, DC, 8 April 2014) <foreignpolicy.com/articles/2014/04/09/special_report_darfur_united_nations_peacekeeping_investigation_part_3>.

Political agreement is necessary to return legitimate authority and ensure stability, which cannot be enforced by military means. International troops can use force to clear villages of rebel groups, forcibly disarm, and deter attacks, but without a peace process, the rebels will return after the troops leave. The presence of the Force Intervention Brigade in the DRC in 2013, for instance, played an important role in neutralizing the threat from rebel groups. However, the withdrawal of international political support for the groups, combined with a comprehensive dialogue, mutually reinforced the military action. Indeed, all modern peacekeeping missions recognize the primary importance of political engagement.[81]

V. Political Challenges

The UN, through the Security Council, authorizes the use of force to protect civilians in peacekeeping operations under Chapter VII of the Charter. However, mandates do not always specifically mention the use of force; instead, the euphemism 'all necessary means' is used. This constructive ambiguity affords Member States and troop-contributing countries the latitude to implement the mandate within national parameters, interpreting rather than adhering to explicit language. While the ambiguity of the 'all necessary means' formulation can be useful for securing Member State agreement to the mandate, it results in a lack of clarity regarding the expectation to use force for mandate implementation. While some consider that 'United Nations peacekeepers—troops or police—who witness violence against civilians should be presumed to be authorized to stop it in support of basic United Nations principles',[82] others consider the same principles to circumscribe the use of force. It remains unclear to what extent pre-emptive or proactive force is authorized or expected, and if the use of force is at all obligatory.[83]

When the MONUSCO Force Intervention Brigade was created, in addition to authorizing 'all necessary means to protect civilians', the mandate included authorization to conduct 'targeted offensive operations'. While the additional instruction was intended to remove any room for interpretation and any ambiguity, it may have created confusion in other missions regarding the scope of the original language. The original mandate language and the ROE already provided sufficient authority to use force: the issue was that the *will* to use it was lacking.

The 2014 OIOS report found that 'the reasons [why peacekeeping missions were not intervening with force when civilians were under attack] include different views in the Security Council and among troop-contributing countries and, importantly, a *de facto* dual line of command involving mission leadership and troop-contributing countries that regulates the use of force by missions'.[84] This was illustrated in eastern DRC in 2003 when peacekeepers deployed to Bunia did not act to stop a massacre of more than 400 civilians because they 'were convinced that they

[81] Capstone Doctrine, see n 8, 23.

[82] Brahimi Report, see n 2, x.

[83] See Siobhán Wills, Chapter 10 in this volume.

[84] OIOS Report, see n 16, 2.

were not operating under Chapter VII and therefore assumed that they were not allowed to use force. Instead of undertaking action the peacekeepers waited for authorization from [their national] parliament.'[85]

In order to effectively protect civilians, military operations need to occur, in part, before the threat becomes imminent. Such preventive operations require political will at the strategic and operational levels. When political will is not forthcoming, peacekeepers arrive too late to protect. In addition to the tragic humanitarian consequences of delayed action, the reputational damage to the UN is often greatest when it has failed to act. As the Brahimi Report noted, 'no failure did more damage to the standing and credibility of United Nations peacekeeping in the 1990s than its reluctance to distinguish victim from aggressor'.[86]

The policy framework for using force to protect civilians is still evolving and the scale of the UN's failures to physically protect civilians has led some commanders and commentators to conclude that not only are peacekeeping operations operationally justified in using force, they are also morally compelled to do so.[87] However, moral compulsion cannot substitute for 'clear, credible and achievable mandates' and 'comprehensive operational guidance', as called for in the Brahimi Report.[88] Peacekeepers face many challenges in the implementation of their mandates; the lack of clear consensus of when and how to use military force remains one of them.

VI. Future of the Use of Force in Peacekeeping Operations

If the use of force to protect civilians is to remain a viable option for the UN, the Organization will require well trained and capable troops, adequate resources, timely intelligence, political will, and for contingents to be held to account. Peacekeeping mandates have become more aggressive, and the adversaries that peacekeepers face have grown more dangerous. By taking proactive and pre-emptive action, the UN risks being increasingly targeted by armed groups. But despite this, while many peacekeepers have died in the course of their duty, the DPKO data suggests that 'no casualties have resulted from interposition between a vulnerable population and hostile elements attacking civilians'.[89]

Having capable troops that can be rapidly deployed to protect civilians in volatile situations is also essential. In the absence of a UN reserve force, mission capability to protect civilians could be enhanced by greater inter-mission co-operation, allowing missions to share scarce resources when faced with sudden crises. This would enable a surge capacity to quickly insert troops with current operational experience into critical conflict areas, as occurred in 2011 when the UN Mission in

[85] Reynaert, see n 65, 15.
[86] Brahimi Report, see n 2, ix.
[87] Ibid., para. 50.
[88] Ibid.
[89] OIOS Report, see n 16, para. 20.

Liberia (UNMIL) reinforced the UN operation in Côte d'Ivoire (UNOCI) with Pakistani troops and Ukrainian attack helicopters.[90]

The challenges with the UN's use of force are multiple and in some cases, where more aggressive or pre-emptive military action has been necessary, have been sidestepped and delegated to regional organizations or coalitions of Member States. This has been the case in Somalia where the African Union has led the kinetic fight against Al-Shabaab, and in Afghanistan where a North Atlantic Treaty Organization (NATO) coalition countered the threat from the Taliban. In several instances, the African Union, authorized by the Security Council, has led the initial, offensive phase of a deployment, and then handed over to a UN peacekeeping mission.[91] The international community will need to decide whether it is preferable for the UN to continue outsourcing the use of force to regional organizations and coalitions of willing states because the UN peacekeeping instrument is incapable of effectively addressing such challenges, or to improve the capability of the UN peacekeeping instrument.

VII. Conclusion

Although a different manifestation of the use of force than that envisaged by the drafters of the UN Charter, peacekeeping has evolved as a core activity of the UN, and one of the Council's primary tools for addressing threats to international peace and security. With the evolution of peacekeeping has come a recognition that when peaceful means fail, force can be used to create a secure and stable environment to allow space for the implementation of a political solution to a conflict.[92] While a political solution may be reached without the use of force, the use of force will not resolve a conflict in the absence of a political solution.

Deploying military force to support a peace process can prevent political activities being derailed by spoilers. While peace cannot be imposed by force, it can be reinforced by the physical security that the use of force can create. UN commentator Richard Gowan observed the value of Brazilian marines determinedly cleaning up the slums of Haiti, and Indian and Pakistani troops and attack helicopters pursuing militia groups in the eastern DRC.[93] UN peacekeeping has also played an important stabilization role in Sierra Leone, Liberia, and Côte d'Ivoire, where the use of force by peacekeepers has led to significant decreases in civilian deaths.[94]

[90] United Nations, 'UN Security Council Meetings Coverage: Force Commanders Dwell on New Technology, Pre-deployment Training, Inter-mission Cooperation in Briefing Security Council on Peacekeeping Operations' (26 June 2013) UN Doc SC/11047.

[91] For example, the African-led International Support Mission to Mali (AFISMA) preceded the UN Multidimensional Integrated Stabilization Mission in Mali (MINUSMA), see UNSC Res 2100 (2013) UN Doc S/RES/2100, para. 7, and the African-led Support Mission to the Central African Republic (MISCA) preceded the UN Multidimensional Integrated Stabilization Mission in the Central African Republic (MINUSCA), see UNSC Res 2149 (2014) UN Doc S/RES/2149, para. 21.

[92] Capstone, see n 8, 23.

[93] Richard Gowan, 'Send in the Blue Helmets', *The World Today* (London, June 2014) <wiltonpark.org.uk/wp-content/uploads/UN-on-the-frontline-Richard-Gowan.pdf>.

[94] See generally, Willmot and Mamiya, n 5.

The strategic authorization to use force by the Security Council does not mean that operationally it should always be used. The judgement and professionalism of soldiers at all levels is critical. Officers throughout the chain of command need to have a thorough understanding of the mission mandate and ROE in order to effectively exercise judgement on the use of force for the protection of civilians.

The review of UN peacekeeping currently underway[95] should address some of the challenges to the protection of civilians by UN peacekeepers outlined herein. Above all, effective protection requires leadership and political commitment from the Security Council, the Secretariat, the mission, and troop-contributing countries. Without this, the UN may once again find itself 'standing by, in impotent horror, while the most appalling crimes [are] committed'.[96]

[95] Statement of Secretary-General Ban Ki-moon, in UNSC (2014) UN Doc S/PV.7196, 3.

[96] United Nations, 'Press Release: Fifty Years of United Nations Peacekeeping has Helped Pave the Road to Peace, Secretary-General tells Special Commemorative Meeting of Assembly' (6 October 2000) UN Doc SG/SM/6732.

15

The Utility of Force for Protecting Civilians

Stian Kjeksrud

I. Introduction

This chapter investigates how military force has been utilized to successfully protect civilians in United Nations (UN) peacekeeping operations. The UN Office of Internal Oversight Services (OIOS) recently found 'a persistent pattern of peacekeeping operations not intervening with force when civilians are under attack'.[1] Several explanations were identified, including

> different views in the Security Council and among troop-contributing countries, a *de facto* dual line of command of mission leadership and troop-contributing countries, a weak understanding of peacekeepers' obligations to act when host governments are unable or unwilling to protect civilians, a perception among peacekeepers of having insufficient resources to respond to force with force and a concern about possible penalties if their use of force is judged inappropriate.

Although met with some internal criticism regarding the validity of its findings, the report provided profound insights, the consequences of which are now being debated at the highest levels of the UN.[2]

While the OIOS report found that UN peacekeepers have mostly shied away from using force, it did not provide any insight on the effectiveness of military protection efforts when force had been employed. UN peacekeepers have used military force to protect on several occasions. In some instances they have done so successfully, while in others they have failed.

Investigating UN operations in Africa between 1992 and 2011, Lisa Hultman, Jacob Kathman, and Megan Shannon found that an increased number of UN peacekeepers correlated with reduced battlefield deaths.[3] This chapter, however, asserts that being present is not enough; understanding how peacekeepers can best meet the specific threat posed is critical for improving civilian protection.

[1] United Nations General Assembly (UNGA), 'Report of the Office of Internal Oversight Services, Evaluation of the Implementation and Results of Protection of Civilians Mandates in United Nations Peacekeeping Operations' (2014) UN Doc A/68/787, 1 (OIOS Report).

[2] Security Council Report, 'Public Briefing by UN Force Commanders' (*What's in Blue*, 8 October 2014) <www.whatsinblue.org/2014/10/public-briefing-by-un-force-commanders.php>.

[3] Lisa Hultman, Jacob Kathman, and Megan Shannon, 'Beyond Keeping Peace: United Nations Effectiveness in the Midst of Fighting' (2014) 108 American Political Science Rev 737–53.

The chapter seeks to develop insights about the utility of the use of force to protect civilians, drawing on an assessment of 188 military protection operations across ten UN peacekeeping missions in Africa during the period 1999–2014.[4] The majority of the information has been extracted from reports of the UN Secretary-General to the Security Council, which are seen as 'the most regular and visible reporting on mission operations'.[5] Based on these reports, a dataset has been developed, which captures most of the cases where UN military personnel have used force to protect. The examination is limited to African conflicts, where the majority of UN operations have been deployed over the past fifteen years, and where almost all have been mandated to protect civilians. It is also in Africa that some of the most complex protection challenges have arisen.

The chapter provides an overview assessment of the success of protection operations, based on the actual outcome compared with a counterfactual. Those findings are then examined against a theory developed by Alexander Beadle, in which he asserts that unlike traditional warfare, in which militaries are primarily trained to fight an enemy directly, successful protection operations rely on a different logic, requiring a more nuanced understanding of how and why perpetrators attack civilians.[6] This analysis provides a picture of how often UN peacekeepers have effectively matched their use of force with that of the perpetrator, and whether it resulted in a successful outcome. The chapter then proceeds to identify the most common civilian protection scenarios encountered by the UN in Africa, and the use of force most effective to combat those. Finally, three brief case studies offer additional insights to the conditions favouring effective military protection.

The analysis presented in this chapter seeks to move beyond the debate of why the UN seldom uses force to protect and whether it should. Instead, it examines how force can be best utilized for the protection of civilians, finding that the UN is successful in using force to protect civilians in fewer than four out of ten operations. There is significant room for improvement. One aspect of improving the effectiveness of the use of force for the protection of civilians is the selection of appropriate countermeasures, based on a proper understanding of the perpetrators' methods and intent.

[4] These are United Nations Multidimensional Integrated Stabilization Mission in Mali (MINUSMA), United Nations Mission in the Republic of South Sudan (UNMISS), United Nations Interim Security Force for Abyei (UNISFA), United Nations Organization Mission in the Democratic Republic of the Congo (MONUC)/United Nations Organization Stabilization Mission in the Democratic Republic of the Congo (MONUSCO) (together counted as one mission), United Nations Mission in the Central African Republic and Chad (MINURCAT), African Union/United Nations Hybrid operation in Darfur (UNAMID), United Nations Mission in the Sudan (UNMIS), United Nations Operation in Côte d'Ivoire (UNOCI), United Nations Mission in Liberia (UNMIL), and United Nations Mission in Sierra Leone (UNAMSIL). The UN mission in the Central African Republic (CAR) also has a protection mandate, but there had been no official reporting from the Secretary-General on the activities of this operation at the time of writing.

[5] UNGA, 'Evaluation of the Implementation and Results of Protection of Civilians Mandates in United Nations Peacekeeping Operations' (2014) UN Doc A/68/787, para. 16.

[6] Alexander William Beadle, *Finding the 'Utility of Force to Protect'—Towards a Theory on Protection of Civilians* (Kjeller: Norwegian Defence Research Establishment (FFI), 2011); Alexander William Beadle, *Protection of Civilians—Military Planning Scenarios and Implications* (Kjeller: Norwegian Defence Research Establishment (FFI), 2014).

II. Using Force to Protect

The insights of General (retired) Rupert Smith, in his seminal work *The Utility of Force: The Art of War in the Modern World*, provide the first steps towards understanding how military force can be employed more wisely in contemporary intra-State conflict.[7] One of his core arguments is that in 'wars amongst the people' the appropriate 'functions of force' must be employed in order to achieve the intended effect. Smith states that military force has only four functions in achieving goals in current operations:

1. **Amelioration.** When troops assist in delivering humanitarian aid, put up refugee camps, observe ceasefires, etc. Military force is only employed in self-defence. Traditional UN peacekeeping would fall into this category. Tasks such as manning observation posts and checkpoints, patrolling, outreach, and engagement would be included in this category.[8]
2. **Containment.** When military forces prevent something, such as arms, planes, and troops, from spreading or passing through a barrier. This can be done through maintaining arms embargos and no-fly zones. This category would include inter-positioning UN forces between armed opponents, or between attackers and a civilian population, as well as the establishment of buffer zones. Rules of engagement would usually limit and control the use of force.
3. **Deterrence/coercion.** Involves a 'wider use of force', according to Smith. Military forces are used to pose or carry out a threat, in order to 'change or form' the opposition's intentions. When force is actually employed, it is used to coerce. UN forces sometimes undertake cordon and search operations, and perform joint military operations with host nation security forces, both of which would fall into this category. Such activities are based on the logic of deterrence and potential coercion as a last resort.
4. **Destruction.** Using military force to attack the opposing combatants in order to destroy their ability to achieve their objective. This is a rare function of force in UN missions. However, the Force Intervention Brigade, which is part of the UN operation in the Democratic Republic of the Congo (DRC), is mandated to 'neutralize' armed groups through 'targeted offensive operations'.[9] Destruction was part of the UN's operations against the insurgent group M23, in the DRC, in 2013.

Beadle asserts that knowing why and how armed groups use violence against civilians is necessary in order to identify the appropriate countermeasures.[10]

[7] Rupert Smith, *The Utility of Force: The Art of War in the Modern World* (New York: Penguin Books, 2006).

[8] UN Department of Peacekeeping Operations (UN DPKO) and UN Department of Field Support (UN DFS), *United Nations Infantry Battalion Manual: Volume 1* (New York: United Nations).

[9] UN Security Council (UNSC) Resolution (Res) 2098 (2013) UN Doc S/RES/2098, para. 12(b).

[10] Beadle (2011), see n 6; and see Beadle (2014), n 6.

Drawing on Smith's four functions of force, he argues that perpetrators employ four 'types of violence' against civilians:

1. **Impairment.** Perpetrators foster insecurity that threatens civilian life without actually physically targeting them. They may impair civilian security by virtue of their threatening presence or by using civilians as human shields.
2. **Incitement.** Violence is used against civilians to spread fear and insecurity, including through improvised explosive devices and suicide bombers. Perpetrators are not seeking to kill as many civilians as possible, but rather to undermine the government's ability to protect its own citizens.
3. **Deterrence/coercion.** Violence and brutality are used to change civilian behaviour, often to deter collaboration with the opposition.
4. **Destruction.** Violence is used to directly destroy civilians (or civilian installations), such as during genocide and mass killings.[11]

Beadle's core argument is that there is little utility of force to be found if the function of force employed by the protector does not match the type of violence chosen by the perpetrator.[12] For example, if a perpetrator aims to 'destroy' an ethnic group, there is little utility in the protector choosing to 'ameliorate' the situation by merely supporting the delivery of humanitarian aid. In this situation, greater utility of force would be derived from 'destruction' of the perpetrator's ability to conduct mass killings. Conversely, if a perpetrator uses 'impairment' or 'incitement' to undermine the legitimacy of a government, using 'coercive' or 'destructive' force against them would probably lead to stronger incentives to scale up attacks against civilians. Instead, 'amelioration' and 'containment' are better suited to protect civilians in such scenarios. Consequently, to maximize the utility of force, protectors must *match* the perpetrator's violence against civilians.[13] Only then will protectors be able to effectively influence the will and ability of the perpetrator to attack. The following section explores these theoretical claims further by applying them to a comprehensive dataset of protection operations in UN peacekeeping missions.

III. Measuring Protection

A. Limitations

As the progress of stabilization operations worldwide has at times proven ambiguous, measuring the effects of military efforts has become increasingly important, although it remains challenging. Assessing the impact of the use of force by UN peacekeepers carries particular difficulties due to inconsistent levels of political support; the composition of UN missions; the principles, mandate caveats, and practical limitations of UN peacekeeping; and the paucity of reliable information.[14]

[11] Beadle (2011), see n 6, 27. [12] Beadle (2014), see n 6. [13] Ibid.

[14] Thierry Tardy, 'A Critique of Robust Peacekeeping in Contemporary Peace Operations' (2011) Intl Peacekeeping 18(2) 152–67; Stian Kjeksrud, *Matching Robust Ambitions with Robust Action in*

As detailed in other chapters in this volume, political support for the protection of civilians by UN peacekeepers plays a critical role in the effectiveness of mandate implementation.[15] Influential factors include: support from the Security Council for robust mandate execution; support from troop-contributing countries for their military personnel to put themselves at risk and use force; support from the host State to facilitate the mission carrying out its work, or at least not obstruct it doing so; and financial support from the General Assembly Fifth (Administrative and Budgetary) Committee, translating into crucial resources. The level of political support for the protection of civilians can vary across missions. Additionally, regional political initiatives can prove particularly powerful. For example, the establishment of the MONUSCO Force Intervention Brigade was premised on a South African Development Community (SADC) initiative.[16]

Resources are also a critical factor. Despite the fact that the UN deploys more than 100,000 uniformed personnel to some of the world's harshest conflict environments, UN peacekeeping suffers from significant practical limitations. The Organization lacks key capabilities, such as proper intelligence and sufficient airlift—critical enablers which many military organizations take for granted.

UN peacekeeping operations are mostly organized as multidimensional integrated missions, comprising a range of components, including military, police, political affairs, civil affairs, and human rights. Almost all mission components play a role in protecting civilians.[17] Most UN missions work alongside a UN Country Team, comprising humanitarian and development agencies, many of which are also involved in protection efforts.[18] Given the combined activities of multiple UN actors, it is difficult to isolate the effects of military force on civilian protection, especially at the operational level. At the tactical level, however, it is easier to identify the immediate impact of a military intervention.

Due to the traditional principles of UN peacekeeping,[19] there are also limitations upon what UN military components are expected to achieve in terms of protecting civilians. According to the principles, they are supposed to operate impartially, with the consent of the host State, and only use force at the tactical

UNPeace Operations—Towards a Conceptual Overstretch? (Kjeller: Norwegian Defence Research Establishment (FFI), 2009).

15 See Mona Ali Khalil, Bruno Stagno Ugarte, Jean-Marie Guéhenno, and Fiona Blyth and Patrick Cammaert, in this volume.

16 For information on the Peace, Security and Cooperation Framework for the Democratic Republic of the Congo and the region, see UNSC (2013) UN Doc S/2013/131, and 'MONUSCO Background' (*United Nations Peacekeeping*, Undated) <www.un.org/en/peacekeeping/missions/monusco/background.shtml>.

17 UN DPKO and UN DFS, *Protection of Civilians—Coordinating Mechanisms in UN Peacekeeping Missions—Comparative Study and Toolkit* (New York: United Nations, 2012) <www.peacekeepingbestpractices.unlb.org/PBPS/Library/Protection%20of%20Civilians%20Coordination%20Mechanisms%20in%20UN%20Peacekeeping%20Missions,%20DPKO-DFS%20Comparative%20Study%20and%20Toolkit%20(2012).pdf>.

18 'UN at Country Level' (*United Nations Development Group*, 18 February 2015) <undg.org/home/country-teams/unct-home>.

19 UN DPKO and UN DFS, *United Nations Peacekeeping Operations: Principles and Guidelines* (New York: United Nations, 2008).

level, in self-defence or in defence of the mandate.[20] Additionally, UN mandates usually include caveats that direct peacekeepers only to protect civilians 'under imminent threat of physical violence' and 'within [the mission's] capacities and areas of deployment'.[21]

Reliable statistics on the conflict areas in which the UN is involved are difficult to obtain, and there is a lack of systematic reporting on the performance and outcomes of UN military protection efforts.[22] The DPKO Office of Military Affairs does hold detailed situational reporting on the activities of UN military contingents, however, the analysis in this chapter is limited to that information publicly available through Secretary-General's Reports. While the day-to-day military activities in many missions, such as patrolling and manning checkpoints and observation posts, may have a deterrent effect on potential perpetrators of violence against civilians, if there is nothing significant to report, often information on such activities is not included in public reporting. However, as the UN is sensitive to the use of military force, it is likely that the majority of operations in which UN military personnel actually used force to protect have been reported to the Security Council through the Secretary-General's reports.

A further challenge for measuring the outcome of any protection effort is the need to assess outcomes counterfactually. This analysis takes on the challenge of comparing the actual outcome of an operation with what is likely to have happened if UN forces had not intervened, or had not been there at all.

B. Methodology

In light of the foregoing challenges, it is only possible to estimate the effectiveness of military efforts to protect. The assessment of UN protection operations in this chapter is based on a combination of counterfactual reasoning and case-specific knowledge. The typical *modus operandi* of any given perpetrator is used as a baseline for assessing how a situation would have developed if the UN had not intervened. This approach clearly has limitations, and the findings must, therefore, be considered in that context.

Only a small subset of the spectrum of military operations undertaken by UN peacekeeping forces are included in the dataset. UN military activity is considered a 'protection operation,' and included, when the following criteria are met:

[20] The 'tactical level' is the level of warfare 'where we find battles, engagements and fights'. Smith points out that the 'essence of all tactics is fire and movement, and the basic tactical dilemma is to find the correct balance between how much effort to apply to striking the opponent to achieve the objective and how much to countering his blows'. It is exactly this dilemma that UN military personnel face when trying to protect a civilian population threatened by a perpetrator of violence, with the additional element of a third actor—the civilians themselves.

[21] UNGA, 'Evaluation of the Implementation and Results of Protection of Civilians Mandates in United Nations Peacekeeping Operations' (2014) UN Doc A/68/787.

[22] Alex Dewaal, 'The UN's Darfur "Cover-Up" and the Need for Reliable Conflict Data' (*Reinventing Peace*, 7 November 2014) <sites.tufts.edu/reinventingpeace/2014/11/07/the-uns-darfur-cover-up-and-the-need-for-reliable-conflict-data/?utm_content=buffer3e66f&utm_medium=social&utm_source=twitter.com&utm_campaign=buffer>.

1. UN forces are deployed by the Security Council with a specific mandate to protect civilians, either unilaterally or in support of host State or regional security forces;
2. Armed groups constitute an imminent physical threat to civilians; and,
3. One or more of Smith's functions of force (amelioration, containment, deterrence/coercion, or destruction) are employed by UN forces for the purpose of protection.

Only operations in which the threat or use of force was employed are included. Those situations where peacekeepers were mandated to protect but failed to deploy are not incorporated in the analysis. In 2010, for example, at least 387 civilians were raped by combatants in North Kivu, in the DRC, without UN intervention.[23] This study focuses not on when and why force is used or not used, but rather, when force is used, how it is effectively employed to protect.

In assessing each protection operation the following questions are addressed:

1. What is likely to have happened to the civilians under threat if UN military forces had not intervened to protect at that time?
2. How does the expected outcome compare to the actual outcome following the UN military intervention?

For the sake of simplicity, a dichotomous variable is employed, with operations being assessed as 'mostly successful' or 'mostly unsuccessful'.

Operations are assessed as 'mostly successful' where UN forces effectively protect a high level of potential victims in a specific area at a certain time. This could occur, for example, when a perpetrator is denied access to a contested area by the UN's use of force. To illustrate, in late January 2013, following a period of heightened cattle rustling and accompanying violence against civilians in Unity, Lakes, and Warrap states in South Sudan, over 3,000 armed Nuer youth mobilized, purportedly to launch cattle raids in Warrap and Lakes States.[24] An armed group of that size, in an area where communal tensions were already high, presented a direct and imminent threat to civilians. The UN mission in South Sudan (UNMISS), in collaboration with the Sudan People's Liberation Army (SPLA) and South Sudan Police Service (SSPS), reacted immediately and managed to push the armed youths back to their places of origin. The military efforts included blocking food and water supplies to the Nuer armed group, making further raids unfeasible. Based on the *modus operandi* of cattle raiders in that conflict, it is highly likely that such a raiding party would have led to many casualties among civilians.

Operations are assessed as 'mostly unsuccessful' where UN forces fail to effectively protect a high level of potential victims in a specific area at a certain time,

[23] MONUSCO and the UN Office of the High Commissioner for Human Rights (UN OHCHR), *Final Report of the Fact-finding Missions of the United Nations Joint Human Rights Office into the Mass Rapes and other Human Rights Violations Committed by a Coalition of Armed Groups Along the Kibua-Mpofi Axis in Walikale Territory, North Kivu, From 30 july to 2 August 2010* (July 2011) 4 <www.ohchr.org/Documents/Countries/CD/BCNUDHRapportViolsMassifsKibuaMpofi_en.pdf>.

[24] UNSC (2013) UN Doc S/2013/140.

despite a military intervention. In many cases, such failures occur because UN forces and/or their local security partners are not able to respond in time or the tactics employed have little effect on civilian security. For example, in early May 2013, more than 250 Ngok Dinka youth arrived in Abyei town and began causing unrest.[25] Misseriya traders, who usually sold their goods in the Abyei market, had fled the previous night. Troops from the UN mission in Abyei (UNISFA) and Ngok Dinka civil society representatives intervened after the fact to calm the situation. However, they were not able to deter the youths from burning down the market. Later that evening, another group of Ngok Dinka destroyed most of the Abyei town mosque.[26] No casualties were reported arising from these incidents, mostly due to the fact that the potential victims had saved themselves by fleeing in advance. In this instance, the military response of UNISFA was not particularly effective, resulting in widespread material destruction of the market and the mosque, and a high number of civilians fleeing from physical threats.

In many cases the outcome of a protection operation is complicated. To assist the determination of its success, the assessment methodology relies not only on the specific outcome of a given case, but also on how each case compares to others in the dataset. To illustrate, the following case describes a situation from 2005 in the DRC, where UN efforts to protect civilians with military force were assessed as 'mostly unsuccessful' despite the fact that many civilians were probably protected. In July 2005 the UN Organization Mission in the DRC (MONUC) and the *Forces Armées de la République Démocratique du Congo* (FARDC) ran a series of joint military operations in South Kivu to limit the movement of the *Forces démocratiques de libération du Rwanda* (FDLR) and protect the civilian population.[27] They destroyed several FDLR camps in an effort to compel fighters to repatriate or relocate to more remote areas. Destroying the camps most likely protected civilians in the vicinity, as many FDLR fighters moved on. However, the threat was not completely expunged, as the village of Ntulamamba was attacked during the operations, and forty-seven civilians were killed.[28] There is no other case in the fifteen-year period analysed by this study in which more people were killed in a single attack by the FDLR (and where UN forces were deployed to protect). For that reason, the operation was assessed as 'mostly unsuccessful'.

An example of an ambiguous case being assessed as 'mostly successful' is taken from the DRC in July 2013, when the Mayi-Mayi Nyatura and the militia *Forces de défense des intérêts du peuple congolais* (FDIPC), attacked the insurgent group M23. On 6 July, more than thirty Mayi-Mayi fighters attacked the M23 in Kanyaruchinya, firing on the local population and killing one person.[29] According to the Secretary-General's report, 'in response to the imminent threat posed to the civilian population, [MONUSCO] engaged the Mayi-Mayi elements, killing one, injuring two and arresting another'.[30] In this case, it is assessed that the UN intervention likely protected many civilians, as continued armed clashes would

25 UNSC (2013) UN Doc S/2013/294.
26 Ibid.
27 UNSC (2005) UN Doc S/2005/506.
28 Ibid.
29 UNSC (2013) UN Doc S/2013/581.
30 Ibid.

have put the local population under imminent threat of physical violence. Interestingly, the M23 was soon to become the main opponent for coercive UN operations, and as such the UN effectively defended its future adversary.

It is recognized that the employment of the dichotomous variable 'mostly successful' or 'mostly unsuccessful' risks missing important nuances. It is also recognized that the assessment of situations requires a level of subjective judgement. While the methodology is acknowledged as imperfect, it serves to render the inherently complex subject matter manageable, and enables the production of an overarching empirical picture of the situation.

IV. Finding the Utility of Force to Protect

The following overview presents a broad indication of where the UN protects through force, and to what effect. Table 15.1 demonstrates that 69 out of 188 operations were assessed as 'mostly successful' in using force to protect civilians, 50 were assessed as 'mostly unsuccessful', and 61 did not include sufficient information to determine an outcome. This indicates that protection operations have been successful more often than not. However, the remaining operations, for which there was insufficient information to determine an outcome, could significantly influence that finding.

Table 15.1 Overview of UN protection operations in Africa and their outcomes, 1999–2014

	Number of protection operations	Mostly successful	Mostly unsuccessful	Unknown protection effect	N/A
Total	188 (100%)	69 (37%)	50 (27%)	61 (32%)	8 (4%)

A. Distribution of protection operations by UN mission

Table 15.2 demonstrates that the highest number of UN protection operations (eighty-one) were conducted in the DRC, where the UN mission (MONUC and its successor MONUSCO) has had a protection mandate since 2000. The second-highest number of protection operations was carried out in South Sudan, with the UN mission (UNMISS) undertaking twenty-nine operations in only three and a half years. As few as five missions were responsible for 87 per cent of the use of force by the UN to protect civilians in Africa: MONUC/MONUSCO (DRC), UNMISS (South Sudan), UNMIL (Liberia), UNISFA (Abyei), and UNAMID (Darfur).

Table 15.2 Distribution of protection operations across ten UN operations in Africa, 1999–2014

UN mission	Number of UN military protection operations in Africa (percentage)
MONUC/MONUSCO (DRC, 2000–)	81 (43%)
UNMISS (South Sudan, 2011–)	29 (15%)
UNMIL (Liberia, 2003–)	19 (10%)
UNISFA (Abyei, 2011–)	19 (10%)
UNAMID (Darfur, 2007–)	17 (9%)
UNMIS (Sudan, 2005–7)	7 (4%)
UNOCI (Ivory Coast, 2004–)	7 (4%)
UNAMSIL (Sierra Leone, 1999–2005)	4 (2%)
MINURCAT (CAR/Chad, 2007–10)	3 (2%)
MINUSMA (Mali, 2013–)	2 (1%)
Total	188 (100%)

Table 15.3 demonstrates that 'mostly successful' outcomes vary considerably across missions. At 57 per cent, the UN Mission in Sudan (UNMIS) had the highest percentage of 'mostly successful' protection operations, with only 14 per cent of operations 'mostly unsuccessful'. However, only seven operations were conducted by UNMIS over three years, which constitutes a very small sample. A similar issue arises with a number of missions.

Table 15.3 Protection outcomes across ten UN operations in Africa

	Mostly successful	Mostly unsuccessful	Unknown protection effect	N/A	Total
MONUC/ MONUSCO (1999–)	22 (27%)	19 (23%)	40 (49%)	–	81
UNMISS (2011–)	9 (31%)	8 (28%)	11 (38%)	1 (3%)	29
UNMIL (2003–)	10 (53%)	3 (16%)	4 (21%)	2 (11%)	19
UNISFA (2011–)	9 (47%)	7 (37%)	2 (11%)	1 (5%)	19
UNAMID (2007–)	9 (53%)	7 (41%)	–	1 (6%)	17
UNMIS (2005–7)	4 (57%)	1 (14%)	2 (29%)	–	7
UNOCI (2004–)	3 (43%)	2 (29%)	2 (29%)	–	7
UNAMSIL (1999–2005)	1 (25%)	1 (25%)	–	2 (50%)	4
MINURCAT (2007–10)	1 (33%)	1 (33%)	–	1 (33%)	3
MINUSMA (2013–)	1 (50%)	1 (50%)	–	–	2
Total	69	50	61	8	188 (100 %)

B. Matching perpetrator violence

To explore Beadle's claim about the utility of force to protect, the following section examines cases in which the specific function of force employed by UN peacekeepers matched the type of violence employed by the perpetrator. The analysis is based on first determining which function(s) of force were employed by the UN (amelioration, containment, deterrence/coercion, and destruction) and comparing it to the type(s) of violence employed by the perpetrator (impairment, incitement, deterrence/ coercion, and destruction). Cases in which the function of force employed by the protectors was appropriate for addressing the type of violence exercised by the perpetrators were assessed as a 'match'. Cases in which the function of force, type of violence, or outcome were unknown were excluded from this part of the analysis.

As set out in Table 15.4, the analysis indicates that in 59 out of 112 operations, or 53 per cent, UN peacekeepers matched the type of violence employed by the perpetrator. When matching occurred, the protection operation was 'mostly successful' in 92 per cent of cases. This observation clearly supports Beadle's claims that matching leads to more effective civilian protection.

In 5 out of 112 operations, or 6 per cent, UN peacekeepers matched the type of violence of the perpetrator, but the operation was 'mostly unsuccessful'. These are interesting cases for further research, as they might contain insights that can be used to refine Beadle's theory.

Conversely, UN peacekeepers' function of force mismatched the perpetrators' types of violence in 53 of the 112 protection operations, or 47 per cent. The outcome was 'mostly unsuccessful' in 72 per cent of those cases. It appears, therefore, that mismatching correlates significantly with unsuccessful protection operations. There are, however, exceptions to the rule. In fifteen operations where UN forces mismatched the perpetrator, a 'mostly successful' outcome was identified. The vast majority of these cases seem to be explained by the fact that UN missions opened their gates to civilians on the run from threats and violence, in particular UNMISS.

Table 15.4 Protection operations assessed on matching the protector's function of force with the perpetrator's type of violence

	Match/ mismatch	Mostly successful	Mostly unsuccessful
Match	59 (53%)	54 (92%)	5 (8%)
Mismatch	53 (47%)	15 (28%)	38 (72%)
Total	112	69	43

V. Variations in the Functions of Force

In an effort to determine which functions of force are most relevant for effective protection operations, the pie charts in Figure 15.1 reflect the relative prevalence of each function of force in operations where peacekeepers matched the perpetrator's type of violence, and which led to successful outcomes. The analysis indicates that the two dominant functions of force employed by UN peacekeepers in this context were deterrence and coercion. Amelioration, containment, and destruction were much less prevalent. While deterrence clearly plays a major role in UN peacekeeping operations, the entire spectrum of functions of force has been employed with success.

MONUC/MONUSCO

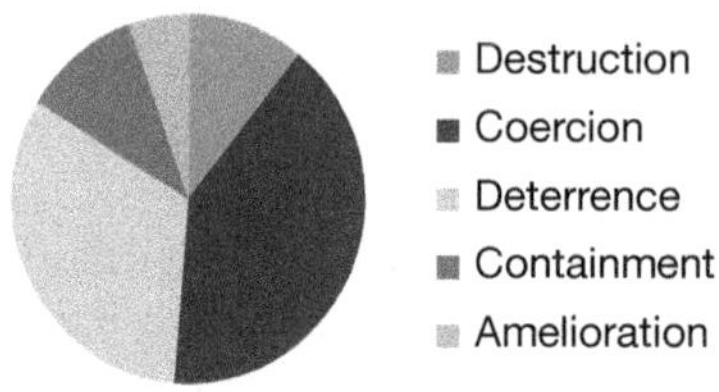

MONUC/MONUSCO has had a protection mandate since 2000. In only 21 out of 81 operations have the perpetrator's types of violence been matched and led to mostly successful outcomes. In these 21 operations coercion and deterrence have been most prevalent. Of the ten missions analysed, MONUC/MONUSCO and UNOCI are the only missions to utilise destruction.

UNMIL

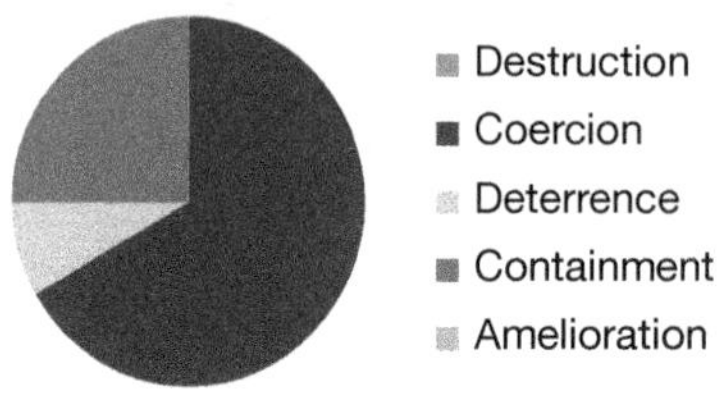

UNMIL has had a protection mandate since 2003. In ten out of 19 operations, the perpetrator's type of violence has been matched and led to mostly successful outcomes. Coercion is clearly the dominating function of force. Containment, however, has also been often employed. Deterrence has had a less prominent role.

UNISFA

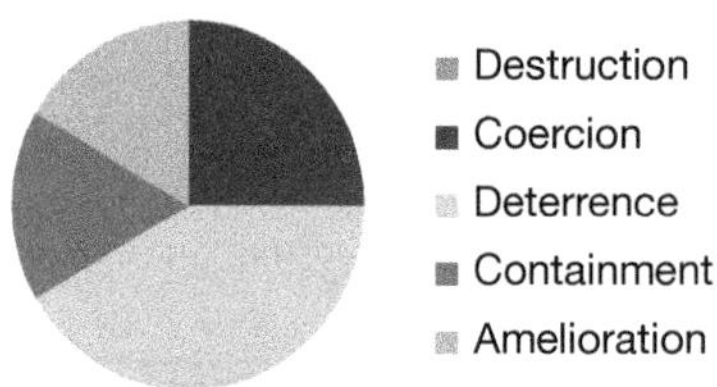

UNISFA has had a protection mandate since 2011. Out of 19, nine operations have matched the perpetrator's type of violence and led to mostly successful outcomes. Deterrence is clearly the function of force most employed, while coercion is also quite common. Containment and amelioration have also been a significant part of UNMIL's military efforts to protect.

Total (10 UN missions)

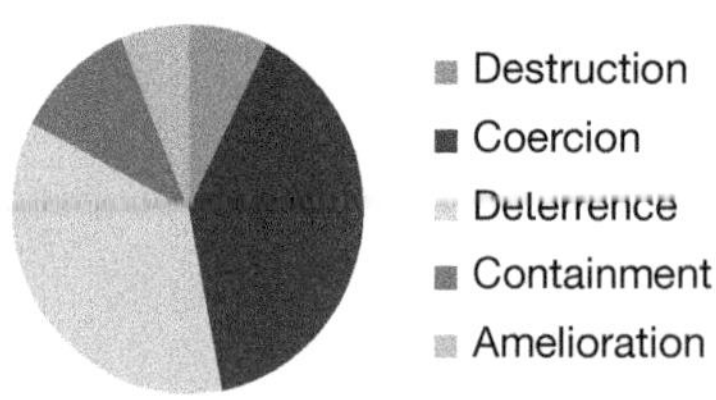

The two clearly dominant functions of force in 54 protection operations that matched the perpetrator's types of violence and led to mostly successful outcomes were deterrence and coercion. Amelioration, containment, and destruction were much less prevalent. This demonstrates that deterrence still plays a major role in UN peacekeeping operations, although the entire spectrum of the functions of force have been employed with success.

Figure 15.1 Functions of force in selected UN protection operations that have matched perpetrators' types of violence and led to mostly successful protection outcomes

VI. Protection Scenarios

To help differentiate among threats to civilians, Beadle has also developed seven generic scenarios:[31]

1. **Genocide**—where perpetrators seek to exterminate a national, ethnic, racial, or religious group;
2. **Ethnic cleansing**—where perpetrators seek to expel a certain group from specific territory;
3. **Regime crackdown**—where regimes use violence to repress resistance;
4. **Post-conflict revenge**—where former victims take revenge against previous perpetrators;
5. **Communal conflict**—where whole communities engage in continuous cycles of violence seeking both revenge for previous violence and deterrence of future retaliation;
6. **Predatory violence**—where predators attack the local population to ensure their own survival or for profit;
7. **Insurgency**—where government forces or rival groups are the primary targets, but perpetrators still target civilians as a tactic, including to prevent collaboration with the enemy, weaken confidence in the government, or provoke an overreaction by government forces.

The utility of military force for protecting civilians varies significantly across the seven scenarios. For example, in communal conflicts, force may be effectively used to deter or defend against attacks by both sides. In particular, force can be used to engage attackers, provide physical security for civilians and their means of survival, and coercively disarm militia.[32] In situations of predatory violence, offensive military operations may be the only way to effectively protect civilians, as the perpetrators are likely to continue committing acts of brutality, abductions, and killings as long as they are able to operate.[33] In insurgencies, the role of military forces in protecting civilians will probably be limited, as most civilian casualties will likely result from attacks against government targets or retribution for suspected

[31] Alexander William Beadle and Stian Kjeksrud, *Military Planning and Assessment Guide for the Protection of Civilians* (Kjeller, Norway: Norwegian Defence Research Establishment (FFI), 2014). The scenarios are described based on five parameters that describe key characteristics of the perpetrators: (a) strategic rationale for attacking civilians, (b) types of perpetrators, (c) strategies and tactics, (d) capabilities needed to attack civilians, and (e) the expected outcome when perpetrators succeed. The scenarios are categorized according to the perpetrators' rationale, because it is the perpetrator's motivation that first and foremost will determine the nature of threat to civilians. Together, these scenarios seek to capture the scope of fundamentally different types of physical threats that civilians may be under.

[32] Ibid. [33] Ibid., 21.

collaboration with the enemy. However, force may be used to support non-military stabilization efforts, holding and defending areas of tenuous government influence, and expanding government control.[34]

By analysing the dataset of UN protection operations against the typology of scenarios, it is possible to identify the threats to civilians against which UN military personnel in Africa have most often used force. As set out in Table 15.5, communal conflict,[35] predatory violence,[36] and insurgency[37] have been the three main scenarios, accounting for 92 per cent of situations that UN forces have addressed. The regime crackdown scenario occurs only twice in the dataset—both operations conducted in Côte d'Ivoire during the 2011 conflict.

Some situations are difficult to place within Beadle's typology and have been grouped together as 'other'. In addition to those scenarios identified, UN military personnel have employed force to protect civilians in a number of instances, including mob violence,[38] attempted coups,[39] criminal activity (murders, etc.),[40] and targeted assassinations.[41]

Table 15.5 Distribution of scenarios across all 188 protection operations 1999–2014

Scenarios	Number of operations (%)
Communal conflict	73 (39%)
Predatory violence	55 (29%)
Insurgency	45 (24%)
Other	13 (7%)
Regime crackdown	2 (1%)
Total	188 (100%)

[34] Ibid., 22.

[35] UN forces have employed force to protect civilians in communal conflict scenarios in South Sudan; Abyei and Darfur, Sudan; Ituri, Democratic Republic of the Congo (DRC); Chad; Ivory Coast; and Liberia.

[36] UN forces have employed force to protect civilians from predatory violence in Abyei, DRC, Darfur, Liberia, and Sierra Leone.

[37] UN forces have employed force to protect civilians from insurgencies in Mali, South Sudan, DRC, Chad, Darfur, and the Ivory Coast.

[38] UN forces have employed force to protect civilians from mob violence in Liberia and Sierra Leone.

[39] Two possible coup attempts in DRC, one in 2011 (see UNSC (2011) UN Doc S/2011/298, para. 11) and one in 2013 (see UNSC (2014) UN Doc S/2014/157, para. 3).

[40] Burundi, for example, saw a significant increase in criminal activity in the second half of 2009 (see UNSC (2004) UN Doc S/2004/902, para. 18).

[41] According to UNSC (2014) UN Doc S/2014/403, para. 15, a sixty-year-old man was shot in Kidal town in May 2014, reportedly because of his alleged co-operation with Operation Serval and Malian forces. This might also be seen as insurgent tactics.

The most prevalent scenario, communal conflicts, is one of the more deadly for civilians. However, it is also one of the types of situations in which military force can be effectively utilized to deter or defend against attacks that feed cycles of violence. Recent examples include military protection efforts to deter violence between communities in South Sudan[42] and between the Misseriya and Ngok Dinka in Abyei.[43]

The second most common scenario is predatory violence, in which perpetrators strike opportunistically at civilian targets and often avoid confrontation with intervening forces. Deterrence through UN presence may improve local security, but if the perpetrators are not targeting a specific population, they may simply attack elsewhere. The threat to civilians is likely to persist until the perpetrator is neutralized. The Lord's Resistance Army is the archetypal predatory armed group, which has long lost its political agenda but still preys on local populations for survival and profit.[44] Several of the armed groups in eastern DRC, including the Allied Democratic Forces (ADF), also display predatory behaviour.[45]

The third most common scenario is insurgency, in the context of which military force usually plays a minimal role protecting civilians, because they are not the primary target. However, where control over territory is contested, such as in some areas of Afghanistan and Nigeria, insurgents have temporarily increased attacks against civilians. UN missions have been and continue to be deployed in conflict areas with active insurgencies, including in Mali (MNLA),[46] the DRC (M23/

[42] For example, UNMISS support to SPLA patrols to deter conflict in the Tri-State Area through Operation Longhorn in 2013. See UNSC (2013) UN Doc S/2013/366, paras 45–6. Also, UNMISS launched a sustained foot and vehicular patrol campaign in Pibor County, Jonglei, in August 2013, which 'gradually restored confidence among the civilian population, facilitated freedom of movement into Pibor and Gumuruk for food distribution and fostered a more secure and safe environment'. See UNSC (2013) S/2013/651, para. 40.

[43] UNISFA blocked thousands of armed Misseriya from entering Makir Awed in Abyei in March 2014. See UNSC (2014) UN Doc S/2014/336, para. 9.

[44] Tim Allen and Koen Vlassenroot (eds), *The Lord's Resistance Army: Myth and Reality* (New York: Zed Books, 2010).

[45] International Crisis Group, *Eastern Congo: The ADF-NALU's Lost Rebellion* (Brussels: International Crisis Group, 2012); Daniel Fahey, 'New Insights on Congo's Islamist Rebels' *Washington Post* (Washington, DC, 19 February 2015) <www.washingtonpost.com/blogs/monkey-cage/wp/2015/02/19/new-insights-on-congos-islamist-rebels/>; Jason Stearns, Judith Verweijen, and Maria Eriksson Baaz, *The National Army and Armed Groups in Eastern Congo—Untangling the Gordian knot of Insecurity* (London: Rift Valley Institute, 2013).

[46] The UN terminology on armed actors in Mali includes references to 'extremists', 'armed groups', and also 'insurgents'. See, for example, United Nations, 2015, S/2015/219, para. 27. Those armed groups that seek political influence and/or self-determination in parts of Mali accord with the description of insurgency found in the US Headquarters of the Army, *Counterinsurgency*, FM 3-24, (2006), para. 1–2: 'an organized, protracted politico-military struggle designed to weaken the control and legitimacy of an established government, occupying power, or other political authority while increasing insurgent control.'

CNDP),[47] South Sudan (David YauYau),[48] and Sudan/Darfur (JEM/SLA-AW/SLA-MM).[49]

Several scenarios may unfold in parallel, with the motivations of armed groups evolving and their methods changing. The former M23 in the eastern DRC is an example of such mixed motives and methods. Primarily fighting for political influence in parts of the east, the M23 was also responsible for rapes and other exactions that are not easily reconciled with a military campaign to further a political agenda. The M23 can also be seen as providing the last line of defence of the Congolese Tutsi against both real and perceived threats from the FDLR, originally consisting of ethnic Hutu and other armed groups.[50] Where protection operations came up against such mixed scenarios, the analysis was based on the primary defining circumstance.

Table 15.6 indicates the effectiveness of UN military protection efforts in each of Beadle's scenarios. In the most common scenario, communal conflict, UN protection operations seem to be 'mostly successful' as often as they are 'mostly unsuccessful'. Once again, the significant number of unknown outcomes may influence this finding. In the case of predatory violence, there are a very substantial number of unknown outcomes, making it difficult to draw conclusions for this particular scenario. In the case of insurgencies, close to half of the operations have led to 'mostly successful' outcomes, but in this case also, a high proportion of outcomes are unknown.

Table 15.6 Outcome of protection operations in different scenarios 1999–2014

Scenarios	Many protected	Few protected	Unknown	N/A	Total
Communal conflict	28 (38%)	29 (40%)	13 (18%)	3 (4%)	73
Predatory violence	13 (24%)	9 (16%)	33 (60%)	–	55
Insurgency	21 (47%)	9 (20%)	14 (31%)	1 (2%)	45
Other	5 (38%)	3 (23%)	1 (7%)	4 (31%)	13
Regime crackdown	2 (100%)	–	–	–	2
Total	69	50	61	8	188

[47] Jason Stearns, *From CNDP to M23: The Evolution of an Armed Movement in Eastern Congo* (London: Rift Valley Institute, 2012).

[48] Small Arms Survey, 'David YauYau's Rebellion', Human Security Baseline for Sudan and South Sudan, 2012.

[49] Julie Flint and Alex de Waal, *Darfur: A New History of a Long War* (London: Zed Books, 2008).

[50] Stearns, see n 47.

VII. Protection Successes and Failures in Contemporary UN Missions

The following section illustrates, through three brief case studies, how more case-specific analysis may offer additional insights into the conditions favouring effective military protection. These three cases correspond to the most common scenarios: insurgency and predatory violence in the DRC (M23) and communal conflicts in Abyei (Misserya vs. Ngok Dinka) and South Sudan (Murle vs. Lou Nuer).

A. Neutralizing the M23 in the DRC (2013)

In 2013, MONUSCO's Force Intervention Brigade (FIB) and the national army of the DRC (FARDC) employed military force in joint operations that combined 'initiative, surprise, unity of effort, leadership, and discipline' to destroy the capability of the M23.[51] The M23 was the most potent armed group in eastern DRC and had threatened to march on Kinshasa, the capital, after having secured Goma, the most important Congolese town in the east.[52] Although ambitions to attack Kinshasa were probably unrealistic at the time, the group exercised common insurgent logic, seeking influence in parts of eastern DRC and thereby directly challenging the Congolese authorities.

The M23 also displayed predatory behaviour against the civilian population. The group both used physical violence to coerce the population into supporting them in their campaign against Congolese authorities, and attacked them directly for personal gain. The MONUSCO investigation into human rights violations committed by the M23 in North Kivu during the period April 2012 to November 2013 established that the group killed 116 people and was responsible for 161 instances of rape, and hundreds of other violations, such as abductions, forced recruitment, forced labour, and arbitrary arrests.[53] The report also noted that the actual number of violations was probably much higher.

At the end of July 2013, MONUSCO established a security zone around Goma.[54] A month later, the M23 retreated from positions around the town as a direct result of FIB/FARDC coercive operations which included artillery, attack

[51] US Army Peacekeeping & Stability Operations Institute (PKSOI), *UN Force Intervention Brigade against the M23* (Stability Operations Lessons Learned & Information Management System SOLLIMS Lesson # 1307) (*PKSOI*, 2013) <pksoi.army.mil/LL/Lessons/LMS-AF_1307_UN_FIBde_M23.pdf>.

[52] 'DR Congo's M23 Rebels Threaten to March to Kinshasa', *BBC News* (London, 21 November 2012) <www.bbc.com/news/world-africa-20427682>.

[53] MONUSCO and UN OHCHR, 'Report of the Joint Human Rights Office on Human Rights Violations Committed by the M23 in North Kivu Province between April 2012 and November 2013' (2014) 9. <www.ohchr.org/Documents/Countries/CD/UNJHROOctober2014_en.pdf>.

[54] 'UN Mission Sets Up Security Zone in Eastern DR Congo, Gives Rebels 48 Hour Ultimatum', *UN News Centre* (New York, 30 July 2013) <www.un.org/apps/news/story.asp?NewsID=45535#.VY3KCRPBzGc>.

helicopters, special forces (including snipers), and infantry units.[55] In late October, the M23 was attacked by the FIB/FARDC on several fronts, which split the armed group in three.[56] FIB units blocked possible escape routes and the FARDC forced the M23 to retreat towards the Ugandan and Rwandan borders, during which many fighters were captured.

Both coercion and destruction were dominant in these operations. The functions of force employed by the protectors clearly matched the perpetrators' type of predatory violence, and resulted in a successful outcome. The operations ultimately put an end to the M23 by overrunning their positions and expelling them from the DRC. While there is a correlation between the successful outcome and the matching of the functions of force with the types of violence, establishing a causal relationship would benefit from further investigation.

What is clear, however, is that by defeating the M23, MONUSCO and FARDC protected many civilians from violence. Additionally, following the defeat of the M23, over 6,000 fighters belonging to other armed groups surrendered.[57] While choosing the right functions of force was an important factor in the success of MONUSCO/FARDC operations against the M23, several factors contributed to making such a robust approach viable. These included the specific language of the mission mandate, a regional initiative from core troop contributors, improved conduct of operations on the part of the FARDC, and international pressure on Rwanda and Uganda to cease their support to the M23.[58]

B. Avoiding large-scale communal conflict in Abyei

The conflicts in Abyei include both 'traditional' inter-communal violence between the nomadic Misseriya and the agro-pastoralist Ngok Dinka and elements of the more recent inter-State conflict between Sudan and South Sudan over the future status of Abyei (whether it should remain part of Sudan or become part of South Sudan). The inter-communal conflict between the Misseriya and Ngok Dinka tends to flare up every year during Misseriya migration through Dinka lands, and is exacerbated by the fact that both Sudan and South Sudan use the two parties as proxies.

55 Martin Guy, 'DRC Sniper Revelation Compromising SANDF Troops', *Defence Web* (Johannesburg, 5 September 2013) <www.defenceweb.co.za/index.php?option=com_content&view=article&id=31797:drc-sniper-revelation-compromising-sandf-troops-expert&catid=111:sa-defence&Itemid=242>; Stephan Hofstatter, 'South Africa at War in DRC', *The Times Live* (Johannesburg, 22 August 2014) <www.timeslive.co.za/local/2014/08/22/south-africa-at-war-in-the-drc--the-inside-story>.

56 Darren Oliver, 'How M23 Was Rolled Back', *African Defence Review* (London, 30 October 2013) <www.africandefence.net/analysis-how-m23-was-rolled-back>; PKSOI, see n 511; Jason Stearns, 'A Year After Its Defeat, Could the M23 Make a Comeback?' (*Congo Siasa*, 9 November 2014) <congosiasa.blogspot.com/2014/11/a-year-after-its-defeat-could-m23-make.html>.

57 UNSC (2014) UN Doc S/2014/450.

58 Stian Kjeksrud and Lotte Vermeij, 'Protecting Governments from Insurgencies: The DRC and Mali', in Cedric de Coning and Chiyuku Aoi (eds), *UN Peacekeeping Doctrine Towards the Post-Brahimi Era? Adapting to Stabilization, Protection and New Threats* (Oxford: Oxford University Press, forthcoming 2016).

Communal conflict peaks during the Misseriya's seasonal migration southward in search of grazing and water for their cattle. The migration occurs through several natural 'migration corridors' into the Abyei area, which often brings them in close contact with the Ngok Dinka. The migration also occurs in reverse when the Misseriya return. The movement creates opportunities for cattle raids, as the herds of both communities are in close proximity. The raids are usually carried out by a small group of youths from either community, and most commonly involve few casualties, but a large number of cattle stolen.

UNISFA has often been able to deter opportunities for large-scale, inter-communal violence through inter-positioning. For example, in March 2014, 4,000–5,000 armed Misseriya militia entered the Abyei area from Western Kordofan state in Sudan. UNISFA troops deployed to block their progression, following which the militia withdrew from the area.[59] In this case, the potential type of violence employed by the perpetrator must be assessed counterfactually, since no one was harmed. Based on former *modus operandi* of such columns of communal fighters, force is often applied to coerce the opponent into fleeing or at least to deter future attacks on their own community. UNISFA matched the likely type of violence employed by the perpetrators through effective deterrence. More coercive measures may have been needed if the Misserya militia had been determined to proceed.

In many instances deterrence has been combined with amelioration, especially through dialogue and direct negotiation with the parties. In February 2012, for example, UNISFA 'requested a group of Misseriya nomads with approximately 12,000 cattle in Cwein not to proceed with their migration towards the Kiir/Bahr el-Arab River' because they had not obtained prior authorization.[60] At the same time, SSPS elements arrived at the southern edge of the river with heavy machine guns and threatened the Misserya nomads. UNISFA's intervention deterred violence: it calmed the situation and the SSPS withdrew.

C. Failing to understand the Lou Nuer White Army (2011–12)

In late 2011–early 2012, approximately 6,000–8,000 armed youth of the Lou Nuer White Army gathered in Jonglei state and launched a series of attacks over twelve days against the ethnic Murle population. While those attacks were ongoing, Murle militia launched reprisal attacks against Lou Nuer areas. More than 900 civilians were killed.[61]

Before these attacks, UNMISS was aware of the build-up of the White Army, the development of which was closely linked to Murle attacks on the Lou Nuer earlier that year. As the White Army moved south towards Murle population centres, UNMISS military forces deployed pre-emptively into positions in key population

[59] UNSC (2014) UN Doc S/2014/336. [60] UNSC (2012) UN Doc S/2012/175.

[61] UNSC (2012) S/2012/140; UN Mission in South Sudan, 'Conflict in South Sudan: A Human Rights Report' (2014) <unmiss.unmissions.org/Portals/unmiss/Human%20Rights%20Reports/UNMISS%20Conflict%20in%20South%20Sudan%20-%20A%20Human%20Rights%20Report.pdf>.

centres, providing deterrence and early warning, and allowing civilians to move out of harm's way.[62] UNMISS' efforts allowed tens of thousands of civilians to escape, saving many from physical violence. The UN's use of force did not, however, have a full deterrent effect. The White Army continued its march south and many villages were burned along their route. In this case, presence in itself was not a sufficient deterrent. That said, the UN peacekeepers were heavily outnumbered by the White Army, and confronting them directly was not a viable option.

On New Year's Eve, the White Army reached Pibor, the main population centre in Jonglei. Because of the UN's efforts, the majority of the population had fled. The SPLA used coercion when, on 2 January 2012, they fired on the advancing column that was attempting to enter Pibor. UNMISS supported the deterrent efforts by blocking the White Army's entrance into the town. Following this repulsion, the White Army crossed the Pibor River and proceeded to attack Murle populations living to the east and south of the town, without any interference from the SLPA or UNMISS. Before the White Army retreated, Murle militia retaliated against Lou Nuer areas, during which approximately 300 people were killed. As the Murle operated in much smaller units, they were more difficult to locate.

UNMISS was not prepared for the reprisal attacks. While the failure to address the attacks can be attributed partly to resources, the cycles of violence common to communal conflicts were known. Counter-attacks should have been expected and warning efforts should have been extended to both parties.

UNMISS' military efforts protected many, as most civilians in danger were able to flee the impending threat due to the mission's warning efforts. The mission protected several of the main population centres, and provided shelter to 3,500 civilians in its compounds. However, this case is, arguably, an example of the protector not understanding, and therefore not matching, the perpetrator's type of violence. It appears that UNMISS and the SPLA assumed that taking Pibor town was the White Army's ultimate objective. However, the target was not the town per se but the Murle population, wherever they were. As few Murle remained in Pibor town after UNMISS' early warning efforts, the White Army proceeded southward, attacking many more unprotected Murle targets. Exacerbating the situation, the Murle living beyond Pibor were not given advance warning, and were caught unawares by the White Army.[63]

Given that UNMISS was outnumbered and outgunned by the White Army, providing amelioration, through providing warning, was a relevant response, although it mismatched the type of violence employed by the perpetrators. Defending Pibor town may have been important militarily, but in terms of providing protection, early warning efforts should have been prioritized to include Murle living south and east of the town.

[62] UNSC (2012) S/2012/140.

[63] UN Mission in South Sudan, 'Incidents of Inter-communal Violence in Jonglei State' (2012) <unmiss.unmissions.org/Portals/unmiss/Human%20Rights%20Reports/June%202012%20Jonglei%20 Report.pdf>.

VIII. Conclusion

This chapter demonstrates that despite a number of previous UN protection failures, there is reason to be optimistic about the ability of UN military forces to protect civilians, provided that certain criteria are met. The empirical analysis of data indicates that civilians are more successfully protected when the UN uses the appropriate functions of force to meet the types of violence employed by specific perpetrators. If UN peacekeepers' military responses are based on a thorough understanding of the perpetrators' methods and intent, more civilians are likely to be protected.

Over the past fifteen years, a little less than half of all UN military protection operations have been conducted in the DRC. Lessons from MONUC/MONUSCO have, rightly, been influential and are likely to remain so. However, more recently established missions, such as UNMISS (South Sudan), MINUSMA (Mali), and MINUSCA (Central African Republic), may surpass UN efforts in the DRC, both in terms of the tempo of protection operations and the lessons learned from them. Given that the effectiveness of using force to protect civilians has been shown to be closely associated with the methods and intent of particular perpetrators, merely copying a successful approach from one mission to another should be avoided. Instead, planning of future protection operations would benefit from being informed by the protection scenarios prevalent in the mission area and on the *modus operandi* employed by known perpetrators.

Troops in UN missions in Africa are likely to be engaged in at least one of three scenarios: communal conflict, predatory violence, and/or insurgency. Each of the scenarios requires different functions of force to be employed to effectively protect civilians. Troop-contributing countries would benefit from being aware of the requirements of each scenario, in order to inform the pre-deployment training, preparation, and equipping of their troops.

This chapter presents an overarching picture of the situation. The findings would benefit from further analysis and refinement, and future research would be well served by complementary qualitative analysis of relevant cases. This chapter seeks to move beyond the debate regarding whether the UN has or should use force to protect. Instead, it has begun identifying and exploring the conditions under which force can be used successfully and most effectively. In doing so, it has found that despite the limitations that UN military components face, force can and has been effectively used to protect civilians. However, there is significant room for improvement, something which may be achieved partly through better tailoring the military response to the threat posed.

16

The Contribution of Human Rights to Protecting People in Conflict

Michael Keating and Richard Bennett[1]

I. Introduction

Human rights work is central to protecting civilians in conflict situations. Early warning, through human rights monitoring and reporting, contributes to preventing and responding to violent conflict. Human rights advocacy and investigations strengthen accountability. They play an essential role in preventing the recurrence of violence, as well as serving a deterrent function during conflict. Human rights actors also provide some of the most accurate information about the effects on civilians of ongoing violence. Their monitoring considers the causes and consequences of harm to civilians and attempts to identify perpetrators responsible for the harm, thereby helping to shape more targeted prevention as well as protection responses and interventions.

These activities are widely recognized as critical, and they are anchored in internationally agreed legal frameworks for the protection and promotion of human rights. Yet human rights actors in the field sometimes face tensions with other actors undertaking protection activities due to divergent objectives with different time frames. Such tensions manifest primarily with political actors, but also to a lesser extent with humanitarians.

Within the United Nations (UN), much progress has been made on human rights at the strategic level. The 'Human Rights Up Front' initiative, along with other tools such as commissions of inquiry and the voice of the High Commissioner for Human Rights, are all playing an important role in increasing the prominence of human rights in the UN's approach to conflict situations. Strong political support by UN leaders is critical for improving field-based human rights work.

[1] The authors are deeply indebted to Ms Regina Fitzpatrick for her substantial assistance in the preparation of this chapter. From her experience serving as a human rights officer in South Sudan and Afghanistan, Ms Fitzpatrick made an invaluable contribution to this work. When writing this chapter, Michael Keating was a Director at Chatham House. He now serves with the United Nations Assistance Mission in Somalia. The views expressed herein are his personal views and do not necessarily reflect the views of, nor should they be attributed to, the United Nations.

Drawing upon three case studies, this chapter attempts to demonstrate that UN human rights protection practice can significantly contribute to overarching civilian protection objectives, before, during and after conflicts. However, despite a strong normative basis and renewed determination by the UN, serious challenges persist with regard to operationalizing human rights and ensuring that human rights work plays a full part in protection strategies on the ground.

II. Human Rights in Context

The UN Charter explicitly includes 'promoting and encouraging respect for human rights and fundamental freedoms' as objectives of the Organization.[2] The establishment of the UN Commission on Human Rights in 1946 and the adoption of the Universal Declaration of Human Rights in 1948 were among the Organization's early initiatives. Both demonstrated the commitment of Member States to human rights principles and the role of the UN in promoting and protecting human rights. Over the past sixty years, the international community has generally continued to embrace the principles of human rights, while developing their content and the architecture to implement and enforce them. The maturation of international human rights principles—as exemplified by the proliferation of human rights treaties, standards, and jurisprudence—has had an impact at the policy level, but this has not always been equally evident on the ground.

The UN has developed a human rights architecture at both the strategic level (generally at headquarters) and the operational level (generally in the field). The former now includes the UN Human Rights Council and the UN Office of the High Commissioner for Human Rights (OHCHR). In addition to the advocacy role of the High Commissioner, OHCHR serves as a secretariat for the Human Rights Council, supporting the Universal Periodic Review process,[3] Special Procedures,[4] treaty bodies established to enforce human rights treaties, and commissions of inquiry.[5] In addition to these specialized entities, the office of the Secretary-General has taken on an expanded role, including by appointing special representatives and rapporteurs[6] and providing briefings to the Security Council and

[2] Charter of the United Nations (adopted 26 June 1945, entered into force 24 October 1945) 1 UNTS 16, Article 1(3) (UN Charter).

[3] The Universal Periodic Review (UPR) is a process under the auspices of the Human Rights Council through which the human rights records of all member states are reviewed. See UN General Assembly (UNGA) Resolution (Res) 60/251 (2006) UN Doc A/RES/60/251, para. 5(e).

[4] Special Procedures, also under the auspices of the Human Rights Council, include independent experts and working groups with thematic and country-specific mandates.

[5] For an overview of these mechanisms, see Philip Alston and Ryan Goodman, *International Human Rights* (Oxford: Oxford University Press, 2013), 691–4, 704–8, 728–9, 735–7, 762–3.

[6] These include the Special Representative of the Secretary-General (SRSG) on Children in Armed Conflict, the SRSG on Conflict-Related Sexual Violence, and the Special Rapporteur on the Situation of Human Rights Defenders. See, respectively, UNGA Res 51/77 (1997) UN Doc A/RES/51/77, paras 35–8; UN Security Council (UNSC) Resolution (Res) 1888 (2009) UN Doc S/RES/1888, para. 4; Commission on Human Rights Resolution 2000/61 (2000) UN Doc E/CN.4/RES/2000/61, para. 3.

General Assembly on human rights issues.[7] At the operational level, OHCHR and UN field missions deploy Human Rights Officers to conduct human rights activities. As human rights mechanisms flourish, human rights actors abound.

A. The link between human rights and the protection of civilians

In 1999, the Inter-Agency Standing Committee, the co-ordinating mechanism for international humanitarian assistance, adopted a rights-based approach to its work, articulating a broad concept of protection: 'The concept of protection encompasses all activities aimed at obtaining full respect for the rights of the individual in accordance with the letter and the spirit of the relevant bodies of law (i.e. human rights law, international humanitarian law and refugee law).'[8] This broad formulation followed from the principle of the indivisibility of human rights.[9]

Such a broad concept of 'protection', however, is not synonymous with the concept of 'protection of civilians' during conflict. In such situations, the human rights relevant to the protection of people from violence are a smaller subset of the full panoply of rights. These focus on the right to life, freedom from torture, and freedom from arbitrary detention.[10] Contributing to recent efforts to define the protection of civilians in peacekeeping, OHCHR has explained that 'PoC [the protection of civilians] is more narrowly focused than, but complementary to, the broader human rights mandate, which encompasses not only the rights to life and physical integrity, but also deals with the wide range of civil, cultural, economic, political, and social rights.'[11]

The UN Departments of Peacekeeping Operations (DPKO) and Field Support (DFS) have adopted a three-tiered approach to the protection of civilians that includes: (a) protection through political process, (b) protection from physical violence, and (c) establishing a protective environment.[12] Human rights work is often relegated to the third tier, which includes the promotion of legal protection, human rights advocacy, the facilitation of humanitarian assistance, and support to national

[7] This has become an increasingly strong role following the Secretary-General's 2005 report 'In Larger Freedom': 'Accordingly, we will not enjoy development without security, we will not enjoy security without development, and we will not enjoy either without respect for human rights.' See UNGA, 'In Larger Freedom: Towards Development, Security and Human Rights for All' (2005) UN Doc A/59/2005, para. 13.

[8] Inter-Agency Standing Committee, *Protection of Internally Displaced Persons* (New York: Inter-Agency Standing Committee, 2000) 4 <www.humanitarianinfo.org/iasc/downloaddoc.aspx?docID=4415&type=pdf>.

[9] 'All human rights are universal, indivisible and interdependent and interrelated.' World Conference on Human Rights, 'Vienna Declaration and Programme of Action, Report of the World Conference on Human Rights' (1993) UN Doc A/CONF.157/23, 32 ILM 1661, 23.

[10] International Covenant on Civil and Political Rights (adopted 16 December 1966, entry into force 23 March 1976) 999 UNTS 171, arts 6, 7, and 9.

[11] OHCHR, *Human Rights and the Protection of Civilians in Peacekeeping: Approaches, Methodologies and Tools*, 2015, p. 3.

[12] UN Department of Peacekeeping Operations and Department of Field Support, 'Draft Operational Concept on the Protection of Civilians in United Nations Peacekeeping Operations' (2010), 1 <www.peacekeeping.org.uk/wp-content/uploads/2013/02/100129-DPKO-DFS-POC-Operational-Concept.pdf>.

institutions.[13] However, there is a role for human rights in all three tiers, including, importantly, tier two—protection from physical violence.

B. Human rights protection practice

Significant developments in human rights protection practice have taken place at the strategic level. In several cases, the UN Security Council has authorized military deployments on the grounds of mass violations of human rights.[14] Increasingly, human rights provisions are incorporated into international peace agreements.[15] The UN, regional organizations, and individual States have all used various tools to hold governments and individuals accountable for serious human rights violations, including embargos, sanctions, and criminal responsibility mechanisms.[16] Thus, both international human rights and humanitarian law and their application at the global, strategic level have evolved and spread.

At the operational level, human rights protection practice has also evolved and deepened. Human Rights Officers have been increasingly deployed in UN field presences—peacekeeping operations, special political missions, UN Country Teams, and stand alone OHCHR country offices. They often have a wide presence across the relevant territories and good contacts amongst local NGOs and other civil society actors. As such, they play a critical role in UN protection efforts.[17]

Human rights actors contribute to the protection of civilians in conflict through a number of activities on the ground. Most prominent is regular human rights monitoring, reporting, and analysis, before, during, and after violence. The High Commissioner for Human Rights has emphasized the importance of human rights indicators as early warning signs of crisis.[18] Additionally, civilian casualty tracking and recording have become useful tools in discerning conflict dynamics

[13] Ibid., 9.

[14] See Jon Western and Joshua S Goldstein, 'Humanitarian Intervention Comes of Age: Lessons from Somalia to Libya', *Foreign Affairs* (November/December 2011); Jennifer M Welsh, 'The Security Council and Humanitarian Intervention' in Vaughan Lowe, Adam Roberts, Jennifer Welsh, and Dominik Zaum, *The United Nations Security Council and War: The Evolution of Thought and Practice since 1945* (Oxford: Oxford University Press, 2010).

[15] Leslie Vinjamuri and Aaron P Boesenecker, *Accountability and Peace Agreements: Mapping Trends from 1980 to 2006* (Geneva: Henry Dunant Centre for Humanitarian Dialogue, 2007) 9, 11, Appendix 1.

[16] For an overview of these mechanisms, see Philip Alston and Ryan Goodman, *International Human Rights* (Oxford: Oxford University Press, 2013), 1117–224.

[17] OHCHR, n 11, p. 4.

See also Liam Mahony, *Proactive Presence: Field Strategies for Civilian Protection* (Geneva: Henry Dunant Centre for Humanitarian Dialogue, 2006); Liam Mahony and Roger Nash, *Influence on the Ground: Understanding and Strengthening the Protection Impact of United Nations Human Rights Field Presences* (Brewster, USA: Fieldview Solutions, 2012).

[18] Statement of the High Commissioner for Human Rights, in UNSC (2014) UN Doc S/PV.7247, 3–5. See also Samantha Power and Graham Allison, *Realizing Human Rights: Moving from Inspiration to Impact* (New York: St. Martin's Press, 2000) 329; A Walter Dorn, 'Early and Late Warning by the UN Secretary-General', in Albrecht Schnabel and David Carment (eds), *Conflict Prevention from Rhetoric to Reality: Organizations and Institutions* (Lanham, USA: Lexington Books, 2004) 326.

and for pressuring parties to adjust their methods of warfare to mitigate civilian harm.[19]

Human rights actors conduct discreet advocacy through dialogue with governments and non-State actors, as well as public reporting. The reputational risks of being identified as a human rights violator make the latter a powerful tool. Direct engagement with parties prior to publication can be effective for encouraging both policy and behaviour change.

Further, the physical presence of human rights and other actors can deter violations and instil confidence among civilians.[20] When combatants and perpetrators know that their actions are being witnessed, they may be less likely to commit violations.[21] Along with others, human rights actors can escort populations under threat to the nearest safe haven. They also frequently contribute to protecting individuals at risk—particularly victims, witnesses, and human rights defenders—through dedicated presence, advocacy, and even extractions and relocations. Early warning provided by human rights actors can be critical for informing effective and preventive physical protection, through identifying vulnerable populations and anticipating violations.

Human rights actors also support the protection of civilians through building local capacity, including of civil society and human rights defenders, security services, and justice actors.[22] Through advocacy and the provision of credible information from investigations, human rights actors promote accountability for violations of human rights and humanitarian law, which can contribute to deterrence.[23]

Finally, human rights work at the operational level can also inform the development of prevention and response strategies by other protection actors, and persuade UN leaders in the field to take specific actions in the face of violent threats to civilians. By working collaboratively with UN military and police and advising senior UN officials, human rights actors influence the Organization's overarching protection approach.

The following case studies consider the challenges of human rights protection practice in the field and the imperative of focusing attention on enhancing activities at the operational level. These case studies cover three settings: one in a UN Country Team, the second a special political mission, and the third a peacekeeping operation.

[19] See Ellen Policinski, 'Civilian Harm Tracking: An Important Tool During Armed Conflict' (*Völkerrechtsblog*, 12 January 2015) <http://voelkerrechtsblog.com/2015/01/12/civilian-harm-tracking-an-important-tool-during-armed-conflict/>; UNSC, 'Report of the Secretary-General on the protection of civilians in armed conflict' (2013) UN Doc S/2013/689, paras 36–7.

[20] Mahony, see n 17, 16–24.

[21] Office of the High Commissioner for Human Rights (OHCHR), *OHCHR Report 2013* (Geneva: United Nations, 2013) 3.

[22] OHCHR, *Rule of Law Tools for Post-conflict States: Mapping the Justice Sector* (Geneva: United Nations, 2006) v.

[23] OHCHR, *Manual on Human Rights Monitoring* (New York and Geneva: United Nations, 2011), Chapter 30.

III. Case Studies

A. Sri Lanka

Following more than twenty-five years of cyclical conflict and ceasefire agreements, the Government of Sri Lanka definitively routed the rebel movement, the Liberation Tigers of Tamil Eelam (LTTE, commonly known as the Tamil Tigers), by military means in May 2009. Although the UN Human Rights Council initially praised Sri Lanka for defeating terrorists, subsequent reviews by the Secretary-General and reconsideration at the Human Rights Council acknowledged deep and credible concerns about the protection of civilians and the human rights approach of the UN.[24]

According to retrospective accounts, UN human rights actors provided repeated and ample warnings of human rights violations by both sides to the conflict from 2002 to 2008.[25] In 2007, the government formally launched its military campaign in an area in the north of Sri Lanka known as the Vanni, to root out the remaining LTTE elements, and over the following eighteen months the conflict escalated at a devastating cost to civilians.[26] From January 2009 to May 2009, government forces carried out an intense shelling campaign directed at this small region, where many civilians were trapped—in part by the LTTE as human shields.[27] By May 2009, most of the LTTE leadership had been reported killed, and the government claimed victory in the war.[28] As surviving civilians emerged, in destitute condition, from the conflict zone during the final stages and after the fighting, they were screened and detained en masse in military internment camps as the government sought to identify and isolate LTTE elements.[29] According to the findings of the Secretary-General's Panel of Experts on Sri Lanka, there could have been as many as 40,000 civilian deaths during those final stages of the conflict.[30] At the time, the government termed its operation 'humanitarian' and denied killing, let alone targeting, any civilians.

24 See the Human Rights Council resolution mandating a 'comprehensive investigation': Human Rights Council Resolution 25/L.1/Rev.1 (2014) UN Doc A/HRC/25/L.1/Rev.1. This resulted in a report (A/HRC/30/CRP2) finding 'reasonable grounds to believe that gross violations of international human rights law, serious violations of international humanitarian law and international crimes were committed by all parties': p. 6.

25 'Several reports were prescient in predicting events to come.' UN Secretary-General's Internal Review Panel on United Nations Action in Sri Lanka, 'Report of the Secretary-General's Internal Review Panel on United Nations Action in Sri Lanka' (2012), para. 7 (Petrie Report). See also Norah Niland, *Inhumanity and Humanitarian Action: Protection Failures in Sri Lanka* (Medford, USA: Tufts University, 2014), 11–12.

26 Petrie Report, see n 25, para. 14.

27 Ibid., para. 20; David Keen, 'Compromise or Capitulation: Report on WFP and the Humanitarian Crisis in Sri Lanka', in World Food Programme, *Humanitarian Assistance in Conflict and Complex Emergencies* (Rome: World Food Programme, 2009) 50; Human Rights Watch, *Trapped and Mistreated: LTTE Abuses against Civilians in the Vanni* (New York: Human Rights Watch, 2008) 2–3.

28 Petrie Report, see n 25, paras 31, 34.

29 Ibid., para. 32.

30 UN Secretary-General, Report of the Secretary-General's Panel of Experts on Accountability in Sri Lanka (31 March 2011), para. 137 (Sri Lanka Panel of Experts Report).

During the relevant period, the UN presence in Sri Lanka consisted solely of a UN Country Team, headed by a Resident Coordinator/Humanitarian Coordinator and with representatives from various UN agencies, funds, and programmes.[31] There was no political or peacekeeping mission, and no uniformed UN personnel. The only human rights presence was a single Human Rights Adviser, supported by two national staff; repeated requests to the government by the UN to establish an OHCHR presence in the country were denied.[32] The UN actors in-country had primarily humanitarian and development roles, with no explicit human rights or protection of civilians mandate. Protection work was only conducted via humanitarian activities.[33] As the conflict escalated, the UN evacuated out of the Vanni conflict zone in mid-September 2008,[34] except for some national staff who stayed behind with their families.[35] Senior UN officials conducted a series of visits to Sri Lanka during this time,[36] but the deteriorating situation did not make it onto the Security Council agenda.[37]

In such circumstances, UN activities related to protecting civilians were limited. Most emphasis was placed on humanitarian responses, including running humanitarian convoys into the Vanni from October 2008 through February 2009, until it became too dangerous.[38] There was no dedicated monitoring and reporting capacity in the UN Country Team, but as the significant human toll of the government assault on the Vanni became apparent, individual UN staff members began collecting and verifying casualty figures.[39] This cross-organization initiative became known as the UN Crisis Operations Group and was supported by the Resident Coordinator/Humanitarian Coordinator. However, despite the rigorous methodology of the Crisis Operations Group and the ample information compiled, the data was never used for advocacy purposes, either internally with UN Headquarters, discreetly with Member States, or publicly. The sole exception was a public statement by the High Commissioner for Human Rights in March 2009, citing casualty figures and calling for an immediate suspension of hostilities to allow for the evacuation of civilians.[40] This deafening silence was in part due to the reluctance of any UN actors in Sri Lanka at the time to advocate vociferously on principles enshrined in human rights law. Rather, the approach was one of soft advocacy, behind closed doors, with government officials.[41] UN actors on the ground prioritized the preservation of humanitarian access (minimal though it was) over the human rights imperatives relating to deterrence and accountability. In the end, the UN failed to protect civilians from the violence.

[31] Petrie Report, see n 25, paras 10–11.

[32] Petrie Report, see n 25, Annex III, para. 9.

[33] The 2008 Consolidated Humanitarian Appeal Process for Sri Lanka included a protection strategy, but the relevant projects generally overlapped with issues covered by humanitarian clusters such as food and health. See ibid., Annex III, para. 13.

[34] Petrie Report, see n 25, Annex 3, para. 35.

[35] Ibid., Annex 3, paras 14, 34.

[36] Ibid., para. 62; Keen, see n 27, 78.

[37] Ibid., Annex III, paras 127–30.

[38] Ibid., Annex III, paras 39–68.

[39] Ibid., paras 21, 51, 75, Annex V, paras 19–21.

[40] OHCHR, 'Press Release: Serious Violations of International Law Committed in Sri Lanka Conflict: UN Human Rights Chief' (Geneva, 13 March 2009). The HC spoke out despite attempts at dissuasion by other senior UN officials. See Petrie Report, n 25, paras 81–8.

[41] Petrie Report, see n 25, Annex II paras 89–90.

The Sri Lankan example exhibits many of the fundamental challenges to the operationalization of human rights protection practice in the field. First, the UN presence had no clear and distinct mandate to protect civilians, or even to monitor and report on the situation.[42] This stemmed, in large part, from the type of UN presence on the ground, with neither a security nor a human rights role, and with no UN entities clearly mandated to conduct civilian protection activities. The absence of a human rights presence—beyond a single adviser—also clearly impeded protection work.[43] There was no technical human rights contribution to ground communications with the government in international human rights and humanitarian law and obligations,[44] and there was no monitoring and reporting presence tasked to collect information.[45] The UN Country Team was simply not equipped or mandated to deal with the situation it faced. Although admirable efforts were made to overcome the deficiencies, they were ad hoc rather than institutional, which necessarily limited their impact. The UN had no strategy to protect civilians in Sri Lanka.[46]

In the absence of a dedicated human rights presence, humanitarian and other actors did not feel it was their place to take up human rights advocacy and did not want to jeopardize their aims, particularly the delivery of humanitarian assistance. This lack of political will and leadership at the field level was no doubt influenced by the silence emanating from the highest political levels.[47] Throughout the last stages of the conflict, the Security Council held no formal dialogue on the Sri Lanka situation,[48] the Human Rights Council did not consider the situation until the war was won,[49] and Member States for the most part remained aloof.[50] Meanwhile, UN Headquarters provided little consistent or strategic political engagement. The only strategy was a series of high-level UN visits intended to convey messages to the government.[51] The mixed messages of these visits alternately prioritized security concerns, humanitarian access, and human rights principles. This lack of political will and failure of leadership at all levels resulted in poor support to the UN team on the ground.[52]

[42] Ibid., Annex III, para. 9.

[43] According to the Petrie Report, this single Adviser 'lacked the capacity and stature of a human rights operation'. Ibid., Annex III, para. 9.

[44] Ibid., Annex V para. 5.

[45] According to the Petrie Report, the UN had recognized early on, since at least 2003, that there was an urgent need for independent human rights monitoring in Sri Lanka. Petrie Report, see n 25, Annex III, para. 9.

[46] Niland, see n 25, 17, 22.

[47] Keen, see n 27, 89–90.

[48] Petrie Report, see n 25, Annex III, paras 127–30; Keen, see n 27, 78.

[49] Although there was an attempt at the Human Rights Council within a month of the end of the conflict to pass a resolution to establish an investigation, the result was the opposite, congratulating the Sri Lankan government for vanquishing the terror threat of the Tamil Tigers. See Human Rights Council Resolution S/11-1, 'Assistance to Sri Lanka in the Promotion and Protection of Human Rights' (2009) UN Doc S/11-1. This was regarded by many as the nadir of the UN Human Rights Council. See Petrie Report, n 25, Annex III, paras 131, 153–5.

[50] Petrie Report, see n 25, Annex 3 paras 127–8.

[51] From January 2007 to December 2009, there were at least nineteen such high-level visits to Sri Lanka. Petrie Report, see n 25, para. 62.

[52] See Julian Vigo, 'Independent Report on Sri Lanka and UN Human Rights Violations', *Sri Lanka Guardian* (Online, 11 April 2012) <www.srilankaguardian.org/2012/04/independent-report-on-sri-lanka-and-un.html>.

In the aftermath of the violence, the Secretary-General took up the human rights issues that had been so ignored during the conflict by appointing a Panel of Experts to advise on the accountability process for violations of international humanitarian and human rights law in the final stages of the conflict.[53] In its final report, the Panel found credible allegations that both sides of the conflict had committed 'a wide range of serious violations'.[54] In addition to recommending investigations into the violations, the Panel recommended a comprehensive review of the UN's implementation of its humanitarian and protection mandates during the conflict.[55] This recommendation stemmed from the Panel's unequivocal finding: 'During the final stages of the war, the United Nations political organs and bodies failed to take actions that might have protected civilians.'[56]

Such a soul-searching exercise was conducted when the Secretary-General established an Internal Review Panel on UN actions in Sri Lanka in 2010. Finding a 'systemic failure' of the UN, the Panel 'conclude[d] that events in Sri Lanka mark a grave failure of the UN to adequately respond to early warnings and to the evolving situation during the final stages of the conflict and its aftermath, to the detriment of hundreds of thousands of civilians and in contradiction with the principles and responsibilities of the UN'.[57] In the end, the judgment was that even if the UN could not have actually protected civilians in Sri Lanka, it had an obligation to try, and it failed. Today, efforts to overcome the legacy of Sri Lanka are visible in the Human Rights Up Front initiative. Whether the initiative lives up to expectations will become clearer over time and will depend on the success of implementation efforts.

B. Afghanistan

Following the launch of US military operations in Afghanistan and the ousting of the Taliban regime, in 2001 the UN authorized an international force—the International Security Assistance Force (ISAF)—with a mandate to help the Afghan national security forces maintain security in and around Kabul, the nation's capital.[58] Since then, armed conflict has never abated, as a multiplicity of actors have, at various points, joined as parties to the conflict. Throughout, civilians have borne the brunt of the violence, in particular due to the parties' adoption of imprecise methods of warfare such as improvised explosive devices and aerial attacks.[59] As the conflict widened and deepened throughout 2007 and 2008, a corresponding rise in

[53] The Secretary-General did so with his authority, pursuant to Article 99 of the UN Charter, to collect information to bring to the attention of the Security Council regarding threats to the maintenance of international peace and security.

[54] Sri Lanka Panel of Experts Report, see n 30, ii.

[55] Ibid., vii–viii.

[56] Ibid., vi. In particular, in its memo covering the report, the Panel noted that the UN 'did not adequately invoke principles of human rights that are the foundation of the UN but appeared instead to do what was necessary to avoid confrontation with the government'. Cited in Petrie Report, see n 25, para. 1.

[57] Petrie Report, see n 25, para. 80.

[58] UNSC) Res 1386 (2001) UN Doc S/RES/1386.

[59] See UN Assistance Mission in Afghanistan (UNAMA) Protection of Civilians in Armed Conflict annual and midyear reports 2009 through 2014 for trends and details on various tactics of killing and injuring civilians, available at <www.unama.unmissions.org/Default.aspx?tabid=13941&language=en-US>.

civilian casualties was observed;[60] to date, civilian casualties continue to increase.[61] A gradual drawdown of international forces with a transfer of security operations to Afghan forces was formalized in June 2013.[62] The drawdown was paused in October 2015 when the United States government announced that the existing 9,800 US troops (out of a NATO total of 17,000) would remain in Afghanistan until the end of 2016, at least, due to the incapability of Afghan security forces to stem attacks and advances by anti-government elements.[63]

The UN Assistance Mission in Afghanistan (UNAMA), a special political mission, was established in 2002.[64] Reviewed annually, the mission's mandate has been altered over time to reflect the changing context and priorities, but it has consistently emphasized human rights and, more recently, the protection of civilians.[65] The mandate now authorizes UNAMA to

> monitor the situation of civilians, to coordinate efforts to ensure their protection, to promote accountability, and to assist in the full implementation of the fundamental freedoms and human rights provisions of the Afghan Constitution and international treaties to which Afghanistan is a State party, in particular those regarding the full enjoyment by women of their human rights.[66]

As a political mission, UNAMA has no military or other uniformed personnel.[67] Protection of civilians work is co-ordinated by a team within UNAMA's Human Rights Unit. UNAMA human rights personnel are present nationwide in eight regional and five provincial offices, as well as the mission's headquarters in Kabul.[68] National staff working on human rights issues are particularly strong in the mission.

In implementing its mandate, UNAMA's Human Rights Unit has identified four priority areas: (a) protection of civilians in armed conflict, (b) violence against women, (c) peace and reconciliation, and (d) detention practices.[69] Within the protection of civilians area of work, Human Rights Officers undertake various activities, including

[60] UNAMA, *Afghanistan: Annual Report on Protection of Civilians in Armed Conflict, 2008* (Kabul: United Nations, 2008) 1.

[61] UNAMA, *Afghanistan: Mid-Year Report on Protection of Civilians in Armed Conflict, 2015* (Kabul: United Nations, 2015) 1–9.

[62] Emma Graham-Harrison, 'Afghan Forces Take Over Security from NATO', *The Guardian* (London, 18 June 2013).

[63] *New York Times*, 15 October 2015.

[64] UNSC Res 1401 (2002) UN Doc S/RES/1401.

[65] The Secretary-General's March 2002 report on Afghanistan, adopted as the initial mandate of UNAMA by Security Council Resolution 1401, ibid., did not specifically mention protection of civilians, but said 'human rights . . . will be central to the purposes and functions of the mission', para. 103, and laid out tasks of 'monitoring, analyzing and reporting on the overall political and human rights situation' and 'investigating human rights violations and, where necessary, recommending corrective action'. See UNGA and UNSC, 'The Situation in Afghanistan and Its Implications for Peace and Security, Report of the Secretary-General' (2002) UN Doc A/56/875– S/2002/278, paras 103, 104(a), 104(g) (Secretary-General's 2002 Report on Afghanistan). Protection of civilians was first raised in the 2007 mandate, tasking UNAMA with monitoring the situation of civilians in armed conflict as part of its human rights work. UNSC Res 1746 (2007) UN Doc S/RES/1746, para. 4.

[66] UNSC Res 2145 (2014) UN Doc S/RES/2145, para. 6(e).

[67] Secretary-General's 2002 Report on Afghanistan, see n 64, para. 100.

[68] Ten provincial offices were recently closed due to budget cuts.

[69] UNAMA, 'Human Rights' (UNAMA, undated) <unama.unmisssions.org>.

independent and impartial monitoring, documentation and reporting of incidents involving loss of life or injury to civilians; advocacy activities to strengthen protection of civilians affected by the armed conflict; and initiatives to promote respect for international humanitarian and human rights law, and the Afghan Constitution among all parties to the conflict.[70]

The primary focus of this work is documentation, analysis, reporting, and advocacy related to incidents of violence that result in civilian casualties caused by all parties to the conflict. UNAMA independently verifies each incident with three different types of sources, and documents each case in a custom-designed database. Since 2007 the Human Rights Unit has compiled civilian casualty data and publicly released the information with corresponding analysis and recommendations in regular reports.[71] UNAMA then uses the information to conduct advocacy efforts with all parties to the conflict, both discreetly and publicly, to reduce civilian casualties and improve the protection of civilians, increase respect for the laws of war, and effect change in the conduct of hostilities.

Several factors contribute to these protection efforts, albeit that security conditions represent a major impediment. First, UNAMA has a meaningful human rights capacity, being well resourced with staff in field offices throughout the country. In particular, the capacity and involvement of Afghan national human rights staff enables access to sources and information, as well as contextual analysis, that international staff alone would not be able to provide.[72] Further, UNAMA has benefited from strong leadership of the Human Rights Unit, both in setting direction with clear priorities and strategies and in motivating, training, and supporting the human rights team, notably the national staff.[73]

Nor is the strong leadership in Afghanistan limited to the Human Rights Unit. In recent years human rights staff have been explicitly supported by mission leadership and have earned the respect of national and international stakeholders. In an unusual move among UN missions, and because of the Human Rights Unit's achievements, UNAMA leadership declared protecting and promoting human rights for all Afghans to be one of three priorities for the entire UN family in Afghanistan.[74] Echoing the clear, consistent mandate language on human rights, this declaration demonstrates a link between strong political leadership at the

[70] Ibid.; UNAMA, see n 61, 7.

[71] Annual reports in 2007 and 2008 were then increased to biannual reports since 2009.

[72] 'The presence of national staff with local language and cultural knowledge is a clear advantage for accessing information and building trust in communities.' Jacob Beswick and Elizabeth Minor, *The UN and Casualty Reporting: Good Practice and the Need for Action* (London: Oxford Research Group, 2014) 26 <www.oxfordresearchgroup.org.uk/sites/default/files/ORG-UN-and-CR.pdf>. UNAMA HRU also benefits from 'accidental activists' and local networks of Afghan civilians frustrated with the devastating toll of the conflict who contribute to casualty monitoring. See Norah Niland, 'Civilian Casualties—What Counts?' (*Transconflict*, 16 April 2011) <www.transconflict.com/2014/04/civilian-casualties-counts-164/>.

[73] Beswick and Minor, see n 71, 38–9.

[74] The other two priorities are facilitating a reconciliation process and linking development and security. UNAMA, 'Featured News: New Head of UNAMA Lays Out Priorities at First Press Conference in Kabul' (UNAMA, 25 January 2012) <unama.unmissions.org/Default.aspx?tabid=12330&ctl=Details&mid=15756&Itemid=33538&language=en-US>.

strategic and operational levels. In this way political and human rights agendas are shown to be mutually supportive and practically integrated.

In addition to being integrated into the wider work of the UN family, including political, humanitarian, and development efforts, one of the strongest attributes of the approach to human rights protection practice in Afghanistan has been the multidimensional and integrated approach adopted by human rights actors. After setting clear human rights objectives,[75] holistic strategies have been developed. For example, civilian casualty recording is not considered an end in itself. The information and analysis is leveraged for both discreet engagement with all parties and timed and targeted public information and advocacy efforts. This multidimensional approach is further enhanced by the collaborative attitude of human rights actors towards other actors whose work is relevant to human rights. In addition to relationships with the humanitarian protection cluster[76] and the national human rights commission, the UNAMA Human Rights Unit has benefited from the confidence and co-operation of various national and international sources, from the health community to the security services.[77]

Such strong attributes have enabled human rights actors to overcome considerable challenges. Despite significant security and access constraints caused by the unending armed conflict, and a particular difficulty engaging with opposition forces,[78] UNAMA's human rights and protection of civilians activities have effectively changed the discourse about civilian casualties in Afghanistan. Through regular, respected reports and constructive engagement with the warring parties, human rights advocacy has led to a discernible impact on the conduct of hostilities. An early example of this success was in 2008, when UNAMA's documentation and advocacy concerning the effects of an airstrike in Shindand district, Herat province, contributed to changes in an ISAF tactical directive on airstrikes; the policy change was then shown by UNAMA's data to have subsequently reduced civilian casualties from such incidents.[79] Following a 2012 airstrike in Logar province, UNAMA conducted several meetings with ISAF, informing that such incidents would be highlighted in an upcoming public Protection of Civilians in Armed Conflict report. Subsequently, ISAF issued an order on airstrikes limiting aerial attacks on civilian residences to situations of self-defence and as a last resort; no similar incidents were recorded by UNAMA after the order was issued.[80]

[75] Beswick and Minor, see n 71, 38, citing focus and purpose as key factors contributing to UNAMA's success in effective casualty recording.

[76] Under the cluster system, different agencies take the lead on particular activities in accordance with their mandates and expertise. UNHCR is the global protection cluster lead; at the country level the lead can be UNHCR, OHCHR, or UNICEF. Inter-Agency Standing Committee, Guidance Note on Using the Cluster Approach to Strengthen Humanitarian Response, November 24, 2006, 3.

[77] See, for example, UNAMA, n 61, 50, 56; Beswick and Minor, see n 71, 38, citing alliance building and co-operation with other actors in Afghanistan as a component of UNAMA's success.

[78] Beswick and Minor, see n 71, 40.

[79] 'Other ISAF policy changes aimed at reducing civilian casualties can be attributed to similar factors, including ISAF's own casualty tracking and interaction with UNAMA Human Rights and others' evidence-based advocacy.' Beswick and Minor, see n 71, 37. 'International military forces showed themselves more willing than before to institute more regular and transparent inquiries into specific incidents': UNAMA, see n 60, Executive Summary, para. 7.

[80] UNAMA, see n 61, 6–7, 36–8; Beswick and Minor, see n 71, 37–8.

The impact of UNAMA's monitoring and advocacy work has been most significant with regard to international and other pro-government forces, which cause only a small fraction of the harm to civilians in Afghanistan. But even anti-government forces are sensitive to UNAMA's reporting. As noted in one external report, 'In terms of the attitudes of opposition groups, the political Taliban feels the need to respond to UNAMA's [human rights] reports using the language of the protection of civilians, and to make statements on measures taken to avoid and mitigate casualties.'[81] The Taliban have responded to UNAMA's reports by setting up their own civilian casualty mitigation committee, compiling monthly 'war crimes' reports, publicly stating that their members do not use certain types of improvised explosive devices, and seeking regular dialogue on human rights with UNAMA.[82]

Although these impacts are limited, some of the responses may be cynical, and far too many Afghan civilians continue to suffer the effects of armed conflict, the prioritization and implementation of human rights protection practice in Afghanistan has begun to contribute to mitigating harm against civilians.[83] However, the situation of civilians continues to be of enormous concern and may deteriorate.

C. South Sudan

Following decades of conflict, South Sudan realized independence in July 2011. The newly independent State, buoyed by international goodwill and assistance, began with serious capacity, resource, and infrastructure deficits. Moreover, from independence South Sudan continued to struggle with various low-intensity conflicts and inter-communal violence. Then, in December 2013, a political struggle between the President and the former Vice President erupted into widespread violence that quickly played out along ethnic lines. Notwithstanding multiple peace agreements between the conflicting parties including the latest in August 2015, outbreaks of violence continue in South Sudan.

At independence, a new UN peacekeeping mission was born along with the new State: the UN Mission in South Sudan (UNMISS).[84] With an authorization of 7,000 troops and 900 police, the Security Council granted UNMISS a wide-ranging mandate, focused on state building.[85] The mandate included strong human rights and protection of civilians provisions, but the latter were framed

[81] Beswick and Minor, see n 71, 37.

[82] See references in UNAMA, *Afghanistan: Annual Report on Protection of Civilians in Armed Conflict, 2013* (Kabul: United Nations, 2013) 5, 36, 72–3.

[83] 'Though these changes are focused on the reduction of civilian casualties, rather than their elimination or the end of hostilities, and though the most effective advocacy is with the conflict party that now causes the minority of harm, these changes are still highly significant to people living through conflict in Afghanistan.' Beswick and Minor, see n 71, 38.

[84] UNMISS was preceded by the UN Mission in Sudan (UNMIS), which monitored implementation of the peace agreement between Sudan and (then-called) Southern Sudan. See UNSC Res 1997 (2011) UN Doc S/RES/1997, paras 1, 3.

[85] UNSC Res 1996 (2011) UN Doc S/RES/1996, paras 3(a), 3(b), 3(c). For discussion on the questionable nature of this approach, see Jean-Marie Guéhenno, 'The United Nations and the Protection of Civilians', Chapter 11 in this volume.

primarily as supporting the State's protection activities.[86] In response to the conflict that began in December 2013, the Security Council first authorized the deployment of more uniformed personnel to protect civilians,[87] and then gave UNMISS a new mandate listing only four priority tasks: (a) protecting civilians; (b) monitoring and investigating human rights; (c) enabling the delivery of humanitarian assistance; and (d) supporting the peace process.[88] UNMISS' protection of civilians work is co-ordinated by a few Protection of Civilians Advisers, while nearly 100 UN human rights staff are deployed across the ten states of South Sudan.[89]

Given the context of continuing armed conflict, UNMISS' strong mandate, and its expansive presence, a great deal of the work of the mission's Human Rights Division is focused on the protection of civilians. Several of the Division's activities contribute directly to the protection of civilians, including: (a) monitoring and reporting on human rights violations, (b) analysing the threats against civilians and feeding into the mission's early warning mechanism, (c) providing protection through presence, (d) building the capacity of local protection actors, (e) advocating for accountability as a deterrent, and (f) intervening in individual cases. Further, the Human Rights Division works closely with the Protection of Civilians Advisers to co-ordinate mission-wide protection strategies and responses, guided by human rights standards and principles.

The tenure of UNMISS has been marked by moments of significant success as well as failure in fulfilling its protection of civilians mandate, particularly in the strategic state of Jonglei. During the Government's civilian disarmament campaign in Jonglei in 2012, the mission engaged proactively and consistently, negotiating a voluntary rather than forcible disarmament process, deploying integrated teams throughout the state to monitor human rights violations, and advocating for accountability for violations by government security forces.[90] During the height of armed rebellion and corresponding government counter-insurgency operations in Jonglei in 2012–13, the mission invested considerable political resources in facilitating a local peace process, while also providing physical protection to civilians within UN bases when violence erupted. It launched a proactive military patrolling campaign to improve security and boost confidence of civilians and comprehensively monitored, investigated, and reported on human rights violations, including several massacres of civilians by government forces.[91] Although civilians suffered

[86] See UNSC Res 1996 (2011) UN Doc S/RES/1996, para. 3(b).

[87] UNSC Res 2155 (2014) S/RES/2155, para. 8, authorizing 12,500 troops and 1,323 police.

[88] Ibid., para. 4.

[89] Increasingly in UN peacekeeping missions, protection of civilians work is co-ordinated by Protection of Civilians Advisers, rather than led by human rights components.

[90] Such advocacy was discreet and political, as well as public. See, for example, UN Mission in South Sudan (UNMISS), 'Press Release: UNMISS Calls for Action to Safeguard Peace Process in Jonglei State' (UNMISS, August 24, 2012) <reliefweb.int/sites/reliefweb.int/files/resources/LinkClick_22.pdf>.

[91] Reminiscent of Sri Lanka, the mission's prioritization of political considerations meant that none of these reports were released publicly, and the public statements that were made always emphasized that both sides were committing violations against civilians, when in fact extensive human rights reporting and investigations showed that the vast majority of violations against civilians were committed by government forces.

considerably from violence in both cases, the examples nonetheless represent attempts by UNMISS to take multidimensional approaches to its protection of civilians mandate. In contrast, during two large-scale waves of intercommunal violence in Jonglei, in December 2011/January 2012 and July 2013, the mission was unable to provide physical protection to civilians and was unsuccessful in any political engagement to prevent the killing of thousands of civilians and the destruction of whole villages.[92]

When widespread, ethnically targeted violence broke out in South Sudan in December 2013, UNMISS reacted immediately, opening its gates to protect civilians, saving tens of thousands of lives in the first days. Although widely lauded, it can be argued that the need to open the gates resulted from a failure of protection of civilians strategies and interventions in the first instance. Moreover, the opening of the gates, followed by the establishment of protection of civilians sites within the UN bases where, as of August 2015, nearly 190,000 civilians continue to stay, soon gave rise to new protection challenges. These included the need for UNMISS to project force rather than retreat into a fortress mentality; to proactively patrol so as to protect displaced and vulnerable civilians outside UN bases;[93] and to monitor and protect within the protection of civilians sites, in particular where internally displaced persons (IDPs) were of mixed ethnicities. Extensive monitoring by the UNMISS Human Rights Division fed into early warning mechanisms and co-ordinated responses, including successful escorts of hundreds of civilians to safety in Unity and Upper Nile states; extractions and other specific efforts to protect victims, witnesses, and human rights defenders; and the adoption of rights-based approaches to the UN's management of the protection of civilians sites. Unfortunately, coordinated responses were not always forthcoming. Tragedies such as the attack on the UNMISS base in Jonglei State in April 2014, resulting in the deaths of nearly fifty IDPs, and the targeted killings by a local militia of at least six humanitarian aid workers in Upper Nile State in August 2014 might have been averted had early warning signals been heeded. These examples emphasize the criticality of sustained commitment, proactive efforts, and dynamic responses to operationalize protection of civilians strategies in ongoing conflict, all of which require senior leadership at the field level. Since the onset of the current conflict, UNMISS has increasingly spoken out strongly and publicly about human rights and international humanitarian law violations committed by both parties to the conflict.[94]

[92] *See* UNMISS, 'Incidents of Inter-Communal Violence in Jonglei State' (UNMISS, June 2012) <unmiss.unmissions.org/Portals/unmiss/Human%20Rights%20Reports/June%202012%20Jonglei%20Report.pdf>.

[93] More than 2,400,000 South Sudanese have been displaced by the conflict; many fled violence but others were forced to move in search of basic subsistence: Report of the UN Secretary-General to the Security Council on South Sudan, 21 August 2015, s/2015/655, p. 8. At least initially, displaced persons in UN protection of civilians sites were unique from other displaced populations in that they remained in a dangerous territory, only protected by the UN walls and soldiers.

[94] See UNMISS, 'Interim Report on Human Rights: Crisis in South Sudan' (UNMISS, 21 February 2014) <http://unmiss.unmissions.org/Portals/unmiss/Documents/PR/Reports/HRD%20Interim%20Report%20on%20Crisis%202014-02-21.pdf>, and UNMISS, 'Conflict in South Sudan: A Human Rights Report' (UNMISS, May 8, 2014) <www.unmiss.unmissions.org/Portals/unmiss/

Provided with a robust mandate, a significant human rights capacity, and uniformed personnel to execute physical protection, UNMISS has nonetheless struggled to protect civilians from violence. Access and security constraints have proven significant challenges, as have the simple logistics of movement across the vast and undeveloped terrain of South Sudan. However, the single most influential factor in the failures of the UNMISS protection of civilians efforts has been the emphasis on state-building at the expense of principled political engagement and a focus on the protection of civilians and human rights. Before the December 2013 crisis, most of the mission's protection efforts were tailored towards establishing a protective environment. The efforts gained little traction, however, and were premature.[95] There were also warning signs, including the shooting down of a UN helicopter by the army, the expulsion of a Senior Human Rights Officer, and numerous government violations of the Status of Forces Agreement, as well as dilemmas over human rights reporting. Prior to the December 2013 crisis and subsequently, UNMISS experienced some success protecting civilians from physical violence. Going forward, the challenge for UNMISS and the entire UN in South Sudan will be whether, while sustaining physical protection efforts, it can enhance a multidimensional protection of civilians strategy to include greater emphasis on political engagement and advocacy grounded in human rights principles.

IV. Viability of Human Rights Protection Activity

A. Challenges

As illustrated by these case studies, human rights actors encounter many and varied challenges in conducting their work. Tensions often arise between human rights activities, particularly advocacy, and other objectives being pursued by the international community. In these cases, the human rights agenda frequently suffers, as political, military, and humanitarian objectives generally trump human rights concerns in situations of armed conflict.

One of the areas of tension is the widely held view that advocating for human rights will jeopardize the international community's relationship with the host government. In situations where host governments are complicit in the perpetration of violence against civilians, raising human rights concerns may result in access and movement constraints, the denial of visas for staff to take up work in the country, expulsion of staff declared *personae non gratae*, or more severe consequences.[96] The dilemma of whether to speak up or risk being expelled, though, may be a false dichotomy:[97] in Sri Lanka, once the humanitarian convoys ended in February 2009, the UN had so little access and ability to deliver aid that there was very little

Human%20Rights%20Reports/UNMISS%20Conflict%20in%20South%20Sudan%20-%20A%20 Human%20Rights%20Report.pdf>, as well as various press statements and releases.

95 See Guéhenno, Chapter 11 in this volume.

96 All international organizations, and UN presences in particular, must maintain the consent of the host nation to remain in country and function.

97 See, for example, Keen, n 27, 101.

left to risk.[98] In many cases, the risk of running afoul of the government may be overstated. In some cases, the government may not be willing to sacrifice international political support and assistance; in others, its behaviour will not be affected one way or the other by UN condemnation.[99]

Due to the tensions with the government that can result from human rights advocacy, international actors, including the UN, often prioritize other areas of work, such as political, humanitarian, and development agendas. While such activities are critical, they ignore a key comparative advantage of the UN: other entities deliver aid and assistance, but the UN has unique global moral authority to uphold human rights principles. To focus on political, humanitarian, and development aims to the exclusion of human rights not only undermines the foundational principles of the UN but also sacrifices long-term goals for short-term gains.[100] Political resolutions that fail to address the root causes of conflict fail to prevent the recurrence of conflict. Further, focusing on state-building while ignoring early signs of conflict leaves the international community unprepared, and then compelled to take urgent and more costly action once widespread violence has erupted.

Tensions can also arise between the work of human rights and humanitarian actors. Humanitarians need to distinguish themselves from human rights actors, as from all political and military elements, in order to maintain access to affected populations. Humanitarians aspire to be both impartial and neutral, providing assistance to all in need; in contrast, human rights actors are impartial but not necessarily neutral, speaking out against human rights violations and their perpetrators. These distinctions emphasize the need for a dedicated human rights capacity, to provide an advocacy voice, so humanitarians themselves need not endanger their access to alleviate suffering. In the field, humanitarian actors are often the most supportive of human rights work, even providing evidence and information to human rights monitors and investigators, as long as their space is maintained and their confidence kept.

Many of these tensions are exacerbated by institutional challenges within international, particularly UN, presences. Human rights objectives, though nominally mandated at the highest levels, have often not been prioritized in the field. This can combine with the perception of those outside the human rights community that human rights actors are 'negative', 'pessimistic', or 'critical'. As a result, human rights actors are frequently excluded from fora where policy, planning, and priorities are decided, including on issues of protection. This can lead to strategies not informed by human rights principles, and failure to allocate resources to human rights protection work.

[98] 'In fact, the amount of "humanitarian space" in which aid agencies could operate was perceived as having shrunk alongside a series of concessions to the Sri Lankan government.' Keen, see n 27, 79.

[99] For example, Sri Lanka, see Keen, n 27, 87.

[100] See Keen, n 27, 51, noting that in Sri Lanka, as in earlier crises, the humanitarians adopted relatively short-term time horizons. Alternatively, it can be argued that development organisations sometimes prioritize long-term institutional presence over short-term protection priorities. See Niland, n 25, 16, 19.

B. Enabling conditions

Despite all these challenges, there is ample evidence that human rights protection activities can and do make a crucial contribution to the protection of civilians in conflict. Certain enabling conditions make this result more likely. The case studies suggest that the following elements enable the successful operationalization of human rights activities in the field, contributing to overarching protection of civilians strategies: (a) increased human rights capacity, (b) strong political will and leadership, and (c) multidimensional strategies.

As the case studies reveal and the new UN Human Rights Up Front initiative recognizes, for an effective UN response, human rights principles must be at the heart of the UN's work on peace and security, particularly the protection of civilians during conflict. The promotion and protection of human rights needs to be incorporated into the responsibilities of all UN staff, whether military, political, humanitarian, or other personnel.[101] Limiting the promotion and protection of human rights to human rights officers risks such activities being viewed as a discrete stream of work, when in fact all UN activity should be in line with human rights objectives. Promoting and protecting human rights requires strong leadership. The Sri Lanka case study showed the reluctance of the Resident Coordinator/ Humanitarian Coordinator and humanitarians, as well as senior-level officials, to speak out on human rights due to competing objectives. In the absence of human rights officers, no one stepped in to fill the advocacy role. In South Sudan, protection of civilians imperatives have been effectively mainstreamed in UNMISS but human rights principles have not enjoyed the same status. In contrast, in Afghanistan, UNAMA's credibility was enhanced by embracing and communicating human rights objectives, even though ongoing conflict continues to result in widespread human rights abuse. OHCHR and field human rights components continue to bear the responsibility for appropriate orientation and training of staff in human rights principles and objectives, supported by commitment from senior officials.[102]

In addition to the shared UN responsibility for defining and achieving human rights objectives, a specialized human rights presence is required to provide technical advice and support to senior officials and specialized capacity for protection activity.[103] Such roles include collection and verification of information; legal analysis and related advocacy; the conduct of risk assessments, extractions, and other protection measures for individuals at risk; and implementation of victim-oriented approaches. In Sri Lanka, the failure to obtain or heed technical human rights advice limited the UN's effectiveness, in particular its advocacy and

[101] OHCHR, UN Department of Peacekeeping Operations, UN Department of Political Affairs, and UN Department of Field Support, 'Policy on Human Rights in Peace Operations' (2011) Ref. No 2011.20, paras 81–118 (Policy on Human Rights in Peace Operations).

[102] Ibid., paras 71–6.

[103] 'But technical assistance and long-term institution-building are of little or no value where the basic principle of protection is being actively violated. A greater human rights field presence during times of crisis would provide timely information to United Nations bodies and, when necessary, draw urgent attention to situations requiring action.' 'In Larger Freedom', see n 7, para. 143.

communications with the government. While the UN Crisis Operations Group stepped into the breach to conduct monitoring and reporting, the mechanism was based on personal initiative rather than built into the UN design. Moreover, there was no high-level human rights official to advocate for leveraging the information produced by the Crisis Operations Group. The Afghanistan and South Sudan case studies show the potential effectiveness, particularly in monitoring and reporting, of well-resourced human rights presences. In particular, strong national staff capacity has an exponential effect on the success of human rights work. The case studies further show that real impact requires not only the presence but also the inclusion of human rights actors during policy development, planning, and political processes.

If human rights is to be a central element of protection of civilians strategies, strong political support is needed. The absence of such support in Sri Lanka made it impossible for human rights objectives to be realized. The Security Council never formally met on the issue during the last stages of the war, and the Human Rights Council only belatedly addressed the situation. When it did, it praised rather than condemned the government. No senior UN officials, other than the High Commissioner for Human Rights, spoke out publicly on human rights abuses or the extent of and responsibility for civilian casualties. Further, the UN Headquarters leadership did not advise staff in the field on human rights-related protection activities. This was in sharp contrast with UNAMA and UNMISS, as evidenced in the missions' mandates and the resourcing of their respective human rights components. In South Sudan, the importance of high-level political support was further emphasized with the mission's renewed mandate following the outbreak of conflict in December 2013.[104]

Political will derives from numerous sources, including UN Member States—particularly those serving in the Security Council, the Secretary-General, and senior UN officials both at headquarters in New York and Geneva, and the leadership of UN presences in the field. Without leadership, even the strongest human rights mandates cannot be implemented and are easily overshadowed by political exigencies. In the case of Sri Lanka, the UN Country Team was reluctant, and its leadership not sufficiently knowledgeable about human rights, to implement a rights-based approach to advocacy with the government or to condemn violence against civilians publicly. Even where staff took it upon themselves to conduct monitoring and reporting, the leadership chose not to use such information. In UNMISS, quiet diplomacy was often preferred over public human rights advocacy, particularly when there were allegations of government involvement in violence against civilians.[105] This occurred despite strong external, UN Headquarters, and Security Council pressure for public reporting on human rights

[104] UNSC Res 2155 (2014) S/RES/2155.

[105] In its first two and a half years, the mission's only public human rights reports were on intercommunal violence, while human rights investigations and reports on violations by the Government (including the December 2012 massacre of protesters by security forces in Wau, Western Bahr el-Ghazal State, and 2012–13 atrocities committed during counter-insurgency campaigns in Pibor County, Jonglei State) were never made public.

violations.[106] Of the three case studies, UNAMA seems to be the exception: in recent years senior mission leadership emphasized the central role of human rights in the overarching strategy of the mission. Senior-level support can lead to enablers for human rights work, including recruitment of strong human rights personnel; access of human rights staff to leadership meetings and decision-making processes; and allocation of mission resources such as air assets, security clearances, and other logistical support.

In order to be effective, human rights strategies must be multidimensional, and cannot be limited to what is traditionally perceived as human rights work: 'naming and shaming' (more technically, calls for accountability). It is this element of human rights work that draws the ire of host governments and other parties to conflict, as well as leading other elements of the UN to distance themselves from human rights objectives. The UN's failures in Sri Lanka may have stemmed from a limited conception of human rights work as only publicly blaming the government, and therefore distaste for such work. Even private advocacy with the government was not rooted in international law. In contrast, the protection of civilians work of UNAMA shows the potential for success of a multifaceted approach that includes collection of credible information and constructive engagements with parties to the conflict. Public reports are not issued in a vacuum, but rather are useful as part of a broader strategy to promote and protect human rights. In South Sudan, advocacy efforts were sometimes strengthened by credible information collection, in particular during the 2012 Jonglei civilian disarmament campaign and during the first months of fighting in 2014. However, these approaches have never been holistic enough, with the release of public human rights reports rarely integrated into a comprehensive human rights strategy.

Finally, protection strategies must also be multidimensional in order to be effective, with human rights activities alongside humanitarian and political activities.[107] The more multidimensional a strategy is, the less likely it is that any one dimension will derail the entire enterprise. Trade-offs and judgments inevitably need to be made in terms of which activities are best pursued when and where. Making these judgments will never be easy, and human rights must never be compromised in the process. However, these judgements are likely to be better informed and understood if they are seen in the context of achieving objectives shared and subscribed to by the whole UN system with a view to protecting people.

[106] See, for example, Samuel Oakford, 'Greater Transparency Urged for U.N.'s South Sudan Mission', *Inter Press Service* (Rome, 1 February 2014) <www.ipsnews.net/2014/02/transparency-urged-u-n-s-south-sudan-mission/>; Human Rights Watch, 'They Are Killing Us: Abuses against Civilians in South Sudan's Pibor County' (New York: Human Rights Watch, 2013) 42–3; UNSC Res 1996 (2011) UN Doc S/RES/1996, para. 3(b)(iii). The current conflict has seen an increased willingness for such human rights emphasis by UNMISS leadership (as evidenced by two public human rights reports in 2014, see n 93), likely influenced by the severity of violations and the roughly equal culpability of both sides in the conflict.

[107] As noted by the Internal Review Panel on Sri Lanka: 'In fact, with its multiplicity of mandates and areas of expertise, the UN possesse[s] the capabilities to strive for humanitarian access while also robustly condemning the perpetrators of killings of civilians.' Petrie Report, see n 25, para. 75.

V. The Human Rights Up Front Initiative

The high-profile Human Rights Up Front initiative, introduced earlier, identifies necessary efforts to improve the UN's human rights work, including protection practice.[108] The associated plan sets out six actions to ensure that 'the protection of human rights and of people are at the heart of UN strategies and operational activities'.[109]

The initiative has been welcomed by many Member States and civil society actors as an important step forward. It is informing the regular discussions among UN leaders in New York as to how the system will respond to specific country situations, and has triggered a number of interventions. One example was the decision to open UNMISS compound gates in South Sudan in December 2013;[110] another the statements by the Secretary-General and his Special Envoy for Syria drawing attention to the risk of civilian massacres, for example in Kobani in September 2014.[111] The credibility of the initiative will now depend upon its systematic implementation, particularly where populations are at risk of, or are already experiencing, massive violations of their rights.

From a field perspective, the third Human Rights Up Front action item is key to success, namely the development of coherent and implementable protection strategies on the ground. Hence the initiative in late 2014, supported by New York, Geneva, and field-based leadership, to develop a UN system-wide protection strategy for Syria, to which humanitarian, human rights, and political actors are contributing with a view to progressing a defined set of protection outcomes. These will relate, for example, to reducing violence, improving humanitarian access, strengthening local protection capacities, and addressing the needs of particularly vulnerable groups.[112] Success in implementing the Human Rights Up Front initiative requires leveraging the UN system's diverse mandates and capacities, as well as creativity and boldness in reacting to events and seizing opportunities to protect people.

Success will also require a more systematic approach, including engagement and, where possible, partnerships with other actors, governmental and from civil society, to achieve objectives that will make a real difference to real people. Timely interventions by the UN to save lives and protect people at risk will always be vulnerable to accusations that they are politically motivated, that they prioritize certain situations or population groups over others, or that they reflect cultural or other

[108] One of the authors of this chapter served as head of the team that worked with the Deputy Secretary-General and the Executive Office of the Secretary-General to develop the Plan of Action.

[109] See Andrew Clapham, 'Protection of Civilians under International Human Rights Law', Chapter 6 in this volume, for a more detailed discussion of Human Rights Up Front.

[110] See Andrew Gilmour, 'The Future of Human Rights: A View from the United Nations' (2014) 28 Ethics and Intl Affairs 239.

[111] United Nations, 'Note to Correspondents—Transcript of press conference by UN Special Envoy for Syria (SES) Staffan de Mistura' (Geneva, 10 October 2014) <www.un.org/sg/offthecuff/index.asp?nid=3674>.

[112] Internal UN note entitled 'Agreed Way Forward', shared with participants after a meeting held in Beirut, 4/5 September 2014, on 'Protection in Syria's Armed Conflict'.

prejudices. The more UN action on protection is recognized as being rooted in reliable data and objective assessment of risk, the more credible and effective it will be.

The Human Rights Up Front initiative has raised expectations of the UN. Implementation of the action plan, whether in mission or non-mission settings, requires both leadership and strong teamwork, notably at the field level, to define and pursue collectively agreed, actionable protection objectives. This will be particularly challenging in situations where the UN architecture is unusually complex and responsibilities diffused between humanitarian, human rights, development, and political actors. But it is precisely in such situations where the risk is greatest of failure by the system to mobilize its diverse capacities to protect people. In this regard, the initiative may both highlight and help resolve accountability deficits.

Ultimately, the UN will be judged, fairly or otherwise, by perceived success in doing everything in its power to make a difference not only to prevent massive abuses of rights, but also in situations which are best characterized as crises of protection, including Syria, Iraq, South Sudan, and the Central African Republic.

VI. Conclusion

As this chapter describes, human rights actors regularly contribute to the protection of people in conflict. The UN and its partners have gained valuable experience in this field over the past decades, yet there remains scope for sharing knowledge about the lessons learned and how they can be applied. For the potential of human rights protection practice to be realized, human rights actors need not only capacity and resources, and for their work to be integrated into overarching protection strategies, but also, critically, they need to benefit from strong political support and leadership at both the strategic and operational levels. It remains to be seen whether the promise of the Human Rights Up Front initiative will be fully realized; there is no time to lose.

17

Humanitarian Protection—Moving beyond the Tried and Tested

Sara Pantuliano and Eva Svoboda

I. Introduction

Since the 1990s, norms and policies dealing with the protection of civilians have dramatically expanded. Discourse on protection intensified in the wake of post-Cold War interventions and some conspicuous failures to protect civilian populations, for example in Bosnia and Rwanda. UN Secretary-General Boutros-Ghali's 1992 Agenda for Peace challenged the presumption that civilian suffering was the sole responsibility of the government of their country and laid the policy bedrock for a more interventionist UN approach by promoting an end to absolute sovereignty.[1] In 2001, the International Commission on Intervention and State Sovereignty (ICISS) report proposed a reformulation of this doctrine in the form of the Responsibility to Protect, stressing the sovereign responsibility of the State to protect those within its borders, but also the responsibility of the international community to intervene where a population is suffering serious harm. The Responsibility to Protect doctrine was recognized by the United Nations (UN) through the adoption of the World Summit declaration in 2005.[2] The related but distinct protection of civilians concept, the subject of annual reports by the Secretary-General since 1999,[3] has become firmly established on the UN Security Council agenda and has increasingly featured as an explicit component of peace-keeping mandates. Many UN peacekeeping missions have protection-focused

[1] United Nations General Assembly (UNGA) and United Nations Security Council (UNSC), 'Report of the Secretary-General Pursuant to the Statement Adopted by the Summit Meeting of the Security Council on 31 January 1992, An Agenda for Peace, Preventive Diplomacy, Peacemaking and Peace-keeping' (1992) UN Doc A/47/277— S/24111, para. 17.

[2] Gareth Evans and Mohamed Sahoun, *The Responsibility to Protect: Report of the International Commission on Intervention and State Sovereignty* (Ottawa: International Development Research Centre, 2001). The Responsibility to Protect (RtoP) doctrine was formally recognized through its adoption in the World Summit declaration in late 2005. UNGA Resolution (Res) 60/1, '2005 World Summit Outcome' (2005) UN Doc A/60/L.1, paras 138–40.

[3] See, for example, UNSC, 'Report of the Secretary-General to the Security Council on the Protection of Civilians in Armed Conflict' (1999) UN Doc S/1999/957.

mandates,[4] as have the recent African Union missions in Somalia and the Central African Republic. This has also been accompanied by expansions in UN human rights work and renewed dynamism in international law, including the adoption of standards for internally displaced persons (IDPs).[5] Similarly, growing numbers of non-governmental organizations (NGOs) are specializing in protection issues, and many others have begun 'mainstreaming' protection in their work or setting up specific protection programmes.

This significant legal and policy-level expansion has not, however, been accompanied by a commensurate improvement in protection for civilians on the ground. This becomes evident when looking, for example, at the continuously high prevalence of conflict-related sexual violence in the Democratic Republic of the Congo (DRC) and the associated impunity of perpetrators;[6] the increasing number of refugees and internally displaced in Syria and surrounding countries;[7] and the last weeks of the civil war in Sri Lanka, when the civilian population came under intense attack from government forces.[8]

This chapter examines why the gap between policy and practice exists and its consequences both for protection actors and affected communities, and considers how it can be addressed. It argues that the lack of definitional clarity of the concept of humanitarian protection, a proliferation of protection actors, and differing mandates and objectives have contributed to a disjointed analysis, even as mechanisms such as the Inter-Agency Standing Committee (IASC) aim to counter this effect.[9] Humanitarian actors recognize that an improved collective analysis is critical for protection work if it seeks to influence behaviour of armed actors and thus better protect affected communities. Improved collective analysis also needs to understand the role of local actors who have important knowledge of and networks among communities. It is argued that all too often, local actors are insufficiently incorporated into the humanitarian response. Recognizing the experience and knowledge of local actors, and involving them, should not be a last option when all

4 See, for example, UNSC Res 1996 (2011) UN Doc S/RES/1996; UNSC Res 1925 (2010) UN Doc S/RES/1925.

5 See, for example, Inter-Agency Standing Committee (IASC), *Protection of Internally Displaced Persons* (Geneva: IASC, 1999); African Union Convention for the Protection and Assistance of Internally Displaced Persons in Africa (adopted 22 October 2009, entered into force 6 December 2012) 52 ILM 397; Sorcha O'Callaghan and Sara Pantuliano, *Protective Action, Incorporating Civilian Protection into Humanitarian Response* (London: Overseas Development Institute, 2007) 1–2.

6 Human Rights Watch, 'Democratic Republic of the Congo: Ending Impunity for Sexual Violence' (New York: Human Rights Watch, 10 June 2014) <hrw.org/news/2014/06/10/democratic-republic-congo-ending-impunity-sexual-violence>.

7 See Stephanie Nebehay, 'Syrian Refugees Top 3 Million, Half of All Syrians Displaced: UN', *Reuters* (London, 29 August 2014) <www.reuters.com/article/2014/08/29/us-syria-crisis-refugees-idUSKBN0GT0AX20140829>.

8 *Report of the Secretary-General's Internal Review Panel on United Nations action in Sri Lanka* (November 2012) para. 25, Annex III paras 105, 127, 137, 141, 155, Annex V para. 17 (Sri Lanka Internal Review Panel) <www.un.org/News/dh/infocus/Sri_Lanka/The_Internal_Review_Panel_report_on_Sri_Lanka.pdf>.

9 See IASC, 'IASC Guidance Note on Using the Cluster Approach to Strengthen Humanitarian Response' (Geneva: IASC, 2006) <www.humanitarianresponse.info/system/files/documents/files/IASC%20Guidance%20Note%20on%20using%20the%20Cluster%20Approach%20to%20Strengthen%20Humanitarian%20Response%20(November%202006).pdf>.

else fails, but the default approach. Regardless of protection actors' involvement, the local population will ultimately constitute the first line of defence when people are threatened. Civilians' own activities are frequently the most important element of their survival, based on an often detailed and sophisticated understanding of the threats they face.

II. Lack of Definitional Clarity

There are fundamental definitional issues associated with protection. Not only do international actors have different understandings of the concept; they also differ on how to operationalize it.[10] The humanitarian community generally accepts the IASC definition of protection as 'all efforts aimed at obtaining full respect for the rights of the individual and of the obligations of the authorities/arms bearers in accordance with the letter and the spirit of the relevant bodies of law'.[11] While the definition is legally oriented and comprehensive, it lacks focus and was ultimately unhelpful to many, being seen as confusing and impractical.[12] This resulted in agencies developing their own working definitions, while at the same time accepting that of the IASC. Subsequently, the Sphere Project introduced a Charter and Minimum Standards in Humanitarian Response,[13] and the International Committee of the Red Cross (ICRC) together with others developed the Professional Standards for Protection Work.[14]

There is not a unified view on what humanitarian protection is and what humanitarians can and should do in this regard. Simply put, protection is about ensuring that civilians are safe. The aim of protection is therefore to reduce or minimize the risks to which civilians are exposed. This can be done on three levels: (a) by preventing a particular violation, or at least mitigating its effect (*responsive action*); (b) by restoring people's dignity following abuse (*remedial action*); and (c) by creating an environment where the rights of individuals are respected (*environment building*).[15] Examples of humanitarian protection activity include

[10] International Committee of the Red Cross (ICRC) and Humanitarian Policy Group (HPG), 'Roundtable on Civil–Military Coordination, The Concept of Protection: Towards a Mutual Understanding' (Geneva: ICRC, 2011) 6 <www.icrc.org/eng/assets/files/2012/hpg-icrc-roundtable-summary-note-2011-12-12.pdf>.

[11] In 1999 the ICRC hosted several workshops with human rights and humanitarian organizations, following which this definition was adopted by the IASC. For explicit use of this definition, see Angelo Gnaedinger, 'Address to Humanitarian and Resident Coordinators' Retreat: Protection of Civilians in Conflict—the ICRC Perspective' (Geneva, 9 May 2007) <www.icrc.org/eng/resources/documents/statement/children-statement-140507.html>.

[12] Andrew Bonwick, 'Who Really Protects Civilians?' (2006) 16 Development in Practice 270, 271.

[13] The Sphere Project, 'Charter and Minimum Standards in Humanitarian Response' (Geneva: The Sphere Project, 2011) 19–24, 25–354 <www.sphereproject.org/handbook>.

[14] ICRC, *Professional Standards for Protection Work Carried out by Humanitarian and Human Rights Actors in Armed Conflict and Other Situations of Violence* (Geneva: ICRC, 2013) <www.icrc.org/eng/resources/documents/publication/p0999.htm>.

[15] Sara Pantuliano and Sorcha O'Callaghan, *The 'Protection Crisis': A Review of Field-based Strategies for Humanitarian Protection in Darfur* (London: Overseas Development Institute, 2006) 6.

monitoring violations of international humanitarian and international human rights law and advocating for their compliance with warring parties, including State and non-State actors. It may also include activity such as tracing missing family members and visiting prisoners to ensure they are treated humanely. Humanitarians may contribute to civilian protection by deterring violence due to their presence, although this assertion is contested. Ultimately, all humanitarian agencies endeavour to contribute to a more comprehensive concept of protection through *protection mainstreaming*, even if they do not consider themselves as protection agencies. Through protection mainstreaming, agencies incorporate principles such as dignity into all of their work, seek to ensure access to services by all affected persons, and avoid causing harm by their delivery of aid. The concept puts strong emphasis on the fact that material assistance is not sufficient to achieve protection: it must be provided bearing in mind the imperatives of dignity and access.

The human rights community's conception of protection is broad. Haidi Willmot and Scott Sheeran argue that the human rights framework 'provides a platform for the broadest understanding of the fulfilment of civilian protection ideals'.[16] Finally, the Protection of Civilians Operational Concept developed by the UN Department of Peacekeeping Operations (DPKO) outlines three tiers of action: (a) protection through political processes, (b) providing protection from physical violence, and (c) establishing a protective environment.[17]

The increasingly multidimensional nature of international peacekeeping missions and the growing number of actors working on protection issues has contributed to hampering coherence on the protection of civilians. As a result, interaction on protection issues at an operational level is often extremely problematic. In addition, for many protection actors the concept is treated as an activity or a process rather than an outcome. Despite the creation of guidelines,[18] many humanitarian agencies have failed to develop an outcome-oriented focus to their protection activities. This means that action on the ground may be inadequate, but is very difficult to measure, and in some cases protection 'mainstreaming' appears to be little more than a box-ticking exercise.

It is not just the concept of 'protection' that suffers definitional complexity, but also that of 'civilians'. The distinction between combatants and civilians who at times 'engage in a range of different kinds of agency in war' is not easily made.[19] Frédéric Mégret argues that in the case of Syria the term 'civilian' was often instrumentalized as part of an 'interventionist agenda' that portrayed Syrians as helpless and in need of rescuing.[20]

[16] Haidi Willmot and Scott Sheeran, 'The Protection of Civilians Mandate in UN Peacekeeping Operations: Reconciling Protection Concepts and Practices' (2013) 95 IRRC 517, 533. See also Keating and Bennett, Chapter 16, in this volume.

[17] Ibid., 534; Victoria Metcalfe and Simone Haysom, 'Trends and Challenges in Humanitarian Civil-Military Coordination, A Review of the Literature' (London: Overseas Development Institute, 2012) 24.

[18] See, for example, ICRC, n 14.

[19] Hugo Slim, Chapter 1 in this volume.

[20] Frédéric Mégret, 'Helping the Syrians Help Themselves? The Ambiguities of International Assistance to the Rebellion' (2014) 3 Stability: Intl J Security and Development 10, 1. See also Slim, n 20.

Current approaches to civilian protection are confused, in part, because they make unwarranted assumptions regarding the role of third party protectors, and are often not grounded in analysis of the actual determinants of civilian security. A glaring example exists in the DRC, where different approaches to civilian protection over the past two decades have neglected the Congolese State's primary responsibility, as well as the strategies for self-protection put in place by affected communities.[21] Examples from the response to the 2010 earthquake in Haiti highlight how well-intentioned interventions by international humanitarian actors can have unintended and destructive consequences for civilians.[22] In many cases, the shortcomings of the protection response by the international community stem from their failure to adequately take into account local contexts, priorities, and capacities.[23]

There is a tendency to assume that the protection agenda is essentially about how third parties can intervene to protect civilians. This is unsurprising, perhaps, for organizations that see protection as part of their business and are seeking to define their respective roles. Yet it tends to involve assumptions about the potential of third parties that are at best untested, and often manifestly unfounded. Among humanitarian agencies in particular, protection tends to be discussed as though it were a service that can be delivered—another 'sector' of activity, like health care or food aid. This is fundamentally misleading. While it would be unfair to characterize all such discussions in this way, it is a prevalent enough view to be of concern.

Most humanitarian protection actors would agree that although they may have different operational approaches, the fundamental objectives of protection are to reduce the greatest risk of harm from violence, abuse, or deliberate deprivation, by minimizing the level of threat, limiting civilian exposure to threats, or enhancing the opportunities civilians have to be safe.[24] There are three main factors in civilian safety in this sense. The first, and most critical, concerns the actions and motives of the parties to a conflict: the degree to which warring parties adhere to the rules of war is the fundamental factor in the level of risk facing civilians. The second concerns the steps that civilians take to protect themselves from the direct and indirect consequences of the actions of warring parties. The final factor concerns the interventions of third parties aimed at protecting civilians.[25]

Whether viewed in terms of physical or legal safety, protection of civilians is primarily the responsibility of States or parties to a conflict. Remedial protection action by international actors can rarely address pre-existing threats,[26] and they

[21] J Arthur Boutellis, 'From Crisis to Reform: Peacekeeping Strategies for the Protection of Civilians in the Democratic Republic of the Congo' (2013) 2 Stability: Intl J Security and Development 48, 6–9.

[22] See generally CH Logie, 'Exploring Unintended Social Side Effects of Tent Distribution Practices in Post-Earthquake Haiti' (2013) 2 Stability: Intl J Security and Development 50.

[23] Carla Suarez, 'Survival in the Everyday of Armed Violence' (*OpenCanada.org*, 27 November 2012) <opencanada.org/features/the-think-tank/essays/survival-in-the-everyday-of-armed-violence>.

[24] Aide-Memoire for the Consideration of Issues pertaining to the Protection of Civilians in Armed Conflict, in UNSC Statement of the President (2010) UN Doc PRST/2010/25, Annex, 2–3.

[25] O'Callaghan and Pantuliano, see n 5, 3.

[26] ICRC and HPG, see n 10, 10.

often risk raising expectations beyond what is achievable, both within the international community and among the affected civilian population.[27] Violation of State sovereignty with the intention of civilian protection is highly controversial and intensely debated, including because of the seemingly uneven response of the Security Council to various crises, which appears heavily driven by the preferences of its members.[28]

The emphasis on the use of force to protect civilians sits uneasily with the emphasis in IHL on protection as restraint on the use of force. For instance, the Intervention Brigade in the DRC has a protection of civilians mandate but is also a party to the conflict.[29] There remains, however, a crucial overlap of military and humanitarian agendas. For the most part, humanitarian actors do not have the means to protect directly,[30] although they may have the means to enhance civilian security by reducing vulnerability and exposure to violence. They rightly urge warring parties to respect the IHL principles of distinction, precaution, and proportionality in the use of force. However, most humanitarians also recognize the requirement for force to be deployed on occasion, in order to protect civilians.[31] Here, the interface and relationship between humanitarian and military actors and agendas needs to be better defined.

While the humanitarian civilian protection agenda is not necessarily framed as a *rights* protection agenda—IHL, for example, is not so much a rights-based code as a duty-based one—there is also substantial overlap between humanitarian and human rights concerns with the protection of civilians. That said, the humanitarian and human rights protection agendas may differ both on the priorities they set and the means by which they are pursued. This is evident particularly in the relative emphasis attached in human rights approaches to exposing and publicly denouncing abuse, and in justice processes, whereas the humanitarian approach is generally more low-profile, pragmatic, and focused at the local level. This divergence matters where the means by which the protection agenda is pursued may be in tension, such as the disharmony between public denunciation of abuse and maintaining safe access on the ground.[32]

The divergence among actors points to the value of a pragmatic division of labour and a search for complementarity of action. Perhaps more importantly, divergence matters where it prevents the different actors coming together around a

[27] Ibid., 6; Ditchley Foundation, 'Protecting Civilians in Armed Conflict, A Note by the Director' (*The Ditchley Foundation*, June 2013) <www.ditchley.co.uk/conferences/past-programme/2010-2019/2013/protecting-civilians>.

[28] Alex J Bellamy, 'Libyan Case a Red Herring in Syria Dilemma' (*The Global Observatory*, 13 January 2014) <theglobalobservatory.org/component/myblog/libyan-case-a-red-herring-in-syria-dilemma/blogger/Alex%20J.%20Bellamy>.

[29] Maj. Gen. Patrick Cammaert and Fiona Blyth, 'The UN Intervention Brigade in the Democratic Republic of the Congo' (New York: International Peace Institute, 2013) 1.

[30] Marc DuBois, 'Protection: Fig-leaves and Other Delusions', *Humanitarian Exchange* (London, March 2010) 2–4.

[31] Alex de Waal, 'Military Intervention in Africa' (University of Pennsylvania African Studies Center, 1995) <www.africa.upenn.edu/Hornet/milt_intv.html>.

[32] Sri Lanka Internal Review Panel, see n 8, paras 26, 49.

shared protection agenda—not an agglomeration of their respective agendas, but a common core agenda, representing overlapping concerns. This requires acceptance that urgent and selective priorities for collective action need to be set in such contexts.

III. The Protection Gap

There has often been a tendency to proclaim a 'protection failure' where international action is seen as insufficient to protect civilians, with significant blame often apportioned to the UN. This apparent gap between the rhetoric of protection and its reality stems, in part, from the fact that protection has been treated more as an activity than as an outcome. Aid agencies 'do' protection work, while peacekeeping forces 'implement' protection of civilians mandates. Plans and promises become the focus, rather than outcomes.[33]

The gap between policy and practice also exists because of a lack of comprehensive pre-deployment training for both military and humanitarian actors working on protection. An insufficient understanding of IHL and of the political and military context of a country can result in unrealistic expectations and a poor understanding of which approaches will result in better protection.

Past and current research points to the need for context analysis and yet, more often than not, many organizations are ill-prepared to respond to a particular crisis because they do not invest in thorough analysis, lack adequately skilled staff, and fail to take into account the affected population's assessment of their own needs. Understanding the motives of armed actors is a crucial element of any analysis. Agencies and organizations often compete to produce the leading analysis on a situation, rather than working to develop common analysis and complementary approaches. Monitoring undertaken by integrated UN missions or the UN Office of the High Commissioner for Human Rights (OHCHR) is rarely converted into shared trend analysis. Some NGOs develop socio-political analysis for advocacy, but this is rarely systematized throughout the organization or shared more broadly, including within or through humanitarian protection clusters.

For the military, a lack of training and expertise within peacekeeping missions has proven problematic. There has been great difficulty, for instance, in translating protection of civilians mandates into operational directives that make sense to military leaders.[34] The responsibility of UN Force Commanders to interpret their protection mandate within a complex political and tactical reality should not be

[33] Ashley Jackson, 'Protecting Civilians: The Gap between Norms and Practice' (London: Overseas Development Institute, 2014) 4; see also InterAction, 'Results-based Protection Practitioners' Roundtable, Summary Report' (Washington, DC: InterAction, June 2013) 3–6 <www.interaction.org/document/results-based-protection-final-roundtable-report>.

[34] Ditchley Foundation, see n 27.

underestimated. Additionally, differences between contingents' national doctrines on civilian protection (where in existence) can also lead to a lack of coherence.[35]

For humanitarian actors, greater adherence to ICRC Professional Standards for Protection Work[36] and more comprehensive training may enable better engagement with all armed groups, even those classified as terrorists, to explain their responsibilities of civilian protection under IHL, and to negotiate access. This is particularly important in the context of conflicts such as Syria, where the Free Syrian Army, despite having played a role in protecting civilians, also sees the legitimacy of its cause as reason to relieve it of IHL obligations.[37] As well as more systematic, context-specific training, there is a need for more effective learning. Currently, the protection community as a whole lacks effective ways to measure its impact on protecting civilians,[38] and the lessons learnt by military actors are rarely shared among the wider protection community.[39]

In complex humanitarian emergencies where both humanitarian and military actors are attempting to provide protection, there is a need for a greater degree of mutual understanding and some level of interaction and dialogue. This interaction must not, however, compromise the neutrality and impartiality of humanitarians, who are arguably best placed to ensure community involvement in protection strategies. While in many instances this interaction has been extremely problematic, the most successful examples of co-ordination have evolved organically in response to the specific context without global humanitarian policy.[40]

Humanitarians and civil society actors often have knowledge of relevant social, economic, micro-political, and cultural factors, as well as the perceptions of the affected communities themselves. Such knowledge can and should be used to inform political and (where necessary) appropriate military action. Protected access for relief assistance is only one component of this. The domain of humanitarian action, governed by principles of impartiality and neutrality, may be distinct and limited in scope—but it nevertheless demands a dialogue with military actors, belligerent or otherwise, about factors that have a bearing on the security of civilian populations.[41]

Each set of actors has specific roles to achieve comprehensive protection. It is vital to acknowledge that protection is about not just physical security, but also human dignity and safety. Protecting civilians thus often involves practical steps such as improving infrastructure (e.g. more thoughtful camp construction and layout) and the protection of livelihoods. Prevention should also be at the heart of protection planning, with early warning, early engagement, and contingency planning all essential elements of protection work.[42]

[35] ICRC and HPG, see n 10, 6. [36] ICRC, see n 14. [37] See, e.g., Mégret, n 20, 7.

[38] Ditchley Foundation, see n 277.

[39] Victoria Metcalfe, 'Protecting Civilians? The Interaction between International Military and Humanitarian Actors' (London: Overseas Development Institute, 2012) 5.

[40] Ibid.

[41] HPG, 'Political and Humanitarian Approaches to Civilian Protection, Roundtable Summary Note' (London: Overseas Development Institute, April 2007) <www.odi.org/events/186-political-humanitarian-approaches-civilian-protection#report>.

[42] Ibid.

Political commitment to civilian protection is essential. Some argue that there is a need to try harder and more often to achieve political solutions before automatically deploying a one-size-fits-all UN peacekeeping force.[43] Crises such as Syria, Somalia, Bosnia, and Rwanda have also brought into stark relief the limits of what humanitarian action can achieve in the absence of political action to protect. Ironically, in the process, refugee protection and its core tenets (asylum, *non-refoulement*) seem to have slipped off the humanitarian agenda. Yet for both refugees and IDPs, the issue of safe flight options and non-forcible return remain core humanitarian concerns.[44]

The core protection agenda in situations of armed conflict might be described in terms of defined threats of violence, coercion, and denial of basic subsistence, including access to relief. An approach focused on reducing known risk factors (threats, vulnerabilities) in a given context would point to alternative policy and programme options. Understanding civilians' own responses to violence and facilitating their avoidance of risk—through safe flight options or otherwise—is one essential component of this, as discussed later in the chapter. More generally, it may be helpful to think in terms of establishing a protection regime in the context in question, stressing the primary role and responsibility of the State and warring parties, and recognizing the limits of third party action (military, humanitarian, or other).[45]

IV. Protection Actors—Too Many, Too Few?

Traditionally, humanitarian protection programming was largely seen as the remit of the ICRC and the UN High Commissioner for Refugees (UNHCR). Both organizations share an approach centred on legal obligations and work with national actors to encourage them to abide by such obligations, the ICRC in the midst of conflict and UNHCR initially with refugees in third countries, but now also with IDPs. For some time these remained the only two major organizations committed to protection, although they were joined by the UN Children's Fund (UNICEF) in 1989, after the adoption of the Convention on the Rights of the Child, and OHCHR upon its establishment in 1993.[46]

Several NGOs also began engaging in protection activities and the number of protection actors continued to grow steadily (the Norwegian Refugee Council, International Rescue Committee, Save the Children, Oxfam, etc.) Some focused

[43] Ditchley Foundation and HPG, see n 27.

[44] Sarah Collinson, James Darcy, Nicholas Waddell, and Anna Schmidt, 'Realising Protection: The Uncertain Benefits of Civilian, Refugee and IDP Status' (London: HPG, Overseas Development Institute, 2009) 1.

[45] ICRC and HPG, see n 10, 6.

[46] The two other prominent protection actors, Unicef and the Office of the High Commissioner for Human Rights (OHCHR), assumed this role much later. See Gil Loescher and James Milner, *UNHCR: The Politics and Practice of Refugee Protection in the 21st Century* (London: Taylor and Francis, 2008) 108; and see Aryeh Neier, *The International Human Rights Movement* (Princeton, USA: Princeton University Press, 2012) 111.

their programmes on the rule of law and access to justice, sexual and gender-based violence, and child protection in armed conflict, while others (such as Oxfam and World Vision) combined protection activities with their initial area of expertise of providing assistance. Advocacy, research, and policy work on humanitarian protection is increasingly undertaken by NGOs.

In the context of the proliferation of protection actors and increasingly complex conflicts, one of the key concerns among practitioners in the 1990s was the development of commonly agreed standards to ensure that protection programmes were effective and complementary. These were developed through a consultative process that was led by the ICRC, and also resulted in the definition of humanitarian protection adopted by the IASC.[47]

While it is clear that no single organization has the exclusive monopoly on protection, it has become evident that some of those who claim to 'do protection' in fact have little or no experience identifying protection threats and their likely impacts, designing protection programmes, and employing appropriately skilled staff and resources to pursue protection programmes over an extended period of time. It is more difficult for organizations to acquire expertise on protection than on assistance, which tends to be seen as requiring specific technical skills.[48] In addition, the proliferation of actors has created a risk of duplication and overlap in some areas, while others remain unaddressed.

V. Protection Actors, Protection Challenges

Humanitarian organizations in general, and those working on protection issues in particular, face a number of significant challenges that limit their ability to help civilians reduce the risks they face. Drawing from past and current conflicts, this section will consider some such challenges and how protection actors address or mitigate them.

A. Access

There is no definition of 'humanitarian access' in international law. The Swiss Federal Department of Foreign Affairs uses the following definition: 'Humanitarian access encompasses access by humanitarian organisations to those in need of humanitarian assistance and protection, and access by those in need to the goods and services essential for their survival.'[49] The debate concerning the technical modalities of access has often overshadowed other crucial issues, such as the value of a common analysis of protection needs and the development of a common strategy for all protection actors, addressing immediate as well as long-term needs.

[47] For more information on the process please see Sylvie Giossi Caverzasio, *Strengthening Protection in War* (Geneva: ICRC, 2001).

[48] Sorcha O'Callaghan and Sara Pantuliano, see n 5, 2–3.

[49] Switzerland Federal Department of Foreign Affairs, *Humanitarian Access in Situations of Armed Conflict: Field Manual* (Bern: Federal Department of Foreign Affairs, 2011) 1.

Historically, humanitarian access to populations in need has rarely been straightforward, and claims that at one point in time during the Cold War there was a 'golden age' for humanitarian agencies are unfounded.[50] In many conflicts since the Second World War humanitarian access has been not only challenged but often openly denied, forcing aid agencies to make difficult operational and ethical choices.

Access during the civil war in Biafra is often used as an example of cross-border activities in the absence of consent from the government.[51] However, such operations are not without risk, and in the case of Biafra it meant that the humanitarian flights that were organized to overcome the blockade were attacked by the Nigerian air force. Aid agencies also had to respond to accusations that their operations only prolonged the conflict, and thereby the suffering of the population of Biafra.[52]

Access constraints have frequently been in the news in the context of the Syrian conflict. After several unsuccessful attempts, in July 2014, the Security Council finally passed resolution 2165 authorizing cross-border operations without awaiting the consent of the Syrian government.[53] Although the Syrian government declared that any convoy not authorized by Damascus would be considered a pretext for aggression, humanitarian agencies, acting on the basis of the resolution, have been crossing the border to provide assistance to people who had not previously been reached.[54] While the resolution was a significant development,[55] improvements on the ground have not been as dramatic as was hoped,[56] and at the time of writing, access had not been regular, safe, or unhindered.[57]

The very real challenges of cross-border operations into Syria are rarely mentioned.[58] Arbitrary denial of humanitarian assistance may be a war crime, but the distant threat of such sanctions has little impact on the ground.[59] While the Security Council may provide specific legal authority for humanitarian access, warring parties on the ground may choose to ignore it. In practice, considerations for the safety of aid workers often trump legal arguments.

[50] Sarah Collinson and Samir Elhawary, 'Humanitarian Space: Trends and Issues' (London: Overseas Development Institute, 2012) 1.

[51] See David P Forsythe, *The Humanitarians: The International Committee of the Red Cross* (Cambridge: Cambridge University Press) 66–7.

[52] Michael Barnett, *Empire of Humanity: A History of Humanitarianism* (Ithaca, USA: Cornell University Press, 2011) 31.

[53] UNSC Res 2165 (2014) UN Doc S/RES/2165.

[54] Mark Leon Goldberg, 'A Risky Humanitarian Relief Gambit Pays Off' (*UN Dispatch*, 26 August 2014) <www.undispatch.com/risky-aid-convoy-reaches-besieged-syrians/>.

[55] 'UN Authorizes Syria Aid Delivery across Borders', *Gulf Times* (Doha, 14 July 2014) <www.gulf-times.com/Mobile/Region/216/details/400417/UN-authorises-Syria-aid-delivery-across-borders>.

[56] 'UN Security Convoy Authorizes Syria Aid Convoys', *Channel News Asia* (Singapore, 15 July 2014) <www.channelnewsasia.com/news/world/un-security-council/1263930.html>.

[57] 'UN Reports Improved Humanitarian Access to Syria for First Time in Six Months', United Nations News Centre (New York, 28 August 2014) <www.un.org/apps/news/story.asp?NewsID=48583#.VBVpyq1MvIU>.

[58] Hugo Slim and Emanuela-Chiara Gillard (2013) 'Ethical and Legal Perspectives on Cross-border Humanitarian Operations', *Humanitarian Exchange* (London, November 2013) 7–9.

[59] Al Jazeera and agencies, 'UN Authorizes Cross-border Aid to Syrians' *Al Jazeera* (Doha, 15 July 2014) <www.aljazeera.com/news/middleeast/2014/07/un-authorises-cross-border-aid-syrians-2014714162244894482.html>.

Humanitarian actors, and in particular humanitarian protection actors, maintain that without access, a meaningful response is difficult. Proximity to affected communities is critical to better understand their needs and therefore develop better programming. However, while international actors may be prevented from accessing populations in need, local humanitarian actors may have the required access.[60]

There has always been a need for humanitarians to engage with both States and armed non-State actors, in order to gain access and provide assistance to those in need.[61] While such engagement may not be new, it has traditionally been the remit of the ICRC, yet is increasingly becoming necessary for other humanitarian organizations.[62] Many organizations do not invest in developing the skills and knowledge needed to negotiate with armed non-State actors, leaving their staff inadequately prepared.[63] Negotiating with belligerents is key not only to obtaining access to affected communities but also to discussing the parties' obligations under international law, including to protect civilians. Some organizations will deliberately avoid being in contact with armed non-State actors out of fear of falling foul of counter-terrorism legislation.[64]

B. Tension between international humanitarian law and counter-terrorism measures

Since the events of September 2001, States and intergovernmental bodies have increasingly introduced measures, through the adoption of legislation and policy, to prevent groups and individuals from engaging in terrorism. Many of these measures aim to deprive individuals of the material and financial resources to plan and execute terrorist activities. Security Council resolution 1373, adopted on 28 September 2001, orders States to refrain from providing any form of support to terrorist groups and individuals.[65]

Many of the individuals and groups targeted by sanctions are crucial actors in providing humanitarian access. In Afghanistan, for instance, engagement with the Taliban is necessary for effective and safe humanitarian access to areas under their

[60] The Union of Syrian Medical Relief Organizations is such an example. See Tania Cheung, 'Interview with Dr Nizar Hammodeh, Union of Syrian Medical Relief Organizations', *Humanitarian Exchange* (London, November 2013) 14.

[61] Ashley Jackson and Eleanor Davey, *From the Spanish Civil War to Afghanistan: Historical and Contemporary Reflections on Humanitarian Engagement with Non-state Armed Groups* (London: Overseas Development Institute, 2014) 1.

[62] For a more detailed discussion on the role of the UN and NGOs in negotiating access see Jackson and Davey, ibid., 23–8.

[63] Ashley Jackson and Antonio Giustozzi, 'Talking to the Other Side: Humanitarian Engagement with the Taliban in Afghanistan' (London: Overseas Development Institute, 2012) iv.

[64] Other organizations, such as the Centre for Humanitarian Dialogue, work with non-state armed actors on issues such as protection of civilians and humanitarian access. For more information, see Andrea Bartoli, 'NGOs and Mediation', in Susan Allen Nan, Zachariah Cherian Mampilly, and Andrea Bartoli (eds), *Peacemaking: From Practice to Theory* (Volume 1) (Santa Barbara, USA: ABC-CLIO, 2011) 114–16.

[65] UNSC Res 1373 (2001) UN Doc S/RES/1373, para. 2(a). See also Security Council Report, 'UN Sanctions Special Research Report' (New York: Security Council Report, 2013) 7.

influence or control. Many humanitarians have thus become concerned that engaging with proscribed groups will make them liable to criminal prosecution.[66] Humanitarian actors argue that IHL allows them to offer their services to all parties to a conflict while counter-terrorism legislation limits their engagement.[67] Both IHL and counter-terrorism measures attempt to protect civilians from harm, and yet the latter suggest that helping a victim on the 'terrorist side' might be considered a criminal act.[68] Humanitarian organizations may also be perceived as aligning their actions with the political agendas of States when subjected to conditions about when they are allowed to negotiate with certain groups and when they are not.

The discussion of the impact of counter-terrorism legislation on humanitarian action is not a theoretical one. Following the events of 11 September 2001, Islamic charities felt the immediate impact of counter-terrorism laws, resulting in decreased funding and the freezing of financial transactions.[69] Subsequently, the impact has become more general across the humanitarian sector. In Somalia, for example, funding to humanitarian organizations decreased significantly after Al-Shabaab was declared a terrorist organization,[70] almost certainly exacerbating the effect of the 2011 famine.[71] The pressure to comply with and fear of potentially falling foul of counter-terrorism measures has made agencies reluctant to share information with other organizations.[72] This lack of information exchange has further undermined the capability of agencies to produce collective protection analyses in areas where listed actors control territory.

C. Programmatic and organizational challenges

In most conflict situations, protection actors do not work together to establish a common understanding of protection threats[73] and ways to mitigate or prevent them. The introduction of the 'protection cluster', a country-specific co-ordination mechanism for humanitarian agencies to work together on protection issues, was intended to enhance predictability and facilitate co-ordination among actors. However, better co-ordination does not automatically translate to better protection

[66] Sara Pantuliano, Kate Mackintosh, and Samir Elhawary, 'Counter-terrorism and Humanitarian Action: Tensions, Impact and Ways Forward' (London: Overseas Development Institute, 2011) 5.
[67] Ibid., 6. [68] Ibid. [69] Ibid., 7. [70] Ibid., 9.
[71] Kate Mackintosh and Patrick Duplat, *Study of the Impact of Donor Counter-Terrorism Measures on Principled Humanitarian Action* (Geneva and New York: United Nations, 2013) 103.
[72] Pantuliano, Mackintosh, and Elhawary, see n 66, 8.
[73] Oxfam defines threats as follows: (a) 'Violence', including 'deliberate killing, wounding, torture, cruel and inhuman and degrading treatment, sexual violence including rape, and the threat of any of the above'; (b) 'coercion', including 'forced prostitution, sexual slavery, sexual exploitation, forced or compulsory labour, forced displacement or return, forced recruitment into armed forces, and being forced to commit acts of violence against others'; and (c) 'Deliberate deprivation', including 'deliberately destroying civilian objects such as homes, wells, crops and clinics; preventing access to land and jobs; preventing the delivery of relief supplies; deliberate discrimination in getting jobs, schooling, land, services, etc.; and demanding illegal "taxes" or tolls'. See Oxfam, 'Protection' (*Oxfam*, Undated) <policy-practice.oxfam.org.uk/our-work/conflict-disasters/protection>.

for the affected population, including because co-ordination mechanisms are usually limited to international actors.[74] A comprehensive protection analysis needs to include: a detailed examination of the threats facing civilians, including the motivations and strategies of armed groups, the strategies employed by civilian populations to keep safe, and the role of national and international protection actors. The lack of such comprehensive analysis in many instances results in predetermined approaches by humanitarian organizations, rather than context-specific responses.[75] While participatory assessment is important for all relief interventions, it is critical for protection.[76] However, time, access, and financial constraints can make this difficult.[77]

Funding difficulties are often quoted by humanitarian organizations as a barrier to engaging in protection activities. Securing financial support for protection is undoubtedly more difficult than in other sectors that are perceived to be more life-saving.[78] Protection programming is expensive relative to other activities, as it requires heavy investment in personnel. In Darfur, the first emergency to be labelled a 'protection crisis', agencies reported that when overall funding was cut, protection was the first to suffer due to perceptions that it was not life-saving.[79] A 2007 study by the Humanitarian Policy Group (HPG) highlighted that donors appeared to prefer funding stand-alone protection programming rather than the adoption of protection principles and approaches across the work portfolio.[80] This was confirmed by operational agencies, and many spoke of 'hiding' the costs of mainstreaming a protection approach through their programmes (staff, training activities, etc.), in order to secure funds.[81] This trend does not seem to have been reversed in recent years.

While funding challenges are real, there are deeper organizational challenges that prevent the improvement of humanitarian protection initiatives. Incorporating an appreciation of civilian safety into humanitarian analysis and response requires a significant shift for most humanitarian organizations. The World Food Programme (WFP), for instance, recognized its own knowledge gap on protection issues, acknowledging responsibility not only for the efficient distribution of food, but also for contributing to the safety and dignity of affected populations.[82] Structural

[74] Vance Culbert, 'Protection Cluster Co-facilitation in the Democratic Republic of Congo—Lessons Learned for Oxfam's Protection Cluster Support Project' (Geneva: IASC, 2011) 23 <www.disasterriskreduction.net/fileadmin/user_upload/drought/docs/Oxfam%20DRC%20protection%20cluster%20eval%20-%20lessons%20learned.pdf>.

[75] O'Callaghan and Pantuliano, see n 5, 2–7.

[76] See Bonwick, n 12, 276.

[77] O'Callaghan and Pantuliano, see n 5, 2–7.

[78] Julian Murray and Joseph Landry, *Placing Protection at the Centre of Humanitarian Action* (Ottawa: Global Protection Cluster, 2013) 14. In a review of protection funding over a longer period (2007–12), Murray and Landry found that 'protection is usually underfunded in relation to the amounts requested in the consolidated appeals, and "more underfunded" relative to most other clusters': ibid., 4.

[79] O'Callaghan and Pantuliano, see n 5, 2–6.

[80] Ibid.

[81] Ibid.

[82] Nickolas Crawford, Gina Pattugalan, and Lianna Simmons, 'Protection in Practice: Adaptation and Application in the Context of Food Assistance', in Nickolas Crawford and Gina Pattugalan (eds), *Protection in Practice: Food Assistance with Safety and Dignity* (Rome: World Food Programme, 2013) 20.

divisions within organizations between 'protection' and 'assistance' efforts have been reported to impede integration.[83]

Over the past decade, many organizations have developed training on protection, but this tends not to be institutionalized and many different conceptions of protection continue to prevail, with diverging definitions even within a single organization. The lack of a systemized approach results in ad hoc and inconsistent implementation, with protection efforts expanding and contracting depending on the individual directing the programme or the organization.

VI. Affected Populations

As well as recognizing that various actors understand 'protection' differently, it is apparent that many humanitarian actors lack a detailed understanding of what 'protection' means to civilians themselves. This is one of many reasons why proximity to affected communities is so important. Maintaining dialogue with local people and groups to understand the detailed context and keep abreast of constantly changing conflict dynamics is vital, as is knowing how communities define 'protection' and understanding both their vulnerabilities and their resilience.

Currently, international actors rarely involve civilians in the design and implementation of protection strategies, including failing to understand or build upon pre-existing community protection strategies that may be the first and only line of defence. While not always necessarily right in principle, the strategies of affected communities must be the starting point for any international action.

A. Community-based protection

People are not passive in the face of threats to their safety and subsistence. They look to political and military actors for protection, but they also take action to protect themselves, their families, and other community members. Civilians themselves frequently constitute the first, and sometimes only, line of defence in a conflict and their own activities are frequently the most important element of their survival.

The distinction between physical protection and aspects of livelihood security is often irrelevant for civilians, as both are essential for their survival. The desire to escape violence and coercion is a powerful determinant of behaviour, but so too is the need to secure basic subsistence (food, etc.) in the short term, and other vital interests (livelihoods, health care, etc.) in the longer term. People often face invidious choices between high-risk options. Avoidance through flight may be achieved at the cost of exposure to threats of other kinds: loss of subsistence, disease, destitution, and so on. In Angola, DRC, Sudan, and South Sudan, millions died from the effects of disease and hunger when they fled their homes through fear of violence—far more than were killed in conflict.[84] Elsewhere, situations of 'frozen'

[83] O'Callaghan and Pantuliano, see n 5, 2–4.

[84] See Keith Krause, 'Beyond Definition: Violence in a Global Perspective', in Vittorio Bufacchi (ed.), *Rethinking Violence* (Abingdon, UK: Routledge, 2011) 58–60; see also Human Security Report

insecurity persist, where people keep safe by not doing what they would normally do—going to market, ploughing their fields, and so on. The result may be impoverishment and lack of development, children not being able to go to school, and in more extreme cases, a catastrophic loss of access to the basic means of subsistence.

People may seek protection from a variety of sources. The Cuny Center documented more than 500 different types of self-protection strategies used by individuals and communities in situations of armed violence.[85] They categorized these responses into three main types of strategies: *avoidance* of violence by temporarily or permanently fleeing an insecure area; *accommodation* with armed groups, whereby the security of civilians is guaranteed in exchange for a good and/or service; and *affinity*, whereby civilians mobilize old or new networks to galvanize support.[86] Communities typically use a combination of these strategies.[87]

Most civilians will turn for help to members of the extended family, community, or clan. The community will also play an important role in restoring the dignity of those people subjected to violence. Social cohesion among affected populations can assist in providing social and economic security following attacks.[88] On the other hand, affected communities can be the source of protection threats during a conflict or because negative practices that pre-date a conflict are exacerbated by it, such as domestic violence, neglect of particular categories of people, and harmful traditional practices.[89] Effective protection strategies need to be sensitive to such dynamics.

In some cases, self-protection takes the form of actively confronting the threat (real or perceived) by resorting to arms, which leads to difficulties distinguishing between combatants and civilians, as described by Hugo Slim.[90] In such cases civilians are no longer passive victims of violence, but become perpetrators of it, and provide a recruitment base for armed militia and regular armed forces. Less overtly militarized forms of action include vigilante groups and volunteer forces whose members commit acts of violence against the perceived enemy. Political activity for such activists amongst the general population may lead to vulnerability by association.[91]

B. Role of diaspora, local networks, and associations

Moving beyond the false dichotomy between 'saviours' and 'victims' is essential for a civilian protection framework that avoids disempowering conflict-affected

Project, *Human Security Report 2009/2010: The Causes of Peace and the Shrinking Cost of War* (New York: Oxford University Press, 2011) 105–9.

85 Casey A Barrs, 'Preparedness Support: Helping Brace Beneficiaries, Local Staff and Partners for Violence' (Arlington, USA: The Cuny Center, 2010) 3–6.

86 Ibid. For a similar categorization of self-protection measures in the Democratic Republic of the Congo, see Aditi Gorur, 'Community Self-Protection Strategies: How Peacekeepers Can Help or Harm' (Washington, DC: Henry L Stimson Center, 2013) 4.

87 See generally Barrs, n 85, and Gorur, see n 86.

88 Kate Berry and Sheryl Reddy, 'Safety with Dignity: Integrating Community-Based Protection into Humanitarian Programming' (London: Overseas Development Institute, 2010) 5.

89 Ibid. 90 See Hugo Slim, Chapter 1, in this volume.

91 See Casey A Barrs, 'How Civilians Survive Violence: A Preliminary Inventory' (Cuny Center, 2010) 1–2.

populations.[92] The 'formal humanitarian system'[93] as it stands today cannot respond to all humanitarian needs of affected populations. The gaps are often filled by local actors, and yet the formal system often fails to recognize the vital contributions they make.

Many individuals of diaspora communities retain personal and professional ties with their countries of origin. These ties often translate into tangible financial support as well as active participation in emergency relief, potentially including a return—even if only temporary, as in the case of Syria—to the ancestral country.[94] Diaspora communities from Haiti, Libya, Pakistan, Somalia, and Syria have been a significant source of funds, human resources, and information for humanitarian agencies and policy-makers, which have often resulted in a protective benefit for at-risk communities and individuals.[95] According to the World Bank, remittances sent back to developing countries far exceed official development assistance.[96] In 2014 it was estimated that $436 billion will be sent to home countries, an increase of 7.8 per cent since 2013.[97] Thus, when Barclays Bank decided to close its Somalia accounts in September 2013, citing concerns regarding money-laundering regulations, the loss of $1.3 billion in remittances posed significant food security risks.[98]

Although diaspora groups are generally not considered protection actors per se, their financial support sent to relatives living in conflict areas can make the difference between having to stay while the conflict rages and being able to seek safety elsewhere. Research has also shown that remittances can help those who remain,[99] and decrease the incidence of negative coping mechanisms such as survival sex, early marriage, and forced labour.[100]

From the beginning of the Syrian conflict, individual Syrians living abroad and local groups started organizing their own coping mechanisms, and in many ways social cohesion provided the protection that international actors could not. One

92 Carla Suarez and David Black, 'Surviving Violence: Transgressing Categories and Boundaries in Armed Conflicts' (2014) 3 Stability: Intl J Security and Development 26, 2–3.

93 The UN, the Red Cross/Red Crescent Movement, and INGOs.

94 Alice Fordham, 'Syrian Diaspora in D.C. Area Helps Fight Regime', *The Washington Post* (Washington, DC, 2 September 2011) <www.washingtonpost.com/lifestyle/style/syrian-diaspora-in-dc-area-helps-fight-regime/2011/08/24/gIQAhsGbxJ_story.html>.

95 Africa Renewal online, 'Somali Diaspora's Remittances Cast a Lifeline' <http://www.un.org/africarenewal/magazine/may-2013/somali-diaspora%E2%80%99s-remittances-cast-lifeline>.

96 World Bank, 'Press Release: Remittances to Developing Countries to Stay Robust this Year, Despite Increased Deportations of Migrant Workers, says WB' (Washington, DC, 11 April 2014) <www.worldbank.org/en/news/press-release/2014/04/11/remittances-developing-countries-deportations-migrant-workers-wb>.

97 Ibid.

98 Kevin Watkins, 'Letter to Antony Jenkins Group Chief Executive, Barclays Bank on behalf of ODI' (London, 2 September 2013) <www.odi.org/sites/odi.org.uk/files/odi-assets/publications-opinion-files/8563.pdf>.

99 Patricia Weiss Fagan and Micah N Bump, 'Remittances in Conflict and Crises: How Remittances Sustain Livelihoods in War, Crises and Transitions to Peace' (New York: International Peace Academy, 2006) 14 <www.ipinst.org/media/pdf/publications/remittances_erpt.pdf>.

100 Integrated Regional Information Networks, 'JORDAN: Early Marriage a Coping Mechanism for Syrian Refugees?' *IRIN* (Nairobi, 19 July 2012) <www.irinnews.org/report/95902/jordan-early-marriage-a-coping-mechanism-for-syrian-refugees>.

group assisted others by secretly transporting medicines across checkpoints, knowing that they were less likely to be checked but also conducting this activity at great personal risk.[101] In the early stages of the conflict, networks of activists began secretly connecting with field hospitals that would agree to take the injured following demonstrations, thereby mitigating the risk that wounded demonstrators would be arrested by government forces.[102] With time, these same networks expanded their activities from social and medical support to mediating inter- and intra-communal tensions, often negotiating payment for the release of kidnapped individuals.[103]

VII. Doing Things Differently—the Need for a Creative Way Forward

Protection actors rightly point to the considerable advancements in norms and policies dealing with the protection of civilians, and yet it does not take too much scrutiny to see that these norms and policies are insufficiently translated into effective action on the ground, with devastating consequences for civilians.[104] States bear the primary responsibility for protecting civilians, but humanitarian protection actors do bear some responsibility for addressing violence against civilians when the government is unable or unwilling.

International actors (humanitarian, human rights, peacekeeping) have different understandings of the concept of protection.[105] They also differ on how to operationalize the concept, a divergence that may cause tension.[106] The gap between policy and practice stems in part from a lack of comprehensive pre-deployment training for both military and humanitarian actors, in particular on IHL,[107] and protection threat analysis.

There is a critical need for greater investment in collective situational analysis at the outset of a crisis, to inform the initial response. This analysis must then be sustained as the crisis evolves.[108] Such collective analysis is critical for protection, not only in terms of addressing protection needs, but also to prevent violations by influencing the behaviour of armed actors.[109] If protection actors were to identify a

[101] Dalia Abdelwahid, '"You Got the Stuff?": Humanitarian Activist Networks in Syria', *Humanitarian Exchange* (London, November 2013).

[102] Ibid., 15. [103] Ibid., 16.

[104] See, for example, UN High Commissioner for Refugees, *War's Human Costs: UNHCR Global Trends 2013* (Geneva: United Nations, 2014) 2.

[105] Willmot and Sheeran, see n 16, 535–7.

[106] ICRC, 'The International Committee of the Red Cross's (ICRC's) Confidential Approach' (2012) 94 IRRC 1135, 1136.

[107] Ashley Jackson and Simone Haysom, 'The Search for Common Ground: Civil–Military Relations in Afghanistan, 2002–2013' (London: Overseas Development Institute, 2013) 26.

[108] Global Protection Cluster, 'GPC Seminar on "Protection in Humanitarian Crises: Recommendations to the SG Working Group on the follow-up to the Sri Lanka IRP Report"' (Geneva: Global Protection Cluster, 2013) 5 <www.globalprotectioncluster.org/_assets/files/news_and_publications/GPC_Seminar_Summary_Conclusions_Recommendations_EN.pdf>.

[109] Ditchley Foundation, see n 27.

shared protection strategy based on a collective analysis, it may overcome some of the existing challenges born of divergent approaches.

Many humanitarian actors lack a detailed understanding of what 'protection' means to affected communities, even though much has been learned in recent years about the need to take local perspectives into account, hire local staff, and work with local agencies. However, this way of working is more familiar to development organizations, and most protection actors have so far been slow in looking beyond the kind of response to which they have become accustomed. The Listening Project revealed that local communities perceive the international system as aiming for a quick delivery of goods while underestimating the need to take sufficient time to identify strong local partners and maintain effective partnerships with them.[110] When the formal system does incorporate local actors, it is often because circumstances force agencies to rely on 'remote management', withdrawing expatriate staff and giving national staff or local organizations greater responsibilities, albeit rarely greater decision-making power, with local NGOs often seen as mere service providers.[111] Yet recognizing and strengthening local actors is vital. Perhaps the conflict in Syria, where access for international organizations has been particularly challenging, has given the role played by local actors the necessary prominence to lead to serious and systematic strategies of support and involve long-term investment in resources.

Equally, the self-protection role of affected communities should not be underestimated. They are the first, and often the last, line of defence when violence breaks out. Civilians' own activities are frequently the most important element of their survival, even if invariably they are confronted with difficult choices. Yet recognizing and strengthening affected communities in their efforts to protect themselves is vital.

Protection needs in current and future conflicts cannot be addressed exclusively by local actors, nor can they be met by an exclusively international response. International protection actors as well as donors must seek ways to work with local groups who may not easily fit established requirements, such as an adherence to professional standards, strict financial accountability, or respect for humanitarian principles. International protection actors must be creative and bold in seeking genuine partnerships with local actors and affected communities. They should also be prepared to invest in these partnerships whenever possible before a conflict starts, and long afterwards.[112] If Syria is in any way an indication of how future conflicts will be fought and how contested access for international actors might become, then it is imperative to work with those on the ground and build on their local knowledge and expertise to better protect civilians.

110 Dayna Brown, 'Building Effective Partnerships: Local Views', *Humanitarian Exchange* (London, April 2011) 10–13.

111 Abby Stoddard, Adele Harmer, and Jean S Renouf, *Once Removed: Lessons and Challenges in Remote Management of Humanitarian Operations for Insecure Areas* (London and New York: Humanitarian Outcomes, 2010) 18.

112 Donor money is still predominantly channelled through multilateral agencies while local NGOs receive only a fraction of international funding (1.6 per cent of total humanitarian funding given to local NGOs). Global Humanitarian Assistance, *Global Humanitarian Assistance Report 2014* (Bristol, UK: Development Initiatives, 2014) 64.

18

The Problems and Dilemmas of Helping to Build Protection Capacities

Lise Grande[1]

I. Introduction

This chapter considers the strategies international actors are using to help build States' capacity to protect their own people. Although most of the international community's attention focuses on protecting civilians under threat of violence in conflict situations, whether through military intervention, humanitarian relief, or promotion of human rights, State responsibility for the security and safety of the people who live within their borders is the end-goal of the protection chain. Helping States build protective capacities is a key aspect of international work; it is also one of the most technically difficult, and politically, it presents major reputational risks for the international community. The principle that States are responsible for 'protecting their populations from genocide, war crimes, ethnic cleansing and crimes against humanity'[2] was endorsed at the 2005 United Nations (UN) World Summit. In support of this principle, the international community was called upon to assist States in exercising this responsibility and building their protection capacities.[3] Further support for this idea came in the UN Secretary-General's 2009 report on implementing the Responsibility to Protect, which recognized protection capacity-building as a major area of international engagement and described a range of activities that could be taken to help States uphold their responsibilities.[4]

Although the Responsibility to Protect was limited by the World Summit to four categories—genocide, war crimes, ethnic cleansing, and crimes against

[1] Lise Grande has worked for the United Nations for twenty years, serving in humanitarian, development, and peacekeeping operations, including in South Sudan in the years immediately preceding independence and the first year of statehood. Ms Grande consulted a number of colleagues in the preparation of this chapter. The views expressed herein are those of the author and do not necessarily reflect the views of, nor should they be attributed to the United Nations.

[2] United Nations General Assembly (UNGA) Resolution (Res) 60/1, '2005 World Summit Outcome' (2005) UN Doc A/RES/60/1, para. 138.

[3] Ibid., para. 139.

[4] See the discussion on pillar two on international assistance and capacity building in UNGA, 'Report of the Secretary-General, Implementing the Responsibility to Protect' (2009) UN Doc A/63/677, 15–22.

humanity—the commitment of the international community to help build broader protection capacities has gained traction, particularly in fragile and post-conflict countries where civilian populations are victimized by widespread, systematic violence and brutality. Capacity-building is understood to be the means for achieving the goal of a State capable of and committed to ensuring the safety of its population. In practice, this has meant helping security and justice institutions do what the providers of assistance think they should do. It has included: strengthening the administrative structures of these institutions; training and equipping security personnel; installing modern systems for institutional planning, budgeting, monitoring and co-ordination; installing mechanisms to better manage core institutional functions; and introducing democratic, transparent governance procedures and protocols. The question this chapter seeks to explore is whether the approaches being used by the international community to build these capacities are effective, and, if not, what the preferred alternatives are.

According to guidelines and best practices, the main aim of current capacity-building efforts is to help a State assume responsibility for protecting its population by fundamentally transforming its security and justice systems into effective military, police, and court institutions capable of ensuring citizen safety and protection. This is an exceptionally ambitious goal that involves functions central to a State's sovereignty. It is also a goal that can only be achieved with strong, unwavering political commitment from State elites. In involving itself in this endeavour, the international community finds itself confronted with the dilemma of how to best assist the transformative process. The most common option currently chosen by the international community is to embark on a comprehensive overhaul of the security and justice system, knowing that attempts to do so require the kind of long-term, high-risk, expensive commitment that few partners are willing or able to make, and that while this is underway, civilians will continue to be unprotected and unsafe. A second option is for the international community to accept that in the short term, nothing is more important than building a State's capability to ensure the physical security of its people, even if this means strengthening the powers of *selective* coercive institutions in accordance with core human rights and rule-of-law standards in the absence of comprehensive institutional development. Ideally, the international community should do both simultaneously; in practice, this is unlikely, which is why a choice has to be made—pursue rapidly and rigorously the security and safety of civilians, or work to establish institutions of governance and justice as state-building priorities. Without underestimating the risk, this chapter recommends that priority is given to building the capacity of a State to ensure the safety of its population and communities as a first step in helping it to assume full responsibility, recognizing that selective coercive structures may operate without the full range of optimal oversight and institutional restraints in the short and medium term.

The argument is a pragmatic one, drawing on field realities where comprehensive efforts to reform security and justice systems frequently falter. If the strategies the international community is using to overhaul security systems were faster and more effective, the choice would not have to be made. However, experts and experience show that the approaches are flawed and slow to have an impact, which is why the dilemma exists. It is important to be clear on this point. Whenever possible, the preferred approach is to pursue objectives that build strong security institutions capable of and committed to protecting civilians at the same time as comprehensively building institutions of governance and justice. However, experience strongly suggests that building accountable and effective institutions, separating powers across these institutions, and instilling a culture of respect for law in post-conflict and fragile States is an enormously complex, lengthy, and politically fraught endeavour. Starting this process with steps that significantly improve civilian safety and win the confidence of populations, and then implementing, after extensive trial and adaptation, a modest set of actions designed to incrementally improve the functioning of security institutions makes more sense and is more feasible than far-reaching schemes that attempt to reform whole parts of the security and justice system within the timeframe of a peacekeeping and state-building mission. This chapter argues that a 'security-first' approach is the most pragmatic approach to the achieving the end-goal of the protection chain.

II. Building Protection Capacities in South Sudan

The recent experience of South Sudan illustrates the difficulties of capacity-building and the risks to civilians if efforts falter. Since 2005, when the Comprehensive Peace Agreement (CPA) was signed ending Sudan's civil war, the then semi-autonomous Regional Government of Southern Sudan—now the Republic of South Sudan—has confronted overwhelming challenges in all areas of governance, perhaps none more so than in the security and justice sectors.[5] Committed to helping strengthen core State functions, the international community, including the UN peacekeeping mission and bilateral partners, made transformation of the security and justice system one of its highest priorities during the transition and early years of statehood. In accordance with multilateral guidelines and best practices,[6] a comprehensive approach was adopted, involving technical assistance to military, police, and rule of institutions, as well as the introduction of democratic governance norms. The restructuring and capacity-building of the police service were major areas of effort, involving the co-location of large numbers of international

[5] Following the signing of the Comprehensive Peace Agreement (CPA) in 2005, the Security Council established a new UN peacekeeping operation charged with supporting the six-year transition period. The mandate of the United Nations Mission in Sudan (UNMIS) included reform of the South Sudanese police service; see UN Security Council (UNSC) Res 1590 (2005) UN Doc S/RES/1590, para. 4(vii).

[6] For guidance developed during this period, see, for instance, UNSC, 'Report of the Secretary-General, The Rule of Law and Transitional Justice in Conflict and Post-conflict Societies' (2004) UN Doc S/2004/616; Scott N Carlson, 'Legal and Judicial Rule of Law Work in Multi-dimensional Peacekeeping Operations: Lessons Learned Study' (New York: United Nations, 2006) <www.peacekeeping bestpractices.unlb.org/PBPS/Library/ROL%20Lessons%20Learned%20Report%20%20March%20 2006%20FINAL.pdf>; Anja T Kaspersen, Espen Barthe Eide, and Annika S Hansen, *International Policing and the Rule of Law in Transitions from War to Peace* (Oslo: Norwegian Institute of International Affairs, 2004).

police advisers in all ten of South Sudan's states and a massive training programme.[7] Under the first UN Mission in Sudan (UNMIS) and continuing under the UN Mission in South Sudan (UNMISS),[8] tens of thousands of South Sudan police officers received training in referendum security and general skills, with specialized training for smaller numbers in law and order, riot control, civilian protection, and other tasks.[9] UNMISS, as a peace mission with protection and state-building as core goals, was mandated to strengthen the security and justice sectors by helping to develop strategies for security system reform, promoting rule-of-law reform and strengthening capacities in the justice sector. The mission was also tasked with strengthening the capacity of the national police through advice on policy, planning, and legislative development, as well as training and mentoring in key areas.[10] Major efforts were made to transfer skills and provide formal training to hundreds of police officers on leadership, criminal investigation, and community policing, as well as helping to establish special police protection units for women and children in all states.[11]

As part of a comprehensive approach, UNMISS was involved in other aspects of security system reform as well. Committed to promoting the rule of law and respect for human rights, UNMISS supported the development of a national security policy, with the aim of helping 'national institutions [. . .] assume greater responsibility for protecting civilians, respecting, protecting and promoting human rights and fighting impunity and corruption'.[12] The mission also co-chaired a Joint Mechanism with the government on mandate implementation that included discussions on security system reform, and established the UNMISS Consultative Group, a forum with members from civil society that advised the mission on enhancing the effectiveness of the police and establishing security throughout the country. In 2013, the mission reported that significant steps towards reforming the security system had been taken by the government, assisted by the UN,[13] including personnel changes in senior national posts, technical training leading to consultations on the draft national security policy, and the establishment of two security sector oversight coordination mechanisms.[14] As an integrated mission, the United

[7] In late 2005, UNMIS agreed to the co-location of international police experts (see UNSC, 'Report of the Secretary-General on the Sudan' (2005) UN Doc S/2005/821, para. 41). The UN Security Council approved the deployment of 715 personnel to southern Sudan, eventually increased to 900 in 2011 in the recognfigured UN Mission in South Sudan (UNMISS). (See UNSC Res 1996 (2011) UN Doc S/RES/1996, para. 1). This authorized figure remained constant throughout the presence of the UN in southern Sudan, and then upon independence, in South Sudan, until the outbreak of renewed conflict in December 2013. See UNSC Res 2132 (2013) UN Res S/RES/2132, para. 4.

[8] See UNSC Res 1996 (2011) UN Doc S/RES/1996, para. 16.

[9] UNSC, 'Report of the Secretary-General on the Sudan' (2010) UN Doc S/2010/681, paras 46, 47; UNSC, 'Report of the Secretary-General on the Sudan' (2011) UN Doc S/2011/239, paras 53, 54.

[10] UNSC Res 1996 (2011) UN Doc S/RES/1996, paras 3(c)(i), 3(c)(iii).

[11] UNSC, 'Report of the Secretary-General on the United Nations Mission in South Sudan' (2013) UN Doc S/2013/140, para. 35.

[12] UNSC, 'Report of the Secretary-General on South Sudan' (2012) UN Doc S/2012/820, para. 81.

[13] UNSC, 'Report of the Secretary-General on the United Nations Mission in South Sudan' (2013) UN Doc S/2013/140, para. 3.

[14] UNSC, 'Report of the Secretary-General on the United Nations Mission in South Sudan' (2013) UN Doc S/2013/366, para. 61.

Nations Development Programme (UNDP) was also a key partner for UNMISS in these efforts, focusing on infrastructure and institutional strengthening.[15]

Although significant human and financial resources were channelled into capacity-building initiatives, the behaviour of security personnel was slow to change. This was widely acknowledged, including by UNMISS. In a 2013 document, the mission reported that despite the co-location of mission personnel with security institutions, and mentoring and training initiatives, national security institutions continued to violate human rights.[16] Other prominent organizations noticed the same problems, including the Henry L Stimson Center, which concluded in a report on police programming in South Sudan that capacities remained extremely limited despite six years of training,[17] and Human Rights Watch (HRW), which warned that four years after the signing of the CPA, the government 'had not managed to protect civilians from crimes committed by its security forces'.[18] In a second report in 2012, HRW concluded that due to insufficient resources and training, the police were 'largely unable to protect civilians, maintain law and order and prevent, combat or investigate crime and observed that most police were concentrated in the capitals of the ten states, with few officers present in the vast and sometimes difficult to access rural areas, where 83% of South Sudanese reside'.[19]

The impact on civilian safety while the comprehensive efforts to transform the security and justice system were underway was deeply concerning. Between December 2011 and January 2012, mass inter-communal violence took place in Jonglei state, killing more than 800 people, destroying hundreds of homes, and displacing thousands.[20] There was little, if any, South Sudanese police response to those events, in terms of protection or investigation. According to HRW, 'the government has yet to demonstrate that it will respond to the violence appropriately by actually identifying and prosecuting those responsible ... the absence of justice

[15] For a description of UN efforts to support policing in South Sudan, including by UNDP, see Alice Hills, 'Learning the Hard Way: Implementing SSR in Africa's Post-Authoritarian States', in Mark Sedra (ed.), *The Future of Security Sector Reform* (Waterloo, Canada: Centre for International Governance Innovation, 2010) 177–91.

[16] UNSC, 'Report of the Secretary-General on the United Nations Mission in South Sudan' (2013) UN Doc S/2013/366, paras 92, 93, and 96; see in particular paragraph 96: 'Cases of arbitrary arrest, detention, torture and extrajudicial killings by the security forces and agencies, as well as the inability of authorities to hold those responsible to account, are particularly worrisome.'

[17] The Henry L Stimson Center, *UN Police, Justice and Corrections Programming in South Sudan, A Compact Case Study* (Washington, DC: The Henry L Stimson Center, 2012) 6. In 2009 and 2012, Human Rights Watch (HRW) reached similar findings; see Human Rights Watch, *Prison is Not for Me* (New York: Human Rights Watch, 2012) 23; Human Rights Watch, 'News Release: South Sudan: Step Up Urgent Human Rights Reforms' (New York, 4 July 2012) <www.hrw.org/news/2012/07/05/south-sudan-step-urgent-human-rights-reforms>; Human Rights Watch, 'News Release: South Sudan: No Justice for Protester Killings (New York, 24 May 2013) <www.hrw.org/news/2013/05/24/south-sudan-no-justice-protester-killings>.

[18] Human Rights Watch, *There Is No Protection: Insecurity and Human Rights in Southern Sudan* (New York: Human Rights Watch, 2009) 2.

[19] Human Rights Watch, *Prison Is Not for Me*, see n 17, 23–4.

[20] UN Mission in South Sudan, 'Conflict in South Sudan, A Human Rights Report' (Juba, South Sudan: United Nations, 2014) <www.unmiss.unmissions.org/Portals/unmiss/Human%20Rights%20Reports/UNMISS%20Conflict%20in%20South%20Sudan%20-%20A%20Human%20Rights%20Report.pdf>.

contributes to the cycles of attacks and counterattacks across the country'.[21] In December 2012, police opened fire on a peaceful protest in Wau, killing six people, with two later dying of their wounds in hospital. No investigation or prosecutions occurred.[22] On 16 December 2013, following an eruption of violence triggered by disputes for power among political elites, it was alleged that in the capital, Juba, the South Sudan national police and army corralled civilians belonging to an ethnic group into a police building and killed them.[23] In the following months, the Secretary-General reported numerous human rights violations as well as violations of UN agreements by the police and other security forces.[24] These events demonstrated that the efforts made in the lead-up to and after independence to build the capabilities of the South Sudanese State to protect its population were not having the expected impact quickly enough, at a terrible price to South Sudanese civilians.

Explanations for what went wrong were varied. Some argued that the international community was doing the right things in terms of reform, but that more time was needed to see impact. Others criticized the international community for focusing on the wrong initiatives and for trying to do too many things at the same time.[25] For many, the problem lay in the comprehensive approach itself. Some criticized security reform efforts in South Sudan for being *too* comprehensive, dispersing efforts across multiple complex activities; others for being not comprehensive *enough*, focused too narrowly on training rather than civilian oversight and democratic governance. Almost everyone agreed that the situation in South Sudan pointed to fundamental issues one way or the other; what has not been clear is what should be done In May 2014, after months of inter-communal violence displaced millions and killed thousands, the UN Security Council weighed in, changing the UNMISS mandate to focus on direct protection, human rights, and humanitarian assistance. Capacity-building activities were limited and were expected to be conducted in strict compliance with the UN Human Rights Due Diligence Policy.[26]

III. Institutional Critiques of Protection Capacity-building

Efforts to build State responsibility through comprehensive security system transformation are being undertaken in a number of countries where civilians are at risk. Although the UN Security Council suspended security system transformation in UNMISS, it continues to mandate security capacity-building and reform

21 Human Rights Watch, 'News Release: South Sudan: Step Up Urgent Human Rights Reforms', see n 17.

22 Human Rights Watch, 'News Release: South Sudan: No Justice for Protester Killings', see n 17.

23 Human Rights Watch, 'News Release: South Sudan: Ethnic Targeting, Widespread Killings' (New York, 16 January 2014) <www.hrw.org/news/2014/01/16/south-sudan-ethnic-targeting-widespread-killings>.

24 See UNSC, 'Report of the Secretary-General on the United Nations Mission in South Sudan' (2014) UN Doc S/2014/58, paras 29, 30, 32; UNSC, 'Report of the Secretary-General on the United Nations Mission in South Sudan' (2014) UN Doc S/2014/708, paras 47, 49, 71.

25 Author's discussion and notes.

26 See UNSC Res 2155 (2014) UN Doc S/RES/2155, paras 4(a)(vi), 9.

elsewhere.[27] The recently established UN Multidimensional Integrated Stabilization Mission in Mali (MINUSMA), for example, is charged with helping to rebuild the 'police and gendarmerie, through technical assistance, capacity-building, co-location and mentoring programmes, as well as the rule of law and justice sectors'.[28] Security transformation, which is well underway in several fragile States, including Côte d'Ivoire, Liberia, Somalia, and the Democratic Republic of Congo, among others, is an expensive undertaking.[29] Iraq and Afghanistan prove the point. In 2014, for example, the US Special Inspector-General for Reconstruction in Afghanistan informed Congress that of the USD 104 billion allocated to build the Afghan National Security Forces, promote good governance, conduct development assistance, and engage in counter-narcotics and anti-corruption efforts',[30] the United States had spent USD 15.9 billion since 2002 to 'build, equip, train and sustain the [Afghan National Police]'.[31] According to the former Special Inspector-General for Reconstruction in Iraq, the US has spent similar sums in Iraq, where more than USD 21 billion has been directed to police and army reform as part of the US commitment to rebuild the Iraqi State.[32]

Protection capacity-building is being reviewed and examined by leading institutions. In 2012, for example, at the request of the UN's Department of Peacekeeping Operations, the Henry L Stimson Center was requested to 'study [. . .] the impact that police, justice and corrections components in UN peace operations have on the areas in which they work'.[33] The report acknowledges the positive contributions made by UN police, particularly in operational support for police planning and exercises,[34] but concludes that UN police are 'overextended,

[27] While the Security Council has in past decades provided 'executive mandates' to UN missions, authorizing them to directly undertake security and justice tasks including investigation, arrest, and administration, this discussion focuses on the more narrow capacity-building mandates that have become much more common in modern peacekeeping. See Nina M Serafino, 'Policing in Peacekeeping and Related Stability Operations: Problems and Proposed Solutions' (CRS Report for Congress, RL 3231) (Washington, DC: United States Congressional Research Service, 2004).

[28] UNSC Res 2100 (2013) UN Doc S/RES/2100, para. 16.

[29] See Secretary-General reports on peacebuilding in the aftermath of conflict: UNGA and UNSC, 'Report of the Secretary-General, Peacebuilding in the Aftermath of Conflict' (2012) UN Doc A/67/499-S/2012/746; UNGA and UNSC, 'Report of the Secretary-General on Peacebuilding in the Immediate Aftermath of Conflict' (2010) UN Doc A/64/866—S/2010/466; and UNGA and UNSC, 'Report of the Secretary-General on Peacebuilding in the Immediate Aftermath of Conflict' (2009) UN Doc A/63/881—S/2009/304. For a recent Security Council Resolution on security system transformation see UNSC Res 2151 (2014) UN Doc S/RES/2151. On the funds being channelled into security system reform, see Mark Downes and Robert Muggah, 'Breathing Room: Interim Stabilization and Security Sector Reform in the Post-War Period', in Sedra, see n 15, 144.

[30] Special Inspector General for Afghanistan Reconstruction (SIGAR), *Quarterly Report to the United States Congress* (Arlington, USA: SIGAR, 30 July 2014) 79.

[31] Ibid., 107.

[32] Stuart W Bowen, Jr, 'Learning from 10 Years in Iraq: Can We Develop the Planning, Doctrine, and Personnel to Help in Developing Foreign Rule of Law Oriented Societies?' (Washington DC: Security Capabilities Network, 2013) <www.strategycenter.org/wp-content/uploads/2014/05/Learning-from-10-years-in-Iraq2013.pdf>.

[33] William Durch, Madeline England, and Fiona Mangan, *Understanding the Impact of Police, Justice and Corrections Components in UN Peace Operations* (Washington, DC: The Henry L Stimson Center, 2012) ix.

[34] Ibid., 5.

under-resourced and lacking sufficient institutional support'.[35] It finds that most of the international police who are deployed are 'general-duty police officers, because police with highly specialised operational skills are needed within their own institutions'.[36] The report cautions that UN police frequently have limited capacity-building skills and calls on the UN to review the tools used, and the role of deployed police, to meet mandated goals, including the protection of civilians.[37]

The UN itself acknowledges shortcomings in the approaches being used to build protection capacities. The Secretary-General's first comprehensive report on the role of the UN in security system reform was issued in 2008.[38] It was a frank reflection on the UN's deficits in effectiveness, knowledge, capacities, and resources, acknowledging that many efforts to establish security and protection of civilians, particularly in post-conflict and fragile States, have been largely ad hoc.[39] The report recommended the development of security system reform policies and guidance—work that was undertaken by the UN between 2008 and 2011. In his second report on security system reform, published five years later in 2013, the Secretary-General noted significant steps forward in UN efforts, including additional specialized capacities, expanded partnerships, and improved co-ordination.[40] Reflecting on current gaps, the report noted the increasing importance of non-State actors and the prevalence of traditional, informal leaders in providing civilian protection and delivering security and justice services, and called for fuller engagement with these actors so that civilians are at less risk, particularly in areas where State authority is not yet fully consolidated.[41] In the 2011 Secretary-General's report on the work of UN Police, deficits in international police capacities were discussed and there was frank recognition that 'general skills to transfer knowledge effectively [. . .] are frequently lacking'.[42] These same points were made in a 2011 report by a senior advisory group (SAG) tasked by the Secretary-General with independently reviewing civilian capacities in the aftermath of conflict. The advisory group's report focused on States emerging from conflict and the critical shortage of capacities needed to promote sustainable peace. It concluded that while the UN was often successful in humanitarian and peacekeeping operations, it struggled 'to rapidly deploy the range of expertise required and to transfer skills and knowledge to national actors', increasing the 'risk of relapse into

[35] Ibid., 3. [36] Ibid., 4.

[37] Ibid., 6. The Secretary-General also acknowledged that capacity-building skills are frequently lacking. See UNGA, 'Report of the Secretary-General, United Nations Police' (2011) UN Doc A/66/615, para. 52.

[38] See, UNGA, 'Report of the Secretary-General, Securing States and Societies: Strengthening the United Nations Comprehensive Support to Security Sector Reform' (2008) UN Doc A/62/659.

[39] See UNGA and UNSC, 'Report of the Secretary-General, Securing Peace and Development: The Role of the United Nations in Supporting Security Sector Reform' (2008) UN Doc A/62/659–S/2008/39, 1.

[40] UNGA and UNSC, 'Report of the Secretary-General, Securing States and Societies: Strengthening the United Nations Comprehensive Support to Security Sector Reform' (2013) UN Doc A/67/970 – S/2013/480, 1.

[41] Ibid., para. 11.

[42] UNGA, 'Report of the Secretary-General, United Nations Police' (2011) UN Doc A/66/615, para. 52.

conflict'.[43] The senior advisory group observed that States emerging from conflict frequently requested capacity-building support, particularly in basic security and safety, but it raised concern about 'evidence of many actors making aspirational claims of capacity, perhaps in the hope of generating resources'.[44]

IV. Expert Critiques of Protection Capacity-building

Security system transformation and efforts to build protection capacity are being heavily scrutinized by experts. For an issue of such importance to the international community, it is striking how many experts openly question the approaches being taken. Critics point to the failure of initiatives to achieve demonstrable impact and raise concerns that although resources are being mobilized and deployed, changes seem rarely to happen—not in the order expected and certainly not within the time frame envisioned.[45] Experts identify a range of issues to explain this, from conceptual problems in current approaches to flaws in design and implementation.

The consistent failure of both policy-makers and practitioners to politically situate reforms because of misplaced normative judgments about how States do and should function is one of the sharpest critiques.[46] Experts making this point, and there are many, blame the limited impact of reform initiatives on the mismatch between what the international community expects and wants to happen, and political realities on the ground. Experts exploring this issue point out that in post-conflict and fragile States, power is fragmented across elite structures, formal and informal power brokers, networks, alliances, and institutions.[47] This variability forces citizens to seek protection and safety from a wide range of security actors in

[43] UNGA and UNSC, 'Civilian Capacity in the Aftermath of Conflict: Independent Report of the Senior Advisory Group' (2011) UN Doc A/65/747–S/2011/85, 5.

[44] Ibid., para. 35(e).

[45] Downes and Muggah draw attention to the large numbers of scholars 'calling for a fundamental rethink' of approaches. See Downes and Muggah, n 29, 136.

[46] The lack of political context is touched on by Robert Egnell and Peter Haldén, 'Laudable, Ahistorical and Overambitious: Security Sector Reform meets State Formation Theory' (2009) 9 Conflict, Security and Development 27–54; Eric Scheye and Gordon Peake, 'To Arrest Insecurity: Time for a Revised Security Sector Reform Agenda' (2005) 5 Conflict, Security and Development 295–327; Herbert Wulf, 'Chances, Dilemmas and Obstacles of Security Reform', in Clem McCartney, Martina Fischer, and Oliver Wills (eds), *Security Sector Reform, Potential and Challenges for Conflict Transformation* (Berlin: Berghof Research Center for Constructive Conflict Management, 2004) 71–5 <www.ciponline.org/images/uploads/publications/3363.pdf>; Nicole Ball and Dylan Hendrickson, 'Trends in Security Sector Reform: Policy, Practice and Research' (London: King's College London, 2009) 9–14 <www.securityanddevelopment.org/pdf/CSDG%20Paper%2020.pdf>; Erwin van Veen and Maria Derks, 'The Deaf, the Blind and the Politician: The Troubles of Justice and Security Interventions in Fragile States' (2012) 4 Hague J Rule of L 76–97; Mark Sedra, 'Towards Second Generation Security Sector Reform', in Sedra, see n 15; Paul Jackson, 'SSR and Post-Conflict Reconstruction: Armed Wing of State-building?', in Sedra, see n 15; Paul Jackson, 'Security Sector Reform and State Building' (2011) 32 Third World Q 1803–22; Michael Brzoska, *Development Donors and the Concept of Security Sector Reform* (Geneva: Geneva Centre for the Democratic Control of Armed Forces, 2003); Laurie Nathan, *No Ownership, No Commitment: A Guide to Local Ownership of Security Sector Reform* (Birmingham, UK: University of Birmingham, 2007); and Hills, see n 15, among many others.

[47] Egnell and Haldén, ibid., at 45, underline this point in their discussion of reform in Central Asia.

ways that are difficult to predict and even more difficult to programme for.[48] Experts caution that reforms depend on a careful understanding of political dynamics within the State, society, and polity and warn that because the real structures of power are constantly mutating among elites, particularly in countries emerging from years of fighting, the 'technocratic social engineering' approach commonly taken to reform diverts attention away from the factors and forces that will determine whether reform is successful or not.[49] Robert Egnell makes this point forcefully, arguing that 'over-ambitious normative aims in quasi states are likely to fail as it means meddling with highly complex social and historical processes that are notoriously difficult to predict and more so to socially engineer'.[50] Although a clear understanding of the drivers of change is the first step in security system transformation, international reformers often lack the deep insight into the cultures in which they work[51] and 'tend to look at formal structures and assume that power flows according to those structures, whereas power relations are much more fluid, particularly in fragile and conflict-affected environments'.[52] Experts with long experience in security reform warn that preconceived ideas about what needs to be fixed may elbow out questions about how institutions function and distract from finding politically feasible, workable solutions.[53]

Even with an ideal amount of political and cultural data, conventional technocratic approaches to capacity-building may be oversimplified at best. Experts warn that the path to reform will almost never be linear and caution against assuming that the accurate identification of problems and detailed elaboration of plans is sufficient for moving forward with security transformation.[54] International capacity-builders will want to be wary of the tendency to underestimate the many complex factors working against reform,[55] ranging from the vested interests of local and regional elites and change-resistant institutions to the distorting effect of increasing criminality and violence on political space and options.[56] Because reform is a

[48] On the issue of fragmentation, see also Heiner Hanggi and Vincenza Scherrer, 'Towards an Integrated Security Sector Reform Approach in UN Peace Operations' (2008) 15 Intl Peacekeeping 486; on the role of local security actors see Nathan, n 46; Van Veen and Derks, see n 46; Bruce Baker, 'Non-state Providers of Everyday Security in Fragile African States', in Louise Andersen, Bjørn Møller, and Finn Steputat, *Fragile States and Insecure People* (New York: Palgrave MacMillan, 2007) 123–47; and Downes and Muggah, see n 29.

[49] Egnell and Haldén, see n 46, 46. On the issue of technocratic approaches, Paul Jackson goes further in his critique, arguing in that 'some technocratic interventions make fragile situations worse, or at best, do not improve the security situation'. Jackson, 'Security Sector Reform and State Building', see n 46, 1812.

[50] Robert Egnell, 'The Organised Hypocrisy of International State-building' (2010) 10 Conflict, Security and Development 465–91, 485.

[51] Hills, see n 15, 178.

[52] Louise Anten, Ivan Briscoe, and Marco Mezzera, *The Political Economy of State-building in Situations of Fragility and Conflict: A Synthesis Paper Based on Studies of Afghanistan, Democratic Republic of the Congo, Guatemala, Kosovo and Pakistan* (The Hague: Netherlands Institute of International Relations (Clingendael), 2012) 4–7, 30–6. For a discussion of western bias in security system reform see Hills, see n 15.

[53] Ball and Hendrickson, see n 46, 26.

[54] Egnell and Haldén, see n 46, 47.

[55] For a thoughtful discussion of obstacles to reform, see Wulf, n 46.

[56] The question of ownership is widely discussed among experts; see in particular the work of Nathan, n 46.

'deeply political endeavour' that creates 'winners and losers', many elites, particularly those empowered through their control of illegal elements of the conflict economy, are likely to see changes to the instruments of security as challenges to their position and influence—something they will probably resist, violently if necessary.[57] Security reforms imply 'an ambitious realignment and re-engineering of power and power-holding elites and the strengthening of (non-violent) State-civil society bargaining capacities'[58] which occurs at the expense of actors that have become used to acting under little, if any, legitimate constraints.

Institutional resistance is another major factor impacting negatively on security reforms. Security institutions—often conservative and distrustful of reform initiatives—frequently emerge from conflicts distorted and bloated by fighting the war, unwilling to downsize and unable to move in positive new directions, more so where the institutions are themselves the site of political contestation.[59] Security institutions—the ones which have to change in order to better protect civilians—are sometimes so distrusted by populations, particularly if they have a history of repressive behaviour, that communities actively seek other security providers as better alternatives.[60] There is also the reality of the security environment itself. Violence, insecurity, and crime often increase when fighting ends, leading to the paradoxical situation of civilians feeling more unsafe and at risk than they did during the conflict.[61] Popular opposition to ambitious reformist measures can easily arise when communities are demanding an 'iron hand' to ensure their security and safety.[62]

Efforts to build protection capacities are also hindered by factors internal to the way security system reforms are programmed. Experts point to a number of issues, starting with an over-reliance on approaches designed to fit project templates. Nicole Ball and Dylan Hendrickson blame donors for this, arguing that they

> continue to have a strong preference for discrete projects rather than broader programmes and for activities with concrete outputs (a defence white paper, human rights training for police officers) rather than process-based work (developing consensus on the need for security sector reform, strengthening the capacity of government officials to develop policies.)[63]

Reform initiatives are often ad hoc in nature; a review conducted by the Organization for Economic Cooperation and Development's Development Advisory Committee (OECD-DAC) concluded that programmes frequently lack strategic direction or concept.[64] A number of experts point to the futility of assuming that reform is even possible in the short term. Because fundamental transformations in

[57] Scheye and Peake, see n 46, 308–10. The question of ownership is widely discussed among experts; see in particular the work of Nathan, n 46.

[58] Downes and Muggah, see n 29, 138.

[59] Scheye and Peake, see n 46, 307, referencing Brzoska, see n 46.

[60] Scheye and Peake, see n 46, 310.

[61] Charles Call, 'Introduction: What We Know and Don't Know about Postconflict Justice and Security Reform', in Charles Call (ed.), *Constructing Justice and Security after War* (Washington DC: US Institute of Peace Press, 2007) 3–4. This same point is made by Downes and Muggah, see n 29, 141.

[62] Scheye and Peake, see n 46, 303.

[63] Ball and Hendrickson, see n 46, 15.

[64] Organization for Economic Cooperation and Development, Development Assistance Committee (OECD-DAC), *Security System Reform and Governance: A DAC Reference Document* (Paris: OECD

security and justice institutions have historically taken up to two generations,[65] donors focused on right-sizing military forces and reducing budgets, for instance, have consistently set unrealistic short-term goals, creating a false pace and sense of urgency, and forcing attention on aspects of the problem which are important to donors but less so to national actors.[66]

The monitoring and sustainability of reform efforts are also problematic. Monitoring of development projects is difficult under normal conditions, all the more so in the highly complex environments where security sector reforms are attempted.[67] Mark Downes and Robert Muggah make the striking argument that 'there is virtually no empirical evidence of what works in support of security sector reform and what does not',[68] implying that practitioners and policy-makers are forced to make blind decisions about programme implementation and course adjustment in the absence of dependable data and information. The medium to long-term financial sustainability of security institutions is no less important, particularly in countries where donors fund the early stages of security reform on the grounds that public financial management systems are weak and national budgets over-extended. The assumption that reform initiatives will be financed by national budgets at a later date is not always borne out, leaving donors with the choice of supporting, at high cost, security institutions for an indefinite period, or halting reforms before they have become institutionalized.[69]

Practitioners trying to make reform initiatives successful point to other inhibiting factors. An often overlooked but operationally significant factor is the confusing juncture at which the security sector sits. Practitioners are as likely to have a background in political and security theory as to be domain professionals in security system reform, management, organizational reform, or capacity-building. They prioritize different elements, use dissimilar strategies to accomplish divergent goals, and measure impact with varied, sometimes contradictory metrics.[70] This impacts negatively on the ability to prioritize and contributes to the random nature of efforts often seen and criticized in the field.

Because of the all-encompassing nature of what reformers are trying to achieve, initiatives are highly complex. To achieve the goal of establishing a legitimate, sustainable, democratically managed security and justice system with sufficient capacity to ensure the safety of civilians and protect individual and community rights, partners are advised to adopt an all-encompassing approach involving multiple institutions and multiple stakeholders.[71] OECD-DAC, a leading force in the

Publishing, 2005) 59–60. Egnell and Haldén share this view, warning that 'the practice of SSR is often a mixed bag of ad hoc, small scale projects and activities'. Egnell and Haldén, see n 46, 32.

65 Van Veen and Derks, see n 46, 89.

66 Eboe Hutchful and J 'Kayode Fayemi, in OECD-DAC, see n 64, Annex 4.A1, 71; Ball and Hendrickson, see n 46, 26.

67 Scheye and Peake, see n 46, 302.

68 Downes and Muggah, see n 29, 144.

69 Regarding financial sustainability, see William Byrd, 'The Financial Dimension of Security Sector Reform', in Sedra, see n 15, 301–26; see also Scheye and Peake, n 46, 315.

70 Downes and Muggah, see n 29, 138, observe that many field practitioners have a 'technocratic bias' because they are 'frequently drawn from more formal legal, military and policing backgrounds'.

71 On comprehensive approaches see Urusla C Schröder and Johannes Kode, 'Rule of Law and Security Sector Reform in International State-Building: Dilemmas of Converging Agendas' (2012) 4

security sector, expects that reform initiatives will involve 'the armed forces, the police, [...] intelligence services and similar bodies, judicial and penal institutions, as well as the elected and duly appointed civil authorities responsible for control and oversight'.[72] The principal tasks to be accomplished are equally comprehensive. OECD-DAC's reform agenda includes four pillars: (a) developing a clear institutional framework; (b) strengthening governance and oversight of security institutions; (c) building capacities and professional security forces that are accountable to civil authorities; and (d) promoting sustainability of justice and security delivery systems.[73] The OECD-DAC guidelines advise that security reforms should be: (a) people-centred, locally owned, and based on democratic norms and human rights principles and the rule of law, seeking to provide freedom from fear; (b) seen as a framework to structure thinking about how to address diverse security challenges facing States and their populations through more integrated development and security policies and through greater civilian involvement and oversight; (c) founded on activities with multisectoral strategies, based upon a broad assessment of the range of security needs of the people and the State; (d) developed adhering to basic principles underlying public sector reform such as transparency and accountability; and (e) implemented through clear processes and policies that aim to enhance the institutional human capacity needed for security policy to function effectively.[74]

The UN's approach, as set forth in the Secretary-General's 2008 report on security system reform, observes that effective security systems have at least five common features, including: (a) a legal and/or constitution framework; (b) an institutionalized system of governance and management; (c) capacities; (d) mechanisms for interaction among security actors; and (e) a culture of service.[75] The UN's approach involves a wide range of activities including development of guidance and civilian capacities, co-ordination mechanisms, and collaboration with regional and sub-regional organizations, in particular the African Union.[76]

The insistence on comprehensiveness is justified on a number of grounds. In an article describing the UN's approach, Adedeji Ebo and Kristiana Powell argue that focusing on broad aims helps to ensure that reform initiatives are not merely a 'set of simplistic activities consisting of narrow exercises such as "rightsizing" the security services or "training and equipping" uniformed personnel'.[77] Mark Downes and Robert Muggah, questioning the ambitiousness of all-encompassing approaches, point out that they have been 'driven in large part by development and

Hague J Rule of L 31, 32; and Neil Cooper and Michael Pugh, 'Security Sector Transformation in Post-conflict Societies' (London: King's College London, 2002) 6, 19 <securityanddevelopment.org/pdf/work5.pdf>.

72 OECD-DAC, see n 64, 11.

73 Ibid., 12.

74 OECD-DAC, *OECD DAC Handbook on Security System Reform: Supporting Security and Justice* (Paris: OECD Publishing, 2007) 21–2.

75 UNGA and UNSC, 'Report of the Secretary-General: Securing Peace and Development: The Role of the United Nations in Supporting Security Sector Reform' (2008) UN Doc A/62/659–S/2008/39, para. 15; for a discussion of the UN's approach, see also Hänggi and Scherrer, n 48, 490.

76 UNSC Res 2151 (2004) UN Doc S/RES/2151, preambular para. 12.

77 Adedeji Ebo and Kristiana Powell, 'Why is SSR Important? A United Nations Perspective', in Sedra, see n 15, 47.

security actors, and an assumption that poorly governed and unreformed security sectors can generate instability and undermine the potential for political, social and economic development'.[78]

A main problem with all-encompassing reform approaches, as laudable as they are, is their unmanageability in the contexts where they are being implemented. Experts like Eric Scheye and Gordon Peake describe security system transformation as 'intricate' and involving many moving parts, the management of which 'would challenge even the most richly resourced, high skilled government or multinational corporation'.[79] The problem is particularly acute in situations where multiple actors are providing security and protection in areas where State authority is not yet fully present, if present at all. A senior official working on security system reform in South Sudan echoed this concern, saying 'it doesn't make sense to ask us to help reform so many aspects of the security services so soon after a conflict ends. There are too many places where State authority isn't present and too many actors providing so-called security.'[80] The same official observed that taking a comprehensive approach underestimated on-the-ground realities:

> Let's be frank, most security institutions emerge from conflicts stronger than they were before. The same is not true for democratic institutions, including the ones that are necessary for civilian oversight of the security forces; they are often at their weakest. A comprehensive approach that assumes progress can be made on all fronts doesn't appreciate these realities.[81]

Because comprehensive approaches to building protective capacities are flawed—due to unrealistic objectives, over-complexity, insufficient expertise, lack of deep contextual knowledge, unsustainability, and deficient monitoring[82]—a number of experts, including the International Network on Conflict and Fragility (INCAF), advocate a 'process' approach.[83] Advocates praise the approach for 'provid[ing] a practical lens to improve the way in which interventions deal with the critical challenges of political ownership, programme management, monitoring and the definition of results'.[84] The approach is incremental in nature, envisioning small steps first aimed at creating space for political consolidation, linked over time through experiment and innovation to long-term options for justice and security delivery. It also involves building capacities relevant for the political context, managing political risks, and adopting flexible results and monitoring frameworks so that practitioners and policy-makers can understand what is really working. As a relatively new contribution to programming, there is still little guidance from process advocates on the substantial steps that should be taken to build protection

[78] Downes and Muggah, see n 29, 138–9. [79] Scheye and Peake, see n 46, 305.

[80] Author's notes and discussions. [81] Author's notes and discussions.

[82] Downes and Muggah, see n 29, 150, characterize the problems of security system reform as 'legion'.

[83] Advocates of the process approach include Nicole Ball and Luc van de Goor, *The Challenges of Supporting Effective Security and Justice Development Programming* (Paris: OECD Publishing, 2013); Jackson, see n 46; and Wulf, see n 46.

[84] Van Veen and Derks, see n 46, 93.

capacities or on their sequencing,[85] aside from general recommendations about how the process itself should be organized. The direction of the approach is sensible and promising, however, and because it addresses the problematic ways in which comprehensive reforms are currently being implemented, it is a welcome improvement on conventional strategies. It may, however, not yet go far enough.

V. Conclusion

Perhaps the better way is to build, as a first step, on the basis of a roadmap and as quickly as possible, the capacity and capability of *selective* security forces to physically protect and ensure the safety of civilians. This involves conceptualizing the process approach in a way that front-loads certain kinds of initiatives while delaying others. The types of initiatives that could sensibly be prioritized, depending on political conditions, include establishing, training, reinforcing, equipping, housing, nationally funding, strategically orienting, tactically preparing, administratively situating, and politically ring-fencing protection police units, and locating these in areas where civilians are at high risk or maintaining them on twenty-four-hour stand-by in major population centres for rapid deployment to areas where violence unexpectedly erupts. The problems associated with these kinds of units cannot be under-estimated: who they report to, what criteria is used to trigger their deployment, and what protocols they should follow at the community level are just some of the difficult issues that need to be resolved.

The strength of a 'security-first' approach is the acknowledgement that many parts of a government in post-conflict and fragile States, including parts of the security services, will not meet high standards for efficiency or effectiveness in the short term, and very often will fail to do so for generations. The approach is a recognition that difficult decisions will arise during the lengthy period of capacity-building and that when they do, they will need to be faced in all of their complexity with the security of civilians foremost in mind. For many stakeholders, civilian security is a first-order priority. In its integrated guidance note on security system reform, the UN stresses that 'in the immediate aftermath of conflict, support should go to initiatives that will improve delivery of basic safety and security to the population and build national capacity in key areas of democratic governance'.[86] The World Bank shares this view, arguing that in situations of conflict and violence, development actors should explicitly focus on 'prioritising the institutions that provide citizen security, justice (including controlling corruption), and jobs'.[87]

[85] For thoughtful guidance on the possible sequencing of reform activities, see ibid.

[86] United Nations Interagency Security Sector Reform (SSR) Task Force, *Security Sector Reform Integrated Technical Guidance Notes* (United Nations, 2012) 93. The UN Interagency SSR Task Force was established by the Secretary-General in 2007 and brings together fourteen UN agencies, departments, funds, offices, and programmes, co-chaired by the Department of Peacekeeping Operations and UNDP. Ibid., v.

[87] The World Bank, *World Development Report 2011* (Washington, DC: The International Bank for Reconstruction and Development/The World Bank, 2011) 146–7.

It is important to stress that prioritizing civilian security is not a way of circumventing, ignoring, or in any way diminishing the urgency of fighting human rights violations and corruption. This is a point that cannot be over-emphasized. There is a recognition, now widespread, that the effectiveness of security forces is a function not only of their coercive actions but also of the way communities perceive them, perceptions best improved and maintained when forces are seen to act justly and, where they commit violations, to be held accountable. A firm, unwavering commitment to the rule of law is a fundamental principle for partners helping governments to better protect their civilians and provide security for their populations.[88] This widely shared view is crucial for the UN; under its Human Rights Due Diligence Policy, the UN is prevented from supporting any local security forces 'where there are substantial grounds for believing there is a real risk of the receiving entities committing grave violations of international humanitarian, human rights or refugee law and where the relevant authorities fail to take the necessary corrective or mitigating measures'.[89]

Security-first approaches have been considered for some time, given shape in the early 1990s when the UN Department of Disarmament Affairs recommended a combination of better policing and disarmament to improve civilian safety.[90] Since then, similar security-first approaches have been used in a number of countries, for example the Palestinian occupied territories,[91] with the intention of building civilian confidence and creating space for negotiations on longer-term peace dividends. The steps being implemented vary across countries, contingent on the political context; in other situations initiatives have aimed to build the capacity of civilian work corps after soldiers and irregular forces have been transitioned into them, and to strengthen the capacity of local security structures and actors in support of inter-community solidarity and preparedness.[92]

The security-first approach has its drawbacks and detractors. Where multiple formal and informal actors provide security, for instance, it is difficult to know which provider has the most legitimacy and therefore should be supported, or who, in the absence of a social compact, is in the position to decide this.[93] Experts such as Robert Egnell and Peter Haldén criticize security-first approaches for historical

[88] The World Bank makes this point strongly, arguing that governments that commit human rights violations and tolerate corruption often create drivers of violence, rather than provide security. Ibid., 81–8.

[89] UN Human Rights Due Diligence Policy on UN support to non-UN security forces, in UNGA and UNSC (2011) UN Doc A/67/775–S/2013/110, Annex, paragraph 1.

[90] Brzoska, see n 46, 29.

[91] Schröder and Kode, see n 71, 43.

[92] Downes and Muggah refer to these as interim stabilization measures and mention several examples in Haiti, Kosovo, Iraq, the Philippines, Rwanda, and Central African Republic. See Downes and Muggah, n 29, 146–50. Interesting examples of efforts to strengthen community solidarity have been funded through the South Sudan Recovery Fund, administered by UNDP. See UN Development Programme, 'South Sudan Recovery Fund' (*UNDP*, undated) <www.ss.undp.org/content/south_sudan/en/home/operations/fund-management/south_sudan_recovery_fund-southsudan.html>. Downes and Muggah, see n 29, 143, among others, strongly support the emphasis on civilian security, which they see as helping to consolidate the social compact in the aftermath of conflict and during fragility. They argue persuasively that the 'contribution to tangibly and subjectively improving and well-being is at the heart of forging legitimacy'.

[93] For a discussion of the complexity of local context, see Hills, n 15.

reasons, arguing that 'a relatively narrow focus on security and military reform has meant that while different programmes serve to increase the efficiency and effectiveness of military and police institutions, the accountability, oversight and governance issues are lagging behind'.[94] During the Cold War, security partners paid little attention to democratic control, allowing the security services in many developing countries to act with autonomy—often impunity—undermining the development of participatory democracy and civilian oversight.[95] The same problem exists now. In war-torn Sierra Leone, Paul Jackson points out that more than ten years of international reform efforts have 'effectively created an overdeveloped security force, including intelligence, but without the culture of civil oversight to control it'.[96]

These critiques are important and useful for helping to promote a more mature formulation of the security-first approach. The recommendation to build the capacity of *selective* coercive security institutions is not intended to undermine or in any way diminish the goal that comprehensive approaches seek to achieve. The goal of helping to establish and strengthen the capacities of a transparent, democratically managed, sustainable, legitimate security and justice system stretching across all relevant institutions is the right goal. This is not in dispute. The timing and sequencing of the approaches to do so, however, is. Transformational, comprehensive approaches operate on long timeframes. This key point should be not only acknowledged, but also built into the way in which protection capacity-building is approached. Understanding the norms and values that will form the social contract between those who use legitimate force and the civilians such force is used to protect is critical. Doing so requires understanding a

> broader milieu that includes history, tradition, and culture of a society; its political and economic system; the distribution of wealth and power; the degree of industrialization; the ethnic, language, and religious make-up of society (the presence of group tension); the level of education of the populace; the extent of urbanization; and the geo-political surroundings (hostile or unstable neighbors).[97]

This is not something that can be done quickly, by contractors, under time pressures linked to mission mandates and exit strategies. This takes years, if not generations.

For this reason, it makes sense to de-link the process of building State responsibility from the exit strategies for peacekeeping and State-building missions. Underlying many of the protection mandates issued today is the assumption that States emerging from decades of conflict, if given sufficient support, can establish the necessary capacity to protect their citizens within the time-span of a mission. The belief is that once this capacity is in place, multilateral organizations are justified in drawing down their forces and re-orienting engagement towards development and

94 Egnell and Haldén, see n 46, 44.

95 Ball and Hendrickson, see n 46, 4.

96 Jackson, see n 46, 123.

97 Brian Tamanaha, 'Primacy of Society and the Failures of Law and Development' (2011) 44 Cornell Intl L J 209, 214.

democratization.[98] Getting to this point is seen, rightly, as the end-state of the protection chain. But since getting there is such a confusing and lengthy process, involving complex institutional adaptation and elite realignment, it may not be the best use of limited international resources to insist that peacekeeping troops are present in the country until this is achieved.

This chapter has set forth the argument that the first-order goal in the short term, around which there is unity of vision, purpose, and action, is building the capacity of *selective* coercive security forces so that States can better protect their civilian populations. The democratic control of the security and justice system should likewise be worked towards with diligence and commitment, over the long term and in a way that is incremental and politically aware. Writing about the debates in security reform, Michael Brzoska argued, over a decade ago, that the most difficult dilemma facing policy-makers and practitioners was the 'relative weight given to the provision of physical security versus more democratic control over decision-making in the security sector'.[99] Reaching both of these goals, in sequence and close proximity, remains the aim of the international community, even if doing so requires us to change, perhaps fundamentally, our current approaches.

[98] Ebo and Powell, see n 77, 48.
[99] Brzoska, see n 46, 23.

19

Community Self-protection

Aditi Gorur and Nils Carstensen

I. Introduction

Over the past few years, there has been a growing recognition of the importance of measures that communities employ to protect themselves when faced with conflict. Discussions regarding the protection of civilians frequently focus on what the international community, governments, or armed groups do or fail to do to protect civilians. Yet civilians are often forced to rely on themselves to guarantee their own safety and the safety of their families and communities. Without a nuanced understanding of communities' self-protection activities, external actors risk undermining those measures when they intervene, or missing opportunities to enhance their own protection impact by augmenting or complementing such initiatives.

This chapter draws on research conducted by the Local to Global Protection Initiative (L2GP) on local perceptions of protection. Between 2009 and 2015, local and international researchers undertook in-depth interviews with more than 1,500 people trying to survive and protect themselves in major humanitarian and protection crises in Burma/Myanmar, the occupied Palestinian territories, Sudan, South Sudan, Syria, and Zimbabwe.[1] It also draws on research conducted by the Stimson Center on the importance of community engagement by external protection actors, peacekeeping missions in particular. The Stimson Center research included interviews, surveys, and focus groups conducted between 2012 and 2015 in South Sudan and the Democratic Republic of Congo (DRC).[2]

The chapter focuses on humanitarian organizations and peacekeeping missions—two key external actors that take different approaches to protection, both of which have attempted to support community self-protection strategies. Other types of external actors, such as human rights and development actors, are

[1] Ashley South, Simon Harragin, Justin Corbett, Richard Horsey, Susanne Kempel, Henrik Fröjmark, and Nils Carstensen, *Local to Global Protection in Myanmar (Burma), Sudan, South Sudan and Zimbabwe* (London: Overseas Development Institute, 2012) 1–36.

[2] See Aditi Gorur, *Community Self-Protection Strategies: How Peacekeepers Can Help or Harm* (Washington, DC: The Stimson Center, 2013); Alison Giffen, *Community Perceptions as a Priority in Protection and Peacekeeping* (Washington, DC: The Stimson Center, 2013); Aditi Gorur, Jok Madut Jok, and Augustino Ting Mayai, *Perceptions of Security in Aweil North County, South Sudan* (Washington, DC: The Stimson Center and the Sudd Institute, 2014); Aditi Gorur, *Perceptions of Security Among Internally Displaced Persons in Juba, South Sudan* (Washington, DC: The Stimson Center, 2014).

not specifically covered in this analysis. The chapter also leaves aside the question of how government actors can support self-protection measures taken by populations within their own states, focusing instead on contexts where the state is unable or unwilling to fully implement its responsibility to protect, including situations where state actors are actively perpetrating abuses.

The proposition of external actors supporting self-protection measures is not a simple one. The differences between their protection capacities, priorities, and approaches and those of local conflict-affected communities can be vast. Yet the potential impact if external actors are able to augment and leverage the protection capacities of conflict-affected communities is significant.

The chapter begins by examining the different ways that external protection actors and local communities understand protection. It then provides an overview of community self-protection, illustrated by an example from Syria. Finally, the chapter explores how external protection actors may be able to support self-protection initiatives, considering protection objectives, different approaches, and challenges that might be encountered. This is supplemented by two short case studies demonstrating different approaches: extensive external involvement in community watch groups in South Sudan, and minimal external involvement in civil society groups providing training and advice on individual self-protection measures in South Kordofan.

II. Understanding Protection

Protection activities by external actors (such as humanitarian agencies, peacekeeping missions, human rights groups, or development actors) are, when they work best, crucial for saving lives and supporting longer-term rehabilitation. The approach of such actors tends to be defined by translating international law and operational guidance into protection activities in highly complex environments, where such activities do not always resonate well with local realities. In all crisis situations there are multiple, sometimes competing, understandings of what 'protection' means and of what strategies and actions might bring about a degree of protection and increase people's chances of survival and recovery.

While external protection actors may arrive in a crisis situation with a good understanding of the different definitions of protection used by their own institutions and by colleagues in other fields (e.g. concepts of refugee protection, protection in peacekeeping, or humanitarian protection), they are often much less familiar with the experiences of affected individuals and groups and their assessments of their own needs. Local conceptions of protection may differ significantly from what is provided for under internationally sanctioned protection approaches. Such differences in the understanding of protection can be attributed to several factors, including: (a) different motivations of affected communities and of humanitarian, peacekeeping, and other external protection actors; (b) differences in importance ascribed to relevant laws and values; and (c) different concepts of what being protected means in practice.

The following sections summarize humanitarian and peacekeeping approaches to protection, as well as community protection concepts. They explore why the external actors may have very different understandings of protection compared to the local communities they seek to protect.[3]

A. Humanitarian approaches

Humanitarian actors' understanding of protection is rooted in international law.[4] It is shaped by carefully crafted humanitarian principles and refined in institutional mandates and operational policies and guidance. According to the most widely accepted definition, provided by the Inter-Agency Standing Committee (IASC),[5] protection

> encompasses all activities aimed at ensuring full respect for the rights of the individual in accordance with the letter and the spirit of the relevant bodies of law, i.e., human rights law, international humanitarian law and refugee law. Human rights and humanitarian organisations must conduct these activities in an impartial manner (not on the basis of race, national or ethnic origin, language or gender).[6]

Guidance documents, such as the widely used and referenced Active Learning Network for Accountability and Performance in Humanitarian Action (ALNAP) *Guide to Protection*,[7] which provides an extensive list of violations to address as protection concerns, often reflect the language of international human rights and humanitarian law.

Given this strongly legal foundation, many of the classic examples of humanitarian protection involve advocating with governments to recognize legal rights, such as the United Nations High Commissioner for Refugees' (UNHCR) work to determine refugee status,[8] negotiating with armed groups to secure the rights of affected populations,[9] or sensitizing armed groups to their obligations under international

[3] For a more detailed discussion of the different concepts of protection among humanitarian, peacekeeping, and other actors see Ralph Mamiya, Chapter 3, in this volume, and Haidi Willmot and Scott Sheeran, 'The Protection of Civilians Mandate in UN Peacekeeping Operations: Reconciling Protection Concepts and Practices' (2013) 95 IRRC 517.

[4] On the development of obligations under international humanitarian law with respect to civilians, see Hugo Slim, Jamie Williamson, and Sara Pantuliano and Eva Svoboda, in this volume.

[5] The Inter-Agency Standing Committee (IASC) was established in June 1992 in response to United Nations General Assembly Resolution 46/182 on the strengthening of humanitarian assistance. General Assembly Resolution 48/57 affirmed its role as the primary mechanism for inter-agency coordination of humanitarian assistance. See United Nations General Assembly Resolution (UNGA Res) 46/182 (1991) UN Doc A/RES/46/182, para. 33; UNGA Res 48/57 (1993) UN Doc A/RES/48/57, paras 6, 11–13, preambular para. 13.

[6] IASC, *Protection of Internally Displaced Persons: Inter-Agency Standing Committee Policy Paper* (New York: IASC, 1999) 4. The definition was originally adopted by a 1999 Workshop of the International Committee of the Red Cross (ICRC) on Protection. See Sylvie Giossi Caverzasio, *Strengthening Protection in War* (Geneva: ICRC, 2001).

[7] Hugo Slim and Andrew Bonwick, *Protection, An ALNAP Guide for Humanitarian Agencies* (London: Overseas Development Institute, 2005) 11–23.

[8] UN High Commissioner for Refugees (UNHCR), 'Legal Protection' (*UNHCR*, undated) <www.unhcr.org/pages/49c3646cce.html>.

[9] Slim and Bonwick, see n 7, 85.

humanitarian law, as is frequently undertaken by the International Committee of the Red Cross (ICRC).[10]

Humanitarian protection goes beyond these conventional legal activities, however, drawing in elements of humanitarian assistance—the provision of goods and services to alleviate suffering rather than to protect rights. Humanitarian assistance is generally considered a distinct activity from humanitarian protection, but the distinction is based on the purpose of the activities and there is often overlap. For instance, in 1995 in Bosnia and Herzegovina, communities had to wait for fresh water in long queues, where they were exposed to sniper fire. The International Rescue Committee rehabilitated old pipe infrastructure that allowed people to get their water much more quickly, greatly reducing their exposure to risk.[11]Such water projects are common in humanitarian and development assistance, but in this case the primary objective was protection. Humanitarians have also sought to 'mainstream' protection concerns in their activities, being guided by the imperative to 'do no harm', in an effort to undertake activity in a way that seeks to ensure respect for the rights and dignity of beneficiaries.[12]

B. Peacekeeping approaches

The approach to protection in United Nations (UN) peacekeeping missions flows from resolutions of the UN Security Council, as well as policies and guidance developed by the UN Departments of Peacekeeping Operations and Field Support. Although Security Council mandates have long been issued in support of improving security generally, these mandates 'shifted to support "stronger" protection measures through affirmation of international humanitarian and human rights law and a more explicit emphasis on the physical protection of civilians' after peacekeeping failures in the 1990s, including the failure to protect civilians in Rwanda and Srebrenica.[13] The Council issued its first resolution explicitly mandating a peacekeeping mission to protect civilians in 1999 when it authorized the UN mission in Sierra Leone.

Today, protection of civilians mandates are common for peacekeeping missions—over 97 per cent of UN peacekeeping personnel worldwide serve in missions with protection mandates.[14] Missions that are given explicit mandates to protect civilians are generally instructed to protect them from the threat, or imminent

[10] 'Building Respect for Humanitarian Action and IHL among "Other" Weapon Bearers' (*ICRC*, 29 Oct 2010) <www.icrc.org/eng/what-we-do/building-respect-ihl/dialogue-weapon-bearers/other-weapons-bearers/overview-icrc-other-weapon-bearers.htm>.

[11] Slim and Bonwick, see n 7, 89.

[12] The Sphere Project, *The Sphere Handbook 2011: Humanitarian Charter and Minimum Principles in Humanitarian Response* (Bourton on Dunsmore, UK: Practical Action, 2011)'Protection Principle 1: Avoid exposing people to further harm as a result of your actions', also available at: <www.spherehandbook.org/en/protection-principle-1-avoid-exposing-people-to-further-harm-as-a-result-of-your-actions>.

[13] Victoria Holt and Glyn Taylor, with Max Kelly, *Protecting Civilians in the Context of UN Peacekeeping Operations* (New York: United Nations, 2009) 35.

[14] Figure derived from 'Peacekeeping Statistics' (*UN Department of Peacekeeping Operations*, 30 April 2015) <www.un.org/en/peacekeeping/resources/statistics>.

threat, of physical violence. Protection in the context of UN peacekeeping tends to be more narrowly focused on protection from physical violence, in comparison with humanitarian approaches to protection, which may focus on a broader range of protection threats, such as hunger and disease.

Peacekeeping policy now defines the protection of civilians as comprising three tiers of activities which may be undertaken simultaneously: (a) protection through dialogue and engagement, (b) provision of physical protection, and (c) establishment of a protective environment.[15] All components of a multidimensional peacekeeping mission—military, police, and civilian—have a role to play in operationalizing these three tiers. Peacekeeping operations are expected to fulfil their mandates *impartially*, for example, to protect civilians from physical violence without regard to the identity of the population under threat or the identity of the perpetrator. However, they are not required to be *neutral*, and often provide support to one party to the conflict, namely, the host government.

C. Community approaches

Local communities' approaches to protection are shaped by their cultural and socio-economic environments. In conflict areas, the multitude of understandings held by affected individuals and communities are likely driven by their urgent need to act to protect themselves in the chaos and lawlessness of conflict and war.[16] As such, local communities' perceptions of what constitutes a protection threat and how activities to address different threats should be prioritized may be quite different from those of external actors. For example, in a 2012 focus group study conducted by Oxfam and the Stimson Center in conflict-affected communities in the DRC, participants were asked to identify the most important threats in their communities. While most identified threats such as killings, sexual violence, and arson that are familiar to external actors, a few also identified issues such as promiscuity, public drunkenness, or a general attitude of aggression, which are less likely to be identified by external actors as protection threats.[17] Many communities studied by L2GP identified a close connection between protection and livelihoods, indicating that the ability to protect oneself and one's community is often intimately linked to the kind of resources that can be mobilized or otherwise drawn upon when a crisis hits, but many external actors may not consider livelihoods to be a protection issue.

Even where local communities and external actors are attempting to address the same threats, as is often the case, local communities may be confounded by many of the principles, policies, and practices that restrict external actors from taking certain actions. For example, Article 23(c) of the Fourth Geneva Convention provides that parties are obliged to allow the free passage of humanitarian assistance if they

[15] UN Department of Peacekeeping Operations (DPKO) and UN Department of Field Support (DFS), 'DPKO/DFS Policy: The Protection of Civilians in United Nations Peacekeeping' (New York: United Nations, 2015) § E.2 (UN DPKO and UN DFS Protection of Civilians Policy).

[16] For more detail on the impact of war on civilians, see Hugo Slim, Chapter 1, in this volume.

[17] Data from Stimson Center focus groups with conflict-affected communities in North Kivu, South Kivu, and Orientale provinces, Democratic Republic of Congo, June 2012, on file with authors.

are satisfied that it will not result in advantage to the military efforts or economy of the enemy.[18] The Humanitarian Policy Group has noted that this excludes a 'developmental approach'[19] to humanitarian aid, restricting the capacity-building in which numerous humanitarian organizations engage and which in some cases communities may prefer. Similarly, international legal categories of persons, such as 'civilian', 'refugee', or 'internally displaced person', are important for specific regimes and the actors working to implement them, but are not always helpful for protection in practice.

Humanitarian protection literature and guidance often distinguish between what are described as 'protection needs' and 'pressing needs'.[20] However, communities often do not make similar distinctions,[21] nor do they make a clear distinction between threats to survival, protection, and attempts to recover. On the contrary, people caught up in life-threatening crises often take a holistic perspective where past, present, and possible future threats, challenges, and needs are closely interlinked.[22]

For peacekeeping missions, priorities and restrictions laid out in a mandate may be far removed from what local communities expect, and consider central to their protection. For example, in a 2013 survey conducted by the Stimson Centre and the Sudd Institute in Aweil North county in South Sudan, a number of respondents expressed an expectation that the role of the UN mission in South Sudan (UNMISS) included monitoring and resolving border disputes.[23] Aweil North county borders Sudan and has experienced armed group incursions and bombing from across the border. Although UNMISS had a mandate to protect civilians throughout the country, it was not mandated to monitor or resolve disputes involving the border between Sudan and South Sudan. Similarly, some respondents believed that UNMISS' role included offering humanitarian or development services, such as providing food or mosquito nets, which also fell outside its mandate.[24]

Communities are, of course, not monolithic and different members of a particular community may perceive and prioritize threats and protection differently. For example, the same 2013 survey in Aweil North county found that women were less likely to place trust in government protection actors than men.[25] More broadly, L2GP studies in Myanmar (Burma),[26]

[18] Geneva Convention relative to the Protection of Civilian Persons in Time of War (adopted 12 August 1949, entered into force 21 October 1950) 75 UNTS 287, Article 23.

[19] Kate Mackintosh, 'The Principles of Humanitarian Action in International Humanitarian Law' (London: Overseas Development Institute, 2000) 9.

[20] Slim and Bonwick, see n 7, 11–23.

[21] Justin Corbett, 'Learning from the Nuba: Civilian Resilience and Self-protection during Conflict' (Local to Global Protection (L2GP), 2011) 23 <www.local2global.info/wp-content/uploads/SK_Nuba_L2GP_report_final.pdf>.

[22] Ibid., 23. [23] Gorur, Jok, and Ting Mayai, see n 2, 38. [24] Ibid., 37.

[25] Ibid., 33.

[26] As a Karen Buddhist migrant worker interviewed in Thailand said, 'Migrant workers here don't go to the refugee camps because we don't know people there—we don't have any connection . . . those who enter the refugee camps have money, or family in the camps'. Ashley South with Malin Perhult and Nils Carstensen, 'Conflict and Survival: Self-protection in South-east Burma' (London: Chatham House, 2010) 36 <www.local2global.info/area-studies/burmamyanmar-karen>. Similarly, a representative of the Karen Women Organization stated: 'Despite all the abuses that the women chiefs are

Zimbabwe,[27] Syria,[28] and Palestine[29] found that variables such as sex, age, ethnicity, religion, and location (rural/urban, government/opposition-held) were often a factor in very different perceptions of threats and resulting self-protection activities. For example, women in Sudan's South Kordofan and Burma's Karen State saw themselves as particularly vulnerable to certain threats but also as much stronger 'agents of protection' than male family members in other respects.[30] These findings imply that the realities of community-based protection may be complex, and a thorough understanding of protection threats needs to take into account the situation of a range of 'sub-communities'. External protection actors that bring a predefined focus on specific vulnerabilities based on institutional mandates or experiences may need to reconsider assumed categories in each context.[31]

III. Community Self-protection

Self-protection measures can be defined as 'any activities that conflict-affected communities undertake with the intention of countering, mitigating, deterring or avoiding a threat'.[32] Protection actors and researchers have also used other terms such as 'coping strategies' or 'survival mechanisms', sometimes interchangeably, to describe these activities. There is no clear and widely accepted definition of these alternative terms. Some terms, such as 'coping strategies', may be interpreted to include a wider range of responses to conflict that are undertaken to improve general wellbeing—for example, strategies to earn income to improve quality of life in the aftermath of conflict, or psychological responses to manage conflict-related trauma.[33] Terms such as 'coping strategies' or 'survival mechanisms' may also be

forced to endure, their testimonies are not merely those of passive victims. On the contrary, the women frequently display a remarkable degree of strength and determination to protect the rights of their communities, regardless of all the risks and personal sacrifices.' Ibid., 27.

27 An older woman in Zimbabwe stated: 'Women are most at threat, because the responsibility of feeding the family falls on them. In their pursuit of food, they end up facing different threats, such as rape or being asked for sexual favours in exchange for food, which leads to the further threat of disease. The same predicament applies to children, especially girls.' Richard Horsey, 'Local Protection in Zimbabwe' (Copenhagen: L2GP, 2011) 72; <www.local2global.info/wp-content/uploads/L2GP_Zimbabwe_study.pdf>. A retired Zimbabwean magistrate said: 'Boy children are also vulnerable to sexual abuse, but this is not recognized or understood by most communities, and is very hidden. There is little awareness of paedophilia, and most people are incredulous: "what would anyone want to do with a young boy?" they say.' Ibid., 35.

28 Data from ongoing research on self-protection in the Syria crisis by Kholoud Mansour, Line Urban, and Nils Carstensen for the L2GP initiative, on file with authors.

29 Rafael Eguiguren and Luna Saadeh, 'Protection in the Occupied Palestinian Territories' (Copenhagen: L2GP Initiative, 2014) 12–13, 91–4 <www.local2global.info/area-studies/palestine-opt>.

30 Corbett, see n 21, 19–21; South with Perhult and Carstensen, see n 26, 27.

31 Giffen, see n 2.

32 Gorur (2013), see n 2, 4.

33 See, for example, Gilles Carbonnier, 'Security Management and the Political Economy of War', *Humanitarian Exchange* (London, June 2010), which describes economic 'coping strategies' such as poppy cultivation or diamond prospecting in conflict environments; and Theresa Stichick and Claude Bruderlein, 'Children Facing Insecurity: New Strategies for Survival in a Global Era' (Cambridge, USA: Harvard Program on Humanitarian Policy and Conflict Research, 2001) <www.hpcrresearch.org/sites/default/files/publications/ChildrenFacingInsecurity.pdf>, which uses 'coping mechanisms' to

used to describe responses to non-conflict threats, such as natural disasters or domestic violence.

Self-protection measures exist on a spectrum from *positive* (having only a positive effect on the security of the community) to *negative* (having negative effects in the long term despite some short-term benefit, or exacerbating security problems for some within the community while improving security for others). Examples of the latter have included measures such as sending a son to fight with a particular armed group, giving in to demands for bribes and illegal 'taxation', employing armed self-defence as has occurred in Myanmar,[34] and resorting to child-marriage practices as has occurred in Syria.[35] However negative or unacceptable such measures may appear to outsiders, it should be kept in mind that they are often employed in environments characterized by a near total 'protection vacuum'. Often, these are situations where affected communities perceive themselves to be left with few other options, as national and international actors have failed to provide any meaningful degree of protection.

Self-protection measures also exist on a spectrum from individual to communal. At the individual level, for example, a person might comply with an illegal payment demanded at a checkpoint in order to avoid a violent response.[36] At the communal level, the whole community might meet to share information about security threats.[37] Often, self-protection measures will fall somewhere in between—for example, a family may form a plan to flee as a unit if there is an attack,[38] or individual members of the community may spontaneously form groups with people around them for safety in numbers while walking through a dangerous area.[39] Self-protection initiatives may be led by local civil society organizations or individuals that represent smaller or larger subsets of the community, such as religious organizations, trade associations, or women's and youth groups.[40] In some cases, self-protection measures may deliberately exclude a portion of the community (for example, community security meetings that exclude women).[41]

Over the past half-decade, recognition of the importance of understanding conflict-affected communities' self-protection mechanisms has grown. Reports and

describe a wide range of activities undertaken by children in conflict environments, including developing social networks to provide a sense of connection to others.

[34] South with Perhult and Carstensen, see n 26, 18, 23, 24, 26, and 38.

[35] United Nations Children's Fund (UNICEF), 'A Study on Early Marriage in Jordan' (Amman: UNICEF, 2014) 8–10, 22 <www.unicef.org/jordan/UNICEFJordan_EarlyMarriageStudy2014-E_COPY_.pdf>; see also Save the Children, 'Too Young to Wed—The Growing Problem of Child Marriage among Syrian Girls in Jordan' (London: Save the Children, 2014) 2–11 <www.savethechildren.de/fileadmin/Berichte_Reports/Too_Young_to_Wed.pdf>.

[36] Data from Stimson Center focus groups with conflict-affected communities in North Kivu, South Kivu and Orientale provinces, Democratic Republic of Congo, June 2012, on file with authors.

[37] Ibid. [38] Gorur, Jok, and Ting Mayai, see n 2, 27.

[39] Interviews by Aditi Gorur and Alison Giffen in Bentiu, South Sudan, June 2015, on file with authors.

[40] Data from Stimson Center focus groups with conflict-affected communities in North Kivu, South Kivu, and Orientale provinces, Democratic Republic of Congo, June 2012, on file with authors.

[41] Gorur (2013), see n 2, 9.

studies on self-protection include a 2009 Oxfam report on community-based protection in the DRC,[42] the Cuny Center's inventory of self-protection strategies,[43] and several documented cases in Colombia,[44] as well as the L2GP and Overseas Development Institute–Humanitarian Practice Network (ODI-HPN) studies of self-protection in seven major crises.[45] The past few years have also seen the development of more practice-oriented guidance for protection actors at international agencies[46] and in peacekeeping missions.[47] In its 2009 *Professional Standards for Protection Work*, and again in its revised 2013 edition, the ICRC encouraged protection actors to avoid undermining positive self-protection measures, to consider complementing them, and to be aware of the risks and limitations involved.[48]

Recognition of the importance of self-protection within the UN peacekeeping community has been more modest than in humanitarian fora. Until recently, the importance of self-protection measures was not acknowledged in any UN peacekeeping policy or guidance. In February 2015, the UN Departments of Peacekeeping Operations and Field Support produced guidelines on the protection of civilians for military components of UN peacekeeping missions, which acknowledged the value of 'the mechanisms locals have established to ensure their own protection'.[49] Shortly thereafter, in April 2015, the same UN departments produced a policy on the protection of civilians in UN peacekeeping, which recognized that 'civilians at risk are also protection actors: they organize themselves to support the most vulnerable and implement measures to enhance their physical security.'[50] Both the policy and the military guidelines on the protection of civilians encourage peacekeepers to complement existing self-protection measures when protecting communities, where possible.

[42] Katherine Haver, *Self-protection in Conflict: Community Strategies for Keeping Safe in the Democratic Republic of Congo* (Oxford: Oxfam, 2009) 1–36.

[43] Casey A Barrs, 'How Civilians Survive Violence' (Arlington, USA: Cuny Center, 2012) 1–25 <www.oxfam.org.au/wp-content/uploads/2011/08/casey-barrs-supporting-documentation-how-civilians-survive.pdf>.

[44] Gimena Sanchez, 'Against All Odds: Experiences of IDP Self- Protection Measures in Colombia' (presented at the Brookings Institution seminar 'Exploring Civilian Protection', 28 October 2010) 1–19 <www.brookings.edu/~/media/events/2010/10/28-civilian-protection-two/case-study-columbia-oct-2010-gimena-sanchez.pdf>.

[45] South, Harragin, Corbett, Horsey, Kempel, Fröjmark, and Carstensen, see n 1.

[46] See, for example, Kate Berry and Sherryl Reddy, 'Safety with Dignity: Integrating Community-based Protection into Humanitarian Programming' (London: Overseas Development Institute, 2010) 5; UN High Commissioner for Refugees (UNHCR), 'Protection Policy Paper: Understanding Community-Based Protection' (undated) 1–29 <www.refworld.org/pdfid/5209f0b64.pdf>; ICRC, *Professional Standards for Protection Work Carried out by Humanitarian and Human Rights Actors in Armed Conflict and Other Situations of Violence* (Geneva: ICRC, 2013); The Sphere Project, see n 12.

[47] Gorur (2013), see n 2; Oxfam, 'Engaging with Communities' (Oxford: Oxfam, 2010) 3–4 <www.oxfam.org/sites/www.oxfam.org/files/file_attachments/bp141-engaging-with-communities-221110-en_4.pdf>.

[48] ICRC, *Professional Standards for Protection Work* (Geneva: ICRC, 2009) 24; ICRC, *Professional Standards for Protection Work* (Geneva: ICRC, 2013) 28.

[49] UN DPKO and UN DFS, 'Protection of Civilians: Implementing Guidelines for Military Components of United Nations Peacekeeping Missions' (New York: United Nations, 2015) 3.

[50] UN DPKO and UN DFS Protection of Civilians Policy, see n 15, Annex A.

The following example of community self-protection in Syria highlights a range of measures that communities under threat have taken to protect themselves in an environment where external protection efforts are highly restricted. It demonstrates both the resilience and initiative that conflict-affected communities can demonstrate as well as the limitations and challenges they encounter.

A. Community self-protection in Syria

As the conflict and subsequent humanitarian crisis in Syria has spread and deepened, aid agencies have continued to struggle with access to many of those most in need, and '[t]he lack of physical presence of international aid agencies has shone a spotlight onto what is commonly called "the local response"'.[51] Ongoing interviews with individuals and communities inside Syria, and with families who have sought refuge in neighbouring countries, have revealed the employment of vast and diverse protection strategies.[52]

Community self-protection in Syria has proven effective in addressing a major obstacle to external humanitarian assistance: government consent. Despite the Security Council's authorization of cross-border assistance without the approval of the Syrian government, many areas remain inaccessible to international organizations. Yet inside Syria, community-led protection activities take place regularly in opposition-controlled as well as government-controlled areas. Networks of activists have repaired and tried to maintain life-saving water supply infrastructure. They also organized low-profile food and non-food distributions in war-affected communities across the country. Throughout the crisis, health professionals have continued to provide life-saving services under extremely dangerous and difficult circumstances, often at great risk to their own lives.

Some Syrian self-protection activities face the same potentially negative outcomes that communities face in conflicts elsewhere. Many refugee families consider it necessary to keep girls out of school in order to protect them from sexual abuse or exploitation.[53] Self-taught volunteers try to defuse, move, or otherwise neutralize unexploded cluster and barrel bombs in densely populated areas. Other volunteers undertake equally dangerous rescue work in the ruins of recently bombed buildings.[54] Activists engage in 'risk education messaging', spanning from graffiti warnings against sniper fire at dangerous street corners to using a wide range

[51] Eva Svoboda and Sara Pantuliano, 'International and Local/Diaspora Actors in the Syria Response' (London: Overseas Development Institute, 2015) iii <www.odi.org/sites/odi.org.uk/files/odi-assets/publications-opinion-files/9523.pdf>. On access challenges faced by humanitarian actors in Syria, see also Sara Pantuliano and Eva Svoboda, Chapter 17, in this volume.

[52] This section draws from ongoing research on self-protection in the Syria crisis by Kholoud Mansour, Line Urban, and Nils Carstensen for the L2GP initiative, on file with authors.

[53] A Syrian woman interviewed in Lebanon stated: 'I cannot send my daughter to school because of the harassment and insulting comments we often hear in the streets. Men would tell us: "What is your price?" or "Syrian women are for sale" and other humiliating comments. I do not send my daughter to school in order to protect her.' Ibid.

[54] See for instance the homepage of volunteer rescue workers in Syria, 'The White Helmets' <www.whitehelmets.org>.

of media to alert parents and children to the dangers of touching or just being close to unexploded bombs, grenades, and missiles.

The self-protection strategies of ordinary Syrians also highlight the limits of international legal protection, with some avoiding international protection efforts due to the risks they incur. Some Syrian families, having fled to Lebanon, seek shelter and assistance from extended family networks and exhaust their own resources rather than registering with and seeking assistance from established humanitarian actors.[55] In doing so, they try to avoid the dangers they associate with being registered as refugees, which many view as likely to hinder or complicate their possible future return to Syria.

IV. Supporting Self-protection

The previous section demonstrated that conflict-affected communities can play a critical role in their own protection. External protection actors may be able to augment communities' protection capacities and support self-protection measures, potentially producing more effective protection outcomes. This section examines the conceptual goals of supporting self-protection, identifies different approaches that external actors could take to support such initiatives, outlines some of the major challenges and offers two short case studies of ways in which external protection actors have tried to support self-protection in South Sudan and Sudan. These examples demonstrate both the potential benefits and the complicated challenges that supporting self-protection entails.

A. Goals

Given their different mandates and understandings of protection, various external protection actors may conceptualize their goals differently with regard to complementing self-protection measures. For humanitarian organizations, support for self-protection could be viewed simply as a form of immediate relief—a way of boosting the impact of organizational protection programming by combining international and community capacities and resources. They may proceed on the assumption that once the protection crisis ends, the self-protection mechanisms will no longer be needed. For peacekeeping missions, support for self-protection could be viewed as a way to bridge the gap between the second tier (provision of physical protection, i.e. direct physical intervention by peacekeepers) and the third tier (establishment of a protective environment, i.e. developing capacities that allow the state to fully implement its primary responsibility to protect). This view would take into account the reality that security sector reform is an idealistic and

[55] Data from ongoing research on self-protection in the Syria crisis by Kholoud Mansour, Line Urban, and Nils Carstensen for the L2GP initiative, on file with authors.

long-term goal, and that developing the community's own self-protection capacities may be a pragmatic way to offer improved protection in the interim.[56]

External protection actors may take on more or less modest goals with respect to self-protection, ranging from simply avoiding undermining existing self-protection mechanisms (e.g. ensuring that the organization's presence is managed carefully so as not to undermine agreements or settlements between neighbouring communities that have historically been in conflict), to providing resources and capacities that complement or boost the strength of existing mechanisms. Either goal requires external actors to engage with communities to understand their perceptions of security and protection and the strengths and weaknesses of their existing and potential self-protection measures.[57]

The emerging focus on self-protection should not obscure the fact that national governments are ultimately responsible for the protection of their population.[58] Community self-protection is never itself a satisfying solution to the wide-ranging and serious abuses suffered by people at risk. All the L2GP case studies demonstrate that while self-protection strategies may be necessary for survival, they do not in themselves provide the degree of safety, security, and dignity that people need and to which they are entitled; such protection comes only through an effective and accountable government. Thus, vital as it is, local agency must never be regarded as a substitute for the protection responsibilities of national authorities or, failing that, relevant international actors.

B. Approaches

External protection actors' approaches to supporting self-protection mechanisms can be conceptualized as falling into three categories. First, external actors may support truly community-led protection mechanisms, wherein members of the community define the priority threats and identify the appropriate protection strategies for the community to adopt with the support of the external actors. Second, external actors may help to set up new protection mechanisms in consultation with the community, and both parties may participate in their operation. Third, external actors may learn from communities about their existing self-protection mechanisms and find ways for their own actions to augment or complement those mechanisms such that they meet both the community's and the external actor's objectives and priorities.

All three approaches, to differing degrees, require external actors to cede control to the community under threat. Self-protection is fundamentally concerned with

[56] See further Fairlie Chappuis and Aditi Gorur, *Reconciling Security Sector Reform and the Protection of Civilians in Peacekeeping Contexts* (Stimson Center and Geneva Centre for the Democratic Control of Armed Forces, 2015) <www.stimson.org/images/uploads/research-pdfs/CIC-No3-web.pdf>.

[57] On ways to engage conflict-affected communities, see further Aditi Gorur and Alison Giffen, *Engaging Community Voices in Protection Strategies: Annexes on Lessons Learned* (Washington, DC: The Stimson Center, 2013).

[58] Responsibility to protect populations from genocide, war crimes, ethnic cleansing, and crimes against humanity. See UNGA Res 60/1 (2005) UN Doc A/RES/60/1, paras 138–40.

individuals and communities identifying their own protection threats and needs, and then acting on their own initiative, based on their own knowledge and priorities. From an external actor's perspective, supporting self-protection requires empowering communities, which implies surrendering a significant degree of control over activities and funds.

While many international protection actors ascribe significant importance to the role of affected communities in their policy documents and public statements, protection efforts that are truly locally led are rarely acknowledged or supported by outside agencies.[59] This reluctance was illustrated in a 2014 survey on community-based protection.[60] While the majority of respondents (staff with international agencies) understood community-based protection as activities 'originating from within and being led by communities to protect themselves', only a handful could identify to concrete cases that they knew of, or that their organization had supported. In contrast, the vast majority of respondents could offer examples of community-based protection that originated from an external agency but included engaging communities at different stages of the activities.

Transferring direct control over projects and funding to affected communities presents a particular challenge for many larger humanitarian agencies and other large institutional protection actors answerable to (and constrained by) the politics and policies of host governments, donors, inter-governmental bodies, and often very elaborate in-house procedures and manuals. Many such actors may be able to deepen and expand the manner in which they consult and include the perspectives of local communities, ultimately though, they may find it difficult to go much further. Smaller, more flexible national or international agencies with experience in genuinely nurturing and supporting local initiatives may be better positioned to empower and support local protection efforts on the community's own terms.

Where positive self-protection strategies exist, and fall within the mandates and objectives of external actors, the third approach, taking communities' existing self-protection mechanisms as a starting point for external actors' protection programming, may offer several benefits over the second approach, which involves setting up a new mechanism in consultation with the community. First, it may improve a given programme's chances of success, since working with existing mechanisms can mean that members of the community are more likely to identify culturally with or place trust in the programme. Second, it may help to ensure that the programme causes minimal disruptions or negative side effects for members of the community. Third, it may be an efficient entry-point to protection, since communities that have been dealing with a threat for a long time may have already tried several self-protection measures and identified the most effective one. Finally, it may help to ensure the sustainability of the protection programme after the external actor leaves.

[59] Ashley Jackson, 'Protecting Civilians: The Gap Between Norms and Practice' (London: Overseas Development Institute, 2014) 4.

[60] Joint UNHCR-NGO-Academia team, 'Community Based Protection, Survey Findings and Analysis' (prepared for UNHCR's 2014 Annual Consultation's session on Community Based Protection) 2–3 <www.unhcr.org/ngo-consultations/CBP-Survey-Findings-Final-June2014.pdf>.

One example of how an external actor might try to work with existing local protection mechanisms is through engagement with local laws, norms, and traditions. Customary law, as well as local values and traditions, often matter at least as much as formal rights in local conceptions of protection. The L2GP study of local protection in Jonglei, South Sudan, for instance, found that 'the Dinka concept of *cieng* is the rights framework within which local people operate, and family mediation and the court structure are the institutions that protect their rights if they have behaved "properly"'.[61] This study also found that 'family mediation plays the primary role in seeking a solution for the vulnerable. But for those without any kind of protective family structure, the courts, including those practising both customary and judiciary law, play a vital role in providing "protection" for local people.'[62]

External protection actors may see Dinka customary law as being different from, and in some cases incompatible with, their own approaches. Yet it may be important for external protection actors to acknowledge and accept customary law as a point of departure. It is one of the local protection mechanisms in place, one by which most local people live, and one that frequently offers positive as well as negative elements of protection. The South Sudan case study, below, demonstrates some of the challenges involved in engaging with traditional justice.

C. Challenges

A major challenge for external actors in supporting self-protection measures stems from the fact that local perceptions of protection are often quite broad. When asked to name what they see as the most pressing threats and useful protection strategies, local communities often raise issues related to livelihoods, strengthening social cohesion, local leadership, and psychosocial support. These concerns go well beyond what many external protection actors understand as their mandate, responsibility, or area of competence.

Other difficulties which external actors wishing to support self-protection might encounter include: exclusionary or unrepresentative protection initiatives; disproportionate participation or control by elites; protection measures that might be considered unethical or dangerous; protection measures that might be considered benign or positive but outside the mandate or aims of the external actor; and protection initiatives the benefit of which may be difficult to measure or explain to donors. Communities may also prefer protection measures that present challenges with respect to: monitoring and evaluation or accountability; keeping pace with changing conflict dynamics; and impartiality and/or neutrality, particularly in cases where the community is seeking protection from a government actor.

[61] Simon Haragin, 'South Sudan—Waiting for Peace to Come: Study from Bor, Twic East & Duk counties in Jonglei' (Copenhagen: L2GP Initiative, 2011) 8 <www.local2global.info/wp-content/uploads/L2GP_Jonglei_S_Sudan_TR_FINAL.pdf>.

[62] Ibid., 8.

D. Supporting community watch groups in South Sudan

The messy and complicated reality of external actors' support for community self-protection measures is demonstrated by the recent experience of the UN peacekeeping mission in South Sudan.[63] The mission, UNMISS, operates 'protection of civilians sites' (PoC sites) within several of its bases. These sites are IDP camps that formed after civilians fled to UN bases for protection from fighting, including deliberate violence against civilians, when civil war broke out in December 2013. At the time of writing, there were over 150,000 civilians living in PoC sites around the country.[64]

UN police are responsible for maintaining internal safety and security within the PoC sites, but their numbers are small in proportion to the total population living in the camps. Their capacity is also restricted by their mandate, which does not include most of the functions usually associated with law enforcement, such as the conduct of criminal investigations or arrests. As a result, they worked with communities to establish Community Watch Groups (CWGs). UNMISS' support to CWGs takes an external actor-led approach to supporting self-protection. CWG members are nominated by the community, but UNMISS retains the authority to remove members from the CWG if they violate certain standards. UNMISS helps to train and empower CWG members to intervene in low-level disputes, but CWG members are required to refer cases to UNMISS police if they rise to a level involving the use or threat of violence. The protection efforts of CWGs and UNMISS thus complement one another, with UNMISS establishing roles, responsibilities, standards, and guidelines to define their activities and relationship.

Community Watch Group members serve several protection functions: they patrol and keep watch for dangerous activity; receive complaints by community members of misbehaviour; informally investigate allegations in minor disputes; mediate disagreements between members of the community; and serve as a liaison with and reporting avenue to UNMISS police. To assist them with their activities, UNMISS offers CWG members training on a variety of subjects such as patrolling, child protection, gender-based violence, conflict avoidance and resolution techniques, and fire safety. Although CWGs are instructed not to intervene physically in violent situations or to deal directly with serious crimes, they play important protection roles in preventing situations from escalating to violence and ensuring that such incidents are reported to UNMISS.

Engagement with the CWGs offers UN police significant benefits including enhanced situational awareness and capacity within the PoC sites, cultural knowledge and linguistic skills that increase the ability of UNMISS police to maintain security, and improved legitimacy and trust through the interface with community

[63] The information in this example is drawn from interviews conducted in South Sudan (Juba and Bentiu) by Stimson Center staff in June 2015. The interviews were conducted with protection of civilians site residents and community watch group members, UN personnel including UN police, and others (such as humanitarian personnel working with protection of civilians site residents).

[64] UN Mission in South Sudan (UNMISS), 'UNMISS Protection of Civilians (POC) Site Update No. 81' (7 July 2015) <reliefweb.int/sites/reliefweb.int/files/resources/07-07-Update%2081%20%283%29.pdf>.

representatives. The CWGs provide valuable assistance to UNMISS in dealing with very serious internal safety and security issues, including crowd control, gang violence, weapons possession, and violent crimes.

Working with CWGs also presents UNMISS with complicated challenges. First, there are issues related to representation. Although UNMISS has made efforts to ensure that women participate in the CWGs, cultural barriers and expectations around gender roles have meant that women remain underrepresented. In the PoC site in the capital city, Juba, women are estimated to make up 15–20 per cent of CWG representatives, and in the largest PoC site, near the town of Bentiu, they are estimated to account for only 10–15 per cent. Moreover, as inter-county and intra-tribal tensions rise within the country more broadly, these tensions have been reflected within PoC sites and could complicate the mission's relationship with the CWGs. UNMISS police try to ensure regional diversity within CWGs by seeking representatives from different zones within the PoC sites, which often align with different regions and sub-tribes. However, this measure may not be sufficient if tensions continue to escalate. In the Bentiu PoC site, tensions between IDPs from Mayom County (who are perceived as pro-government) and the rest of the IDP community have grown to the point where the communities have decided to establish separate 'high committees' (community leadership structures) instead of one integrated high committee. Given how important it is to UNMISS to be perceived as impartial, this issue has the potential to present serious difficulties in working with CWGs.

Second, there are issues related to accountability and abuse of power. There have been several instances of CWG members acting beyond their authority, for example, detaining or imposing physical punishments on persons they deemed to have committed offences. There have also been unconfirmed reports that CWG representatives were charging community members for some services. There is no thorough way for UNMISS to vet the CWG representatives nominated by communities. Although UNMISS can and has removed members from CWGs for egregious abuses of power, this kind of accountability can prove difficult; members of the community are often very reluctant to identify specific CWG members who have abused their authority. Moreover, UNMISS police are put in a difficult position of deciding whether specific instances of abuse warrant removal from the CWG. If they were to remove members for even slight abuses of authority, the system might become unworkable altogether.

Third, there are also issues related to different understandings of threats and protection. Residents of the PoC sites in Bentiu[65] and Juba,[66] for example, have frequently expressed dissatisfaction with the fact that UNMISS refuses to punish behaviours that are considered serious infractions of traditional laws and cultural norms, such as adultery, or elopement without paying the bride's family a dowry in cattle. Cultural norms often dictate that this behaviour necessitates detention or physical punishment, and these responses may even be seen as a way of protecting

[65] Interviews conducted by Aditi Gorur and Alison Giffen in Bentiu, South Sudan, June 2015, on file with authors.

[66] Aditi Gorur (2014), see n 2, 13–14.

the perceived victims as well as the wider community by acting as a deterrent. However, the mission's policies and approaches to protection do not permit it to acknowledge these behaviours as threats or to detain or expel the perceived offenders.

The UNMISS's experience with CWGs demonstrates that supporting community self-protection measures is not necessarily a simple proposition for external protection actors, but it can nevertheless offer significant benefits for improved protection programming. Despite the flaws and challenges, the combined efforts of the UN police and the CWGs have likely played an important role in enhancing the capacity and perceived legitimacy of UN police in the PoC sites, and in doing so improved their protection effectivensess.

E. Supporting self-protection in South Kordofan

In contrast to the UNMISS case study, L2GP has worked with a more community-led approach to self-protection in opposition-controlled parts of South Kordofan in Sudan. An estimated one million people remain in the area, trying to survive a civil war that broke out in 2011.[67] The civilian population continues to be targeted by aerial bombardment and ground attacks. At the same time, they are denied any formal humanitarian assistance or public services, despite a severe food crisis, massive displacement, and increased mortality from disease. The Sudanese government was perceived by those interviewed as being the main source of threat, while international actors—be they political or humanitarian—were seen to be paralyzed by the government's continued obstruction of access.[68]

L2GP researchers working with local NGOs and volunteers established and funded a programme to strengthen local communities' self-protection capacities, drawing on earlier research into self-protection responses in the area.[69] With this support, local civil society actors, increasingly led by a local women's association, developed a project that reached several hundred thousand individuals. Volunteers moved between villages offering training and advice on practical individual self-protection skills, including: (a) avoiding injury or death from armed conflict, by hiding from aerial bombings and providing first aid; (b) avoiding life-threatening risks from lack of food, income, basic services, and shelter, including through pre-positioning food and property in safe places; and (c) dealing with fear, a sense of isolation, despair, unhappiness, and the erosion of dignity and core values,

[67] Because of access restrictions related to the conflict, exact figures on the size of the population residing in South Kordofan remain elusive. The opposition's 'Sudan Relief and Rehabilitation Association' in its January–June 2015 report (on file with researchers) lists the total population in conflict areas of South Kordofan as 1.3 million, with some 466,630 displaced by conflict. Based on secondary sources, the June 2015 Humanitarian Snapshot by the UN Office for the Coordination of Humanitarian Affairs (UN OCHA) in Sudan suggests that up to 538,000 people may be displaced in South and West Kordofan and Blue Nile State combined. UN OCHA, 'Humanitarian Snapshot: Sudan, June 2015' (June 2015) <reliefweb.int/sites/reliefweb.int/files/resources/Sudan_Humanitarian_Snapshot_30_Jun_2015_A4.pdf>.

[68] Corbett, see n 21, 1–77.

[69] Justin Corbett, *Protection in Sudan's Nuba Mountains: Local achievements, International Failures* (Copenhagen: L2GP Initiative, 2012) 1–77.

including through building and maintaining psychosocial support within family structures.

Building on existing networks, local civil society actors set up a system of 'training-of-trainers', which gradually expanded to larger areas in South Kordofan. Self-protection messages quickly spread to schools, mosques, and churches. An evaluation of the project based on household interviews demonstrated that the information provided that was perceived to be most helpful was advice on staying safe during aerial bombardment, followed in descending order by information on: health and sanitation; family budgeting and food storage; women's rights and violence against women; traditional medicine and first aid; and finally, dealing with mental trauma and psychosocial issues.[70]

The minimal involvement of external actors demonstrated how much the community was able to accomplish on its own, but also brought some challenges. The difficulties associated with international protection actors not having a local presence limited the ability for external monitoring and evaluation.[71] Access limitations made it difficult to ensure reliable and regular monthly payments to cover programme costs.[72] The limited oversight meant that it was difficult to identify volunteers who needed additional training or who were not a good fit for the programme.[73] Local actors were able to overcome most challenges and the programme continued to develop and considerably expand its reach. However, the limited support from external humanitarian actors did mean that the local volunteers could not adequately address many critical protection concerns, such as severe and prolonged food insecurity.[74]

Despite these challenges, the programme is believed to have reduced casualties from aerial bombardments in the area.[75] The initiative proved to be sustainable over four years of intense war in an area with no international access. Unlike most traditional rights-based, internationally led protection responses, it reflected a holistic understanding of threats and incorporated a wide range of issues, treating them as deeply interconnected.[76] Further, the communities' and local leaders' appreciation of these activities gave the women's association the influence and momentum to go on to address issues such as women's rights and violence against women, with both civil and military leaders.

V. Conclusion

While many external protection actors now recognize that communities affected by conflict often take measures to keep themselves safe, there is still considerable confusion about how they might be able to support community self-protection measures. Some external actors may be able to adopt a truly community-led approach

[70] Justin Corbett, 'Experiences with Local and Global Responses to the Protection Crises—South Kordofan and Blue Nile, Sudan 2010–2015' (Copenhagen: L2GP Initiative, October 2015) 9–10 <http://www.local2global.info/wp-content/uploads/L2GP_SK_BN_2015_final.pdf>.

[71] Ibid., and Corbett, see n 69, 5–6.

[72] Corbett, see n 69, 3, and Corbett, see n 70, 5–6.

[73] Corbett, see n 69, 6.

[74] Ibid.

[75] Ibid.

[76] Ibid., 3–4.

to supporting self-protection, while others may be constrained from doing so by their existing mandates, policies, and practices. However, there are other ways that external actors can engage positively with community self-protection: by incorporating local communities' understandings of protection into their own protection activities; by ensuring that they have a nuanced understanding of local self-protection mechanisms to avoid inadvertently undermining them; by working with communities to design protection programmes that leverage both the external actor's and the community's strengths; and by identifying ways to complement or strengthen any positive self-protection mechanisms that are already in place.

For external actors, working to empower communities to protect themselves can present diverse and serious challenges. External actors and local communities may perceive protection differently, and may not share the same assessment of the most appropriate self-protection measures to employ. These challenges echo the complexities, constraints, and roadblocks that protection actors encounter in their work more broadly. Any effort to protect civilians from conflict will necessarily be complicated by varying expectations of how host state governments, parties to the conflict, external protection actors, and civilians should behave; which threats should be prioritized; and how limited resources should be allocated. Decisions about who to protect and how always involve trade-offs, and as a result, full or even adequate protection is rarely accomplished.

Yet the pursuit of protection is still of fundamental importance, given the impact it can have for people whose lives are devastated by conflict. Support to community self-protection is riddled with challenges, but as recognition of the importance of self-protection grows, and as external actors make more attempts to engage with and support self-protection, organizations may be able to learn from each other's experiences. Over time, the protection field can draw lessons from its successes and failures and reshape its approach to strive for a less imperfect response to civilians under threat.

Conclusion

Haidi Willmot, Ralph Mamiya, Scott Sheeran, and Marc Weller

While the protection of civilians holds a place of centrality in international relations, it remains a somewhat unclear concept. Significant confusion persists between the Responsibility to Protect doctrine, the protection of civilians peacekeeping mandate, humanitarian protection activities, and the protection and promotion of human rights. There is no common understanding of the concept, even within the UN, and the absence of a unified legal framework results in a complicated patchwork of normative overlaps and lacunae. This matters because it undermines political consensus at the strategic level and co-operation and implementation of practical activities in the field.

Over the past sixty years, the protection of civilians has proven a dynamic concept, taking on a range of meanings and encompassing a spectrum of activities as it has been adopted and adapted by various elements of the international community. From moral and ethical prescriptions of just war, through to the formal establishment of a body of international humanitarian law (IHL), the idea that civilians—persons distinguished from combatants—should not be unduly affected by hostilities has a long history. The protection idea was powerfully advanced and reinforced by developments in international human rights law (IHRL) and the range of special legal regimes dealing with the treatment of individuals and groups, although much of this normative development failed to grapple with conflict situations. Following the tragedies in Rwanda and the former Yugoslavia during the 1990s, there was a drive within elements of the international community to strengthen and develop a more active concept of protection. This led to the mandating of the use of force to protect civilians in UN peacekeeping missions and the development of the humanitarian intervention and responsibility to protect doctrines. Alongside these political and security developments, humanitarian relief activity came to be framed in a protection paradigm.

This wide range of activities led to a splintered evolution of the protection-of-civilians concept, with many strands developing independently despite a common foundation. In order to effectively protect civilians, efforts need to be made to holistically conceive the concept, clarify the legal framework, and bring coherence to the disparate streams of effort it comprises. The succeeding sections seek to do so.

I. Protection of Civilians Concept and Definition

In the armed conflict context, the concept of protection derives from the humanitarian tradition, which seeks to preserve the most fundamental aspects of human life and dignity including in times of chaos and existential threat. The compassionate view of war, centring on the distinction between civilians and combatants, has a long history based in ethics codes across cultures. Many people in a conflict situation are implicated in hostilities at some level and in some way, at times making the distinction between civilians and combatants somewhat complex and artificial. Nevertheless, the distinction remains important and widely accepted, and forms a core tenet of IHL.

In the human rights context, the responsibility for protecting civilians, whether borne by a State or the international community, derives from the social compact underlying the forming of a polity, and the relation of authorities to the people. Social compact theory was part of ancient Greek and Stoic philosophy and later folded into concepts in major religions, including the covenants of Judaism and Christianity and the concept of bay'ah in Islam. Enlightenment thinkers drew upon these ancient and religious ideas when considering the legitimacy of the State and the relationship between natural and legal rights. This, in turn, formed a key foundation of modern human rights law concepts.

The protection of civilians concept bridges these traditions, and draws the two ideas together with the rights and responsibilities to use force to protect civilians, which have evolved through the development of the *jus ad bellum* and the UN Charter. It attempts to create a coherent approach to rights and responsibilities of sovereigns to protect people within their territorial jurisdiction, responsibilities of belligerents to refrain from targeting civilians and minimise civilian casualties in conflicts, and the broader responsibility of the international community to protect civilians from the most serious crimes. In doing so, it attempts to overcome issues associated with the application of different bodies of law in times of war and peace, requirements to meet legal thresholds of 'non-combatant' and 'armed conflict', and barriers to intervention on the basis of human rights and humanitarian concerns.

While the various traditions and bodies of law maintain their own concepts of protection, a holistic understanding asserts that in times of conflict, harm to civilians should be minimised and humanitarians have the right to provide relief, but when the life or physical integrity of civilians is being threatened, States and the international community have rights and responsibilities to actively and forcefully protect civilians. In this way, the protection of civilians concept resides at the nexus of human rights, *jus ad bellum* and *jus in bello*, drawing from each of the traditions and bodies of law. While disagreements between military, humanitarian, and human rights actors remain, at the end of the day the Responsibility to Protect doctrine, the humanitarian intervention idea, the UN peacekeeping civilian protection mandate, the non-derogable human rights, the principle of *non-refoulement*, the prohibition against targeting civilians, the provision of humanitarian relief, and certain development activities all derive from the same fundamental idea—the recognition that in times of conflict the life and dignity of civilians should be preserved. While they may go about it in different ways, protection actors all strive to achieve that same fundamental objective.

The protection of civilians concept focuses on the fundamental dimensions of life and physical integrity, and does not seek to defend the panoply of human rights.

It is intimately tied to action, which may be undertaken by a range of actors, including local, national, and international, in the military, humanitarian, human rights, and development spheres. Protection activity is often limited by political constraints and may carry with it costs to protectors and risks to civilians. These need to be well understood and carefully managed, guided by the imperative of not causing greater harm. While many actors undertake activities that ultimately contribute to civilians being protected, some actions will more directly result in that outcome than others. For example: the threat or use of military force to halt or prevent violence and rape; the provision of food, shelter, and medical assistance; the extraction of human rights and humanitarian actors who are being threatened; and, the non-return of people to countries in which they will be tortured, all act to directly preserve civilian life and physical integrity. Indirect protection activities require intervening steps between the action and civilians being protected. For example: ongoing political engagement with local authorities; raising awareness of IHL; building the capacity of national governance institutions; and, monitoring and reporting on human rights abuses all act to indirectly preserve civilian life and dignity.

In an effort to give real meaning to the protection of civilians terminology, it is important that it is not used as a catch-all phrase for the plethora of activities undertaken in conflict situations that might ultimately contribute to a broad concept of protection. Both direct and indirect protection activities are of immense value, both require a proximate causal nexus, but the qualitative difference between the two should be acknowledged.

Many of the chapters in this volume identified that the definitions of 'protection of civilians' variously employed by peacekeeping,[1] humanitarian, and human rights communities[2] have complicated the discourse and manipulated the concept well beyond its natural meaning. The peacekeeping definition has been criticized for failing to provide sufficiently detailed guidance, and the humanitarian/human rights definition has been condemned for being too broad and theoretical. Definitions are important. A recent report on humanitarian protection noted: 'The diverse interpretations of what protection means, coupled with varied uses of this terminology by relief workers has detrimental consequences for affected

[1] The protection-of-civilians mandate for civilian, military, and police components in UN peacekeeping is defined as follows: 'all necessary means, up to and including the use of deadly force, aimed at preventing or responding to threats of physical violence against civilians, within capabilities and areas of operations, and without prejudice to the responsibility of the host government.' UN DPKO and UN Department of Field Support (DFS), *Policy, The Protection of Civilians in United Nations Peacekeeping* (New York: United Nations, 1 June 2017) <http://www.ccopab.eb.mil.br/biblioteca/documentos/150323%20POC%20policy%20final.pdf>.

[2] The Inter-Agency Standing Committee (IASC), established by the UN General Assembly to strengthen the co-ordination of its humanitarian emergency assistance, adopted the definition of 'protection' as 'all efforts aimed at obtaining full respect for the rights of the individual and of the obligations of the authorities/arms bearers in accordance with the letter and the spirit of the relevant bodies of law'. The definition was originally adopted by a 1999 Workshop of the International Committee of the Red Cross (ICRC) on Protection.

populations and the delivery of an effective response at the system level. In other words, it is not a question of semantics.'[3]

A shared understanding of the term would facilitate the spectrum of protection actors working together to achieve complementary objectives. In order to overcome the challenges and shortfalls of existing definitions, the development of a common definition should aim to address the following:

- Reconcile the various concepts of protection into a single coherent definition.
- Apply with equal relevance to military, humanitarian, human rights, development, and local actors.
- Use plain English, not technical terms of art.
- Give real meaning to the term, by avoiding an overly broad, vague, or catch-all concept.
- Be clear about whether the noun 'protection' is being used as 'an act of protecting' (activities) or 'state of being protected' (objective).
- Clarify elements of the legal regimes from which the concept derives, including key issues such as: delinking the term 'civilian' from the ascribed meaning under IHL so as not to be tied to the threshold of 'armed conflict'; identifying relevant human rights, to avoid the unmanageable assumption that protection requires the fulfilment of all human rights; and clarifying whether there is a need for host-state consent, to ensure that the definition is not assumed to be based on the 'principles' of peacekeeping or the aspirations of the responsibility to protect.

The international community would be well served by adopting a common definition of the protection of civilians along the lines of the following:

> 'Protection of civilians' is the act of protecting from violence and minimizing harm toward those not directly participating in hostilities, in conflict situations. Such acts are undertaken pursuant to the rights and responsibilities of national authorities, belligerents, and the international community, and are governed by a legal framework of positive and negative obligations based on the UN Charter, IHL, IHRL, and refugee law. In this context, the state of being protected manifests primarily as fulfilment of the rights to life and physical integrity, whether citizen or alien. Direct protection activities are those that have a proximate casual connection resulting in the immediate and direct physical protection of civilians. Indirect protection activities are those that have a less proximate casual connection vicariously resulting in the protection of civilians.

[3] Norwegian Refugee Council, *Independent Whole of System Review of Protection in the Context of Humanitarian Action*, May 2015, https://interagencystandingcommittee.org/system/files/final_whole_of_system_protection_review_report_corrected_v2.pdf

II. Protection of Civilians Legal Framework

Various bodies of law use the term 'protection' in different manners and seek to achieve different types of protection in different ways. However, the protection of civilians, as holistically conceived above, lies at the intersection of these bodies of law, the interaction of which provides a framework of positive and negative obligations. See diagram below:

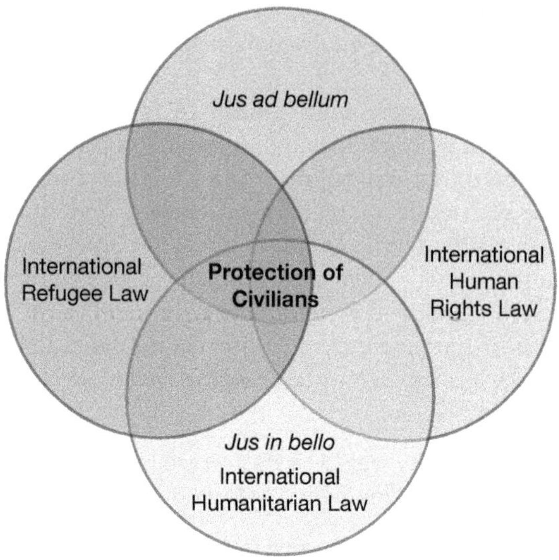

Protection of Civilians under international law

A. Positive obligations

Through requiring States to respect and ensure respect for the spectrum of human rights, IHRL provides a positive obligation upon States to protect their people from violence, in accordance with the rights to life and physical integrity (e.g. freedom from torture and slavery), which are non-derogable, including in times of conflict. This includes people who are internally displaced and those from another country who have sought refuge. The UN Security Council has built up a general right to intervene in internal conflicts, either with the consent of the host State (UN peacekeeping) or without it (peace enforcement), where there are gross violations of international human rights or humanitarian law. This represents an evolution of the collective security agreement, which has manifested through progressive interpretations of the UN Charter. The Security Council, arguably, also has an obligation or duty to intervene in specific circumstances, namely serious breaches of peremptory norms of international law, according to both customary international law and the International Law Commission's Draft Articles on the Responsibility of States for

Internationally Wrongful Acts. The Council, however, has not yet assumed or accepted a general obligation upon the UN to intervene, which inter alia would require the Responsibility to Protect doctrine to both crystallize into a binding norm and also override the Permanent Members' veto.

IHL provides the distinction between civilians and combatants, prohibiting attacks against civilians in armed conflict. To the extent that Article 1 of the Geneva Conventions obliges States to 'ensure respect for' the provisions of the conventions, this can be understood as contributing to the legal authority for the UN or States to intervene in other States where serious or systematic IHL violations are occurring, but is not generally interpreted in that way—although, once deployed, States with troops in theatre have a greater expectation to ensure respect for IHL. IHL also provides some modest positive obligations in respect of allowing humanitarian access and delivery of humanitarian relief.

At the operational level, the protection of civilians mandate provided by the UN Security Council to UN peacekeeping operations, regional organizations, and coalitions of, or individual Member States, creates a strong requirement to protect civilians against violence perpetrated by all parties, including the host government, through all necessary means, including the use of force. However, this obligation is circumscribed—missions are only required to protect civilians when they know, or should know, that they would be subject to violence, and have the means to carry out protection activity. Even in the absence of a specific protection of civilians mandate, UN peacekeeping operations have the right and possibly even duty to use force to protect civilians from violence.

In UN-authorized peacekeeping operations, the use of force to protect civilians is governed by the Security Council mandate, the mission's Rules of Engagement, the SOFA/SOMA, and customary international law, including relevant aspects of IHL and IHRL. Force Commanders have significant legal scope to use force, including pre-emptively. They may use force against an individual or group if they commit or threaten to commit physical violence against civilians, or if the Force Commander has reasonable belief that a potential aggressor has the intent and capacity to inflict physical violence.

B. Negative obligations

IHL provides the primary obligations, which may be understood as negative obligations, in the context of the protection of civilians. Its rules apply in both inter-State and intra-State armed conflicts, to all States and the UN by virtue of the Geneva Conventions, customary international law, and, in the case of the UN, the Secretary-General's Bulletin on the observance of IHL. IHL distinguishes between civilians and combatants and obliges parties (and the UN) to conduct their activities in a manner that minimizes harm to civilians by limiting the means and methods of warfare and respecting the principle of distinction. However, in this context, a certain level of harm to civilians (collateral damage) can be deemed acceptable. The Geneva Conventions prohibit arbitrary displacement of civilians, except where the security of the civilians involved or military imperatives require it.

While personnel of UN-authorized missions generally enjoy the status of non-combatants under IHL, the use of force (including in targeted offensive operations or even for self-defence) may result in UN military personnel losing the protection of IHL, becoming party to the conflict and therefore a legitimate target. While this is not the case with protection of civilians mandates generally, the ongoing protection of IHL will depend on the intensity and duration of the activity and the likelihood and justification of losing such protection may be increased by a UN force supporting a host government who is a party to the conflict. A foundation stone of IHL is reciprocity and non-differentiation amongst those fighting in armed conflict. The direct application to UN peacekeepers arguably misconceives the status of UN troops implementing Security Council resolutions (more akin to world policing than impartiality among belligerents); however, it is the current state of the law.

When a situation cannot be considered an armed conflict, and also in particular circumstances when IHL applies, the activities of combatants and UN troops are constrained by IHRL. While IHRL provides the basis for obligations and rights that protect civilians, it must also be observed by those acting to protect civilians, and in this way provides both negative and potentially positive obligations regarding the conduct of protection activities. Both the UN Organization and internationally deployed troops are obliged to observe core international human rights norms, including those relevant to the protection of civilians. Armed non-State actors must also observe human rights norms. In this context, the UN has a negative obligation to refrain from supporting host-nation security services that commit human rights abuses, pursuant to the Draft Articles on the Responsibilities of International Organizations, customary international law, and Charter obligations, as manifest in the UN Human Rights Due Diligence Policy.

Also of relevance to the protection of civilians is the principle of *non-refoulement* enshrined in international refugee law and read into IHRL, along with related customary international law. It prohibits the expulsion or return of a refugee to States or territories where his/her life or freedom would be threatened on account of his/her race, nationality, membership of a particular social group, or political opinion. The principal requires refraining both from returning a refugee to a country where his/her life or safety would be at risk and from rejecting and turning away an asylum-seeker at the border.

C. Accountability

Individuals, States, and international and regional organizations can all be held accountable for breaches of both positive and negative international obligations relating to the protection of civilians. This is as a matter of State or international organization responsibility or international criminal responsibility, as well as national legal and UN administrative responses. However, it has proven very challenging to consistently hold the UN and its personnel to account because of its immunities, which commonly act as a shield to legal proceedings.

In addition to the regime of war crimes in IHL and as reflected in the International Criminal Court, there are circumstances in which Force Commanders (and possibly Heads of Mission) can be held responsible for failing to use force to protect civilians, and contingents for not following orders to use force; although, as members of national contingents, they remain under the exclusive jurisdiction of their national criminal legal system. Responsibility of troop-contributing States and/or the UN will depend, to some extent, on the level of control exercised over an operation.

D. Further work

There remain a number of lacunae in the legal framework for the protection of civilians. The instances in which the international community is obliged to intervene remain unclear. If and where the residual responsibility to act resides following the casting of a veto in the Security Council is unsettled and challenging. While the UN Security Council has assumed a right to intervene to protect civilians under the UN Charter, the requirements for assessing people as 'civilians' and situations as 'armed conflict' remain unaddressed.

The body of IHL was developed prior to the advent of UN peacekeeping, resulting in fraught application to contemporary UN missions. The application of IHL fails to fully account for the unique role of UN peacekeepers executing the collective security agreement, and the relationship between IHL and the UN Charter. While peacekeepers should not act with impunity and must adhere to IHL in their conduct, treating them in an equivalent manner to any other armed group fails to recognize the legitimacy of their actions carried out in pursuit of the implementation of Security Council mandates. Allowing that UN peacekeepers are a legitimate target also raises legal inconsistencies with the Convention on the Safety of UN and Associated Personnel and Security Council sanctions regimes. The awkward and somewhat unpredictable application of IHL to UN peacekeepers leads to problems in decision-making on the use of force by UN peacekeepers and undermines its effective employment for civilian protection.

Perhaps of most concern is the lack of concrete avenues for ensuring accountability, and the unwillingness, at times, of the UN to waive its immunity in instances where the substance of the claim goes beyond the foundations for the existence of such legal privilege.

Given the importance of the protection of civilians in the maintenance of international peace and security today, the international community would benefit from clarification of the legal framework through the development and conclusion of a clear unified statement of the normative framework, perhaps something akin to the Guiding Principles on Internal Displacement. Such should address the following:

- Obligations of national authorities for the protection of non-combatants in conflict situations.
- Rights and obligations of the UN, and other international actors, to intervene to protect non-combatants in conflict situations.

— The substance of the rights and obligations attaching to the protection of civilians mandate, including the proactive use of force against all belligerents, including host State authorities.
— The rights and obligations of UN peacekeepers to protect civilians in the absence of a specific mandate to do so.
— The substance of the requirements of UN and non-UN missions to observe IHRL.
— The substance of the requirements of UN and non-UN missions to observe IHL.
— The substance of the protection of UN missions, premises, and personnel under IHL.
— Accountability mechanisms and avenues for claims and redress of the above.

III. Protection of Civilians Activities

Achieving conceptual and legal coherence has inherent value. However, its greatest importance is the cascade effect in supporting the practice of protecting civilians in the field. The survey of practice in this volume reveals a number of key issues being raised time and again. The most pervasive is the need for greater political will and accountability for lack of action. Without these two things, the statements of the Security Council are empty, the resources are not forthcoming, the use of force is half-hearted and transitory, and the work of humanitarians is impeded.

Another issue that is raised on more than one occasion is the need for co-ordination among protection actors to ensure that their activities are complementary and do not undermine one another. A further issue is the need to consult local communities when developing protection strategies, as they are best placed to understand the conflict dynamics, their own protection needs, and the activities likely to achieve the protection objective.

The combined analysis in this volume suggests that protection practice would benefit from being guided by the following general principles, which are drawn from the challenges and solutions that the various authors have identified.

Principle 1. ***The Security Council must avoid selectivity in addressing the protection of civilians in conflict situations.*** All of the Council's members, permanent and elected, play an important role introducing and dealing with issues on the Council's agenda. When the Council is unable or unwilling to address a situation, including through the casting of the veto, the General Assembly must take up its residual responsibility for the maintenance of international peace and security. The Council should utilize all tools at its disposal (coercive and non-coercive) and be clear about its intent regarding the protection of civilians. When mandating protection activities, the Council should be cognisant of the need for rebuilding after intervention and the reputational risks for the Organization, and should acknowledge the risks to the safety of peacekeepers.

Principle 2. ***States must demonstrate political support for the protection of civilians in conflict situations.*** Security Council members should contribute finance, equipment, and personnel, commensurate with their ability and responsibility, to implement the protection of civilians mandates that they provide. Member States of the UN should provide sufficient resources to carry out direct protection activities, including financing sufficient troop levels and enabling equipment in UN peacekeeping missions. Troop and police-contributing governments should acknowledge that their contingents will be required to use force and operate in high threat environments to protect civilians, and ensure that they have the technical capacity and political support to do so. Pressure must be brought to bear on host States to ensure that they support and not obstruct UN efforts to protect civilians.

Principle 3. ***Protection of civilians activities must be accompanied by a political process.*** The mandate to use force to protect civilians, common to most UN peacekeeping operations, does not of itself constitute a political strategy. The impact of military and humanitarian protection activities will be transitory if they do not take place within the context of a political process seeking a longer-term solution to underlying conflict issues.

Principle 4. ***Protection actors must co-ordinate to develop a unified protection strategy for each country/conflict area.*** In order to ensure that protection actors share the same ultimate objectives, and that their activities are complementary and do not undermine one another, they should co-ordinate to develop a unified and cohesive protection strategy for a conflict area. This should include political, humanitarian, military, human rights, and development aspects. Civilians themselves often play an important part in ensuring their own safety and the safety of their families and communities. It is critical that protection strategies incorporate the knowledge and activities of the local population and local actors.

Principle 5. ***Protection strategies must be based on a collective analysis of the threat environment and protection needs.*** Too often protection strategies are based on limited or imperfect information and analysis. A collective analysis of the threat environment and protection needs should be undertaken and include input from political, humanitarian, military, human rights, and development actors. Civilians themselves often have a detailed and sophisticated understanding of the threats they face and their own protection needs; it is critical that the collective analysis includes the knowledge of the local population and local protection actors.

Principle 6. ***The use of force employed to protect civilians must be calibrated to the type of violence exerted by the perpetrators.*** The effectiveness of the use of force to protect civilians will be improved by UN forces better understanding the intent, capabilities, and *modus operandi* of potential perpetrators, and tailoring their military response to meet that.

Principle 7. ***For force to be effectively employed, troops must be well trained and equipped, supported by adequate capabilities, and led by proactive commanders at all levels.*** Troop and police-contributing countries should also refrain from including operational caveats on their deployments and intervening in UN command decisions. Troops and police need to be assured that they have the political support of their government to use force to protect civilians as necessary.

Principle 8. ***The legal parameters and practical expectations for the use of force must be clear.*** The use of force to protect civilians can be inhibited by concerns or confusion regarding the legal parameters of using force. Military leaders and commanders need to be made aware of the legal framework for the use of force to protect civilians, including the potential accountability for failing to use force.

Principle 9. ***Capacity-building activities by development actors should employ a 'security first' approach.*** Recognizing the importance of fulfilling the whole protection chain, where necessary, state-building should prioritize rapidly and rigorously pursuing the security and safety of civilians over working to establish institutions of governance and justice.

Principle 10. ***International and regional organizations, States, and individuals must be held accountable for failing to protect civilians.*** The responsibilities of senior leaders in UN missions must be clarified, including for the use and non-use of force. UN missions should assess the probability, seriousness, and location of likely attacks against civilians; prepare plans to counter the assessed risks to civilians; document those plans; and pass the intelligence and planning information up the chain of command. This will facilitate accountability of senior leaders.

IV. Final Remarks

The protection of civilians lies at the heart of global peace and security, which is no longer a concept limited to conflict among nations, but extends to the well-being of populations. There has been a growing acceptance that the international community holds an interest in, and responsibility for, the safety of civilians in conflict situations, irrespective of their polity. Civilians have become recognized as legitimate actors of the UN collective security system.

While the international community's engagement on the protection of civilians has inched toward this cosmopolitan concept, often the action has fallen well short of the rhetoric. Showcasing the best and worst of international relations, self-serving, disingenuous actions have sat side by side with progressive, humane efforts. Yet there has been significant progress, and now is the time for the international community to take advantage of this positive trajectory. Civilian protection efforts would be well served by a clear and common understanding of the protection of civilians concept, a comprehensive and cohesive normative framework, and a co-ordinated and complementary implementation approach. Yet above all, what is required is real political commitment underwritten by a willingness to act, ensuring that those in power are held accountable for matching the action to the rhetoric, and that civilians are protected without prejudice to their nationality.

History will judge the UN, and the international community more broadly, on our ability to 'save succeeding generations from the scourge of war', as promised in the UN Charter. We have myriad tools at our disposal to do so—political, diplomatic, military, humanitarian, human rights, and development. Aside from preventing conflict, actively protecting civilians is the most powerful way of delivering on that promise.

Index

abduction 151, 230n, 342, 345
Abyei
communal conflict 342n, 345–7
displaced persons 184n
Human Rights Watch 131n
Misseriya 343, 346–7
Ngok Dinka 336, 343, 346–7
physical violence 103
predatory violence 342n
seasonal migrants 184n
UN operations 88, 103
UN resolutions 124n, 129n, 184n, 299n, 373n *see also* UN Interim Security Force for Abyei (UNISFA)
Active Learning Network for Accountability and Performance in Humanitarian Action (ALNAP)
Guide to Protection 411
acts of aggression 117, 120, 122, 125–7
accountability
abuse of power 424
Afghanistan 359
community self-protection 422
criminal 4, 149–50, 170, 206, 214–18, 222, 257
deficits in 371
deterrence 363
financial 390
government security forces 363
human rights advocacy 350
human rights norms 148n
human rights violations 3, 142, 145–6, 170n, 204, 280–1, 354, 358
ICTR 297
impartiality 231
individual 270
international responsibility 4, 149–50, 170n, 247–51, 434–5, 438
lack of action 436
legal mechanisms for 152, 259, 435–6
'naming and shaming' 369
OECD–DAC 403
Pan-African Parliament 282
security-first approaches 406–7
South Sudan 363
Sri Lanka 355–6
transparency 403
troop-contributing countries 322
UN peacekeepers 152–3, 232n, 435
use of force 47, 438 *see also* Human Rights Up Front initiative
advocacy
campaigns 284
High Commissioner for Human Rights 351, 352, 356
human rights 20, 74, 79, 286, 350, 354, 357, 360–9
NGOs 378, 381
RtoP 40, 128
aerial bombardment 15, 16, 18, 161, 191, 425–6
Afghanistan
airstrikes 172n
civilian casualties 361–2
civilians at risk (1980s) 306
Constitution 359–60
counterinsurgency operations 93–4
human rights investigations 100
human rights protection 6, 358–62
insurgency 343–4
invasion (2001), justifications for 84n, 118n
ISAF 125n, 261, 358–62
National Security Forces 397
NATO operations 88, 100, 104, 106, 267n, 327
non-military special political missions 269
reconstruction and development 397
Taliban 260, 383–4
terrorism as threat to the peace 124
UN Crisis Operations Group 368
US soldiers and resources 319
war, British involvement in 22 *see also* UN Assistance Mission in Afghanistan; UN Mission in Afghanistan(UNAMA)
African Commission on Human and Peoples' Rights 280n, 284–5, 287
African Committee of Experts on the Rights and Welfare of the Child 285–6
African Court on Human and Peoples' Rights 5, 282–7
African-led International Support Mission to Mali (AFISMA) 96, 104–5, 127n, 300, 317, 327n
African-led Support Mission to the Central African Republic (MISCA) 96, 104–5, 153, 300, 327n
African Union (AU) 101
African-led International Support Mission to Mali (AFISMA) 96, 104–5, 127n, 300, 317, 327n
African-led Support Mission to the Central African Republic (MISCA) 96, 104–5, 153, 300, 327n

African-led Support Mission to the Central African Republic (MISCA) (*cont.*);
  AU Assembly of Heads of State and Government 281–2
  AU Commission on International Law 285
  AU Economic, Social and Cultural Council 286
  AU Mission in Burundi (AMIB) 104, 123, 125n, 278n
  AU mission in Somalia (AMISOM) 95–6, 104, 107, 127n, 261, 266, 268, 275–6, 300n
  AU mission in Sudan (AMIS) 95, 104–5, 130n, 278n
  AU Pan-African Parliament 282
  AU Peace and Security Council (PSC) 95, 101n, 259n, 268n, 277–82, 286–7
  AU Peace Support Operations 95
  AU–UN Hybrid Operation in Darfur (UNAMID) 44n, 46, 129n, 131n, 133n, 134, 184, 220–1, 278n, 299n, 300, 310n, 314, 320, 321, 324n 330n, 337–8
aggression, definition of 115, 117 *see also* acts of aggression
Al-Qaida 305
Alawites 174n
Albania 123, 125n *see also* Operation Alba
amelioration 160–1, 167–8n, 171, 386, 331–2, 335, 339–41, 347–8
Amnesty International 6, 69, 230–1, 288n
anarchy 111–12, 114, 165
Angola 123, 386
Arab League 127n, 287
arbitrary arrest 180, 230n, 345, 395n
Argentina 22, 171n, 296n, 297
area security 312
Armenia 174n
assassination 276n, 277, 342
asylum seekers 178, 192–3, 284 *see also* displacement; refugees
AUCISS, *see* Report of the Commission of Inquiry on South Sudan (AUCISS)
Australia 78n, 125n, 134n, 242, 249, 266n, 301–2, 305
Balkans, the 33–4, 76, 105
Bangladesh 35, 266n, 294, 298, 306
basic subsistence 364n, 380, 386
Battle of Mogadishu (1993) 294–5
Belarus 35n
belligerency 67–8, 174
Biafra 294, 382
bombardment, *see* aerial bombardment
bombs
  cluster and barrel 418
  laser-guided 261
  petrol 22
  unexploded 419
Bosnia and Herzegovina 19, 57, 72n, 84n, 239–40, 258, 294, 296–7, 300, 303, 310, 320, 372, 380, 412
Brahimi Report 43–4, 46–7, 90n, 169n, 231n, 233, 251, 262, 264, 300, 309n, 320, 325n, 326
Brazil 47, 291, 297, 306, 327
breach of the peace 32n, 121n, 117, 122, 124–7, 310n
buffer zones 312, 331
Burma, *see* Myanmar
Burundi 44n, 90n, 124n, 129n, 268n, 294, 299n, 342n *see also* African Union Mission in Burundi (AMIB)
camps, *see* PoC sites; prison camps; refugee: camps
Canada 76, 78, 82, 182, 266n, 298, 318
capacity building, *see* development/national capacity building
Capstone Doctrine 43n, 44n, 51n, 52, 80n, 82n, 84n, 91, 93n, 98–9, 126n, 218n, 268n, 300, 311n, 312n, 325n
ceasefires 43, 71, 102, 208n, 219, 288, 312, 331, 355
Central African Republic (CAR)
  AU missions 104–5, 125n, 276, 278n, 279, 373
  Christian militias 174
  civilian killings 290
  civilian protection mandate 144, 208, 276, 330n, 371
  EU operations 88, 105
  French forces 267, 290
  human rights protection 145, 153
  interim stabilization measures 406n
  Pan-African Parliament 282
  rapid deployment 317–18
  refugees 175n, 184, 196
  sanctions 270
  Séléka, emergence of 307
  threats to the peace 123
  UN peacekeeping deployments 1, 88, 216, 219n, 267–8
  uniformed personnel 263 *see also* African-led Support Mission to the Central African Republic (MISCA); *see also* Operation Sangaris; UN Mission in the Central African Republic and Chad(MINURCAT); UN Multidimensional Integrated Stabilization Mission in the Central African Republic (MINUSCA)
Chad
  communal conflict 342n
  EU operation 130n
  human rights violations 268n
  insurgency operations 342n
  refugees 196 *see also* UN Mission in the Central African Republic and Chad (MINURCAT)

charitable donations 385, 390n, 402, 421, 422
Charter of the United Nations, *see* UN Charter
checkpoints 19, 312, 331, 334, 389, 416
chemical weapons 301–2
child soldiers 151–2, 230n
China 34, 35n, 120, 292–3, 296n, 297, 301, 302n, 306
Christianity 13–14, 31, 174, 429
civil rights, *see* International Covenant on Civil and Political Rights (ICCPR)
civilian, definition of 2, 12, 64, 79, 431 *see also* protection of civilians
coercion 331–2, 335, 339–41, 346, 348, 380, 384n
Cold War 33, 71–2, 77, 120, 124, 372, 382, 407
collateral damage 93–6, 100, 104, 107, 164, 174–5, 211, 433
collective security system 3, 30, 32–7, 42, 48, 54, 60–2, 70, 86, 109–37, 234, 244, 280, 432, 435, 438
  collective security 114–16
  international relations theory 110–14
  protection of civilians 127–35
    peacekeeping mandate 128–31
      impact 134–5
      implementation of 132–4
  UN system 116–18
    aggression 120–2, 125–7
    breaches of the peace 125–7
    evolution of 119–27
    response measures 120–7
    threats to the peace 122–7
communal conflict 341–9
Community Alert Networks (CAN) 323
community self-protection 409–27
  self-protection measures 415–19
    Syria 418–19
  support for 419–26
    approaches 420–2
    challenges 422
    goals 419–20
    South Kordofan 425–6
    South Sudan, community watch groups 423–5
  understanding protection 410–15
    community approaches 413–15
    humanitarian approaches 411–12
    peacekeeping approaches 412–13
compassionate view of war 2, 12, 13, 11–28
  arguments for civilian protection 27–8
  civilian experience in war 11–12, 18–23
    civilian agency 20–3
    civilian victims 18–20
  principle of distinction 23–7
  traditional approaches 12–14
  World War I 16–18
  wounded and combatants first 14–16
Comprehensive Peace Agreement (CPA) 393, 395
Concept of Operations (CONOPS) 102, 312
conduct of hostilities 1, 13, 24, 67, 164, 360–1
consolidation 99–101, 213
constitutionalism 30, 61, 109, 115, 118–19, 136, 227n, 230, 244, 284
containment 61, 331–2, 335, 339–41
contingent/mission command structures 4, 206, 222
corruption 284, 394, 397, 405–6
cosmopolitanism 113, 137
Costa Rica 5, 303, 305
Côte d'Ivoire/Ivory Coast
  armed forces 165n
  civilian deaths 327
  civilian protection 208, 229–30
  ECOWAS 125n, 130n
  French forces 267
  Gbagbo camp's abuses 230–1
  regime crackdown 342
  security transformation 397
  threats to the peace 123, 124n *see also* Operation Licorne; UN Operation in Côte d'Ivoire (UNOCI)
counterinsurgency theory 15, 93, 100, 107
crimes against humanity 37n, 39–40, 49n, 50, 58, 79n, 83, 95, 128, 146, 156–7, 170, 187, 210, 231n, 276–8, 284, 287, 391, 420n
Croatia 248n
cultural norms 424
Cyprus, *see* UN Peacekeeping Force in Cyprus (UNFICYP)
Czech Republic 297
Darfur 29n, 46, 50–1, 59, 82, 124, 129–31nn, 134, 150, 170, 184, 219n, 220, 263, 278, 282, 303, 324, 337–8, 342n, 344, 385, *see also* African Union–United Nations Hybrid Operation in Darfur (UNAMID)
DARIO (Draft Articles on the Responsibilities of International Organisations) 227–8, 231, 236–8, 241, 247, 251–2
DARSIWA (Draft Articles on the Responsibility of States for Internationally Wrongful Acts) 56n, 57n, 156–7
defence policy, *see* EU Common Security and Defence Policy (CSDP)
demobilization 102, 315
democracy 116, 120, 276n, 277, 282, 287, 407
Democratic Forces for the Liberation of Rwanda (FDLR) 316, 336, 344
Democratic Republic of the Congo (DRC)
  amnesty pact 226n
  armed conflict 216
  armed groups 133
  civilian protection 88, 208, 342n
    failure to protect 130n, 131
  conflict-related sexual violence 373
  destruction 331

Democratic Republic of the Congo (DRC) (*cont.*);
  EU missions 125n, 130n, 267n
  Force Intervention Brigade 331
  freedom of movement 312n
  peacekeeping deployments 263
  PoC mandates 45
  refugees 175
  self-protection 387n
  stabilization mission 90n, 103n, 169n, 184n, 209n, 214, 299–300, 310, 323n
  threats to the peace 123, 124n
  UN military forces 133
  UN patrols 313
  UN peacekeeping deployments, *see also* FARDC; Operation Artemis; UN Organization Mission in the Democratic Republic of the Congo (MONUC); UN Organization Stabilization Mission in the Democratic Republic of the Congo (MONUSCO)
Denmark 318
Department of Field Support, *see* UN Department of Field Support (UN DFS)
Department of Peacekeeping Operations, *see* UN Department of Peacekeeping Operations (UN DPKO)
destruction 15, 19, 25, 164, 287, 301–2, 331–2, 335, 339–41, 346, 364
detention 16, 148, 150, 154–9, 166–7, 199–200, 207, 352, 359, 395n, 424
deterrence 56, 91, 114, 262–4, 307, 331–2, 335, 339–41, 343, 347–8, 354, 356
development/national capacity building 391–408
  expert critiques 399–405
  institutional critiques 396–9
  South Sudan 393–6
development projects 177n, 190n, 402
dignity 21, 38, 142, 175, 190–1, 201, 374–5, 379, 385, 387, 412, 420, 425–6, 428–30
disarmament 102, 264, 315, 363, 369, 406
discrimination 154, 157, 384n
disease 16, 19–20, 38n, 124, 180, 181n, 386, 413, 415n, 425
disengagement, *see* UN Disengagement Observer Force (UNDOF)
displacement 177–204
  international legal framework 184–202
    act of displacement 185–92
    IDP protection 196–200
    protection of displaced persons 192–
    refugee protection 192–6
    solutions 200–2
  protection of civilians 179–84 *see also* asylum seekers; internally displaced persons (IDPs); refugees
distress 20, 180
Djibouti 268n, 297n
doctrine of civilians 1, 12, 26–8 *see also* protection of civilians
domestic violence 387, 416
drones 261
Druze 174n
Dumbarton Oaks Conference 120
East Timor 154
  Australian-led International Stabilization Force (ISF) 125n *see also* UN missions in East Timor (UNTAET, UNMISET, UNMIT); UNTransitional Administration in East Timor (UNTAET)
economic rights, *see* International Covenant on Economic Social and Cultural Rights (ICESCR)
education rights 199, 261n, 279, 407
effects-based force generation 6, 311
enforced disappearance 144n, 148, 150
English School 111–12
Enhanced Rapidly Deployable Capacity (ERDC) 318
Eritrea 129n *see also* UN Mission in Ethiopia and Eritrea (UNMEE)
ethics of war 2, 2, 13–18, 20, 23, 25–7, 29, 429
Ethiopia 129n, 266n, 268, 294 *see also* UN Mission in Ethiopia and Eritrea (UNMEE)
ethnic cleansing 24, 39, 128, 156, 177n, 178n, 188, 190, 210, 294, 297, 305, 341, 391, 420n
European Union (EU) 2, 88, 96–8, 153, 231, 267, 306
  CAR (EUFOR RCA) 88, 105
  Common Security and Defence Policy (CSDP) 96–7, 105
  DRC (Operation Artemis) 125n, 129n, 130n, 267n
  missions and operations 102
extra-judicial killing 230n, 237
family tracing 194, 375
family unification 178, 187–91, 387, 415n, 416, 419
famine 16, 180, 384
FARDC (national army of the DRC) 217, 226–7, 336, 345–6
field support, *see* UN Department of Field Support (UN DFS)
first aid 425–6
food provisions 335, 343n, 356n, 376, 385, 386, 388, 414, 415n, 418, 425–6, 430 *see also* World Food Programme (WFP)
Force Intervention Brigade (FIB) see UN Organization Stabilization Mission in the Democratic Republic of the Congo (MONUSCO)
forced labour 16, 230n, 345, 388
forced recruitment (military) 180, 345, 384n
forceful population clearance 19

France 15–16, 40, 97, 231, 267, 295–6, 298n, 301, 302n, 307, 318n
game theory 111, 271
Geneva Conventions 3, 14–15, 18, 24, 55n, 56, 65–8, 73, 160–71, 187–201, 241, 243–7, 252, 306, 413–14, 433 *see also* international humanitarian law (IHL)
genocide 3, 16, 18–19, 37n, 39–40, 43, 47n, 49n, 50, 52, 56–9, 69, 76, 79n, 83, 88, 95, 127–8, 142, 146, 150, 156–7, 170, 177, 207, 208n, 210, 247, 249, 251, 258, 276–8, 284, 294–8, 305, 324n, 332, 341, 391, 420n
Georgia 40, 296
Ghana 268n
global governance 2, 48–9, 61
global society 3, 110, 113, 270
Great Lakes, Africa 73, 76, 127n, 316–17
Greek philosophy 429
Guinea-Bissau 270n
Haiti 33, 66n, 67n, 72n, 84n, 90n, 124, 153n, 208, 250, 260, 264, 299n, 310n, 313n, 327, 376, 388 *see also* Operation Uphold Democracy; UN Stabilization Mission in Haiti (MINUSTAH)
Handbook of the International Law of Military Operations 155
health care 191, 376, 386
High Readiness Brigade, *see* UN Standing High Readiness Brigade (SHIRBRIG)
Holy Roman Empire 31
hospitals 151, 161, 293, 316, 389
host State co-operation 324
hostage taking 16, 130n, 157, 199, 236n, 241
human rights 350–71
  case studies 355–65
    Afghanistan 358–62
    South Sudan 362–5
    Sri Lanka 355–8
  context 351–4
    PoC, link with 352–3
    protection practice 353–4
  Human Rights Up Front Initiative 370–1
  logic of 68–9
  viability of protection activity 365–9
    challenges 365–6
    enabling conditions 367–9
Human Rights Up Front initiative
  Central African Republic 371
  credibility 370
  field-based human rights work 350, 370–1
  impact and success 370–1
  Iraq 371
  mission settings 235
  Plan of Action 55, 158, 203–4, 235–7, 252, 304, 371
  responsibility to protect 142–3, 156–8
  South Sudan 370, 371
  Sri Lanka 358
  Syria 370, 371
  UN accountability 250, 252
Human Rights Watch (HRW) 5, 395
humanitarian access 381–3
humanitarian affairs, *see* Office for the Coordination of Humanitarian Affairs (OCHA)
humanitarian approaches 411–12
humanitarian intervention 29–62
  constraints 54–60
    definitional ambiguity 54–5
    obligation to act 55–8
    political selectivity 58–60
  historical development 30–48
    concept 34–7
  State sovereignty 53–4, 58–60
Humanitarian Policy Group (HPG) 63n, 374n, 376n, 379n, 380n, 385
humanitarian protection 372–90
  affected populations 386–9
    associations 387–9
    community-based protection 386–7
    diaspora 387–9
    local networks 387–9
  creative approaches 389–90
  definitional clarity 374–8
  protection actors, numbers of 380–1
  protection challenges 381–6
    access 381–3
    counter-terrorism measures 383–4
    organizational 384–6
    programmatic 384–6
  protection gap 378–80
hunger 19, 38n, 386–7, 413
hygiene 187–91
idealism 111
imminent threat, definition of 211
impairment 332, 339
impartiality 39, 43, 49, 58, 59, 63–74, 80–2, 86, 93, 126, 132, 150, 171, 207, 218, 220–1, 251, 268–9, 270, 379, 422, 434
imprisonment 12
improvised explosive devices (IEDs) 19, 27, 332, 358, 362
India 7, 35, 208n, 266n, 306, 315, 327
  infrastructure destruction 19, 289 *see also* UN Military Observer Group in India and Pakistan (UNMOGIP)
inhumane treatment 236–7, 240n, 241, 251–2
intelligence 131, 253, 259n, 265, 320, 323–4, 326, 333, 403, 407, 438
insurgency 15, 228, 263n, 342–5, 349 *see also* counterinsurgency theory
Inter-Agency Standing Committee (IASC) 7, 19n, 43n, 74, 352, 361n, 373–4, 381, 385n, 411, 430n
internal oversight services, *see* UN Office of Internal Oversight Services (OIOS)
internally displaced persons (IDPs) 20, 43n, 82, 143, 158, 176, 177, 181–5, 196–202, 259, 283, 313, 323, 352n, 364, 373, 411n *see also* displacement; refugees

International Commission on Intervention and State Sovereignty (ICISS) 36n, 37–44, 48n, 50n, 52, 57, 82–3, 128, 156, 372
International Committee of the Red Cross (ICRC) 3, 17–18, 27, 65, 66n, 67–8, 73–6, 85–6, 97, 102, 160n, 161n, 162, 175n, 180, 209n, 215, 238, 374n, 389n, 411n, 412, 430n
  Conference 18n, 65–6n, 162, 165n, 167n, 171n, 172
International Conference on the Great Lakes Region (ICGLR) 127n, 316–17
International Conference on the Protection of Civilians 135n
International Court of Justice (ICJ) 35, 121, 147, 228n, 238–9, 241, 243–9
International Covenant on Civil and Political Rights (ICCPR) 56n, 143n, 144, 147, 157, 236–40, 352n
International Covenant on Economic Social and Cultural Rights (ICESCR) 144
International Criminal Tribunal on Rwanda (ICTR) 170n, 229, 297, 307
International Criminal Tribunal for the former Yugoslavia (ICTY) 170n, 297, 307
International Crisis Group 226n, 268n, 271n, 343n
international human rights law (IHRL) 141–9
  extraterritorial effect 147–9
  Human Rights Up Front initiative 156–8
  obligations of armed non-state actors 149–52
  obligations of UN peacekeepers 152–6
  relevance for PoC 143–7
  responsibility to protect 156–8
international humanitarian law (IHL) 160–76
  challenges 173–5
  compliance with 169–73
  framework 163–5
  implementation 165–9
  operational dialogue 165–9 *see also* conduct of hostilities
International Law Commission (ILC) 5, 56, 146, 156, 246, 249, 432–3
International Network on Conflict and Stability (INCAF) 404
international organisations, responsibility of, *see* DARIO
International refugee law (IRL), *see* refugees
international relations (IR) theory 1, 3, 14, 29–32, 70, 85–6, 110–15, 122, 136, 257, 428, 438
international responsibility 224–54
  accountability 247–51
  complicity 226–8
  independent legal obligation 228–33
  obligations of UN missions under IHL 241–7
    Common Article 243–7
    law of occupation 241–3
  obligations of UN missions under IHRL 233–41
    protection 234–38
    troop-contributing States 238–41
International Security Assistance Force (ISAF) 93, 125n, 261, 358, 361
international society theory 1, 12, 27, 36, 112
International Stabilization Force (ISF) 125n
Iran 305
Iraq
  crisis of protection 371
  displacement 191–2
  first war (1991) 12
  humanitarian situations 33, 124
  ISIS 173n, 174, 260n, 302
  Kurdish movement 72
  Kurds, attacks on 181
  military intervention 33, 73
  no-fly zones 84n
  non-military special political missions 269
  refugees 182, 191–2, 196
  sanctions 270–1, 305n
  security and stability 229, 397
  stabilization measures 406n
  UK forces in 239
  US-led invasion (2003) 84n, 125n, 130
  violence 94
  wars in 12, 22 *see also* UN Assistance Mission in Iraq
Islam 429
Islamic charities 384
Islamic militants 173–4, 260n, 267n, 290, 302
Islamic radicalization *see* radicalisation
Islamic State in Syria and the Levant (ISIL) 178
Islamic State of Iraq and al-Sham (ISIS) 173–4, 191, 260n, 302
Israel 22, 34n, 123, 147, 165n, 244–6, 293
Ivory Coast, *see* Côte d'Ivoire
Joint Mission Analysis Centre (JMAC) 265, 323–4
Judaism 18, 429
jus ad bellum, see Just War theory; UN Charter; use of force
jus in bello, see conduct of hostilities; Geneva Conventions; international humanitarian law (IHL)
Just War theory 13–14, 25–7, 30–4, 37, 54, 61, 83, 428
Kampuchea 35, 294
Kenya 170, 174, 266n, 268, 284n
Korea, Democratic People's Republic of 120–1, 305
Korean War 306
Kosovo 35–7, 61, 78n, 104, 154, 239, 298, 406n *see also* UN Mission in Kosovo (UNMIK)
Kurds 72, 174n, 181, 182n, 191

leadership 4, 158, 206, 210, 222, 322–3, 328, 329, 345, 357, 360, 364, 367–71, 394, 422, 424
Lebanon 124n, 165n, 208, 260n, 263n, 418n, 419 *see also* UN Interim Force in Lebanon (UNIFIL)
legitimacy 61, 69, 168
liberalism 110–13, 117, 119, 124
Liberation Tigers of Tamil Eelam (LTTE) 149, 355
Liberia 23, 123, 124n, 129n, 131n, 208, 263, 327, 342n, 343n, 397 *see also* UN Mission in Liberia (UNMIL)
Libya 1, 2, 5, 41, 45, 47–8, 54, 59–61, 63–4, 84–6, 88, 93–4, 100, 104, 106–7, 123–5, 127n, 128, 150, 229, 231n, 269, 270, 275, 283, 286–99, 306, 377n, 388 *see also* Operation Unified Protector
Lieber Code 15, 66n, 163n, 164n, 186
limited war 1, 12, 162n
Local to Global Protection Initiative (L2GP) 409, 413–26
Luxembourg 301–2
Mali 1, 45, 88, 98, 104–6, 123, 124n, 129n, 131n, 134, 208, 216, 220, 267–8, 282n, 316–18, 323, 338, 342n, 343, 349 *see also* African-led International Support Mission to Mali (AFISMA); Operation Serval; UN Multidimensional Integrated Stabilization Mission in Mali (MINUSMA)
medical assistance 430
medicine 197, 389, 426
mercenarism 284
Middle Ages/ Medieval Europe 13, 15–18, 23, 31
military force
civilians under threat 89
compliant practice 27
Constitutive Act 277-8
deterrent against civilian violence 310, 343, 430
early intervention 84
effects 333
ethics 27
humanitarians and 92
IHL protection 133
implementation by peacekeepers 107–8, 326
intra-State conflict 331
as last resort 99
minimal role 343
NATO 100
non-compulsion to provide 60
operational activities 311-12, 333
peace process 327
physical protection 88
PoC concept 75
positive contribution 262
prohibition of arbitrary use 114
provision of standing 117, 119, 127, 317
Security Council decisions 136
State consent 33
UN peacekeeping operations 89, 103, 310, 329-50
utility of 6 *see also* use of force
MINURCAT, *see* UN Mission in the Central African Republic and Chad (MINURCAT)
MINURSO, *see* UN Mission for the Referendum in Western Sahara (MINURSO)
MINUSCA, *see* UN Multidimensional Integrated Stabilization Mission in the Central African Republic (MINUSCA)
MINUSMA, *see* UN Multidimensional Integrated Stabilization Mission in Mali (MINUSMA)
MINUSTAH, *see* UN Stabilization Mission in Haiti (MINUSTAH)
MISCA, *see* African-led Support Mission to the Central African Republic (MISCA)
mobility 263–6, 321
Model Status of Forces Agreement 215–16, 220, 222, 235n, 243n, 249, 312, 433
money 21, 197, 414n
money laundering 284, 388
Mozambique 276
Myanmar 40, 409, 414, 416
murder 12, 28, 79, 180, 186, 206, 237, 241, 301, 342
Nalu Allied Democratic Forces—National Army for the Liberation of Uganda (ADF) 268n, 316, 343
Napoleonic Wars 15
natural disaster 177n, 190n, 196–7, 279, 416
natural law 31
natural resources, exploitation of 284
Netherlands 36, 153n, 215n, 228–9, 240, 251n, 318
neutrality 17, 63–74, 81, 86, 194, 207, 208n, 251, 268n, 379, 422
New Zealand 2, 294n, 295n, 296n, 297
Nigeria 68, 174, 268, 280, 296–7, 343, 382
non-governmental organizations (NGOs) 23, 29, 64, 73, 150–1, 175n, 183n, 198, 250, 261, 283, 353, 373, 378, 380–1, 383n, 388n, 390, 425
non-refoulement 194–5, 199, 429, 434
North Atlantic Treaty Organization (NATO)
Afghanistan, intervention in 88, 94, 104, 267n, 327, 359
civilian protection 89–90, 97, 104–7, 246
avoidance of casualties 98, 104
indirect approach 93–4, 96
collateral damage 104
counterinsurgency logic 100–1, 107
J-3 166
Joint Operational Guidance 94, 100
Kosovo, intervention in 35–7, 61, 104, 239

North Atlantic Treaty Organization (NATO) (*cont.*);
  Libya, intervention in 5, 60, 88, 94, 104, 106, 125n, 127n, 229, 288–9, 306
  partnership arrangements 266–7
  peacekeeping deployments 1, 2
  SACEUR 260
  Serbia, intervention in 76
  use of force 2, 89
  Yugoslavia, bombing of 82, 84n, 125n, 298
Northern Ireland 118n, 253n, 309n
Norwegian Defence Research Establishment (FFI) 2, 6, 81n, 88n, 100n, 330n, 333n, 341n
nutrition 181, 187–91
observation posts 312, 331, 334
Organization of African Unity (OAU) 95n, 143n, 276, 277n, 283n, 284n
Oman 104, 297
Operation Alba (Albania) 125n
Operation Allied Force (Yugoslavia) 298
Operation Artemis (DRC) 105, 129n, 130n, 267n
Operation Licorne (Cote d'Ivoire) 125n, 129n, 130n, 267n
Operation Longhorn (South Sudan) 343n
Operation Sangaris (CAR) 125n, 130n, 267n
Operation Serval (Mali) 125n, 127n, 130n, 267n, 317, 343n
Operation Turquoise (Rwanda) 125n, 295–6
Operation Uphold Democracy (Haiti) 125n
Operation Unified Protector (Libya) 93
Operations Plan (OPLAN) 102
Organization for Security and Cooperation in Europe (OSCE) 102
Overseas Development Institute (ODI) 7, 180n, 388n, 417
Oxfam 75n, 261n, 380–1, 384n, 385n, 413, 417
Pakistan 208n, 266n, 297, 315–16, 327, 388
  see also UN Military Observer Group in India and Pakistan (UNMOGIP)
Palestinian Occupied Territories 22, 34, 123, 181, 244–6, 406, 409, 415
party to the conflict 4, 81, 131–3, 166, 171, 174, 194, 206, 216, 222, 377, 413, 434
patrols/patrolling 101–2, 144, 169n, 202, 221, 265, 272n, 312, 313–15, 331, 334, 343n, 363, 423
peace agreements 70–1, 102, 135, 151, 201, 269, 293, 310, 312–13, 316, 333, 362, 393
peace process 6, 23, 99, 273, 311, 324–5, 327, 363
peacekeeping
  approaches 412–13
  basic principles 218–22
    host State consent 218–20
    impartiality 220–1
    self-defence 221–2
  effective 262–4
  leadership 322–3
  legal framework 218–22
  limitations on missions 324
  mandate, Security Council 128–31
    failure to fulfil 213–15
    impact 134–5
    implementation of 132–4
  operational concept 91–2, 94, 98–9, 101, 213n, 269–70, 375
  policy 300, 413, 417
  protection of civilians 77–82
    confusion 80–2
    discretion 78–80
    principles of protection 80–2
  resources 319–21
  robust 207–8
  rules of engagement 71, 95, 141, 165, 167, 209, 211n, 252, 312, 331, 433
  UN deployments 1, 88, 216, 219n, 267–8
  use of force 309–28
    military force 311–13
    political challenges 325–6
    seldom use of force 103–4
Philippines 406n
philosophical approaches 29, 31–2, 38n, 68, 112, 429
physical assault/attack 18–19, 424
physical integrity 92, 116, 122, 144, 153, 195, 199, 186, 352, 429–32
physical protection 5, 46, 52, 55, 88, 92, 93, 95, 98, 99, 101–3, 107, 129, 131, 145, 184, 257–8, 269, 272, 273, 310, 354, 363–5, 386, 412–13, 431
pillage 12, 15, 28
piracy 284
places of worship 161, 293
political participation 199, 143
political peace process 6, 311
political rights, *see* International Covenant on Civil and Political Rights (ICCPR)
positivism 31–2, 34, 41
post-conflict revenge 341
poverty/impoverishment 18–19, 38n, 180, 387
predatory violence 341–6, 349
pre-emption 99–101, 213, 263–6
prevention 99–101, 213, 263–6
prison camps 16
property rights 112, 175n, 185–6, 190, 202, 210, 280, 287, 425
protection chain 7, 391, 393, 408, 438
protection of civilians (PoC)
  activities 436–8
    accountability 438
    community self-protection 409–27
    development 257, 275–7, 287–90, 298, 322–3, 366, 370–1, 381–2, 387–8, 390, 408, 412, 414, 428–31, 437–8

diplomatic 58, 66–7, 116, 135, 161n, 162, 236, 288–9, 292–308, 438
human rights 350–71, 438
humanitarian 366, 369, 370, 372–90, 438
military 309–49, 438
peacekeeping 257–91
political process 437
political support 437
security-first approach 438
selectivity 436
threat environment and protection needs 437
troops 437
unified protection strategy 437
use of force, legal parameters 438
use of force and violence 437
concept and definitions 7, 8, 54, 64, 66, 73–5, 77, 79, 91–2, 95, 97–9, 102, 114, 257–9, 273, 299, 373–8, 381, 410–11, 428–31
constraints 54–60
definitional ambiguity 54–5
financial 258, 383, 385, 390
legal 34n, 37, 49–51, 65–9, 152, 184–202, 209–22, 228–33, 259, 432–8
material 197, 258, 269, 375, 383
obligation to act 55–8
political 49–51, 58–60, 325–6, 437
practical 29, 42, 55, 59, 61, 163
enforcement, evolution of 75–85
protection and intervention 82–5
Security Council framework 76–7
historical development 30–48, 63–87
concept 42–7
human rights 68–9
international humanitarian law 65–8
international refugee law 65–8
legal protections, rise of 65–9
humanitarian intervention 29–62
legal framework 432–6
accountability 434–5
further work 435–6
negative obligations 433–4
positive obligations 432–3
under international law 432
organisational approaches 88–108
AU, see African Union (AU)
EU 2, 88, 96–8, 153, 231, 267, 306
ICRC 66n, 74, 76, 175n
NATO 2, 88–9, 100, 104, 106, 267n, 327
UN OCHA 196
UN OHCHR 147
UN Office of Legal Affairs 79, 205n, 210, 214n, 235n, 312
UN peacekeeping 89, 103, 309–50
UN Security Council 69–72, 76–7, 292–308
UNHCR 66n, 67–8, 174n, 177n, 181, 192n, 193n, 195–6, 380, 389n, 411, 417n
PoC sites 272n, 364, 423–5
political and legal relationships 49–51
responsibility to protect 29–62
Security Council 69–72
abbreviated history 293–303
diplomacy 292–308
framework for PoC 76–7
impartiality 70–1
neutrality 70–1
Rwanda (1994) 293–302
Syria (2014) 293–302
threats 72
tools 302–6
State sovereignty 53–4, 58–60
United Nations 257–74
alternatives to force 269–72
changing nature of conflict 260–1
force 262–9
partnership arrangements 266–9
pre-emption and prevention 264–6
UN concept of PoC 258–60
protection threats 3, 381, 384, 413–16, 420–7, 437 *see also* threats (to civilians)
psychological support 415
psychosocial support 422, 426
public order management 102, 115, 193
Quakers 17
racial discrimination 157
radicalization 168, 173–5, 289
ransom 12
rape 12–13, 15, 16, 18–19, 28, 39, 150–1, 154, 180, 210n, 241, 315, 345, 384n, 415n, 430
rapid deployment 265, 317–18, 405
realism 36, 62, 109–13, 116–18, 221
Red Cross, *see* International Committee of the Red Cross (ICRC)
refugees/refugee law
AU approach 101
asylum protection 192–6, 380
Bosnia, Srebrenica 76, 240, 259, 380
camps 184, 331
Cartagena Declaration on Refugees 193n
Central African Republic (CAR) 175n, 184, 196
children 177–8
Colombia 175n
community cohesion 414n
condition and sanitation 181n
Convention Governing the Specific Aspects of Refugee Problems in Africa 193n, 277n
Convention relating to the Status of Refugees 55n, 192–5
diplomatic protection, definitions of 66–7
displacement 175n, 176, 180–1, 204
eligibility for refugee status 193

refugees/refugee law (*cont.*);
EU guidelines 102
family tracing 194
fear of persecution 193
freedom of movement 102
freedom to choose one's residence 200–1
Guiding principles on IDPs 183, 186, 190, 192, 198–201
Geneva Conventions 66, 193–4
High Commissioner for Refugees 67
humanitarian assistance 21, 181, 182, 240
ICRC 66n, 74, 76, 175n
Integrated Regional Information Networks 388n
internally displaced persons (IDPs) 175n, 177, 196, 197, 199
international protection regime 178–204
International Rescue Committee 380
Iraq 72, 181–2, 192, 196
land and property of 202
local integration into country of asylum 201
legal recognition/status 178, 193, 198, 411, 414
loss of domestic protection 66n
loss of property and livelihood 175n, 202
neutral nations 68
non-forcible return 380, 434
non-refoulement principle 194–5, 199, 280
Norwegian Refugee Council 177n, 178n, 179n, 380, 431n
occupied territories 194
Oxfam 380
Palestine 181
physical abuse, risk of 175n, 184
protection of refugees, definitions of 66, 74, 97, 410–11, 431
Protocol relating to the Status of 192–3
Regional Refugee Response 178n
resettlement in another country 201
reunion of dispersed families 194
right to return to one's country 200–2
risks and dangers 418–19
Rwanda 76, 177, 182, 251, 259, 380
safety of 182–4
Save the Children 380
self-protection strategies 418–19
sexual abuse and exploitation 175n, 418
Somalia 72, 102, 196, 300
South Sudan 315
State obligations 192–6
Syria 174–5n, 178–9, 192, 195–6, 373, 380, 388n, 418–19
UN High Commission for Refugees (UNHCR) 66n, 67–8, 174n, 177n, 181, 192n, 193n, 195–6, 380, 389n, 411, 417n
Yemen 196
Yugoslavia, former 177, 182 *see also* asylum seekers; internally displaced persons (IDPs)
regime crackdown 341–2
regional support 316–17
reintegration practices 102, 198, 201–2, 315
relief and works, *see* UN Relief and Works Agency (UNRWA)
religious minority communities 174n
Report of the Commission of Inquiry on South Sudan (AUCISS) 281
resettlement 198–9, 201–2
resources, mobilization of 6, 45–6, 80, 103, 131–4, 206–8, 211, 231, 237, 253, 258–60, 320–1, 326, 329, 333, 348, 369, 371, 413, 419–20, 437
responsibility to protect 29–62, 64, 79, 82–5, 372n
commonalities with PoC 48–9
constraints 54–60
definitional ambiguity 54–5
obligation to act 55–8
political selectivity 58–60
historical development 30–48
concept 37–42
political and legal relationships 49–51
State sovereignty 53–4, 58–60
responsibility while protecting (RwP) 30, 47–8
restraint 1, 2, 11–15, 26, 37, 377
revisionism 25–7
right to life 143n, 144, 148, 155, 186, 190, 195, 199, 228, 233, 236–40, 251–2, 352, 431–2
rules of engagement (ROE) 71, 95, 141, 165, 167, 209, 211n, 252, 312, 331, 433
Russia 34, 35, 40, 82, 120n, 238n, 290, 292, 296, 301, 302n, 306 *see also* Soviet Union
ruthless war 1, 11–12, 24, 27
Rwanda 3, 33, 34, 37, 43, 44n, 47, 58, 61, 72n, 74, 76, 78, 84n, 119, 123, 124, 125, 127, 135n, 142, 156, 170, 177, 182, 190, 205-7, 226n, 249, 251, 258-9, 276, 292, 295-300, 304, 306, 310, 320, 346, 372, 380, 406n, 412, 428 *see also* Democratic Forces for the Liberation of Rwanda (FDLR); International Criminal Tribunal on Rwanda (ICTR); Operation Turquoise; UN Assistance Mission in Rwanda (UNAMIR)
San Francisco Conference 117, 120–2
Save the Children 17, 380, 416n
sectarian violence 174n, 253n
security-first approach 7, 393, 405–7
security policy, *see* EU Common Security and Defence Policy (CSDP); Organization for Security and Cooperation in Europe (OSCE)

self-defence 4, 31–2, 35, 43, 76, 78, 80, 84n, 117, 126, 148, 154–5, 205–6, 216, 218–19, 221–2, 264, 310, 312, 315, 334, 361, 416, 434
self-determination 109, 116, 157, 343n
self-protection 1, 7, 8, 21, 376, 387, 390, 409–27
Serbia and Montenegro 57, 76
sexual abuse 175n, 230n, 253n, 415n, 418
sexual violence 18–19, 144–5, 150–1, 154, 180, 232, 314–15, 321, 351n, 373, 384n, 413
shelter 21, 23, 86, 103, 188, 191, 197, 206n, 251–2, 272n, 348, 419, 425, 430
Shia 174n
SHIRBRIG, *see* UN Standing High Readiness Brigade (SHIRBRIG)
Sierra Leone 44, 72n, 76, 129, 170, 208, 268n, 276, 313, 327, 342n, 343n, 407 *see also* UN Mission in Sierra Leone (UNAMSIL)
slavery 143n, 150, 157, 384n, 432
smart weapons 261
smuggling, *see* trafficking
social compact theory 406, 429
social rights, *see* International Covenant on Economic Social and Cultural Rights (ICESCR)
Somalia 19, 33, 37, 42n, 72, 73, 77, 84n, 88, 95–6, 104–5, 123–4, 125n, 127n, 129n, 174, 175n, 182, 242, 260n, 261, 266–9, 275–6, 278–9, 282, 291, 294, 300, 310, 327, 350n, 373, 380, 384, 388, 397
South African Development Community (SADC) 333
South Africa 268, 277n, 289, 290n, 306, 333
South Kordofan 410, 415, 425–6 *see also* Sudan
South Korea 120
South Sudan
- advocacy efforts 369
- armed groups 154
- communal conflict 342n, 345
- community watch groups 410, 423–5
- crisis of protection 371, 409
- disease and hunger 386
- ethnic minority killings 396
- human rights protection 6, 7
- human rights violations 59, 280–1
- humanitarian programmes (2014) 19, 184
- insurgencies 342n, 343–4
- inter-State conflict 346
- internal displacement 103
- physical violence 103
- PoC sites 103, 183–4, 221
- political support 368
- protection capacities 393–6
- recovery fund 406n
- refugees 175n
- Security Council visiting mission 303
- security system reform 404
- self-protection 419, 422
- South Sudan Police Service (SSPS) 335, 347
- State-building 272
- threats to the peace 123–4
- UN peacekeeping deployments 1, 82, 88, 132n, 203, 208, 221, 362–5, 368
- uniformed personnel 263 *see also* Operation Longhorn; Report of the Commission of Inquiry on South Sudan(AUCISS); UN Mission in South Sudan (UNMISS)

Soviet Union 68, 120, 306 *see also* Russia
Spain 296n, 297
Special Representative of the UN Secretary-General (SRSG) 6, 7, 212–13, 319, 322, 351n
Srebrenica 3, 37, 43, 57, 61, 74, 76, 78, 127, 142, 153n, 156, 205–7, 215n, 228–9, 239–41, 251, 258–9, 292, 296–8, 300, 412
Sri Lanka 3, 6, 142, 149, 152, 157, 159, 200, 235, 303, 306, 355–8, 363n, 365–9 *see also* UN Action in Sri Lanka
starvation 15, 16–17, 19–20, 185
Status of Force Agreement (SOFA) 215–16, 220, 222, 235n, 243n, 249n, 312, 433
Stimson Center 7, 395, 397, 409, 413, 416n, 420n, 423n
Stoic philosophy 113, 137, 429
Sudan
- AU Mission 95, 104, 125n, 278n
- communal conflict 344
- crisis of protection 409
- disease and hunger 386
- humanitarian crisis (2008–9) 42n
- inter-State conflict 346
- international criminal justice 271
- limitations on peacekeeping missions 324
- Pan African Parliament 282n
- population density 319
- refugees 175n
- return of displaced persons 184
- self-protection 419
- terrorism 124
- threats to the peace 123–4
- UN peacekeeping missions 208, 221
- women 415 *see also* Darfur; South Kordofan; UN Mission in the Sudan (UNMIS)

Sudan People's Liberation Army (SPLA) 335, 343, 348
suicide bombers 332
Supreme Allied Commander Europe (SACEUR) 260
Syria
- access constraints 382, 390
- armed groups 150, 154, 191
- chemical weapons 301–2
- civil war 21, 22, 42, 58, 86, 191, 191n, 270, 292, 301–2, 306
- civilian massacres 370
- Commission of Inquiry 173n, 174n

Syria (*cont.*);
community self-protection 409, 410, 415n, 418–19
Council (in)action 65, 77, 84–5, 122, 301, 306
crisis of protection 371, 380
cross-border operations 382
diaspora communities 388
displacement crisis 178–9, 373
economy 19
fact-finding missions 270n
family networks 418–19
Free Syrian Army 379
human rights violations 150
humanitarian assistance 34n
humanitarian programmes 19
international community, failures of 1
interventionist agenda 375
ISIS 174, 191n
Israel, agreement with 293
local knowledge 390
medical relief organizations 383
military intervention in 34
refugees 175n, 178–9, 195–6, 373, 388
sanctions 270
threat to the peace 301
UN Mission (UNSMIS) 129n
UN resolutions 63
UN Special Envoy for Syria (SES) 370
UN system-wide protection strategy 370
use or threat of veto 33–4, 48
Taliban 150, 260, 305, 327, 358, 362, 383–4
Tamil Eelam, *see* Liberation Tigers of Tamil Eelam (LTTE)
Tanzania 16, 35, 268, 278n
Tehran Conference on Human Rights 244
terrorism 124, 167, 261, 267, 276n, 277, 282, 284, 304–7, 383–4
threats (to civilians) 155, 184, 205, 211–15, 218, 231, 232, 237, 250–3, 265, 271, 287–8, 315–16, 336, 341–2, 354, 363, 374, 376, 380–1, 385–7, 430n *see also* protection threats
threats to the peace 3, 42, 110, 117–27, 135, 182, 309, 310n, 327
concept 72
determination 122–4
response measures 125–7
Timor-Leste 303
torture 18, 28, 55n, 56n, 143n, 144, 148, 150, 154, 157, 171n, 195n, 210n, 228, 230, 233, 236–7, 239–41, 246, 249n, 251–2, 352, 384n, 395, 430, 432
trafficking 289, 323
arms 290
drugs 284
hazardous waste 284
persons 284
smuggling 384
training 91, 98, 100, 101, 102, 107, 132n, 153, 156, 165, 167n, 176, 215–16, 261, 266, 279, 317, 319, 321–3, 349, 367, 378–9, 385–6, 389, 392, 394–6, 403, 405, 423, 425–6
Troop contributing countries (TCCs) 45–6, 62, 81, 86, 103, 132–3, 149n, 207, 213, 215–18, 222, 308, 319–22, 325, 328, 329, 333, 349
troop professionalism 318–19
troop levels 318–19, 437
truce supervision, *see* UN Truce Supervision Organization (UNTSO)
unconstitutional change of government 284
Uganda 35, 181n, 241, 268, 276, 316, 346
see also Nalu Allied Democratic Forces—National Army for the Liberation of Uganda (ADF)
Ukraine 34, 306
Universal Declaration of Human Rights (UDHR) 144, 158, 192n, 200n, 234, 236, 351
UN Action in Sri Lanka 6, 158n, 200n, 303n, 355n
UN Assistance Mission in Afghanistan 6, 150, 299n, 359
UN Assistance Mission in Iraq 7
UN Assistance Mission in Rwanda (UNAMIR) 76, 251, 295–6
UN Charter 2, 6, 30, 32–7, 41, 46n, 49, 53, 61–2, 69–70, 79, 90, 109–10, 117–18, 142, 153, 208, 209, 219, 222, 242, 245, 247, 257–8, 262, 291, 293, 297, 302, 304–6, 309, 317, 327, 429, 431–2, 435, 438
UN Children's Fund (UNICEF) 151n, 361n, 380, 416n
UN Crisis Operations Group 356, 368
UN Department of Field Support (UN DFS) 43n, 56, 79n, 80n, 90–1n, 100n, 132n, 210, 213n, 218n, 220n, 226n, 250n, 265n, 268n, 269, 270n, 299n, 300n, 311n, 312, 331n, 333n, 352n, 367n, 413n, 417n, 430n
UN Department of Peacekeeping Operations (UN DPKO) 2, 43n, 52, 56, 63n, 79n, 80n, 90n, 91, 94, 100n, 103n, 109n, 126n, 132, 210, 213n, 218n, 220n, 230, 235n, 250, 261, 263n, 265–6n, 268n, 270n, 299n, 300n, 311n, 312, 331n, 333n, 352n, 367n, 375, 397, 412n, 413n, 417n
UN Development Programme (UNDP) 7, 394–5, 405n, 406n
UN Disengagement Observer Force (UNDOF) 208n
UN General Assembly Special Committee on Peacekeeping Operations (C-34) 45, 134, 218, 257, 318

UN High Commissioner for Refugees (UNHCR), *see* Refugees
UN High Level Panel on Peace Operations 59, 169n, 170
UN Interim Force in Lebanon (UNIFIL) 44n, 90n, 129n, 133n, 208, 220–1, 263n, 299n, 310n, 319–20
UN Interim Security Force for Abyei (UNISFA) 44n, 90n, 129n, 133n, 184, 220, 299n, 330n, 336–8, 340, 343n, 347
UN Military Observer Group in India and Pakistan (UNMOGIP) 208n
UN Mission in Afghanistan (UNAMA) 6, 100, 150, 208n, 299n, 358n, 359–62, 367–9
UN Mission in the Central African Republic and Chad (MINURCAT) 44n, 90n, 129n, 131n, 184n, 299n, 330n, 338
UN Mission in Ethiopia and Eritrea (UNMEE) 129n
UN Mission in Kosovo (UNMIK) 154, 208n
UN Mission in Liberia (UNMIL) 44n, 90n, 129n, 131n, 133n, 154n, 184n, 220, 299n, 326–7, 330n, 337, 338, 340
UN Mission for the Referendum in Western Sahara (MINURSO) 208n
UN Mission in Sierra Leone (UNAMSIL) 44, 77–8, 90n, 129–30, 205, 208, 298, 330n, 338
UN Mission in South Sudan (UNMISS) 44n, 90n, 129n, 131n, 133n, 134, 150, 183–4, 203, 210n, 212n, 220–1, 232, 293, 299n, 310, 315, 330, 335, 337–8, 341, 343n, 347–9, 362–70, 394–7, 414, 423–5
UN Mission in the Sudan (UNMIS) 44n, 46, 90n, 129n, 330n, 338–9, 362n, 393n, 394
UN missions in East Timor (UNTAET, UNMISET, UNMIT) 129n
UN Multidimensional Integrated Stabilization Mission in the Central African Republic (MINUSCA) 45n, 46, 81, 129n, 131n, 133n, 134, 144, 153, 184, 210n, 217, 220, 300, 327n, 349
UN Multidimensional Integrated Stabilization Mission in Mali (MINUSMA) 45n, 46, 81, 129n, 131n, 133n, 134, 144, 153, 184, 210, 217, 220, 300, 327n, 349
UN Office for the Coordination of Humanitarian Affairs (OCHA) 77n, 90–2, 97, 130, 196, 425n
UN Office of Internal Oversight Services (OIOS) 45–6, 48n, 59n, 79n, 80n, 93n, 103, 133, 141–2, 205–6, 265n, 213n, 215n, 216n, 218n, 221, 265n, 299n, 313–14, 325–6, 329
UN Office of the High Commissioner for Human Rights (OHCHR) 74, 75n, 145n, 146–7, 150, 151n, 154n, 155n, 232, 335n, 345n, 351–6, 361n, 367, 378, 380
UN Operation in the Congo (ONUC) 71
UN Operation in Côte d'Ivoire (UNOCI) 44n, 46, 81, 129n, 133n, 220, 230–1, 327, 330n, 338, 340
UN Organization Mission in the Democratic Republic of the Congo (MONUC) 44n, 45, 102, 129n, 131n, 226–7, 233–4, 263, 268n, 309n, 315–16, 322n, 330n, 336, 337–8, 340, 349
UN Organization Stabilization Mission in the Democratic Republic of the Congo (MONUSCO) 44n, 46, 81, 86, 90n, 92, 129n, 133–4, 169n, 209n, 214, 217, 220, 226, 259, 299, 310, 311, 315–17, 319, 323–5, 330n, 333, 336–8, 340, 345–6, 349
  Force Intervention Brigade (FIB) see 46, 86, 99n, 103, 127n, 133, 169n, 217, 316–17, 319, 325, 331, 333, 345–6
UN Peacekeeping Force in Cyprus (UNFICYP) 208n
UN Protection Force for the Former Yugoslavia (UNPROFOR) 76, 77, 128n, 228
UN Relief and Works Agency (UNRWA) 181
UN Security Council (UNSC) 12, 90–1, 95, 141, 163, 169, 179, 181–4, 191, 200–1, 203, 230–2, 241, 246, 257, 287–91, 353, 396, 432–3, 435
UN Stabilization Mission in Haiti (MINUSTAH) 44n, 129n, 133n, 208n, 220, 250, 299n
UN Standing High Readiness Brigade (SHIRBRIG) 318
UN Transitional Administration in East Timor (UNTAET) 78, 129n
UN Truce Supervision Organization (UNTSO) 208n
UNAMID, *see* African Union–United Nations Hybrid Operation in Darfur (UNAMID)
United Kingdom 34, 36, 120, 171n, 296n, 296–7, 298n, 301, 302n, 304, 309n
United States 99n, 100n, 104n, 118n, 120, 132n, 147–8, 164n, 172n, 186, 231, 238–9, 242, 245n, 250n, 263n, 294–7, 301, 302n, 304, 306–7, 311n, 319, 345n, 359, 397
Universal Periodic Review (UPR) 173, 351
use of force 31–4, 51–3, 205–23, 331, 436–8
  accountability 47, 438
  basic peacekeeping principles 218–22
    host State consent 218–20
    impartiality 220–1
    self-defence 221–2
  collective security 32–4
  Just war theory 31–2
  legal framework 209–18
    basic peacekeeping principles 218–22
    criminal accountability, fear of 215–18
    failure to fulfil the mandate 213–15
    Force Commander 212–13

legal parameters 438
legal terminology 209–12
host State, primary responsibility of 212
protected status, loss of 215–18
robust peacekeeping, *raison d'être* of 207–8
Special Representative of the Secretary-General 212–13
measuring protection 332–7
limitations 332–4
methodology 334–7
NATO 2, 89
practical challenges 314–25
guidance on who is to be protected and from whom 314–16
host State co-operation 324
intelligence 323–4
leadership 322–3
mobility 321
peace process 324–5
rapid deployment 317–18
regional support 316–17
resources 320–1
training 321–2
troop levels 318–20
troop professionalism 318–20
proactive and pre-emptive 56, 96, 134–5, 215, 221, 264–5, 313–14, 317, 325, 326, 363–4, 436
protection scenarios 341–4
communal conflict 341
ethnic cleansing 341
genocide 341
insurgency 342
post-conflict revenge 341
predatory violence 341
regime crackdown 341
protection success and failure 345–8
Abyei, avoiding communal conflict 346–7
Lou Nuer White Army (2011–12) 347–8
neutralizing the M23 (2013) 345–6
refugees 182
role of 313–14
UN peacekeeping operations 309–28
military force 311–13
political challenges 325–6
seldom use of force 103–4
utility of force 329–49
matching perpetrator violence 339–41
UN protection operations, distribution of 337–9
unwillingness to use 218
using force to protect 331–2
amelioration 331
containment 331
destruction 331, 332
deterrence/coercion 331, 332
impairment 332
incitement 332 *see also* military force
victimhood 1, 12, 20
Vietnam 35
Vietnam War 11, 68
vulnerabilities 178, 180, 184, 197, 200, 203, 380, 386, 415
war crimes 20, 37n, 39–40, 49n, 50, 58, 79n, 83, 95, 128, 141, 146, 150, 156, 170, 187, 189, 191, 193, 210, 216n, 217n, 226, 231n, 268, 276–8, 284, 305, 362, 382, 391–2, 420n, 434–5
warfare
aerial attacks 358
civilians as targets 261
contemporary 260
'conventional' 173
imprecision 358–9
individualization of 261
land 186
methods of 163, 261, 353–4, 433
regulation of 160, 163, 433
siege 177
starvation 185
tactical level 334n
traditional 89, 330
water 20, 21, 197, 252, 335, 347, 412, 418
weapons of mass destruction (WMDs) 304–5
weapons searches 272n
Western Sahara, *see* UN Mission for the Referendum in Western Sahara (MINURSO)
World Conference on Human Rights 352n
World Food Programme (WFP) 355n, 385
World Summit 39–41, 48–50, 57–8, 83, 128, 200, 210n, 307, 309n, 372, 391–2
World War I 16, 17, 22, 178, 205, 309
World War II 18, 64, 162, 186–7, 192, 205, 309, 382
wrongful acts 227, 247 *see also* DARSIWA
Yugoslavia, the former 43, 44n, 73, 76, 82, 84, 119, 123, 125n, 170, 177–8, 182, 189–90, 258n, 266n, 297–8, 320, 428 *see also* International Criminal Tribunal for the former Yugoslavia (ICTY); UN Protection Force for the Former Yugoslavia (UNPROFOR)
Zaïre 123
Zimbabwe 409, 415